PORTRAITS OF THE PTOLEMIES

PORTRAITS OF THE PTOLEMIES

Greek Kings as Egyptian Pharaohs

PAUL EDMUND STANWICK

University of Texas Press
AUSTIN

This book has been supported by an endowment dedicated to classics and the ancient world and funded by the Areté Foundation; the Gladys Krieble Delmas Foundation; the Dougherty Foundation; the James R. Dougherty, Jr. Foundation; the Rachael and Ben Vaughan Foundation; and the National Endowment for the Humanities. The endowment has also benefited from gifts by Mark and Jo Ann Finley, Lucy Shoe Meritt, the late Anne Byrd Nalle, and other individual donors.

Printed in the United States of America
First edition, 2002

⊗The paper used in this book meets the minimum requirements of ANSI/NISO Z39.48-1992 (R1997) (Permanence of Paper).
ISBN 0-292-77772-8

LIBRARY OF CONGRESS
CATALOGING-IN-PUBLICATION DATA

Stanwick, Paul Edmund.
Portraits of the Ptolemies : Greek kings as Egyptian pharaohs /
Paul Edmund Stanwick.
p. cm.
Includes bibliographical references and index.
ISBN 0-292-77772-8 (hardcover : alk. paper)
1. Ptolemaic dynasty, 305–30 B.C.—Portraits. 2. Portraits, Hellenistic—Egypt.
3. Portrait sculpture, Egyptian—Themes, motives. I. Title.
NB1296.2.S73 2003
731'.82'0932—dc21
2002013478

This book is dedicated to Hetty,
with whom I have shared a lifelong interest in scholarship,
and without whom this book would not have been possible.

CONTENTS

PREFACE

IN WRITING ABOUT EGYPTIAN-STYLE PORTRAITS OF THE Ptolemies in 1961, Hans Wolfgang Müller described the field as *terra incognita* ("unfamiliar land").[1] Only a few pioneering studies had appeared by that time, limiting an understanding of the sculptures. Much has changed in the intervening decades with the appearance of important treatments by Egyptologists and classicists. Moreover, the underwater archaeological teams of Jean-Yves Empereur and Franck Goddio have discovered spectacular examples of royal portraits from the coastal waters near Alexandria. From a position of relative obscurity, Egyptian-style portraits of the Ptolemies have gained a new prominence.

My approach to Egyptian portraits of the Ptolemies has diverse roots. These range from basic observations about physical appearance and archaeological context, to more conceptual opinions about ideology and aesthetics. Each has a value in telling the story of the sculptures. Just as one needs to examine a statue from all angles to understand it, so, too, do varied forms of research create a more insightful view.

The distinctive appearance of Ptolemaic royal portraits first sparked my interest in them. Opposing cultural orientations—an Egyptian emphasis on continuity and a Greek bias toward change—create a powerful visual impact. I began my research with a thorough examination of the physical aspects of the portraits, from measurements, inscriptions, and materials to characteristics of the faces, bodies, and back pillars. This research now underpins many parts of this book. Sculptural details are important in isolation and in how they reflect broader iconographical trends, both of their own time and of more ancient periods.

Architectural context likewise intrigued me. A reconstruction of the portraits' original settings posed a challenge because such information was unfortunately not preserved in most cases. Numerous sculptures are labeled "provenance not known," and others have provenances that cannot be verified. Additionally, museum settings alter our perceptions of the portraits. Using archaeological reports, inscriptions, and other records, I built a basic understanding of original architectural context. The role of geography in influencing the characteristics of the portraits was an important outcome of these efforts. There is a startling contrast between the vibrantly Greek capital of Alexandria and the tradition-bound regions of Egypt to the south.

Ancient viewpoints are crucial to my approach. Though we necessarily see Ptolemaic royal sculptures in modern terms, historical texts and documentation provide some glimpses through ancient eyes. I initially became interested in this direction after reviewing the priestly decrees, ancient inscriptions that are extraordinary in providing information about the viewpoints of the Ptolemies and their priestly advisors. I expanded on the approach by collecting other ancient documentation from Egyptian, Greek, and Roman sources. Of special interest were the Egyptian royal titulatures of the Ptolemies, whose elaborate phrasings were revealing about the ideological intent of specific statues and groups of them. I also let the sculptures themselves inform my thinking. Royal regalia and other details yield much information about how the ancients comprehended the confrontation between Egypt's remote antiquity and the new concepts of the Hellenistic Greeks.

Chronology is the bane of scholars of Ptolemaic sculpture as well as the topic that excites the most interest and debate. I therefore approached chronology with careful consideration. I gathered the best-dated evidence to make judgments about the most effective methods for dating Ptolemaic royal portraits. As a result, I focused on portrait characteristics, principally hair and facial features, to build my chronological framework. Around this, I layered the social, political, and religious developments that formed the backdrop for changing tastes and concepts in royal portraiture.

Stylistic and aesthetic analysis both began and completed my work. Initially, I had hoped that stylistic development—the study of how a sculpture's details are rendered—would be an organizing principle for Ptolemaic royal portraits. Though valuable in this respect, the approach had several pitfalls, principally its subjectivity and reliance on modern constructs. Therefore, I embarked on other forms of analysis, as outlined here, to reach a more comprehensive understanding. Stylistic and aesthetic development then became much more comprehensible as the outcome of my broader research and as the concluding chapter of this book.

A number of potentially fruitful paths lie ahead for research on Ptolemaic Egypt and its royal portraiture. Further finds in Alexandria and Canopus will help redress the uneven archaeological record. Continued publication of the abundant hieroglyphic and demotic texts will provide ever more insight to the Egyptian side of Ptolemaic Egypt. Further explorations of the great Ptolemaic temples of Upper Egypt will clarify the nature of royal representation in these areas. New discussion of the art-historical significance of the period's Egyptian sculptures will highlight their place in Egypt's millennia of sculptural achievements. Though the study of Egyptian-style portraits of the Ptolemies has not yet reached *terra firma,* it nonetheless has advanced enormously.

NOTES

1. H. W. Müller 1961, 27.

ACKNOWLEDGMENTS

THE ORIGINS OF THIS BOOK LIE IN THE TALENTS AND energies of Professor Bernard V. Bothmer of the Institute of Fine Arts at New York University. I learned from him the value of the careful observation of a sculpture's stylistic details and discovered the means to appreciate the aesthetic principles of Egyptian sculpture. Under his guidance and encouragement, I began my study of Ptolemaic royal sculptures. Through seminars, discussion, and travel, I benefitted from the breadth of his knowledge. Most importantly, Professor Bothmer provided generous access to his bibliographic and photographic opus, the Corpus of Late Egyptian Sculpture, which includes many of the statues catalogued here. The Corpus formed the basis for my research and has served as an important resource to this day.

In my ten years of research on Ptolemaic royal portraits, I have been fortunate to benefit from the knowledge and support of many individuals. Professor David O'Connor of the Institute of Fine Arts read my Ph.D. dissertation through its innumerable incarnations, offering crucial comments and criticisms. He particularly helped me develop ideas about the significance of the physical contexts of royal sculpture and how to interpret the priestly decrees that describe them. I thank him for his openness to looking at ancient statuary from multiple perspectives. Professor R.R.R. Smith of Oxford University was enormously insightful on how to organize and argue the wide-ranging topic of Ptolemaic royal portraiture. His knowing comments on specific sculptures still resonate with me. He enthusiastically supported my research from its inception. Professor Ogden Goelet of New York University helped me navigate through the sometimes difficult interpretations of ancient texts. I owe to him my appreciation of the richness of the ancient Egyptian language. My other advisors at New York University also deserve many thanks: Dr. Donald Hansen, Dr. Evelyn Harrison, and Dr. Katherine Welch.

Mrs. Brunilde Sismondo Ridgway, emerita of Bryn Mawr College, freely shared her considerable knowledge of ancient art as well as of the workings of scholarly publishing. Her extensive comments and advice sharpened my understanding of the classicist's perspective on my topic. Bruni's unforgettably enthusiastic lecture style first drew me to the study of archaeology and art. I am grateful to Miss Machteld Mellink, emerita of Bryn Mawr College, for her guidance over many years.

Jack Josephson provided help, encouragement, and keen observations. Jack taught me the importance of distinguishing Ptolemaic portrait styles from others, an essential subject for the imperfectly understood Ptolemaic Period. Jack has helped me avoid missteps and has opened new opportunities.

Several individuals reviewed the manuscript and generously gave criticisms, comments, and additional bibliography. They are: Dr. Herman De Meulenaere, Ms. Biri Fay, Ms. Emma Swan Hall, and Dr. Zsolt Kiss. Dr. Klaus Parlasca periodically provided information during my research as well as critiqued the text. Dr. Helmut Kyrieleis graciously and promptly responded to my inquiries and helped shape the scope of my revised text. I thank my anonymous readers sponsored by the University of Texas Press, who provided both praise and fruitful criticism. Laurel Bernstein and Beatrice Rehl gave nonspecialist readers' viewpoints on the manuscript and its outline, respectively. I thank Mrs. Norma Jean Bothmer for her continuing friendship.

Some scholars contributed to my understanding of specific aspects of Ptolemaic royal portraits. I thank Dr. Sabine Albersmeier, for many thoughtful conversations about statues of Ptolemaic queens; Dr. Dieter Arnold, for discussion about the erection of royal statuary in Egyptian temples; Dr. Dorothea Arnold, for important clarifications on how to interpret statue bases; Dr. André Bernand, for translations of Greek inscriptions on statues; Dr. Giuseppina Capriotti Vittozzi, for helpful insights on statues of queens and sculptures in Italian collections (and photographs of them); Dr. Sylvie Cauville, for information on the Dendera temple treasure horde; Dr. Janet Johnson, for access to the preliminary draft of "The Chicago Demotic Dictionary"; Dr. Eva Rogge, for her assistance in understanding sculptures in the Kunsthistorisches Museum; Dr. Christophe Thiers, for many significant comments on my interpretation of the priestly decrees and other inscriptions; and Ms. Nadja Toumoum for information on sculptors' studies/votives. Any errors or omissions, however, are entirely my own. Ms. Madeleine Cody, Dr. Jean-Yves Empereur, Dr. Christa Landwehr, Dr. Karol Myśliwiec, and Dr. Dietrich Raue helped obtain photographs. Mr. Sherif Sonbol was my excellent photographer in the Cairo Museum.

Many museum directors and curators patiently facilitated my sometimes repeated examinations of sculptures, and provided important background information and photographs. Other members of the Egyptological community likewise gave assistance. They are: Dr. G. Ali Gaballa, Secretary General of the Supreme Council for Antiquities; Dr. Ahmed Abd el-Fattah and Dr. Mervat Seif el-Din of the Graeco-Roman Museum, Alexandria (as well as their team of curators and assistants); Dr. Jean-Yves Empereur and Dr. Marie-Dominique Nenna of the Centre d'Études Alexandrines of Alexandria; Dr. Willem M. van Haarlem of the Allard Pierson Museum, Amsterdam; Dr. Angeliki Ziva of the Benaki Museum, Athens; Dr. Ioannis Touratsoglou and Dr. Nikolaos Kaltsas of the National Archaeological Museum, Athens; Dr. Ellen Reeder (formerly) and Ms. Kate M. Lau of The Walters Art Museum, Baltimore; Dr. W. D. Heilmeyer and Dr. Ilona Trabert of the Antikensammlung, Berlin; Dr. Dietrich Wildung, Dr. Katje Lembke, and Dr. Ingeborg Müller of the Ägyptisches Museum und Papyrussammlung, Berlin; Dr. Phil Watson of the Birmingham Museums and Art Gallery; Dr. Adriana Calinescu and Ms. Kathy Henline of the Indiana University Art Museum, Bloomington; Dr. Cristiana Morigi Govi of the Museo Civico Archeologico, Bologna; Dr. John Herrmann and Mr. Christopher Atkins of the Museum of Fine Arts Boston; Mr. Richard Fazzini, Dr. James Romano, Dr. Edna R. Russmann, Ms. Madeleine Cody, and Dr. Bojana Mojsov (formerly) of the Brooklyn Museum of Art; Ms. Diane Bergman (formerly) and Ms. Mary Gow of the Wilbour Library at the Brooklyn Museum of Art; Dr. L. Masschelein-Kleiner of the Institut Royal du Patrimoine Artistique, Brussels; Dr. Edith Varga and Dr. Péter Gaboda of the Szépmüvészeti Múzeum, Budapest; Dr. Mohamed Abdel Hamid Shimy (formerly), Mme. Soheir el-Sawy, and the team of curators at the Cairo Museum; Ms. Amy Brauer of the Harvard University Art Museums, Cambridge; Dr. Emily Teeter of The Oriental Institute at The University of Chicago; Dr. Bodil Bundgaard Rasmussen and Ms. Anne Haslund Hansen of the

National Museum, Copenhagen; Dr. Mogens Jørgensen of the Ny Carlsberg Glyptotek, Copenhagen; Dr. Angelo Bottini of Il Regio Museo Archeologico, Florence; Dr. Harald Schulze of the Archäologisches Institut of the Johann Wolfgang Goethe-Universität, Frankfurt; Dr. Rosemarie Drenkhahn of the Kestner Museum, Hannover; Ms. Sue Davies and Dr. H. S. Smith of Huntingdon (North Saqqara excavations); Dr. Peter Gercke of the Staatliche Museen Kassel; Dr. M. J. Raven of the Rijksmuseum van Oudheden, Leiden; Dr. W. V. Davies, Dr. A. J. Spencer, and Mr. James Putnam of the British Museum, London; Dr. M. A. Leahy and Dr. Patricia Spencer of The Egypt Exploration Society, London; Dr. Barbara Adams, Dr. Stephen Quirke, Ms. Sally MacDonald, and Mr. Hugh Kilmister of the Petrie Museum of Egyptian Archaeology, University College London; Ms. Helen Dorey of Sir John Soane's Museum, London; Dr. María del Carmen Pérez Die of the Museo Arqueólogico Nacional, Madrid; Dr. Genvième Galliano of the Musée de Beaux-Arts, Lyon; Dr. Ugo Bazzotti of the Museo Civico di Palazzo Te, Mantua; Dr. Claire Derriks of the Musée Royal de Mariemont; Dr. Gisèle Piérini of the Musée d'Archéologie Méditerranéenne, Marseille; Dr. Ermanno A. Arslan and Dr. Francesco Tiradritti of the Civico Museo Archeologico, Milan; Dr. Alfred Grimm and Ms. Claudia Walke of the Staatlichen Sammlung Ägyptischer Kunst, Munich; Professor Stefano De Caro, Soprintendenza Archeologica delle province di Napoli e Caserta; Dr. Susan Matheson of the Yale University Art Gallery, New Haven; Dr. Roger Colten and Ms. Maureen Da Ros of the Peabody Museum of Natural History at Yale University, New Haven; Dr. Carmen Arnold-Biucchi (formerly) and Dr. Ute Wartenberg of The American Numismatic Society, New York; Dr. Dorothea Arnold, Dr. Marsha Hill, Dr. Elena Pischikova, and Dr. Catharine Roehrig of the Metropolitan Museum of Art, New York; Dr. William Kelly Simpson; Mr. Leonard Stern; the Department of Antiquities, Nicosia; Dr. Jaromir Malek, Dr. Diana Magee, and Ms. Elizabeth Miles of the Porter-Moss archives at the Griffith Institute, Oxford University; Mme. Mathilde Avisseau-Broustet of the Bibliothèque National, Paris; Mme. Christiane Ziegler and M. Christophe Barbotin of the Egyptian department of the Musée du Louvre, Paris; M. Alain Pasquier and Mlle. Agnès Scherer of the Greek and Roman department of the Musée du Louvre, Paris; Mme. Claudic Judrin, Mme. Bénédicte Garnier, and M. Jérome Manoukian of the Musée Rodin, Paris; Mrs. Nashwa Hussein of the National Museum, Port Said; Dr. Maria Teresa Nota of the Museo Barracco, Rome; Dr. Loredana Sist, Rome; Dr. Rosanna Friggeri and Dr. Marina Sabelli of the Museo Nazionale, Rome; Dr. Francesco Buranelli, Dr. Paolo Liverani, and Dr. Giandomenico Spinola of the Vatican Museums, Rome; Ms. Lisa Schwappach of the Rosicrucian Egyptian Museum, San Jose; Dr. Claude Traunecker of the Institut d'Egyptologie at the Université Marc Bloch, Strasbourg; Dr. Margret Honroth of the Württembergisches Landesmuseum, Stuttgart; Dr. Emad Bedair of the Tanta Museum; Mrs. Alison Easson, Dr. N. B. Millet, and Dr. Roberta Shaw of the Royal Ontario Museum, Toronto; Prof. Dr. K. Zibelius-Chen of the Ägyptologisches Institut der Universität, Tübingen; Dr. Anna Maria Donadoni Roveri of the Museo Egizio, Turin; Dr. Helmut Satzinger, Dr. Elfriede Haslauer, and Dr. Alfred Bernhard-Walcher of the Kunsthistorisches Museum, Vienna; Ms. Susan Boyd of the Dumbarton Oaks Byzantine Collection, Washington, D.C.; Mrs. Henrietta Ryan and Miss Siân Smith of the Royal Collections, Windsor Castle; and Dr. Khaled Aly Elsayed of the Orabi Museum, Zagazig.

This book has been supported by an endowment dedicated to classics and the ancient world and funded by the Areté Foundation; the Gladys Krieble Delmas Foundation; the Dougherty Foundation; the James R. Dougherty, Jr. Foundation; the Rachael and Ben Vaughan Foundation; and the National Endowment for the Humanities. The endowment has also benefited from gifts by Mark and Jo Ann Finley, Lucy Shoe Meritt, the late Anne Byrd Nalle, and other individual donors.

I thank the business, editorial, and design staffs at the University of Texas Press, particularly Jim Burr and Sherry Wert for their editorial guidance, and Joanna Hitchcock for deciding to sponsor this book.

I thank Dr. William Kelly Simpson and the board of the Michela Schiff Giorgini Foundation of the United States for their generous support for obtaining new photographs. While there is much that can be written about Ptolemaic royal portraits, it is the sculptures themselves that form the essence of this book.

DEFINITIONS AND CONVENTIONS

SEVERAL CONVENTIONS ARE EMPLOYED IN THE BOOK. "Egyptian-style" or "Egyptian" refers to hard stone and other statues created by native craftsmen, even those that display strong Greek influence. "Greek-style" or "Greek" describes statues made by Greeks, typically in marble or bronze. Like terminology denotes whether a temple displays predominantly Greek or Egyptian features. When an Egyptian sculpture has "Greek hair" (Fig. 105), it means that the hair is patterned after Greek-style works (Fig. 260), even though it may be rendered in a stylized Egyptian manner. The same is true for "Roman hair."

For the hieroglyphic and demotic texts, I use the European system of transliteration,[1] regardless of whether it was used by authors in the citations for these texts. For the Greek, I provide a transliteration unless an anglicized form is better known, such as "Ptolemy." For common Egyptian terms, I use established transliterations, such as the *shendyt*-garment or *heqa*-scepter. Egyptological convention is inconsistent in using a Greek, Roman, or Arabic name for sites.[2] Although I prefer the Greek or Roman designation, I often employ the Arabic one because it is more commonly cited. For example, I use the Arabic Medinet Madi rather than the Greek Narmouthis, because Medinet Madi typically appears in major publications on the site.

Table D.1 gives the conventions employed for the purpose of classifying sculptures into broad categories of size. In addition, some special terminology describes the depiction of the eyes and eyebrows:

- Eyebrows in relief = indicated in relief edged by incision, generally in a hieroglyphic, symmetrical manner (Fig. 20).
- Natural eyebrows = rendered as raised contours that are not edged by incision (Fig. 52).
- Single-arc versus semicircular eyebrows = executed as a continuous, single curve versus in two separate semicircles (Fig. 199).

TABLE D.1 HEIGHT CONVENTIONS
(in centimeters)

	Height of Head (= HeadH)	*Height of Face (= FaceH)*[a]
Well under life-size	Up to 9.1	Up to 6.2
Under life-size	9.2–21.1	6.3–13.3
Life-size	21.2–27.3	13.4–18.6
Over life-size	27.4–40.0	18.7–26.0
Colossal	40.1 and up	26.1 and up

[a]Forehead hair, if any, is excluded from the height of face measurements.

- Rimmed eyes = upper lid of the eye is rendered plastically, with both of its edges indicated by incision. Only the upper edge of the lower lid is marked with incision (Fig. 138).
- Fully rimmed eyes = both upper and lower lids are rendered plastically, with both edges of each lid indicated in relief edged by incision (Fig. 158).

Catalogued sculptures are arranged into Groups A–J and designated by a number, such as A3 or D8. The sequence of groups, which is mostly chronological, is explained at the beginning of Chapter 7 and in Table 7.1. Every effort has been made over the last several years to obtain photographs, but not all statues are illustrated. Catalogued sculptures generally are referenced by their catalogue numbers (such as A3), whereas other objects are labeled by their figure numbers (as in Fig. 240). Left and right sides refer to a statue's own left and right. Exceptionally, the viewer's left or right is used in reference to inscriptions, reliefs, or temple entrances.

Question marks (?) next to a sculptural reference, transliteration, date, or another word indicate that the description, reading, dating, or interpretation is uncertain. Thus, in citing a list of sculptures with double crowns, the number of a catalogued sculpture is followed by a question mark (as in "B7?"), if it is not certain that the crown was originally present. I use the traditional B.C. and A.D dating designations. When neither is specified, B.C. should be understood. Despite attempts at standardizing to these conventions, inconsistencies undoubtedly persist in the text.

NOTES

1. James P. Allen, *Middle Egyptian: An Introduction to the Language and Culture of Hieroglyphs* (Cambridge, 2000), 14–15.
2. See comments of Di. Arnold 1999, 4.

DYNASTIC CHRONOLOGY

THE CHRONOLOGY IS SELECTIVE, BASED ON RULERS AND periods mentioned in the text. Dates mostly follow Ian Shaw, ed., *The Oxford History of Ancient Egypt* (Oxford, 2000), 480–482, and Hölbl 2001.

Early Dynastic Period (Dynasties 1–2)	c. 3000–2686 B.C.
Old Kingdom (Dynasties 3–6)	c. 2686–2181
Middle Kingdom (Dynasties 11–13)	c. 2055–1650
New Kingdom (Dynasties 18–20)	c. 1550–1069
Third Intermediate Period (Dynasties 21–25)	c. 1069–664
Late Period (Dynasties 26–30)	c. 664–332
Dynasty 29	399–380
Dynasty 30	380–343
Second Persian Period	343–332
Macedonian Period	332–306 B.C.
Alexander the Great	332–323
Philip Arrhidaios	323–317
Alexander IV	317–310/309
Ptolemaic Period	306–30 B.C.
Ptolemy I Soter	306–283/282
Ptolemy II Philadelphos	285/284–246
Arsinoe II	279/274–270
Ptolemy III Euergetes I	246–222/221

Berenice II	246–221
Ptolemy IV Philopator	221–204
Arsinoe III	221–204
Ptolemy V Epiphanes	204–180
Cleopatra I	194/193–176
Ptolemy VI Philometor	180–145
Cleopatra II	175–116
Ptolemy VIII Euergetes II	170–163, 145–116
Cleopatra III	141/140–101
Ptolemy IX Soter II	116–107, 88–80
Ptolemy X Alexander I	107–88
Ptolemy XI Alexander II	80
Ptolemy XII Neos Dionysos	80–58, 55–51
Cleopatra VII Philopator	51–30
Ptolemy XIII	51–47
Ptolemy XIV	47–44
Ptolemy XV Caesarion	44–30
Roman Period	30 B.C.–A.D. 395
Octavian-Augustus	30 B.C.–A.D. 14
Caracalla	A.D. 198–217

PORTRAITS OF THE PTOLEMIES

CHAPTER 1

A UNIQUE VANTAGE POINT

THE PTOLEMIES OF EGYPT HAD A UNIQUE VANTAGE POINT. From their fabled capital of Alexandria, these Greek rulers looked north to Greece, east to Asia, west to Rome, and south to Egypt. As beneficiaries of the conquests of Alexander the Great, the Ptolemies were closely connected with the Hellenistic empires of the eastern Mediterranean, stretching in a broad sweep from Macedonia in northern Greece, through Turkey and the Near East, and to Egypt. In later years, the Ptolemies became alternatively allies or enemies of Rome and its charismatic leaders, Julius Caesar, Marc Antony, and Octavian-Augustus. As inheritors of one of the oldest civilizations, the Ptolemies joined a long line of pharaohs reaching back thousands of years. They governed a land of great antiquity, rich in monuments with a resolutely Egyptian character.

The forces that drew together Egypt, Rome, and Greece in the last centuries before the Common Era were fertile ground for the creation of a remarkable brand of royal portraiture. War, larger-than-life personalities, luxurious wealth, and grandiose religious beliefs were the key ingredients. Starting with the bold conquests of Alexander the Great, and ending with the crushing force of Rome, the Ptolemaic era was driven by armed conflict and its consequent political machinations and social upheavals. Royal portraiture takes on a strongly propagandistic nature, based on its use as a tool to further the aims of its sponsoring leaders. The Ptolemaic dynasty was one of distinguished individuals, who managed as a group to keep their grip on power longer than any preceding dynasty in Egypt, and whose names still linger with us today. Some of their sculptures dramatically reflect their powerful personas. One of the reasons the Ptolemies, and ultimately Rome, coveted Egypt was the wealth originating from its agrarian economy, its strategic location on trade routes, and its access to mineral resources. The lavish lifestyle that the Ptolemies enjoyed, and that the Romans vilified as decadent, financed a renewed output of colossal and ostentatious sculptures. Egypt's long-lasting focus on religion and the resultant economic and social clout of the native priests impressed many foreign visitors to the country. An elaborate native royal cult was developed for the benefit of the Greek rulers. Religious beliefs and practices shaped how royal images would look and where they would be placed.

The most distinctive aspect of Ptolemaic royal portraiture, however, was its blend of Egyptian and Greek cultures. The arrival of the Ptolemies fostered the creation of Greek buildings and sculptures on a large scale, one of the most pervasive foreign artistic intrusions during Egypt's millennia of history. Yet, the rulers also sponsored a major program of Egyptian temples and sculptures, which remain among the most enduring monuments in the country today. For sources of inspiration, Ptolemaic royal portraits could draw on the ideas of Greece, Rome, and Egypt itself. The complex political and social fabric of Italy and the eastern Mediterranean during Hellenistic times produced some of the most provocative marble and bronze portraits known from the ancient world. At the same time, Egypt possessed an enormous legacy extending from sculptures such as the Great Sphinx at Giza of the third millennium B.C. to the accomplished statues of the native pharaohs of Dynasty 30 in the fourth century B.C.

AN EVENTFUL 300 YEARS

Developments in Ptolemaic royal portraits were set against an eventful 300 years.[1] The period was full of strife. There were wars with the neighboring Seleucid kingdom, bloody conflicts among royal siblings, and native Egyptian uprisings. It was also a time of significant achievement. The new city of Alexandria was founded and quickly became the most important center of the eastern Mediterranean, possessing the Pharos lighthouse, one of the seven wonders of the ancient world. For one of the few times in Egypt's history, women had highly visible governing roles. The political tactics and strong-arm maneuvers of the Cleopatras rank as some of the most daring and ruthless acts ever undertaken by rulers of either gender.

The Ptolemaic Period began with a lively exuberance. Alexander the Great freed Egypt from oppressive Persian rule and founded Alexandria. A few decades later, one of Alexander's former generals declared himself sovereign of Egypt and became Ptolemy I. The ancient capital of Memphis, with its high-ranking native priests and rich, millennia-long history, retained a key role for the next three centuries, though it was quickly eclipsed by Alexandria, which emerged as an extraordinary metropolis. Ptolemy II built the famous library and embellished his court with influential writers and intellectuals from the Greek world. From the beginning, the rulers established a relationship with native priests, who had a dominant leadership role in the country. Ptolemy II founded the highly successful native cult honoring his wife and sister Arsinoe II. This powerful woman became an enduring model for subsequent queens. The Egyptian priest Manetho wrote his famous history of Egypt—in Greek, for Greek readers—in these first years.

By the second half of the third century, there were signs that the early success was about to unravel. Ptolemy III built Alexandria's most honored temple, the Serapeum, and he extended Ptolemaic Egypt to its greatest geographic reach through military conquest and strategic alliance. His wife, Berenice II, was celebrated in the work of the Alexandrian poet Callimachus. During a campaign abroad, however, Ptolemy III was forced to return home in 245 B.C. to quell a native rebellion. His son, Ptolemy IV, triumphed against the Seleucid king Antiochus III at the Battle of Raphia in 217 B.C., but he was unable to overcome continuing internal unrest, which culminated in the declaration of an Egyptian counterpharaoh called Haronnophris in Thebes in 206 B.C. The rebellion was not suppressed for two decades.

Developments in the second century demonstrated both the powerful potential of the Ptolemaic dynasty and its tendency toward self-destruction. The century began with two boy-kings, Ptolemies V and VI. Ptolemy V married the Seleucid princess Cleopatra I, the first in a series of like-named queens. During his rule, Egypt lost most of its foreign possessions. The king was poisoned by his generals in 180 B.C., leaving the young Cleopatra I to serve as regent over the boy Ptolemy VI until she died a few years later. The teenaged Ptolemy VI's rule was threatened when the Seleucid king Antiochus IV invaded Egypt twice, in 170/169 B.C. and again in 168 B.C. Ptolemaic sovereignty was maintained only with the help of Rome, whose military might was beginning to cast a shadow over the eastern Mediterranean. Ptolemy VI married his sister, the formidable Cleopatra II. Their subsequent triple monarchy with rival-brother Ptolemy VIII soon dissolved into a conflict that initiated a long line of bitter intradynastic feuds. After partially restoring the tarnished fortunes of the Ptolemaic state, the mature Ptolemy VI died from wounds sustained in battle against the Seleucid king Alexander Balas.

The reign of Ptolemy VIII, one of the dynasty's longest, was also its most notorious. Nicknamed Physkon ("fat man" or "pot belly"), this king married his sister (and former sister-in-law) Cleopatra II and then his niece and stepdaughter Cleopatra III. The three shared the throne, alternating between proclamations of dynastic unity and highly public, vicious attacks against each other. During a civil war in 132–124 B.C., Ptolemy VIII and Cleopatra III fled to Cyprus, and Cleopatra II became sole ruler in Alexandria. In revenge, Ptolemy VIII murdered his son by Cleopatra II and sent the dismembered remains to his sister-wife, for delivery the night before her birthday. Despite these vicissitudes, the second century was a time of much temple-building in Upper Egypt. Projects at Dendera, Edfu, Kom Ombo, and Philae were initiated or continued. Like the early Ptolemies, those of the second century cultivated relations with the native priesthood, now with a more urgent need to forestall periodic intervals of native unrest. Another Egyptian counter-pharaoh, Harsiese, arose in Thebes in 131/130 B.C.

Following the demise of Ptolemy VIII in 116 B.C., Cleopatra III became the dominant royal power for about fifteen years. The dead king's will left the Ptolemaic kingdom to her and the son of her choice. The queen initially selected Ptolemy IX, forcing him to divorce his first wife and later conspiring to have him sent into exile in 107 B.C. Cleopatra III then ruled with Ptolemy X until she was murdered at his behest in 101 B.C. She was enormously powerful and assumed many royal male prerogatives, including going to battle.

Egypt gradually slid into Rome's grasp during the final century of Ptolemaic rule. Roman intervention was needed to place Ptolemy XII on the throne, to reinstate him after his subjects drove him out of the country, and to settle the succession among his four children. Cleopatra VII brilliantly succeeded in her relationships with two of the most powerful Romans of her time, Julius Caesar and Marc Antony, and bore children by both of them. She had high aspirations for her son by Caesar, Ptolemy XV Caesarion.

Strong cultivation of relations with the native population continued under the last rulers. Ptolemy XII had an Egyptian-style coronation at Memphis in 76 B.C. Cleopatra VII was the first Ptolemaic ruler to learn to speak Egyptian. In a final bid to secure the fortunes of the Ptolemaic kingdom, Cleopatra VII and Marc Antony fought Octavian at the sea battle of Actium in 31 B.C. The couple's defeat marked the end of Ptolemaic rule.

EARLIER STUDIES

The study of Egyptian-style, Ptolemaic royal portraiture has its roots in a chapter in Friedrich Wilhelm von Bissing's seminal *Denkmäler ägyptischer Sculptur,* published in the early twentieth century. For the first time, this Egyptologist gathered together many sculptures and studied differences between purely Egyptian examples and those having Greek features. Since Bissing's work, no Egyptologist has attempted a comprehensive examination of Ptolemaic royal portraits, though some broad-based studies have analyzed selected sculptures. In 1960, the highly influential exhibition catalogue *Egyptian Sculpture of the Late Period, 700 B.C. to A.D. 100* dated a handful of Ptolemaic royal sculptures using a rigorous stylistic analysis. Now known as *ESLP,* the book argued for Greek influence on Egyptian sculptures, building on ideas from historians of Greek art. In 1988, Robert S. Bianchi's *Cleopatra's Egypt* critically reappraised the existing body of scholarship. This exhibition catalogue's polemical rejection of Greek influence on Egyptian sculpture was extreme, but it was instrumental in fostering a more balanced view of these interactions. Bianchi layered religious and historical information on top of stylistic analysis. In 1997, Jack Josephson published *Egyptian Royal Sculpture of the Late Period, 400–246 B.C.* He made significant progress in isolating portraits of Dynasty 30 and the early Ptolemaic Period, and clarified the dating of some works erroneously placed in the fourth century. During these decades, other scholars wrote articles on individual sculptures. H. W. Müller expanded on *ESLP*'s stylistic analysis techniques, and Klaus Parlasca innovatively compared Greek- and Egyptian-style sculptures and used clay sealing portraits as an attribution tool.[2]

Classicists have produced the most comprehensive studies of Ptolemaic royal portraits, approaching the material from a Greek rather than an Egyptian viewpoint. Helmut Kyrieleis's *Bildnisse der Ptolemäer* of 1975, which treated primarily marble portraits, was a breakthrough study in its scope, identification techniques, and ideas about Greek and Egyptian interaction. Stylistic and portrait analysis formed the core of the approach. Kyrieleis continues to publish important treatments, particularly in the promising and abundant field of clay sealing portraits.[3] R.R.R. Smith dealt extensively with the Ptolemies in his 1988 book, *Hellenistic Royal Portraits,* a far-reaching analysis that did much to define the purpose of portraiture, as well as to debunk a plethora of attributions. Smith generally eschewed stylistic analysis in favor of a sociopolitical approach based on the study of ancient texts.

Though the contributions of classicists have been valuable, their perspective has led to an incomplete understanding of the Egyptian nature of the material. First and foremost, Egyptian-style portraits of the Ptolemies, even those with Greek features, remain strongly rooted in native conventions. The sculptures need to be viewed in this light. Furthermore, classicists have focused on the Egyptian portraits with Greek hair and faces, leaving the remaining majority of statues in obscurity. This analysis seeks to correct that imbalance.

AN EXPANDED METHODOLOGY

The present study uses prior ones as a foundation, but seeks to expand the methodology with two important aims. First, it looks to develop an integrated approach spanning ancient texts, archaeological evidence, royal attributes, kingship ideology, and portrait and stylistic analysis. Second, it aims to construct an Egyptological framework for understanding sculptures that have been predominantly viewed from a classicist perspective. Succeeding chapters are arranged to build toward these goals. Chapter 2 examines the textual evidence of the priestly decrees such as the one on the Rosetta Stone, which is famed for its role in the modern decipherment of Egyptian hieroglyphs.[4] These texts are precise in defining why royal images should be created, where they should be placed, and how they should function. Chapter 3 uses archaeological information to critically reexamine assumptions about the physical context of Ptolemaic sculpture. New excavations in Alexandria and Canopus are providing increasing clarity on where royal statues were set up, particularly on how images in the capital may have differed from those in other parts of Egypt. Statue types, poses, scale, material, attributes, and inscriptions are surveyed in chapter 4 to understand how these contributed to the visual impact and meaning of royal imagery. The significance of Egyptian royal headdresses such as the double crown is studied in relationship to Greek additions, such as the cornucopia, the horn of plenty. Chapter 5 explores the Ptolemaic dynasty's ideological aims, as outlined in their Egyptian royal titularies and other sources, to determine how well they were integrated with royal portraits. Individual sculptures are examined to understand how they reflected the conceptions of their time, most importantly why "Greekness" was highlighted through the addition of Greek hair and faces. Chapter 6 establishes a chronological framework by gathering together Ptolemaic royal portraits, both Greek- and Egyptian-style, that can be dated by inscription, archaeological context, or comparative analysis. Previously established chronological points are reviewed and new ones introduced. Criteria for dating other portraits are established.

Chapter 7 comprises attributions of sculptures to specific rulers and time frames. This exercise was both rewarding and difficult. Unlike other periods in Egyptian royal portraiture, the Ptolemaic era is curiously susceptible to the scholarly inclusion of works from other eras, including the modern one. Estimating conservatively, about one-quarter of the Egyptian royal sculptures identified as Ptolemaic in current scholarly literature do not belong there, in my view. If one adds the opinions expressed in auction catalogs, the number rises to half! What is responsible for this astounding situation? First, there is a willingness to read oddities in a sculpture as the product of Egyptian and Greek cultural interactions rather than modern workmanship. Second, there is a related misunderstanding of the possible range of portraits and sculptural styles for the Ptolemaic Period. Though most scholarship to date has focused on assigning sculptures to individual rulers, progress has been slow. Attributions have suffered from a piecemeal approach and an uneven methodology.

This book seeks to rectify this state of affairs by questioning Ptolemaic dates for many sculptures, and by relating portraits to the sociopolitical and religious developments of their time. Ptolemaic royal sculptures are alternatively youthful/aged, trim/corpulent, and benign/forceful in support of a ruler's or the dynasty's ideological viewpoints. Stylistic analysis—a detailed examination of how eyes, mouth, body, and other features are sculptured—is employed, albeit with caution. There is much stylistic diversity in the Hellenistic era, suggesting that a clear, singular path of development should not be expected. Instead, there is a multilayered progression. Stylistic analysis is also useful in exposing sculptures that do not belong in the Ptolemaic Period, particularly modern imitations (Appendix B). The resulting series of attributions, though imperfect because of the incomplete state of our knowledge, nonetheless provides an increased clarity that can serve as the foundation for future research.

The final chapter takes a look at royal sculptors and stylistic trends of the Ptolemaic Period. Although textual sources give an impression of how the rulers and their priestly advisors viewed royal imagery, we have scant written evidence of what ideas and talents sculptors contributed. Nevertheless, their achievements are visible in preserved sculptures. Like the Ptolemies, the sculptors had a strong vantage point. They looked back to Egypt's long history of achievement and around them at the new ideas emerging from the Greek Hellenistic milieu. By combining elements of disparate cultures, these sculptors masterfully portrayed Greek kings who were Egyptian pharaohs.

NOTES

1. Ptolemaic history: Turner 1984, Bowman 1986, D. J. Thompson 1994a, Chaveau 2000, Lloyd 2000, and Hölbl 2001. Werner Huss published a new history (2001) as I was finalizing the manuscript.

2. H. W. Müller 1955 and 1961. Parlasca 1967, 1976, and 1978.

3. Kyrieleis 1990 and 1996.

4. Quirke and Andrews 1989.

CHAPTER 2

THE PRIESTLY DECREES

FROM THE EARLIEST YEARS OF THEIR RULE, THE PTOLEMIES realized that a strong relationship with the native clergy was necessary for a successful dominion over Egypt. A number of early documents attest to this. According to the Satrap stele, the future Ptolemy I made overtures to the priests with two important acts:[1] he repatriated images appropriated by the Persians, Egypt's archenemies, and he made benefactions to the temple of Uto (*Wadjyt*) in Buto. From the viewpoint of Ptolemy's royal ambitions, these acts were shrewd, because Uto was one of the "Two Ladies" (*Nebty*), the goddesses of Egypt's northern and southern halves, who were intimately connected with pharaonic kingship. Another early text, the Mendes stele, recounts how Ptolemy II convened a national synod of native priests for the inspection and enthronement of the sacred ram of Mendes.[2] These actions astutely played to native interests, given the persistent and fanatical interest in animal cults during the Late and Ptolemaic periods.

We likewise possess some texts that describe how the Ptolemies and native clergy interacted in the creation of royal images. A series of priestly decrees and related inscriptions—such as the Rosetta Stone's Memphis decree—are a rich source of information on many points:

- Setting and purpose: where images should be placed and how they should function and be attended.
- Physical characteristics: pose, material, scale, attributes, and manner of inscription.
- Ideology: what aspects of kingship should be conveyed.
- Design and creation: who is responsible for managing the creation of royal images and the reasons why they should be made.

The texts establish a framework in which Ptolemaic royal sculptures can be analyzed profitably, and help us to view them in a manner consonant with ancient perspectives.

THE DECREES AND RELATED TEXTS

Each priestly decree records the decisions of a national synod of native priests convened under royal auspices at a temple center such as Alexandria or Memphis. The texts are lengthy—the Greek version on the Rosetta Stone is fifty-four lines long—and they exist in copies from various temples, attesting to wide dissemination. They represent one type of information conveyed to priests and officials all over Egypt about the nature and purpose of royal images. The texts can be written in as many as three scripts, Egyptian hieroglyphic, Demotic, and Greek, and their introductions mention precise dates. Important events trigger the decrees, such as a coronation, a major victory in battle, a royal anniversary, or the deification of a royal family member.

Two texts from the reign of Ptolemy II provide information on the national synods, the Sais stele[3] and the previously mentioned Mendes stele. Both make note of synods in a list of royal activities. The texts also mention Ptolemy II's deified wife-sister Arsinoe II, with the Mendes stele noting how her cult images (*ꜥẖmw*[4]) should be set up next to divine ones in all temples as "temple-sharing gods" (*sunnaoi theoi*), meaning that the queen's images were entitled to honors and attendance equivalent to those of the gods.[5] The texts are important documents regarding the highly successful Egyptian royal cult established for Arsinoe II by Ptolemy II.

Later texts transcribe decrees that are the outcome of such national synods:[6] the Canopus (Ptolemy III), Raphia (Ptolemy IV), Memphis (Ptolemy V), and Philensis I and II (Ptolemy V) decrees (see Table 2.1).[7] They follow highly similar formats, with Canopus displaying the most variance: they begin with a date, royal titulature (except for Canopus), and a place and reason for the synod; a middle section explains why the specific Ptolemy merits his kingship; and a final section describes the honors accrued to the king, including the royal imagery set up in all temples. The Raphia, Memphis, and Philensis decrees (not the Canopus one) share nearly identical phrasing, as though sourced from a common template, and then they "fill in the blanks" and add wording to suit the decree's particular circumstances. Previous scholars have discerned three categories of royal likeness in the decrees; these are discussed in the next sections.

The Victorious King

The Raphia, Memphis, and Philensis decrees[8] describe one category of royal image that is placed in highly visible positions in the temple complex and depicts the king's all-important protective role over the country. Called "Ptolemy, protector of Egypt,"[9] this image is placed in a "conspicuous place in the temple" and made in "the Egyptian manner."[10] The decrees note that the king should be presented with a sword of victory (*ḫpš*) by a god, and perhaps be accompanied by the queen. As part of their duties, the priests need to attend to these images and perform appropriate rituals.[11]

Various words denote these images, *ẖntj* in the hieroglyphic, *twtw* in the Demotic, and *eikōn* in the Greek, all of which many scholars translate as "statue."[12] Nevertheless, the scene described—the king acting as the protector of Egypt and receiving the sword of victory—is not attested in Ptolemaic statuary, though it is known in relief examples.[13] A major one appears on the massive pylon of the Horus temple at Edfu, where a colossal figure of Ptolemy XII grasps a group of foes and prepares to smite them in front of Horus, who presents the sword of victory (Fig. 202). Thus, while these images are often called statues, they might have been reliefs.[14]

Other supportive evidence for the interpretation as reliefs can be cited. The Demotic version of the Raphia decree, immediately after describing the afore-

TABLE 2.1 PRIESTLY DECREES

Ruler	*Modern Name*	*Synod Location, Date*	*Reason for Synod*	*Royal Images Decreed*
Ptolemy III	Canopus decree	Canopus, 238 B.C.	Royal jubilee and deification of princess	Deified Princess Berenice
Ptolemy IV	Raphia decree	Memphis, 217 B.C.	Victory at Raphia	King and queen
Ptolemy V	Memphis decree	Memphis, 196 B.C.	Coronation of the king	King
Ptolemy V	Philensis II	Alexandria, 186 B.C.	Supression of rebellion	King and queen
Ptolemy V	Philensis I	Memphis, 185 B.C.	Enthroning of Apis bull	King and queen

mentioned image as *twtw,* uses the same word for a smiting scene to be placed on a stele, which must be in relief.[15] This text is even more explicit in its instructions for this image, which are followed fairly closely in the scene atop the Tell el-Maskhuta stele of the Raphia decree: a spear-wielding Ptolemy IV is mounted on a rearing horse and wears a double crown and Greek armor; behind him stands Queen Arsinoe, and before him, a kneeling, bound captive and Atum proffering the sword of victory.[16] Moreover, the decrees typically conclude by directing that copies of them should be set up near the king's image, and use *ẖntj* for the hieroglyphic text, *twtw* for the Demotic, and *eikōn* for the Greek;[17] placement of such decrees on a stele or wall near a temple pylon—and hence the king's relief image—fits what is known of ancient practice. The Dodekaschoinos stele of Ptolemy VI, which records the grant of tax revenues to the Isis temple of Philae, is set against the temple's second pylon under a relief image of Ptolemy XII (Fig. 204).[18] Finally, the Greek word used, *eikōn,* is best translated as "likeness" and could refer to either a two- or three-dimensional image.[19]

Thus, this first category of royal imagery may refer to highly visible temple reliefs. Even if it does not, however, the reliefs give tangible expression to the intent of the *ẖntj.* The "conspicuous place" cited in the decrees likely refers to a highly public part of a temple complex, most probably an area in front of the entrance through the enclosure wall or a court within the enclosure that was at least partly accessible to the public. Both the *ẖntj* and copies of the decree are to be placed here: *wsḫt mšʿw* (?) ("[in] the court of the people") in the hieroglyphic text, *n p3 m3ʿ nt wnḥ* ("in the public part") in the Demotic, and *en tōi epipha[nestatōi topōi]* ("in the most conspicuous place") in the Greek.[20] Evidence from the Isis temple at Philae strongly confirms the position of this prominent place. As one approaches the temple through a large, colonnaded court, one sees a smiting Ptolemy XII on the first pylon ahead (Fig. 203). Then, as one passes through this pylon into a court leading to the second pylon, one can see copies of the Philensis decrees inscribed on a wall to the left (the outer face of the wall of the birth house).[21] Both the king's image and the decrees are located in positions considered "conspicuous."

The Godlike Sovereign

A second category of royal images described in the decrees comprises cult statues kept in the innermost parts of temples and carried around in public processions during religious festivals.[22] The hieroglyphic and Demotic texts of the Memphis decree call them *sḫm,* whereas the Greek uses *xoanon,* which connotes a wooden, and hence portable, image.[23] In the Raphia decree, *sḫm* are taken from Egypt by its enemies, repatriated by Ptolemy IV, and subsequently carried in procession.[24] For a queen's statue with similar purpose, Philensis I and II's hieroglyphic texts use *sšmt,* while Philensis II's Demotic version says *sḫm.*[25]

The Canopus decree elaborately describes how the deceased princess Berenice is honored with *sḫm,* called "Berenice, mistress of maidens" in the hieroglyphic text.[26] This "image" is often rendered as *agalma* in the Greek,[27] meaning "glorious offering," which is appropriate because the first of these images is described as *m nbw* ("golden") and decorated with *ʿ3t* ("semiprecious stones").[28] Much verbiage is devoted to describing this statue's crown, which is specified as being "different from" (rendered in Greek as *diapherousan*[29]) the one on images of her mother, Queen Berenice, and a means to provide identification.

The Raphia, Memphis, and Philensis decrees focus on providing details about the shrine enclosing the king's *sḫm.* Temple relief images show priests bearing the rectangular shrine of the *sḫm* and its curved bark with horizontal poles on their shoulders; small royal and divine sculptures in attitudes of attendance decorate the bark.[30] The Memphis decree specifies how the shrine should be constructed with precious materials, and decorated with the double crown, uraeus, papyrus, and sedge plants.[31] These attributes, like those on the crown of Princess Berenice's *sḫm,* are meant to "distinguish" (*tn*) the royal naos from divine ones, and the decree further instructs that both types of naos should be carried together in procession on major festivals.[32] As with Arsinoe II's images in the Mendes stele, the king's *sḫm* is treated as a *sunnaos theos.*

Some archaeological finds most likely belong to the *sḫm* category, particularly the precious-metal statues found at Dendera (Figs. 185–186; E22). Such a group of divine images and instruments is described in the Raphia decree.[33] A bronze and gold bust of a king found in a horde at Tukh el-Karamus served as the finial for cultic equipment (A7).[34] In addition, Dendera reliefs catalogue a large corpus of cult statues, mostly of divinities, although some royal ones are included. Highly specific information about scale (generally less than life), material, attributes, appearance, and pose are communicated via a relief depiction of the statue and an accompanying hieroglyphic text;[35] these reliefs mirror the decrees' purposefulness in conveying details about physical appearance when describing sacred imagery.

The Shrine and the People

A third category of royal images described by the decrees is directed at the general public, called *wnnyw* ("people") in the hieroglyphic, *rmṯ.w* ("people") in the Demotic, and *idiōtai* ("private individuals") in the Greek.[36] The texts specify the means of facilitating the people's participation in relevant festivals, referring back to the shrine in the second category, but not mentioning an image. The hieroglyphic uses *mjtt k3r* ("the likeness of the shrine") and the Demotic *p3 smt (n) t3 g3(.t)* ("the likeness of the shrine"), whereas the Greek says *proeirēmenos naos* ("the aforementioned shrine").[37] Since the hieroglyphic text indicates that the shrine is *m pr.sn,* which is typically translated as "in their [i.e., the people's] homes," scholars consistently have interpreted this passage as referring to royal cult activity in domestic settings: "It will be possible for those who so wish to set up a likeness of this shrine . . . and to cause it to be in their homes."[38] The Demotic text, however, indicates that the shrine is at *n3y=w m3ᶜ.w,* possibly meaning "their [i.e., the people's] places,"[39] and the Greek *par' autois,* meaning "beside themselves [i.e., the people],"[40] and thus perhaps something other than home worship is indicated. Proof that the Demotic *m3ᶜ* does not necessarily translate as "home" is found earlier in the Memphis decree, where the word, in the phrase *p3 m3ᶜ nt wnḥ,* refers to "the conspicuous place" in a temple complex.[41]

An alternative interpretation is that the third category is not a separate one at all, but instead describes how the general public interacts with the enshrined *sḫm* images. This is a more convincing explanation for several reasons. The texts perhaps intend to say that they are referring to the same shrine because the Greek text specifies that the shrine is "previously mentioned." So, instead of worship in a home, the decrees could refer to how people will be able to interact with the sacred shrine at appointed places when it is brought out from the temple by the priests for major holidays. The lack of a specific mention of an image for the third category fits well with this interpretation, because we know from relief representations and a description of Herodotus that the image remained enclosed in its shrine during these processions.[42]

The hieroglyphic *m pr.sn* might then be interpreted as "in their [the people's] places," referring to locations where people could attend such a procession. Lanny Bell has proposed that the Ramses II court in the temple at Luxor was just such a place, because the lower parts of columns in the court (only the eastern part) are decorated with the bird hieroglyph for *rḫyt* ("common folk").[43] The bird has its limbs raised in adoration, as would those witnessing the ceremony. Thus, the priests bearing the *sḫm* shrine periodically would set it down, allowing for petitioning by the common people. An Egyptian alabaster altar of Amenhotep III imbedded in the Ptolemaic dromos at Hermopolis Magna is a possible example of such a resting place (Chapter 3).

Some Conclusions

The decrees describe two categories of royal likeness, highly visible smiting figures (*ḫntj*) and small-scale cult images (*sḫm*). Similar preoccupations are betrayed for both, in that the decrees catalogue the pose, material, scale, attributes, and name of the image as well as where it should be placed, how it should function, and how it should be attended. The *ḫntj*'s aggressive depiction of the king as a defender of Egypt and its highly public display indicate its importance to the positioning of Ptolemaic kingship. Such a protective role has a long tradition in Egypt, but it was also apt for a dynasty that fought many territorial wars abroad (Raphia decree) and dealt with repeated internal rebellion (Memphis and Philensis II decrees). In contrast, the *sḫm*'s ideological focus is on the king's divine nature: its golden shrine produced a radiant aura and was treated like those of the gods. This programmatic development of the king's public image is part of the decrees' stated purpose.[44]

The priestly decrees' vision for royal imagery is strikingly echoed in a Greek papyrus of the first century A.D., which records the emperor Claudius' agreement to have statuary (*andrias*) erected in his honor in Egypt.[45] There are some golden statues to be carried in processions, paralleling the idea of the *sḫm.* There are also three *quadriga* (four-horse-drawn chariot) images to be placed at Egypt's key entrance points—Taposiris, Pharos, and Pelusium—which, like the *ḫntj,* can be interpreted as "conspicuous" depictions of the triumphant emperor as the protector of Egypt.

The Karnak Decree

A decree found at Karnak describes yet another category of royal likeness, over-life-size stone statuary.[46] This fragmentary text may date from the time of Ptolemy V or VIII and is preserved only in its Greek version. Its wording implies that the decree was issued by the Theban priesthood rather than by a national synod.[47] Most of the initial portions are lost, but the remaining words do not contain the same formulaic language regarding royal images as is found in the national decrees. The final portions, which are better preserved, describe religious rituals and royal benefactions, and conclude by saying that a stele describing the king's deeds should be set up "in a conspicuous place on the dromos of Amun" (*en tōi epiphanestatōi tiopōi* [sic] *epi tou dromou tou Ammonōs*), and that "images" (restored as *eikonas* from the remaining *nas*) of the king and queen, "five cubits high" (*pentapēcheis*) and "in black stone" (*ek tou melanos lithou*), should be set up there as well.

This measurement of five cubits would result in an over-life-size statue between two and three meters tall, a height similar to some statuary in the catalogue. In particular, the king set up at the end of a temple dromos at Tebtunis (E3) seems to be the type of statue to which the decree refers, although this example is in limestone. The fragmentary limestone Cleopatra II from Karnak (B14), found in front of the temple's first pylon, is of similar scale,[48] as are the granite statues of Ptolemy II and Arsinoe II in the Vatican (A3, A4).

Implications of the Decrees

The priestly decrees can be used to define the key elements that constituted the conception of Egyptian-style royal portraits in Ptolemaic Egypt. In addition to stipulating setting and purpose (such as the protective *ẖntj*), physical characteristics (the height and material of the royal statues in the Karnak decree), and ideology (the divine nature of the *sẖm*), the decrees provide information on the design and creation process, in terms of who is responsible for it and the reasons why images should be made.

For the national and Karnak decrees, the priests—acting under royal auspices—initiate the creation process. As noted in the Memphis decree, *ʿq.s m jb n wʿbw . . . sʿḥʿ ẖntj* ("It entered the heart of the priests . . . to set up an image").[49] Use of the word "heart" implies a conceptualization process based on the intellect and a remembrance of tradition, because Egyptians regarded the heart much as the brain is understood today: as the seat of wisdom and memory.[50] Another text, a Demotic inscription on a bronze tablet from Dendera that lists the accomplishments of its dedicator-priest, is particularly descriptive of the role outlined in the decrees: the priest is *sẖ wt* (?) ("scribe of the decrees"), and among his accomplishments, he lists how he constructs a "naos . . . according to the instructions" (*g3 . . . r ẖt t3 sb3jt*) and gilds an "image" (*sšm*) of Isis, which is described as "hidden" (*ḥp*).[51]

For the Mendes and Pithom steles of Ptolemy II, the king is portrayed as ordering or setting up images, though priests or local officials must have carried out his directives: *wḏ.n ḥm.f* ("His majesty ordered . . .") in Mendes and *sʿḥʿ.f* ("He [i.e., the king] had set up . . .") in Pithom.[52] Indeed, Senoucheri, a high official at Koptos in the third century B.C., considered the setting up of royal images (*mnw*) as one of his duties.[53] The Famine stele, perhaps dating to the reign of Ptolemy V, mentions various steps in the creation of imagery, from quarrying stones and obtaining precious metals to sculpting and smithing, giving priests a controlling role, and also describing the involvement of a gamut of officials, administrators, and laborers.[54] Thus, the creation of the king's images was overseen by the sovereign, the clergy, and high officials.

REASONS FOR CREATING IMAGERY

The decrees and related inscriptions establish reasons for the creation of royal imagery. In general, such actions are tied to the proper performance of the duties of pharaonic office and to a significant point during a reign: the deification of a member of the royal family (Mendes stele and Canopus decree), a coronation (Memphis decree), a royal anniversary (Canopus decree), or the defeat of enemies, both foreigners and native rebels (Raphia and Philensis II decrees). Particular benefactions to a temple can also result in statuary (Karnak decree).

A few other reasons can be pinpointed. When a new temple was built, or an old one refurbished, it needed to be outfitted with the king's image. This may be what the Pithom stele describes: *qd.tw ḥwt-nṯr n mrt-sn.f sʿḥʿ.f nṯrw-snw jm*; "A temple was built for (Arsinoe) Philadelphos. He had (images of) the brother-sister gods set up there."[55] Celebration of a *sed*-festival, the traditional Egyptian rite of renewal for a long-reigning king, is another potential reason that has pre-Ptolemaic precedent.[56] The festival's persistence is attested by a Ptolemy II gateway with reliefs illustrating his jubilee,[57] and Ptolemy IX had such a celebration in Memphis during his second rule.[58] Statues memorialized the king and his deeds, provided a vehicle for his cult, and thanked him for gifts.

WORKSHOP LOCATIONS

Ptolemaic sculptors likely worked at both quarries and major temple centers, continuing established Egyptian practice.[59] Some portion of the effort, from the initial rough hewing of a statue to its final polishing, was accomplished at either location, though the relative division of labor is uncertain. The sculptor Psenamunis traveled to the Wadi Hammamat quarries during the reign of Ptolemy II to make an "image" (*twt*) of the pharaoh and an "image" (*rpj*) of Arsinoe,[60] according to a Demotic graffito at the site. Two Ptolemaic structures within the great temple enclosure at Tanis (Appendix A) may have been sculptors' studios because they contained incomplete or grid-marked items as well as tools and materials. Hieroglyphic texts in the Hathor temple at Dendera attest to the presence of a gold- and silversmithing studio that made cult statues.[61]

Ptolemaic royal sculptures reveal similar practices. Quality can vary greatly at a single provenance, though the most outstanding works are concentrated at major temples. The important religious centers of Canopus and Tanis and their surrounding areas have high-end (A34, A35) and low-end (A9, E20) works, whereas Zawiet el-Amwat and Wannina have only medium- to low-quality ones (A41, D21). Fig. 198 depicts the distribution of finds in limestone and granite, the two most frequently used stones (Chapter 4). Results are summarized in Table 2.2. For the limestone sculptures, these observations suggest the existence of multiple workshops throughout the country, associated with major and minor temple centers, with highly variable levels of technical ability, as supported by the fact that limestone was widely available in quarries all over Egypt.[62] The more specialized use of granite, particularly for high-quality works at major temple centers in Lower Egypt, points to a more elite group of ateliers. The division of labor between the granite quarries in Upper Egypt[63] and the temple centers is uncertain. For the highest-quality, hellenized sculptures, however, the hair and facial features may have been executed close to the sculptures' final destinations in Alexandria and Canopus, given their close adherence to Greek-style sculptures that were prevalent in those areas.

CONCLUSIONS

The priestly decrees and related inscriptions provide the basic tools with which Ptolemaic royal sculpture can be examined and understood. The texts outline how pose, material, scale, and placement are used to support time-honored ideological programs. A conspicuous representation of the smiting king receiving the sword of victory demonstrates his all-important role of protecting Egypt, while a hidden image of the godlike ruler embodies his or her ability to act as an intermediary between the divine and human realms. Attributes are particularly highlighted as a means to provide potency, as well as to set apart one sovereign's image from another's or the gods'. According to the Memphis decree, the double crown and other regalia distinguish the royal naos from divine ones. The decrees also set a national agenda for royal imagery, in that they are formulated by a geographically diverse synod and their resulting instructions are broadly disseminated. Sculptures are created to commemorate the Ptolemaic dynasty's rightful dominion, august stature, and specific benefaction.

A closer look at the vocabulary of the national decrees—the Canopus, Raphia, Memphis, and Philensis decrees—provided new ideas about the images they enumerate. A review of the *ẖntj* of the victorious king questioned whether it might be a relief instead of a statue, as it is generally interpreted. Did Egyptians perceive differences between two- and three-dimensional sculpture the way that we do? Discussion of the *sḫm* proposed that the relevant passages do not describe home worship, but instead outline how the general

TABLE 2.2 COMPARISON OF LIMESTONE AND GRANITE STATUES

	Limestone Statues	*Granite Statues*
Geographical spread	Broadly across the country	Concentrated in Lower Egypt
Importance of temple	Highly varied	Focus on major centers
Quality of sculptures	Tend to be low to medium	Tend to be medium to high
Sculptural style	Highly varied	Many with Greek hair

public can interact with the shrines enclosing portable royal images when they emerge from temples during periodic festivals. Succeeding chapters will take a closer look at different aspects of royal representation, using the information gained from the priestly decrees.

NOTES

1. Cairo CG 22182 (JE 22263), granite, from Cairo, but perhaps originally from Sais, H: 185 cm; Robert S. Bianchi, "Satrapenstele," *LÄ* 5, cols. 492–493; and Hölbl 2001, 80, 83, fig. 3.2. Repatriation of sacred images: Winnicki 1994; and Hölbl 2001, 81.

2. Cairo CG 22181 (JE 37089), quartzite, from Tmai el-Amdid, H: 147 cm; De Meulenaere and Mackay 1976, 173–177, 205–206, cat. no. 111, pl. 1a; Quaegebeur 1998, 74, 83, 87, cat. no. 7; Thiers 2000, cols. 90–91; and Hölbl 2001, 84, 101, fig. 3.3.

3. Paris, Louvre C 123 (with Naples, Museo Nazionale 1034 and a fragment known from the Codex Ursinianus), dark stone; Thiers 1999.

4. Sethe 1904, 41.16; *Wb:* 1, 225–226; and Wilson 1997, 178.

5. Arsinoe II deification: Quaegebeur 1971; D. J. Thompson 1988, 126–133; and Hölbl 2001, 101–104. *Sunnaos theos:* Nock 1930; and Schmidt-Dounas 1994.

6. Discussion of decrees: Daumas 1952; Huss 1991; Lanciers 1991; C. Johnson 1995; Simpson 1996, 1–24; Clarysse 2000; Minas 2000, passim; and Hölbl 2001, passim.

7. Canopus: A. Bernand 1970b, 989–1036; Onasch 1976; Dunand 1980; Heinz-Josef Thissen, "Kanopusdekret," *LÄ* 3, col. 321; A. Bernand 1992a, 22–35; A. Bernand 1992b, 30–36, nos. 8–10; and Simpson 1996, 2–3, 224–241. Raphia: Gauthier and Sottas 1925; Thissen 1966; A. Bernand 1992a, 36–43; A. Bernand 1992b, 37–44, nos. 12–14; and Simpson 1996, 3–4, 242–257. Memphis: Quirke and Andrews 1989; A. Bernand 1992a, 44–56; A. Bernand 1992b, 46–56, nos. 16–18; and Simpson 1996, 4–5, 258–271. Philensis: W. Müller 1920; Erich Winter, "Philensis-Dekrete," *LÄ* 4, cols. 1027–1028; and Simpson 1996, 5–6.

8. Unless otherwise noted, line numbers for the Canopus decree refer to the Tanis stele (Sethe 1904 for the hieroglyphic, Simpson 1996 for the Demotic, and A. Bernand 1992a, no. 9, for the Greek), for the Raphia decree to the Tell el-Maskhuta stele (Simpson 1996 for the Demotic and A. Bernand 1992a, no. 14, for the Greek), for the Memphis decree to the Rosetta Stone (Quirke and Andrews 1989 for the hieroglyphic, Simpson 1996 for the Demotic, and A. Bernand 1992a, no. 16, for the Greek), and for the Philensis decrees to the Philae verions (W. Müller 1920 for the hieroglyphic and Demotic). Translations are taken from the sources noted.

9. Memphis decree: *(Ptwlmjs) nḏ B3qt* in the hieroglyphic (line 6; Quirke and Andrews 1989, 13, 20), *(Ptlwmy3s) nḏ Bqy* in the Demotic (line 23; Simpson 1996, 266–267), and *Ptolemaiou tou epamunantos tēi Aiguptōi* in the Greek (line 39; A. Bernand 1992a, 46–47).

10. This appears as *k3t msntyw nw Bqt* in the hieroglyphic (line 14 of Philensis II; W. Müller 1920, 80), *jpy.t n rmṯ (n) Kmy* in the Demotic (line 33 of Raphia [Simpson 1996, 252–253], and similarly in line 23 of Memphis [Simpson 1996, 266–267] and line 11 of Philensis II [W. Müller 1920, 80]), and *kateskeuasmen[a ton tōn Aiguptiōn]* in the Greek (line 39 of Memphis; A. Bernand 1992a, 46–48).

11. Lanciers 1991, 135–136.

12. *Ḫntj:* line 6 of Memphis (Quirke and Andrews 1989, 13); lines 9 (mostly restored) and 10 of Philensis I (W. Müller 1920, 40–41), and perhaps line 14 of Philensis II (W. Müller 1920, 81). *Twtw:* lines 32 and 34 of Raphia (Simpson 1996, 252, 254); line 22 of Memphis (Simpson 1996, 266); and line 11 of Philensis II (W. Müller 1920, 80). *Eikōn:* line 38 of Memphis (A. Bernand 1992a, 47). Translation as "statue": Quaegebeur 1989, 102–103; Quirke and Andrews 1989, 20; Lanciers 1991, 135–136; and Simpson 1996. See Daumas 1952, 175–176. Ockinga (1984, 126) believes that *twt* is a generic term for image, while *ḫntj* is an image more specifically defined by its function. For *twt,* CDD provides "statue, image."

13. Ptolemaic examples: Hall 1986, 43–44. Some earlier statues show the king grasping a prisoner in his left hand, but these are rare and do not match the full scene of the decrees. An example is Cairo JE 37175 (= CG 42152), a granite statue of Ramses VI, from the Karnak cachette, H: 104 cm; Saleh and Sourouzian 1987, cat. no. 227. Other examples: Hall 1986, 40–41.

14. A. Bernand (1970b, 1027) makes a similar distinction, quoting earlier sources. I wish to acknowledge Dr. David O'Connor for stimulating discussions on the meaning of the priestly decrees. Cultic significance of temple reliefs: Traunecker 1991.

15. Lines 35–36 (Simpson 1996, 254). Line 17 of Raphia (Simpson 1996, 246) also uses *twtw* for royal images created to recognize the king's proper performance of his duties. Philensis II draws a similar parallel to an image on a stele, although its vocabulary is less consistent: *sšm* in line 15 of the hieroglyphic version and *twtw* in line 12 of the Demotic (both W. Müller 1920, 82).

16. Cairo CG 50048 = 47806; Gauthier and Sottas 1925, 8–19, pls. 1–2. The presence of the queen in such scenes is unusual, though there are New Kingdom precedents (Hall 1986, figs. 40, 41), and a protective goddess can sometimes appear (Hall 1986, figs. 34, 66).

17. *Ḫntj:* line 14 of Memphis (Quirke and Andrews 1989, 14) and line 17 of Philensis I (W. Müller 1920, 55). *Twtw:* line 32 of Memphis (Simpson 1996, 270) and line 16 of Philensis I

(W. Müller 1920, 56). *Eikōn:* line 19 of the Elephantine version of Memphis (A. Bernand 1992a, 57).

18. Hölbl 2001, 189, 258–260, figs. 9.1D, 9.2.

19. Smith 1988, 16. When the Greek historian Diodorus Siculus describes colossal statues in Egyptian temples, he uses *andrias* (1.47.3, 1.48.5). He may sometimes use *eikōn* to refer to statues (1.47.5, 1.57.5, 1.58.4), but for others, relief is clearly meant. While detailing a scene *toichōn eggegluphthai* ("carved on a wall"), he refers to an *eikōn* (1.48.6); elsewhere, he writes about depictions of the king offering to one god after another (1.49.3) and the king armed with bow, arrows, and spear (1.55.9), both of which would more likely have referred to Egyptian reliefs rather than to statues.

20. Line 14 of Philensis II (W. Müller 1920, 79) for the hieroglyphic text; line 33 of the Raphia decree (Simpson 1996, 252), line 23 of Memphis (Simpson 1996, 266), and line 11 of Philensis II (W. Müller 1920, 79) for the Demotic; and line 38 of Memphis (A. Bernand 1992a, 47) for the Greek. See Lanciers 1991, 136. The same phrase is used in Greek decrees stipulating the erection of statues of Hellenistic rulers; Smith 1988, 17.

21. Hölbl 2001, 258, fig. 9.1F, shows the Philensis decrees on a Philae plan.

22. Wolfgang Helck, "Kultstatue," *LÄ* 3, cols. 859–863; Rainer Stadelmann, "Prozessionen," *LÄ* 4, cols. 1160–1164 and "Stationsheiligtum," *LÄ* 5, cols. 1258–1260; and Karlshausen 1998.

23. *Sḫm:* line 7 in the hieroglyphic text (Quirke and Andrews 1989, 13) and line 24 in the Demotic (Simpson 1996, 266, Elephantine version); Lanciers 1991, 137; and Wilson 1997, 903–904. *Xoanon:* line 41 (A. Bernand 1992a, 49). Strabo (17.1.28) uses the same Greek word to refer to an Egyptian cult image of a sacred animal. Discussion of *xoanon:* Donohue 1988; and Smith 1988, 16 n. 10. For the Demotic *sḫm*, CDD provides "divine power, divine image."

24. Lines 6 and 14 of the Kom el-Qala'a fragment (Simpson 1996, 248, 250).

25. *Sšmt:* lines 10 and 16 (W. Müller 1920, 42, 86). *Sḫm:* line 13 (W. Müller 1920, 86).

26. In a series of references to images of the princess, *sḫm* appears in both the hieroglyphic (Sethe 1904, 147.5, 148.6, 151.4) and the Demotic (Simpson 1996, 236 [line 58], 238 [line 61], 240 [line 69]); *rpyt* appears alternatively as well in the hieroglyphic (Sethe 1904, 148.7, 149.10) and the Demotic (Simpson 1996, 238 [lines 62, 65]). For the naming as "Berenice, mistress of maidens," see Sethe 1904, 148.4, 149.11.

27. In addition to *agalma* (A. Bernand 1992a, 33 [lines 59, 65, 68]), *eikōn* appears (A. Bernand 1992a, 33 [lines 61, 62]) in a series of references to royal images. Raphia renders the Demotic *sḫm.w* (Simpson 1996, 250 [line 14 of the Kom el-Qala'a fragment]) as *agalma* (A. Bernand 1992a, 39 [line 12]).

28. Sethe 1904, 147.5–6.

29. Line 61 (A. Bernand 1992a, 33).

30. Example: Karlshausen 1998, 869, fig. 1.

31. Lines 8–10 in the hieroglyphic (Quirke and Andrews 1989, 13–14), supplemented by the better-preserved lines 24–27 in the Demotic (Simpson 1996, 268).

32. Line 8 of the hieroglyphic (Quirke and Andrews 1989, 13); *ṯn:* Wilson 1997, 1165–1166.

33. Lines 28–29 in the Demotic (Simpson 1996, 250, 252).

34. Pfrommer (1987, 147) suggests "Räucherarm."

35. Cauville 1987, 109: "Autour d'une moyenne majoritaire d'une coudée (52,5 cm), les statues anthropomorphes vont de 22,5 cm à 2,10 m." See also Quaegebeur 1989, 101. Waitkus 1997, 233–234 gathers examples from other temples.

36. *Wnnyw:* line 13 of Memphis (Quirke and Andrews 1989, 14). *Rmṯ.w:* line 31 of Memphis (Simpson 1996, 270) and line 15 of Philensis I (W. Müller 1920, 54). Raphia uses *rm[ṯ];* line 27 of the Kom el-Qala'a fragment (Simpson 1996, 256). *Idiōtai:* line 52 of Memphis (A. Bernand 1992a, 49).

37. Hieroglyphic: line 13 of Memphis (Quirke and Andrews 1989, 14) and line 16 of Philensis I (W. Müller 1920, 54). Demotic: line 31 of Memphis (Simpson 1996, 270) and line 16 of Philensis I (W. Müller 1920, 54). Greek: line 52 of Memphis (A. Bernand 1992a, 49).

38. Line 13 of Memphis (Quirke and Andrews 1989, 22); and line 16 of Philensis I (W. Müller 1920, 54).

39. Line 31 of Memphis (Simpson 1996, 270); and line 16 of Philensis I (W. Müller 1920, 54). Daumas (1952, 197) notes that the Demotic *m3ʿ* may have become the Coptic *ma* (Vycichl 1983, 103: "lieu, place"), which is variously modified to indicate different places. For *m3ʿ*, Erichsen (1954, 149) provides "Ort, Platz," and CDD translates "place."

40. Line 52 (A. Bernand 1992a, 49, translating as "chez eux").

41. Line 23, translated by Quirke and Andrews (1989, 15, 20) as "the (most) conspicuous place" and by Simpson (1996, 266–267) as "the public part."

42. Herodotus 2.63, using *agalma* for "image" and *naos* for "shrine." A prime example of a relief representation is inscribed for Philip Arrhidaios in the Amun temple at Karnak (PM 2^2 [1972], 99–102).

43. Bell 1997, 163–172.

44. For example, lines 31–32 of the Demotic of the Memphis decree (Simpson 1996, 270–271).

45. Rose 1997, 185–188.

46. Wagner 1971, 1–21, pls. 1–2. Commentary: Lanciers 1991, 136–137; and Criscuolo 1995, 23–24 n. 20.

47. Huss 1991, 200 n. 71.

48. I am grateful to Christophe Thiers for information on this statue.

49. Lines 5–6 of Memphis (Quirke and Andrews 1989, 13, 20).

50. Andrews 1994, 72–73.

51. London, British Museum EA 57371; Shore (1979) dates the tablet to the end of the Ptolemaic/early Roman Period

based on the "occasional regnal date and from general circumstantial evidence" of the objects with which the tablet was purportedly found.

52. Sethe 1904, 41.11 for Mendes and 100.8 for Pithom (Cairo CG 22183, a granite, hieroglyph-inscribed stele from Pithom, H: 128 cm; Quaegebeur 1998, 87–88, cat. no. 8). Wilson (1997, 281) defines *wḏ* as "a wish uttered by the king which became inviolable and had to be acted on by those below him."

53. Cairo CG 70031, dark stone slab, H: 107 cm; Petrie 1896, 19–21, pl. 20; Traunecker 1992, 312–315; and Quaegebeur 1998, 105, cat. no. 83. *Mnw:* Petrie 1896, 20, pl. 20, col. 1; *Wb:* 2, 71; and Wilson 1997, 426.

54. Hieroglyphic inscription on the face of granite rock on Sehel Island near Aswan; Barguet 1953; Goedicke 1994; and Hölbl 2001, 167–168.

55. Sethe 1904, 100.7–8; Lanciers 1991, 118 n. 7.

56. Amenhotep III: Kozloff and Bryan 1992, 195–196.

57. Sambin and Carlotti 1995; and Quaegebeur 1998, 92, cat. no. 31.

58. D. J. Thompson 1994a, 317; and Hölbl 2001, 212.

59. Eaton-Krauss 2001, 138–139.

60. Thissen 1979, 83–84, no. 35; *CE* 1988, 41, 47, 63; Lanciers 1991, 118 n. 7; and Quaegebeur 1998, 95, cat. no. 45.

61. Cauville 1987, 110–111.

62. Lucas 1989, 52; and Nicholson and Shaw 2000, 8–9, 12–14, fig. 2.1.

63. Granite quarries: Lucas 1989, 58–59; and Nicholson and Shaw 2000, 8–9, 12, fig. 2.1. Locations of workshops: Kozloff and Bryan 1992, 136–138; and Eaton-Krauss 2001, 139. Peter Dorman (*AJA* 98 [1994], 361) questions Kozloff and Bryan's thesis that statues were largely completed at quarries.

CHAPTER 3

"CONSPICUOUS" AND OTHER PLACES

THE DISCOVERY OF THE ROYAL COLOSSI NEAR THE SITE of the Pharos lighthouse (C21) in 1994–1995 was a watershed in the history of Ptolemaic royal sculpture. The finds were surprising in their massive scale and quantity, their appearance near Pharos, and their Egyptian style. Up until that time, well-documented discoveries of such statues were few, especially in Alexandria. The colossi started a debate about whether the Ptolemies would have sponsored such statuary in the city, or whether they were brought at a later date, perhaps the Roman Period. Was Ptolemaic Alexandria not as purely Greek as some had thought? What might have been the setting and role of such huge Egyptian statues in the capital? Were similar works erected in other parts of Egypt? Besides the "conspicuous" places cited by the decrees in the last chapter, where else were statues placed, and why?

To explore these questions, this chapter gathers evidence on several fronts. On the archaeological side, there are a few excavations and surveys, not only in the Alexandria area, but also at Medinet Madi and Tebtunis, where a number of sculptures were found in situ.[1] In addition, ancient authors, decrees, and biographical inscriptions can provide much information. The *Geographia* of Strabo, a Greek historian and geographer who lived and traveled in Egypt, is a rich source regarding Egypt during the late first century B.C.[2] Moreover, the sculptures themselves, by virtue of their pose, material, scale, attributes, and manner of inscription, can be revealing about their original placement and function.

The discussion begins with Alexandria, nearby Canopus, and the "second city" of Memphis. It then proceeds geographically north to south, from the Delta to Upper Egypt. Provenanced works are summarized in the map on Fig. 197, with dealer-provenanced objects excluded unless confirmed by other evidence. Numerous Egyptian-style sculptors' studies/votives (Appendix A) come from many sites to be discussed, as well as others; only catalogued examples are cited on the map.[3]

ALEXANDRIA "BY EGYPT"

Ancient authors portray Alexandria in its Ptolemaic heyday as an ostentatious city and a major economic, cultural, and political force in the Hellenistic world. It was intrinsically Greek, filled with Greek buildings, temples, and sculptures, despite its location in Egypt. This idea is embodied in the city's ancient naming as *Alexandria ad Aegyptum,* that is, Alexandria "by" or "toward" Egypt,[4] implying proximity to Egypt, not integration with it.

Several key characteristics of Alexandria are relevant for our discussion. Because of the dearth of archaeological information on the ancient city, these are mostly known from textual sources. First and foremost, Alexandria had innumerable temples, which is important information because Egyptian royal sculptures traditionally had religious settings. Both Diodorus and Strabo remark on this profusion, and a fourth-century A.D.(?) text lists over 2,000 temples and shrines.[5] Some of the Ptolemaic ones were related to the royal cults, portraying the rulers as *sunnaoi theoi:* a temple of Serapis, Isis, Ptolemy IV, and Arsinoe III is known from a gold foundation plaque; and a temple of Isis and Ptolemies II–V and their wives is noted in Ptolemy V's Philensis II decree.[6] Strabo indicates that royal edifices, including the palace and tombs, occupied much of the city, providing ample opportunity for royal display.[7]

Alexandria emphasized grandiosity in scale and appearance, as well as richness and exoticism. Diodorus speaks of the city's monumental architecture, and Julius Caesar mentions "lofty towers."[8] Alexandria had wide boulevards, colossal statuary, and the huge Pharos lighthouse, estimated to have been about 100 meters high.[9] The Greek writer Athenaeus transcribes an account of a lavish Dionysian procession in the city during the time of Ptolemy II. The parade included sumptuously costumed marchers, images of the god Dionysos, large-scale paraphernalia (such as statuary, a lance, a winepress, and a phallus), exotic animals (such as peacocks, a giraffe, and a rhinoceros), and many silver and gold objects, including divine and royal statuary (*agalma*).[10]

Ancient authors mention a few Egyptian-style objects in Alexandria and note the presence of a native population, which presumably included priest-advisors to the crown.[11] The Latin writer Pliny relates that Ptolemy II went to great lengths to transport an obelisk—hewn for a Dynasty 30 Nectanebo—to Alexandria to decorate the Arsinoeum dedicated to his wife and sister. Pseudo-Callisthenes records the presence of hieroglyph-inscribed obelisks at the Serapeum, though it is uncertain whether they were erected in the Ptolemaic Period. Moreover, two obelisks of Thutmosis III of Dynasty 18 decorated the emperor Augustus' Caesareum in Alexandria, perhaps representing a continuance of a tradition of obelisks in the city.[12] Athenaeus describes a riverboat of Ptolemy IV having both Greek and Egyptian architectural elements.[13] The Potter's Oracle, a Greek text referring to events of the second century B.C., prophesizes that Egyptian cult images (partially restored as *agalma*) transferred to Alexandria will return to Egypt after the city's downfall.[14] The text, which is preserved on several fragmentary Roman papyri, is based on an original likely composed by native priests. The city's collective royal tomb had a pyramidal superstructure.[15]

Characteristics of Sculptural Finds

Alexandria is the provenance for a major group of Egyptian-style portraits of the Ptolemies, including several associated with two of the city's most visible landmarks, the Serapeum (A33) and the Pharos lighthouse (C21). All sculptures are high in quality and large in scale, and they are the most concentrated find of such monumental, highly public works in Egypt. Almost all are made of granite, and many have Greek hair.

To examine setting and function, we will look at the archaeological evidence, and then at two thorny issues regarding Egyptian-style statues in Hellenistic Alexandria. First, there is the large presence of pre-Ptolemaic *aegyptiaca* (Egyptian statues, building components, and other objects) in the city, which many argue were brought by the Romans. Second, there is the question of setting: If Egyptian statues occupied Ptolemaic Alexandria, were their immediate surroundings primarily Greek or Egyptian in style?

Alexandria Serapeum Sphinxes

A closely matched pair of pink granite sphinxes was excavated near the Alexandria Serapeum at the turn of the last century (A33). These finely executed and colossal images may have belonged to the temple dromos, along with other pre-Ptolemaic sphinxes found in the area,[16] or they could have protectively fronted a gateway. Their original placement is not certain, given the great number of new constructions at the site from the Ptolemaic through Roman Periods, and the temple's eventual destruction. The site's decimation over time was such that when Alan Rowe explored it in the early 1940s, he relied mostly on foundation deposits and traces cut in the bedrock to suggest the original plan of Ptolemy III's Serapeum and Ptolemy IV's temple of Harpocrates.[17] Fragments of widely varying dates were found at the site, including pre-Ptolemaic, Egyptian-style royal sculptures and Greek-style marbles.[18]

There is little evidence regarding the architectural style of Ptolemy III's Serapeum. Traditional speculation has focused on a Greek-style reconstruction, possibly with some Egyptian elements.[19] Jean Yoyotte has proposed, however, that this early construction was more intrinsically Egyptian than generally thought. He cites the native priestly involvement implied by the temple's bilingual Greek/hieroglyphic foundation plaques, and the temple's hypothetical layout, which he argues is comparable to Egyptian layouts.[20] Two fragmentary, Egyptian-style naophorous statues found at the site are inscribed for Psenptais I, a high priest of Ptah at Memphis under the Ptolemies and one of the most important native religious professionals of his day.[21] Psenptais I likely would have periodically traveled to Alexandria to advise the crown, in addition to planning and managing royal activities in Memphis. A naophorous statue of Petobastis I, another high priest of Ptah, was also found near the Serapeum.[22]

Discussions in Chapter 7 will use portrait and stylistic analysis to argue that the sphinxes date to the third century, corresponding to the time of the original Serapeum. Though the site's decimation argues for caution, its Egyptian elements, particularly the statues of priests who would have advised the king on his Egyptian-style images, could mean that the sphinxes were originally erected there. They would reflect early Ptolemaic efforts to build relations with the native clergy, paralleling documents such as the Satrap stele, the Mendes stele, and the Canopus decree (Chapter 2). The Alexandria Serapeum itself elevated Serapis, who was partly derived from Egyptian sources.[23] The sphinxes, as Egyptian elements in a Greek setting, would form a counterpart to the Saqqara Serapeum, which incorporated Greek works into a predominantly Egyptian context (see below).

Pharos Colossi

A series of colossal royal statues was recently rescued by Jean-Yves Empereur's team from the Alexandrian harbor near the site of the Pharos lighthouse (C21).[24] There are portions of several Egyptian-style statues in granite, one removed from the harbor after its discovery in the early 1960s (C27), and the rest recovered by Empereur: a king with *nemes* and Greek forehead hair (C22), a queen with a Hathor headdress, corkscrew locks, and draped costume (C27), a female torso in a draped garment (C25), two royal male heads (C23, C24), and a hips/thighs fragment (C26). Additional fragments remain underwater and continue to be recovered. The large, nearly cubic bases have Greek-style molding and are separately worked.[25]

The underwater explorations have catalogued granite architectural elements: pre-Ptolemaic Egyptian elements (papyrus columns inscribed for Ramses II of Dynasty 19), Greek or Roman elements (Corinthian capitals), and a large number of blocks, which Empereur believes may have belonged to the Pharos itself.[26] He found many pre-Ptolemaic sphinxes (Middle Kingdom to Dynasty 26) and three fragmentary obelisks of Seti I of Dynasty 19.

Other than the lighthouse, there are bits of information about what was built on Pharos island. Julius Caesar mentions that *in hac sunt insula domicilia Aegyptiorum et vicus oppidi magnitudine* ("on this island there are houses of Egyptians and a settlement the size of a town").[27] Portions of the rock-cut Ras el-Tin and Anfushy tombs on Pharos contained both mummified bodies and Egyptian-influenced decoration. There is little objective evidence on which to date the tombs, though scholarly opinion has focused on the second and first centuries B.C.[28] There may have been an Isis Pharia temple on the island.[29]

In terms of statuary on Pharos, several Greek images, possibly of colossal scale, are attested in glyptic and other representations: a statue of Zeus (?) atop the lighthouse, and near it, statues of Poseidon with a trident and Isis holding a billowing sail in front of her.[30] As noted in Chapter 2, a Greek text records that the emperor Claudius agreed to be honored by three *quadriga* statues, including one on Pharos.[31]

As large-scale royal images, the Pharos colossi conceptually correspond to these divine and imperial statues. The colossi could be envisioned as representing *sunnaoi theoi* for an island temple, in much the same way that we have inscriptional evidence for Ptolemies sharing temples of Isis and Serapis in the city. Similar statues stood before temples with royal cult activity in pre-Ptolemaic times. A major example is the rock-cut sanctuary of Ramses II at Abu Simbel, which is fronted by four colossal seated statues of the king.[32] The Pharos statues could also have a notable Greek parallel: Hellenistic rulers commissioned displays of *progonoi* ("ancestors"), consisting of statues of dynastic couples who were important forebears of the king and a means to promote legitimacy and power.[33]

Related Finds

Two other finds from Alexandria point to a connection between royal cults in the city and Egyptian sculptures. The first is a fragment of an over-life-size group (A10), which was found on land to the south of the underwater find spots of the Pharos colossi. The seated group, likely Amun flanked by Ptolemy II and Arsinoe II, is the only certain Ptolemaic example of this traditional type.[34] Its hieroglyphic inscription mentions royal cult activities, particularly images (*sḫmw*) of Arsinoe to be used in processions honoring her, and says that Amun has given her divine status.[35] The group can be associated with the highly successful native cult established by Ptolemy II for Arsinoe II (Chapter 2).

The second related find is a colossal granite head of a king from the eastern harbor (G1). Zsolt Kiss has ascribed the sculpture to Augustus because of the forehead lock arrangement.[36] The find spot is near the Caesareum, a temple completed under Augustus and dedicated to his imperial cult,[37] whose precinct possessed two obelisks, as noted above. In addition, the Greek-Jewish philosopher Philo describes a large complex—with "porticos, libraries, chambers, groves, gateways, and wide open courts" and "a girdle of pictures (*graphai*) and statues (*andriantes*) in silver and gold."[38] The Egyptian-style colossus may have been erected in a "conspicuous" place near the Caesareum in connection with the establishment of Augustus' imperial cult. Its reconstructed height of about 5 meters[39] is almost double that of the 2.8-meter-high Karnak Augustus (G2).

Hadra Colossi

In Alexandria's eastern suburb of Hadra, a colossal granite male/female dyad (E1, E2) was discovered near the ruins of a sizable, poorly documented structure, traditionally identified as the Telesterion of Demeter and Persephone mentioned by the Greek historian Polybius.[40] A nineteenth-century account notes, "Granite blocks, and the remains of columns at this spot, show it to have been the site of a building of some consequence."[41] Hadra has some of the city's oldest tombs, including the "Alabaster Tomb," a lavishly constructed edifice.[42] The royal male figure has a *nemes* with Greek hair, plus attributes linking him with Osiris—the *hm-hm*-crown and the *heqa*-scepter—a combination unknown in other colossal Ptolemaic royal statues.[43] The accompanying female has wholly Egyptian attributes: a tripartite wig and vulture cap, surmounted by a Hathor headdress, now mostly broken off.

Traditionally, this pair has been ascribed to Marc Antony and Cleopatra VII based on the Greek senator Dio Cassius' comment that statues depicted the two as Osiris and Isis.[44] The king's varied forehead locks, however, do not agree with Antony's coin profiles, which show short, orderly locks (Fig. 243).[45] In addition, there are no inscribed representations of Antony with royal Egyptian attributes, nor any Egyptian titulature.[46]

A more persuasive interpretation is that Ptolemy XII is portrayed, because he was specifically called *Wsjrj ḥwnw* ("young Osiris") in his Egyptian titulature[47] and *neos Dionusos* ("young Dionysos") in Greek. The connection between these two gods is noted by ancient authors.[48] A comparison to Ptolemy XII's coin profile (Fig. 240) supports an attribution to him: the king's asymmetrically arranged, bushy hair compares favorably on both, as does the small, rounded chin.[49] The female figure can be interpreted as the goddess Isis. She is placed on the king's right side, which is unusual, but this positioning is documented in some New Kingdom statues where a goddess appears with a god.[50] The female figure's vulture cap further points to an interpretation as a goddess, since this is often a divine headdress. Isis is the archetypical companion for Osiris, and Ptolemy XII's birth name calls him "beloved of Isis" (*mrj-3st*).[51]

The Hadra dyad can be viewed as a major representation of Ptolemy XII as the young Osiris in the company of the great goddess Isis. This colossal and thus highly public demonstration of the king's divinity would have complemented Greek-style statues of Ptolemy XII in the guise of Dionysos.

Other Sculptures

Several other important Egyptian sculptures may be from Alexandria, but the evidence on these is less certain. Anton Ritter von Laurin, a diplomat and collector, reportedly found several sculptures while digging in the garden of his house in Alexandria in the nineteenth century, including a colossal granodiorite king with Horus sidelock now in Vienna (C2).[52] The reliability of this account is questionable, though the sculpture, by virtue of its high quality, large scale, and style, fits into the context of Alexandrian finds discussed so far. A colossal, nummulitic limestone head of a queen (C19) was acquired by the Graeco-Roman Museum via purchase, but it is allegedly from the Mazarita district in the eastern part of the city. A hieroglyph-inscribed granite fragment of a colossal statue of Ptolemy VI perhaps comes from Alexandria (B10).

The Aegyptiaca *Question*

There is significant, ongoing debate about when Egyptian-style objects found in Alexandria were first placed in the city. In addition to Ptolemaic sculptures of this type, many pre-Ptolemaic ones have been discovered in the capital, obviously removed from other sites, notably Heliopolis.[53] According to Strabo, Heliopolis was sacked and left in ruins by the Persian king Cambyses in the late sixth century B.C., thus creating an ample "quarry" for *aegyptiaca,* including obelisks, which he notes were taken to Rome and Thebes.[54] Ptolemaic activity at the site is attested by textual and archaeological evidence. The Greek historian Arrian notes that Alexander the Great passed through Heliopolis on his way to Memphis.[55] An early Ptolemaic royal facial fragment (A37) was found at Heliopolis, and a Greek-style architectural fragment from there may be Ptolemaic as well.[56] The obelisk brought by Ptolemy II to decorate the Arsinoeum in Alexandria may have been from Heliopolis, because Pliny mentions it in the context of other obelisks from the site.[57]

One side of the debate sees Egyptian sculptures being moved to Alexandria during the Roman Period, as part of the creation of cult establishments similar to Rome's Iseum Campense, which incorporated comparable objects in its sculptural program[58] The other side sees some or all of these sculptures being set up under the Ptolemies, the Ptolemaic royal ones with temples connected to the royal cults and the pre-Ptolemaic ones as part of a deliberate selection by the Greek rulers and their Egyptian advisors (much as the dynasty showed interest in Egypt's past by having Manetho write a history of the pharaohs for Greek consumption[59]). Indeed, Barbara Tkaczow's catalogue of a substantial sample of ancient objects from Alexandria lists a number of Egyptian sculptures and inscriptions for prominent pharaohs, including Thutmosis III, Amenhotep III, Seti I, and Ramses II of the New Kingdom, and the Nectanebos of Dynasty 30.[60]

Given the Roman predilection for *aegyptiaca,* the movement of some portion of these objects to Alexandria should be attributed to that period. But a few considerations argue that the city's Ptolemaic royal statues should not be considered as *aegyptiaca* from another site. The sculptures are very few in number relative to Alexandrian *aegyptiaca* as a whole, and they are highly consistent as a group in terms of size, quality, and material. All examples have strong divinizing elements: the large scale, the presence of the attributes of Osiris (E1) and Horus (C2), the companionship of Amun (A10) and Isis (E1, E2), and a deification text (A10). The statues make major ideological statements that are unique in the corpus of preserved sculptures: the bold display of the Pharos colossi (C21), the proclamation of the "young Osiris" in the Hadra Ptolemy XII (E1), and the elevation of the cult of Arsinoe II in the triad (A10). One of the less certain finds, the king with Horus sidelock in Vienna (C2), will be discussed in Chapter 5 as an important image of Ptolemy VIII as *z3-Wsjrj msj-n-3st* ("son of Osiris, born of Isis"), as he was named in his titulature.[61] Conceptually, these outsized and allusion-rich images could find a place in a city whose architecture is described by ancient authors as monumental, temple-laden, and suffused with royal structures, and the scarcity of these images compared with Greek-style fragments also matches these authors' relative silence on Egyptianizing elements.

Greek or Egyptian Settings?

What types of architectural settings in Alexandria housed Egyptian-style portraits of the Ptolemies? At the crux of this issue is whether the city possessed Egyptian temples and/or Egyptian-infused Greek ones in addition to purely Greek structures. Egyptian architecture in the city is sparsely documented. Patrizio Pensabene's far-reaching study of architectural fragments from Alexandria contains a limited number of Ptolemaic, Egyptian column capitals, all stylistically dated.[62] Barbara Tkaczow's catalogue of a substantial sample of ancient objects from Alexandria lists few Egyptian architectural fragments, particularly examples of Ptolemaic date (stylistically dated), among a fair number of Greek architectural fragments and

Egyptian sculptures.[63] An intriguing Egyptian-style example is not included in these studies: a partial, nummulitic limestone column, found in the Sharia Khedive el-Awal, north of the Serapeum, and decorated with cartouches of a second-century Ptolemy and a Cleopatra.[64] One also would expect that Egyptians living in the city, including priests advising the crown, would have had Egyptian temples or shrines for carrying out native rituals.[65] Additional evidence for such structures is offered by *loculus* closing slabs and funerary steles from the Alexandria area, which depict native architecture,[66] and Alexandrian coins from the time of Trajan and later, which depict façades with Egyptian columns and pylons.[67] Available facts could support but do not prove the presence of native temples in Ptolemaic Alexandria.

Evidence for the inclusion of Egyptian-style elements—specifically sculptures in the round—in Greek settings under the Ptolemies is similarly inconclusive. The colossal royal statues of the Pharos—huge Egyptian statues erected near the lighthouse, a major Greek landmark—are a potential but controversial instance. In addition, there are the previously cited testaments from ancient authors, particularly Pliny's anecdote that Ptolemy II went to great lengths to transport Nectanebo's obelisk to Alexandria to adorn the Arsinoeum.

Conclusions

There is strong evidence that Egyptian-style, Ptolemaic royal sculptures were set up in Hellenistic Alexandria. The group's consistency in terms of scale, quality, and material points to a common provenance, and similar statues were found in nearby Canopus. The ideological richness of the images argues for a setting like the cosmopolitan Alexandria, though the Greek or Egyptian style of their specific settings is indeterminate. The phrase *Alexandria ad Aegyptum* underscores the city's predominantly Greek nature, but it does not mean that Egyptian elements were entirely excluded.

CULT CENTER OF CANOPUS

Canopus (Abuqir) and its environs are a rich source of Egyptian-style portraits of the Ptolemies. The site had a number of important temples, including some devoted to the royal cults. Its longevity and strength as a center of pagan religion are attested by Rufinus, a Christian writer of the late fourth/early fifth centuries A.D., who wrote that Canopus had surpassed Alexandria in this respect.[68] About 22 kilometers east of the capital, Canopus is also the find spot for Greek sculptures, and for Egyptian works from pre-Ptolemaic through Roman times.[69]

Egyptian-style, Ptolemaic royal sculptures from Canopus display some characteristics similar to the Alexandrian sculptures, but those from Canopus are much more varied in terms of scale, material, and quality. Their scale ranges from under life-size (D7) to the colossal (B7, D13). Granite is the most frequent material, though a few examples are in quartzite (C13, C14) and limestone (B22, E20). The quality of these sculptures varies from low- or medium-level examples in limestone (B22, E20) to high-quality granite works (such as A34, B7). Over half of the sculptures have Greek-style hair. Their dates span the whole Ptolemaic Period, though there is a concentration in the second and first centuries.

Until the recent underwater explorations of Franck Goddio,[70] systematic excavations have never been undertaken at Canopus, so the original settings of the sculptures must largely be inferred. Older reports contain few details about architectural remains and do not provide reconstructions and layouts of buildings. Travel accounts from the last several centuries paint a similarly sketchy picture.[71] Nevertheless, descriptions of architectural fragments point to Greek-style buildings, occasionally infused with native decorative elements. In discussing Canopus, Evaristo Breccia notes: "I tre principali ordini greci—dorico, ionico, corinzio—sono tutti più o meno abbondantemente rappresentati . . . e che è caratterizzato dalla giustapposizione o dalla fusione di forme greche e di elemente egiziani."[72]

Ancient sources provide more information about Canopus in its Ptolemaic heyday. Strabo writes about a temple of Serapis famous for its curative powers; he also cites a shrine of Aphrodite Arsinoe at the Zephyrium, a promontory near Canopus.[73] A votive rhyton offered by the Greek engineer Ctesibos in the latter temple incorporated an image of the Egyptian god Bes, according to the poet Hedylus of Samos.[74] The Canopus decree of Ptolemy III mentions a few temples at the site: "the temple of the Benefactor Gods,"[75] where the synod took place; "the temple of Canopus,"[76] where the native priests propose to deify the dead princess Berenice with Osiris (hence, the Osiris temple); and "the temple of Amun-Gereb,"[77] which is likely near Canopus. The decree indicates that the Amun and Osiris temples were Egyptian ones, for two reasons. First, they are cited as the origination and end points for the journey of the divine bark of Osiris on appointed holidays; a male standing naophorous statue at Yale University,[78] inscribed as a "prophet of Amun-Gereb" and "scribe of Osiris of the temple of Canopus," may represent an officiant at these temples. Second, the Osiris temple is described as being honored by the king and all Egyptians.[79]

In the 1930s, Evaristo Breccia preliminarily identified some ruins at Canopus with an Osiris (or Isis) temple, though he could not prove his theory. He described the ruins as "une vaste esplande, ainsi que de puissantes lignes de fondations en gros blocs cubiques de calcaire, bien taillée et parfaitement joints" and found there "plusieurs bases de colonnes cannelées de très grand dimension."[80] He also found many sculptures, including Egyptian-style Ptolemies (B22, D6, D24, E19), pre-Ptolemaic kings, sphinxes, and faience oinochoae fragments of Ptolemaic queens. A bit to the north, a granite statue base inscribed in Greek for Arsinoe III was recovered (A19). These finds are consistent with royal cult activity and resemble others found in Alexandria.

At Maamura, a site just to the west of Canopus, a colossal, Egyptian-style, limestone dyad (G5) was discovered in 1954 near the ruins of an Egyptian temple enclosure, where a quartzite Ramses II sphinx was found as well. Not much about the temple is recorded, except that it possessed a limestone pylon about 28 meters long, with recesses for flagpoles, the type of native architecture that appears on Alexandrian bone tesserae (labeled in Greek as Canopus) and on Alexandrian coins from the Roman Period.[81] No relief fragments or other architectural details are published. The sculpture's reconstructed height is over 5 meters.[82]

The Maamura dyad consists of a headless, standing nude male with a much smaller-scale female figure at his left side in a knotted, draped ensemble. The statue may be of Roman date, given that a similar example is known from the early Roman Period, an under-life-size, granite statue of an emperor with *nemes* and hair, genitalia visible, and a diminutive female attendant figure, found near Rome (G6). The Maamura pair most likely represents a ruler or deity accompanied by a priestess. As such, it could be an example of a large-scale, Egyptian-style image made in connection with a ruler cult, but it is the first from the Alexandria area that can be placed in an Egyptian architectural context. The dyad may represent the continuance of a tradition in which colossal, Egyptian statues of the Ptolemies were placed external to native temples at Canopus.

What we can draw from the above analysis is that the Canopus area had major temples associated with the royal cult (such as the temple of Aphrodite Arsinoe at Zephyrium and the one of the Benefactor Gods at Canopus); important activities connected with the royal cult (e.g., the deification of Princess Berenice); Egyptian-style temple(s) (the Canopus decree temples, Maamura ruins, and related pictorial examples);[83] and Greek-style temple(s), possibly with native infusions (note Breccia's description of the Doric, Ionic, and Corinthian architectural remains; the rhyton with the Bes image). The numerous Ptolemaic royal statues found at and near Canopus could be envisioned as part of the sculptural programs of temples or shrines connected with the royal cults. These Egyptian sculptures included colossal images placed in highly visible positions outside of temples (B7, D13), sphinxes forming parts of dromoi or flanking entranceways (A34, B22, C13, D24), and smaller-scale, nonsphinx statues serving as cult objects within temples or shrines (D7).

"SECOND CITY" OF MEMPHIS

In view of the important position of Memphis under the Ptolemies, the city must have had numerous royal images and important edifices. Writing in the early Roman Period, Strabo commented, "The city is both large and populous, ranks second after Alexandria, and consists of mixed races of people, like those who have settled together at Alexandria."[84] This "second city" served as the original seat of government under Ptolemy I when he was satrap, had a royal residence, and hosted Egyptian-style coronations.[85] In contrast to Alexandria and Canopus, ancient Memphis was deeply and visibly Egyptian, tracing its roots back to its role as capital of Old Kingdom Egypt, when the great pyramids were built at nearby Giza. Memphis was also an "international" city well before the Ptolemies arrived, having a multiracial identity based on a long history as a political power and trade center. Unlike its northern neighbors, Memphis' archaeological remains are primarily Egyptian in style, with some Greek objects found as well.

Very little remains of the great temple of Ptah, which dominated Memphis' religious structures and was described by Herodotus as "large and most noteworthy" and by Strabo as having colossal statuary (*kolossos*) and a dromos.[86] This temple complex, built up over many centuries, was surrounded by a huge trapezoidal enclosure wall, having sides varying in length from about 400 meters to over 600 meters.[87] It was here that national priestly synods met under Ptolemies IV and V, promulgating the Raphia and Memphis decrees. The complex must have contained important Ptolemaic royal sculptures, though only one tantalizing fragment of an unusual statue is preserved: a near-life-size, granite statue of a king in a draped garment (F1). This Egyptian sculpture may have once stood in the Ptah temple, because the god's Memphite form, *Ptḥ rsj jnb.f* ("Ptah-south-of-his-wall"), is cited on the back pillar. The draped garment is royal ceremonial garb known mostly from relief representations and is closely connected to the eternal renewal of the king's reign (Chapter 4).

The sculptural milieu of Memphis is better attested at Saqqara, an important religious center to the west of the city, famous for its elaborate animal cults, particularly the Apis bull. Both Greek and Egyptian limestone sculptures lined the dromos between a group of temples and the Apis bull tombs of the Serapeum. The Dionysiac theme of the Greek examples—fantastic and real beasts, the peacock, panther, lion, sphinx, siren, and perhaps a griffin, some ridden by a child-figure of Dionysos—finds striking parallels in the Greek writer Athenaeus' description of Ptolemy II's lavish parade in Alexandria.[88] A nearby hemispherical exedra included Greek-style statues of notables such as Homer, Pindar, and Protagoras.[89] A few of the originally hundreds of Egyptian sphinxes noted by Strabo are preserved today (Fig. 200).[90]

The intermixing of sculptures at Saqqara was a natural extension of the exchange that developed between selected Egyptians and their Greek overlords. The high priests of Ptah at Memphis enjoyed a strong relationship with the crown: they sponsored royal events at Memphis, traveled to Alexandria and Canopus to advise the king, and perhaps had statues of themselves at the Alexandria Serapeum. They therefore must have been familiar with Greek-style royal sculptural programs.

A fair number of sculptors' studies/votives come from Saqqara, and some are Ptolemaic. Depending on how one interprets these objects (Appendix A), they attest to a high degree of sculptural and/or cultic activity. During excavations at North Saqqara's sacred animal necropolis, a well under life-size, plaster bust of a king in a double crown (E9) was found in clean sand in front of the main entrance of a Dynasty 3 mastaba tomb.

THE DELTA

Egyptian-style sculptures of the Ptolemies from the Delta have commonalities with those of Alexandria and Canopus, but they also display notable contrasts. Though many Delta finds are made of granite and are high in quality, they are smaller in scale (over-life-size and less), none have Greek features, and all date to the third century, except for two examples near Alexandria (E8, E11), which are dated in this book to the first century B.C. The most significant finds are three statues from Tanis (A9, A28, A35) and an early temple treasure horde from Tukh el-Karamus (A6, A7, A8).

Sunnaoi Theoi *at Tanis*

In contrast to the extensive building of native temples in Upper Egypt under the Ptolemies, few constructions were undertaken in the Delta.[91] Tanis, a sizable metropolis that had been the royal residence of Dynasties 21 and 22, was an exception, undoubtedly in part because of its strategic importance for the defense of Egypt's northeastern frontier. A dark stone statue of Panemerit, governor of Tanis and military commander under Ptolemy XII, is indicative of such a role for the city. On his chest, he holds a small statue of Horus of Mesen, the *msn pr-ʿ* ("great harpooner") who battled the evil god Seth, paralleling the king's ability to act quickly and powerfully against Egypt's enemies.[92]

Ptolemy IV, who defeated the Seleucid king Antiochus III in the famous battle of Raphia east of the Delta, dedicated a temple at Tanis to Mut, Khonsu, and the deified Ptolemies II–IV and their wives.[93] This dedication, like similar ones for Alexandrian temples, portrays the Ptolemies as *sunnaoi theoi*. The Ptolemy IV temple was a sizable 33.2 × 53 meter building and had its own enclosure outside the site's great enclosure.[94] Nearby, on the north side of the western processional way, W. M. Flinders Petrie excavated a small brick chapel in the late nineteenth century that contained finds indicative of the worship of early Ptolemies.

The chapel's western wall contained a recess with a gilded stele showing Ptolemy IV, Arsinoe III, and Tanite deities (Fig. 206). Petrie found a variety of other Egyptian-style limestone objects on the ground, including a stele of the deified Ptolemy II and Arsinoe II and a well under life-size standing king with *nemes* and double crown (A9).[95] The chapel may have facilitated petitions to the deified Ptolemies by private persons, because the structure was located outside the great temple enclosure and its contents were of adequate, but certainly not superior, quality, with simple or no inscriptions.

In 1961, two Egyptian-style statues of kings were unearthed in a trial pit dug in connection with road construction at Tanis (A28, A35). Compared with the king from the chapel (A9), these examples are higher in quality, perhaps pointing to their original placement within one of the major Tanis temples. The first is a limestone seated king (A28). The well under life-size figure may have been intended to receive offerings or petitions (seated position) or may have served as a sculptor's model (presence of grid lines). The second is a fragment of a slightly under life-size, quartzite statue, perhaps proffering some now-missing object(s) in its hands (A35);[96] the scale and gesture perhaps indicate that the statue was placed near a divine cult image within a temple.

Treasure Hoard at Tukh el-Karamus

A treasure hoard unearthed at the turn of the twentieth century at Tukh el-Karamus in the eastern Delta is significant for its inclusion of cultic objects possibly related to *sḫm* images. The find is dated by coins of Ptolemies I–II found with the treasure, which included items of both Egyptian and Greek workmanship. They probably came from the nearby temple, which had a foundation deposit inscribed for the Macedonian ruler Philip Arrhidaios.[97] Among them is an Egyptian-style bronze-and-gold bust of a king (A7). This well under life-size work served as a finial for cultic equipment. An under-life-size gold and partly gilded silver *nemes* with *hm-hm*-crown (A8) was found, as well as a small gold broad collar with stone inlays (A6). Both may have formed parts of composite statues or served as votive gifts.

THE VIBRANT FAYOUM

The Fayoum was a focal point of early Ptolemaic economic and social policies because of the area's arable land, which was a valuable commodity in desert-covered Egypt. Located south of Memphis, the Fayoum was irrigated by an arm of the Nile that led to the area's Lake Moeris. Reductions in the lake's size during the Ptolemaic Period freed new tracts of fertile land, which the Ptolemies then doled out to Greek officials as well as to soldier-veterans to use as a source of income. One beneficiary was Apollonius, *dioikētēs* ("chief minister") under Ptolemy II, whose large estate was managed by Zenon; the latter's huge archive of papyrus documents was discovered in Philadelphia.[98] The Fayoum had a relatively high population of Greeks, who helped create a distinctive cultural milieu encompassing temple-building projects and unusual sculptures.[99]

Excavations at Tebtunis and Medinet Madi represent two of the best-documented finds of Ptolemaic royal sculptures. These works are consistently in limestone and form the largest concentration of Egyptian-style Ptolemies with Greek hair outside of Alexandria and Canopus. Unlike the refined and calculated sculptural style of the latter areas, the Fayoum style is vivid and lively, with wide-eyed visages.

At Tebtunis, an over-life-size standing king was found in situ at the end of a sphinx-lined dromos during the 1930s excavations of Carlo Anti (E3).[100] A Greek inscription for Ptolemy XII, which may have belonged to the statue's base, was found nearby. It identifies the king as the *Neos Dionusos* ("young Dionysos") and thus forms a counterpart to Ptolemy XII's depiction as the young Osiris in the Hadra colossus (E1). The inscription contains a date corresponding to April 15, 55 B.C., very late in Ptolemy XII's reign.

The statue flanked the left side of the outer face of the entranceway through an enclosure wall surrounding a temple dedicated to the crocodile-god Soknebtunis. This was one of several temples in the Fayoum dedicated to a crocodile-god, reflecting the reptile's pervasive presence in the water-rich area. The temple was initiated under Ptolemy I (over pre-Ptolemaic remains) and modified at intervals through the Roman Period.[101] The statue may have been erected in thanks for some royal favors bestowed on the temple, such as economic benefits that may have financed the repair or augmentation of the temple complex. On the opposite side of the entranceway was a recumbent lion.

Achille Vogliano's excavations at Medinet Madi during the 1930s recovered perhaps the best-preserved example of an Egyptian-style, Ptolemaic royal statuary program (C3). The sculptures were part of the Ptolemaic expansion of a small temple for the cobra goddess Renenutet built by Amenemhat III and IV of Dynasty 12.[102] Two pronaoi were added, as well as a dromos, lined with both Egyptian and Greek sculptures, as at the Saqqara Serapeum. Among the Egyptian sculptures are over-life-size male sphinxes with *nemes* and hair, female sphinxes with corkscrew locks, and recumbent lions. Among Greek-style sculptures are human-headed, winged sphinxes. Middle Kingdom royal statues were preserved within the Middle Kingdom temple, as was a statue of Merenptah of Dynasty 19.[103] A distinctive under-life-size, Egyptian-style, limestone head of a Ptolemy with diadem and hair (D19) was recovered from a refuse pile within the temple. Greek dedications for Ptolemies VIII and IX were also discovered.[104]

Medinet Madi's mixture of sculptures of varied styles and dates—Greek and Egyptian, as well as Middle Kingdom, New Kingdom, and Ptolemaic—is striking. It must be a provincial reflection of similarly diverse statuary programs at major sites such as Memphis. The Medinet Madi program demonstrates the continuing reverence accorded to the Middle Kingdom temple, as well as some specific benefaction under the Ptolemies and/or a private initiative that supported the architectural additions and sculptures.

GREEK TEMPLE AT HERMOPOLIS MAGNA

The Middle Egyptian site of Hermopolis Magna (el-Ashmunein) evidences a strong Greek presence and a relationship with the crown from the beginnings of Macedonian rule. Petosiris, high priest of Thoth in the second half of the fourth century, had a mortuary chapel at the nearby Tuna el-Gebel necropolis, whose walls were decorated with figural scenes using a unique mixture of Greek and Egyptian elements.[105] Construction of the main Thoth temple at Hermopolis Magna, begun in Dynasty 30, was continued under the early Macedonian rulers.[106] The site was also an important military base.[107]

Hermopolis Magna has special significance because it provides a rare glimpse of how one city handled the physical positioning of Greek and Egyptian temples. For the Greek temple built under Ptolemy III, a Greek inscription establishes that the temple and its temenos were erected by Greek cavalry settlers in honor of Ptolemies II–III and their wives, and that the soldiers set up statues (*agalma*) as well.[108] The temenos was built next to a much larger Dynasty 30 enclosure for a group of Egyptian temples, including the main Thoth one. At some point during the Ptolemaic Period, a north-south dromos was constructed, leading past the Greek temenos and through the Egyptian enclosure past the main Thoth temple.[109] It was called the Dromos of Hermes, the Greek god associated with the Egyptian Thoth. An altar of Amenhotep III of Dynasty 18 was imbedded in the processional way, within the Egyptian enclosure and to the south of the Thoth temple, perhaps as a resting place for the *sḫm* shrine during religious celebrations (Chapter 2).[110] This raises some important but currently unanswerable questions: Did a mixture of Greek and Egyptian sculptures line the dromos (as at the Saqqara Serapeum and Medinet Madi)? How did the dromos function in relationship to both temple areas?

A limestone standing statue inscribed for Nectanebo I was found at Hermopolis Magna (Fig. 201a).[111] No Egyptian-style Ptolemies are known, but a fragment of a large-scale Roman emperor with *nemes* (G8) once sat outside the site's Antiquities Department storeroom; the granite statue's original provenance, if known, has not been published.

UPPER EGYPT

Finds from Upper Egypt are diverse. They are consistent only in lacking Greek hair or facial features, except for the Karnak Augustus (G2), which is about half the scale of its possible Alexandrian counterpart (G1). There is a group of life-size and smaller statues at Koptos (A5, A12, A16, F3), mostly third century in date. The Theban area has the only large-scale statuary in Upper Egypt, one of Cleopatra II (B14) and another of Ptolemy VI (B11). They differ from the colossal examples of the Alexandria and Canopus area in being made of limestone; the extent of preservation does not allow a full judgment regarding Greek features, but the queen does have an Egyptian tripartite wig. Despite having plentiful reliefs, the great Ptolemic temples of Upper Egypt have only a few, highly fragmentary statues in granite, all life-size and smaller (B12, B13, F2), as well as a treasure horde with precious-metal divine and royal figures (E22).

Early Ptolemies at Koptos

Koptos enjoyed special favor under the first Ptolemies, likely because it was at the crossroads for trade routes to the Red Sea ports and the Wadi Hammamat quarries.[112] A major temple of Hathor/Isis and Min was built here in the third century.[113] It was to Koptos as well that Ptolemy II's first wife, Arsinoe I, was banished upon

Arsinoe II's return to Egypt, and where Senoucheri, a high official under the same king, considered the setting up of royal images (*mnw*) as one of his duties.[114]

Egyptian royal statuary from Koptos are of medium to high quality and consistently have hieroglyphic back-pillar inscriptions. In the late nineteenth century, W. M. Flinders Petrie found two fragments at the site, a queen's headdress (F3) and a partial limestone statue of Ptolemy III (A16). A fine, under-life-size, schist torso of Ptolemy II may come from Koptos: the belt inscription mentions Min, and the king's throne name is given in a particular form (A12). The back-pillar inscription of another under-life-size dark stone statue of the same king mentions Koptos (A5).

Venerable (and Rebellious) Thebes

Thebes, the once-glorious capital of Egypt during the New Kingdom, was greatly overshadowed by Alexandria and Memphis during the Ptolemaic Period. Writing in the early Roman Period, Strabo dwells on the fame of Thebes' wealth and expanse, but notes the partial ruin and shrinkage that had occurred by his time.[115] The Ptolemies had a relationship of contrasts with the city. On the one hand, major building projects were undertaken at the Karnak temple center, starting with the decoration of the Amun temple's central sanctuary in the name of Alexander the Great.[116] The importance of Amun, the *nsw-nṯrw* ("king of the gods"), was acknowledged by his mention in the throne names of many Ptolemies.[117] On the other hand, the city's primacy was undercut when Ptolemy I founded the Greek settlement of Ptolemais Hermiou to the north, which then grew to be the area's largest city, according to Strabo.[118] Ptolemais was the Upper Egyptian home for senior government officials (the strategos and epistrategos) and a Greek-style royal cult, and the city presumably possessed Greek temples and sculptures, though almost all traces have vanished.[119]

In the light of Thebes' proud past and its conflicted relationship with the Ptolemies, it was inevitable that the city became the focal point for rebellions. The most persistent of these revolts, one that began late in Ptolemy IV's reign, saw a native counterdynasty controlling the Theban area.[120] It is perhaps from one of these troubled times that we have a "killed" royal statue from Karnak (A36). The chipping marks that obscure the nose and mouth of this under-life-size standing king indicate that the dark stone statue was deliberately mutilated, rather than accidentally damaged by a fall.[121] These actions were intended to extinguish the life given to the statue during its original creation; the Egyptian word for "sculptor" is *sꜥnḫ*, literally meaning "the one who makes live."[122] A canonical scene in countless reliefs shows a deity proffering the life-giving *ankh*-sign to the pharaoh's nose and mouth.[123]

The "killed" royal statue was found in 1904 among hundreds of sculptures unearthed by Georges Legrain in the famous Karnak cachette, where objects were buried, probably under the direction of priests.[124] This means that the mutilation and burial occurred in antiquity. Who would "kill" a royal statue, and why? Perhaps the actions were taken by seditious priests during one of the native revolts: the Memphis decree notes that rebels damaged the temples, and other texts and archaeological evidence point to similar actions.[125]

A few other Egyptian-style royal statues are known from the Theban area. A fragmentary over-life-size(?) limestone statue of Cleopatra II was found just outside Karnak's first pylon during the excavations of J. Lauffray (B14). Two large-scale royal male statues, an over-life-size(?) headless and legless limestone torso of Ptolemy VI (B11) and an over-life-size granite statue of Augustus (G2), are recorded as from Karnak, without more specific find-spot information. A black basalt base of a standing statue inscribed in Greek and hieroglyphs for Arsinoe II (A14) is likely from the Theban area, because the inscription mentions Amun-Re of Karnak, Mut, and Khons, three major gods of the region. An under-life-size dark stone standing king with *nemes* and Greek hair, traditionally identified as Marc Antony (D14), reportedly comes from Karnak, because Alexandre Barsanti of the Antiquities Service worked in Karnak during the period he sent the statue to Cairo. The provenance is only presumed, and the Cairo Museum's Journal d'Entrée does not record it.

The Great Temples of Upper Egypt

A few Ptolemaic royal sculptures are known from the great temples of Upper Egypt. The fragments are concentrated in the second and first centuries B.C., when ambitious temple projects were initiated and completed at Dendera, Edfu, Kom Ombo, Philae, and elsewhere. The extensive building activities, the carving of an extraordinary number of reliefs, the production of cult equipment, and the ongoing maintenance costs must have required sizable financing by some combination of royal grant, income from property or industry, and private initiative. The Hathor temple at Dendera, for example, had 12.5-meter-high external walls that provided surfaces for large-scale reliefs, and an elaborate system of crypts that housed scores of cult images of precious and other materials (E22). This is also the time of the creation of the two largest-scale reliefs of the smiting pharaoh known from the Ptolemaic Period, both inscribed for Ptolemy XII, on the first pylon of the Isis temple at Philae (Fig. 203) and the pylon of the Horus temple at Edfu (Fig. 202).[126]

The construction boom perhaps related to the ruling house's efforts to secure the loyalty of Upper Egypt and provide economic stability in the face of the destructive rebellions that periodically broke out from the late third century on. A series of amnesty decrees not only documents the Ptolemies' public stance to buttress the native temples, but also tacitly acknowledges their clout. One well-preserved decree of Ptolemy VIII and Cleopatras II–III declares that the temples will retain the land and revenue belonging to them and that the crown will finance burial costs for the Apis and Mnevis bulls.[127] The decree forbids government officials to exploit the native population.

For their part, the native clergy perceived its relationship with the crown as valuable. An exchange of letters, presumably originally on papyrus, between the priests at Philae and Ptolemy VIII and Cleopatras II–III was considered so important that they were carved in Greek on a stone pedestal for an obelisk before Philae's Isis temple. The priests appeal for royal intervention regarding expenses related to visits of government functionaries, which were draining resources to an extent that threatened the continuance of cult activities.[128] The implication is that, in exchange for protection and financial aid, the priests will perform appropriate rituals, including those for the native royal cult, which the inscription identifies as one role of the priests in question. Other second-century inscriptions at the Philae and Kom Ombo temples document honors due to several generations of Ptolemies stretching from the third through first centuries.[129]

Dendera Temple Treasure Horde

The Hathor temple at Dendera was constructed from the reign of Ptolemy XII through the time of Augustus, and it remains one of the most impressive Ptolemaic buildings to this day.[130] A cache of cult objects was discovered in 1918 near Dendera's sacred lake, within the enclosure wall to the southwest of the Hathor temple (E22). The find included several Egyptian-style royal images: a well under life-size silver sphinx (Fig. 185), a well under life-size gilded stone sphinx (Fig. 184), and a gilded silver naos inscribed for Ptolemy XII(?). Coins of the same ruler reportedly were found as well.[131] The chest of the stone sphinx has traces of a royal titulary starting with the *nfr* sign, a typical beginning for Middle Kingdom royal inscriptions; the statue's style belongs to this time as well.[132] As at Medinet Madi, Middle Kingdom sculptures are revered and intermixed with Ptolemaic sculptures.

The rest of the horde comprises statues of deities (Fig. 186), vessels, ritual instruments, jewelry, and mirrors. The finds originally were used in the Hathor temple as votive offerings, cult instruments, or venerated images.

Edfu Falcon Statue

The temple of Horus at Edfu, begun under Ptolemy III, underwent successive enlargements through the reign of Ptolemy XII.[133] On the left side of the outer face of the doorway of Ptolemy XII's entrance pylon, a granite falcon stands protectively over a male figure in a draped garment (F2). A similar falcon statue, but without the human figure, flanks the right side (Fig. 202, lower left). The positioning on the left side of an entrance and the lack of a duplicate human figure on the right parallel the case of the Tebtunis pharaoh (E3). I am unaware of any published account, however, that documents that this was the original location of the statues. The human figure's identification as a king is uncertain because of his weathered state, but this is a typical position for Nectanebo II in similar statues.[134]

Ptolemy VI at Philae

The island of Philae lies just to the south of the extensive quarries that supplied the Ptolemaic kingdom with ample amounts of granite. Among a variety of religious structures, the island housed the main Isis temple and a birth house, which were particularly augmented under Ptolemies VI and VIII.[135] Two Egyptian-style, Ptolemaic royal statue fragments can be associated with second-century Philae (B12, B13). Made of granite, both were found near the island, and both have inscriptions indicating that the statues were set up by Isis and Horus, major deities at the site. The gods' names are a slightly later addition, perhaps to cover the name(s) of the original dedicator(s), erased during a fall out of favor (such as an adherent of Ptolemy VI might have experienced under Ptolemy VIII).[136] A Greek-inscribed statue base of Ptolemy VI for an approximately life-size statue was purchased by Gaston Maspero in Aswan,

TABLE 3.1 GEOGRAPHIC VARIATIONS IN THE ROYAL IMAGE

	Material	*Scale*	*Quality*	*Greek Hair*	*Appearance*	*Date Range*
Alexandria	Almost all are granite	Over life to colossal	High	Medium to high concentration	Highly ideological	Mostly 2nd and 1st centuries
Canopus	Mostly granite	Under life to colossal	Low to high	Medium to high concentration	Highly varied	Mostly 2nd and 1st centuries
Delta (with Memphis area)	Many granite	Well under life to over life	Low to high	None	Mostly traditionally Egyptian	Mostly 3rd century
Fayoum	All limestone	Under life to over life	Medium	Medium to high concentration	Lively, provincial	All 2nd and 1st centuries
Koptos	Limestone and dark stones	Under life to life	Medium to high	Uncertain because of poor preservation	Traditionally Egyptian	Mostly 3rd century
Karnak/Thebes	Limestone and dark stones	Under life to over life or colossal	Medium to high	One certain example, for Augustus (G2)	Uncertain. Abundant relief examples, however, are traditionally Egyptian.	3rd and 2nd centuries
Rest of Upper Egypt	Mostly granite	Under life to life	Uncertain	Uncertain because of poor preservation	Uncertain. Abundant relief examples, however, are traditionally Egyptian.	All 2nd and 1st centuries

just north of Philae (B12). A second statue base, with a bilingual Greek/Demotic dedication to Ptolemy VI, Cleopatra II, and their son, was found on the nearby island of el-Hesa (B13). The fragment has three rectangular holes on top, which supported Egyptian-style statues that were about life-size or somewhat smaller.

OUTSIDE OF EGYPT

Ptolemaic royal sculptures have been unearthed in Italy, presumably brought there after the Roman takeover of Egypt (A3, A4, B16). Egyptian royal, divine, and private statues of various dates usually are found in the same context, from pre-Ptolemaic through Roman. Roman interest in Egyptian sculptures is well documented.[137]

An over-life-size granite head of Ptolemy VI reportedly was found in the nineteenth century in the Mediterranean Sea near Aegina, Greece (B6). Some suggest that the sculpture was originally set up in nearby Methana, an important Ptolemaic military base on the Peloponnese, but the almost total lack of knowledge about Hellenistic Methana prevents proof of this idea.[138] It is equally possible that the head fell into the sea during the Roman Period antiquities trade, or even at some later time.

A dark stone head of a queen (B30) was found by chance at Panticapeion on the Bosporus (now Kerch in the modern Ukraine), which was ruled by the Spartocid dynasty until conquered by Mithradates VI of Pontus in the late second century B.C. Without better documentation on the archaeological context, it is not possible to determine when the head reached Panticapeion.

CONCLUSIONS

There are clear geographical differences for Ptolemaic royal sculptures, as displayed in Table 3.1. At the top end of the scale are the high-quality, colossal, granite sculptures with Greek hair in Alexandria and Canopus, some with strong ideological messages, such as the Hadra dyad's (E1, E2) proclamation of Ptolemy XII as the "young Osiris." These two sites combined represent the largest concentration of Ptolemaic royal statuary finds, and, except for the Fayoum and perhaps Karnak/Thebes, they have the only known Ptolemaic royal statues with Greek hair and faces (Fig. 197).[139] The Delta, including the "second city" of Memphis, has the second largest number of finds, mostly in granite and many of high quality, but these sculptures are smaller in scale than those of the Alexandria/Canopus area, and their appearance is more traditionally Egyptian and conservative. Other parts of Egypt are highly idiosyncratic. The Fayoum possesses limestone statues in a lively provincial style (C3). Thebes has two large-scale examples in limestone (B11, B14). The Upper Egyptian temples have very little statuary preserved, all lifesize and under, though they do possess abundant relief (Figs. 202–205) and precious-metal images (E22).

Available evidence is clear regarding Egyptian statues of the Ptolemies within Egyptian-style architectural contexts, but not regarding Greek contexts. Alexandria's poor record of preservation does not permit us to get a full picture (though the situation at Canopus is more comprehensible). Compounding the problem is the almost total disappearance of Greek temples in Egypt, apart from stray architectural elements.

Greek-style images in Egyptian-style contexts, meanwhile, are well documented in two situations, which have differing levels of sophistication. At the high end, the dromos at the nationally important sanctuary at Saqqara possessed statues of famous Greeks and Dionysian sculptures alluding to the Ptolemies' purported divine ancestry. This is a careful and deliberate program resulting from collaboration between highly placed religious and government officials, both Egyptian and Greek. Of more modest ambitions, the dromos at the provincial Middle Kingdom temple at Medinet Madi combined Greek sphinxes with Greek-haired, Egyptian ones in a lively but less refined style. The program again represents an Egyptian and Greek collaboration.

Ancient statues were treated with reverence during the Ptolemaic Period. A royal sculptural program at Medinet Madi combined Middle Kingdom, New Kingdom, and Ptolemaic images, and a temple treasure horde at Dendera combined Middle Kingdom and Ptolemaic objects. These examples are reflections of the millennia-spanning sculptural assemblies at major sites such as Memphis, Thebes, and Tanis, which placed the Ptolemies squarely in the line of Egypt's royal traditions. Similar ideologically driven sculptural programs may have been assembled at Alexandria and Canopus by importing statues from other sites, but the archaeological and literary evidence is not conclusive in this respect.

The Ptolemies took a strategic approach to how they provided benefactions to key Egyptian sites that resulted in temple-building and royal image creation. From early on there is a focus on influential religious centers (Memphis and Saqqara) and on locations providing essential advantages like national defense (Tanis) or access to lucrative trade (Koptos). There is also a careful cultivation of native Egyptian royal cults (Tanis). This situation changes in the second and first centuries B.C., when statues with Greek hair and features are produced for the Alexandria and Canopus area, and selectively for other locations. At the same time, increased temple-building in Upper Egypt can perhaps be connected with a royal benefaction policy intended to promote peace and loyalty in areas vulnerable to native rebellion. This was also the time of the creation of large-scale relief images in Upper Egypt showing a Ptolemy as a conquering and powerful pharaoh (Figs. 202–203).

NOTES

1. Bagnall 2001 surveys recent archaeological work on Hellenistic and Roman Egypt.

2. Yoyotte and Charvet 1997.

3. Hostens-Deleu 1977, 9–11, summarizes provenance information on studies/votives.

4. Strabo 5.1.7 and others; Geraci 1995 and Haas 1997, 33.

5. Diodorus 17.52.3 and Strabo 17.1.10; for the list: Fraser 1951, 104. Possible temples in the city: Haas 1997, 141–150; and A. Bernand 1998, 139–155.

6. Foundation plaque: Fraser 1972b, 410–411 n. 557; Bricault 1999, 337, 343, doc. 5; and É. Bernand 2001, 53–56, no. 18. Philensis II: W. Müller 1920, 59, line 4.

7. Strabo 17.1.8.

8. Diodorus 17.52.3; Caesar *De bello Alexandrino* 18.

9. Pharos' height: Clayton and Price 1988, 147; *Gloire* 1998, 98. Wide boulevards: Strabo 17.1.8. A colossal statue: Plutarch *De Iside et Osiride* 28. Colossal processional image: Athenaeus 5.198e–199a. See Habicht 1980, 4–5, on a Greek papyrus that may mention a colossal statue of Ptolemy III at the Alexandria Serapeum.

10. Athenaeus 5.197c–203b. Dionysos as forebear: Smith 1988, 44.

11. Strabo 17.1.12 says that Polybius noted three types of city inhabitant: native Egyptians, foreign mercenaries, and Alexandrians.

12. Nectanebo obelisk: Pliny *Naturalis historia* 36.14.67–69. Serapeum obelisks: Pseudo-Callisthenes 1.33; they are also noted in Aphthonius' early fourth-century A.D. description of the Serapeum, *Progymnasmata* 12.49 (Rabe 1926, 40). Caesareum obelisks: Pliny *Naturalis historia* 36.14.69; one is now in London and the other is in New York (the Greek inscription on a claw support indicates that the obelisks were set up in the eighteenth year of Augustus; A. Bernand 1998, 153; and Hölbl 2001, 292. Obelisks front a Greek-style shrine in the Nile Mosaic of Palestrina; Meyboom 1995, 28–29, fig. 15.

13. Athenaeus 5.205c (Corinthian capitals) and 5.206a–c (columns with Egyptian elements).

14. Lines 34 and 57: Koenen 1968, 206–207; and Kerkeslager 1998, 77; also see Lloyd 1982a, 50–54; Huss 1994, 165–179; D. J. Thompson 2000, 78–79; and Hölbl 2001, 199. Winnicki (1994, 186) analyzes the text relative to others describing the return of Egyptian cult images removed by foreigners.

15. Lucan 8.697; Fraser 1972a, 16; and Hölbl 2001, 169.

16. Tkaczow 1993, 233–235, cat. nos. 122 (Apries), 122A (Horemheb), 127 (Dynasty 19?), 128 (Dynasty 26?).

17. Rowe 1946.

18. Breccia 1907; Rowe 1957, 493, 507–508; Tkaczow 1993, 68–70, 338, site no. 15; and Yoyotte 1998, 212 n. 59.

19. Fraser 1972a, 266; Pensabene 1993, 62; and Tomlinson 1996, 159.

20. Yoyotte 1998, 210–212. See also Kessler 2000, 192–214. Plaques: Rowe 1946, 1–13, 51–59, figs. 1–3, pls. 1–2, 16; D. J. Thompson 1993; and *Gloire* 1998, 95, cat. nos. 51–52, entries by Jean-Yves Empereur. Layout: Sabottka (1989) reconstructed the temple's plan.

21. Alexandria 17533 and Alexandria 17534, limestone, H: 64.5 cm and 62.5 cm, respectively; Breccia 1907, 64–67; Quaegebeur 1980, 53–59, 68, 77–78; Reymond 1981, 27–30, 105–112, nos. 13–14, pl. 8; Maystre 1992, 404–406, no. 198; and Yoyotte 1998, 209, 212.

22. Alexandria 27806, limestone, H: 60 cm; Quaegebeur 1980, 53–59, 64, 65; and Reymond 1981, 27–30, 112–115, no. 15.

23. Kessler 2000, 172–192; and Hölbl 2001, 99–101.

24. Empereur 1996. Reconstructed statue heights: Empereur 1998, 76–77.

25. Frost 1975, 129, fig. 3; and Corteggiani 1998, 39.

26. The catalogue contains citations for archaeological reports, presumed provenances, and supporting inscriptional evidence for these and other sculptures in this chapter.

27. Caesar *Bellum civile* 3.112.

28. McKenzie 1990, 67–68.

29. Fraser 1972a, 20–21; A. Bernand 1998, 151; and Bricault 2000.

30. Clayton and Price 1988, 148–152; and *Gloire* 1998, 98–104. Possible Roman copy of the Isis statue: Ridgway 1990, 366.

31. Rose 1997, 185–188.

32. Di. Arnold 1994, 10–11.

33. Smith 1988, 24–26.

34. Yoyotte 1998, 209.

35. Sauneron 1960.

36. Kiss 1998, 175–177.

37. Kiss (1998, 168) provides a map indicating the head's find spot (no. 1015); the Caesareum is marked, but not explicitly labeled, to the south. Information on the Caesareum: Fraser 1972a, 24; Tkaczow 1993, 128–129, site no. 81; and A. Bernand 1998, 152–154. Augustus' imperial cult in Egypt: Heinen 1995.

38. Philo *Legatio ad Gaium* 151; translation: F. H. Colson, *Philo*, vol. 10 (Cambridge, 1962), 77.

39. Kiss 1998, 175, reconstructs this height.

40. Polybius 15.29.8 and 15.33.8; Van de Walle 1949, 25; and Bruwier 1989, 28–29.

41. Wilkinson 1843, 172. Tkaczow (1993, 177–178, site no. 148) synthesizes historical accounts. See also el-Fattah and Gallo 1998, 12–13.

42. A. Bernand 1998, 246–248; *Gloire* 1998, 92–93; and Adriani 2000.

43. The *hm-hm*-crown is not well preserved today, but it is visible in a nineteenth-century sketch: Van de Walle 1950, 32, fig. 1.

44. Dio Cassius 50.5.3. Plutarch (*Antony* 60.3) notes that Antony was called young Dionysos (*Dionusos neos*), who was equated with Osiris in antiquity. Bothmer et al. (*ESLP* 1960, 132–133) suggest that Ptolemy VI and Cleopatra II could be depicted, but the Hadra head lacks Ptolemy VI's characteristic hairstyle (Chapter 6).

45. Smith 1988, 136–137, pls. 79: 14 and 80: 9.

46. A dark stone base for a statue dedicated to Marc Antony was found in Alexandria (Alexandria, Graeco-Roman Museum 10, H: 29.3 cm, W: 74.9 cm, D: 68.7 cm; two oval holes on the top, both about 4 cm deep). Five lines of Greek on the front mention a date of December 28, 34 B.C. Tkaczow (1993, 203, cat. no. 43) speculates that the statue may have been Egyptian in style. The holes on top argue against this interpretation. Also see *OGIS* 1 (1903), 280–281, no. 195; Fraser 1957; É. Bernand 1982, 37–38, no. 195; Walker and Higgs 2001, 232, cat. no. 213; and É. Bernand 2001, 102–105, no. 36, pl. 20.

47. Beckerath 1999, 244–245, 12T4; Hölbl 2001, 223.

48. Herodotus 2.42; Diodorus 1.25.2; and Dio Cassius 50.5.3; *CE* 1988, 155–156.

49. Kiss (1975, 296, pl. 88a–b; 1984, 23, 119, fig. 3; and 1998, 173–174) attributes the Hadra head to Ptolemy XII by comparison to the king's coin profile.

50. Examples: Cairo CG 39210, a granite seated dyad of Mut and Amun, H: 78 cm; and New York, Metropolitan Museum of Art 17.2.5, a limestone standing dyad of Hathor and Upwawet, H: 129 cm; Vandier 1958, pls. 122: 4 and 137: 4,

respectively. See Kozloff and Bryan 1992, 206–207. Kyrieleis (1975, 73–74) interprets the female's right-side positioning as a sign of dominance and concludes that a mother-regent and a son-king must be represented, but the female's entirely Egyptian attributes more persuasively identify her as a native goddess.

51. Beckerath 1999, 244–245, 12E2.

52. Two colossal, Egyptian-style heads of kings (J8) were also supposedly unearthed.

53. Yoyotte 1998 deals persuasively with arguments regarding the transport of Egyptian sculptures to Alexandria. See also D. J. Thompson 2000.

54. Strabo 17.1.27.

55. Arrian *Anabasis* 3.1.3–4; Hölbl 2001, 9.

56. Architectural fragment: Raue 1999, 136 n. 6. Also, Josephson (1995, 12) discusses how the Vatican Ptolemy II and Arsinoe II (A3, A4) could be from Heliopolis because the queen's back pillar inscription mentions the Heliopolitan Atum. Di. Arnold (1999, 342 n. 72) argues against this idea "because Late Period temples of Atum and Reharakhte were built in Sais, Bubastis, and Pithom."

57. Pliny *Naturalis historia* 36.14–15.

58. Lembke 1994.

59. Donald B. Redford, "Manetho," in *OEAE* 2: 336–337.

60. Tkaczow 1993, 230–242.

61. Beckerath 1999, 240–241, 8H3.

62. Pensabene 1993, 144, 348–351.

63. Tkaczow 1993, 207–242.

64. Alexandria, Graeco-Roman Museum S.G. 727, H: 45.0 cm (c. 90 cm in diameter); Rowe 1948, 42–43, pl. 4. A recent examination confirmed that cartouches of a second-century Ptolemy and Cleopatra are incised, though not all the signs transcribed by Rowe are still visible. Rowe's transcription omitted two cup signs (Gardiner W10) between the two cloth-wound-on-pole signs (Gardiner R8) in the Ptolemy's throne name.

65. Argued by Yoyotte (1998, 218–219). Tomlinson (1996, 159) counters: "An Egyptian style temple in Alexandria . . . seems unlikely."

66. Pensabene 1983; and *Gloire* 1998, 253, cat. no. 195.

67. Handler 1971; and *Gloire* 1998, 248–249.

68. Rufinus *Ecclesiastical History* 2.26; A. Bernand 1970a, 200–201.

69. Breccia 1926, 57–67.

70. Latest information: www.franckgoddio.org. Zsolt Kiss will publish the royal finds. Previous excavations: A. Bernand 1970a, 268–294; and Pensabene 1993, 217–218.

71. A. Bernand 1970a, 259–268.

72. Breccia 1926, 56.

73. Strabo 17.1.16–17. Other ancient sources: A. Bernand 1970a, 164–257.

74. Athenaeus 11.497d–e; Yoyotte 1998, 218.

75. *ḥwt-nṯr nt nṯrwj mnḫwj* in the hieroglyphic (Sethe 1904, 127.5), *ḥ-nṯr n n3 nṯr.w mnḫ.w* in the Demotic (Simpson 1996, 224, line 8), *ierōi tōn Euergetōn Theōn* in the Greek (A. Bernand 1992a, 29, line 7). See A. Bernand 1970a, 306–307.

76. *ḥwt-nṯr n P-gw3t* in the hieroglyphic (Sethe 1904, 143.9), *ḥ-nṯr (n) Pr-gwṯ* in the Demotic (Simpson 1996, 234, line 13 of Kom el-Hisn), *Ka[n]ōpōi ierōi* in the Greek (A. Bernand 1992a, 33, line 50). See Malaise 1999. A gold foundation plaque, having a Greek inscription naming Ptolemy III and Berenice II as dedicators of an Osiris sanctuary, was found at Canopus (London, British Museum, 17.1 cm × 5.8 cm); A. Bernand 1970a, 236–237, no. 7; and Bailey 1984.

77. *ḥwt-nṯr nt Jmn Grb* in the hieroglyphic (Sethe 1904, 144.3), *ḥ-nṯr n pr Jmn-Grb* in the Demotic (Simpson 1996, 236, line 51), *Ērakleiōi ierou* in the Greek (A. Bernand 1992a, 33, line 51). That the Greek text ascribes the temple to Heracles may indicate that the structure was pre-Ptolemaic, because Herodotus (2.113) writes that a like-named temple was located at the mouth of the Nile's Canopic branch at least since the time of Helen of Troy, and Strabo (17.1.18) mentions the temple; Yoyotte 1958, 427–430. Malaise and Winand (1993) argue that *grb* refers to an aspect of Amun under which he guides sailors to a safe landing.

78. New Haven, Peabody Museum of Natural History, Yale University YPM.264191 (= 6277), black granite, H: 102 cm; Malaise and Winand 1993, 13; and Yoyotte and Charvet 1997, 266–267.

79. Simpson 1996, 234–235, lines 49–50.

80. Breccia 1932, 17. Meyboom (1995, 53–55, 75–77, fig. 18) proposes that an Egyptian temple in the Nile Mosaic of Palestrina represents the Osiris temple at Canopus; reviewed by Michel Malaise in *CdE* 71 (1996), 379–383, and by Fabienne Burkhalter in *Topoi* 9 (1999), 229–260.

81. Meyboom 1995, figs. 41a–42d.

82. Leclant 1956, 263.

83. There are also the remains of a Ptolemaic(?), Egyptian-style temple enclosure dedicated to Osiris at Taposiris Magna (Abusir), 45 km to the west of Alexandria; Aufrère and Golvin 1997, 277–278; and Di. Arnold 1999, 193–194, fig. 144.

84. Strabo 17.1.32, translated by H. L. Jones, *The Geography of Strabo,* vol. 8 (Cambridge, 1932), 89.

85. D. J. Thompson 1988, 106 (capital), 16–17 (royal residence), and 118–119 (Ptolemy V coronation). Pseudo-Callisthenes 1.34 purports that Alexander the Great was so coronated; Capriotti Vittozzi 2000, 38–39.

86. Herodotus 2.99 and Strabo 17.1.31. Herodotus (2.153 and 2.176) also mentions large-scale statuary. See D. J. Thompson 1988, 17–18.

87. Di. Arnold 1994, 197–198.

88. Athenaeus 5.197c–203b.

89. Ridgway (1990, 131–134) summarizes theories on this exedra. See also Lauer and Picard 1955; D. J. Thompson 1988, 27–29; Kessler 2000, 217–219; and Hölbl 2001, 281–283.

90. Strabo 17.1.32.

91. Di. Arnold 1999, 144.

92. Cairo CG 27493 (head) and Paris, Louvre E 15683 (torso), from the Amun temple at Tanis, H: 83.5 cm; Desroches Noblecourt et al. 1981, 288–289, cat. no. 320; and *Gloire* 1998, 284, cat. nos. 227a–b. For *msn pr-ʿ*, see Wilson 1997, 462–463.

93. As indicated by the hieroglyph-inscribed foundation plaques; Desroches Noblecourt et al. 1981, 284–287, cat. nos. 287–319; Minas 2000, 39, 47–48; and Hölbl 2001, 160.

94. Di. Arnold 1999, 6, 173–174, plan 1.

95. Petrie 1889, 31, pl. 15. Ptolemy II and IV steles (London, British Museum EA 1056 and EA 1054, respectively): *CE* 1988, 103–105, cat. nos. 14–15. For EA 1054: Walker and Higgs 2001, 76–77, cat. no. 56. Favard-Meeks 1998, 110, 170–172, republishes Petrie's finds.

96. Myśliwiec 1992 on the gesture.

97. Coins: Edgar 1906a, 60–61; and Pfrommer 1987, 150. Foundation deposit: Naville and Griffith 1890, 29, pl. 8b.

98. Hölbl 2001, 58–59.

99. Ethnic composition: Bagnall 1997, 18. Archaeology of Hellenistic and Roman Fayoum: Davoli 1998. Fayoum overview: Terry G. Wilfong, "Faiyum," *OEAE* 1, 496–498.

100. Photo of statue in situ: Bastianini and Gallazzi 1989, 208, fig. 5. Aerial site map: Gallazzi 1989, 181.

101. Aufrère and Golvin 1997, 199; and Di. Arnold 1999, 155.

102. Aufrère and Golvin 1997, 201, illustrates a reconstruction of the end of the dromos.

103. Middle Kingdom royal fragments: Vogliano 1937, 54–56, pls. 38–41, including one of Amenemhat III (Milan E. 922, limestone seated figure, H: 150 cm, without base; Lise 1979, 28, cat. no. 80, pls. 109–113). Merenptah statue: Vogliano 1937, 56–57, pl. 42 (Cairo JE 66571, granite standard-bearer, H: 1.96 m; Sourouzian [1989, 107–109, cat. no. 61, pl. 19] believes the statue was erected during Rameside repairs of the Middle Kingdom temple).

104. É. Bernand 1981b, 72–80; and Leone 1995, 136–137. A Greek dedication for Ptolemy VIII, in large letters on a limestone fragment, was found on the *kôm*, its relationship to the site's monuments uncertain. A Greek-inscribed Egyptian stele mentioning Ptolemy IX and Cleopatra III (Cairo JE 66326) was associated with the temple addition (Vogliano 1937, 65, pl. 48). Two Greek inscriptions for Ptolemy IX (Alexandria, Graeco-Roman Museum 24491 and 24492) were carved on the temple itself.

105. Susanne Nakaten, "Petosiris," *LÄ* 4, cols. 995–998.

106. Spencer et al. 1989, 72–73; and Di. Arnold 1999, 111–113, 138, 140.

107. Fraser 1972a, 234.

108. Temple: Pensabene 1993, 248–253. Inscription: É. Bernand 1999, 16–17, no. 1, pls. 1–2.

109. Spencer et al. 1989, 74, pl. 92: "The first reference to the *Dromos* in the papyri dates from 89 B.C., but it is very likely that the street had been in existence for some time prior to this date, perhaps as early as 240 B.C. when the sanctuary of Ptolemy III and Queen Berenike was constructed."

110. The altar was deliberately incorporated into the dromos. Spencer et al. 1989, 33: "The bottom of this pedestal lay deeper than the pavement, the slabs of which had been arranged around it by turning two of the larger stones to lie along the sides of the block."

111. Cairo JE 87298, limestone statue, H: 2.65 m; Roeder 1959, 286, no. 252/VII, pl. 57b–c.

112. Recent treatments: Traunecker 1992; and Gabolde, Galliano et al. 2000.

113. Di. Arnold 1999, 160–161; and Hölbl 2001, 86.

114. Arsinoe I's banishment: Hölbl 2001, 36. Senoucheri: Petrie 1896, 19–21, pl. 20; Traunecker 1992, 312–315; and Quaegebeur 1998, 105, cat. no. 83.

115. Strabo 17.1.46.

116. Alexander the Great decoration: Di. Arnold 1999, 140.

117. For example, Beckerath 1999, 234–235, 1T1 (Ptolemy I) and 2T1 (Ptolemy II).

118. Strabo 17.1.42.

119. Bagnall 1998. A few Greek decrees from Ptolemais are preserved, mentioning a theatrical association, a city council, a people's assembly, and perhaps a gymnasium, all traditional elements of a Greek city; A. Bernand 1992a, 16–21, 74–77, nos. 3–7, 27.

120. Hölbl 2001, 153–157. Counterkings: Pestman 1995.

121. Russmann 1989, 3, 139, cat. no. 63, on a "statue killing" from the New Kingdom.

122. *Wb* 4: 46–47; and Wilson 1997, 803.

123. Ptolemy II examples: Vassilika 1989, pls. 20a–b, 21d, 22c.

124. Gaston Maspero (in Legrain 1904, 266) speculates that the cachette was filled under Ptolemies III–IV, while Bothmer et al. (*ESLP* 1960, 151–152) argue that additions were made in earlier centuries as well as later in the Ptolemaic Period. Legrain (1905, 66, 82) lists Ptolemaic finds: a bronze Harpocrates, two female statues, two Ptolemaic coins, and draped male statues. See Erika Feucht, "Cachette," in *LÄ* 1, col. 893; and De Meulenaere 1999.

125. Memphis decree: line 16 of the Demotic, *jw=w gmʿ r n3 jrpy.w* ("harming the temples;" Simpson 1996, 262–263), and line 23 of the Greek (A. Bernand 1992a, 46–47). Other textual/archaeological evidence: J. Johnson 1984, 116; Pestman 1995, 103; and Vandorpe 1995, 222, 232.

126. Hölbl 2001, 271–272, 275, 289.

127. Lenger 1964, 128–158, no. 53, and 1990, 15–16, 26, no. 53.

128. A. Bernand 1992a, 60–63, no. 22; Minas 2000, 7–11; and Hölbl 2001, 259–260, 280, 284.

129. Minas 2000, 6–23.

130. Di. Arnold 1999, 212–216.

131. Abdalla (1995, 22–26) says Ptolemy XI, though presumably means Ptolemy XII. Some scholars exclude the

ephemeral Ptolemy VII in their chronologies, reducing each succeeding Ptolemy by one Roman numeral (Ptolemy XII becomes Ptolemy XI); see Huss 1994, 10.

132. Abdalla (1995, 25) says the sphinx has a Ptolemy XI cartouche, though the faint inscription is clearly not Ptolemaic. Inscribed examples of Middle Kingdom royal sculpture: Fay 1996. I am grateful to Biri Fay for assistance with interpreting this sphinx.

133. Di. Arnold 1999, 169–171, 200–202, 209, 216–220.

134. Dynasty 30 falcon statues: Yoyotte 1959; and Josephson 1997a, 9–10.

135. Di. Arnold 1999, 190–193, 202–204.

136. A. Bernand 1969, 113–115, 121–126, nos. 10, 12.

137. Roullet 1972; Lembke 1994; Lollio Barberi et al. 1995; and *Iside* 1997.

138. Six 1887, 220 (based on an Isis sanctuary at Methana mentioned in Pausanias 2.34.1). Site overview: Gill, Foxhall, and Bowden 1997.

139. Egyptian-style statues of Roman emperors with hair and with documented Egyptian provenances are fewer in number than the Ptolemaic examples, and have widely distributed find spots. There is one sculpture of Augustus from Karnak (G2), and possibly another from Alexandria (G1), as well as statues of Caracalla or a second-century A.D. predecessor from Tanis (G10), Mendes (G11), Sheikh Fadl (G12), Terenouthis (G13), and Koptos (G14). Caracalla in Egypt: É. Bernand 1998. The small size and chronological skewing of the Roman sample argue against drawing substantive conclusions.

CHAPTER 4

A VISUAL VOCABULARY

IF PTOLEMAIC ROYAL SCULPTURE WERE A WORK OF literature, what would it be about, and to what genre would it belong? It would be a composition that gathered ideas about religion, propaganda, and magic, not into a narrative, but into a hymn extolling Ptolemaic Egyptian kingship. It would quote heavily from ancient sources, sometimes adding new turns of meaning. It would also sample from contemporary themes, though it would greatly subordinate these to long-established ones.

Egyptian statues, like this imaginary literary composition, are meant to be "read," with each individual component of a sculpture providing words and phrases that can be assembled into larger concepts. In looking at the head of Ptolemy VI from Aegina (B6), one can think of "Greek" (hair and face), "Egyptian" (hieroglyphic inscription), "king" (crowns), as well as of ideological qualities such as "powerful" (double crown), "protective" (uraeus), and "eternally ruling" (granite material), and then join these into an encomium praising the rule of Ptolemy VI.

The ancient visual vocabulary of Egyptian royal imagery was both remembered and altered over the course of the Ptolemaic Period. Careful selections were made among the statue types, materials, royal regalia, and inscriptional practices from Egypt's past, and new ideas were introduced, both subtle and overt. The granite material, *nemes* and double crown headdresses, and inscribed back pillar of the Aegina Ptolemy VI follow millennia-long traditions, but they are startlingly altered by the fresh additions of Greek hair and facial features. This chapter examines the visual vocabulary of Ptolemaic royal statuary to determine what was repeated, altered, or newly developed.

THE TIGHT EMBRACE OF TRADITION

Despite the changed ideas that Ptolemaic rule brought, native royal sculptures stayed strongly and fundamentally Egyptian. Materials, scale, statue types, and royal regalia are overwhelmingly consistent with past traditions. Most preserved statues are made of granite or limestone (each material comprises about 30 percent of Groups A–F in the catalogue, excluding sculptors' studies/votives), though a few are made of marble (B25, B27, C12, E13?, E14?) like Greek-style works.[1] The range in scale mirrors pre-Ptolemaic practice: 30 percent of Groups A–F are over-life-size and colossal, 22 percent life-size or very near, and 48 percent under-life-size or well under life-size, all excluding sculptors' studies/votives. As in prior periods, standing male figures with the left foot forward and male sphinxes with a human head on the body of a recumbent lion make up the vast majority of Ptolemaic royal sculptures.[2] Other types are rare—seated (A10, A28), kneeling (A1, not assuredly royal; A42) and a falcon statue perhaps standing over the king (F2)—but in many cases only heads are preserved, and one cannot judge the original statue type.[3] There is also the vast category of works known as sculptors' studies or votives, which contains Ptolemaic examples (Appendix A).

Most nonsphinx sculptures have a back pillar or the remains of one. Square, trapezoidal, or triangular tops are the most frequent. Though some heads do not show traces of a support at the nape (such as C6, D3), which is unusual, the pillar may have ended lower down, on the back of the figure (as in A23). These examples also maintain a strict frontality consonant with Egyptian tradition, in contrast to the head turns apparent in Greek-style portraits, including one made of Egyptian limestone (Fig. 273).[4]

Attributes—crowns, garments, and hand-held objects—are mostly customary Egyptian ones. Native symbols of power such as the uraeus, *nemes,* and Egyptian diadem are frequent, and many statues originally had elaborate crowning headdresses—ram horns, double crowns, or other combination crowns visible in royal reliefs[5]—that are usually not preserved today. For example, an under-life-size head of a king in Turin (A20) has three holes for several missing attachments, perhaps of precious materials, given the sculpture's fine quality: on top of the *nemes* for an additional crown, at the base of the uraeus for the snake's rearing body, and under the chin for a false beard. These and other traditional attributes give us the visual vocabulary with which we can "read" the royal statuary.

Uraeus

One of the most ancient and ubiquitous of Egyptian royal symbols, the uraeus evokes the essential meaning of kingship in Egypt—the pharaoh as rightful ruler and protector against chaos.[6] It takes the form of a snake whose head rears up on the brow of its wearer, protecting him or her against enemies. The uraeus appears on most Ptolemaic royal statues, normally with a coil on either side of the rearing body (uraeus with loops) for kings, and no coils (loopless) for queens. Most portraits lacking the uraeus (B1, C6, C7, C20, D4, D8, D12, D14, D19, E6, E9, E17, F4) are hellenized, suggesting that the omission mimicked a similar absence in Greek-style works, and that other attributes provided the basis for royal identification. For E9, which has no hellenizing features, the uraeus' absence perhaps parallels pre-Ptolemic instances of the same.[7] In addition, the uraeus may have been present on a now-missing attribute (as with E17, which may have had a double crown).

Nemes

The *nemes* is the most common headdress on Egyptian-style statues of Ptolemaic kings, continuing its dominance as a royal male symbol evident throughout Egypt's history.[8] The Ptolemaic *nemes* has its typical curved shape with frontlet, pigtail, and lappets, though it usually lacks the headdress's characteristic banding. According to Middle Kingdom coffin texts, the *nemes* was white and had red banding and a gold frontlet.[9] Most likely the original headdress was made primarily of fabric, which is a connotation of the Egyptian term *nms.*[10] The Ptolemaic *nemes* is often surmounted by other attributes: a *hm-hm*-crown that associates the king with Osiris (E1) or perhaps Horus (A8),[11] a beetle scarab that points to the god Khepri (B9), or double crowns (such as B6).

Double Crown

The double crown combines the red crown of Lower Egypt and the white one of Upper Egypt into a potent symbol of the unification of the two lands under a single king.[12] Egyptians called the crown *sḫmtj,* meaning "the two powerful ones," the goddesses *Wadjyt* and *Nekhbet* of Lower and Upper Egypt.[13] According to the Memphis decree, the *sḫmtj* prominently marked Ptolemy V's processional shrine.[14] The double crown is worn alone (B23, C1, E9), tied with a diadem (E10), or placed atop a *nemes* (A9, B6, B7?, C2?, C8?, C22, D13) or a diademed head (B1, E17?). Goddesses can wear the crown (Fig. 186). It is one of the few Egyptian attributes to appear in Greek-style royal images (Fig. 223).

Blue Crown

The blue crown, or *ḫprš*,[15] derives its modern name from the fact that some representations of the crown are so colored. Its precise meaning is elusive, but some think that the crown relates either to war or to the king's legitimacy.[16] In its familiar form—a tall, curved shape whose profile view is bisected by a diagonal fold—the blue crown is known on royal statues as early as the New Kingdom. Though the crown appears regularly on Late Period royal statues, it seldom occurs on Ptolemaic statues (D15).[17] The crown frequently appears in reliefs (Fig. 208).

Ram Horns

Ram horns are added to the royal regalia to associate the wearer with gods having these horns, such as Amun, Horus, Osiris, and Khnum.[18] The horns are of two varieties: one that curls around the ears, and a second twisted type that sticks straight out, away from the head. The first has no certain examples among Egyptian-style, Ptolemaic royal statues,[19] though it frequently occurs in Egyptian relief as well as in Greek-style images, particularly coins (Fig. 215).[20] The second can form part of several crowns, including the *hm-hm* (A8, E1), the *atef*, and Arsinoe II's combination crown (E12; see below), and often appears in reliefs (Fig. 211).[21]

Diadem

The Egyptian diadem occurs in royal representations at least as far back as the Old Kingdom.[22] Under the Ptolemies, the *sšd* ("headband") is elevated to new importance because the separately developed Greek version[23] becomes the headdress of choice for the rulers' Greek-style portraits. Both Egyptian and Greek diadems are present in Egyptian-style sculpture, and they can be difficult to distinguish from each other. Assuredly of Greek origin are the wide (C10, C11) or rolled (C7, D4) varieties. More ambiguous are the thin diadems. Those that are horizontal in profile and worn on Egyptian wigs relate well to native models (A43, B29). Thin diadems having a tilted angle in profile (E13, E16),[24] encircling Greek-style hair (C19), and particularly those going under the occipital bulge (B1) are more closely related to Greek models.

The diadem is much less prevalent on Egyptian statues of kings than on those of queens. When the headdress does appear on kings, the statues usually possess hellenizing features, principally Greek hair. Diadems also are worn by boy-kings and princes (B1, B3, E15, E16, E17). In one exceptional case, a diadem encircles a *kausia,* a Macedonian cap (E18).[25]

Queens' Crowns

As the *nemes* is the most prevalent headdress for kings, the diadem is the most popular for queens. The diadem binds the tripartite or corkscrew lock wig, and it is often augmented with a second crown placed on top of the head, usually in a circular modius, either plain (C18) or decorated with uraei (A46, B28, C19, E2). In the few cases where the added attribute is preserved, there are various combinations of cow horns, sun disks, feathers, and uraei (D3, F3), which have divinizing qualities.[26] There are ample precedents for the diadem/modius combination among pre-Ptolemaic images of queens.[27]

A few queens and goddesses wear the vulture cap (A45, E2, E12, F5), whose royal and divine usage extends back to the Old Kingdom. The vulture hieroglyph (*mwt*) means "mother," and the cap alludes to Isis as the mother of Horus, and the queen as the mother of the future king.[28] The headdress has particularly strong divine connotations: it is, for example, exclusively worn by goddesses in the reliefs of the Isis temple at Philae.[29] One sculpture with the cap portrays Isis (E2), whereas the others likely represent deified queens (A45, E12, F5).

Hand-held Attributes

Virtually all standing statues of Ptolemaic kings and some queens hold small objects in the clenched hands at their sides, a gesture having substantial precedent. Usually, the objects appear as rounded knobs emerging from either side of each fist, and they have been interpreted as folded cloths or truncated staffs.[30] Here, they will be called enigmatic objects. The Vatican Arsinoe II (A4) clearly has a cloth in her right hand, since a fold is marked in front of the fist and two ends of unequal length emerge from behind. In addition, the object held in each hand of the Tebtunis king (E3) curves downward behind each fist. One king held a *heqa*-scepter (now commonly called a "crook"), as indicated by the remains of its curved top on the left *nemes* lappet (E1). The crook hieroglyph (*ḥq3*) meant "to rule" or "ruler," as befits a scepter of kings and gods, particularly Osiris.[31]

Queens hold several other royal and divine symbols known from earlier periods. The so-called lily scepter (A45, B14, B29), with a curved, stemlike handle surmounted by a floral finial holding several thin strips of cloth or animal pelts, can be read as *ḫwj,* meaning "to protect."[32] The *ankh*-sign (B29, D10), signifying "life" in Egyptian, points to the queen's role in bearing children to continue the royal line.[33] The *menat* (A4) could be ceremonially shaken to make noise, similar to the better-known sistrum rattle. Transliterated from Egyptian hieroglyphs as *mnjt,* it meant "bead necklace" and symbolized Hathor's protective and procreative powers.[34]

Garments

Several familiar Egyptian royal garments are carried into the Ptolemaic Period. Most kings wear the *shendyt* (from the Egyptian *šndwt,* "skirt"), the belted royal skirt that is the most common garment on statues of kings throughout Egypt's history.[35] The skirt has its typical appearance, with the left side overlapping the right at the front and a center panel hanging between the legs. Usually plain, it can also be pleated (A1, A11, A18, A36, A42, C22, E3), and its belt can be inscribed (A12, E4). Egyptian-style queens often wear plain, close-fitting sheath dresses, whose presence is mostly indicated by collar and hem lines (such as A4), and sometimes pleated outfits with fringed edging (A10, B14, B29) and ribbon-like sashes (A10, B14).[36]

IMPORTANT NEW TRENDS

Though the language of Ptolemaic royal portraits remained resolutely Egyptian, Greek rule spurred fresh adaptations and innovations. Sculptural groups mixed royal and divine figures and depicted the royal family, paralleling types particularly known from the New Kingdom. Statues of queens appeared in large numbers in recognition of the powerful roles of the Arsinoes and Cleopatras. Attributes were altered or newly introduced, principally the triple uraeus and cornucopia for queens, and draped garments and Greek hair for both kings and queens. Greek texts were carved on Egyptian statues, changing inscriptional practices.

Statue Pairs and Sculptural Groups

Statue pairs and sculptural groups receive renewed emphasis under Ptolemaic rule. Two dyads and one triad—multiple figures carved from the same block of stone—portray the Ptolemies as *sunnaoi theoi.* The king appears with Isis (E1, E2), a crocodile-headed god (B23), and probably Amun and the queen (A10). In all three cases, the royal and divine figures are of similar scale, giving the king and queen a status equal to that of the gods. To contrast, Nectanebo II of Dynasty 30 is frequently portrayed as a diminutive figure beneath a towering Horus falcon,[37] similar to one Ptolemaic example (F2). The best parallels for Ptolemaic royal/divine dyads and triads are from the New Kingdom, when such sculptures were common.[38]

Some sculptures originally formed a pair or group portraying the royal couple or family. The Vatican Ptolemy II and Arsinoe II (A3, A4)—of like scale, style, material, and provenance—are one example of what must have been more common pairs that the Karnak decree directed to be set up in thanks for benefactions (Chapter 2). The Pharos colossi provide additional examples (C21). King, queen, and royal son groups are attested in two second-century bases that supported Egyptian-style statues, one found near Philae (B13) and a similar one from Elephantine.[39] A third example from the time of Ptolemy V may have supported Greek- or Egyptian-style statues (B4). A seventeenth-century drawing of a lost sculpture depicts a standing triad with a back slab that gives an impression of how to reconstruct these groups, although this example is carved from a single block of stone. A king (the head is missing, though the figure wears the royal male draped ensemble) and a queen or goddess with Hathor headdress flank a boy in a draped costume (Fig. 207).[40] Royal pairs and groups are unattested for Dynasty 30, but are frequent in the New Kingdom.[41] The Ptolemaic examples, however, are unusual in the way that the royal parents visually frame and present their son.

The Powerful Status of Queens

Statues of queens are produced in unusually high numbers and on a monumental scale, propelled by the highly successful cult of Arsinoe II established by Ptolemy II (Chapter 2) and subsequent queens' major roles as rulers and regents. About one-quarter of Group A–F sculptures depict women. A new visual vocabulary—including the cornucopia, the combination crown of Arsinoe II, the triple uraeus, and the draped ensemble—is created and is added to a few special statues.

The cult of Arsinoe II provided initial direction for the iconography of royal female statuary. A combination crown—a vulture cap, red crown, horizontal ram's horns, and Hathor horns with sun disk—may have been created for the queen's divinization by Ptolemy II.[42] The headdress boldly combines divine attributes with the crown of Lower Egypt, where Alexandria was located. There are relief depictions,[43] as well as one definite example in the round (E12). The Greek cornucopia reportedly was added to Arsinoe II's representations at Ptolemy II's request.[44] This horn of plenty, brimming with cakes and fruits symbolic of wealth and abundance, is cradled by queens (C28, D10, E14) and appears on the reverse of Ptolemaic coins.[45]

The triple uraeus appears on a few statues likely connected to the cults of the deified queens (D9, D10, E13, E14, F3, F5). Some have explained the attribute as an allusion to a triple regency (such as Cleopatra II with Ptolemies VI and VIII)[46] or to land gained by marriage to a rival kingdom's princess (such as Cyrenaica with Berenice II).[47] "Goddesses" (*nṯrwt*) is the best interpretation, however, because that is how three uraei can be literally read in Egyptian hieroglyphs.[48] Moreover, the attribute derives from a vulture head/double uraeus combination[49] that referred to goddesses in pre-Ptolemaic times,[50] and other special attributes on Ptolemaic statues express an association with a deity, such as the *hm-hm*-crown with Osiris (E1, E2) and the sidelock with Horus (B1, C2). The triple uraeus was a powerful addition to statues of queens to recognize their goddesslike status.

Some queens wear a draped ensemble consisting of a tunic undergarment and a fringed overmantle knotted distinctively at the breast (C25, C27, C28, D5, E11, E14).[51] Two Greek features, the cornucopia and corkscrew locks, often appear on the same statues. The overmantle has Egyptian origins[52] and perhaps imitates garments draped over precious-metal cult images of Ptolemaic queens, similar to fringed linen ones found knotted around gilded cult statues of Tutankhamun.[53] It is also a ceremonial dress. In relief, queens wear the ensemble when portrayed as *sunnaoi theoi* (Fig. 206), and when conferred with the right to divine queenship.[54] The costume's elevated connotations led to its identification with Isis during the Roman Period.[55]

Draped Kings

The royal male draped ensemble consists of a bulky, fringed mantle, short-sleeved tunic, and long skirt.[56] It appears on a lost statue (Fig. 207), a fragment from the lower part of such a draped statue (F1), a head with a bit of drapery on the shoulder (E10), a falcon with a draped figure beneath it (F2), as well as better-preserved relief depictions (Figs. 205–206). Typically, the king wears a double crown encircled with a diadem (Fig. 206), as preserved on one statue (E10). Other statues may have worn the draped ensemble, though the state of preservation does not allow a judgment. The Brussels Ptolemy VIII (C1) is a good candidate because it is unusual in wearing the double crown alone.

The ensemble has Egyptian origins, because comparable combinations—heavy mantle, sometimes with a white crown and diadem—appear in pre-Ptolemaic reliefs of *sed*-festivals, the traditional Egyptian celebration of a king's rejuvenated reign.[57] Ptolemaic examples similarly commemorate the eternal renewal of divine kingship.[58] On the gateway of Amun-Re-Montu at Karnak, the draped Ptolemy III and Berenice II stand before the god Khonsu-Thoth, who records the decree bestowing the right to rule.[59] The inscription notes: *k3.wj n nṯr.wj mnḫ.wj m ḏt ḥntj ḥḥ ḥbw-sd ḥḥw*, "the two *ka*s of the Benefactor Gods eternally, forever and ever: tens of millions of jubilees."[60] The *ka* is a legitimacy-conveying life force. The draped garment is thus tightly bound to the king's right to rule. Ptolemy VI and Cleopatra II appear in a similar relief at Kom Ombo (Fig. 205).[61]

The Potency of Greek Hair

Greek hair is the most common hellenizing feature of Egyptian-style Ptolemaic royal sculptures. Such hair, so identified because it is patterned after Greek-style depictions, appears on 35 percent of Group A–F sculptures; 50 percent do not have it, and the rest are too fragmentary to judge (calculations exclude sculptors' studies/votives).[62] The power of Greek hair perhaps derives from the prominence of Alexander the Great's *anastolē*—hair standing up from the forehead with an off-center part—which is a trademark of his portraits.[63] Hair can identify specific rulers in their portraits: four heads of Ptolemy VI (B6, B7, B8?, Fig. 254) have very similar forehead coiffures. Hair can also provide a strong deifying quality: corkscrew locks on queens (C19, C20, C27, C28, D3, D4, D5, D6, D7, D8, E13, E14) descend from similar ones on archaic korai and pre-Hellenistic statues of goddesses.[64]

Literature of both cultures portrays hair as enormously potent. In the Tale of Two Brothers from the New Kingdom, the sea carried a lock of a woman's hair to Egypt, where it fell into the king's laundry and bewitched him.[65] According to the ancient writer Lucian, residents of Memphis displayed the locks of Isis as a treasured relic, and Plutarch wrote that Isis dedicated a tress of her hair at Koptos while mourning for her husband Osiris.[66] In the musings of the Alexandrian poet Callimachus, a lock of Berenice II ascended into the heavens and became a celestial constellation soon after she dedicated it at the shrine of Aphrodite Arsinoe at the Zephyrium near Canopus.[67] An epigram of the Greek poet Damagetus celebrated Arsinoe III's sacrifice of a lock of hair to Artemis.[68]

A usurpation illustrates the critical importance of Greek hair for Ptolemaic royal statuary. In looking at the profile view of an under-life-size dark stone statue of a king with *nemes* and hair in Cairo (D14), the outline of the forehead and front of the *nemes* conspicuously recedes relative to the chin, instead of being on the same plane with it or the forehead being dominant, both of which would be more typical. There is also a shallow depression on the forehead under the current hairline. This suggests that the hair and the front of the *nemes* were cut back as the result of reworking. Additional evidence of this recarving is present on the right and left sides of the jaw, where traces of a natural beard are preserved (Fig. 137).

The alterations signal that the statue's identity was changed from that of a king with a certain forehead hairstyle and beard to that of another king with a different coiffure and no beard. Similar usurpations appear among Greek-style marble portraits of the late Ptolemies, particularly in terms of the presence or absence of a beard.[69] Leaving aside the specifics of who is represented in the first or second version (Chapter 7), the Cairo statue clearly follows the prior Egyptian practice of usurpation, where kings recut and reinscribed statues of their predecessors.[70] In this case, the forehead hair and beard were considered essential elements for establishing identity.

Changes in Inscriptional Practices

Inscriptions on Ptolemaic royal statues are unusual in two respects: they are comparatively rare, and they include Greek texts. Despite the longstanding Egyptian propensity to carve hieroglyphic inscriptions on statuary, such texts mostly are not preserved for Ptolemaic royal examples, and sometimes are complemented or replaced by Greek inscriptions, in keeping with this language's rising importance in official documents of the Ptolemaic Period.

Of the approximately 150 sculptures of Groups A–F, only about twenty-five preserve at least a partial royal text (see Table 4.1). (This figure excludes nonroyal texts, such as C3, and bases for Greek statues, such as D1.) In contrast, inscribed statues, including sphinxes, for the much briefer Dynasty 30 exist in much greater numbers.[71] The circumstance may in part reflect chance, but also indicates a shift in inscriptional practices.[72] More texts may have been placed on an attached base (B12) or a separately worked one (B13), rather than the back pillar, a practice that is consonant with Egyptian custom[73] and exactly mirrors Greek practices. These bases may then have disappeared because they are conveniently sized and shaped for reuse: one base became a support for an altar in a Coptic sanctuary (B13), another served as the back of a stone bench for a boutique (B12), and others became building materials (A15, A19, B4). Missing bases may have carried a statue's main or only inscription.

The addition of Greek texts to Egyptian statue bases (A14, A41, B12, B13, E3?) is another significant change in inscriptional practice. In their placement, wording, and function, these texts are similar to those on Greek statue bases (D1, D2).[74] For example, an Egyptian base from el-Hesa (B13) and a Greek one from Canopus (D1) have comparable phrasing: they state the sovereign's name and Greek royal epithet, followed by the name(s) of the person(s) setting up the statues. Both dedications create an identity for the portrait in a highly visible way. Hieroglyphic inscriptions on bases and belts of Egyptian statues (such as A3, A12, A17) also provided identification, but were complemented by less (or not) visible back pillar inscriptions (such as A3, A12) that imbued the statue with magical puissance. Reflecting the bilingualism of Ptolemaic Egyptians, some Egyptian statues have combined Greek/hieroglyphic (A14) or Greek/Demotic (B13) inscriptions.[75]

CONCLUSIONS

The visual vocabulary of Ptolemaic royal sculpture is mostly an Egyptian one. Statue types, materials, scale, and attributes largely conform to time-honored norms.

TABLE 4.1 ROYAL STATUES WITH INSCRIPTIONS

Description	Statue Style	Script(s)[a]	Inscription Location	Ruler Named
A1. Fragmentary kneeling male statue	Egyptian	H	Back pillar	Alexander the Great or his son
A2. Separately worked statue base	Egyptian?	D, G	Front of base	Ptolemy I
A3. Standing statue of king with attached base	Egyptian	H	Back pillar, belt	Ptolemy II
A4. Standing statue of queen with attached base	Egyptian	H	Back pillar, base	Arsinoe II
A5. Fragmentary statue of king	Egyptian	H	Back pillar	Ptolemy II
A10. Triad of king, queen, and deity	Egyptian	H	Back and sides of seat	Ptolemy II
A11. Standing statue of king	Egyptian	H	Back pillar	Ptolemy II
A12. Torso of king	Egyptian	H	Back pillar, belt	Ptolemy II
A13. Attached(?) statue base	Egyptian	H	Base	Arsinoe II
A14. Attached base for statue of queen	Egyptian	H, G	Front (G), top (H) of base	Arsinoe II
A15. Statue base	Uncertain	G	Front of base	Arsinoe II
A16. Fragmentary standing statue of king	Egyptian	H	Back pillar	Ptolemy III
A17. Attached base for statue of king	Egyptian	H	Front, sides, top of base	Ptolemy III
A18. Torso of king	Egyptian	H	Back pillar	Ptolemy III
A19. Statue base	Uncertain	G	Front of base	Arsinoe III
A41. Sphinx with attached base	Egyptian	G	Front of base	None
A46. Head of goddess	Egyptian	H	Back pillar	None remaining
B4. Separately worked statue base	Uncertain	G	Front of base	Ptolemy V, parents Ptolemy IV and Arsinoe III
B5. Statue base	Uncertain	G	Front of base (?)	Ptolemy V
B6. Head of king	Egyptian	H	Back pillar	Ptolemy VI
B10. Fragment of statue of king	Egyptian	H	Back pillar	Ptolemy VI
B11. Fragment of statue of king	Egyptian	H	Back pillar	Ptolemy VI
B12. Attached base for statue of king	Egyptian	G	Front of base	Ptolemy VI
B13. Separately worked statue base for three statues	Egyptian	D, G	Front of base	Ptolemy VI, Cleopatra II, and son
B14. Fragmentary statue of standing queen	Egyptian	H	Back pillar	Cleopatra II
C3. Sphinxes with attached bases	Egyptian	D	Base	None
C28. Standing statue of queen with attached base	Egyptian	H	Back pillar	Arsinoe II
D1. Separately worked statue base	Greek	G	Front of base	Cleopatra III
D2. Separately worked statue base	Greek	G	Front of base	Ptolemy IX
D15. Head of king with a blue crown	Egyptian	H	Back pillar	None remaining
E3. Standing statue of king with attached base	Egyptian	G	Front of separately worked(?) base	Ptolemy XII
E4. Standing statue of king	Egyptian	H	Back pillar, belt	Ptolemy XII/XV
F1. Standing king	Egyptian	H	Back pillar	Ptolemy XII?
F3. Queen's headdress	Egyptian	H	Back pillar	Uncertain

[a]H = hieroglyphic; D = Demotic; G = Greek.

The typically Egyptian standing and sphinx poses predominate, most preserved statues are made of granite or limestone, and scale ranges from well under life-size to colossal. Regalia, including the *nemes,* uraeus, double crown, and ram horns, largely repeat established ideas.

Several important trends emerge, however. Statue groups combining royal and divine figures depict the Ptolemies as *sunnaoi theoi,* and dynastic pairs and triads bring together king, queen, and royal son. Statues of queens multiply, paralleling the high-profile, influential roles of these women. Royal female attributes receive fresh impetus from new adaptations, notably the triple uraeus and Arsinoe II's combination crown. Status-enhancing draped garments of Egyptian origin appear on representations of kings and queens.

Greek elements come into the vocabulary in a highly selective manner. The cornucopia, the Greek wide diadem, and the *kausia* are added to a few Egyptian statues, as are Greek texts. Greek hair is the most common addition, however, perhaps because of its historical associations with potency, contemporary resonance with Greek ideas, and strong ability to create identity.

NOTES

1. I am not aware of any published tests that shed light on these marbles' possible source(s). The marbles vary in quality and appearance, suggesting multiple sources for the material. The material of E13 and E14 sometimes is identified as limestone, but museum curators for both call the sculptures marble, based on a visual judgment. Marble in Egypt: Lucas 1989, 414–415; Di. Arnold 1994, 146; and Nicholson and Shaw 2000, 44–45. Marble is rarely used for royal statues prior to the Ptolemaic Period (see Cairo JE 43507A, a marble statue of Dynasty 18's Thutmosis III, from Deir el-Medina, H: 26.5 cm; Saleh and Sourouzian 1987, cat. no. 135).

2. In looking at the inscribed stone sculptures of Dynasty 29 and 30 kings, single standing male figures and sphinxes predominate, though there is a higher concentration of kneeling figures, particularly for Dynasty 29 (Traunecker 1979, 409: B1, 414–415: B2, B4), and falcon statues for Dynasty 30 (Josephson 1997a, 9 n. 62).

3. For example, a fragmentary king in the British Museum (A23) may be from a seated statue, because better-preserved pre-Ptolemaic works with a similar hand gesture and cloak have this pose (Chapter 5).

4. A possible late Ptolemaic representation of Alexander the Great (Alexandria, Graeco-Roman Museum 3242, provenance not known, H: 34.0 cm; Wildung and Grimm 1978, cat. no. 78) is exceptional in being made of granite and having a head turn. The standing emperor in Rome (G6) is unusual in lacking a back pillar. A headless, dark stone female statue with corkscrew locks, draped ensemble, and cornucopia (Cairo CG 27473, provenance not known, H: 141 cm; Capriotti Vittozzi 1995, 415, no. 6 as CG 27471) also lacks a pillar and may be Roman as well.

5. Vassilika 1989, 84–95, 293–325.

6. Karl Martin, "Uräus," *LÄ* 6, cols. 864–868; and Shaw and Nicholson 1995, 67, 302–303.

7. For example, Boston, Museum of Fine Arts 11.1738, a pair statue of Mycerinus in a *nemes* (Aldred 1980, fig. 35), and Cairo JE 36195, a seated statue of Mentuhotep II in a red crown (Saleh and Sourouzian 1987, cat. no. 67). Bothmer et al. (*ESLP* 1960, 177) propose that the absence of the uraeus on D14 designated a nonroyal person associated with the crown, such as Marc Antony. For this particular statue, however, the uraeus may have been removed in a recutting (discussed later in this chapter).

8. Christa Müller, "Kopftuch," *LÄ* 3, cols. 693–694.

9. Jéquier 1921, 8–11.

10. *Wb* 2:269; and Wilson 1997, 518–519.

11. Horus and the *hm-hm*-crown: Yoyotte and Chuvin 1988, 171–173.

12. Strauss 1980, col. 813.

13. *Wb* 4:250–251; and Wilson 1997, 904–905.

14. Quirke and Andrews 1989, 14, 21, line 9.

15. *Wb* 3: 268; and Wilson 1997, 722.

16. Strauss 1980, cols. 814–815; and Vassilika 1989, 92.

17. Late Period examples: Josephson 1997a. Robert S. Bianchi (*CE* 1988, 143) suggests that native denial of Ptolemaic legitimacy explains the blue crown's disappearance, though Leahy (1992, 226–227) rightly argues against this proposal by pointing to the continued appearance of the crown in Ptolemaic relief.

18. Strauss 1980, cols. 814–815.

19. Bell (1985, 270 n. 90) identifies two statues wearing such horns as Ptolemies, but they represent deities and are unlikely to be Ptolemaic. The first is Cairo CG 38021, a life-size, limestone standing statue from Karnak, H: 2.05 m; Hornemann 1951–1969, 1: no. 165. The second is Cairo CG 693, an under-life-size limestone head, provenance not known, H: 24 cm; Borchardt 1930, 37, pl. 127; and PM 8 (1999), 203, no. 800-942-200.

20. Egyptian-style reliefs: Vassilika 1989, 86. Greek-style images: Svenson 1995, 14–19, 74–75, 81–82, 84–85, 112–114.

21. Vassilika 1989, 86.

22. Ebba Kerrn-Lillesø, "Stirnband und Diademe," *LÄ* 6, cols. 45–49.

23. Smith 1988, 34–38.

24. The tilted angle should be attributed cautiously to Greek influence, since pre-Ptolemaic examples are known

(Bianchi 1978, 99–100). Bianchi (*CE* 1988, 153) points out that the way the band goes underneath the occipital bulge on B1 compares well to Ptolemy V's coins (Fig. 220), thus bolstering an interpretation of the diadem as a Greek one.

25. *Kausia:* Saatsoglou-Paliadeli 1993, 122–142.

26. Irene Grumach-Shirun, "Federn und Federkrone," *LÄ* 2, cols. 142–145; and Emma Brunner-Traut, "Horn," *LÄ* 3, cols. 9–10. Cow horns and goddesses: Troy 1986, 70; and Vassilika 1989, 94.

27. Troy 1986, 121–122.

28. Emma Brunner-Traut, "Geierhaube," *LÄ* 2, col. 515; and Troy 1986, 116–119. Vulture hieroglyph: *Wb* 2:54; and Wilson 1997, 419.

29. Vassilika 1989, 93.

30. Fischer 1975 presents strong evidence that the shape represents a cloth. Robert S. Bianchi (*CE* 1988, 70) supports Fischer's ideas.

31. Peter Kaplony, "Zepter," *LÄ* 6, cols. 1376–1377; *ḥq3*: *Wb* 3:170–173; and Wilson 1997, 680–681.

32. Geoffrey Graham, "Insignias," *OEAE* 2:165; *ḫwj*: *Wb* 3:244–245; and Wilson 1997, 710.

33. Vassilika 1989, 98–99; and Andrews 1994, 86–87; *ʿnḫ*: *Wb* 1:193–198; and Wilson 1997, 155–157.

34. Elisabeth Staehelin, "Menit," *LÄ* 4, cols. 52–53; and Andrews 1994, 41–42; *mnjt: Wb* 2:75–76; and Wilson 1997, 423–424.

35. Skirts and aprons: Vogelsang-Eastwood 1993, 32–71. *šndwt*: *Wb* 4:522. Nonroyal men also wear this skirt.

36. Dresses: Vogelsang-Eastwood 1993, 95–129; and Lyn Green, "Clothing and Personal Adornment," *OEAE* 1:276–277.

37. Such as New York, Metropolitan Museum of Art 34.2.1, graywacke, H: 72.0 cm; Josephson 1997a, 9–10, pl. 3d.

38. New Kingdom and earlier examples: Seidel 1996.

39. Herwig Maehler will publish this granite base, which is inscribed for Ptolemy VI and Cleopatra II and was recently excavated at Elephantine. Like B13, the base has rectangular holes on top for the placement of three statues, though in this case, the center hole (for the royal son?) is cut into a small, elevated base atop the larger one (as in Fig. 207).

40. Windsor Castle RL 8580, drawing from the collection of Cassiano dal Pozzo; Roullet 1972, 64, cat. no. 46, pl. 49, fig. 65; and *Iside* 1997, 398.

41. Examples: Vandier 1958, pls. 103: 1, 108: 1, and 111: 1.

42. Crown's origins: Dils 1998. Usage by later queens: Quaegebeur 1983, 112–113; Dils 1998, 1309–1312; and Albersmeier and Minas 1998, 14 n. 30. An exclusive identification of the double uraeus with Arsinoe II (Sally-Ann Ashton, in Walker and Higgs 2001, 151–152) does not agree with the attribute's long history and varied associations (Russmann 1974, 35–44).

43. *CE* 1988, 169–170, cat. no. 65; and Vassilika 1989, 94, 322.

44. Athenaeus (11.497b–c) writes *keras* ("cornucopia") rather than *dikeras* ("double cornucopia"). Discussion: D. B. Thompson 1973, 31–33; and Plantzos 1992, 124–126.

45. Kyrieleis 1975, pl. 70: 3.

46. *ESLP* 1960, 147. Vandier (1961, 250) likewise cited the triple regency theory. See varied ideas gathered by Sally-Ann Ashton, in Walker and Higgs 2001, 154–155. The female in a blue glass gem (London, British Museum GR 1923.4-1.676, L: 1.3 cm) wears a *hm-hm*-crown, not a triple uraeus (Walker and Higgs 2001, 143, 155, 156, cat. no. 153). The attribute has straight horns as its base, and three conical elements topped with circular ones, as in the *hm-hm*-crown (Vassilika 1989, 302); Serapis wears this crown on a Vienna gem (*Iside* 1997, 248, cat. no. IV.258). I owe these observations to Giuseppina Capriotti Vittozzi.

47. Capriotti Vittozzi 1995, 427–431.

48. *Wb* 2:362; and Wilson 1997, 558. See *CE* 1988, 176.

49. For example, on Cairo CG 609, a granite head of Queen Tiy, H: 48 cm; Borchardt 1925, 158, pl. 110; and Vandier 1958, 330, pl. 108: 3.

50. Russmann 1974, 35–44; and Russmann 1997. Though some see three uraei on Queen Tiy in the colossal limestone statue from Amenhotep III's funerary temple at Thebes (Cairo JE 33906, H: 700 cm; *ESLP* 1960, 147; *CE* 1988, 176; and Kozloff and Bryan 1992, 203 n. 2), it is a vulture head/double uraeus combination (Tait 1982, col. 86; and Russmann 1989, 98, 100–101, cat. no. 45). The combination also appears on one Ptolemaic example (A45; a broken-off vulture head and holes for two metal uraei).

51. Walters 1988, 4–11, fig. 1, illustrates the two garments. Bianchi (1980) proposes a tripartite ensemble (tunic, robe, and fringed mantle), but this is not visible on statues I have examined. Albersmeier and Minas (1998, 19 n. 47) also question Bianchi's proposal.

52. Walters (1988, 5, 8) gives an overview of research connecting the Ptolemaic ensemble with knotted dresses of the New Kingdom. Though she sees the ensemble as Egyptian, she notes that the undergarment could be the Egyptian sheath dress or the Greek chiton. Bianchi (1980) argues that the Ptolemaic ensemble derives from a Late Period costume.

53. Nicholas Reeves, *The Complete Tutankhamun* (London, 1990), 130, below left.

54. *DPA*, 254, fig. K.

55. Walters 1988; Tran Tam Tinh, "Isis," *Lexicon iconographicum mythologiae classicae* 5, 1 (Munich, 1990), 761–796; Eingartner 1991; and *Iside* 1997.

56. Draped costume: Bruyère 1952; Bianchi 1976a, 1976b, 1978, and 1992b. Bianchi (1976a, 25) sees three garments (a short-sleeved tunic, wrap-around skirt, and shawl) or sometimes four (an additional tunic) depicted in royal reliefs.

57. Amenhotep III: Theban Tomb of Kheruef (Sourouzian 1994, 499–500; and Hodel-Hoenes 2000, 206–207, figs. 143–144). Akhenaten: limestone relief fragment (Cambridge, Fitz-

william Museum E.G.A.2300.1943, provenance not known, 23 cm × 53 cm; Vassilika 1995, 60–61, cat. no. 26). Osorkon II: granite relief fragment (Philadelphia, University of Pennsylvania Museum of Art and Archaeology E 225, from Bubastis, 103.6 cm × 114 cm; Myśliwiec 1988, 114, pl. 20c).

58. Bianchi 1978, 101–102; *CE* 1988, 48, 66–67, 105; and Quaegebeur 1989, 97–98.

59. Redford 1986, 65–96, is a major study of such scenes.

60. Aufrère 2000, 233–241, no. 13a, figs. 36–37.

61. Quaegebeur 1989, 100, pl. 1b.

62. Though Greek hair under the *nemes* on the forehead is a Ptolemaic development, a few earlier examples combine Egyptian-style hair with the headdress: a statue of Djoser (Cairo JE 49158; Saleh and Sourouzian 1987, cat. no. 16), with a heavy ceremonial wig; and an Egyptian alabaster head of Mycerinus (Cairo JE 40705; Reisner 1931, 111, pls. 50–51) with stylized locks. In addition, Egyptian-style plain sideburns (called "tabs") emerge from underneath the *nemes* on most statues of kings throughout Egypt's history.

63. Smith 1988, 47–48.

64. Smith 1988, 94; and Bothmer 1996, 225. Walters (1988, 12) sees a relationship with the heavy wigs of New Kingdom queens.

65. Miriam Lichtheim, *Ancient Egyptian Literature,* vol. 2 (Berkeley, 1976), 207–208. Archaeological remains also attest to the potent connotations of hair. See Robert Kriech Ritner, *The Mechanics of Ancient Egyptian Magical Practice* (Chicago, 1993), 223–224, for a magician's box of talismans that contained a bronze uraeus wrapped in hair; and Nicholas Reeves, *The Complete Tutankhamun* (London, 1990), 168–169 (below right), for a braid of Queen Tiy's(?) hair found in a coffin-shaped box in her grandson Tutankhamun's tomb.

66. Plutarch *De Iside et Osiride* 14; Hölbl 2001, 105. Lucian *The Ignorant Book Collector* 14.

67. Koenen 1993, 89–113; and Hölbl 2001, 105.

68. *Anthologia Palatina* 6.277; Koenen 1993, 109.

69. Smith 1988, 95–97.

70. Kozloff and Bryan (1992, 172–175) discuss how the facial features, inscriptions, and other elements of Amenhotep III statues were altered for Ramses II. See also Claude Vandersleyen, "Porträt," *LÄ* 4, col. 1075; and Brunner 1984.

71. Myśliwiec 1988, 70–71, 73; and Josephson 1997a, 1–12.

72. Russmann (in Russmann et al. n.d., 8) suggests that the paucity of inscriptions resulted from Egyptian resistance to foreign rule. It is difficult to imagine, however, that native priests would have found the complete omission of texts to be acceptable.

73. Thutmosis III statue inscribed on base and not the back pillar: Luxor, granite, H: 59 cm; Mohammed el-Saghir, *The Discovery of the Statuary Cachette of Luxor Temple* (Mainz, 1992), 69–70, figs. 149–152. Separately worked base of Nectanebo II: Paris, Louvre E 11220, Egyptian alabaster, from Koptos, 26 cm × 60 cm × 41 cm; Desroches Noblecourt et al. 1981, 275–277, cat. no. 286.

74. D1 and D2 have round support holes on top, likely indicating the former presence of bronze statues; Willer 1996 discusses such bases. See also Schmidt 1995.

75. Bilingual Egyptians: Peremans 1982; D. J. Thompson 1994b; and Rochette 1996.

CHAPTER 5

IDEOLOGY AND THE ROYAL VISAGE

LIKE THE PHARAOHS BEFORE THEM, THE PTOLEMIES TOOK on Egyptian royal names that expressed the essence of their kingship.[1] These multipart titularies extended and revitalized older themes as well as brought in new concepts. First and foremost, the names emphasized the king's duty to protect Egypt, provide for its people, and honor its gods, the oldest and most traditional ethical roles of a pharaoh. Distinctively, however, Ptolemaic titularies highlighted godlike status and legitimacy, a major conceptual shift from Dynasty 30 ideals that was tied to the specific ideological aims of the Ptolemies. Most significantly, Greek epithets were incorporated among Egyptian phrases, signifying the melding of the two cultures' ideas about kingship. In describing how the ruler should act, how he should be regarded, and how he had both Greek and Egyptian identities, the resulting titularies encapsulated Ptolemaic royal ideologies.

The four concepts—ethics, godliness, legitimacy, and "Greekness"—pervade Ptolemaic imagery. Via technical execution, material, pose, inscriptions, and other devices, royal portraits express the ideological aspects of the dynasty and its rulers. Some examples have already been described. The enemy-smiting *ḫntj* of the priestly decrees (Chapter 2) graphically depicts the king's role as defender of Egypt and is the ultimate symbol of his moral duties. At the same time, the *sḫm,* which had a place among like images of deities as a *sunnaos theos,* epitomizes the king's godliness (Chapter 2). Some of the changes in the visual vocabulary discussed in the prior chapter can be linked to the programmatic development of Ptolemaic ideologies. Notably, sculptural groups of the royal family depict legitimate descent, and Greek hair and facial features proclaim "Greekness." In addition, several special statues to be discussed in this chapter are remarkable for the sophistication with which they embody ideological messages. Ancient texts and their associated images provide perspectives on how the Ptolemies and their advisors wanted the royal house to be perceived by their subjects.

ETHICS

The ethical aspects of kingship dominate the first three names of most Ptolemaic royal titulatures, demonstrating the crucial importance of these roles. The names describe principles of conduct as well as moral duties and obligations. Not only are the themes close to those of Greek Hellenistic kingship, they also substantially follow cherished Egyptian concepts. Not surprisingly, Ptolemaic royal names show significant continuity with Dynasty 30 names on matters of ethical roles, particularly with regard to safeguarding Egypt. Nectanebo II is *mk-B3qt* ("protector of Egypt"), Alexander the Great is *mk-Kmt* ("protector of Egypt"), and Ptolemy IV is *nḏtj-n-ḥnmmt* ("protector of the sun people").[2] Ethics can be defined in three areas: protectiveness over Egypt, beneficence and justice for its people, and piety toward its gods. Each had specific expressions in royal imagery.

The King as Protector

Probably the most ancient ethical role of the pharaoh was to defend his country against its enemies and maintain the order of the land. Ptolemy II's military might is presented in elaborate detail in the text on the Sais stele.[3] In the Canopus decree, Ptolemy III is accorded kingship because he campaigns abroad to prevent war from coming to Egypt.[4] The Memphis decree likewise proclaims Ptolemy V as king because he provides soldiers, battle strategy, supplies, and money to defeat the enemies of Egypt.[5]

The enemy-smiting king (Figs. 202–203) was the most ostentatious expression of his protective role. Some statue inscriptions also describe the sovereign's ability to defend Egypt, thus imbuing the statue with such powers. A few notable examples come from the reign of Ptolemy II: the text on a triad in Alexandria (A10) extols the strength of the king's armies; foreigners who tremble before the king are described in the back pillar of a statue in Rome (A11); and the Nine Bows—the traditional enemies of Egypt—are cited on the back pillar of a torso in Cairo (A12).[6] Egyptian and Greek agreement on this military theme must have been strong, as demonstrated by the appearance of the spear-wielding ruler on horseback in images of both cultures.[7] For the Greeks, Egypt was "spear-won" land.[8]

Beneficence and Justice

Concomitant to the pharaoh's duty to subdue the enemies of Egypt was the need to provide for the well-being of his subjects. Many of the deeds listed by the Canopus and Memphis decrees as requisite to effective monarchs relate to beneficence. According to the Canopus text, Ptolemy III merited his office by granting benefits to the temples and providing Egyptians with justice and food provisions.[9] The Memphis decree paints the ruler's position in similar terms, and Ptolemy V's Golden Horus name calls him *w3ḏ-ʿnḫ-n-ḥnmmt* ("the one who provides a prosperous life for the sun people").[10]

The smiling visages of some monumental statues (such as A3), accentuated by the deeply drilled corners of the lips, express the king's benevolent attitude toward his people. The careful carving of the ears, and the way they sometimes stick out (A3, C2), indicate the king's ability to hear petitions and administer justice. Listening ears appear on the reverse of some royal relief plaques (Figs. 208–209). Royal accessibility in these respects is demonstrated by statues in public parts of the temple complex. In addition, processions of naoi containing the royal image allowed for pauses in which people could approach and make petitions (Chapter 2).

Piety

Various accounts describe Alexander the Great's and his successors' active participation in Egyptian religious rituals, bearing testimony to the king's need to possess piety. Alexander reportedly made a sacrifice to the Apis bull at Memphis, Ptolemy II visited Mendes to petition the ram-headed god Banebdjedet, and Ptolemy IV burnt offerings to images of Egyptian gods recaptured from Egypt's enemies.[11] An appropriate attitude toward Egyptian deities is promoted in the Ptolemic titulary. *Mnḫ-jb-ḫr-nṯrw* ("perfect of heart before the gods") connotes piety.[12]

Relief representations of the king offering to Egyptian gods or participating in religious rituals demonstrate his piety (Fig. 204). Such scenes are a dominant form of wall decoration for Ptolemaic Egyptian-style temples. A statue's pose could convey a similar attitude. Standing statues placed within temples could serve as the king's surrogate in ritual acts. Small bronzes of the king in a ritual pose (A26?, A42) may have been positioned near a divine figure or other important cultic objects. Inscriptions make piety explicit as well. The hieroglyphs on the back pillar of the Ptolemy III torso in Paris (A18) describe how he protects divine images and makes offerings to the gods.[13] A statue base of the same king from Bânûb (A17) includes the phrase *ʿḥʿ.f m-b3ḥ 3st,* "placed before Isis," perhaps indicating that the figure was offered as a votive gift to the goddess.[14]

GODLINESS

Comparisons to Egyptian gods are interspersed liberally throughout Ptolemaic titularies. The proliferation of divinizing phrases is a major shift from Dynasty 30 practice. Some Ptolemies are *smn-hpw-mj-Ḏḥwtj-ʿ3-ʿ3* ("the one who establishes the laws like the twice-great Thoth"), whereas Nectanebo II is only *smn-hpw* ("the one who establishes the laws").[15] Similarly, various Ptolemies are said to be "king like the Sun (Ra)"[16] as well as "like" Ptah-Tatenen, Apis, and Horus, great gods associated with the duties and rights of kingship. Whereas these phrases suggest an intermediary role (for example, in being "like" Thoth, the king was fair in applying the law), other phrases directly refer to the rulers as gods. The epithets of all Ptolemies call them *nṯr(w),* "god(s)," and Ptolemy XII's throne name identifies him as the *Wsjrj ḥwnw* ("young Osiris").[17]

Native royal cults flourished in Egypt under Ptolemaic rule[18] and were a major means for the Ptolemies and native clergy to build and maintain their relationship. Some cults focused on individual rulers, such as Arsinoe II (Chapter 2), and others celebrated the dynasty as a whole. Many Egyptian priests had titles associated with these cults, implying various roles in performing rituals and conducting festivities. The national synods, where king and clergy met on important occasions, produced decrees proclaiming that royal images should be set up alongside divine images in all temples (Chapter 2).

Several elements could contribute an impression of a godlike aura to royal statuary.[19] The pairing of the king with a like-sized figure of a god or goddess was one explicit method (A10?, B23, E1, E2). Other means were attributes such as the beetle of Khepri (B9), the sidelock of Horus (B1, B2, B3, C2), the *hm-hm*-crown of Osiris (E1), and the horned headdress of Isis or Hathor (D3). Technical execution could provide brightness via a highly polished (A3) or gilded surface (C28; traces only) to reflect sunlight. Unusual materials could impart a precious quality that set the king's or queen's statue apart from others. A king from Tanis (A35) is made of quartzite, which was called *bj3t* ("marvelous thing"[20]) by the Egyptians, and some statues were made of Egyptian alabaster, with its rich off-white color and luminous qualities (A23, B1). Setting must have contributed to aura. Statues in "conspicuous places" set against the backdrop of richly textured, monumental temple reliefs must have created a striking impression.

"Son of Isis and Osiris"

Two royal sculptures use similar attributes to convey godlike status, but with contrasting purposes and results. The small scale and Egyptian alabaster material[21] of a Ptolemy V or VI head in Berlin (B1) suggest that it was a cult object for Egyptian ritual, and thus under the close stewardship of the native clergy. For this special audience, the attributes showed the king to be the ruler of Upper and Lower Egypt (double crown), Greek (Greek diadem[22] and hair), and "like" the god Horus (youthful face and sidelock). The Memphis decree, which was issued for Ptolemy V's coronation, similarly described this divine status: "He being a god, the son of a god and a goddess, and being like Horus, son of Isis and Osiris."[23] The sculpture may have been originally housed in a Ptolemaic birth house, which equated the birth of a young god with the sunrise and the eternal renewal of kingship.[24]

A grandiorite statue in Vienna also bears the Horus sidelock and has Greek hair, and perhaps had a double crown (C2). Unlike the Berlin head above, however, this was a highly public and visible proclamation of status, as indicated by the statue's colossal scale. The addition of the Horus sidelock to a large-scale royal statue is not only unique for the Ptolemaic Period, it is relatively unknown in preceding dynasties.[25] The attribute shows the king to be Ptolemy VIII, whose titulature sometimes calls him *z3-Wsjrj msj-n-3st* ("son of Osiris, born of Isis"), a direct allusion to Horus.[26] The facial features and hairstyle support this attribution (Chapter 7). The sculpture perhaps was created in connection with the inauguration of Ptolemy VIII's renewed rule in 145 B.C., as part of an ideological positioning program. The choice of Horus not only associates Ptolemy VIII with the quintessential god of rightful kingship, it also proclaims the king's mastery of the all-important role of defending Egypt, paralleling Horus' defeat of the forces of chaos to gain the throne.

A Series of Dark Stone Statues

A distinctive series of standing kings was created to serve the needs of the native royal cults. The sculptures are notable for their similar scale (under life- to life-size), attributes (*nemes* and *shendyt*), and dark stone material (A36, B15, B16, B17, B18, D22, E4, E5, E7, J1?). The manner of carving the faces and bodies of these images can vary, but the underlying consistency of the type points to a common function, perhaps a private one in a temple because of the smaller scale. The dark stone material has a wealth of meaning. Paint applied to the statues, if any, would not have changed the underlying nature of the stone.

For Egyptians, *km* ("black") connoted the renewal of life for eternity.[27] This was the color of the silt that covered the land every year during the inundation, enabling rich harvesting in *Kmt* ("the black land"), as Egypt was called.[28] Representations of Osiris sometimes have black skin, signifying the god's revival by the Nile's thick silt after his dead body was thrown into the river. The skin of a seated sandstone statue of Mentuhotep II of Dynasty 11 from Deir el-Bahari is painted black, and he crosses his arms in an Osirian pose, perhaps magically enabling the eternal renewal of his life.[29]

Aspects of a few exceptional statues in the series suggest a ritual function. The previously discussed "killing" of one example (A36) would have negated the life-promoting rites performed on it (Chapter 3). Another statue held objects inlaid in another, perhaps precious, material (B16), a unique feature among Ptolemaic royal sculptures that is paralleled by a similar treatment on an exceptionally fine Egyptian alabaster statue of Seti I of Dynasty 19, which likely was a major cult image of the king.[30] A third example is distinguished by its marble material (C12), the relative rarity and whiteness of which recall Egyptian alabaster cult statues; this sculpture likely belongs to the group because of its similar scale, attributes, and pose, despite the different material. Finally, the series is concentrated in the late third through the early first centuries (Chapter 7), when there is significant activity in the native royal cults, as demonstrated by temple inscriptions recording honors due to several generations of Ptolemies at Kom Ombo, Philae, and elsewhere.[31] This is also the time of the Karnak decree (Chapter 2), which specifies that royal statues be made of black stone. Thus, the dark stone statues may have served to embody the king in life-enhancing ceremonies performed by priests.

LEGITIMACY

The term *jwʿ* ("heir") is absent from Dynasty 30 titularies, but is nearly ubiquitous among Ptolemaic ones. Ptolemy III, for example, is *jwʿ-n-nṯrwj-snwj* ("heir of the brother-sister gods," i.e., Ptolemy II and Arsinoe II),[32] and the throne names of most Ptolemies identify them as the "heir" of their deified royal parents. Similarly, the Memphis decree specifies that the king's dutiful performance will accord kingship, not only to him, but to his *ẖrdw* ("children") as well.[33] The legitimate descent implied by these written sources was essential to Ptolemaic royal ideology. Legitimacy buttressed the dynasty's supremacy in the face of claims from rival Hellenistic rulers and native Egyptian rebels.

Facial resemblances among statues of succeeding rulers was perhaps the most important means of demonstrating legitimacy. These similarities can be so strong that they obscure individual identity, particularly when inscriptions are absent. An inscribed statue of Ptolemy II in the Vatican (A3) is close in appearance to an inscribed statue of Nectanebo I of Dynasty 30 (Fig. 201a), establishing the Ptolemy as the legitimate descendant of the respected king (Chapter 7). Hereditary monarchy also was essential to Greek Hellenistic kingship.[34] Theocritus' panegyric for Ptolemy II states that the king was born "in the likeness of his father."[35]

Egypt's Rightful Heir

A life-size statue of a king in the British Museum (A23) positions him as the rightful "heir" in a long line of venerable pharaohs. He wears a *nemes* over a tripartite wig, a false beard, and a traditional *sed*-festival cloak, and he clasps his right hand over his chest, a combination that has very ancient prototypes. A painted limestone seated statue of King Djoser of Dynasty 3 has the same elements and is of similar scale.[36] Several concepts are evoked by the Ptolemaic fragment. First, the use of Egyptian alabaster, an unusual material typically reserved for cult images, highlights that this is an important statue and possibly a cult image. Second, by following the type exemplified by the Djoser statue, this Ptolemy is placed in a long line of Egyptian kings. Third, the choice of a *sed*-costume from the ancient rite celebrating the renewal of a reign portrays the king as the upholder of sacred traditions. This ideological positioning agrees with the assessment—to be discussed in Chapter 7—that the British Museum statue may depict Ptolemy II, who had a demonstrated dialogue with the native upper classes and priests who would have supported him in the creation of such traditional imagery. The famous history of Egypt written by the Egyptian priest Manetho—in Greek for a Greek audience—may have been composed during the time of the second Ptolemy, and he founded a highly successful Egyptian cult honoring his wife, Arsinoe II (Chapter 2).

The Djoser statue was found sealed in a chapel attached to the king's step pyramid in his funerary complex at Saqqara. Two small holes in the chapel's facade allowed the king (embodied in his statue) to look out and receive offerings. Another king in a jubilee costume, a seated sandstone statue of Mentuhotep II of Dynasty 11, was unearthed in a chamber below the terrace of his funerary temple at Deir el-Bahari.[37] Like the Djoser and British Museum examples, this statue is life-size, wears a cloak, and has a false beard, but it differs in that a red crown is worn and both hands are clasped across the chest. The find spots of the Djoser and Mentuhotep II figures, as well as their strong commonalities with the British Museum king, suggest that the latter work had a private ritual function among native priests who would have understood the sophisticated references to the past.

A Ptolemy and His Heir

A seventeenth-century drawing of a lost sculpture depicts a young Ptolemy as the *jwꜥ* ("heir") of his godlike parents (Fig. 207).[38] The adult couple wears divinizing attributes: the draped costume for the king and the Hathor horns, vulture cap(?), and feathered dress for the queen. The boy stands on a slightly elevated base and carries the club of Heracles, a demigod whom the Ptolemies claimed as a forebear.[39] The forearms and hands of the adult figures appear to have been incorrectly restored into awkward gestures. For such groups, one would expect that the inner arms of the adults would cross in an embrace behind the boy, with the king's right arm and clenched fist over his abdomen and the female's left arm by her side.

Similar family groups appear in Ptolemaic temple reliefs. In the birth house at Edfu, Ptolemy VIII in a draped ensemble is followed by a similarly attired son on an elevated base, and then by Cleopatras II and III with Hathor headdresses.[40] Some statue bases refer to family groups as well. One example from the reign of Ptolemy V (B4) depicts that king as the heir of his deified parents, affirming his sovereignty in the face of external (Seleucid kings) and internal (rebels) threats. A second example from the time of Ptolemy VI (B13) confirms his son as successor, countering his rival-brother Ptolemy VIII's claim to the throne. Comparable explanations could be envisioned for the drawing's triad.

"GREEKNESS"

"Greekness" sparked a gamut of reactions in Egyptian written sources, from cooperation to outright rejection. The royal titulary integrates Greek elements seamlessly by adding an Egyptian translation of the king's Greek royal epithet as the sixth part of the classic five-part name (such as *nṯr mnḫ* for *Euergetēs,* both meaning "benefactor god" for Ptolemy III). The priestly decrees portray the Ptolemies as traditional pharaohs who protect Egypt by defeating enemies (including native rebels), glossing over the king's non-Egyptian origins. The Potter's Oracle, another priestly text, instead evinces great hostility toward "Greekness" and prophesizes the downfall of the Ptolemaic dynasty.[41] The text depicts the Ptolemies as the enemies of Egypt who, like other foreign conquerors, have removed sacred images from Egypt to a non-Egyptian place (i.e., Alexandria). These negative attitudes had their most violent expression in the periodic native revolts against Ptolemaic rule.

In light of these contrasting views, why did "Greekness" become such a visible ideology in the Egyptian portraits of the Ptolemies? Why highlight this "otherness" and make such a strong intrusion into native tradition? Was it an expression of Greek superiority over Egyptians, or an indication of cultural integration? To whom was it meant to appeal, and what messages was it supposed to convey? As the most visually dynamic feature of Egyptian portraits of the Ptolemies, Greek hair and faces must have had a special ideological significance.

Greek or Egyptian Influence?

The question of "Greekness" in Egyptian sculptures is traditionally defined in terms of influence. The hair and face of a colossal nummulitic limestone head of a queen in Alexandria (C19) create an immediate impression that the Greek has strongly influenced the Egyptian. Yet, this cause-and-effect relationship is not necessarily as simple as it seems. The idea that the Greek has affected the Egyptian is quickly confounded if one hypothetically places the queen (C19) in a Greek-style building, thus Egyptianizing the context. Now the Egyptian influences the Greek.[42] We have no definite example of such a setting, yet the exercise highlights the fallibility of reflexive assumptions about the direction of influence. In examining the broader sociopolitical trends of Ptolemaic Egypt, a case can be made for mutual "influence," perhaps better expressed as mutual dependence.

On the Egyptian side, various studies have documented a process of hellenization in Egyptian society that gathers strength as the Ptolemaic Period progresses and becomes particularly visible during the second century. Pinpointing Egyptian or Greek ethnicity from a person's name is more readily accomplished for the early years of the Ptolemaic dynasty, but such distinctions become increasingly blurred from the second century onward, as Egyptians take on hellenized or dual Greek/Egyptian names. An important instance occurs in the names of holders of the basilikos grammateus office, a high-ranking position in the Ptolemaic bureaucracy that was held by Egyptians. No Greek names are documented for the third century, whereas a mix of Greek, Greek/Egyptian, and Egyptian names appear during the second and first centuries.[43] The duties of the basilikos grammateus changed over time, but they included measuring and recording all land and crops as well as collecting taxes.

Similar tendencies can be demonstrated for the scribal profession. Surviving papyri indicate that scribes become so hellenized after the third century that it becomes difficult to distinguish, on the basis of grammar or calligraphic technique, whether an Egyptian or a Greek is writing a Greek text; an important change is that native scribes use the *kalamos* (a Greek writing instrument) at this time.[44]

Dorothy J. Thompson has built up several theories regarding various economic and legal incentives supporting hellenization.[45] A Greek education would allow a local villager to have an administrative career, which in turn allowed him to change his name and elevate his status. Thompson also points to a legal-system requirement instituted in 146 B.C. directing that all Egyptian contracts drawn up in Demotic had to be registered in Greek in an official registry office, accelerating the system's hellenization. Egyptian scribes had all to gain by becoming fluent in Greek.[46]

For the Greek side, there is much evidence of the Ptolemies' efforts to cultivate the support of the native Egyptian population out of political and economic necessity. The early Ptolemies played to native interests via strategic benefactions and carefully crafted propaganda (Chapter 2), and their portraits visually followed those of the preceding Dynasty 30 (Chapter 7). The nature of this positioning undergoes a marked shift following the disastrous rebellion under Ptolemies IV–V. The priestly decrees have their floruit under Ptolemy V (Chapter 2), evidencing a strong outreach to the native priesthood. During the balance of the second century, there is a temple-building boom in Upper Egypt, accompanied by a surge in royal cult activity in these temples, and amnesty decrees of the time acknowledge the power of the native temple institutions. Royal policy at this time could be characterized as trading economic and related benefactions for ideological support in the form of the royal cults. Egyptians are increasingly appointed to top administrative posts: under Ptolemy VIII, the Egyptian Paos was made epistrategos of Upper Egypt.[47]

Thus, while aspects of Egyptian society became hellenized under the Greeks, the Ptolemies were "Egyptianized" in that, to preserve their hegemony, they needed to more aggressively position themselves as legitimate pharaohs in the eyes of the native population. "Greekness" in Egyptian royal portraits would have been one means of accomplishing that goal.

Reasons for Introduction of the New Image

Theories regarding the reasons for the introduction of the new image depend significantly on which way the "influence" proceeded and thus on the original context of the sculptures. As noted in Chapter 3, the only Egyptian-style Ptolemies with Greek hair that have a secure and precise context are the sphinxes (C3, C4) and diademed head (D19) from Medinet Madi. Virtually all other examples come primarily from the Canopus area and secondarily from Alexandria itself, and in all cases, the style and purpose of the associated temples are uncertain. We are back to the original question on the head of a queen from Alexandria (C19). Was her original setting Greek or Egyptian in style, and what were the resulting implications?

If the new portraits were associated with Greek-style temples in the capital and Canopus, they could be envisioned as part of the Ptolemaic repertoire of powerful and authoritative Greek-style images in marble and bronze that originated in the Hellenistic Greek emphasis on public display of large-scale royal imagery.[48] In such a light, statues like the Pharos colossi (C21) may have enhanced Ptolemies' aura and legitimacy by connecting them with an ancient and respected civilization. The choice also would reflect an awareness of the awe-inspiring colossi of more ancient kings set up throughout Egypt. Indeed, some Greek historians equate the erection of larger-scale statuary with the might of earlier kings. Diodorus Siculus describes colossal statuary (*andrias*) of Ramses II inscribed with the words, "King of kings am I, Osymandyas. If anyone would know how great I am and where I lie, let him surpass one of my works."[49] In the midst of enumerating the exploits of a legendary pharaoh named Sesostris, Herodotus notes how the king set up colossal sculpture (*andrias*) to commemorate his name.[50] Nevertheless, all of these ideas must be labeled speculative until it can be proven that Egyptian-style Ptolemies occupied prominent positions in Greek-style contexts in Ptolemaic Alexandria and Canopus.

We are on much firmer ground for interpreting the new portraits in Egyptian-style settings, given the Medinet Madi example and the Memphis Serapeum sculptural program combining Egyptian and Greek sculptures (Chapter 3). For such cases, the new images may have been a response to the highly visible Greek-style sculptures that must have been prevalent in areas with heavy Greek populations. Just as native high officials and priests became hellenized, a similar trend might have evolved for sculpture as well. Thus, the new portraits may have developed as a more appropriate means to depict the pharaoh for Egyptians conversant in Greek language and customs. Native sculptors, particularly those in Lower Egypt, may have acquired more expertise in creating hellenized statues given the abundant proximity of Greek sculptors making Greek-style portraits of the Ptolemies.

Yet, the strength of the images suggests specific intent in concert with organic evolution. What was this intent? One aspect of the sculptures provides some answers: they tend to be distinctive, singular images. While groups of portraits can be associated with each other and recognized as portraits of a particular Ptolemy, they have more individualized treatments and are less likely to exist in close copies than those without noticeable Greek elements.[51] This suggests that the hellenized statues were special commissions for very particular settings. Several other observations contribute to this view. As a group, these statues tend to be large in scale and high in quality, with much care expended in the rendering of the face and hair. In addition, despite plentiful examples of Egyptian-style reliefs of the Ptolemies, particularly from Upper Egypt, I know of only one depicting Greek hair,[52] again arguing that the hellenized images were created under highly defined circumstances.

What might have been the particular settings? One possibility is that the hellenized images were created for temples associated with the royal cults. There is a high concentration of hellenized royal images at Canopus, which was an important site for such cult activities (Chapter 3). Two images have particularly strong divinizing attributes: the Hadra Ptolemy XII (E1) and the Vienna Ptolemy VIII (C2). A more speculative example is the colossal head, possibly of Augustus (G1), found near a temple devoted to the emperor's imperial cult. In addition, the Pharos colossi (C21) may have paralleled pre-Ptolemaic examples of colossal statues fronting a royal cult temple (Chapter 3).

Given their focus in the Delta, the new portraits may have been a way to promote the royal cults (and Ptolemaic rule) in this region, just as temple-building was a strategy for garnering support in the south. This would explain a curious geographic dichotomy. In Lower Egypt, we have high concentrations of portraits with Greek-style hair and faces, including the largest-scale ones, but almost no new Egyptian temples. In Upper Egypt, we have the opposite: limited or no evidence of hellenized royal statuary, but abundant temple-building. Although we cannot know how closely this reflects the ancient distribution, the sheer strength of the contrast implies a deliberate choice. As arguments in chapters 6–7 will show, the quality, quantity, and scale of hellenized images reach a high point in the second century through the early first, a time frame that corresponds to both increased temple-building and a flowering of the royal cults.

Who and When?

The priestly decrees describe a relationship between king and native clergy in the formulation of the royal image. Lacking direct evidence, we cannot know definitively how the two parties interacted to create the hellenized Egyptian-style statues. Certainly the original models inspiring the faces and hair on these images would have been devised in the Greek sphere under the king's supervision. The fact that the Greek face was inserted into a statue whose overall format remained strongly Egyptian, however, suggests significant control by native priests. Hellenizations remain confined to the face, hair, and selected attributes, whereas the rest of the statue closely adheres to Egyptian conceptions, with its material, standing pose, and back pillar; some examples have hieroglyphic (B6, C28) or Demotic (C3) inscriptions. Likewise, there is ample pre-Ptolemaic precedent in Egypt for using facial features and attributes as a means of specifically identifying a ruler in his statuary.[53] Thus, the use of the face as a defining feature is consistent with prior practice.

As for the timing of introduction, discussions in Chapter 6 will show that the earliest and most securely attributed examples of hellenized, Egyptian-style royal portraits fall in the reigns of Ptolemies V–VI (B1, B2, B3, B6, B7), coinciding with the disastrous native rebellion of 206–186 B.C. and its aftermath. The new portraits therefore could represent a renewed effort to integrate the Greek rulers into the traditional pharaonic office. Indeed, the statues themselves are a visual means of showing the successful fit of a Greek face into the guise of a native king. Given the highly fragmentary sculptural record, earlier experimentations cannot be entirely ruled out. It is clear, however, that the trend was strongly in place during the time of Ptolemies V–VI.

Thus, the small Egyptian alabaster head in Berlin (B1)—which wears a Greek cloth diadem as well as the double crown—would be a visual attempt to position the Greek rulers in the role of traditional pharaohs and affirm Ptolemaic legitimacy at a time when their rule was threatened. A distinctive aspect of some hellenized images is that they wear the double crown (C1), often as an added element on top of the head (B1, B6, B7?, C2?, C8?, C22, D13, E17?), emphasizing Ptolemaic dominion over both Upper and Lower Egypt. An origin in and focus on Ptolemaic strongholds in Lower Egypt would explain why Egyptian-style Ptolemies with Greek hair are in the minority among catalogued examples, and why they are concentrated in the Alexandria and Canopus area.

Callimachos Decree

A bilingual Demotic/Greek decree by the Theban priesthood during the reign of Cleopatra VII in honor of the strategos Callimachos may refer to an instance where an Egyptian version of a Greek-style work was made.[54] Callimachos' extremely powerful role in Upper Egypt is underscored by the fact that the decree is inscribed on a recarved royal stele.[55] In thanks for the benefactions this powerful official has bestowed, the priests propose to set up several "images" (restored as *eikonas*) of Callimachos "in the most conspicuous place in the temple of the great god Amun-Ra, king of the gods"[56] (*en episēmois topois tou ierou tou megistou Theou Amonrasōnthēr*). Among these images are "one offered by the priests, in hard stone" (*[mian] men tous iereis ek sklērou lithou*), and "two by the city, one in bronze and the other in a similar way in hard stone" (*duo de tēm polin, ēn men chalkēn, ēn de [o]moiōs sklērolithon*).[57] What is significant is that the decree is emanating from the Theban priests, who, by implication, are also involved in the process of managing the creation of the images, especially since they were to be set up at the Amun temple.

What kinds of images were these? The bronze one sounds very much like an honorific statue in Greek style, because it follows the formula repeated many times for such images elsewhere in the Hellenistic world: made of bronze, voted by the city in thanks for some benefaction, and set up "in the most conspicuous place."[58] The one of hard stone offered by the native priests surely was Egyptian in style, as was perhaps the stone image from the city. The decree implies parallel efforts by Egyptian and Greek sculptors, which perhaps extended to making similar faces and hair on all three images. The Egyptian-style Augustus with *nemes* and hair (G2) found at Karnak perhaps indicates that the site was another exceptional area for hellenized Egyptian-style royal images.

Imitation or Instruction?

Prior to the Ptolemaic Period, Egyptian sculpture had recognized "foreignness" through the addition of attributes. Representations of the Kushite rulers of Dynasty 25, for example, have two uraei and ram's head necklaces as well as distinctive facial features.[59] What is different from the Kushite circumstance, however, is that Greeklike sculptural techniques are employed in the Ptolemaic Period, so that both attributes and appearance can be close to Hellenistic models. This correlation is usually visible only in the faces, whereas the bodies of the Egyptian-style statues adhere to native canons and traditions. How closely did Greek and Egyptian interact to make these faces? Did Egyptians see Greek sculptures and imitate them, or was there cross-cultural instruction in techniques?

The questions are particularly relevant for Egyptian-style sculptures with a high degree of hellenization in the face and hair (such as B6, C2, C11, C19). These follow Greek models so closely that one would have difficulty recognizing them as Egyptian if they were more fragmentary and made of marble or bronze. In observing the face of the Aegina Ptolemy VI (B6), Helmut Kyrieleis went so far as to suggest that a Greek might have sculpted it.[60] Despite damage, one can still see fine modulations in the facial surface, especially the diagonal furrows extending down the face from the tear ducts, closely resembling the same in the king's marble portrait in Alexandria (Fig. 254). Likewise, the manner of carving the asymmetric eyebrows and the eyelids of the colossal queen in Alexandria (C19) matches the same of the marble Ptolemy VI (Fig. 254). She has an incised line along the outer edges of both lips, mimicking a line created on some Greek bronzes when the lips were inlaid with copper.[61] A few other sculptures display Greek ideas in the depiction of the bony brow (C10), fine facial folds (C11), and curved lips (C1, C10, C18). Nevertheless, these works strongly adhere to Egyptian sculptural methods, including frontality, materials, and back-pillar use. Despite Greek hair and sideburns, the colossal head from Canopus (D13) was likely sculpted in two halves: the head's left forehead hairline, eyebrow, eye, ear, and mouth corner are all higher than their counterparts on the right. Much the same technique can be observed in the series of dark stone statues without hair or other hellenizations (B15, B16, B17, B18).[62] Similarly, the idea of rendering bronze statues in stone has Egyptian precedent. Two limestone sculptures appear to imitate Egyptian bronzes because of the atypical removal of support screens: between the arms and body of a queen in Cairo (A45) and between the *nemes*-pigtail and the back of a royal bust in Cairo (A24).[63]

If cross-cultural instruction in techniques occurred, strongly hellenized Egyptian-style statues would have been the most likely locus, particularly the highest-quality examples (such as C11, C19, D4, D18). Egyptian sculptures were created by teams of craftsmen who specialized in different parts of the process, from rough hewing to final polishing and painting.[64] Thus, there may have been face and hair specialists who worked closely with their Greek counterparts. This would explain why Greek techniques remain confined to these areas on hellenized Egyptian-style statues. The difference in material—hard and soft stones used by the Egyptians and marble and bronze used by Greeks—suggests collaboration rather than instruction, because these materials must be worked differently to achieve a comparable appearance in individual facial features. Egyptian sculptors changed the hair of the Cairo statue (D14) from that of Ptolemy IX to Ptolemy X (Chapter 7), just as Greek sculptors altered marble portraits of the same time frame (Figs. 265, 268, 269), pointing to collaboration and communication. Egyptian priests likely facilitated such dialogue. They had responsibility for the conceptualization of the sculptural programs combining Greek and Egyptian works at the Saqqara Serapeum and Medinet Madi (Chapter 3). They also managed the creation of the strategos Callimachos' possible Greek- and Egyptian-style images at the Amun temples at Thebes (see above).

CONCLUSIONS

As reflected in the Egyptian titularies, priestly decrees, and other sources, Egyptian royal ideology under the Ptolemies emphasized ethics, godliness, legitimacy, and "Greekness." Similar ideas are reflected in the dynasty's portraits. Generously bowing to tradition, ethical roles are defined in terms of the king's relationship to Egypt, its people, and its gods. The enemy-smiting *ḫntj* image exemplifies these moral duties. Such protectiveness toward Egypt is based on remotely ancient native precedent, but it also finds echoes in Greek ideas about military superiority that were intrinsic to Hellenistic monarchy.

Two other ideological themes—godliness and legitimacy—are newly elevated, deviating from Dynasty 30 ideals. The king is likened to a variety of divinities, paralleling the rise of the native royal cults, and he is named as the rightful heir of his deified royal parents, countering claims from rival Greek and Egyptian rulers. Sculptural manifestations for both concepts exploit a range of options in the Egyptian repertoire, including precious materials, divinizing attributes, larger-than-life scale, statue groups, and distinctive gestures. The depiction of these themes had varied levels of sophistication. The outsized, public image of Ptolemy VIII in Vienna (C2) incorporated the Horus sidelock, a common attribute whose filial and divine connotations could be understood by the general public. To contrast, the cloaked king in Egyptian alabaster (A23) required a more sophisticated audience to comprehend how the attributes and gesture richly evoked long-dead monarchs as part of the Ptolemaic quest for legitimacy.

The introduction of "Greekness" was a bold and controversial ideological move. With their long history of native rule, Egyptians had divergent attitudes toward foreign dominations, from hostile to accepting. In highlighting this "otherness" in sculptures, the differences between the two cultures were strikingly displayed. The replacement of the visage, the most significant part of an Egyptian royal statue, with a Greek face must have evoked varied responses. Depending on one's perspective, this change could represent a hellenization of the Egyptian pharaoh or an Egyptianization of the Greek king. It speaks to the Ptolemies' efforts to dominate Egypt, as well as to their recognition of their need for at least partial acceptance by the native population. Even sculptural techniques evince a duality—though Greek in appearance, hellenized statues nonetheless remain firmly rooted in Egyptian artistic methods, such as carving in two halves. "Greekness" was an ideological experiment that signified the clash as well as the integration of Egyptian and Greek ideas under Ptolemaic rule.

NOTES

1. The building of this traditionally five-part name started at birth, when *Ptwlmjs* ("Ptolemy") was given to each potential king. The other four parts, added upon ascent to the throne, created an individual identity for each ruler. These are the Horus, Two Ladies, Golden Horus, and throne names. A sixth part, newly created in the Ptolemaic Period, was an Egyptian translation of the king's Greek royal epithet. Titulary: Ronald J. Leprohon, "Titulary," *OEAE* 3:409–411. Ptolemaic titulary: Hölbl 2001, 79–80, 85, 166–167, and 239; and Huss 2001. Egyptian kingship: O'Connor and Silverman 1995. Ptolemaic kingship: Walbank 1984; Koenen 1993; Samuel 1993; and Hölbl 1997.

2. Beckerath 1999, 228–229, 3H3, 3H4 (Nectanebo II), 232–233, 1H1 (Alexander), and 236–237, 4N (Ptolemy IV). Similarities between Nectanebo II's and Alexander's titulatures: Hölbl 1997, 23–24.

3. Thiers 1999.

4. Lines 6–7 for the hieroglyphic (Sethe 1904, 129.7–10), lines 13–14 for the Demotic (Simpson 1996, 226–227), and line 12 for the Greek (A. Bernand 1992a, 28–29).

5. Lines 1–5 for the hieroglyphic (Quirke and Andrews 1989, 13, 19–20), lines 12–21 for the Demotic (Simpson 1996, 262–267), and lines 20–36 for the Greek (A. Bernand 1992a, 46–47).

6. A10: Sauneron 1960, 87. A11: Curto 1985, 39–40; and Bol 1994, 466. A12: Borchardt 1930, 30.

7. Smith 1988, 33; and Laubscher 1991.

8. Diodorus Siculus 18.43; Hölbl 2001, 90. Greek views of military might: Walbank 1984, 81–82; and Smith 1988, 49.

9. Lines 4–11 for the hieroglyphic (Sethe 1904, 128.2–132.9), lines 10–20 for the Demotic (Simpson 1996, 224–229), and lines 8–20 for the Greek (A. Bernand 1992a, 28–29).

10. Lines 1–5 for the hieroglyphic (Quirke and Andrews 1989, 13, 19–20), lines 6–21 for the Demotic (Simpson 1996, 260–267), and lines 9–36 for the Greek (A. Bernand 1992a, 44–47). Golden Horus name: Beckerath 1999, 236–237, 5G.

11. Alexander: Arrian *Anabasis* 3.1.4. Ptolemy II (Mendes stele): Sethe 1904, 36.10–37.7. Ptolemy IV (Raphia decree): Simpson 1996, 248–249, line 23.

12. Beckerath 1999, 236–237, 4N (Ptolemy IV), 236–237, 5N (Ptolemy V), and 242–243, 9N3 (Ptolemy IX). Wilson 1997, 434.

13. Thiers 1998, 263.

14. Gallo 1990, 227–228. *Wb* 1:420 for *m-b3ḥ*.

15. Beckerath 1999, 236–237, 4G (Ptolemy IV), 240–243, 9N2, 9G2 (Ptolemy IX), 244–245, 12N1 (Ptolemy XII), and 228–229, 3G1, 3G2 (Nectanebo II).

16. Beckerath 1999, 236–237, 3G, 4G, 5G (Ptolemies III–V), and 240–241, 8G (Ptolemy VIII).

17. Ptolemy XII: Beckerath 1999, 244–245, 12T4.

18. Ptolemaic royal cults in Egypt: Winter 1978; Walbank 1984, 87–99; D. J. Thompson 1988, 125–138; Quaegebeur 1989; and Minas 2000.

19. Divine attributes in portraits of Hellenistic kings and Roman emperors: Bergmann 1998.

20. *Wb* 1:440–441; and Wilson 1997, 308. Discussion: Kozloff and Bryan 1992, 138; and Clair Ossian, "Quartzite," *OEAE* 3:104–105.

21. Dendera reliefs mention Egyptian alabaster cult statues of queens; Cauville 1987, 108, referring to Chassinat 1934, 55, X–XIII, *ʿ3t ḥḏt* ("semi-precious white stone," Wilson 1997, 138, 695).

22. Bianchi (*CE* 1988, 153) argues the diadem is a Greek one because its position underneath the occipital bulge matches Ptolemy V's coins (Fig. 220).

23. Translated from the Demotic by Simpson (1996, 260–261, line 6); Hölbl 2001, 166.

24. François Daumas, "Geburtshaus," in *LÄ* 2, cols. 462–475; and Di. Arnold 1999, 285–288.

25. Ramses II example: Cairo JE 64735, a granite and limestone statue from Tanis, H: 231 cm; Saleh and Sourouzian 1987, cat. no. 203.

26. Beckerath 1999, 240–241, 8H3.

27. Black: *Wb* 5:122–123. Symbolism: Emma Brunner-Traut, "Farben," *LÄ* 2, col. 123; and Gay Robins, "Color Symbolism," *OEAE* 1:293.

28. *Wb* 5:126–127.

29. Cairo JE 36195, from Deir el-Bahari, H: 138 cm; Russmann 1989, 49–52, cat. no. 18. Parlasca (1973, 96–97) argues that statues such as B15 may represent Osiris. While some de-

pictions of males wearing the *nemes* and *shendyt* can be so interpreted, the examples in this section should be seen as kings. The regenerative powers attributed to the statues as part of the royal cults may be a reason why such statue forms evolved into depictions of Osiris.

30. Cairo JE 36692 (CG 42139), from Karnak, court of the cachette, H: c. 238 cm; Saleh and Sourouzian 1987, cat. no. 201.

31. Minas 2000.

32. Beckerath 1999, 236–237, 3T1.

33. Line 5 of the hieroglyphic (Quirke and Andrews 1989, 13, 20).

34. Smith 1988, 49.

35. Theocritus 17.63.

36. Cairo JE 49158, from Saqqara, H: 142 cm; Saleh and Sourouzian 1987, cat. no. 16; and Russmann 1989, 14–16, cat. no. 3.

37. Cairo JE 36195, from Deir el-Bahari, H: 138 cm; Saleh and Sourouzian 1987, cat. no. 67.

38. Windsor Castle RL 8580, drawing from the collection of Cassiano dal Pozzo. Interpretations of the group as Sarapis, Isis, and Harpocrates (Merkelbach 1995, 603, fig. 133) or a priestly family (Eingartner 1991, 82–83, 167, cat. no. 140, pl. 87) lack supportive parallels.

39. Smith 1988, 44.

40. Chassinat 1910, 14–15, pl. 13 (second row of relief from the bottom), where the inscription identifies the boy as the "king's son." See also Quaegebeur 1989, pl. 3a (lower scene).

41. Kerkeslager 1998, with bibliography.

42. Ptolemaic luxury goods present an analogous situation. Some Greek-style glyptic portraits show Ptolemies in Egyptian regalia: a gold ring profile of a Ptolemy in a double crown, Paris, Musée du Louvre Bj 1092 (Fig. 223; Kyrieleis 1975, 63, pl. 46: 6); and a gem profile of a Ptolemaic queen wearing a diadem and Hathor horns, Boston, Museum of Fine Arts 27.711 (Kyrieleis 1975, 117, 120, pl. 100: 2). The Tazza Farnese (Naples, Museo Archeologico Nazionale 27611) has an Egyptian sphinx in strict profile view; La Rocca 1984, pls. 2, 7.

43. Oates 1995, 114–115; reviewed by Willy Clarysse, in *CdE* 72 (1997), 367–369.

44. Clarysse 1993, 193.

45. D. J. Thompson 1994b.

46. Depauw 1997, 24: "[Greek] gained the upper hand. From the end of the third century B.C. the immigrants' idiom became the most important one in public life. The crucial factor probably was the prestige it enjoyed. . . . [Demotic] offered progressively fewer career opportunities."

47. Hölbl 2001, 198, 307.

48. Smith 1988, 15–31; and D. J. Thompson 2000, 77–78.

49. Diodorus 1.47.4. Translation: C. H. Oldfather, *Diodorus of Sicily*, vol. 1 (Cambridge, 1933), 169.

50. Herodotus 2.110; Malaise 1966.

51. This is not to suggest that multiple copies of such hellenized sculptures were never made. Sphinxes lining the Medinet Madi dromos have similarly puffy faces with Greek hair (C3). Even here, however, a distinctive and singular image of a youthful ruler (D19) was found.

52. Sharpe (1855, 5, no. 61, pl. 61) illustrates a drawing of a votive relief plaque(?), i.e., probably *not* a temple wall fragment, with a profile of a king with *nemes* and hair.

53. Kozloff and Bryan 1992, 128–129.

54. Turin 1764, granite stele, 112 cm × 65 cm, Drovetti Collection; *OGIS* 1 (1903), 275–279, 653–654, no. 194; Daumas 1952, 264, 283; Curto 1984, 296–300, 358; A. Bernand 1992a, 106–109, and 1992b, 109–115, no. 46; and Hölbl 2001, 239–240. Greek text: Hutmacher 1965. According to Vandorpe (1995, 235 n. 242); Adel Farid is studying the Demotic text.

55. Burstein (1985, 144–146, no. 111) suggests that the original stele dates to the New Kingdom.

56. Bianchi 1976a, 113: "With few exceptions, examples [of Egyptian-style, striding, draped male statues] with known provenances were erected near temple pylons. Their owners, judging from their inscriptions, were powerful officials who used their influence to embellish the temples in which their statues were dedicated." This is perhaps "the most conspicuous place" where the statues of Callimachos were to be set up.

57. A. Bernand 1992a, 108–109, lines 27–28.

58. Smith 1988, 16–18.

59. Russmann 1974, 25–44.

60. Kyrieleis 1975, 62.

61. Examples: Carol C. Mattusch et al., *The Fire of Hephaistos: Large Classical Bronzes from North American Collections* (Cambridge, 1996), 196 (fig. 5e) and 308 (fig. 1).

62. Diodorus (1.98.6–7) describes this technique as Egyptian.

63. A few small-scale royal bronzes are known from the Ptolemaic Period (A7, A26, A42). Hill (2000, 225–249) proposes other examples.

64. Drenkhahn 1995, 336–338.

CHAPTER 6

CHRONOLOGY

THE CHRONOLOGY OF HELLENISTIC SCULPTURE IS A much-debated topic.[1] Egyptian-style portraits of the Ptolemies are no exception. A dark stone head of a king at Yale (D18) has been dated to both the early Ptolemaic Period and the early Roman Period. A nummulitic limestone head of a queen in Alexandria (C19) has been attributed to the third, second, and first centuries B.C.[2] These are but two examples. Despite the existence of some well-established points in the chronology of Ptolemaic royal portraits, scholars often differ on the identification of specific sculptures because systematic and consistent dating methods are few, and because opinions are often based on subjective observations. To address this situation, this chapter assembles the most solidly identified portraits into a framework to establish what can be said with relative certainty about chronology.

There are a number of ways to date portraits. An inscription on a portrait or its excavation with well-dated material provides the simplest and most direct method. The statue of Ptolemy II in the Vatican is the best preserved of the inscribed royal sculptures of the Ptolemaic Period (A3). Another means is to examine unusual aspects of the royal regalia for clues regarding identity. The Horus sidelock on the Vienna king (C2) showed him to be Ptolemy VIII because his titulature alludes to this god (Chapter 5). A final means is to use well-dated works as a basis for dating others, examining portrait features and stylistic details. For the Ptolemaic Period, this approach includes comparing Egyptian- and Greek-style sculptures to each other as well as to portraits on coins and clay seals, which are impressions of royal intaglio rings used for sealing papyrus rolls.[3] Many ascribe a head in Berlin (B1) to Ptolemy V because it matches the king's coin profile (Fig. 220).

The comparative method is the best tool available because of the nature of the evidence. Though inscribed sculptures are few and many statues have lost their royal regalia, glyptic evidence, mostly coins and clay sealings, is preserved for almost all Ptolemies. These provide a rich source of comparative material. There are, nevertheless, advantages and disadvantages to this approach. On the negative side, glyptic images are small in size, differ in technique from sculpture in the round, and almost invariably focus on the profile view of the head. On the positive side, glyptic images preserve their royal regalia and hair, and can be so abundant that they help define possible ranges of variation in a single ruler's portraits. While Egyptologists often use the comparative method to identify portraits of earlier pharaohs, the Ptolemaic Period is unusual because non-Egyptian materials, namely Greek marbles and glyptic, are used to attribute Egyptian-style portraits.

Using all three methods, about 15 percent of Group A–F sculptures with heads and about fifteen Greek-style portraits can be assembled into a chronological framework that pinpoints portrait types over the entire Ptolemaic Period. This framework, and the comparative methodology underlying it, will be used in the next chapter for dividing the remaining 85 percent of the corpus of portraits into groups and proposing attributions to rulers and time frames.

THE THIRD CENTURY

Our understanding of third-century portraiture is based on a few Greek- and Egyptian-style sculptures and an extensive series of coin portraits. From early on, royal images incorporate tendencies that persist for the duration of the dynasty. Faces are fleshy, with full cheeks and a fold under the chin; eyes are expressively large; and hairstyles change from one ruler to the next. Unlike some later examples, however, the appearance and styles of Egyptian-style portraits are strongly distinguished from their Greek-style counterparts. It is difficult to identify Egyptian statues by using Greek evidence.

Coins provide the most complete evidence for the first four Ptolemies and their wives. Faces are full, often with wide-open eyes, straight nose bridges, prominent chins, and thick necks with fat folds (Figs. 213–219).[4] Portraits are particularly distinguished by hairstyle: brushed forward asymmetrically over Ptolemy I's receding hairline (Fig. 213), symmetrically curled across Ptolemy II's brow (Fig. 214), asymmetrically curled on Ptolemy III's forehead (Fig. 216), and tightly curled all over Ptolemy IV's head (Fig. 218). Ptolemies II and IV have long sideburns as well (Figs. 214, 218). Queens have a melon coiffure with a bun at the back (Figs. 215, 217), except for Arsinoe III (Fig. 219), who has her hair pulled back from the forehead and gathered into a roll at the nape.

Although numerous marble portraits are called early Ptolemies based on comparisons to the coins, most are at best only partly convincing because they lack strongly distinguishing features, such as well-defined hair or unusual attributes. Two marble heads, one in Copenhagen and another in Paris (Fig. 245), can be attributed to Ptolemy I.[5] They depict a mature man with a heavy brow, round eyes, and a large chin, just like the king's coin portraits (Fig. 213). A bronze head in Mantua (Figs. 252–253) can be assigned to Arsinoe III, because the facial profile and hair arrangement, particularly the roll of hair at the nape, compare well to the queen's coin portrait (Fig. 219).[6] An under-life-size, diademed marble head of a king in Paris (Figs. 246–247) depicts an early king, perhaps Ptolemy II. Its bony brow and large dimpled chin compare well to the king's coins (Fig. 214), though the head's forehead locks are more varied.[7] Other attributions are more tenuous. Although two marble heads in Boston are often named as Ptolemy IV (Figs. 248–249)[8] and Arsinoe III (Figs. 250–251),[9] these assignments are not fully convincing. The Boston king is reworked: the profile shows recutting on the forehead, sideburns, and jaw, and there are traces of a wide diadem at the top and a narrow one at the back. The facial profile of the Boston queen is a reasonable match for Arsinoe III's coins (Fig. 219), but the marble head has rows of a melon coiffure on top, unlike the coin portrait.

Egyptian-style Portraits of the Third Century

Information about Egyptian-style portraits of the first Ptolemies is based on five sculptures, either inscribed or excavated with well-dated evidence (A3, A4, A5, A7, A9). These early images are quite unlike their Greek-style counterparts, because their facial features adhere so strongly to native approaches and because Greek elements, particularly hair, are lacking. These ideas are illustrated by two inscribed statues of Ptolemy II: an over-life-size, red granite statue in the Vatican (A3), and an under-life-size, dark stone statue in Strasbourg (A5). Though the Strasbourg example has more open eyes and fuller cheeks, the two sculptures are highly similar in appearance. Both have a robustly fleshy tone, and both are executed in a refined style characterized by symmetric eyebrows, slanted eyes, noses with narrow roots and wide bases, and smiling, protruding lips with strong corner drill holes. Tripartition is emphasized in the Vatican statue—meaning that the sculpting brings out the horizontal lines defining the lower edge of the pectoral muscles and the bottom of the rib cage—and the rounded abdomen has a deep teardrop-shaped depression surrounding the navel.

Two other sculptures, excavated with third-century material, closely resemble the Vatican and Strasbourg works. A well under life-size bronze and gold bust of a king (A7), found with coins of Ptolemies I–II at Tukh el-Karamus (Chapter 3), is a strong match for the Vatican Ptolemy II, with its single-arc eyebrows, fleshy cheeks, and full lips. A well under life-size limestone king (A9), discovered in a Tanis chapel with steles inscribed for Ptolemies II and IV (Chapter 3), has a full face, arching upper eyelids, and smiling lips like the Strasbourg Ptolemy II. The Tanis king's body is thick, with almost no neck or waist, perhaps a clumsy execution of the robust body type exemplified by the Vatican Ptolemy II.

When these early Egyptian-style Ptolemies are placed beside the contemporary marble head in Paris (Figs. 246–247), not much resemblance can be noted: eyes, nose, and mouth are sculpted differently. The single-arc eyebrows, almond-shaped eyes, fleshy nose, and semicircular lips of the Vatican face contrast with the semicircular eyebrows, oval eyes, bony nose, and naturally shaped lips of the Paris king. A comparison to Ptolemy II's coins (Fig. 214) brings the same result. Though both the Egyptian sculptures and the Greek coin have full faces and open eyes, their manner of conception is entirely different.

Representations of third-century kings and queens resemble each other closely. An inscribed statue of Arsinoe II (A4), found with the Vatican Ptolemy II (A3), is similarly executed, but in slightly smaller proportions.[10] Her facial features are like the king's, except for the long cosmetic extensions at the outer canthi. The queen's body exudes a healthy fleshiness, with ample, round breasts, tight waist, and soft abdomen, all of which emphasize her fecundity.

A few other sculptures, fragmentary and headless, are inscribed for third-century rulers. The largest concentration is associated with Ptolemy II, which is not surprising in the light of his nearly forty-year rule (A10, A11, A12, A13, A14).[11] An under-life-size schist torso in Cairo (A12) is notable for its similarity to the Vatican Ptolemy II (A3): the curve of the pectoral muscles, the favoring of tripartition, and the rounded abdomen with a teardrop-shaped depression. For Ptolemy III, there are two small fragments (A16, A17), as well as a near-life-size limestone torso in Paris (A18), which has fleshy pectorals and a prominent abdomen like Ptolemy II's images.[12] Fragments for (possibly) Alexander the Great or his son (A1), Ptolemy I (A2), and Ptolemy IV (B4) are known, but are not informative relative to sculptural styles.[13]

THE SECOND AND FIRST CENTURIES

During the second and first centuries, Greek-style evidence becomes critical to the identification of Egyptian-style portraits, because works of both cultures strongly resemble each other. Despite differences in material and technique, one can often recognize when the same ruler is represented in Egyptian or Greek style. This visual relationship is the largest source of attributions. Inscriptions or unusual royal regalia also identify a few statues, and there is a series of glyptic portraits, some coins, and many clay sealings.

More individualized portraits emerge as well. Boys, overweight men, and powerful queens are depicted. It becomes easier to distinguish one sovereign from the next by comparing facial features and hairstyles. Ptolemy VI's lean and bony face, for example, stands apart from the corpulent one of his brother Ptolemy VIII.

Ptolemies V–VI

Coins with profiles of Ptolemies V and VI help define possible features of their portraits. These are the dynasty's first boy rulers, both ascending to the throne at age 5 or 6, and both dying young, about 30 for Ptolemy V and 40 for Ptolemy VI. One coin portrait type is known for Ptolemy V (Fig. 220). This shows a young face with a broad forehead, a large eye, a virtually straight nose slope, and a small, pointy chin.[14] Short, C-shaped forehead locks curl toward the ear, and similar locks cover the head. Two basic coin portraits are known for Ptolemy VI.[15] One, minted during the regency of his mother Cleopatra I (Fig. 221), is closely modeled on his father's type (Fig. 220). A second coin portrait, from late in his reign, has a longer, more mature face, lacking fleshiness, with wavy locks, a narrow eye, a prominent nose with an arched bridge, and a large, thrusting chin (Fig. 222).

Three sculptures match the youthful coin portraits of Ptolemies V–VI. A well under life-size Egyptian alabaster head with Horus sidelock, diadem, and double crown in Berlin (B1) has a boyish appearance, compact hairstyle, circular eyebrows, straight-sloped nose, and pointy chin like Ptolemy V's coin profiles (Fig. 220), and is similar as well to Ptolemy VI's (Fig. 221). Other striking features are the elongated, downward-slanting eyes with puffy lids, the hollowed orbital cavity that brings out the cheeks and lower face, as well as the straight, small lips. Two additional small Egyptian alabaster heads in Berlin with the sidelock (B2, B3) have similar features but are more exaggerated, with low cheekbones, pursed lips, and narrow chins.[16] The thick lidded eyes (B3) and elongated faces (B2, B3) are like those of a Ptolemy VI head (Fig. 254) to be discussed below.

Several heads can be assigned to the mature Ptolemy VI via inscriptions and comparisons. The key example is an over-life-size granite head from Aegina (B6), whose back pillar is inscribed for Ptolemy VI. The lean, angular face strongly follows Greek-style works. It has a horizontal forehead furrow, natural, semicircular eyebrows, deeply set eyes, diagonal furrows extending from the tear ducts down the face, and a broad mouth. The outline of the broken nose has a thick bridge between the root and the base, with a rounded depression by each nostril. There is no fold of flesh under the thrusting chin. A double tier of forehead locks is distinctively arranged, with a thick wave of hair (curling left) in the center, framed on either side by spaced locks curling symmetrically inward. Roughening below both curly sideburns indicates a light beard or sideburns extension.[17]

Two uninscribed sculptures, a colossal, Egyptian-style granite head from Canopus (B7) and a life-size, Greek-style marble one in Alexandria (Fig. 254),[18] also belong to Ptolemy VI. Their forehead hair is patterned closely after the Aegina example, and their features resemble the king's profile on his late coins (Fig. 222). The Alexandria heads have longer faces with larger chins than the Aegina image, and their hairstyles diverge slightly: though the Alexandria heads have the centered, thick wave of hair, the surrounding locks lack the Aegina example's precise symmetry, and the roughening below the sideburns is lacking. Despite the differences, however, all three heads have lean, bony faces with deeply set eyes, large nose outlines, and thin, broad lips that hint at a smile. A dark stone head in a private collection (B8) also has Ptolemy VI's hairstyle, though rendered rather schematically. The long face resembles the two Alexandria sculptures (B7 and Fig. 254), and the chin is like the one from Aegina (B6). The nose and lips, however, are smaller than the Alexandria and Aegina examples. The head (B8) can be tentatively attributed to Ptolemy VI.[19]

One head without forehead hair can be associated with Ptolemy VI and gives an impression of alternative portrait styles from the first half of the second century. The scarab atop a well under life-size limestone head with *nemes* in New York (B9) points to the beetle-god Khepri, and thus to Ptolemy VI, whose throne name was *stp-n-Ptḥ-Ḫprj* ("chosen by Ptah-Khepri").[20] Unlike the representations above, the oval face lacks strong characterizations, though it does have low, puffy cheeks like the Berlin heads (B1, B2, B3). The formerly inlaid eyes have evenly semicircular lids, and the nearly straight, protruding lips have strongly drilled corners. A few other Egyptian-style fragments document a wide geographic dispersion of Ptolemy VI's images: a partial back pillar from a colossal granite figure, perhaps from Alexandria (B10), a headless large-scale limestone statue from Karnak (B11), a base for a granite, near-life-size, standing statue, probably from Philae (B12), and a granite statue base from el-Hesa, which supported approximately life-size figures of Ptolemy VI, Cleopatra II, and their son (B13).

The Physkons

Portraits of Ptolemy VIII and his sons Ptolemies IX–X reflect their naming as Physkons, or "fat men." The faces known from coins and clay sealings are distinguished by their heaviness, and their noses can have arched bridges, flattened, hanging tips, and flaring nostrils. A different type of headdress becomes frequent, the Greek wide diadem, and it is known in both Greek-style (Figs. 235–238, 272) and Egyptian-style (C10, C11) portraits through Cleopatra VII (Fig. 278). Though many images are youthful, others show advanced age through sagging facial features and receding hairlines. These kings came to the throne in their twenties and thirties and ruled through their fifties and sixties.[21]

Ptolemy VIII One coin portrait type is known for Ptolemy VIII.[22] It shows an overweight man with varied forehead locks, prominent brow, large eye, flaring nostril, thick lips, and a round chin with significant fleshiness underneath (Fig. 225). A similar portrait, on a clay sealing bearing the Greek numeral for 50, has thicker hair and a protruding lower lip, a distinctive feature that appears in the king's marble portrait (Figs. 258–259). The "50" may signal a regnal year and thus indicate that the portrait dates to circa 121/120 B.C. (counting from the start of his joint rule with Ptolemy VI in 170 B.C.), when Ptolemy VIII would have been about 60.[23] Various other glyptics, including a sealing in Toronto (Fig. 227) and an engraved garnet in Bloomington (Fig. 226),[24] are part of this series. Some have slight beard stubble,[25] continuing a practice of light facial hair seen in the Ptolemy VI head from Aegina (B6).

A Greek-style marble head in a private collection (Figs. 258–259)[26] and a dark stone Egyptian-style head in Brussels (C1) match each other as well as Ptolemy VIII's coin profile (Fig. 225) and clay sealing with the "50" numeral. All have puffy faces with wide-open eyes, flaring nostrils, fleshy lips, and rounded chin, though the eyebrow shapes differ slightly for the two sculptures. Those of the marble head slant downward to the nose root from peaks at the outer canthi, while those of the dark stone head peak near the tear ducts. The marble face has a dense mass of forehead locks, thick hair at the sides, and a space for a wide(?) diadem. A well under life-size plaster head in Hildesheim surely belongs to Ptolemy VIII as well, with its wide-open eyes and bulging fleshiness.[27]

As noted in Chapter 5, the Horus sidelock on a colossal granodiorite sculpture in Vienna (C2) identifies the king as Ptolemy VIII, whose titulature alludes to Horus in the phrase *z3-Wsjrj msj-n-3st* ("son of Osiris, born of Isis"). This sculpture is an alternate portrait type for Ptolemy VIII, however, because its hairstyle and face differ from the sculptures above. The forehead locks curl symmetrically inward from either side toward a center median line, unlike the marble face (Fig. 258). Although the Vienna king has a comparably heavy face and two fat folds on the neck, his facial features are less exaggerated, with flatter eyebrows and smaller eyes. The visual reference to the titulature may indicate that the portrait was created near the start of Ptolemy VIII's renewed rule in 145 B.C., after the death of Ptolemy VI.

A similar hairstyle appears on an over-life-size head from a limestone sphinx (C4) excavated in a Medinet Madi temple addition where Greek dedications for Ptolemies VIII and IX were also discovered (Chapter 3). The forehead hair has a center portion with locks curling inward to the middle. In contrast to prior examples, the facial features are highly Egyptian, particularly the slanted eyes with arching upper lids and smiling lips with drilled corners. Both the Medinet Madi and Vienna portraits have more elongated faces compared to the Brussels head (C1), recalling a similar difference between the Aegina (B6) and Canopus (B7) heads of Ptolemy VI. The diademed ruler (D19) from Medinet Madi will be discussed in the next chapter.

Ptolemies IX–X Coin portraits are lacking for Ptolemies IX–X, though some clay sealings represent these kings because the profiles do not match those of Ptolemies known from coins.[28] These Physkon brothers alternated rules, with Ptolemy IX reigning for about ten years after the death of their father, then Ptolemy X for nearly twenty, and finally Ptolemy IX returning to rule for about eight more years. One group of seals shows a fleshy but compact face with asymmetrical, often tightly curled locks and a thick, under-the-chin beard. These seals display a divergent age range, with some having youthful features (Fig. 234)[29] and others showing an older, thicker-faced individual with a beaked nose (Fig. 235).[30] This age divergence fits Ptolemy IX because the youthful portraits would belong to his first reign and the older ones to his second. Another group of seals shows a fuller-faced man with a large nose, and often a jutting lower lip and light facial hair. Though this type recalls those of Ptolemy VIII, it is distinguished by its smaller chin and thinner forehead hair, especially in more aged versions of the face. This second group of seals displays a more continuous age range, pointing to Ptolemy X. Some youthful examples have slightly thick forehead hair (Fig. 236), some show a heavier face with thinner hair (Fig. 237), and still others depict an older man with thinner hair and forehead wrinkles (Fig. 238).[31] A king paired with a queen on one sealing has long sideburns and represents Ptolemy IX or X (Fig. 239).[32]

Various portraits can be associated with Ptolemies IX–X based on comparisons with the seal profiles. The most convincing are a life-size, Egyptian-style granite head in Berlin (D12) and a fair number of Greek-style examples. These include a colossal marble and plaster head in Boston (Figs. 265–266);[33] an over-life-size marble head from Mersa Matruh (Figs. 269–270);[34] an over-life-size limestone statue from Aphroditopolis in Cairo (Figs. 271–273);[35] a life-size marble head in the Getty;[36] a well under life-size bronze head in Stuttgart (Fig. 267);[37] and an under life-size marble head in Stuttgart (Fig. 268).[38]

The Boston (Fig. 265), Stuttgart bronze (Fig. 267), and Berlin (D12) heads are particularly strong matches to each other and to seals from Ptolemy IX's first rule (Fig. 234). All the sculptures have richly curled forehead hair, heavy brows, deeply set eyes, flaring nostrils, broad lips, and thick, under-the-chin beards. The Boston portrait is especially forceful (Figs. 265–266), with its large eyes, nose, and lips. In profile view, the sharply indented nose root accents the convex bridge and flattened nose tip, and the lower lip noticeably protrudes. The Berlin head is distinctive for its two tiers of tightly curled forehead locks and the thick V-formation of its brow.

The Boston (Fig. 265), Getty, and Stuttgart marbles (Fig. 268) are reworked from earlier portraits: their necks bear traces of the originally larger faces.[39] The Boston and Getty marbles originally may have depicted Ptolemy VIII (as in Fig. 258), with the lower parts of the face being narrowed for the Boston work's second version and transformed into a beard for the Getty one. Also similar to the Ptolemy VIII marble are the Boston head's wide-open eyes and protruding lower lip, and the Getty head's originally larger eyes (visible between the current upper lids and brow) and full lips.

In addition, a limestone head of a king (D21) was found at a Ptolemy IX temple for Triphis at Wannina (Athribis). Though heavily damaged, one can still see the full face and a heavy double chin indicative of a Physkon identification. The sculpture is important evidence of the continuance of traditional Egyptian styles in the late Ptolemaic Period because hellenizations, including Greek hair, are lacking. Instead, the face is highly Egyptian, with citrus-segment-shaped eyes, a broad nose base, and drilled mouth corners.

Second-Century Queens

A few coins and sealings document portraits of the powerful and long-lived queens of the second century. Cleopatra I appears on a coin minted late in her reign (Fig. 228).[40] The profile shows a youthful face with wavy(?) forehead locks, a bun at the back of the veiled head, a wide-open eye, a slightly concave nose slope, and a rounded chin with fleshiness underneath. Several coin types depict Cleopatra Thea, daughter of Ptolemy VI and Cleopatra II, sister of Cleopatra III, and wife of various Seleucid kings (Fig. 232).[41] She is shown with a nose having a concave bridge with upturned tip, full lips, and a doubled chin. Her corkscrew coiffure can be two-tiered.

Various uninscribed glyptic portraits can be attributed to second-century queens by comparisons to images of Cleopatra I, Cleopatra Thea, and Ptolemies VI–X. A profile of a queen on a seal in Amsterdam has her hair pulled into a bun at the back (Fig. 229).[42] Her wide diadem and resemblance to the coin profile of Cleopatra I (Fig. 228) point to the second century, and her comparatively lean physiognomy suggests a pre-Physkon date, either Cleopatra I or II. A seal in Athens displays a queen in front of a young king in a double crown (Fig. 230), in contrast to the more prevalent arrangement where the queen is in the background (Figs. 213, 214, 239).[43] The queen, whose profile resembles Cleopatra I's (Fig. 228), wears a plumed Hathor headdress vulture cap, corkscrew locks, and ram horn, which all proclaim her deified status. Cleopatra I and II (with Ptolemies VI and VII, respectively) have been suggested,[44] but Cleopatra III is possible as well, in the light of this queen's ostentatious naming as Isis (Chapter 4) and her politically charged bearing of male heirs for her uncle Ptolemy VIII. Two additional examples have heavy, Physkon-era faces. A queen on a Toronto seal has an unusual lock of hair at the side of her head (Fig. 231), a coiffure associated with Cleopatra II during the time of Ptolemy VIII (Chapter 7).[45] A bone finger ring from Cyprus (Fig. 233) has a multilayer corkscrew hairstyle identified with Cleopatra III (Chapter 7).[46]

Inscriptional and comparative evidence indicates that a well under life-size limestone statue in New York is a posthumous representation of Arsinoe II from the Physkon era (C28). The back pillar's hieroglyphic inscription includes the phrase, "Arsinoe, the goddess Philadelphos," connecting the statue with the cult of Arsinoe II established by Ptolemy II. Her facial features repeat those of the Brussels Ptolemy VIII (C1): puffy contours, wide-open eyes, cupid's bow lips with downward incisions at the corners, and rounded chin. In addition, the queen's row of forehead corkscrews compares well to Cleopatra Thea's (Fig. 232). The body is plumper than that of the third-century Arsinoe II in the Vatican (A4), with its fat neck, slightly sagging breasts, and thick waist.

A few sculptures can be linked to second-century Cleopatras on archaeological or inscriptional grounds. The Medinet Madi temple addition (Chapter 3), which had inscriptions for Ptolemies VIII and IX, possessed female sphinxes with puffy faces framed by corkscrew locks (C3). The round, open eyes are similar in appearance to the Brussels Ptolemy VIII (C1), though they slant downward. There are deep nasio-labial furrows on either side of the large, level mouth, suggestive of corpulence. The fragmentary large-scale Cleopatra II from Karnak is unfortunately faceless (B14). The limestone statue's tight waist, fleshy abdomen, and ample thighs mimic third-century ideals (e.g., A4, A45).[47]

Ptolemy XII

One basic coin type is known for Ptolemy XII (Fig. 240).[48] In it, he has thick hair with multidirectional curls, a nose with a convex bridge and flaring nostrils, and a small, round chin lacking significant fleshiness underneath. The bushy hair and hooked nose recall Ptolemy IX's (Fig. 235), though Ptolemy XII is differentiated by his beardlessness. Since Ptolemy XII's birth date is not known, the age range for his rule is uncertain.[49]

Two sculptures, one Greek and the other Egyptian, alternatively depict Ptolemy XII in his counterpart identities as the "young Dionysos" and "young Osiris." A well under life-size bronze bust in a private collection wears the ivy and bull horns of Dionysos,[50] while the colossal granite king from the Hadra dyad (E1) has the *hm-hm*-crown and *heqa*-scepter of Osiris (Chapter 3). The Greek-style bronze's convex nose bridge, flaring nostrils, and round chin are very similar to the coin profile (Fig. 240), and the Egyptian-style granite king's thick, multidirectional hair matches as well. In front view, both faces have broad foreheads and cheekbones that narrow to a small, round chin. The bronze, however, has incised forehead folds that impart an aged appearance, whereas the granite king has a youthfully smooth face. The Hadra dyad is remarkable for its manipulation of contrasting mannerisms: the female has Egyptian single-arc eyebrows and tripartite wig, while the male has "hellenized" eyebrows in two semicircles and Greek hair, thus carefully differentiating the Egyptian goddess from the Greek Ptolemy beside her.

The over-life-size limestone Tebtunis king (E3), found with a Greek inscription for Ptolemy XII (Chapter 3), has a fuller face than the two examples above, but other details are the same. Like the bronze, the Tebtunis king has an incised forehead fold, convex nose bridge, flaring nostrils, and broad mouth, and like the Hadra king (E1) has wide-open eyes. A few other sculptures may belong to Ptolemy XII. A near-life-size Greek-style marble head in Paris (Figs. 274–275)[51] has a sharply indented nose root like the king's coin profile (Fig. 240), but it shows signs of reworking on the brow, nose, and mouth. Thus, the fidelity of the facial features to Ptolemy XII is uncertain.

Other Egyptian statues can be cited. The back pillar of a fragmentary, near-life-size figure in a draped costume (F1) may be inscribed in hieroglyphs for Ptolemy XII.[52] A slightly under life-size headless basalt standing king in New York is inscribed with hieroglyphs for Ptolemy XII or one of his successors (E4), whose known titulatures are extremely similar.[53] A closely matched statue, also headless and in New York has no inscription (E5).

The Dendera treasure horde (E22) likely dates to the first century B.C., because the Hathor temple crypts that housed such images were built at that time.[54] The Ptolemy XII coins and inscribed material reportedly found with the horde (Chapter 3) support this date as well. The goddess and sphinx (Figs. 185–186) are traditionally Egyptian in their facial features and lack hellenizations. Like the head from Wannina (D21), these statues point to the persistence of established Egyptian styles in Upper Egypt in the late Ptolemaic Period. The goddess (Fig. 186) has an echeloned, tripartite wig, natural, single-arc eyebrows, citrus-segment-shaped eyes, and a broad nose base. The face of the silver sphinx (Fig. 185) is similarly styled.

Cleopatra VII

Several coin types bear Cleopatra VII's image (Figs. 241–242).[55] The queen ruled for about twenty years, from her late teens through late thirties, usually in conjunction with a male ruler, such as her brothers Ptolemies XIII–XIV and her son Ptolemy XV. An early coin shows the queen with a melon coiffure with a chignon at the back, a wide diadem, a nose with depressed root, a small, pointy chin, and sometimes fat folds on the neck (Fig. 241). In a later series with the queen on one side and Marc Antony on the other (Figs. 242–243), Cleopatra still has the melon coiffure, but its rows are slightly more numerous and the chignon is smaller or absent. Her features are more exaggerated, with the nose more pendulous, and fat folds on her elongated neck.[56]

Three Greek-style marble heads (Figs. 276–280) can be associated with Cleopatra VII by comparison to her coin portraits. All wear the wide diadem and have a melon coiffure with a center-parted layer of hair at the front, and two preserve the chignon at the back (Figs. 276 [not visible], 278). The most complete of the three, a head in Berlin (Fig. 276),[57] has an egg-shaped face, a slightly convex nose bridge, rather broad lips, and a somewhat undershot chin. Heads in the Vatican (Figs. 277–278)[58] and Cherchel (Figs. 279–280)[59] are similar, but their eyebrows slant noticeably to the root of the nose, and their lower faces are fuller, particularly the Cherchel one. In addition, the Cherchel head has fourteen melon rows, compared with eight on the Vatican portrait and a similar number on the Berlin one. Some scholars associate the Cherchel head with Cleopatra Selene, Cleopatra VII's daughter by Marc Antony. Even if this identification could be definitely proven,[60] the portrait is nonetheless highly dependent on Cleopatra VII's type. A distinctive aspect of all three heads is the presence of small curls on the forehead, which curve outward from a center part toward either temple.[61]

Ptolemy XV Caesarion

While no coins are inscribed for Ptolemy XV Caesarion, Cleopatra VII's son by Julius Caesar, some uninscribed clay sealings can be attributed to him because of their distinctive features.[62] These seals show a boy or a young man with a diadem or *kausia,* thick bangs of forehead hair, sometimes an under-the-chin beard and mustache, and a peculiarly undershot chin. Unlike the nose bridges on other late Ptolemies, the one here is relatively straight. A sealing from this series was found at Tanis (Fig. 244).[63] Caesarion ruled with his mother as a boy and teenager.

Two Egyptian-style sculptures can be ascribed to Caesarion because of their correspondence to the sealing profiles: an under-life-size gabbro head in Bologna (E15), and a well under life-size graywacke statue in Brooklyn (E16).[64] The profiles of both, with undershot chins and forehead locks curling slightly toward the ear, can be likened to the same on the sealing profiles (Fig. 244).[65] The sculptures have narrow diadems, forehead hair parted at the center, rounded faces, and thin, small, downturned lips.

Augustus

An over-life-size granite king from Karnak (G2) has forehead hair that follows Augustus' so-called Actium type known from numerous Greek-style marbles.[66] A group of centered hair locks curling to the right forms a pincer over the right eye and a part over the left eye. The tapered shape of the face and convex nose bridge with indented root also follow Augustus' official type. Compared to the Vatican Ptolemy II (A3), the body is proportionally taller, particularly in the head and neck, and it is more tightly muscled. The *shendyt* is short, like that of the two late Ptolemies in New York (E4, E5). The colossal granite head with *nemes* and hair recently found in the Alexandrian harbor may represent Augustus (G1). The forehead locks are worn, but there appears to be a pincer over the right eye and a part over the outer corner of the left eye.

CONCLUSIONS

Inscriptions, distinctive regalia, excavation evidence, and comparative material can be used to construct a basic chronology of Greek and Egyptian portraits for the Ptolemies. A few broad trends become apparent. Egyptian-style portraiture undergoes a fundamental change from the third to the second and first centuries through the introduction of Greek elements. The refined and quintessentially Egyptian appearance of third-century statues like the Vatican Ptolemy II (A3) is very different from contemporary Greek marbles (Figs. 246–247) as well as from later Egyptian-style examples with Greek hair and facial features (such as B6). This is not, however, a simple trend of increasing hellenization with the passage of time. Rather, it is a shift from an Egyptian approach that excludes Greek ideas to one that selectively incorporates them. Numerous examples of the second and first centuries show this eclecticism. Sculptures can have Greek hair and facial features (B6) or lack them both (B9, E2). Sculptures can also have Greek hair and Egyptian facial features (C4), or Greek facial features but not hair (C1).

Concomitant with the infusion of Greek elements, Egyptian sculptural styles multiply. Examples from the time of Ptolemies II–III (A3, A4, A5, A12, A18) show much the same stylistic features, such as single-arc eyebrows, even when executed on a small scale (A7). On the other hand, portraits of Ptolemies V–VI—the small-scale Egyptian alabaster heads in Berlin (B1, B2, B3) and the larger-scale heads of Ptolemy VI (B6, B7, B8?)—have differing renderings of eyebrows, eyes, and mouths. Similarly, three heads of Ptolemy VIII have contrasting treatments (C1, C2, C4). Rather than a consistent line of stylistic development in the second and first centuries, there are diverse sculptural hands. Therefore, stylistic analysis needs to be applied with caution.

Despite the proliferation of hellenized sculptures in the second and first centuries, traditional Egyptian styles persist at this time. Portraits of Ptolemy VI, some hellenized (B6, B7) and another highly Egyptian (B9), demonstrate the strong contrast between the two modes. Similarly, Upper Egyptian finds from the late second or first century B.C. (D21, E22) are entirely Egyptian in appearance, and lack the Greek elements that infuse other sculptures from this time, such as the posthumous Arsinoe II in New York (C28) and the two Caesarion portraits (E15, E16).

From the beginning, Ptolemaic royal portraits emphasize features that accentuate wealth, power, and sensuality. Full faces and fleshy bodies evince a well-fed, privileged existence, whereas large eyes, flaring nostrils, and curvaceous lips give an impression of sensing and absorbing life. At the same time, there are alternative ideals. Ptolemy VI's face is lean-featured (B6, B7), for example, and Ptolemy XII's sometimes has an age-lined forehead (E3). These variations contribute to the individualization of royal portraiture and visually separate one ruler from another. The origins and goals of the diverse ideas about portraiture will be examined in the next chapter.

In constructing the chronological framework, hairstyle and the appearance of the face emerged as strong definers of identity. Hairstyle's success as a criterion deserves highlighting. Third-century coins showed changing coiffures from one king to the next. Distinctive hair arrangements enabled the assignment of sculptures to Ptolemy VI (B6, B7, B8?, Fig. 254), Ptolemy VIII (C2, C4), Cleopatra VII (Figs. 276–278), Ptolemy XV (E15, E16), and Augustus (G2). Though hairstyle is typically used for dating Roman Imperial portraits, it has not been systematically applied to Ptolemaic images. A single king's facial characteristics were not as consistent as might be expected, but his portraits did retain some underlying commonalities. The face of the Canopus head of Ptolemy VI (B7) is more elongated than in his Aegina sculpture (B6), but both have lean, bony contours. The face of the Brussels Ptolemy VIII (C1) is much rounder and his lips much smaller than in his Medinet Madi sculpture (C4), but both have large eyes and plump contours. Rather than careful copying, there are individualized treatments. In addition, portraits possess idiosyncratic elements, such as Ptolemy VI's large, thrusting chin (Fig. 255), Ptolemy VIII's protruding lower lip (Figs. 258–259), and Ptolemy XV's undershot chin (E15, E16). Both hairstyle and facial features will be applied more broadly in the next chapter as criteria for naming and dating portraits.

NOTES

1. Recent treatments: Ridgway 1990 and 2000; Smith 1991.

2. See catalogue entries for details.

3. Vandorpe 1996.

4. Kyrieleis 1975, passim; Smith 1988, 90–92, pl. 75.1–10; Mørkholm 1991, 63–70, 101–111, pls. 17–21; and Hazzard 1995, 1–7, 102–111. Pantos (1985, 309–339, pls. 33–38) ascribes selected clay-seal impressions to the early Ptolemies.

5. Copenhagen, Ny Carlsberg Glyptotek 2300, provenance not known, H: 26 cm; Kyrieleis 1975, 13–16, 129, 165–166, A 3, pls. 4–5; and Smith 1988, 90, 111, 164, cat. no. 47, pl. 34: 4–6. Paris, Louvre Ma 849, marble head, provenance not known, H: 24 cm (ancient part); Kyrieleis 1975, 12, 41, 126, 165, A 1, pl. 2; Smith 1988, 90, 111, 164, cat. no. 46, pl. 34: 1–3; and Hamiaux 1998, 70–71, cat. no. 73.

6. Mantua, Museo Civico di Palazzo Te, formerly in collection of Giuseppe Acerbi, Austrian Consul in Alexandria, 1826–1834, and therefore possibly from Egypt, H: 31 cm; Kyrieleis 1975, 105–112, 182, L 3, pls. 92–93, 94: 1; and Smith 1988, 92, 165, cat. no. 50, pl. 35: 7–9.

7. Paris, Louvre Ma 3261, reportedly from Hermopolis (purchased in 1896), H: 25.5 cm. Kyrieleis (1975, 21–24, 136, 167, B 10, pl. 15) and Hamiaux (1998, 71–72, cat. no. 74) place the head with Ptolemy II, and Smith (1988, 150, App. V) in the third century.

8. Boston, Museum of Fine Arts 01.8208, purchased in Alexandria with Boston 01.8207 in 1901, H: 27.5 cm; Kyrieleis 1975, 44–49, 55, 170–171, D 1, pls. 31–32; and Smith 1988, 30, 91–92, 112, 165, cat. no. 48, pl. 35: 1–3.

9. Boston, Museum of Fine Arts 01.8207, purchased in Alexandria with Boston 01.8208 in 1901, H: 35 cm; Kyrieleis 1975, 104–112, 129–130, 133–135, 181–182, L 1, pl. 89; and Smith 1988, 91–92, 165, cat. no. 49, pl. 35: 4–6.

10. An over-life-size granite queen (Rome, Vatican, Museo Gregoriano Egizio 22683, H: 266.6 cm) was found with those of Ptolemy II and Arsinoe II. Some see a third-century work (Botti and Romanelli 1951, 25–26, 137, cat. no. 33, pls. 22–23), and others a Roman copy (Roullet 1972, 109, cat. no. 181, pl. 146, fig. 204; Grenier 1989, 21–33, figs. 11–12; and Quaegebeur 1998, 74, 104, cat. no. 81).

11. In addition, Bernard V. Bothmer and Herman De Meulenaere tentatively attributed a right leg of a dark stone royal statue with a hieroglyph-inscribed back pillar to Ptolemy II (Petrie Museum of Egyptian Archaeology, University College London 14630, H: 45.6 cm, reportedly from Memphis); H. M. Stewart 1983, 38, cat. no. 145, pl. 27. Bothmer ascribed to Ptolemy II a green schist, left third of an armless chest with plain *nemes* lappet, pigtail, and hieroglyph-inscribed back pillar (New York art market, H: ?); unpublished, but recorded as no. 2288 in Corpus of Late Egyptian Sculpture at the Brooklyn Museum of Art.

12. Heinrich Brugsch, *Thesaurus inscriptionum aegyptiacarum,* vol. 5 (Leipzig, 1891), 1234, illustrates a hieroglyph-inscribed granite fragment containing a partial throne name of Ptolemy III and mentioning Behbeit el-Hagar, similar to A17. This may be a back-pillar fragment of a royal statue. I am grateful to Herman De Meulenaere for this information.

13. An Egyptian royal statue recently acquired by the Liebieghaus in Frankfurt (granite; H: 162 cm) has been attributed to Alexander the Great (Peter Bol, "Alexander der Grosse als Pharao im Liebieghaus in Frankfurt am Main," *AW* 32 [2001], 65–69). I am unable to form an opinion about the date of this sculpture from the published photos.

14. Kyrieleis 1975, 52, pl. 40; Smith 1988, 92, pl. 75: 11; Mørkholm 1991, 109–111, pl. 21, figs. 319–320, 323–324, 329; and Hazzard 1995, 7–8, 111–112, figs. 15, 16, 18, 134.

15. Kyrieleis 1975, 58–59, pl. 46: 1–3; Smith 1988, 93, pl. 75: 13–15; and Hazzard 1995, 9–10, 113–115, figs. 20, 22, 23.

16. Two other Ptolemy V attributions should be questioned: Berlin, Ägyptisches Museum 16699, H: 12 cm, provenance not known (Kyrieleis 1975, 54, 172, E 4) is an Old Kingdom head in Egyptian alabaster; and a terra-cotta from Athribis, H: 20 cm (Kyrieleis 1975, 54, 172–173, E 5, pl. 42: 5) is too general in execution for attribution to a ruler.

17. Two gold ring portraits often attributed to Ptolemy VI have roughening below the sideburns, though it extends under the chin: Paris, Musée du Louvre Bj 1092 (3.4 cm × 2.5 cm) and Bj 1093 (Dia: 2.5 cm; Figs. 223–224); Kyrieleis 1975, 63, pl. 46: 5–6; and Boussac 1989, 333, figs. 8–9. Walker and Higgs (2001, 67, cat. nos. 44–45) suggest a late Ptolemy.

18. Alexandria, Graeco-Roman Museum 24092, provenance not known, H: 41 cm; Kyrieleis 1975, 59–60, 120–121, 127, 174, F 3, pls. 49: 2, 50, 51; and Smith 1988, 28 n. 133, 93, 166, cat. no. 55, pl. 38: 1–2. Another marble head (Alexandria, Graeco-Roman Museum 26038, provenance not known, entered collection in January 1953, H: 17 cm, unpublished) may belong to Ptolemy VI (or V?) because of its long face and large chin; hair and sideburns were completed in plaster, and their pattern is not preserved.

19. I thank Dr. Klaus Parlasca for asking me to study this head. The attribution to Ptolemy VI is based on photos of the sculpture. A physical examination of the head is needed for confirmation.

20. Beckerath 1999, 238–239, 6T1–2.

21. Ptolemy VIII ruled with his brother and sister as a boy/teenager, but likely was in his thirties when he succeeded Ptolemy VI.

22. Kyrieleis 1975, 63, pl. 52: 1; Smith 1988, 94, pl. 75: 17; and Hazzard 1995, 11, 115–116, fig. 24.

23. Kyrieleis 1996, 319, pl. 58 (top rightmost).

24. Toronto, Royal Ontario Museum 906.12.141, from Edfu(?), H: 1.7 cm; Milne 1916, 93, cat. no. 161, pl. 5; Parlasca 1967, 180–185, fig. 4 (Ptolemy X); and Kyrieleis 1975, 69, pl. 54: 9 (Ptolemy IX). Bloomington, Indiana University Art Museum, Burton Y. Berry Collection 76.85.13, 1.33 × 1.17 × 0.28 cm; Spier 1989, 23, 25, cat. no. 2, fig. 6 (Ptolemy IX); and Plantzos 1999, 45, 113, cat. no. 8, pl. 2: 8 (Ptolemy VIII).

25. Kyrieleis does not mention any stubble in his article (Kyrieleis 1996), but confirmed its presence in a private correspondence (on Kyrieleis 1996, pl. 57, top rightmost, bottom rightmost).

26. New York, William Kelly Simpson collection, provenance not known, H: 23.5 cm; Smith (1996, 207–208, fig. 5) associates the head with Ptolemy VIII. It is worked from the front and cut off behind the preserved left ear; a hole is drilled into the back at brow level.

27. Hildesheim 2160, reportedly from Memphis, H: 12 cm; Kyrieleis 1975, 64, 71, 174, G 1, pl. 52: 2–3; and Smith 1988, 94.

28. In addition to Kyrieleis 1975, 64–69; Kyrieleis 1990; Kyrieleis 1996; and Smith 1988, 95–96; see Milne 1916; Parlasca 1978; Spier 1989; and Plantzos 1996a and 1996b. Parlasca (1967, 181), Kyrieleis (1975, 68), and Krug (1978, 17–18) attribute some seals to Ptolemy XI, but Maehler (1983, 10) and Smith (1988, 95 n. 61) rightly argue that one is unlikely to find portraits of someone who ruled less than three weeks.

29. Toronto, Royal Ontario Museum 906.12.125, from Edfu(?), H: 1.7 cm; Milne 1916, 93, cat. no. 134, pl. 5; Kyrieleis 1975, 68, pl. 55: 11 (Ptolemy XI); and Smith 1988, 95–96, pl. 75: 18 (Ptolemy IX?).

30. Toronto, Royal Ontario Museum 906.12.121, from Edfu(?), H: 1.2 cm; Milne 1916, 92, cat. no. 125, pl. 5. Kyrieleis (1996, 319–320) proposes this type as Ptolemy IX.

31. Listed respectively. Toronto, Royal Ontario Museum 906.12.86, from Edfu(?), H: 1.5 cm; Milne 1916, 91, cat. no. 83, pl. 4; and Kyrieleis 1975, 67, pl. 55: 5 (Ptolemy X). Toronto, Royal Ontario Museum 906.12.84, from Edfu(?), H: 1.7 cm; Milne 1916, 91, cat. no. 81; and Kyrieleis 1975, 67, pl. 55: 6 (Ptolemy X). Toronto, Royal Ontario Museum 906.12.100, from Edfu(?), H: 1.5 cm; Milne 1916, 92, cat. no. 96, pl. 4; and Kyrieleis 1975, 66, 68, pl. 54: 1 (Ptolemy IX).

32. Toronto, Royal Ontario Museum 906.12.192, from Edfu(?), H: 2 cm; Milne 1916, 95, cat. no. 214, pl. 5; Kyrieleis 1975, 115–116, pl. 100: 5 (Ptolemy X with Cleopatra III or Cleopatra Berenice III); and Smith 1988, 96 (Ptolemy X?).

33. Boston, Museum of Fine Arts 59.51, from Egypt, H: 64 cm; Parlasca 1967; Kyrieleis 1975, 69–73, 120–123, 127, 133, 175–176, H 6, pls. 62, 64; and Smith 1988, 96, 124, 167, cat. no. 57, pl. 39: 1–2.

34. Alexandria, Graeco-Roman Museum 24660, from Mersa Matruh, H: 38 cm; Krug 1978, 18–19, figs. 29–33; and Smith 1988, 97, 124, 167, cat. no. 60, pl. 40: 3–4.

35. Cairo JE 42891, from Aphroditopolis, H: 2.05 m (without the base); Kyrieleis 1975, 70–71, 175, H 3, pl. 59: 3–4; Smith 1988, 30, 84, 97, 124, 168, cat. no. 61, pl. 41: 1–3, and Fröhlich 1998, 206–211, 274–275, cat. no. 14, fig. 20.

36. Malibu, The J. Paul Getty Museum 83.AA.330, H: 34 cm, reportedly from Alexandria; Smith 1988, 96, 124, 167, cat. no. 59, pl. 40: 1–2; and Varner 2000, 92–93, cat. no. 3.

37. Stuttgart, Württembergisches Landesmuseum 3.827,

from Egypt, H: 2.1 cm; Kyrieleis 1975, 73, 78, 176, H 9, pl. 65: 2–3; and Smith 1988, 96 n. 65.

38. Stuttgart, Württembergisches Landesmuseum 1.6, reportedly from Athribis (Tell Atrib), H: 23 cm; Kyrieleis 1975, 45, 72–73, 176, H 8, pl. 65: 1; and Smith 1988, 96 n. 65.

39. Parlasca (1967) proposed that the Boston head was reworked from an older portrait. Smith (1988, 96, 167), Varner (2000, 92), and others discuss the reworkings as well.

40. Smith 1988, 94, pl. 75: 16; and Hazzard 1995, 9, 113, fig. 20.

41. Smith 1988, 76, 94, pl. 76: 19; and Hazzard 1995, 11–12, fig. 25.

42. Amsterdam, Allard Pierson Museum 2550, from Edfu(?), H: 1.8 cm; Plantzos (1996a, 308–309, pl. 48: 2, and 1999, 47, pl. 86: 9) proposes Cleopatra I.

43. Athens, National Archaeological Museum MN 2447 (Benaki collection), from Alexandria, H: 2.17 cm.

44. Boussac (1989, 327–332, fig. 3) prefers an identification with Cleopatra I. See also Plantzos 1996a, 309, pl. 48: 5.

45. Toronto, Royal Ontario Museum 906.12.187, from Edfu(?), H: 1.8 cm; Milne 1916, 95, cat. no. 209, pl. 5; and Svenson 1995, 78–79, 245, cat. no. 174, pl. 35 (as Toronto 906.12.167).

46. Nicosia, Cyprus Museum J 745, found in a grave near Kyreneia on Cyprus, 3.6 cm × 3.1 cm; Marangou 1971, 164, 168–171, pl. 81: 4.

47. Despite Bianchi (1978, 98–99, fig. 65), there is no reason to assume a usurpation from the New Kingdom for B14. The body's forms are consonant with third-century types; Quaegebeur 1989, 103.

48. Kyrieleis 1975, 75–76, pl. 68: 1–2; Smith 1988, 97, pl. 75: 20; and Hazzard 1995, 12, 119, fig. 152.

49. Bennett (1997, 46–66) proposes a birth date of 117 B.C.

50. Paris, private collection, reportedly from Alexandria, H: 4.8 cm; Seyrig 1968; Kyrieleis 1975, 77–78, 178, I 2, pl. 68: 6–7; *CE* 1988, 155–156, cat. no. 58; and Smith 1988, 97 n. 67.

51. Paris, Louvre Ma 3449, reportedly from Alexandria, H: 36 cm; Kyrieleis 1975, 69, 76–77, 121, 127, 134, 178, I 1, pl. 69; *CE* 1988, 154–155, cat. no. 57; Smith 1988, 97, 168, cat. no. 62, pl. 42: 1–2; *Gloire* 1998, 274, cat. no. 218; and Hamiaux 1998, 81–82, cat. no. 83.

52. Bothmer 1959, 107 n. 26.

53. Hieroglyphic names of Ptolemies XII and XV are known, but none are certain for Ptolemies XIII and XIV. Traunecker (1992, 315–324) argues that cartouches of Ptolemy XIV can be distinguished from his father's by the presence or absence of Cleopatra VII in the same text. He believes that a Koptos chapel is inscribed for Ptolemy XIV because Cleopatra VII is described as royal wife, which would not apply if Ptolemy XII were meant.

54. Building history: Di. Arnold 1999, 212–216.

55. Kyrieleis 1975, 124–125, pl. 107: 1–4; Smith 1988, 133–134, pl. 75: 21–24; Hazzard 1995, 12–14, 119–120, figs. 27–32; and Walker and Higgs 2001, 177–178, 233–235, cat. nos. 177–186, 214–231.

56. Smith (1988, 133–134) and others propose that the portrait change for the later series—toward one closer to the Roman Republican style—indicated Cleopatra VII's pro-Roman stance following Marc Antony's territorial grants to her.

57. Berlin, Antikensammlung 1976.10, provenance not known, H: 29.5 cm; Vierneisel 1980; *CE* 1988, 187–188, cat. no. 77; Smith 1988, 35, 97–98, 133, 169, cat. no. 68, pl. 44: 4–6; and Walker and Higgs 2001, 204–207, 220–221, cat. no. 198.

58. Rome, Vatican 38511, from Rome, H: 39 cm; Kyrieleis 1975, 125, 128, 185, N 1, pl. 107: 8–9; *CE* 1988, 184–186, cat. no. 76; Smith 1988, 35, 97–98, 133, 169, cat. no. 67, pl. 44: 1–3; and Walker and Higgs 2001, 203–204, 218–219, cat. no. 196.

59. Cherchel S 66 (31), from the harbor area of Cherchel, H: 31 cm.

60. Fittschen (1983) proposed an attribution to Cleopatra VII, followed by Smith (1988, 97–98, 169, cat. no. 69, pl. 45: 1–3) and Walker and Higgs (2001, 207–208). Mafoud Ferroukhi (Walker and Higgs 2001, 219, cat. no. 197) argues for Cleopatra Selene. In a forthcoming publication, Christa Landwehr (*Caesarea* 4, cat. no. 280) suggests Selene as well.

61. Although forehead curls are present on some coin profiles (for Arsinoe II, Berenice II, and Cleopatra VII; figs. 215, 217, and 242, respectively), these are loosely spaced and circle *inward* rather than outward, and hence do not duplicate the type plastically rendered on Cleopatra VII's marbles. These inward curls may have been painted (not sculpted) on some portraits, as in Musée royal de Mariemont B.264, a marble head reportedly from Hermopolis Magna, H: 33 cm; Kyrieleis 1975, 181, K 5, pls. 86: 4, 87.

62. Kyrieleis 1990; and Kyrieleis 1996, 318, pls. 54–56.

63. London, British Museum EA 15932, H: 1.7 cm; Petrie 1889, 34, pl. 12: 14. Coins, possibly tetradrachms of Cleopatra VII, were found in the same building, all of whose finds had been burnt by fire; Favard-Meeks 1998, 114, 164 n. 102.

64. Kiss (1984, 47, 49, 143, figs. 81–82) proposes Nero for E15, but the depiction of a Roman emperor in a diadem would be unlikely (G14 is an exception); Smith 1988, 38.

65. Examples with undershot chins: Kyrieleis 1996, pl. 54 (bottom leftmost) and pl. 56 (bottom rightmost).

66. Strocka (1980) made the assignment to Augustus. Boschung (1993, 202, cat. no. 268) disagreed, based on the somewhat anomalous hairstyle, arching eyebrows, and full lips. The facial details, however, reflect late Ptolemaic mannerisms (Chapter 8). Recent discussion of Augustus' hairstyle: Pollini 1999, 726, 729.

CHAPTER 7

POWERFUL TRADITIONS, NEW DYNAMICS

THOUGH THE PRIESTLY DECREES AND RELATED ANCIENT sources tell us much about Ptolemaic royal imagery, they are silent on a number of topics of great interest. They do not explicitly tell us why certain portrait features, such as hair and face, were chosen for a particular ruler or series. Why is Ptolemy VIII represented with a plump face, large eyes, flaring nostrils, and full lips? The ancient sources also do not explain variations in sculptural style. Why are the brows, eyes, and mouths of two portraits rendered in a different manner? Why do some lips have a protruding V-shape, while others are plump cupid's bows? Though we have little or no direct knowledge of what the king, priests, or sculptors thought about these matters, other evidence does remain. The preserved statues are revealing, as are the historical events, political ambitions, and religious propaganda surrounding them. These can be used to understand how royal sculpture developed under the Ptolemies into a potent combination of millennia-strong traditions and the fresh energies of Hellenistic Greek portraiture.

Creating a chronology for Egyptian portraits of the Ptolemies was like assembling a large jigsaw puzzle, starting with the knowledge that many pieces would not belong, many would be missing, and others would not directly join to the remaining portions. The overall appearance of the fully assembled puzzle was also unknown, though there were several conflicting hypotheses about it. The only real clues were some pieces that were definitely known to belong, and whose relative placement was preserved. These were the Egyptian sculptures discussed in the previous chapter, which comprise 15 percent of Group A–F examples with heads. After arranging these statues in a framework, the process of sorting through the other examples began.

First came the setting aside of pieces that possibly or definitely did not belong to the puzzle's original composition. For the sculptures, this process involved a detailed stylistic analysis of the entire corpus of portraits attributed to the Ptolemies. By isolating examples that did not conform to the group's norms, then comparing these to sculptures of other time frames, including the modern one, the analysis excluded portraits from the Ptolemaic Period. Some of these became Group H, and others are mentioned in the text. Selected Roman examples were also isolated into Group G for comparative purposes. Next came the "easy fits" among the pieces—finding obvious joins that would further rebuild the puzzle. These were sculptures that could be associated using the most effective techniques evident from the chronological framework, namely, hairstyle and distinctive facial characteristics. Matching Greek hairstyles alone increased the assembled corpus from 15 percent to 40 percent of statues with heads. Additionally, the faces of the Physkon era of Ptolemies VIII–X proved to have some particularly strong traits that allowed the placement of some portraits without Greek hair, bringing the total to nearly 50 percent.

This provided enough progress to begin to discern the puzzle's overall composition and thus start to join the rest of the pieces. Some of these strays did not directly adjoin the larger assembly, but interlocked with each other. The resulting mini-compositions made it easier to form strong hypotheses about where they might belong. For the royal portraits, this involved creating small groups of sculptures sharing common stylistic, facial, and physical traits, and then comparing these mini-groups to each other and the existing framework to decide where to date them. Information about religious, ideological, and political trends was compared to the sculptures' visual evidence to support the decision-making process. The few remaining pieces, which appear to belong, but whose position is less certain, became Group F. The partly assembled puzzle, while still missing large portions, nevertheless provided much information about the complete composition. The same is true for the royal portraits. Though our knowledge of the sculptural output of the Ptolemaic Period remains highly incomplete, its partial reconstruction provides important ideas about its scope and development. The results are discussed in approximate chronological order, and sculptures are grouped according to the convention shown in Table 7.1.

TABLE 7.1 PORTRAIT GROUPS DEFINED

Group A	Macedonian rulers
	Ptolemy I
	Ptolemy II
	Ptolemy III
	Ptolemy IV
Group B	Ptolemy V
	Ptolemy VI
Group C	Ptolemy VIII
Group D	Cleopatra III
	Ptolemy IX
	Ptolemy X
Group E	Ptolemy XII
	Cleopatra VII
	Ptolemy XV
Group F	Ptolemaic, date uncertain
Group G	Roman
Group H	Date uncertain
Group J	Miscellanea

THE HEIRS OF DYNASTY 30

If one did not know the facts of the historical accounts and simply looked at the visual evidence of royal portraiture, one might conclude that the early Ptolemies were the direct descendents of the last native pharaohs of Dynasty 30. The faces of the Egyptian-style sculptures of the first Greek rulers closely follow those of the Nectanebos.[1] They portray a fleshy-faced sovereign with a benign expression in highly abstract terms. Faces are fold-free, eyebrows are arranged in a pleasing but unnatural single arc, eyes closely follow their hieroglyphic forms, noses have wide bases, and mouths perpetually smile. Symmetry is near-perfect, and individualizing features are few.

Nowhere is this resemblance more apparent than in the best-preserved statues of the early Ptolemaic Period, those of Ptolemy II and Arsinoe II in the Vatican (A3, A4). The faces of these statues look like that of an inscribed limestone statue of Nectanebo I from Hermopolis Magna (Fig. 201a).[2] The single-arc eyebrows, the broad nose base, and the full, smiling lips are all characteristics shared by the Vatican and Hermopolis works. What is slightly different is that the Vatican statues have less elongated, wider open eyes and rounder cheeks. Another inscribed Nectanebo I sculpture, a life-size granite head in Paris, provides an additional reference point (Fig. 201b).[3] Here, the resemblance is still apparent, but not as strong. The single-arc eyebrows and slanting eyes relate to the Vatican faces, but the Paris head's eyes are narrower and more elongated.[4] A sandstone sphinx in Paris inscribed for Nectanebo I (Fig. 201c) has a full face with features similar to those of the Hermopolis statue.[5]

The visual association between the Vatican statues and those of the preceding native dynasty is both organic and deliberate. It is an outgrowth of the handing down of traditions by generations of sculptors from the fourth through third centuries.[6] It also makes the statement that the Greek rulers were the legitimate successors to the Nectanebos.

That the Ptolemies and Egyptian high officials and priests collaborated in this effort is evident from what we know of the personalities of the early Ptolemaic courts who were connected to, or familiar with, the Nectanebos. These span a variety of important professions and roles and provide a glimpse of the interactions that occurred during these formative years. An early Ptolemaic military and administrative official was called Nectanebo and was the grandson of a sister of Nectanebo I.[7] Manetho, the famous Egyptian historian who was sponsored by the early Greek rulers, came from Sebennytos, the legendary "hometown" of the Nectanebos. Anemhor II, high priest of Memphis in the mid-third century B.C. and thus an influential religious professional of his day, played roles in Dynasty 30 ancestor cults and the newer ones of the early Ptolemies, and cult statues for both must have been in his care. Anemhor records on his stele that he had roles in the cults of both a Nectanebo and Arsinoe II.[8] The fictitious Nectanebo ancestry concocted in the third century is reflected in the Alexander Romance's assertion that Nectanebo II fathered Alexander the Great, and in Pliny's anecdote relating how Ptolemy II went to great lengths to obtain an obelisk of a Nectanebo to decorate the Arsinoeum dedicated to his wife and sister in Alexandria.[9] The line of descent was given tangible form in the royal portraits and in temple-building programs that continued constructions begun under the Nectanebos. For example, at Behbeit el-Hagar, near Sebennytos, the decoration of a major Dynasty 30 temple was continued under the early Ptolemies.[10]

As we look across the now mostly anonymous heads of the early Ptolemies, highly similar faces are the norm (Group A). There is a concerted attempt to adhere closely to a type and style of royal portraiture that ignores the Greek origins of the ruling house, emphasizes dynasty continuity, and largely eschews individuality. Despite diversity in terms of scale, quality, and material, the sculptures have a "sameness" of appearance. A group of sculptures that are virtual copies of the Ptolemy II in the Vatican (A3) illustrates this point. In particular, an under-life-size schist head in Turin (A20) is a close parallel in terms of its single-arc eyebrows, slanted, rimmed eyes with small cosmetic extensions at the outer canthi, well-preserved nose with a broad base and philtrum indicated underneath, and protruding smile. Their *nemes*-headdresses are of similar proportions, and both are decorated with alternating roughened and polished stripes, as well as an additional headdress on top, now missing. An under-life-size plaster head in the Rodin collection in Paris (A21) is nearly a feature-for-feature match for the Turin head, as is a well under-life-size limestone bust in New York (A22). A life-size Egyptian alabaster statue in the British Museum (A23) belongs here, though the sculpture's cheeks are puffier, and the nose tip is fleshier. A number of other sculptures are looser copies of the same type (A24, A25, A26, A27, A28, A29). Among these, a well under life-size limestone king found at Tanis (A28) has a fleshy torso like that of the Vatican Ptolemy II (A3).

Identical observations can be made about statues of early queens. A well under life-size limestone head in Brooklyn (A43) has a fleshy face, puffy cheeks, and a rounded chin, all as in the Vatican Arsinoe II (A4). Likewise similar are the slightly slanted, rimmed, almond-shaped eyes with long cosmetic extensions, the eyebrows in relief, and the nose outline that flares sharply from root to nostrils. The face of a well under life-size limestone head from Abu Rawash (A44) also resembles that of the Vatican statue, but is more delicately carved.[11] An under-life-size limestone standing figure in Cairo (A45) has a similarly featured oval face with more open eyes. Like the Vatican statue, this queen has ample breasts, a tight waist, a fleshy abdomen with deep navel, and bulging thighs. A near-life-size limestone head in Baltimore (A46) has a long face akin to the Strasbourg Ptolemy II (A5), and the two have large, rimmed eyes, full cheeks, and strongly smiling, protruding lips. The head likely represents a goddess because of the divine epithets inscribed on the back pillar. An under-life-size dark stone queen in Paris (A47) has facial features and ample breasts like those of the Vatican Arsinoe II, though both eyebrows and eyes were once inlaid. The single-arc eyebrows and narrow eyes of a finely executed, dark stone queen in the Miho Museum (A48) recall those of the Ptolemy II bronze bust (A7). Her fleshy body has squatter proportions in comparison to the Vatican Arsinoe II.

Early royal portraits also reveal a desire to selectively reach back to models earlier than Dynasty 30. These efforts effectively position the Ptolemies, despite their Greek origins, in a long line of native pharaohs, again reflecting collaboration between the king and highly placed Egyptians. An Egyptian alabaster king wears a *nemes,* ceremonial wig, and cloak, and clasps his hand over his chest (A23), evoking very early royal prototypes (Chapter 5). A granite seated triad of the royal couple and a god (A10) is unique for the Ptolemaic Period in its recollection of a prevalent New Kingdom type (Chapter 4).

Who's Who?

Among the numerous heads with portrait types and styles close to those of Ptolemy II, it is probable that there are representations of other early rulers, including possibly Alexander the Great and dynasty founder Ptolemy I. Because critical information (particularly an inscription) is lacking, these sculptures can only be labeled as rulers of the late fourth and third centuries for now. By close observation, however, a few can be picked out for distinctive facial details that allow them to be associated with each other and set apart from known portraits of Ptolemy II. Each of these mini-groupings may be attributed to a specific early Ptolemy as more discoveries are made.

An over-life-size granodiorite head in Brooklyn (A30) has a particularly stout face, with heavy cheeks brought out by deep cutting under the eyes and near the nose and mouth. The narrow eyes and large, flattened nose add distinctiveness to a face having single-arc eyebrows and puckered lips with deeply drilled corners characteristic of other early portraits. An under-life-size dark stone head in Naples (A31) has a comparably puffy face and similar features, particularly the flattened nose, although the eyes are more open and slanted. A slightly over life-size quartzite head in Turin (A32) is heavy in the lower two-thirds of its face and can be grouped here as well.

Two colossal granite sphinxes from the Alexandria Serapeum (A33) have faces characterized by strong cheekbones and chinbones that push out from beneath the skin's surface. High arching upper eyelids make for a wide-eyed look, and the smiling lips are very puckered, accentuated by deep drill holes at the corners. A colossal granite sphinx head from Moustapha Pasha (A34) shares many characteristics with the Serapeum sphinxes, including facial shape, smile, and prominently modeled chinbone. The open eyes are similar, with strongly curving upper lids and nearly straight lower ones, and there are long cosmetic extensions from the outer canthi. The face of a slightly under life-size quartzite king found at Tanis (A35) can be compared favorably with the Moustapha Pasha head, in terms of its large chin and flattened, smiling lips with noticeable corner drill holes, though the eyes are narrower. The bottom edge of the pectorals is more rounded and deeper than in Ptolemy II's inscribed examples. A well under life-size bronze kneeling king in Marseille (A42) has a smiling face, prominent chin, and chest muscles like the Tanis king, and perhaps belongs here as well.

Two sculptures are distinguished by narrow faces with de-emphasized cheekbones and a triangular, pressed-in chinbone: an under-life-size dark stone king from Karnak (A36) and a life-size graywacke facial fragment from Heliopolis (A37). The undercutting of the lower lip is strong for both, creating a deep, highly distinctive, bow-tie-shaped depression between mouth and chin. There are slight differences between the two faces. The Heliopolis one has larger eyes, eyebrows that dip in toward the root of the nose rather than form a single arc, and a horizontal fold above each corner of the upper lip. The Karnak king has thickly muscular pectorals, a tight waist, and an avocado-shaped abdomen with a deep median line. An under-life-size plaster half-face in Amsterdam (A38) resembles the Heliopolis fragment,[12] though the distinctive triangular chinbone is lacking.

Three sphinxes also belong in the late fourth or third century, but their specific relationship to one of the types outlined above, or to those of Ptolemy II, is not clear-cut. Two examples of a similar scale, style, and limestone material (A39, A40) have single-arc eyebrows, elongated eyes, broad nose bases, and full-lipped smiles comparable to other early portraits.[13] An under-life-size limestone sphinx from Zawiet el-Amwat (A41) has a more distinctive appearance, with its puffy face, single-arc eyebrows, and open eyes. The Greek lettering on its base, particularly the slanting upper and lower lines of the sigma, parallels the same on the third-century statue base of Arsinoe II in Chicago (A14).[14]

Fourth or Third Century?

The strong similarities between fourth and third century portraits can make it difficult to decide where selected examples belong. A major case in point is the Saqqara Serapeum sphinxes, hundreds of which originally lined the processional way to the tombs of the Apis bulls, on the same route that included Greek-style sculptures (Chapter 3). The fifteen-plus surviving examples (including Fig. 200) form a close group in that they are made of limestone, comparably life-sized, and identically styled (plain *nemes* with formerly inlaid uraei and eyes).[15] They differ, however, in the treatment of the facial features: some have puffy, heavy faces, whereas others are relatively lean, and some lips smile broadly, whereas others are pursed.[16]

A Vienna example (Fig. 200) has a fleshy face whose single-arc eyebrows, slanted and almond-shaped eyes, and broad smile resemble those of the Vatican Ptolemy II (A3). The sphinx's chest bears a Greek graffito that can be paleographically dated to the third century B.C. or slightly later.[17] Does this mean that a series of early Ptolemies is represented?[18] Possibly, but this interpretation is complicated by the fact that Ptolemy II sculptures resemble those of Nectanebo I. Moreover, the shapes of the faces, eyes, and mouths of some examples look remarkably close to those of inscribed sphinxes of Nepherites I and Hakoris, other fourth-century rulers.[19] The Saqqara sculptures therefore either date to the fourth century or are early Ptolemaic imitations of types from the preceding century.

EXPERIMENTATION UNDER THE BOY-KINGS

A distinctively Ptolemaic brand of royal portraiture comes to the fore strongly under the dynasty's first boy-kings, Ptolemies V–VI. In comparison to the homogeneity of the early Ptolemies, some portraits of the initial decades of the second century experiment with distinctive and unusual characterizations, such as the exaggerated features of the Egyptian alabaster heads in Berlin (B1, B2, B3) or the lean-faced depictions of Ptolemy VI with Greek hair and features (B6, B7). At the same time, a second layer of portraits follows an idealizing style derived from the third-century approach, and excludes Greek features. The limestone head identified with Ptolemy VI because of the Khepri beetle attribute (B9) was an example discussed in the prior chapter.

The high priests of Ptah in Memphis likely had a defining influence on the two different directions for the royal image, which persisted for the balance of the Ptolemaic Period. These native priests would have numbered among the various adult advisors of the kings as they matured. Harmachis, who crowned the 13-year-old Ptolemy V in Memphis in 196 B.C., also had responsibilities for the cults of the deified Ptolemies III–V and their wives, and for the deified Arsinoe II in her Memphite temple. Two statues of his successor, Psenptais I, were found at the Alexandria Serapeum (Chapter 3).[20] The Berlin heads of Ptolemies V–VI (B1, B2, B3), which combine Egyptian and Greek ideas in an Egyptian alabaster material and small scale indicative of their ritual use in a native temple (Chapter 5), reflect the decisions of these priests.

Heightened Youthfulness and Other Developments

Heightened youthfulness is a hallmark of many sculptures of the early second century. For statues without Greek features, the king's face is fold-free, like those of the third century, but its contours are more rounded, suggestive not so much of fleshiness, but of the less-defined facial features of boys and young men. The more evenly oval outlines of these faces contribute to this effect, as do the robust contours of the torsos. This is also the time of the earliest documented statue bases dedicated to Ptolemaic princes or kings and their royal parents (B4, B13).

Stylistic diversity increases sharply, implying new workshops, or changes in how existing ones were managed. Such developments would have logically accompanied the increased temple-building and royal cult activity that sought to redefine Ptolemaic legitimacy in a new way following the ruinous revolt under Ptolemy V. The "sameness" of third-century portraiture is replaced by a more eclectic approach that still recognizes dynastic continuity, but has more diverse treatments, particularly those incorporating Greek features. Mannerisms of the third century are variously repeated, changed, or discarded. Single-arc eyebrows in low relief appear, but in other cases are transformed by thickening, or replaced by eyebrows in two semicircles. Lips continue to smile, but their edges are more softly defined, and corner drill holes are more pronounced. In comparison to the highly symmetrical portraits of the third century, asymmetrical treatments multiply.

Four dark stone kings typify these trends (B15, B16, B17, B18). These standing figures belong to a special class of sculptures likely made in support of the royal cults (Chapter 5). They are linked to each other by their dark color, under-life-size scale, similar proportions, and style, particularly the high polish on three (B15, B16, B17) and the inlaid eyes and bold torso modeling on all. Executions are curiously asymmetric: for the Yale example (B15), the top of the crown, the ear, and the bottom fold of the *nemes* wing are lower on the left than on the right, and the left eye is higher than the right one.

The faces of the dark stone kings have a highly youthful quality. They are oval and have either a slight fold of flesh under the chin or none. Orbital cavities are hollowed out, making the cheeks and the lower part of the faces stand out, like the three Egyptian alabaster heads of Ptolemy V or VI in Berlin (B1, B2, B3) and the head with the Khepri beetle of Ptolemy VI (B9). The latter's oval eyes also match two examples (B15, B18). Though united as a group, the four kings do show some differences. Although the faces of the Yale (B15) and Rome (B16) examples are treated similarly, the first has slightly thickened, natural eyebrows in two gentle semicircles, and the second has single-arc ones. The Munich king's (B17) mouth is very broad and straight and the chin large, resembling the same on the Ptolemy VI head from Canopus (B7), but it differs from the Yale king's (B15) smaller, slightly smiling mouth with large drill-hole corners. The Copenhagen king (B18) also has a broad mouth.

A similar youthful type appears in a few additional kings of varying materials, scale, and quality. An under-life-size graywacke head of a king has an oval face with rounded contours and a pleasant expression (B19). Its rather narrow and elongated eyes, featured in other contemporary sculptures (B15, B20, B21), are placed close to the natural, single-arc brow. The outline of its nose is streamlined in comparison to third-century noses, which have wide bases (such as A23). The lower lip is thickened, and there is no fold of flesh under the chin. The king in a well under life-size dyad is a less-precise version of the same type (B23). His eyes are again long and narrow, and the natural eyebrows are shallow semicircles that closely follow the contours of the upper eyelids. He has soft, sloped shoulders, rather prominent pectorals, and thin arms. Three other under-life-size examples are a limestone head in Brooklyn (B20) with semicircular eyebrows, narrow eyes, and a skewed face (the left half is higher than the right), a granite head in Rome (B21) with narrow eyes and a pronounced smile, and a limestone head from Canopus (B22) with single-arc eyebrows, fully rimmed eyes with arching upper lids, and pursed lips.[21] The Brooklyn head was acquired in Upper Egypt, and its distinctive appearance may reflect its origins in a studio in that region.

The First Cleopatras

Sculptures of the first two Cleopatras are patterned strongly after those of their husbands, but they add a layer of fleshiness to the face. An under-life-size quartzite head in a plain tripartite wig has an oval face with gently semicircular, slightly thickened eyebrows, narrow eyes, and a slightly smiling mouth with drilled corners (B28) that compare particularly well to the kings from the dark stone series (B15, B16, B17, B18). The face is fuller, however, and there is a fold of flesh under the chin. The sculpture's weathered and broken state belies its original appearance, which must have been striking with the eye inlays and the large uraeus modius surmounted by a now-missing crowning headdress. An under-life-size sandstone queen in Turin (B29) has a puffier face with open eyes. The proportions of the standing statue's body can be compared to the Cleopatra II statue from Karnak (B14), with a similarly soft abdomen and rounded thighs; both are covered with a pleated garment with fringed border. The atypical use of sandstone for the Turin queen suggests an Upper Egyptian provenance, where the stone was the material of choice for temple-building.[22] A dark stone head of a queen in St. Petersburg belongs to one of the first Cleopatras as well (B30). She has slightly thickened eyebrows and oval eyes like the Yale king (B15), though hers were not inlaid.

Two Colossal Sculptures

Two colossal sculptures of the period are remarkable for their interplay of Egyptian and Greek elements (B26, B27). Both depict a long face with delicately rimmed, wide-open eyes, and smiling mouths with drilled corners, but they are dissimilar in their degree of adherence to Egyptian ideas. The marble material, elongated face and neck, broad mouth, and prominent, oval chin framed by the trapezoidal jawbone link the Alexandria example (B27) to Ptolemy VI's Greek-style marble head (Figs. 254–255). Yet the Alexandria face is Egyptian in its regalia (frontlet and side tabs), frontality, and depiction of single-arc brow, eyes, and mouth. The sculpture presents a typological anomaly. As a face cut off at the frontlet and neck and hollowed at the back, it looks like examples from the enigmatic category of sculptors' studies/votives (A21; this example is not hollowed). The sculpture also resembles Greek-style marble portraits from Egypt that were cut off at the brow, back, and neck (such as Fig. 266) for insertion into statues of other materials, typically bronze. Indeed, the marble face has small drill holes on its top surface, suggestive of its original attachment to a composite statue. To contrast, the head in Bloomington (B26) is wholly Egyptian in its conception. It is made of limestone and has low relief eyebrows (dipping slightly at the root of the nose), a nose with a flaring outline, and pursed lips, all strongly suggestive of third-century works (A37 for the brow; A20 for the nose and lips). The two colossal portraits perhaps represent Ptolemy VI, but have contrasting approaches to depicting the details of the king's face. One was likely made for Alexandria or its environs (B27), and the other perhaps for a location elsewhere in the country (B26).

Two other sculptures of kings closely relate to the colossal ones. An under-life-size marble face in Naples (B25) has elongated proportions, single-arc eyebrows, delicately rimmed, wide-open eyes, and a smiling mouth like those of the colossal version (B27). Dissimilarly, however, the top and back of this smaller example are left rough and are not hollowed or drilled. In these details, the face resembles some works in the sculptors' studies/votives category (Appendix A). A life-size limestone head in Brooklyn (B24) has an oval face and a distinctively puckered smile that match the same of the colossal Bloomington head (B26). Its youthful delicacy is highlighted by single-arc eyebrows in low relief and rimmed, slanted eyes.

Ptolemy VI's Mature Portrait Type

While many portraits from the time of Ptolemies V–VI have fleshy-toned faces, a few examples of Ptolemy VI's mature portrait type—the Aegina, Canopus, and Alexandria heads (B6, B7, Fig. 254) and related coin portrait (Fig. 222)—stand out in their angular leanness. After struggling with his brother and the encroachments of Rome, the thirty-something Ptolemy VI seemed on the verge of reversing the Ptolemaic kingdom's half-century of decline, punctuated by the loss of foreign possessions, native revolt, and Seleucid invasion. By marriage and military action, he subdued the Seleucid threat, and even briefly assumed the diadem of Asia.[23] After the bloody internal struggles of his father's reign (culminating in Ptolemy V's poisoning by his generals), Ptolemy VI practiced a policy of tolerance within Egypt. He reportedly did not put any Alexandrians to death, contrary to the practice of his predecessors, and he allowed Jewish immigrants from Syria to settle in the Delta.[24] The dynamic leanness and pleasant facial expression of Ptolemy VI's mature portrait type accompanied this revised and reinvigorated version of Ptolemaic kingship, which was cut short by his death in Coele-Syria after a battle against the Seleucid king Alexander Balas, and the subsequent speedy enthronement of Ptolemy VIII, who had a very different perspective on kingship.

PTOLEMY VIII AND THE SUMPTUOUS EAST

The years of the Physkon ruler Ptolemy VIII produced some of the most ostentatious royal sculptures of the Ptolemaic Period. Unlike the lean visages of his brother Ptolemy VI, those of Ptolemy VIII are conspicuously heavy, embodying his vision of the lavish lifestyle that he considered his right as a king of the Hellenistic East. Distinctive facial features and hairstyles make his portraits the most recognizable of any in the dynasty and give a vivid impression of his presence. Thick folds of flesh at the outer canthi, mouth corners, and under the chin convey girth, while exaggerated facial features—large eyes, flaring nostrils, and pursed, sensuous lips—provide an idiosyncratic expressiveness that the king must have promoted. He is the incarnation of *truphōn,* connoting softness, voluptuousness, and extravagance, a title that he himself adopted. According to Athenaeus, Ptolemy VIII's life of indulgence made his belly so large that it was almost beyond measurement.[25] In his memoirs, the king is a gossipy raconteur of the lives of the Hellenistic elite. He writes about the exotic birds of the Alexandrian zoo, the mistresses of Ptolemy II, the luxurious court of the Numidian king Massinissa, and the buffoonery of the Seleucid king Antiochus IV in Rome.[26] The corpulent face of Ptolemy VIII allies him with the sumptuous East.

The particular power of Ptolemy VIII's Egyptian-style portraits reflects his strong sponsorship of Egyptians. He appointed the Egyptian Paos as epistrategos of Upper Egypt, a kind of governorship that was almost exclusively the province of Greeks.[27] The king's courting of native interests likely had political and cultural motives. A canny survivor, Ptolemy VIII had one of the longest reigns among the Ptolemies, successfully playing Romans, Greeks, Egyptians, and his own family members against each other in his pursuit of power and wealth. Native officials helped him in his struggles against his sister Cleopatra II and rebel forces in Upper Egypt. The king may have also been attracted to what the exoticism of Egyptian culture could add to his grandiose aura. Luxury objects like the Tazza Farnese, which integrates an Egyptian sphinx in profile view into a Greek-style composition with rich and complex divine allusions, typify such royal attitudes.[28]

A Distinctive Portrait Series

Ptolemy VIII can be recognized in a number of portraits, based on his distinctive hairstyle and face. An Egyptian-style granite head in Athens (C5) and a Greek-style marble sculpture in Copenhagen (Figs. 256–257 [nose and lips are restored])[29] both have the remains of forehead bangs curling symmetrically inward to the middle of the forehead. The portraits are of similar scale, and the outlines of their fleshy faces closely resemble each other, as do the semicircular curve of the eyebrows and the styling of the eyes. The granite head's lips are protruding, parted, and downturned. The marble head tilts and turns to the left, and there is a space for a diadem on the right side of the head and a flesh fold on the left side of the neck. Two well under life-size heads in dark stone, one in the Benaki Museum in Athens (C7) and the other in Washington (C6), have Ptolemy VIII's coiffure and fleshy physiognomy, which has large eyes, flaring nostrils, and folds at the corners of the mouth. An under-life-size diorite head in Vienna (C8) has particularly ripe features: thick hair, round, fully rimmed eyes, a heavy fold of flesh under the chin, and deep folds, horizontally from the outer canthi and vertically from the corners of the mouth, emphasizing an impression of girth. An under-life-size limestone head in Tübingen (C9) has similar characteristics. The fleshy face has wide-open, deeply set eyes, semicircular eyebrows, and a thick fold of flesh under the chin.

Ptolemy VIII's persona pervades a number of Egyptian-style sculptures without Greek hair. An under-life-size marble king in Amsterdam (C12) and two large-scale quartzite heads from Canopus (C13, C14) have similarly puffy faces, open eyes with semicircular upper lids and eyebrows, and protruding lips. The marble statue has a short, squat neck and a torso with subtly carved fat folds between the robust pectorals and round abdomen, alluding to the king's Physkon status. The better-preserved of the Canopus heads (C13) has plump cheeks accented on the left side by a raised (rather than the typically sunken) nasiolabial furrow, flaring nostrils (as preserved in the nose's outline), and thick lips (the lower one rises 1.1–1.2 centimeters from the surface of the chin). Three other examples, of differing styles, are variations of the same portrait type: an under-life-size limestone sphinx from Sanhur (C15) with large eyes, an under-life-size granite head at Yale (C16) with fleshy face and slightly protruding lips, and an under-life-size limestone head from a sphinx in Vienna (C17) with heavy cheeks and small lips.

Ptolemy VIII's Alternative Portrait Type

Ptolemy VIII's portrait series offers important evidence that a single Ptolemaic ruler had multiple, distinct types of sculpted portraits. The type described so far shows the king with forehead hair curling inward from both sides, and often with a *nemes* (C2, C5). This likely is an early type, because the Horus sidelock of one example, the Vienna king (C2), associates it with the start of Ptolemy VIII's renewed rule in 145 B.C. after the death of Ptolemy VI (Chapter 5). The Vienna king may be an inaugural portrait type. A second type has a wide diadem and a large mass of forehead hair and is represented in two dark stone examples, a head in Copenhagen (C10) and another in Paris (C11), as well as a Greek-style marble discussed in the last chapter (Figs. 258–259). All have a thick mass of locks over their foreheads, with the dark stone locks generally curling to the left and the marble locks to the right. The over-life-size Paris head (C11) is a particularly fine example. Several folds add refinement to the heavy face, horizontally across the forehead, at the outer canthi, and diagonally down from the tear ducts and nostrils. The wide-open eyes are sunk deeply below the brow and have thin upper lids reminiscent of Greek-style works. A light beard, indicated by roughening on the sides of the face and under the chin, is a feature of selected glyptic portraits of Ptolemy VIII.[30] The life-size Copenhagen head (C10) has a heavy brow, sensuous lips, and thick flesh overhanging the throat.

This new portrait type for Ptolemy VIII likely was introduced at a significant interval in his reign. It may be a jubilee image created in conjunction with the king's fiftieth anniversary of rule, corresponding to the clay sealing with the Greek numeral for 50 (similar to Fig. 227).[31] It would thus be a portrait type of circa 121/120 B.C., when the king was about 60 years old. The remarkable resemblance between the marble head of the second type (Figs. 258–259) and the Brussels

Ptolemy VIII (C1) suggests that the latter belongs here as well. This would explain why the Brussels sculpture is one of the few Ptolemaic royal portraits to wear the double crown alone, which relief representations associate with a king's jubilee and the renewal of his reign (Chapter 4). Ptolemy VIII's alternate wearing of the wide diadem and double crown in portraits of his second type parallels the same in the gold ring profiles in Paris (Figs. 223–224), which likewise may have commemorated an anniversary in another Ptolemy's reign. Although the faces of the four sculptures (C1, C10, C11, Figs. 258–259) differ, they all have Physkon features and are closely related to each other by hairstyle and choice of attributes, again underscoring the importance of these two factors in establishing identity.

Cleopatra II as a Physkon Queen

Three Egyptian-style queens (C18, C19, C20) and one marble head (Figs. 260–261)[32] have closely related coiffures and Physkon facial traits. As examples of the first of two major royal female portrait types from the Physkon era, the three Egyptian sculptures depict Cleopatra II, because their fleshy faces, flaring nostrils, and sensuous lips follow Ptolemy VIII's portraits, whereas those of the second major type, with a different hairstyle, to be discussed below, belong to Cleopatra III, because their facial features resemble those of her co-regent sons, Ptolemies IX–X. Some chronological overlap between the portraits of these two Cleopatras should be expected, because the mother-daughter pair at times occupied triple regencies with Ptolemy VIII, but hairstyles and faces clearly distinguish the queens.

Cleopatra II's portraits have two alternate but highly similar hairstyles. A near-life-size head in Copenhagen (C18) belongs to the first type, with thick, wavy hair parted in the middle with a uraeus and gathered into a bun in the back. Her facial features resemble those of Ptolemy VIII heads, especially the open eyes (C8), flaring nostrils (C1), cupid's bow lips (C1, C10), and fat fold on the neck (C2). An over-life-size marble head of a queen or goddess in Kassel (Figs. 260–261) has a similar wavy hairstyle. Her semicircular eyebrows, oval eyes, and sensuous lips are like those of Ptolemy VIII's faces, both Egyptian-style (C2, C5, C10) and Greek-style (Fig. 256; not the restored lips). Though the marble head has almost universally been identified as Berenice II based on a comparison to the queen's full-faced coin profile (Fig. 217),[33] the hairstyles do not match: the sculpture has wavy locks over the forehead, whereas the coin has the melon coiffure. The Kassel head may date to the second century and is an example of the type of Greek-style work that inspired Cleopatra II's portraits.

Two other sculptures with similar facial traits have a comparable coiffure, but add corkscrew locks and a knot of hair on either side of the head (C19, C20).[34] A colossal, nummulitic limestone head in Alexandria (C19) is a particularly strong example. The queen has thick, wavy hair parted in the middle with a uraeus and gathered into a rolled bun in the back, side knots of hair, and corkscrew locks. Her fleshy face has asymmetrically arranged eyebrows, flaring nostrils, and cupid's bow lips. The same type appears in a much-reduced scale in an under-life-size dark stone head in Alexandria (C20). A well under life-size faience head in the Benaki Museum (Fig. 262)[35] has a fleshy face and a similar hairstyle, but lacks the hair knots.

Locks of hair and corkscrews have strongly deifying connotations for Ptolemaic queens. The poet Callimachus' immortalization of the lock of Berenice II and its apotheosis is the most famous instance that has come down to us (Chapter 4). The change in Cleopatra II's hairstyle to include knots perhaps points to an important elevation, just as the addition of the Horus sidelock to Ptolemy VIII's Vienna portrait (C2) declared him to be the "son of Osiris, born of Isis" when he took the throne in 145 B.C. after the death of Ptolemy VI. For Cleopatra II, the comparable event is her assumption of the deifying titles of *Thea Philometor Soteira* ("Mother-loving Savior Goddess") after 132 B.C., when she was proclaimed in Alexandria as sole ruler of Egypt after Ptolemy VIII fled to Cyprus during a civil war.[36] The naming connected her to the dynasty's founder, Ptolemy I Soter, and to her deceased husband-brother, Ptolemy VI Philometor, and strikingly cast her in the all-important protective role central to kingship (Chapter 5). Symbolic of this role, the queen bears a quiver over her shoulder in a clay sealing of her profile with the sidelock of hair (Fig. 231).[37] Thus, the colossal head from Alexandria (C19) would have functioned as a major statement of the queen's elevation, just as the Vienna sculpture (C2) did for Ptolemy VIII. Both portraits use hair as an attribute to provide divine status.

Colossal Statues of the Pharos

The propagandistic use of Egyptian-style royal portraits during the Ptolemaic Period reaches a major peak with the colossal granite statues found near the Pharos (C21). A king from this group (C22) has the puffy, oval face of Ptolemy VIII, and the forehead locks appear to be his as well. The pattern visible at both sides of the head under the *nemes* is a single row of symmetrical locks that curve slightly forward and extend in an even curve across the forehead, though weathering makes the center configuration unclear. As with other portraits of Ptolemy VIII, flesh folds appear at the outer canthi (C11), the mouth is downturned and has corner drill holes (C5, C12), and the chinbone is round (C1, C9). He wears a *shendyt,* and his broad-shouldered body has a robust, fleshy tone.

Among the queens from the Pharos, a headless one perhaps had a bun coiffure, because no tresses appear on the draped torso (C25), while another more complete figure in a draped ensemble has a single(?) tier of corkscrew locks encircled by a diadem and parted in the center of the forehead with a loopless uraeus (C27). The suggested hairstyle of the first (C25) is that of Cleopatra II without the corkscrew locks (as in C18), whereas the second (C27) is the coiffure of Cleopatra III, to be discussed below. The headless queen's waist (C25) is tighter in comparison to the more complete queen's (C27) fuller figure. A second-century king (Ptolemy VI?) may be represented in the angular-faced head with traces of small Greek-style sideburns under the *nemes* (C23). The third male head (C24), which has no traces of inlaid eyes or Greek hair under the *nemes* like the other examples is too poorly preserved for proper assessment. The hips/thighs fragment (C26) may join the female torso (C25), if confirmed by precise measurements of the fragments.

Given their enormous scale and possible strategic physical positioning, what might have been the purpose of the Pharos statues? As suggested in Chapter 3, the figures may have represented the rulers as *sunnaoi theoi* for an island temple. More complete answers await the recovery of additional fragments of the statues and better documentation of their context. The colossal king (C22) is a highlight of a royal portraiture program under Ptolemy VIII that glorified the sumptuous and exotic East.

When Ptolemy VIII became a priest of Apollo in Cyrene in the mid-second century, he inherited the sponsorship of an annual dinner for a festival called the Artemitia.[38] According to established practice, the current priest would invite all of his predecessors to this dinner and give them ceramic vessels containing a large quantity of game and fish. Ptolemy VIII embraced the tradition, but decided to embellish it greatly and leave his personal mark on it. He presented diners with solid silver bowls, each of which cost as much as the entire dinner and gift-giving in prior years. He also provided horses adorned in gold and equipped with grooms, so that guests could travel home in style. Ptolemy VIII likewise adopted the well-established traditions of Egyptian royal portraiture and sponsored idiosyncratic and extravagant paths of development.

A NEW ROYAL IDEAL

A new royal ideal infuses selected portraits during the reigns of Cleopatra III and her sons Ptolemies IX–X. Though youthful, pleasant countenances persist at this time, other portraits possess furrowed faces and forceful expressions. Two representations of Cleopatra III with nearly identical coiffures—layers of tight curls over the forehead and corkscrew locks around the head—characterize these new ideas. The face of a limestone head in Alexandria (D3)[39] is fleshy and smooth, with wide-open eyes, flat nose bridge, and cupid's bow lips. To contrast, its basalt counterpart in Vienna (D4) has a double tier of bags below her narrow eyes, deep nasiolabial furrows, folds at the mouth corners, a convex nose bridge, a pouting lower lip, a chinbone defined by a deep incision, and a sagging bulge of flesh under the chin. The first face is wholly feminine, whereas the second has a distinctly masculine aspect, with broad cheekbones and a forceful expression in which the eyebrows slant downward from their outer corners to the root of the nose. Not only does the hairstyle distinguish these portraits from those of Cleopatra II (C18, C19, C20), but age and gender indications separate them as well. Similarly, some royal male portraits, both Greek- and Egyptian-style, have numerous facial folds (D16, Fig. 271), incised forehead furrows (D20, Fig. 238), and thin hair (Figs. 237–238), and others adopt a forceful expression, with the king's face being youthful (D13, D14) or more mature (D17).

What is the source of the new ideal? It likely originates in the Greek sphere, because it is heavily concentrated among Egyptian-style images with Greek hair and facial features.[40] Similar age-lined portraits in marble proliferate in the eastern Mediterranean and Italy during the late second and early first centuries, with the heavily furrowed visages and short-cropped hair of the late Roman Republic particularly exemplifying this trend.[41] Forceful expressions also occur in this larger geographic arena. Though Ptolemaic affairs had been strongly tied to the eastern Mediterranean from the beginning of their rule, contact with Italy accelerated from the latter half of the second century onward. Ptolemy VIII appealed to Rome for assistance in settling intradynastic intrigues, both he and Ptolemy X abortively willed their kingdoms to Rome, and there were reciprocal diplomatic visits.[42] Cyrenaica, a Ptolemaic dominion directly to the west of Egypt, passed to Roman control in 96 B.C. according to the terms of the will of Ptolemy Apion, a son of Ptolemy VIII.[43]

At the same time, conflict within Egypt and abroad required ruthless and aggressive behavior. The Greek writer Pausanias recounts how Cleopatra III schemed to get rid of her son Ptolemy IX by denouncing him as her attacker before an angry Alexandrian mob and displaying her guards—bloodied with wounds she had inflicted—as false proof.[44] She was a warrior-queen, traveling with her army by land northeast from Egypt to Coele-Syria to besiege the city of Ptolemais.[45] Her son had like tendencies. At the start of his second reign, Ptolemy IX crushed an Upper Egyptian rebellion with such force that Thebes was reduced to a shadow of its former self.[46] Royal portraits from this time not only acknowledge Egypt's growing ties with Rome, but also position the Ptolemies as forceful monarchs in a time of struggle.

An Imperious Queen and Goddess

The alternately aged, forceful, and youthful portraits of Cleopatra III are preserved in a wide variety of scales, styles, and media, reflecting an exceptional sculptural output during her four decades of reign. Her statues are expressive of her aggressive style of rule and her aspirations to divinity. During the time of Ptolemy VIII, she competed against her mother Cleopatra II, producing heirs with her uncle Ptolemy VIII as her mother had done. After the king's death in the late second century B.C., she became the dominant political power in Egypt and closely managed the fortunes of her sons, Ptolemies IX–X, with whom she successively ruled as co-regent. The queen put her name before theirs in official documents and assumed a position of primacy in Egyptian temple reliefs.[47] As Cleopatra II was venerated as *Thea Philometor Soteira,* Cleopatra III was honored as Isis, both during the rule of Ptolemy VIII and later.[48] Egyptian titulatures of Ptolemies IX–X include the phrase *sḫʿj-sw-mwt.f-ḥr-nst-jt.f* ("whom his mother placed on the throne of his father"), alluding to the queen's political status and to her Isis-like role of empowering her son, the Horus-king.[49] Because Cleopatra III ruled with Ptolemy VIII and then Ptolemies IX–X, her extant portraits probably span this time frame, though her aged, forceful depictions likely date to the time of her sons because of commonalities with their portraits, to be described below.

Cleopatra III's hairstyle consists of one or more layers of corkscrews enveloping the head and neck from crown to shoulders, with wavy locks or curls over the forehead, often parted at the center. The particularly voluminous forehead hair of the Vienna (D4) and Alexandria heads (D3) recalls the cluster of hair on Ptolemy VIII's possible jubilee portrait type (C10, C11) and resembles the thick curls of Ptolemy IX's Berlin portrait (D12), discussed in the last chapter. The corkscrew hairstyle is indebted to images of goddesses, and Cleopatra III's sister, the Seleucid queen Cleopatra Thea, likewise has a multilayered corkscrew coiffure (Fig. 232).

Besides the under-life-size Alexandria head (D3), several other sculptures present Cleopatra III in youthful terms. An under-life-size dark stone statue at Yale (D5) has a single tier of corkscrew locks across the forehead and curved tresses around the head. The oval face has rounded, fold-free surfaces, semicircular eyebrows, wide-open eyes, and an extra-thick fold of flesh under the chin. Her body has especially large breasts and a long, narrow waist. A near-life-size granite head from Canopus (D6) has a similar hairstyle—corkscrew locks around the head, but curved strands of hair over the forehead rather than corkscrews. The sculpture has a heavy face, semicircular eyebrows, downward-slanting, oval eyes, and fat folds on the neck. A chalcedony gem signed by Lykomedes in Boston has a Hathor headdress, diadem, double tier of tight curls over the forehead, and fleshy, fold-free face like the Alexandria head (D3), with a more elaborate arrangement of corkscrew locks at the side of the head.[50]

Several sculptures are closely related to Cleopatra III's aged and forceful portrait in Vienna (D4). A near-life-size Greek-style marble head in Paris (Figs. 263–264)[51] is a strong visual match, particularly the narrow eyes and distinctive eyebrows, which slant down toward the root of the nose from arches at the outer canthi. The figure wears a diadem, and at its crest there is a small, off-center hole for an added attribute. The image lacks the Vienna sculpture's strong facial folds, but the Paris queen's face is similarly un-feminine, with broad cheekbones and a semicircular incision marking the chin. The forehead corkscrews are layered in two tiers over each other and curve slightly outward from a center part, compared to the Vienna queen's triple tier of tight curls. An under-life-size dark stone head from Canopus (D7) with diadem and two uraei has slanting eyebrows in a forceful expression and a particularly heavy face. There is a triple layer of corkscrews around this queen's head, compared to the double layer on the Vienna queen (D4), and the forehead locks curl away from a center part, as in the Paris queen (Fig. 263), but in a more pronounced way. The sculpture has a thick throat and a flesh fold on the neck. A well under life-size green flourite head in Paris (D8), with its corkscrew locks and broad-cheeked, unfeminine face, belongs to this group of portraits, as does a bone finger ring from Cyprus (Fig. 233), which shows a corpulent female face with a triple layer of tight curls over the forehead and three tiers of corkscrew locks at the side of the head.[52]

Distinctive Cult Statues

Where Ptolemy VIII's self-promotion expressed itself in extravagant expenditure, Cleopatra III's manifested itself in grandiose religious conceptions. Multiple priesthoods in Alexandria were devoted to her cult in her lifetime.[53] The series of under-life-size dark stone royal figures (Chapter 5) continues with two distinctive examples depicting Cleopatra III (D9, D10). The statues are unusual for the styles and attributes employed, particularly for their selective incorporation of Greek-style facial mannerisms and their use of the triple uraeus associated with Isis and other goddesses (Chapter 4). This attribute, like the Horus sidelock of Ptolemy VIII (C2) and the hair knots of Cleopatra II (C19), perhaps signified Cleopatra III's divine elevation. The tripling is indicative of the attribute's special potency.

A statue in San Jose (D9) and another in St. Petersburg (D10) have heavy bodies, with large hips and abdomen that give literal emphasis to Cleopatra III's position as the mother of two kings and the incarnation of Isis, the powerfully maternal goddess. The San Jose sculpture has a stocky face with much fleshiness under the dimpled chin and fat folds on the neck (D9). It has the slight brow protrusion above the nose root that appears on the Alexandria head (D3). A "love handle" bulge is depicted on either side above the round buttocks. A closely related statue in St. Petersburg (D10) shows the queen with the double cornucopia symbolic of the dynasty's abundant wealth. The face is more feminine, with slanting, elongated eyes, straight-sloped nose, and slightly downturned, cupid's bow lips. The earlobes have holes for earrings, which must have originally imparted a rich appearance to the statue. A well(?) under life-size queen with a triple uraeus in Paris also belongs here, although the quality of execution is lower (D26). Her fleshy face resembles that of the St. Petersburg statue (D10), and she has a similarly heavy body in a sheath dress. The queen has a pronounced fold of flesh under her chin and a thick neck.

An under-life-size dark stone figure of a standing queen with a plain diadem and plain tripartite wig in Berlin (D11) has a heavy body that is close in proportions to the San Jose and St. Petersburg statues (D9, D10), though has only a single uraeus.[54] The Berlin figure's facial features, particularly the natural brow and large eyes with curved upper lids, follow Upper Egyptian examples from the Physkon era (D21) and the first century (E22; Fig. 186), perhaps indicating that the statue comes from that region as well.

Cleopatra III's Physkon Sons

As the rival brothers Ptolemies VI and VIII had lean- and heavy-faced sculptures that clearly differentiated them, so did the competing sons of Cleopatra III have contrasting portraits. The brothers alternated rules for some thirty-five years, with their mother as co-regent for nearly half of this period until she was murdered by Ptolemy X.[55] Though portraits of Ptolemies IX–X both have fleshy faces in keeping with their naming as Physkons, those of Ptolemy IX have thick, tight curls, whereas those of Ptolemy X have C-shaped, compact locks over the forehead, usually with a single off-center pincer formation. The clay sealings show the same differentiation between Ptolemy IX's thick coiffure (Figs. 234–235) and Ptolemy X's thinner one (Figs. 237–238). Facial hair is also distinguishing, with Ptolemy IX usually having a heavy beard and Ptolemy X having scant or no facial hair. As with Cleopatra III's representations, some royal male ones have forceful expressions or show signs of age.

Several portraits can be associated with Ptolemy IX. A colossal granite head from Canopus with *nemes* and double crown (D13) has a striking face with eyebrows slanted in a forceful expression, huge eyes, puffy cheeks, narrow nose, and puckered lips with large drill-hole corners. Like Ptolemy IX's portrait in Berlin (D12), the head has a double tier of tightly curled locks over the forehead, though very long sideburns replace the under the chin beard, as in a clay sealing of the era (Fig. 239).

Many have identified the Canopus head with Ptolemy IV based on that king's coin profile, which has a full face with kinky hair and long sideburns (Fig. 218).[56] Despite the resemblance in hairstyle, however, the sculpture's facial features do not match the coin's and are entirely unlike third-century portraits, which have benign expressions, single-arc eyebrows, almond-shaped eyes, and broad nose bases (A20, A23). The Canopus head (D13) can be linked to comparably heavy-faced Greek-style portraits of Ptolemy IX, particularly a well under life-size bronze head in Stuttgart (Fig. 267), which has densely curled forehead hair and beard, large eyes, and ponderous cheeks. In addition, the Canopus head has stylistic affinities with other Physkon sculptures: the proportions and decoration of the *nemes* and double crown are similar to those of the Pharos king representing Ptolemy VIII (C22), and the eyebrows and eyes resemble a marble head identified with the same king (Fig. 258).

An under-life-size dark stone king in Cairo (D14) strongly resembles the Canopus Ptolemy IX (D13) in its forceful expression and puffy facial shape—broad cheekbones narrowing to a round chin. Their hairstyles, however, are very different: the Cairo king's thinner, C-shaped strands contrast sharply with the densely curly Canopus hairstyle. Nevertheless, the shallow depression on the forehead under the current hairline, receding outline of the forehead and front of the *nemes,* and traces of a natural beard above the jawline (Figs. 136–137) all indicate that the Cairo sculpture originally possessed a different hairstyle and had a beard (Chapter 5). Its first version represented Ptolemy IX because the facial traits follow his Canopus head (D13) and because the remaining outline of forehead hair and beard traces matches his Berlin portrait (D12), discussed in the previous chapter. His narrow, thick-lidded eyes are also close to those of Cleopatra III's marble portrait in Paris (Fig. 263). The second (and present) version depicts Ptolemy X, because the newer hairstyle, which is arranged to form a pincer over the right eye, matches this king's hairstyle, as will be discussed below. When Ptolemy X came to power after Ptolemy IX fled Egypt in 107 B.C., the sculpture was likewise usurped, with the forehead locks changed and beard removed to conform to the new king's type. The usurpation visually attests to the rivalry between the two brothers and to efforts to differentiate their portraits.

The Cairo sculpture (D14) is often ascribed to Marc Antony because the lack of a uraeus is believed to denote a nonroyal person associated with the Ptolemaic house.[57] Yet some royal statues lack the uraeus (Chapter 4). Moreover, the facial type bears no resemblance to those of Marc Antony's contemporaries, Cleopatra VII (Figs. 276, 277) or Augustus (G2), which have longer proportions, flatter cheeks, and more angular chins.

Ptolemy IX has a second, more mature portrait type, represented in three sculptures with similarly broad faces and thin lips (D15, D16, D17). These may date from the king's second reign, and they correspond to his older-looking clay sealing portrait with a strongly hooked nose (Fig. 235). Indications of age are particularly apparent on the life-size plaster face in Munich (D16), which has many small folds around its eyes and bags underneath them. It has natural eyebrows, rather small, slanted, rimmed eyes, a large nose with a convex bridge, slightly smiling lips with corner folds, and a knobby chin with a pronounced doubling underneath. A well under life-size dark stone head in Paris (D15) and an unfinished, under-life-size granite king in London (D17) have similar facial traits, but lack the folds that make aging explicit. The top-heavy Physkon head of the London king is incongruously placed on a trimly muscled body with flat pectorals. His brow slants in a forceful expression, his left eye is much more open and rounded than the right one, and his chin is heavy and dimpled. Though the Paris and Munich sculptures (D15, D16) were originally identified as Nectanebo I, and later as Ptolemy X, they are more convincingly seen as Ptolemy IX. The portraits do not fit into the sequence for Ptolemy X, to be outlined below, in that the eyes, shape of the face, and lips are not equivalent to any of the sculptures. Instead, the two works can be viewed as mature versions of the Ptolemy IX head in Berlin (D12), because all three have identically small eyes and broad chins, and the facial shapes could be interpreted as younger and older versions of the same person.

More Dark Stone Kings

A few dark stone sculptures of kings have close stylistic affinities with Ptolemy IX's portraits. An under-life-size dark stone king in Berlin (D22) has a youthful face whose semicircular eyebrows and rimmed, oval eyes are rendered just like those on the Ptolemy IX head in Paris (D15). The circular loops of the uraeus and shape of its rearing body are likewise close, but the face lacks the heaviness of the Paris one. Unlike the robustly muscled chests of earlier statues of the second century (B15, B16, B17, C12), the Berlin statue's physique is trim, just like Ptolemy IX's London sculpture (D17): the flat pectorals are modeled in a bow shape without indication of nipples, the rib cage and abdomen modeling is slight, and the buttocks are small and rounded. The strong stylistic match with the Paris head suggests that the Berlin statue, despite its non-Physkon appearance, dates to the time of Ptolemies IX–X. Three granite sculptures, of life-size scale or near it, are highly similar to the Berlin example: a sphinx head in Bloomington has a closely matching face (D23), a sphinx head from Canopus (D24) has a fuller face and broader lips, and a head in Madrid (D25) exceptionally has single-arc eyebrows.

Ptolemy X's Portraits

Ptolemy X's compact, pincer hairstyle marks both his Greek- and Egyptian-style portraits. A particularly strong example is the Greek-style limestone king from Aphroditopolis, which has short-cropped hair and a pincer over the right eye (Fig. 271). The profile of this over-life-size statue—wide diadem, flat hair over a furrowed forehead, indented nose root, deeply set eyes, sideburns, and protruding chinbone (Fig. 272)—matches Ptolemy X clay sealing profiles (Fig. 237). Viewed from the front, the face is comparatively lean and has a thick brow, downward-slanting, lemon-shaped eyes with extra-large tear ducts, elongated lower two-thirds of the face, and plump, cupid's bow lips with a centered depression underneath. The face appears mature because of the horizontal forehead fold and the furrows around the eyes, nostrils, and mouth. While the Aphroditopolis statue has sometimes been assigned to Marc Antony, it is more convincingly seen as Ptolemy X.[58]

The face of an over-life-size Greek-style marble head from Mersa Matruh (Figs. 269–270) closely resembles the limestone Aphroditopolis one (Figs. 271–272), though it lacks folds and furrows. Both have semicircular eyebrows, lemon-shaped eyes, cupid's bow lips with a centered depression underneath, and a large chinbone. There is a space for a diadem on the Mersa Matruh head and a small drill hole (0.5 centimeter in diameter × 0.5 centimeter deep) behind the diadem's crest. The marble portrait appears to have the pincer over its right eye, though damage does not allow full confirmation. Like the Egyptian-style Cairo king (D14), which was usurped for Ptolemy X from Ptolemy IX, this marble head was partly redone for a later ruler, who had more abundant facial hair. The recutting is evident in the contrast between the careful execution of the short sideburns in raised relief and the roughly incised under-the-chin beard, the sharp marking of the beard's cheekside edges, as well as the scratched-on mustache, all of which facilitated plaster additions of fuller facial hair. Thus, this Ptolemy X portrait was recarved for the bearded Ptolemy IX during his second reign, after Ptolemy X fled Egypt in 88 B.C., or for Ptolemy XV, whose representations had beards and mustaches (Fig. 244, beard only).[59]

Two Egyptian-style heads have the pincer hairstyle and possess a youthful, plump-cheeked visage, a life-size dark stone head at Yale (D18) and an under-life-size limestone one from Medinet Madi (D19). The Yale example has a row of short locks under its *nemes,* with a pincer over the right eye. The eyebrows are shallowly semicircular, the lemon-shaped eyes are readied for inlays, the curved lips are slightly downturned, and there is an Adam's apple, which is unusual for an Egyptian-style Ptolemy. It is particularly close in appearance to the Mersa Matruh head (Figs. 269–270). The diademed Medinet Madi head (D19) is covered with short locks, and there is a pincer over the left eye. The face is carved in a lively style characteristic of the Fayoum, where it was found, with thick, semicircular eyebrows, open eyes, and a smiling mouth.

One final Egyptian-style sculpture can be considered in relationship to Ptolemy X, a life-size granite statue found east of Alexandria, toward Canopus (D20). The furrowed face with the heavy brow, lemon-shaped eyes, and large chin is clearly modeled after the Aphroditopolis type (Figs. 271–273). A single fold is incised on the forehead, and shallow diagonal folds appear at the root of the nose. The hairstyle—two rows of short, similarly semicircular locks that curl away from the center of the forehead in an orderly fashion—lacks the pincer, but is similar to the Aphroditopolis coiffure in the shape and sizing of the locks and neat arrangement. The broad shoulders and large chest muscles compare well to the Pharos king (C22) from nearby Alexandria. The differing hairstyle indicates that the Alexandria statue is the single example of a possible alternate portrait type for Ptolemy X.

GRAND AMBITIONS AND WANING FORTUNES

Royal portraiture in the last decades of Ptolemaic rule embodies the era's mixture of grand ambitions and waning fortunes. Ptolemy XII and Cleopatra VII inherited the achievements of their predecessors, but were also burdened with their failings, particularly in terms of managing the growing encroachments of Rome. Ptolemy XII was extolled as a powerful conqueror in the two largest relief examples of the smiting pharaoh known from the Ptolemaic Period (Figs. 202–203; Chapter 3). At the same time, the king was paying enormous sums to the Romans to keep his grip on power, ruinously draining the country's resources and temporarily resulting in his expulsion from Egypt by the Alexandrians.[60] His daughter, Cleopatra VII, depicted herself as Isis and Marc Antony as Osiris,[61] and together they envisioned a powerful new empire of the East, with Egypt as its center. Their boy and girl twins were named after the sun and moon. The couple's plans abruptly collapsed following the victory of Octavian at the sea battle of Actium.[62]

Some sculptures of these final years strategically quote from the established repertoire of royal portraiture. A limestone portrait of Ptolemy XV Caesarion (E18) characterizes this trend in the way it combines Greek and Egyptian attributes and styles to convey a lofty, albeit ill-fated, message. The head, which has Caesarion's center-parted forehead locks and small sideburns, wears the Macedonian *kausia,*[63] Greek diadem, and Egyptian uraeus, a combination that positions the boy-king as the rightful inheritor of both the Greek eastern Mediterranean and Egypt. In a similar way, Prince Ptolemy Philadelphos wore the *kausia* and diadem during a lavish ceremony in Alexandria when he and Cleopatra VII's other children by Julius Caesar and Marc Antony were given enormous grants of land, which figuratively extended the Ptolemaic empire to its greatest geographic reach ever.[64] At the same time, the face of the sculpture—with its single-arc eyebrows, almond-shaped eyes, and smiling mouth—is so reminiscent of early Ptolemaic portraits that it was originally thought to belong in the fourth or early third century.[65] The head is unique in its juxtaposition of cultures and time frames. Though the results are visually satisfying, the political agenda failed. Within five years after the elaborate land-grant ceremony, Cleopatra VII was dead by her own hand, and Caesarion was murdered at the behest of the conquering Octavian.

Declarations of divine status contributed to the elevated sensibilities of the final Ptolemaic years. Ptolemy XII was called the "young Osiris/Dionysos" and Cleopatra VII the "young Isis," the latest incarnations of the dynasty's two most favored gods.[66] Many portraits assume a highly youthful quality and appealing expression. Faces of Ptolemy XII, such as the colossal Hadra one (E1), narrow from a broad forehead to a small chin, recalling the boyish depictions of Ptolemies V–VI (B1, B2, B3). Ptolemy XV's images, such as the Bologna and Brooklyn examples (E15, E16), have youthfully rounded faces and short hair. Eyes are often large and elongated, and lips small and highly puckered, giving the sculptures a sweet, delicate expression that stands apart from earlier idealizing models, particularly the Nectanebo-influenced, benign faces of the third century and the alternatively corpulent and forceful ones of the Physkon era. The portrait mode also stands in sharp contrast to the age-lined, mature faces with receding hairlines on sculptures of contemporary Roman leaders such as Julius Caesar, as well as on some private sculptures in Egypt, such as that of Panemerit, a general and governor of Tanis under Ptolemy XII.[67] The tousled hair and amiable faces of Ptolemy XII identify him as a young god and inheritor of the sumptuous traditions of the Ptolemaic dynasty.

There is some evidence that both Ptolemy XII and Cleopatra VII had alternate portrait types that departed from this youthful ideal. As noted in the previous chapter, later coins of Cleopatra VII during her alliance with Antony give her exaggerated features (Fig. 242) in comparison to a youthful type struck over significant periods of her reign (Fig. 241). Ptolemy XII's Tebtunis statue (E3) has a full face, an incised fold on its forehead, thin, unsmiling lips, and a thick body, and his Greek-style bronze portrait likewise has forehead folds.[68] The Greek inscription associated with the Tebtunis statue contains a date late in Ptolemy XII's reign, perhaps indicating that this more mature portrait type belongs there as well.

The Young Osiris/Dionysos

Several portraits in varied materials and styles, all life-size or smaller, depict Ptolemy XII in highly youthful terms. A granite head with a diadem in Turin (E6) closely follows the king's Hadra portrait (E1) in having tousled forehead locks, a face narrowing to a small chin, semicircular eyebrows, and open eyes. Its thick-lidded oval eyes and cupid's bow mouth are rendered after

Greek models. There is a centered drill hole under the lower lip, a mannerism present on selected Greek-style late Ptolemies (Figs. 268, 269, 271).

Some sculptures without Greek hair have the same small-chinned and petite-lipped face. A dark stone king in the Louvre (E7) has slanting, elongated eyes with high arching upper lids, and puckered, smiling lips that give an impression of sweet adolescence. There is a centered drill hole directly under its lower lip, as in the Turin head (E6). The physique is trim, with broad, muscled shoulders, flat pectorals, a slightly protruding, avocado-shaped abdomen, and a large navel. A dark stone head from Kafr Dawar (E8) and a plaster bust from North Saqqara (E9) have large eyes and pinched lips that make them close visual matches to the Louvre king. A limestone head in Brooklyn (E10) treats the same type a bit differently, with more oval eyes highlighted by cosmetic extensions and less exaggeratedly smiling lips. The king has a false beard and wears the double crown, diadem, and draped costume associated with the eternal renewal of the king's reign (Chapter 4). The traditional attributes agree with the sculpture's reported Upper Egyptian provenance, where such regalia were depicted in relief (Fig. 205).

The Young Isis

Two under-life-size marble(?) sculptures portray Cleopatra VII as the "young Isis," a head in Brooklyn (E13) and a standing statue in New York (E14). Both are identified with the queen by their thick forehead spit curls parted at the center, which match the forehead hairstyle on the queen's Greek-style marble portraits (Figs. 276, 277, 279?). Unlike these, however, the two sculptures wear the triple uraeus and have corkscrew locks surrounding the head from crown to shoulder. The New York queen additionally bears the cornucopia that signifies her gift of abundance. These features not only visually affirm the queen's naming as Isis, but also associate her portraits with those of Cleopatra III, which bore the triple uraeus to commemorate that ruler's identification as the same goddess (see above). Cleopatra VII is thus elevated to divine status and placed in a direct line of descent from her famous namesake, who dominated her male co-regents on the throne of Egypt, as the last Cleopatra did. Like Cleopatra III, Cleopatra VII put her name before her son's in official documents.[69] The Brooklyn and New York sculptures are remnants of a sculptural program that positioned the queen as Isis incarnate, and that likely had more elaborate and monumental expressions than are preserved today.

The two sculptures are stylistically distinct from each other. The Brooklyn example (E13) has an oval face, very rounded eyebrows, wide-open eyes prepared for inlays, and fat folds on the neck. For the New York example (E14), the eyes are elongated, the eyebrows are gentle curves, and the lips are thin and virtually straight. The aggressive curves of the body's narrow frame, with long neck, prominent breasts, and slender waist, suggest youthfulness.

A queen with a triple uraeus in Turin (F5) perhaps belongs to Cleopatra VII as well, but this identification is uncertain. She has a distinctively characterized face, with hollowing under the eyes and folds on either side of the nose and lips. Like the Brooklyn head (E13), the eyes are wide open, the lips are downturned, and the neck has a fat fold. The curvaceous body resembles the New York statue (E14), though here the large breasts are prominently displayed through a tight sheath dress. The vulture cap adds to her divine aura and has large plain lateral feathers, like those of the goddess of the Hadra dyad (E2). The Turin statue can be tentatively attributed to Cleopatra VII.

Other First-Century Queens

Two other statues of queens, a life-size granite one from Fouah (E11) and an under-life-size limestone figure in Leiden (E12), belong in the first century. Both have open eyes and small, pursed lips that are very much like those on royal male portraits of the first century (E7, E8, E9), but that differ from these in having narrower, longer-proportioned faces. The sweet expression of the Fouah statue is particularly akin to the Louvre king (E7), and the queen's narrow-framed body wears the draped ensemble. The Leiden statue (E12) wears the combination crown associated with Arsinoe II and later queens (Chapter 4). Her body has a compressed frame, with peculiarly hunched shoulders, ample breasts pressed together, and softly rounded abdomen. Although the Leiden queen is sometimes dated to the third or second century,[70] her face has no parallels in that period.

A Queen in Copenhagen

A life-size dark stone head of a queen in Copenhagen (F4) is often named as Arsinoe III based on comparisons to a bronze head of Arsinoe III (Figs. 252–253) in Mantua and a marble queen in Boston (Figs. 250–

251).[71] Although there is a typological similarity among the three portraits, the Copenhagen example is nonetheless not the same. It has a more compact face, more rounded eyebrows, larger eyes, and a smaller chin, all of which give the portrait a highly youthful appearance. In addition, the hair is arranged differently. The forehead locks of the Copenhagen head are swept up at an angle, and the strands on top are parted at the center and proceed diagonally down the sides of the head; in the back, the nearly vertical hair at the nape is gathered into a bun positioned high on the rear of the head. On the Mantua head, the wavy forehead locks are pulled downward into a roll placed near the nape. The Boston head has rows of a melon coiffure; the hair at the back appears to be positioned low on the neck and swept upward.

Whom might the Copenhagen head represent? The lean facial characteristics argue against the Physkon era. Cleopatra I or early Cleopatra II are possibilities, though the head is not easily compared to those of Ptolemies V–VI (B1, B2, B6, B7). Instead, the Copenhagen queen has large citrus-segment-shaped eyes and a broad face that narrows to a dainty chin, like other first-century portraits such as the Louvre king (E7) or the Fouah queen (E11). Its hairstyle, however, does not match the melon coiffure of Cleopatra VII (Figs. 276–278), and no portraits of Cleopatra V, the shadowy wife of Ptolemy XII, are known. A specific naming for the Copenhagen head should remain open.

The King of Egypt and Its Possessions

In the grandiose land-grant ceremony of Cleopatra VII and Marc Antony, Ptolemy XV Caesarion was named king of Egypt, Cyprus, Libya, and Coele-Syria, expressive of the high hopes invested in the adolescent and his combined Ptolemaic and Roman lineage. Caesarion's comparatively large number of extant portraits, and their varied styles and attributes, attest to Cleopatra VII's considerable efforts to demonstrate his great potential. In a pointed show of her devotion to the succession, the queen petitioned Octavian to allow her children to continue to rule as she plotted her suicide by poison.[72] Though Caesarion was said to resemble his father, Julius Caesar,[73] his portraits are based on Ptolemaic royal ideals for depicting boys, and they incorporate late Ptolemaic mannerisms evident in the sculptures of Ptolemy XII and Cleopatra VII.

Besides the Bologna and Brooklyn representations discussed in the previous chapter (E15, E16) and the head in the *kausia* described above (E18), several other sculptures can be attributed to Caesarion. An under-life-size dark stone head in Athens (E17) strongly resembles the Bologna and Brooklyn portraits in having a diadem, center-parted forehead bangs, short sideburns curled toward the ears, and a boyishly round face with oval eyes. A square hole and flattened, oval area on top of the head likely supported the double crown. Two other sculptures have the same hairstyle, but have expressively large eyes and a different headdress: a well under life-size faience head with a wide diadem in the Benaki Museum (Figs. 281–282),[74] and an under-life-size granite head from Canopus with a *nemes* (E19). A life-size granite head in a private collection (E21), with open eyes and a pleasant expression, belongs in the first century as well.

A battered, life-size limestone head from Ras el-Soda (E20), an area between Alexandria and Canopus, represents an alternative portrait type for Caesarion. It has a square hole on top of the *nemes,* possibly for the addition of the double crown. Like the Benaki (Figs. 281–282) and Canopus portraits (E19), the Ras el-Soda head has a highly curved left eyebrow and wide-open eye. Unlike them, however, the forehead locks of the hair are more varied, and there is a beard from sideburns to the chin, matching the clay sealings showing a bearded and maturing Caesarion (Fig. 244). The hurried execution of the sculpture in soft limestone—particularly apparent in the rough marking of the hair and the lopsided and poor execution of the ears—is an apt metaphor for the harried state of affairs that must have characterized the final moments of the Ptolemaic kingdom.

CONCLUSIONS

Egyptian portraits of the Ptolemies evoke the shifting political dynamics and propagandistic aims of the ruling house and its advisors. Early on, sculptures promoted the simple concept that the new Greek kings were legitimate dynasts in the grand native tradition. Portraits of the first Ptolemies strongly resemble those of indigenous kings of the fourth century. The ideological message is overwhelmingly consistent. Sculptures found in places as diverse as Alexandria (A33), Tanis (A28), Tukh el-Karamus (A7), and Karnak (A36) closely follow an established formula. They convey the idea of Ptolemy as Egyptian pharaoh, hardly signaling who specifically is portrayed.

In the second century, the intent of royal images becomes more complex, selectively incorporating Greek ideas, tailoring facial features in support of each ruler's individual ideology, and proclaiming ever-loftier religious conceptions. Portraits progress from the lean-featured visages of Ptolemy VI's reinvigorated kingship, to Ptolemy VIII's plump-faced vision of the sumptuous East, to Cleopatra III's age-lined, masculine expression of forcefulness, to Ptolemy XII's and Cleopatra VII's respective incarnations as the "young Osiris/Dionysos" and "young Isis." Ideological messages not only become more tightly honed, they become multichanneled as well, varying in emphasis and sophistication. A range of inventiveness is particularly apparent under the Physkons. For Ptolemy VIII, there is the imposing show of dynastic strength from the Pharos colossus (C22), the "son of Osiris," replete with Greek hair and facial features, perhaps from Alexandria (C2), a big-eyed, thick-cheeked, full-lipped portrait for Canopus that embodies the *truphōn* title (C13), a Medinet Madi sculpture that signals Greekness by including hair (C4), and a marble figure that subtly uses Egyptian sculptural conventions to show a Physkon as an Egyptian pharaoh (C12). Likewise, Cleopatra III's portraits radically revise the definition of royal female ideals. While some of her images build on prior portrait types by having fleshy, petite-lipped, feminine faces (D3), other images aggressively break these trends by adopting age-lined, broad-lipped, masculine faces (D4). After an initial period of careful conservatism, royal portraiture became diverse and dynamic. Greek ideas provided the spark, but the energy generated by royal sponsorship and Greek/Egyptian collaboration provided the momentum.

NOTES

1. Josephson 1995, 10–11; and 1997a, 12, 43–44.

2. Cairo JE 87298, limestone statue, H: 2.65 m; Roeder 1959, 286, no. 252/VII, pl. 57b–c; Myśliwiec 1988, 70; Josephson 1995, 10, fig. 8; and Josephson 1997a, 8, 13, 26, 35, 43, pl. 3b.

3. Paris, Louvre E 27124, provenance not known (acquired in 1972; formerly Flameng and Allez collections), H: 56 cm; Myśliwiec 1988, 70; Berman and Letellier 1996, 84–85, 98, cat. no. 26; Josephson 1997a, 7–8, 13 pl. 2d; and PM 8 (1999), 150–151, no. 800-858-700.

4. Josephson (1997a, 23–26) distinguishes three separate portrait types for Nectanebo I, numbering them in chronological order. He believes that the Paris head belongs to the second group and the Hermopolis head to the third.

5. Paris, Musée du Louvre A 29 (N 29), provenance not known, H: 76 cm?; Lauer and Picard 1955, 7 n. 1; Myśliwiec 1988, 70, no. 6; and PM 8 (1999), 152, no. 800-858-880.

6. Dieter Arnold (1999, 310) discusses a list of generations of "royal overseers of the works" at the Wadi Hammamat quarries that displays continuity in this role between the end of native rule in Dynasty 26 and the succeeding Persian Dynasty 27.

7. As evidenced by the text on a sarcophagus, Berlin 7: Sethe 1904, 24–26, no. 11; Hölbl 2001, 27.

8. Vienna, Kunsthistorisches Museum ÄS 153, a limestone stele, H: 72 cm. See De Meulenaere 1960, 94; Reymond 1981, 71–77, No. 4 pl. 2; Maystre 1992, 393–396, no. 192; and Quaegebeur 1998, 75, 99–100, cat. no. 63.

9. Alexander Romance: Pseudo-Callisthenes 1.1–14; Huss 1994, 129–133; Capriotti Vittozzi 2000, 32–38, 41–42; and Hölbl 2001, 78–79. Herodotus 3.2 relates a similar tale for another foreign dynasty, the Persians: an Egyptian princess of Dynasty 26 marries Cyrus and bears Cambyses, the Persian pharaoh of Dynasty 27; Lloyd 1982b, 175. Obelisk: Pliny *Naturalis historia* 36.14.67–69.

10. Favard-Meeks 1991.

11. This resemblance was first noticed in *ESLP* 1960, 125–126. Quaegebeur (1983, 116; and 1998, 104, cat. no. 80) argues for a fourth-century date because a Nectanebo II architectural block was found near the head and because of the stylistic closeness between Dynasty 30 and the early Ptolemies. Absent an inscription, one cannot rule out the earlier date, though the resemblance to the Vatican Arsinoe II suggests a Ptolemaic one.

12. Josephson (1995, 12 n. 47, as inv. no. 54) points out this similarity.

13. Franke 1992, photo no. II/2059 (fiche 44), includes a handwritten note, by Hans Wolfgang Müller(?), indicating A40 as "ähnlich Alex 11425" (i.e., A39). There is another closely matching limestone sphinx (Alexandria, Graeco-Roman Museum 11426, H: 78 cm, W: 30 cm [damaged], D: 152 cm, provenance not known) whose face and right side are heavily abraded.

14. Date of Arsinoe II base: Quaegebeur 1998, 86, cat. no. 3. See also Albersmeier and Minas 1998, 13–14, where a Greek text on an Egyptian-style relief depicting Arsinoe II has a sigma similar to the one on the Cairo sphinx (A41); the authors' paleographic analysis indicates a date during the time of Ptolemy II or III.

15. Recent publications: Lembke 1998 (early Ptolemaic); and Rogge 1999, 1–50 (Dynasty 30 or early Ptolemaic). *Minerva* 12 (March/April 2001), 37, fig. 1, illustrates one of a pair recently sold at auction.

16. Lembke 1998 illustrates many of the sphinxes.

17. Vienna ÄS 5758: Rogge (1999, 16: mid-third century) reads *Anouireis,* whereas Nachtergael (1999, 355: 225–175 B.C.) sees *Panouireis.* Many (all?) extant sphinxes have Greek graffiti.

18. Proposed by Lembke 1998. To distinguish the Saqqara sphinxes from fourth-century works, particularly a series of Luxor sphinxes inscribed for Nectanebo I, Lembke notes the absence of false beards and the lack of royal inscriptions, as well as stylistic and proportional differences, which are reasonable, though not definitive, criteria for identification. Lembke separates the sphinxes into portrait types labeled as Groups A–E.

19. Paris, Louvre A 26 (N 26) (Nepherites I) and A 27 (N 27) (Hakoris), basalt sphinxes, from Rome, 87.5 × 47.4 × 150.4 cm and 78.5 × 44 × 151 cm, respectively; Myśliwiec 1988, 67, 68; and Lollio Barberi et al. 1995, 200–202, 248–249, cat. no. 47. Rogge (1999, 14) sees similarities between the Louvre basalt sphinxes and the Saqqara sphinxes. Josephson (1997a, 3) notes that the basalt sphinxes underwent post-antique repairs, particularly to their noses and mouths, and suggests that both sculptures were made under Nepherites I.

20. Harmachis and Psenptais I biographical inscriptions: Reymond 1981, 92–112; Lanciers 1991, 143–144; and Maystre 1992, 186–190. See also *CE* 1988, 229–230.

21. Based on Franke 1992, photo no. I/552–555, II/1631 (fiche 43), an uninscribed limestone sphinx with plain *nemes* and uraeus from Sanhur (Cairo JE 42896, H: 43 cm) has a face similar to that of the Canopus head (B22).

22. Suggested by Capriotti Vittozzi (1998). She convincingly assigned the Turin queen (B29) to Cleopatra II or III, based on an analysis of other statues of queens, relief representations, style, and the use of sandstone material. Sandstone usage: Di. Arnold 1994, 219.

23. Years of decline: Hölbl 2001, 134–148. Subduing the Seleucid threat: Hölbl 2001, 192–194.

24. Tolerance toward Alexandrians: Polybius 39.7.2–5. Jewish immigrants: Hölbl 2001, 190.

25. Athenaeus 12.549d–e.

26. Fraser 1972a, 515; and Hölbl 2001, 203.

27. Hölbl 2001, 198.

28. Naples, Museo Archeologico Nazionale 27611; La Rocca 1984, pls. 2, 7.

29. Copenhagen, National Museum ABb 290, acquired by the museum in 1860 from Thomas Reutze, a teacher for a Danish nobleman's son, who traveled in the Near East and possibly Italy for many years, H: 32.0 cm. The nose and lips are restored and have been removed since the photographs used in Figs. 256–257 were taken. I thank Anne Haslund Hansen at the National Museum for the provenance information. The head is worked from the front, and the back is cut off; there are two drill holes on the rear surface at brow level and a large, triangular depression with two drilled holes at the back of the neck. Kyrieleis (1975, 21–24, 167, B 8, pl. 13) attributes the head to Ptolemy II based on comparisons to other sculptures he associates with that ruler.

30. See Kyrieleis 1996, pl. 57 (top rightmost and bottom rightmost).

31. Kyrieleis 1996, 319, pl. 58 (top rightmost).

32. Kassel Sk 115, marble, reportedly from Alexandria, H: 38 cm; Smith 1988, 48 n. 20, 91, 166, cat. no. 54, pl. 37: 4–5, and other citations in note 33 below. A dark stone female head in London (British Museum GR 1926.4–15.15) is a Roman goddess, not a Ptolemaic queen (Walker and Higgs 2001, 52–53, cat. no. 16, as indicated by the rendering of the hair and eyes.

33. Attributions to Berenice II include: Kyrieleis 1975, 98–102, 128, 132, 135, 180, K 1, pls. 83, 84: 1–3; *CE* 1988, 172–173, cat. no. 67; *Gloire* 1998, 83, cat. no. 45; and Felgenhauer 1996, 204–208, cat. no. 98.

34. Kyrieleis (1975, 185) describes the arrangement as "eine mit Rosetten oder Knotten verzierte Binde," whereas Brunelle (1976, 92–93) describes them as "ein über das Haarband fallendes Lockenbündel wurde zu einer Rosette gelegt." Since the knots are marked with wavy incisions like the rest of the coiffure, hair is the most logical reading.

35. Athens, Benaki Museum 12552, reportedly from Alexandria, H: 3.3 cm; D. B. Thompson 1973, 200, cat. no. 275, pl. 65; Fotopoulos and Delivorrias 1997, 132–133, cat. no. 197.

36. Minas 2000, 150–151; and Hölbl 2001, 197.

37. Toronto, Royal Ontario Museum 906.12.187, from Edfu(?), H: 1.8 cm; Milne 1916, 95, cat. no. 209, pl. 5; and Svenson 1995, 78–79, 245, cat. no. 174, pl. 35 (as Toronto 906.12.167).

38. Athenaeus 12.549e–550a; Hölbl 2001, 188–189.

39. I am grateful to Sabine Albersmeier for calling my attention to this sculpture.

40. This is not a general comment on the origins of the aged and furrowed faces in Egyptian private portraits during the Late and Ptolemaic periods, which is a considerably more complex topic.

41. Smith 1988, 128–132 (reviewed by A. Stewart 1990, 509); and Smith 1991, 255–258. See also Giuliani 1986; and Ridgway 2000, 303–304.

42. D. J. Thompson 1994a; Lampela 1998, 196–232; and Hölbl 2001, 186–188, 196–197, 207, 211.

43. Lampela 1998, 227–229; and Hölbl 2001, 210.

44. Pausanias 1.9.2; and Hölbl 2001, 207.

45. Hölbl 2001, 209.

46. Pausanias 1.9.3; Hölbl 2001, 211.

47. Hölbl 2001, 204–210, 275, 280.

48. Minas 2000, 151–153, 157–160; and Hölbl 2001, 199, 286.

49. Beckerath 1999, 240–243, 9N1 (Ptolemy IX) and 10H (Ptolemy X).

50. Boston, Museum of Fine Arts 27.711, reportedly found in Phoenicia or near Tarsos, H: 3.3 cm; Kyrieleis 1975, 117, 120,

pl. 100: 2; Smith 1988, 76; Svenson 1995, 235–236, cat. no. 127, pl. 40; and Plantzos 1999, 52–54, 115, cat. no. 48, pl. 9.

51. Paris, Louvre Ma 3546, reportedly from Egypt, H: 37 cm; Kyrieleis 1975, 120–123, 128, 185, M 12, pl. 104; Smith 1988, 94–95, 166–167, cat. no. 56, pl. 38: 3–4; and Hamiaux 1998, 87–88, cat. no. 89.

52. Nicosia, Cyprus Museum J 745, found in a grave near Kyreneia on Cyprus, 3.6 cm × 3.1 cm; Marangou 1971, 164, 168–171, pl. 81: 4.

53. Minas 2000, 157–161; and Hölbl 2001, 208.

54. I am grateful to Sabine Albersmeier for calling my attention to this statue.

55. Athenaeus 12.550a.

56. See catalogue entry.

57. See catalogue entry.

58. H. Jucker (1981, 675–677) and G. Grimm (1998, 144–146) argue for Marc Antony, whereas Kyrieleis (1975, 70–71), Smith (1988, 97) and Fröhlich (1998, 211) see a late Ptolemy.

59. Kyrieleis (1990, 457) suggests that Ptolemy XV could be represented in the later version of the Mersa Matruh head, given the presence of the mustache, a feature seen on clay sealings that likely depict this young ruler (Kyrieleis 1990, pl. 67f).

60. Hölbl 2001, 223–230.

61. Dio Cassius 50.5.3. Plutarch *Antony* 54.6; Hölbl 2001, 292. A coin minted at Patras in the Peloponnesos has the melon-coiffed Cleopatra VII (obverse) and an Egyptian headdress of Hathor horns, sun disk, and double plumes (reverse) that is associated with goddesses such as Isis (Dunand 1973, 21).

62. Lives of Cleopatra and Antony: Hölbl 2001, 239–251.

63. Glyptic portraits with the *kausia:* Kyrieleis 1996, pl. 59 (top leftmost); Plantzos 1996a, pl. 48: 1, and 1996b, figs. 4–5. Literary sources: Saatsoglou-Paliadeli 1993, 137–138.

64. Plutarch *Antony* 54.5; Josephson 1997a, 21; and Hölbl 2001, 244.

65. Bianchi 1992a.

66. Young Osiris: Beckerath 1999, 244–245, 12T4; Hölbl 2001, 223. Young Isis: Plutarch *Antony* 54.6; Hölbl 2001, 292.

67. Caesar's portraits: Johansen 1987. Panemerit: Cairo CG 27493 (head) and Paris, Louvre E 15683 (torso), from the Amun temple at Tanis H: 83.5 cm; Desroches Noblecourt, et al. 1981, 288–289, cat. no. 320; and *Gloire* 1998, 284, cat. nos. 227a–b.

68. Paris, private collection, reportedly from Alexandria, H: 4.8 cm; Seyrig 1968; Kyrieleis 1975, 77–78, 178, I 2, pl. 68: 6–7; and *CE* 1988, 155–156, cat. no. 58.

69. Hölbl 2001, 239.

70. See catalogue entries for details. Although Robert S. Bianchi (*CE* 1988, 180–181, cat. no. 72) suggested Cleopatra II or III, he noted that the facial characteristics could belong to the first century B.C.

71. See catalogue entry for details. I am grateful to Sabine Albersmeier for first suggesting to me that the Copenhagen head might be later than the third century.

72. Plutarch *Antony* 71.4–72.1.

73. Suetonius *Divus Iulius* 52.2.

74. Athens, Benaki Museum 12548, reportedly from Alexandria, H: 4.4 cm; D. B. Thompson 1973, 204, cat. no. 288, pl. 67; and Fotopoulos and Delivorrias 1997, 132–133, cat. no. 199.

CHAPTER 8

A GENERATION OF INNOVATORS

IN THE FAMINE STELE FROM THE PTOLEMAIC PERIOD, the king has a fantastic dream after listening to a priest's teachings.[1] He has a vision about the god Khnum, who was famed as a maker of gods, people, and animals, and whose home was Elephantine in Upper Egypt, an area rich in the stones used for royal statuary. Khnum presents the king with an incredible gift—the god's fabulous mineral wealth. Vitalized by the dream, the newly wakened king takes a number of momentous steps, including empowering sculptors to fashion the stones and minerals into statues.

Some similar instance of priestly inspired ideation must have been behind the transformation that Greek rule brought to Egyptian-style royal portraits. After centuries of measured and subtle development during the Late Period, royal portraiture was decisively altered with the introduction of Greek features, seemingly in the span of a generation. A group of important native sculptors shaped this aggressive break with the past, giving tangible form to the new ideas of the king and his priestly advisors. Like the sculptors of the Famine stele, they are mostly anonymous, but their accomplishments are still visible in their statues.

The obvious achievement of these innovators was the provocative melding of Greek and Egyptian forms. More significant, however, was their attainment of highly individualized artistic expressions based on Greek ideas. Royal portraits not only possess an ideological presence specific to their subjects, but they spotlight the mastery of individual sculptors' studios. For the reigns of Ptolemies V–VI, there are the idiosyncratic heads in Berlin (B1, B2, B3), the contrasting facial treatments of two granite heads (B6, B7), and the colossal marble face in Alexandria (B27), which is unusual in its mix of Greek and Egyptian and its design for use in a composite statue. These diverse sculptures date within decades of the perfectionist copying of the early Ptolemaic

Period, which muted the individual expression of both its subjects and its sculptors. The face of the granite statue of Ptolemy II in the Vatican (A3) imitates fourth-century types and is faithfully repeated in representations in schist (A20), plaster (A21), bronze (A7), limestone (A22), and Egyptian alabaster (A23).

There is a veritable explosion of sculptural styles in the second century. Three different yet interrelated modes can be distinguished.[2] The most recognizable is the hellenized mode that uses Greeklike hair and faces to create at least one type for each ruler. The Athens Ptolemy VIII (C5) looks like its marble counterpart (Figs. 256–257). A second mode incorporates Greek ideas, but renders the eyebrows, eyes, and lips in abstract Egyptian terms. The sphinx heads of Ptolemy VIII from Medinet Madi (C3, C4) are examples of this *mezzo* ("middle") style, so named because it occupies a middle ground between the hellenized style and more purely Egyptian ones. The third mode builds on native ideas from the fourth and third centuries and avoids Greek interpolations such as hair. Many statues from the dark stone series keep to this traditional style (such as B15, B16, B17). The contemporary presence of the hellenized, *mezzo*, and traditional styles in the second and first centuries is remarkable. Although physiognomical and ideological similarities among portraits of a single ruler suggest that they are rooted in common models, there is much diversity of sculptural interpretation.

The stylistic transformation of Ptolemaic royal portraiture away from its early traditional mode must have been accompanied by major changes in the royal ateliers. In the third century, the visual association with fourth-century types suggests the continuing power of established workshops. By the second century, the profusion of styles points to the emergence of new sculptors' studios and the reshaping of older ones.

THE HELLENIZED STYLE

Egyptian sculptors engaged to create sculptures for Alexandria and Canopus likely led the introduction of the hellenized style and shaped its course. Despite great destructions since antiquity, more Ptolemaic royal sculptures were found here than elsewhere in Egypt (Fig. 197), attesting to their original abundance. Also, the location is unique in its range of hellenized examples (B7, C21, D13, D20), as well as traditional ones of the third century (A33, A34) and later (B22, E2, E8).

Alexandria and its Canopus satellite afforded the impetus and funding: image-laden dynastic cults, royal patronage, plentiful Greek sculptures, and highly placed Egyptians, including priests attached to the royal cults. This environment of ideas must have attracted inventive native sculptors who were sponsored by the Ptolemies through priestly intermediaries, just as they elevated selected Egyptian religious, political, and military officials in the second century.

Particularly for the largest-scale statues, some of the sculptors' work may have been completed at the quarries, though details of the hair and faces may have been finished at locations near the statues' final destinations, where Greek models would have been abundant. Hellenized-style images may have also been created for other major centers such as Memphis,[3] Tanis, Ptolemais Hermiou, and Thebes, though the archaeological record is unclear in this respect.

These native studios of the second and first centuries completed important commissions such as the Pharos colossi (C21) and major programmatic images like the Horus-imbued Ptolemy VIII in Vienna (C2) and the Hadra dyad of Ptolemy XII as the "young Osiris" (E1, E2). They inherited a tradition of carving colossal royal statues in hard stones that can be traced from the fourth and third centuries: huge granite statues of Nectanebo I were found at Delta sites,[4] and three colossal early Ptolemaic ones are known from the Alexandria and Canopus area (A33, A34). As proponents of the new hellenized style that dominated royal portraits for the rest of the Ptolemaic Period, these artists were the vanguard among native royal sculptors of their day.

The colossal statues of the hellenized style form a small, cohesive group. They stretch from the Canopus Ptolemy VI (B7) to the possible head of Augustus from Alexandria (G1), suggesting a specialized group of ateliers involved in this endeavor in successive generations through the early Roman Period. These sculptures are mostly from Alexandria and Canopus, and many are made of granite. The gap in the time of Cleopatra VII may reflect the accidents of preservation as well as deliberate destruction of her images following her downfall.[5] With their large scale, elaborate regalia, and ample proportions, the colossal statues transform the Ptolemies into superhuman figures. Kings have extra-wide shoulders and prominent pectorals (such as C22), whereas queens have robust bodies with prominent breasts (such as C27).

Smaller-scale hellenized statues are much more varied in materials and stylistic approach, suggesting a diverse group of studios, perhaps more geographically dispersed. The images progress from the Egyptian alabaster heads of Ptolemies V–VI in Berlin (B1, B2, B3), to the dark stone heads of Ptolemy VIII (C6, C7), to the dark stone head of Cleopatra II (C20), to the limestone Arsinoe II of the Physkon era (C28), to the fluorite (D8) and limestone (D3) heads of Cleopatra III, to the marble(?) representations of Cleopatra VII (E13, E14), to the dark stone sculptures of Caesarion (E15, E16). The same studio (or closely related ones) likely produced some examples, such as the dark stone heads of Ptolemy VIII (C6, C7). To contrast, two unrelated ateliers appear to have created the visually divergent fluorite (D8) and limestone (D3) heads of Cleopatra III.

Studios working in the hellenized style had their particular flowering during the Physkon era. Starting with the puffy, wide-eyed, ample-lipped visages of Ptolemy VIII (such as C8) and continuing with the heavy, age-lined, thin-lipped faces of Cleopatra III (D4), royal portraits capture the political ambitions and religious conceptions of their time. Despite the fragmentary record, preserved statues exhibit a range of sculptural expressiveness, attesting to multiple studios and a high level of achievement. Ptolemy VIII's portraits alone show a more exuberant variety than the whole corpus of third-century works, and his Paris head (C11) ranks among the finest royal portraits ever produced in Egypt. The exceptional basalt portrait of Cleopatra III (D4) also dates to this period.

By incorporating Greek ideas into traditional statues, Egyptian sculptors altered the meaning of the borrowed elements and created a new style of portraiture. In present-day terms, these elements were transplanted from a naturalistic portrait style to a symbolic one. The associations that "Greekness" had in its original context were thus changed and expanded. Likewise, Egyptian royal portraiture progressed to a new mode that could be termed eclectic symbolism. Ptolemy X's face and hair have an organic relationship with the naturalistically rendered body of his Greek-style Cairo statue (Fig. 273). Though godlike in his large scale, nakedness, and pose, the figure is nonetheless concretely human in the way that his head turns and his body moves in space. The sculptor mimics nature to achieve his effects and convey the essential aspects of his subject. The king's presence is tangible.

When the same king's face and hair are inserted into an Egyptian-style statue (D20), they take on iconic status. Despite naturalistic rendering, these Greek elements are altered by strict frontality, rendering in hard stone, and framing by Egyptian regalia. By adding "Greekness" to the repertoire of Egyptian royal symbols like the *nemes* and uraeus, the sculptor imbues his subject with the remote and intangible aspects of pharaonic kingship.

THE *MEZZO* STYLE

The *mezzo* style is an offshoot of the more common hellenized one. Its exponents used Greek portraits as a basis for their work but took an expressive, Egyptian approach to evoking them. This is a provincial style, as demonstrated by examples from Medinet Madi such as the Ptolemy VIII sphinx head (C4), which has a strongly Egyptian appearance, but a coiffure and puffy, elongated face that clearly echo the same Greek models that inspired the Vienna Ptolemy VIII (C2). The same can be said about the Yale Cleopatra III (D5), which combines stylized native forms of face and body with the hairstyle seen on the queen's marble portrait (Figs. 263–264). Studios practicing the *mezzo* style may have sprung up in selected regional centers such as the Fayoum in concert with the rise of hellenized Egyptian officials and priests strongly allied with the Greek ruling class, who sought to be *à la mode* with the hellenized images in the Alexandria and Canopus area and perhaps other major centers such as Memphis.

Unlike the hellenized style, the *mezzo* style never appears to have gained much momentum. It is relatively rare, and its sculptures seem to be isolated experiments in the preserved corpus. An extraordinary example of the *mezzo* style, the *kausia*-wearing head of Caesarion (E18), is iconographically and stylistically unique in combining a Greek cap and hair and characteristically Egyptian facial features. The style's possible provincial origins, however, did not detract from the sophistication of its ideological message: the Caesarion head powerfully positioned the king as the inheritor of the Greek East and Egypt (Chapter 7).

By restyling Greek ideas in Egyptian terms, *mezzo*-style sculptors created expressive portraits that relied on exaggeration for their effects. Once likely brightly painted, the Medinet Madi sphinxes (C3, C4) must have created a vivid impression with their outsized, wide-eyed, and smiling faces. The female sphinxes from the site boldly express their corpulence. Similarly, the Yale Cleopatra III (D5) displays a potent sexuality with her full breasts, large navel, long waist, and wide hips.

Whereas hellenized-style portraits have a lofty and complex presence, *mezzo* examples have an immediacy and directness.

THE TRADITIONAL MODE

Royal portraits in the traditional mode took third-century ideas as a point of departure. By the first century, however, the style had evolved away from third-century ideas. Though sculptures of the traditional style are strongly Egyptian, they can have small details in common in Greek-style works. The Egyptian-style puckered lips of the first-century king in Paris (E7) have a centered drill hole underneath that is repeated in several Greek-style late Ptolemies with cupid's bow lips (Figs. 268, 269, 271). Workshops specializing in the traditional style likely flourished with commissions throughout Egypt, given the broad geographic spread of finds: Alexandria and Canopus area (A33, A34, E2, E8), Saqqara (E9), Sanhur (C15), Wannina (D21), and Dendera (E22). During the third century, the visual homogeneity of the royal image suggests strong central control over its appearance. In the second and first centuries, some sculptures strongly resemble each other (such as E7 and E8), but precise copies are mostly lacking, pointing to a looser central control that may have accompanied the declines in Ptolemaic power and the disruptive force of the native rebellions.

Leadership in the traditional style likely originated at an established city like Memphis and/or other Lower Egyptian sites. Most early Ptolemaic portraits were found in the Delta (Fig. 197), which was also the stronghold of fourth-century kings, whose portraiture was so influential in the third century. As the hellenized style gained prominence by the early second century, the traditional style's importance ebbed. Nevertheless, Upper Egypt likely remained a stronghold for the style at this time. Abundant temple reliefs from this region do not show hellenizing features such as Greek hair (Chapter 5), nor do statues from Wannina (D21) and Dendera (E22). A few other strong candidates for an Upper Egyptian provenance were cited in Chapter 7: the limestone head of a king that was acquired in Upper Egypt (B20); the Turin queen (B29), whose sandstone material suggests such a provenance; the Berlin queen (D11), whose traditional forms contrast sharply with contemporary hellenized examples; and the limestone head of a king (E10), which has the double crown, false beard, and draped costume depicted in Upper Egyptian temple reliefs, and which reportedly comes from that region. All of these examples are life-size or smaller, which agrees with the archaeological evidence regarding the scale of statues from Upper Egyptian temples (Table 3.1). Traditional sculptures continued to be created in the late Ptolemaic Period for the Alexandria and Canopus area as well, as demonstrated by the Hadra dyad's Isis figure (E2) and the king's head from Kafr Dawr (E8).

Though the traditional mode started out as the premier style under the early Ptolemies, it became secondary over time. While third-century examples masterfully evoke fourth-century portraits, those of the next two centuries mostly lack the complex allusiveness of the hellenized portraits and the bold expression of the *mezzo* examples. Instead of individualized treatments, these later traditional statues portray the Ptolemies in much more generic terms.

THE TRANSFORMATION OF ROYAL PORTRAITURE

Egyptian sculptors of the Ptolemaic Period culled many of the strongest elements from their country's tradition of royal portraiture and transformed them with new ideas drawn from the turbulent context of the Mediterranean world in the closing centuries before the Common Era. In doing so, these artists took an inward-looking art form and thrust it into the international milieu of their day. In bringing together Egyptian and non-Egyptian, the sculptors created a distinctive type of portraiture that stood apart from contemporary marble and bronze Greek-style works.

Royal portraits of the hellenized style did not copy Greek works. Rather, they invented a new idiom that creatively combined disparate cultural elements. By the time of Augustus, the style embraced Egyptian, Greek, and Roman. The Karnak Augustus (G2) epitomizes these trends. The granite material, monumentality, and *shendyt*-clad standing pose give the statue the strength and permanence of Egyptian tradition, while the face distinctively quotes from Egyptian sculptures of the hellenized style. The semicircular eyebrows, wide-open eyes, and sensuous lips follow Ptolemaic royal portraits, rather than adhere to the flatter eyebrows, narrower eyes, and thinner lips typical of Augustus' marble portraits.[6] Nevertheless, the Egyptian statue has the forehead hairstyle, tapered face, and convex nose bridge, characteristic of some of the marble examples. By successfully assembling contrasting forms, Egyptian sculptors created an image of the Roman conqueror who was the new pharaoh as well as the inheritor of the Ptolemaic state.

As the Ptolemies looked outward to the powers and cultures of Italy and the eastern Mediterranean, so, too, did the hellenized style ambitiously juxtapose Egyptian, Greek, and then Roman. The strength of the style was such that it was subsequently imitated in Rome (G6) and practiced in Egypt on a monumental scale as late as the third century A.D. (G11, G13, G14).

NOTES

1. Hieroglyphic inscription on the face of granite rock on Sehel Island near Aswan; Barguet 1953; Goedicke 1994; and Hölbl 2001, 167–168.

2. Smith (1988, 87) alternatively suggests four modes.

3. Smith 1996, 210.

4. Mansoura 25, fragmentary statue from el-Bakliya (Hermopolis Parva), H: 107 cm (Josephson 1997a, 6, 24, pl. 2a); and Cairo JE 46438, fragmentary statue from Kafr Manaqir (near Athribis), H: 222 cm (Josephson 1997a, 9 n. 60, as Nectanebo II).

5. Such destruction may have occurred despite the account (Plutarch *Antony* 86.5) that Cleopatra's friend Archibios paid Octavian-Augustus a ransom to leave her statues standing.

6. Eyebrows and eyes: e.g., E3; lips: e.g., C10. Augustus' marble portraits: Fittschen and Zanker 1985, pls. 1–10.

APPENDIX A

SCULPTORS' STUDIES OR VOTIVES?

SCULPTORS' STUDIES AND VOTIVES ARE TERMS THAT loosely describe an enigmatic group of Egyptian sculptures typically dated to the fourth or third century.[1] It is not clear whether these objects have a similar purpose, but many are alike in material (limestone or plaster), relatively small scale, and/or marking with grid lines. A portion of this group represents royal figures, and these can be broadly categorized as follows:

1. Heads and busts, typically with flat backs and bottoms (A22, A29).
2. Relief plaques depicting a partial or complete figure (Figs. 208–209).[2] These plaques, as well as the heads and busts of Category 1, are the most common of all the categories representing royalty.
3. Faces (full front or partial profile) depicted from the forehead through some portion of the neck (A21, A38, B25), often with hollowed backs.
4. Full or partial figures. These include standing[3] and seated figures (A28), as well as deliberately headless ones,[4] and are the least common of the categories.

The purpose of the sculptors' studies/votives is much debated, centering on whether they were preparatory models for sculpture or whether they functioned as ritual or votive objects in shrines or large temple complexes. Trying to interpret the sculptures involves explaining their appearance, including their unfinished states, incompleteness (lack of head and arms on some torsos, for example), and grid lines; and interpreting the find spot, inscriptional, and pictorial information. This discussion focuses on the royal categories outlined above and presents arguments on both sides of the debate.

APPEARANCE

The outward appearance of the objects is a strong argument for seeing them as sculptors' models. As shown by C. C. Edgar and then Gay Robins, the grid lines on the heads and busts of Category 1 can be correlated with the placement of different parts of the face and regalia.[5] These sculptures could then be interpreted as master models either distributed to various workshops from major sculptural centers or created within a workshop for the training of junior artisans, and/or as the works of apprentices preparing to execute full sculptures.

Unfinished states, incompleteness, and grid lines are more difficult to explain relative to a ritual or votive function, but pre-Ptolemaic examples provide a few ideas. So-called reserve heads from private tombs of the Old Kingdom are "complete" sculptures, even though they are cut off at the neck and sometimes are incised with lines on the cranium and base of the neck. These are not the same as the grid lines under discussion, but they may be an instance where incised lines had a magical significance.[6] A life-size, wooden half-figure of Tutankhamun of Dynasty 18, found in his tomb at Thebes, was certainly considered complete despite the lack of arms and legs.[7] Royal male busts likewise appear in temple reliefs atop a staff carried by a figure depicting the king's *ka* (Fig. 211).[8] In Egyptian royal ideology, the *ka* is a means of conceptualizing the king's life force that is passed from one ruler to the next.

The presence of ears on some relief plaques of Category 2 is indicative of a votive function. A limestone example in Baltimore (Figs. 208–209) has a figure of a king on one side and multiple ears, a uraeus, and a vulture beak(?) on the reverse.[9] The ears could be interpreted as those of the king receiving the petitions of someone addressing the plaque, with the uraeus and beak adding to the plaque's efficacy.[10] In addition, some plaques show the king's right shoulder in profile,[11] with an outline mimicking a like view of a bust, rather than showing both shoulders from the front, as one would expect if the plaque were a model for a relief.

EXCAVATION EVIDENCE

Faces and busts discovered in structures securely identified as workshops at the New Kingdom site of Tell el-Amarna are close to Ptolemaic examples.[12] Günther Roeder has argued that the Amarna faces are casts of clay models developed in preparation for creating sculptures.[13] The limestone busts from Amarna likewise resemble Ptolemaic ones, except that the former are worked in the round, whereas the latter usually have flat, grid-lined backs (A22, flat back; A24, worked in the round). Dorothea Arnold suggested that the deliberate(?) omission of an inlay in the left eye of the famous bust of Queen Nefertiti from an Amarna workshop indicates that the bust was used as a sculptor's model, rather than intended as a cult object.[14]

Among later dated evidence, Katje Lembke proposed that some royal busts may be from a workshop at Saqqara, but her conclusion relies on a speculative interpretation of meager find-spot information.[15] From Ptolemaic times are two structures in the great enclosure at Tanis, which excavator W. M. Flinders Petrie called "houses of craftsmen."[16] The first, built against the northeastern corner of the enclosure wall by the sacred lake, contained an unfinished, grid-marked, private kneeling statue as well as a grid-marked foot, both made of limestone.[17] Against the southern wall of the temenos, Petrie found a second structure with

> *slabs of limestone, ruled in squares, and one of them much worn. . . . Two of the colours were found that were used; a slab of schist having red ochre ground upon it, and a piece of a pot having blue silicate of copper in it.*

An iron chisel was also found.[18] Although the above instances bolster the sculptor's model theory, one could also argue that these workshops were engaged in the production of votives. Thus, despite the interesting information, particularly from Tell el-Amarna, one cannot be entirely sure about the intended use of the faces and busts.

Additional excavation evidence from the Ptolemaic Period may indicate a ritual or votive function.[19] Two busts of kings were found at Karnak, along with relief plaques and offering vessels, some blackened by fire, perhaps indicating ritual burning.[20] One of Petrie's other discoveries at Tanis, the previously discussed Ptolemaic chapel (Chapter 3), contained many objects, including a small standing statue of a king (A9), a royal relief plaque, and several relief images of the Apis bull,[21] which are remarkably close to similar images with grid lines (although the Tanis finds do not have these lines).[22] The setting up of the stele in the wall niche and the arrangement of the other pieces clearly point to a religious rather than a workshop setting, and the sculptures could have been objects for worship or petition. At North Saqqara, a cache of plaster objects—

including a royal bust (E9), partial faces, headless torsos, and human body parts—was unearthed in clean sand at the entrance to a Dynasty 3 mastaba at the sacred animal necropolis.[23] North Saqqara finds are still in the process of being published and may offer more evidence for defining the purpose of the studies/votives.

INSCRIPTIONAL EVIDENCE

Inscriptions on two sculptors' studies/votives point to a votive or ritual function. A limestone plaque of a bust of a goddess has an ink inscription stating *Apollōnios anethēken Isios pr[o]sōpon Apollōniou ē eikōn* ("Apollonios set up this visage [i.e., bust] of Isis as a votive gift. This image was made by Apollonios"),[24] and one limestone bust has the Demotic word "to save" written on its back side.[25] It is possible that other studies/votives originally had ink inscriptions that have disappeared with the passage of time. For example, the Baltimore plaque may have had such a text on the large blank space underneath the king (Fig. 208). Other preserved examples with inscriptions may be informative about their function.[26]

PICTORIAL EVIDENCE

Some pictorial examples from the Ptolemaic Period help define the significance of the royal busts. An Egyptian-style stele from Crocodilopolis inscribed in Greek for Cleopatra VII and Ptolemy XV depicts a bust of a king with *nemes* and false beard, facing front and sitting within a naos on an altarlike stand.[27] The crocodile-god Souchos stands on one side, a worshiping king appears on the other. The text says that Artemidoros has set up this stele for the queen, the king, and their "ancestors" (*progonoi*). The stele would thus conceptually relate the royal busts of Category 1 to similar "ancestral" busts of private persons used for worship, petition, or ritual in New Kingdom homes and temples.[28] The stele depicts the royal bust in the presence of a king and a deity, though use by a private individual is implied by the inscription and by the fact that the bust faces front, presumably toward a person addressing the stele.

Two other examples from Batn Ihrit (Theadelphia) have Greek inscriptions recording Berenice IV's granting of the right of asylum to the site's temple of the crocodile-god Pnepheros.[29] Each has a bust of a king with a *nemes* and false beard in a naos at the center of the relief decoration on top, flanked by a sacred crocodile on either side (Fig. 210). In return for the right of asylum, the temple's priests agree to perform various religious rites for the queen and her "ancestors" (*progonoi*).

CONCLUSIONS

A full-fledged study of the objects known as sculptors' studies/votives is needed to sort through the conflicting evidence. A more definitive conclusion must wait until then. In the interim, however, two observations are relevant. First, as a group, sculptors' studies/votives may need better subdividing according to purpose. It is unclear whether all of the sculptures share a common function, and a more thorough look at classification may improve our understanding. Second, it is harder to refute the evidence showing that at least some of these objects had ritual or votive functions than it is to refute evidence supporting the sculptor's model theory. The Tanis chapel finds, the inscriptional examples, and the pictorial evidence are clear in pointing to a ritual or votive purpose. Arguments favoring an interpretation as sculptors' studies are more ambiguous. Though some studies/votives were found in workshops, one could propose that these studios were engaged in the production of votives. Moreover, arguments about appearance and the artistic process, however attractive, are ultimately subjective and may relate more to present-day conceptions than to actual ancient practices. Indeed, the meaning of Egyptian sculpture in general is much more strongly rooted in a religious and ritual context than in the artistic process. The interpretation of sculptors' studies/votives needs to strike a balance between ancient ideas and modern conceptions.

NOTES

1. Key bibliography: Edgar 1906c; Bissing 1914, nos. 124–125; Young 1964; Hostens-Deleu 1977; Liepsner 1980; Schäfer 1986, 326–334; *CE* 1988, 82, 242–243; Kaiser 1990; Robins 1994, 177–181; and Lembke 1998. Nadja Tomoum is completing a dissertation on this topic under Dr. Regine Schulz at the Institut für Ägyptologie der Universität, Munich.

2. Baltimore, The Walters Art Museum 22.285, limestone, provenance not known, H: 11.8 cm; Steindorff 1946, 95, cat. no. 326, pl. 61.

3. Baltimore, The Walters Art Museum 22.42, limestone, provenance not known, H: 39 cm; Steindorff 1946, 91, cat. no. 294, pl. 57.

4. Seipel (1992, 472–475, cat. nos. 195–196, entries by Elfriede Haslauer) calls such figures sculptors' models.

5. Edgar 1906c, v–viii; and Robins 1994, 177–181. Young (1964, 254) notes that many grid lines are incised (not painted), making them harder to remove when completing a sculpture; he argues that the lines were intended to be permanent because they had an instructional purpose.

6. Tefnin (1991, 85) proposes that the incisions magically rendered reserve heads "inoffensive à l'égard des vivants." Roehrig 1999 provides counterarguments.

7. Cairo T. 16, H: 76.5 cm. Russmann (1989, 124–127, cat. no. 58) interprets the unusual image as a representation of the "king in a spiritual or magical sense" and points to representations on tomb walls of private persons that "occasionally depict, among the objects being carried to the tomb, a half-length figure wearing a crown."

8. Brooklyn Museum of Art 67.69.2, limestone, reportedly from Abydos, H: c. 24.7 cm; "Additions to the Museum Collections," *BMA* 8 (1966–1967), 161.

9. Other limestone examples: Baltimore, The Walters Art Museum 22.266 (H: 21.7 cm) and 22.269 (H: 21.2 cm), both reportedly from Saqqara; Steindorff 1946, 94, cat. nos. 324–325, pl. 60, respectively.

10. Ears on votive plaques: Robert Schlichting, "Ohrenstelen," *LÄ* 4, cols. 562–566.

11. Baltimore, The Walters Art Museum 22.270, limestone, provenance not known(?), H: 23.5 cm; Steindorff 1946, 95, cat. no. 331, pl. 62. A similar limestone relief from the Amarna Period has a bust of Nefertiti with one shoulder on its obverse and a kneeling figure on its reverse, suggestive of the adoration of a votive (Cairo JE 59296, from the Great Aten Temple, Amarna, H: 27 cm); Wildung and Schoske 1984, 76–77, cat. no. 32.

12. Do. Arnold 1996, 46–51 (plaster faces) and 65–70 (royal busts).

13. Roeder 1941.

14. Do. Arnold 1996, 67–68 (Berlin, Ägyptisches Museum 21300, painted limestone with gypsum plaster layers, H: 50 cm). E9 is a plaster Ptolemaic example with a bust shape very similar to Nefertiti's.

15. Lembke (1998, 268–269) cites the brief statement of the excavator, Auguste Mariette (who said they were found in the Saqqara necropolis where "rien n'indique le voisinage d'une tombe"), and proposes that the context could not have been votive and might have been a sculptor's studio.

16. Petrie 1889, 32–33; and Favard-Meeks 1998, 110–111.

17. Kneeling statue: Cairo CG 33314, H: 43 cm; Edgar 1906c, 5, pl. 4; and Favard-Meeks 1998, 110, 173, pl. 27a–b. Foot: London, British Museum EA 22063.

18. London, British Museum EA 27656; Favard-Meeks 1998, 111. This find was not listed in the original publication of the excavation.

19. Liepsner 1980, col. 179, n. 148.

20. Though Seif (1921) publishes these busts as sculptors' models, Liepsner (1980, col. 179, n. 148) believes that the offering vessels point to a votive purpose.

21. Petrie 1889, 31, pl. 15: 5; and Favard-Meeks 1998, 110, 171, pl. 25a.

22. Apis bull relief plaques with grid lines: Cairo CG 33434–33439 (Edgar 1906c, 64–68, pls. 30–32). Some have Tanis provenances. Petrie does not mention whether such lines are present on any of his Tanis chapel finds; none were visible during a recent reexamination of these objects at the British Museum.

23. Emery 1970, 10–11.

24. Formerly Paris, H. Hoffmann collection, H: 21 cm; Legrain 1894, 2, cat. no. 5, pl. 2; Bissing 1914, nos. 124–125, n. 42; Grimm 1974, 22 n. 78; and Liepsner 1980, col. 173, fig. 2.

25. Cairo JE 45905, H: 14 cm; see Liepsner 1980, cols. 173–174, fig. 3, where the Demotic transliteration is not provided, only its German translation, "retten."

26. Liepsner (1980, col. 173) estimates that about fifty inscribed examples are preserved.

27. Cairo JE 40720, limestone, H: 45 cm; É. Bernand 1975, 45–47, no. 14, pl. 12; Heinen 1998; and Minas 2000, 178–179.

28. Friedman 1994, 114–117, figs. 10–11.

29. Cairo JE 40727 and JE 40728, limestone, H: 120 cm (each); É. Bernand 1981a, 50–60, nos. 116–117, pls. 20–21; and Heinen 1998, 342–345, fig. 2.

APPENDIX B

QUESTIONABLE SCULPTURES

THE SUBJECT OF MODERN IMITATIONS IS OF PARTICULAR importance to the study of Egyptian portraits of the Ptolemies because of the high number of imitations that have been falsely attributed. This has occurred for several reasons. First, Ptolemaic royal sculptures have not been well understood, and well-dated comparisons are few, leaving ample room for misattributions. Second, scholars examining some works have correctly noticed non-Egyptian elements, but incorrectly explained them as a function of Greek influence rather than modern workmanship. Third, the Ptolemaic Period has been a convenient catchall for works considered odd or unusual. Two examples of questionable sculptures can be used to bring out the relevant points of discussion and lay the groundwork for identifying further modern imitations: a head of a king in a blue crown in Brooklyn (Fig. 212),[1] and a king with plain *nemes* and uraeus in New York.[2] Both sculptures are under life-size.

Among the most obvious indicators of falseness are anomalous renderings of the uraeus or crown. In the Brooklyn head, the semicircular curve of the top of the blue crown is unusual, as is the zigzagging snake's body of the uraeus and the form of the frontlet with its incised upper edge. For the New York statue, the squat crown of the *nemes* and the "botched," hanging form of the uraeus point to a modern execution.

The manner of rendering the face and body can be indicative. Often a modern imitator tips his hand by carving elements such as the eyes and lips in a "modern" rather than ancient Egyptian manner, or by clumsily rendering the details such as the structure of the ears (which often show careful attention in genuine royal heads, because part of their function was to hear petitions or other forms of address). The facial type of the Brooklyn head—squat, with a pointy chin—finds no clear parallels among works ascribed to the Ptolemaic Period.

The bulging eyes, rounded lip surfaces, vertical depression down the middle of the back, and uncommonly thin upper arms of the New York king are not ancient renderings.

Other elements can be cause for suspicion as well. The material may be unusual, as with the New York king, sometimes described as made of "marbled limestone." Some sculptures have odd areas of breakage that disguise a detail that was completed awkwardly or not at all. For example, the New York king has breaks on the uraeus and *nemes*-pigtail, both of which are strangely rendered. A sculptural pose may be impossible, in the sense that the work cannot be mentally reconstructed in a way that is consonant with known Egyptian types: the backward-leaning position of the bust of the New York king cannot be restored into a comprehensible statue pose. Some sculptures have unusual areas of preservation versus damage. The Brooklyn head has an oddly weathered surface. Certain statue types may be more susceptible to imitation, such as sculptors' studies/votives, which have compact forms, are carved in more easily worked limestone, are incomplete by nature (meaning that the modern sculptor can leave the work unfinished), and are popular items for acquisition (examples of studies/votives are present in many museums and private collections). Though one anomalous detail may or may not be an indicator of a modern date, the multiplication of them increases the odds that a sculpture is problematic.

One must also be cautious of modern alterations of ancient works. In some cases, these changes appear to be deliberate deceptions, such as in the addition of the Cleopatra cartouche on a queen in New York (E14; see catalogue entry). In other instances, however, the intent may have been to restore a damaged work to its ancient form, perhaps as in a much-repolished head in Naples (J4).

As modern imitations are exposed and sculptures that belong to other ancient periods are identified, Ptolemaic royal portraiture becomes much more comprehensible. Further advances in our understanding will critically depend on making more discerning and selective attributions to the Ptolemaic Period.

NOTES

1. Brooklyn Museum of Art 54.68, marble, provenance not known, H: 14.9 cm; Cooney 1956, 17–18, cat. no. 19, pl. 36 (c. 150–80 B.C.); Aldred 1957, 291 (authenticity questioned); *ESLP* 1960, 108, 167–168, 177, cat. no. 128, pl. 119, figs. 320–321 (c. 100–50 B.C.); *CE* 1988, 143 n. 1 (authenticity questioned); Josephson 1997b, 17–18, fig. 20 (authenticity questioned); *Gloire* 1998, 213, cat. no. 159, entry by François Queyrel (Ptolemy V); and PM 8 (1999), 202, no. 800-942-170 (late Ptolemaic or not ancient).

2. New York, Metropolitan Museum of Art 10.176.44, marbled limestone(?), provenance not known, H: 21.3 cm; *ESLP* 1960, 108, 148, 160–161, 167, 177, cat. no. 124, pl. 115, figs. 311–312 (c. 100 B.C.); Josephson 1997b, 16–17, figs. 17–19 (authenticity questioned); and PM 8 (1999), 199, no. 800-940-670 (late Ptolemaic or not ancient).

CATALOGUE

GROUPS A–E ARRANGE THE CORPUS OF EGYPTIAN-STYLE, Ptolemaic royal portraits into a proposed chronological order (see Table 7.1). Egyptian stone bases for Greek-style statues are also included for comparative purposes. Group F includes a few Ptolemaic sculptures of uncertain date. Sculptures within each of these groups are numbered closely after their order of discussion in the text. Groups G–J are discussed almost exclusively in the catalogue entries. Group G is a preliminary list of statues from the Roman Period. There is no attempt to be comprehensive, except to include all examples with Roman hair, loosely grouping them together. Group H contains unusual portraits that are sometimes dated to the Ptolemaic Period, but do not belong there. The letter *I* is not used to name a group because of its potential to be confused with the number 1. A few miscellaneous pieces, most of which are sometimes identified as Ptolemaic, are discussed in Group J.

NOTES ON CONVENTIONS

A material is listed as "dark stone" in instances where sources disagree on the precise identification of the stone. Egyptian alabaster is used to describe calcite, properly known as travertine (Nicholson and Shaw 2000, 59–60). Provenances are listed as not known unless a sculpture was excavated, or unless there is significant inscriptional or other documentary evidence of the find spot. The bibliography is selective for statues having a large number of references. Minor references have also been omitted. Female statues are identified as queens unless there is strong evidence that a goddess is represented. A few goddesses (A46, E2, E22) are included for comparison to queens. Standing (rather than striding) denotes statues having the left leg advanced. Only inscribed fragments are named for a specific king or queen. Sphinx heads are called heads of kings. See the "Definitions and Conventions" section at the front of the book for additional information.

GROUP A: MACEDONIAN RULERS TO PTOLEMY IV

A1. Fragmentary kneeling male statue inscribed for Alexander the Great or Alexander IV. Liverpool Museum M13933 (now lost)

[No figure]

Granite. H: 58.0 cm, W: 25.0 cm.

From Mendes. Inscription mentions Banebdjedet, the god of Mendes, and statue is described in the Mendes travel log of Lord Valentia, a former owner (De Meulenaere and MacKay 1976, 55). Statue lost in May 1941 during Liverpool Blitz.

Lower part of under-life-size(?) statue, with pleated *shendyt.* Not assuredly royal, but kneeling pose fits well with literary references to Alexander's reverence for Egyptian tradition—his purported crowning in the ancient capital of Memphis (Pseudo-Callisthenes 1.34.2), and his pious journey to learn his future from the famous Amun oracle in the Siwa Oasis (Diodorus 17.49–51 and Curtius 4.7), an arduous trek into the Western Desert. Back pillar: Fragmentary only.

INSCRIPTION: One column of hieroglyphs on back pillar contains birth name of Alexander the Great or his son Alexander (i.e., Alexander IV).

De Meulenaere and MacKay 1976, 55, 198, cat. no. 56. Josephson 1997a, 41 n. 277 (not assuredly royal). Capriotti Vittozzi 2000, 42. (All authors: reign of Alexander the Great or his son Alexander by Roxanne.)

A2. Statue base dedicated to Ptolemy I. Alexandria, Graeco-Roman Museum 19

[Figure 1]

Black granite. H: 32.2 cm, W: 58.2 cm, D: 34.5 cm.

Provenance not known. Formerly in Giza Museum; transferred to Graeco-Roman Museum in 1902.

Statue base with bilingual Greek/Demotic dedication, likely to have supported separately worked, Egyptian-style statue. Back of base broken off. Rough hewn cavity (c. 18 cm × c. 36.5 cm × c. 2 cm) occupies much of top. Front, right, and bottom sides are smooth, left and top sides rough, and back side very rough.

INSCRIPTION: Two lines of Greek on front, followed by similar, two-line Demotic text: (Statue of) King Ptolemy Soter (set up by) Diodotos, son of Achaios.

OGIS 1 (1903), 50, no. 19. Breccia 1911, 1, no. 1, pl. 1.1. Breccia 1914, 149, no. 1. *LdR* 4 (1916), 434, an addition for page 219, n. 3. É. Bernand 1982, 15, no. 19. Peremans 1982, 151–152. (All authors: Ptolemy I.)

A3. Standing statue inscribed for Ptolemy II. Rome, Vatican, Museo Gregoriano Egizio 22681

[Figures 2–3]

Red granite. H: 266.0 cm, HeadH: 35.0 cm, FaceH: 21.4 cm. Base: H: 24.2 cm, W: 42.5 cm, D: 96.4 cm.

Found in early eighteenth century at Villa Verospi with A4 in Rome, site of Gardens of Sallust. Possibly originally from Heliopolis, based on back-pillar inscription of accompanying statue of Arsinoe II (A4), which references the god Atum, whose home was Heliopolis. Dieter Arnold (1999, 342 n. 72) argues against this proposed provenance.

Over life-size. Banded *nemes,* uraeus, and plain *shendyt.* Preserved from top of head through attached statue base. Broken on diagonal from left knee to bottom of back pillar and repaired. Round (Dia: c. 7 cm), slightly depressed area on top of head indicates former presence of additional attribute. Enigmatic objects in hands at sides. Back pillar: Square top reaches to shoulders.

INSCRIPTION: Single column of hieroglyphs on back pillar contains Ptolemy II's throne and birth names. Inscription on belt has same.

Sethe 1904, 71, no. 16. *LdR* 4 (1916), 235, no. 56. PM 4 (1934), 63 (probably from Heliopolis). Botti and Romanelli 1951, 24–25, 137, cat. no. 32, pls. 22–23. PM 7 (1952), 413. H. W. Müller 1955, 210, pl. 27. *ESLP* 1960, 98, 122, 126, 128, 141. H. W. Müller 1961, 26, 29, fig. 14. Helbig 1963, 382, cat. no. 482, entry by Klaus Parlasca. Roullet 1972, 102, cat. no. 153, pl. 125, fig. 177. Quaegebeur 1983, 114. *CE* 1988, 47, 49, 63, 82, fig. 20. Myśliwiec 1988, 86, 88. Grenier 1989, 21–33, fig. 9. Grenier 1993, 51, V.12. Lollio Barberi et al. 1995, 148–150, cat. no. 12. Josephson 1997a, 24 n. 172, 29, 41, 43–44, pl. 13c. (All authors: Ptolemy II.)

A4. Standing statue inscribed for Arsinoe II. Rome, Vatican, Museo Gregoriano Egizio 22682

[Figures 4–5]

Red granite. H: 270.0 cm, HeadH: 32.5 cm, FaceH: 20.5 cm. Base: H: 19.7 cm, W: 42.2 cm, D: 81.5 cm.

Found in early eighteenth century at Villa Verospi with A3 in Rome, site of Gardens of Sallust. Possibly originally from Heliopolis, based on statue's back-pillar inscription, which references the god Atum, whose home was Heliopolis.

Over life-size. Striated, tripartite wig and two loopless uraei. Preserved from top of head (with tenon) through attached statue base. Broken at waist and feet and repaired. Square tenon (H: 7.0 cm, W: 6.5 cm, D: 6.5 cm) in middle of flat, circular area on top of head accommodated additional attribute, now lost. Left hand under breasts clenches *menat,* while right hand at side holds folded cloth. Tight-fitting sheath dress visible in collar and hem lines. Back pillar: Square top reaches top of head.

INSCRIPTION: Single column of hieroglyphs on back pillar contains Arsinoe II's birth name and epithet. One line of text on top of base, perpendicular to left foot, has same.

Sethe 1904, 71–72, no. 16. *LdR* 4 (1916), 241, K. PM 4 (1934), 48, 63 (probably from Heliopolis). Botti and Romanelli 1951, 22–23, 137, cat. no. 31, pls. 22–24. *ESLP* 1960, 120–121, 125, 126, 128, 135, 159 (c. 275–270 B.C., before her deification). Helbig 1963, 382, cat. no. 482, entry by Klaus Parlasca. Quaegebeur 1971, 207, 209, cat. no. 1. Roullet 1972, 109, cat. no. 180, pl. 145, fig. 203. Quaegebeur 1983, 114–115, 117. *CE* 1988, 47, 48, 63, 166–167, fig. 19. Grenier 1989, 21–33, fig. 10. Grenier 1993, 51, V.13. Josephson 1995, 12. Lollio Barberi et al. 1995, 150–151, cat. no. 13. Quaegebeur 1998, 74, 83, 86, cat. no. 5 ("peu après 270 B.C."). (All authors: Arsinoe II.)

A5. Fragmentary statue inscribed for Ptolemy II. Collection de l'Institut d'Égyptologie, Université Marc Bloch, Strasbourg 1585

[Figure 6]

Dark stone. H: 34.9 cm, HeadH: not preserved, FaceH: 8.7 cm.

Probably from Koptos, based on the phrase "words spoken by Osiris of Koptos" in back-pillar inscription. Purchased in Giza in 1905 (Spiegelberg 1909, 12).

Under life-size. Plain *nemes.* Preserved from top of face through pectorals. Uraeus, nose, and most of *nemes* wings missing. Eyes, ears, lips, and chin damaged. Back pillar: Triangular or trapezoid top, perhaps ending at back of head.

INSCRIPTION: Back pillar has two columns of hieroglyphs with Ptolemy II's Horus, Two Ladies, and Golden Horus names.

ESLP 1960, 121–122, 126, 141, 148, cat. no. 96, pl. 90, figs. 239–241. Parlebas 1973, 56, cat. no. 269, fig. 36. *CE* 1988, 82, 98. Myśliwiec 1988, 86, 88. Josephson 1995, 9–12, fig. 6. Josephson 1997a, 41, 44–45, pl. 13d. Gabolde, Galliano et al. 2000, 76, cat. no. 40. (All authors: Ptolemy II.)

A6. Broad collar. Cairo JE 38084

[No figure]

Late fourth or first half of third century B.C.

Gold with stone inlays. Dia: 9.8 cm.

From Tukh el-Karamus. Part of temple treasure horde excavated by C. C. Edgar.

Small broad collar for use as votive gift or as part of composite statue.

Edgar 1906a, 58–62, pl. 22 (c. 300 B.C.). Pfrommer 1987, 142–159, 272, cat. no. KTK 55, pl. 28d. G. Grimm 1998, 56–57, 63, fig. 55c. Pfrommer 1999, 34, 39–40, fig. 58. (All authors except Edgar: late fourth, first half of third century B.C.)

A7. Bust of king. Cairo JE 38123 bis

[Figure 7]

Attributed to Ptolemy II.

Bronze with gold inlay. H: 14.4 cm, D (front of bust to attachment hole at back): 16.0 cm.

From Tukh el-Karamus. Part of temple treasure horde excavated by C. C. Edgar.

Well under life-size. Banded *nemes* and uraeus. Made as finial for ritual equipment. Slight damage to edges of *nemes* wings, but otherwise well preserved.

Edgar 1906b, 206. Pfrommer 1987, 142–159, 271, cat. no. KTK 54, pl. 28b–c. G. Grimm 1998, 56–57, 63, fig. 55b. Pfrommer 1999, 34, 39, fig. 59a–b. (All authors except Edgar: probably Ptolemy II.)

A8. Crown. Cairo JE 38125 (*hm-hm*) and JE 38125A (*nemes*)

[No figure]

First half of third century B.C.

Gold and partly gilded silver. H: 27.0 cm.

From Tukh el-Karamus. Part of temple treasure horde excavated by C. C. Edgar.

Under-life-size *nemes* with *hm-hm* for use as votive gift or as part of composite statue. Some damage to *hm-hm.* Head of uraeus and some *nemes* bands missing.

Edgar 1906a, 58–62 (c. 300 B.C.). Pfrommer 1987, 142–159, 271, cat. no. KTK 51, pl. 28a (275–250 B.C.). G. Grimm 1998, 56–57, 63, fig. 55a (275–250 B.C.). Pfrommer 1999, 34, 39–40, fig. 57 (probably 275–250 B.C.).

A9. Standing king. London, British Museum EA 1190

[Figure 8]

Third century B.C.

Limestone. H: 55.0 cm, HeadH: 8.7 cm, FaceH: 5.4 cm. Base: H: 2.4 cm, W: 12.0 cm, D: 21.1 cm.

From Tanis. Excavated by W. M. Flinders Petrie in early Ptolemaic chapel on north side of western processional way into great temple enclosure.

Well under life-size. Double crown, banded *nemes,* uraeus, false beard, and plain *shendyt.* Preserved from top of crown through attached statue base. Broken in two parts and repaired. Has significantly deteriorated since discovery, obliterating facial features. Holds enigmatic objects in hands at sides. Back pillar: Triangular top reaches top of double crown.

Petrie 1889, 31, pl. 15: 5 (probably Ptolemy II). PM 4 (1934), 24 (Tanis; Ptolemy II?). Favard-Meeks 1998, 110, 171, pl. 25a.

A10. Fragmentary seated triad inscribed for Ptolemy II, Arsinoe II, and Amun. Alexandria, Graeco-Roman Museum 11261

[Figure 9]

Black granite. H: 79.0 cm (with base). Base: H: 34.4 cm, W: 178.0 cm, D: 128.0 cm.

From Alexandria. Found at Châder el-Battikh, shari M[ed] Koraiem, in Anfouchy district; entered museum collection in 1900, according to Graeco-Roman Museum Journal d'Entrée. Botti (1902, 95) provides a provenance near the Drovetti house in Alexandria; see Tkaczow 1993, 184.

Fragment of over-life-size, seated group (lower portions and base only), probably Amun in center, flanked on right by Ptolemy II and on left by Arsinoe II. Ankle-length, pleated garment with fringed edge and two ends of ribbonlike sash visible above feet of queen. Three pairs of feet—each c. 32.5 cm. long—are at equal distance from front edge of base. Though no back slab remains, the sculpture is likely to have had one, like other seated groups.

INSCRIPTION: Multicolumn hieroglyphic inscription in vertical columns on back and two sides of seat, right side containing Ptolemy II's throne name.

Botti 1902, 95. *LdR* 4 (1916), 237, no. 53. PM 4 (1934), 6 (Alexandria, exact find spot unknown). *ESLP* 1960, xxxvi, 122. Sauneron 1960 (argues for Canopus provenance based on evidence of Amun cult there). Quaegebeur 1971, 210, cat. no. 6. Tkaczow 1993, 183–184, cat. no. 2 (third century B.C.). Capriotti Vittozzi 1998, 55–56, fig. 1. Quaegebeur 1998, 75, 85, cat. no. 1 (270–246 B.C.). Yoyotte 1998, 209–210. (All authors: Ptolemy II and Arsinoe II.)

A11. Standing statue inscribed for Ptolemy II. Rome, Villa Albani 558

[No figure]

Dark stone. H: 280.0 cm (without base).

Probably from Bastet temple at Bubastis. Back pillar's hieroglyphic text mentions *B3st,* "Bubastis."

Over life-size. Wears *nemes* and pleated *shendyt.* Enigmatic objects in hands at sides. Heavily restored in post-antique times, including entire head. Back pillar: Triangular (restored?) top reaches shoulder level.

INSCRIPTION: Three columns of hieroglyphs on back pillar contain Ptolemy II's throne and birth names.

Sethe 1904, 70, no. 15. PM 4 (1934), 33 (probably from Bubastis). *ESLP* 1960, 62, 122. Helbig 1972, 336–337, cat. no. 3361, entry by Klaus Parlasca. Roullet 1972, 108, cat. no. 177, pl. 143, fig. 201. Curto 1985, 36–42, cat. no. 7, pl. 8 (c. 265 B.C.). Myśliwiec 1988, 86. Bol 1994, 465–466, cat. no. 547, pls. 276–277, entry by M. de Vos. Lollio Barberi et al. 1995, 141–142, cat. no. 8. Quaegebeur 1998, 102, cat. no. 72. PM 8 (1999), 194, no. 800-900-750 (probably from Bubastis). (All authors: Ptolemy II.)

A12. Torso inscribed for Ptolemy II. Cairo CG 686

[Figure 10]

Green schist. H: 43.2 cm.

Probably from Koptos. Min, major god of site, mentioned on belt inscription. Writing of king's throne name parallels examples from Koptos (*LdR* 4 [1916], 235, no. 53, and 239, no. 71) and nearby Qus (*LdR* 4 [1916], 234, no. 51). Borchardt 1930, 29: "Ankauf [von Datari (*sic*), Kairo]."

Under-life-size torso (collarbone through waist). Plain *nemes* lappets and *shendyt* belt. Arms mostly gone. Back pillar: Extent and top not preserved.

INSCRIPTION: Back pillar has two columns of hieroglyphs with portion of Ptolemy II's Horus name. Throne name on belt.

LdR 4 (1916), 237, no. 65 (Ptolemy II). Borchardt 1930, 29–30, pl. 125 (Ptolemaic). Michalowski 1935, 76–77, fig. 2 (Ptolemy II).

A13. Statue base inscribed for Arsinoe II. Formerly in Boulaq Museum (now in Cairo Museum?)

[No figure]

Material and measurements not known.

From Tell el-Maskhuta (Pithom). Excavated by Édouard Naville.

Fragmentary statue base inscribed in hieroglyphs. Back pillar: None remaining?

INSCRIPTION: Inscription contains Arsinoe II's throne and birth names.

Naville 1885, 5, pl. 7c. *LdR* 4 (1916), 242, N. PM 4 (1934), 54 (Pithom). Quaegebeur 1971, 209, cat. no. 3. Quaegebeur 1998, 86, cat. no. 2 (after 270 B.C.). (All authors: Arsinoe II.)

A14. Statue base inscribed for Arsinoe II. Chicago, Oriental Institute Museum 10518

[Figure 11]

Black basalt. H: 11.0 cm, W: 33.7 cm, D: 56.0 cm.

Probably from temple at Karnak, because inscription mentions Amun-Re of Karnak, Mut, and Khons, three major gods of area. Oriental Institute records note: "Purchased by James Henry Breasted from Yu[s]uf Has[s]an, Luxor, January 23, 1920."

Greek- and hieroglyph-inscribed base of a life-size or smaller standing statue of Arsinoe II, with remains of feet. Front slightly convex. Back pillar: Fragmentary only.

INSCRIPTION: One line of Greek on front: Of Arsinoe Philadelphos. Four column and one-line hieroglyphic inscription on top contains Ptolemy II's throne and birth names, and Arsinoe II's birth name.

Fraser 1960, 133–134, no. 2, pl. 29: 2a–b. PM 1, 2^2 (1964), 787 (Thebes, exact find spot unknown). Quaegebeur 1971, 210, cat. no. 5. Fraser 1972b, 154 n. 234. Peremans 1982, 152. *CE* 1988, 47 (reign of Ptolemy II). Albersmeier and Minas 1998, 14 n. 28. Quaegebeur 1998, 75, 86, cat. no. 3 (after 270 B.C.). (All authors: Arsinoe II.)

A15. Statue base dedicated to Arsinoe II. Alexandria, Serapeum

[No figure]

Granite. Base: H: c. 28 cm, W: c. 87 cm, D: unknown.

From Alexandria.

Rectangular base whose front is visible in substructure of "Pompey's Pillar" at Alexandria Serapeum. Dedicated to Arsinoe II. Much abrasion and cracking. Greek or Egyptian style of statue indeterminate.

INSCRIPTION: Two lines of Greek on front: (Statue of) Arsinoe Philadelphos (set up by) Thestor, son of Satyros, the Alexandrian.

OGIS 1 (1903), 58, no. 32. Fraser 1972b, 129 n. 93. É. Bernand 1982, 16, no. 32. Tkaczow 1993, 200, cat. no. 37 (third century B.C.). Yoyotte 1998, 214 n. 65. É. Bernand 2001, 38–40, no. 10, pl. 4. (All authors: Arsinoe II.)

A16. Fragmentary standing statue inscribed for Ptolemy III. The Manchester Museum 1752

[No figure]

Limestone. H: c. 35.0 cm?

From Hathor/Isis and Min temple at Koptos. Excavated by W. M. Flinders Petrie.

Wears plain *shendyt.* Preserved from waist through most of right thigh and half of left one. Arms at sides mostly missing. Hands hold enigmatic objects. Back pillar: Fragmentary only.

INSCRIPTION: One column of hieroglyphs on back pillar includes Ptolemy III's throne and birth names.

Petrie 1896, 22, pl. 26: 3a. *LdR* 4 (1916), 256, no. 46. PM 5 (1937), 133 (Koptos). (All authors: Ptolemy III.)

A17. Statue base inscribed for Ptolemy III. Cairo JE 41439

[Figure 12]

Black granite. Base: H: 10.0 cm, W: 29.0 cm, D: 68.0 cm.

From Bânûb, but likely originally from nearby Isis temple at Behbeit el-Hagar, because inscription mentions site (Gallo 1990, 227).

From life-size standing statue with hieroglyphic inscription. Minimal remains of two feet and back pillar. Gallo 1990, 226 n. 15: "Sous la base, au milieu, il y a un évidement carré de 6 cm de côté et profound de 4 cm. . . ." Back pillar: Fragmentary only.

INSCRIPTION: One line of hieroglyphs on front and two sides, and two columns on top contain Ptolemy III's throne and birth names.

Chabân 1910, 30, no. 4 (a Ptolemy). *LdR* 4 (1916), 257, no. 52. PM 4 (1934), 42 (Bânûb). Gallo 1990, 226–228, pl. 8a–d. Favard-Meeks 1991, 8 n. 53. (All authors except Chabân: Ptolemy III.)

A18. Fragmentary standing statue inscribed for Ptolemy III. Paris, Musée Rodin Co 1414

[Figure 13]

Limestone. H: 85.0 cm.

Provenance not known.

Fragment (torso, hips, and partial thighs) of near-life-size standing statue with pleated *shendyt.* Remains of false beard(?) on chest. Lack of lappets indicates figure wore crown other than *nemes.* Surface abraded and pitted. Arms at sides mostly missing. Hands held enigmatic objects? Back pillar: Broken off at top and bottom.

INSCRIPTION: Three columns of hieroglyphs on back pillar. Rightmost column contains portions of Ptolemy III's Horus, Two Ladies, and Golden Horus names.

Rodin collectionneur 1967, cat. no. 19 (Late Period). Thiers 1998 (Ptolemy III). PM 8 (1999), 194, no. 800-903-700 (Ptolemy III).

A19. Statue base dedicated to Arsinoe III (now in Alexandria?)

[No figure]

Granite. Base: H: 31.0 cm, W: 98.0 cm, D: 90.0 cm.

From Canopus. Found reused as step in a Christian structure (Breccia 1931a, 276).

Greek-inscribed statue base dedicated to Arsinoe III. Greek or Egyptian style of statue indeterminate.

INSCRIPTION: Four lines of Greek on front: (Statue of) Queen Arsinoe, father-loving goddess, daughter of the benefactor gods (set up by) [. . .] priest of the Nile.

Breccia 1931a, 276–277, no. 2. Breccia 1932, 17. A. Bernand 1970a, 237–238, no. 8. (All authors: Arsinoe III.)

A20. Head of king. Turin, Museo Egizio 1399

[Figure 14]

Late fourth or third century B.C.

Green schist. H: 18.0 cm.

Provenance not known.

Under life-size. Wears banded *nemes.* Attachment holes: on top of head for additional attribute, on uraeus for snake's rearing body, and under chin for false beard. Downward direction of *nemes* pigtail indicates that head is from non-sphinx statue. No back pillar remains.

Bissing 1914, no. 72 (Dynasty 26). H. W. Müller 1955, 208–209 n. 4 (Ptolemy II?). Curto 1984, 292–293, 358 (Ptolemy I). Curto, Donadoni, and Leospo 1989, 178, 183, fig. 270 (probably Ptolemy II). Seipel 1992, 416–417, cat. no. 168 (Ptolemy II?). Josephson 1997a, 24–25 (Ptolemy II). PM 8 (1999), 209–210, no. 800-942-622 (early Ptolemaic). Capriotti Vittozzi 2000, 43–44.

A21. Face of king. Paris, Musée Rodin Co 786

[Figures 15–16]

Late fourth or third century B.C.

Plaster. Incorrectly published as limestone. H: 14.8 cm, FaceH: 6.9 cm.

Provenance not known. Acquired by Auguste Rodin between 1900 and 1916 and given to museum in 1916.

Under life-size. Has frontlet. Back left top broken off, but mostly well preserved. Back of sculpture has shallow, irregular, horizontal depressions and is not hollowed out. Some edges have slight overflows of unmolded plaster.

Rodin collectionneur 1967, cat. no. 23, pl. 7 (Ptolemaic). *Gloire* 1998, 177, cat. no. 126 (third century B.C., Ptolemy II?). PM 8 (1999), 233, no. 800-946-635 (Ptolemaic).

A22. Bust of king. New York, Metropolitan Museum of Art 30.8.79

[Figure 17]

Late fourth or third century B.C.

Limestone. H: 12.1 cm, HeadH. 6.7 cm, FaceH. 4.0 cm.

Provenance not known. Formerly Theodore M. Davis collection.

Well under life-size. Plain *nemes* and uraeus. Flat back and bottom have incised grid lines. Some chips, but virtually intact. Broken through neck and repaired.

PM 8 (1999), 232, no. 800-946-553 (Ptolemaic).

A23. Fragmentary king. London, British Museum EA 941

[Figures 18–19]

Attributed to Ptolemy II.

Egyptian alabaster. H: 60.0 cm, HeadH: 26.0 cm, FaceH: 15.0 cm.

Provenance not known. Presented by Her Majesty Queen Victoria, 1854.

Fragment (head and chest) of life-size king with plain *nemes,* uraeus, plain tripartite wig, and decorated false beard. Holds right forearm over chest, hand clasped over edge of *sed*-festival cloak. Garment lines indicated on neck and right wrist. Uraeus, chin, and false beard damaged. Right shoulder, *nemes* lappet (portion), upper arm, and pectoral missing. Statue unfinished, as indicated by lack of separation between frontlet and tabs of *nemes.* Back pillar: Square top ends at armpit level.

Budge 1914, 24, pl. 53 (c. 200 B.C.). De Meulenaere and Bothmer 1969, 13 n. 1 ("somewhat dubious alabaster bust"). Josephson 1997a, 30, pl. 11a (Nectanebo II?). PM 8 (1999), 198, no. 800-940-600 (Ptolemaic). Walker and Higgs 2001, 42–43, cat. no. 5 (Ptolemy II).

A24. Bust of king. Cairo JE 47932

[Figures 20–21]

Late fourth or third century B.C.

Limestone. H: 23.5 cm, HeadH: 10.5 cm, FaceH: 7.0 cm.

Provenance not known. Reportedly Mendes. De Meulenaere and MacKay 1976, 210, cat. no. 145: "Tell el-Rub'a (purchased in 1923)."

Under life-size. Banded *nemes* and uraeus (partly completed in another material, as indicated by attachment hole on frontlet, and now missing). Ears, lips, nose, and chin damaged. Unlike many sculptors' studies/votives (Appendix A), bust worked in the round, with decorated pigtail at back. Stone support screen atypically removed behind root of pigtail. No grid lines.

De Meulenaere and MacKay 1976, 210, cat. no. 145 (Ptolemaic?).

A25. Head of king. Baltimore, The Walters Art Museum 22.109

[Figure 22]

Late fourth or third century B.C.

Granite. H: 28.5 cm, FaceH: 13.9 cm.

Provenance not known.

Near life-size. Banded *nemes* and uraeus. Nose smashed, right ear badly damaged, and lips abraded. Large hole atop head (Dia: c. 4.5 cm, D: c. 4.5 cm) supported lost attribute. No back pillar remains.

Steindorff 1946, 48, cat. no. 141, pl. 20 (Late Period). Josephson 1997a, 25, pl. 8d (Ptolemy II?). PM 8 (1999), 200, no. 800-942-080 (probably Ptolemy II).

A26. Bronze head of king. New York, Metropolitan Museum of Art 66.99.134

[Figure 23]

Late fourth or third century B.C.

Bronze. H: 6.5 cm, FaceH: 2.2 cm.

Provenance not known.

Well under life-size head with white(?) crown and uraeus. Hollow cast. Top and part of back of crown missing. Uraeus, nose, and left ear damaged.

Cooney 1953, 17, cat. no. 91, pl. 53 (early Ptolemaic). PM 8 (1999), 175, no. 800-892-500 (early Ptolemaic). Hill 2000, 233–234, 603–604, cat. no. 219 (LPPt-25), pl. 81 (early Ptolemaic).

A27. Head of king. New York, Metropolitan Museum of Art 41.6.1.

[No figure]

Late fourth or third century B.C.

Limestone. H: 25.0 cm, HeadH: 20.5 cm, FaceH: 12.6 cm.

Provenance not known.

Slightly under life-size. Banded *nemes* and uraeus. Uraeus, nose, left ear, lips, and chin much destroyed. Possibly from sphinx. No back pillar remains.

PM 8 (1999), 161, no. 800-871-350 (Dynasty 30 or Ptolemaic).

A28. Seated king. Zagazig, Orabi Museum 282

[Figure 24]

Late fourth or third century B.C.

Limestone. H: 49.0 cm.

From Tanis. Accidentally found with A35 in 1961 during road construction near west edge of southern Kom (Myśliwiec 1992, 61 n. 2).

Well under life-size king with plain *nemes*, uraeus, and *shendyt* seated on square throne with low back. Holds hands flat on lap. Nose broken. Most of left forearm and all of right one missing. Incised and/or painted grid lines on back pillar, back of seat, and front of base. Back pillar: Square top ends at armpit level.

Myśliwiec 1992, 61–80, pls. 5–8 (early Ptolemaic?).

A29. Bust of king. Brooklyn Museum of Art 37.37E

[Figure 25]

Late fourth or third century B.C.

Limestone. H: 45.0 cm, HeadH: 24.7 cm, FaceH: 15.9 cm.

Provenance not known. Formerly Dr. Henry Abbott collection. Reported Benha (Athribis) provenance cannot be relied upon because Dr. Abbott built his collection via purchases from antiquities dealers.

Life-size. Banded *nemes* and uraeus. Traces of incised grid lines on back and both sides. Top of head worn and weathered.

Catalogue . . . Henry Abbott . . . 1854, 72, cat. no. 1116 (not attributed). *Catalogue . . . Historical Society* 1915, 68, cat. no. 1112 (not attributed). *ESLP* 1960, 122 (Ptolemy II). Fazzini 1975, 108, 122, cat. no. 105 (Ptolemy II). *CE* 1988, 82–83, 98, 99, 108, 129, 130, 157, 192, 229, 242, 251, cat. no. 1 (Ptolemy II?).

A30. Head of king. Brooklyn Museum of Art 53.75

[Figures 26–27]

Late fourth or third century B.C.

Granodiorite. H: 37.1 cm, HeadH: 28.0 cm, FaceH: 19.6 cm.

Provenance not known.

Over life-size. Plain *nemes* and uraeus. Slight horizontal edge at back left suggests that head comes from sphinx. Top of head and uraeus worn and badly abraded. Chip and scratch marks over face. Recent cleaning removed partial modern restoration of right *nemes* wing.

Cooney 1956, 17, cat. no. 18, pls. 34–35 (probably third century B.C.). Fazzini et al. 1989, cat. no. 86 (305–200 B.C.). Goyon and Gabolde 1991, 24–25, fig. 22 (Dynasty 30?). Josephson 1997a, 19, 43–44, pl. 13b (Ptolemy I?). PM 8 (1999), 202, no. 800-942-160 (early Ptolemaic).

A31. Head of king. Naples, Museo Archeologico Nazionale 321

[Figures 28–29]

Late fourth or third century B.C.

Dark stone. H: 16.7 cm, HeadH: 11.8 cm, FaceH: 7.8 cm.

Provenance not known.

Under life-size. Plain *nemes* and uraeus. Left one-third of face broken off. No back pillar remains.

Cantilena and Rubino 1989, 55, cat. no. 3.6 (Ptolemaic). PM 8 (1999), 206, no. 800-942-480 (Ptolemaic).

A32. Head of king. Turin, Museo Egizio 1396

[Figure 30]

Late fourth or third century B.C.

Quartzite. H: 34.0 cm.

Provenance not known.

Slightly over life-size. Plain *nemes* and uraeus. Horizontal direction of pigtail at back indicates that head likely comes from sphinx. Nose broken off, and uraeus and lips damaged.

H. W. Müller 1961, 26 n. 5 (as "Quarzitkopf in Turin"; Ptolemy II?). Curto, Donadoni, and Leospo 1989, 179, 183, fig. 271 (Ptolemaic). Seipel 1992, 414–415, cat. no. 167 (third century B.C.). PM 8 (1999), 209, no. 800-942-620 (early Ptolemaic).

A33. Sphinxes. Alexandria, Serapeum.

[Figures 31–32]

Late fourth or third century B.C.

Pink granite. *East sphinx* H: 2.20 m, W: 1.12 m, D: 4.11 m, HeadH: 72.0 cm, FaceH: 46.0 cm. Base: H: 32.5 cm, W: 1.12 m, D: 4.11 m. *West sphinx* H: 2.22 m, W: 1.22 m, D: 3.92 m, HeadH: 76.0 cm, FaceH: 48.0 cm. Base: H: 33.0 cm, W: 1.22 m, D: 3.92 m. Measurements approximate.

From Alexandria, near Serapeum. Found in 1906 during Evaristo Breccia's excavations, in Abu Mandur street on south side of Serapeum.

Two colossal sphinxes wearing *nemes* with uraeus. Heads and bodies well preserved. Noses broken off, *nemes* wings damaged, uraei abraded, and corners of base abraded on both. Holes (Dia: c. 2 cm, D: 6.0 cm) drilled on tops of front corners of both bases. Sphinxes sculpted in a similar scale and style, except east sphinx has banded *nemes* and tail curls around right haunch, whereas west sphinx has plain *nemes* and tail curls around left haunch.

Breccia 1907, 72–74. Breccia 1914, 102. Rowe 1957, 493, 508 ("Pharaonic Period"). *ESLP* 1960, 147, 148 (Ptolemy VI). Bothmer 1987, 92 (Ptolemy VI). Tkaczow 1993, 188–189, cat. no. 11 (Ptolemaic). Yoyotte 1998, 212 (Ptolemaic). Rogge 1999, 14 (early Ptolemaic?).

A34. Head of king. Alexandria, Graeco-Roman Museum 23048

[Figure 33]

Late fourth or third century B.C.

Red granite. H: 90.0 cm, HeadH: 90.0 cm, FaceH: 56.0 cm.

From Moustapha Pasha (necropolis east of Alexandria, toward Canopus), according to museum Journal d'Entrée. Entered museum collection in 1912. Tkaczow 1993, 242: "Eastern suburb of Abu Nawatir, found accidentally in 1910, during the digging of foundations for residence of the British Ambassador." Colossal leg of the same material (Alexandria, Graeco-Roman Museum 23049, H: 215.0 cm; Breccia 1932, 20) found with sphinx head is sometimes erroneously thought to belong to the same statue.

Colossal. Wears plain *nemes* with uraeus. Must have come from sphinx, given outward direction of pigtail remains. Uraeus and nose broken off and replaced in antiquity?

Breccia 1932, 20 (New Kingdom). Tkaczow 1993, 242, cat. no. 152 (Dynasty 19). El-Fattah and Gallo 1998, 13 n. 18 (Ptolemaic).

A35. Fragmentary king. Zagazig, Orabi Museum 1411

[Figures 34–35]

Late fourth or third century B.C.

Brown quartzite. H: 52.5 cm, HeadH: 20.8 cm, FaceH: 13.2 cm.

From Tanis. Accidentally found with A28 in 1961 during road construction near west edge of southern Kom (Myśliwiec 1992, 61 n. 2).

Slightly under life-size fragment (head through most of rib cage). Banded *nemes*, uraeus, and false beard. Right angle of left elbow indicates that statue originally proffered some now-missing object(s) with its hands. Back pillar: Trapezoid top extends two-thirds up back of *nemes*.

Montet 1958, 7–8, fig. 3 (Ptolemaic). Myśliwiec 1992, 61–80, pls. 1–4 (early Ptolemaic?). Hill 2000, 667–668 (Ptolemy II or III?).

A36. Standing king. Cairo JE 36708 (now in National Museum, Port Said)

[Figure 36]

Late fourth or third century B.C.

Dark stone. H: 100.3 cm, HeadH: 17.0 cm, FaceH: 11.0 cm.

From Karnak cachette, Amun temple, 1904. Cachette find no. is K.84, according to Cairo Museum Journal d'Entrée.

Under life-size. Plain *nemes,* uraeus, and pleated *shendyt.* Preserved from top of head through most of thighs. Face deliberately defaced, and recent restoration has smoothed over damage (visible in old photographs such as Fig. 36) with filler material(?). Rectangular hole cut into top of head for lost attribute. Enigmatic objects in hands at sides. Back pillar: Triangular top ends at back of head.

No bibliography.

A37. Facial fragment. New York, Metropolitan Museum of Art 12.187.31

[No figure]

Late fourth or third century B.C.

Graywacke. H: 17.0 cm, HeadH: not preserved, FaceH: 13.3 cm (preserved portion).

From Heliopolis. Recovered by W. M. Flinders Petrie during his explorations of site.

Life-size facial fragment of royal quality, but without royal attributes remaining. Right eye and rear of head missing. Nose mostly broken off. No back pillar remains.

Petrie et al. 1915, 6, pl. 6: 3 (Dynasty 26). PM 4 (1934), 60 (Heliopolis, near Sesostris I obelisk). *ESLP* 1960, 59 (Apries). Josephson 1995 (mid-third century B.C.). Josephson 1997a, 44–45, pl. 14a (Ptolemy II?).

A38. Half face of king. Amsterdam, Allard Pierson Museum 1937

[Figure 37]

Late fourth or third century B.C.

Plaster. H: 19.5 cm.

Provenance not known. Purchased in art market.

Under-life-size half face with partial frontlet and tab. Some abrasion, but generally well preserved.

Varga 1960, 7, 9, 13, no. 5, fig. 6 (Ptolemy II). Josephson 1995, 12 n. 47 (as inv. no. 54; early Ptolemaic). PM 8 (1999), 218, no. 800-946-050 (early Ptolemaic).

A39. Sphinx. Alexandria, Graeco-Roman Museum 11425

[Figure 38]

Late fourth or third century B.C.

Limestone. H: 84.5 cm, HeadH: 31.6 cm, FaceH: 19.2 cm. Base: H: 11.5 cm, W: 34.8 cm, D: 152.1 cm.

Provenance not known.

Over life-size. Banded *nemes,* and uraeus. Most of right part of *nemes,* right shoulder, and paw gone. Surface abraded. Tail curls around right haunch.

Franke 1992, fiche 44, no. II/2059 (a similar sphinx, A40, is marked as "ähnlich Alex 11425").

A40. Sphinx. Cairo 8/6/25/1

[Figure 39]

Late fourth or third century B.C.

Limestone. H: 82.2 cm, HeadH: 29.2 cm, FaceH: 18.7 cm. Base: H: 14.8 cm, W: c. 36.0 cm (damaged), D: c. 121.0 cm (damaged).

Provenance not known.

Slightly over life-size. Banded *nemes,* uraeus, and tail curling around right haunch. Head disproportionally large for body. Left side heavily damaged. Front of base and paws missing.

Franke 1992, fiche 44, no. II/2059 ("ähnlich Alex 11425").

A41. Sphinx. Cairo JE 53104

[Figure 40]

Third century B.C.

Limestone. H: 58.8 cm, HeadH: 19.1 cm, FaceH: 12.5 cm. Base: H: 10.5 cm, W: 34.4 cm, D: 104.7 cm.

From dromos leading to sacred enclosure at Zawiet el-Amwat (Weill and Jouguet 1934, 99).

Under life-size. Plain *nemes* and uraeus. Uraeus, chin, right cheek, *nemes* wings, and nose damaged. Tail curls around right haunch.

INSCRIPTION: One line of Greek on front of base: [Set up by] Protos to Apollo.

Weill and Jouguet 1934, 99, pl. 2: 3 (Ptolemaic). Rogge 1999, 15.

A42. Kneeling king. Marseille, Musée d'Archéologie Méditerranéenne 826

[Figure 41]

Late fourth or third century B.C.

Bronze. H: 16.5 cm.

Provenance not known.

Well under life-size. Wears banded *nemes,* uraeus, and pleated *shendyt.* Both arms missing.

PM 8 (1999), 185, no. 800-895-354 (Dynasties 26-31). Hill 2000, 235-237, 580-581, cat. no. 185 (LPPt-26), pl. 82 (third century B.C.).

A43. Head of queen. Brooklyn Museum of Art 86.226.32

[Figure 42]

Third century B.C.

Limestone. H: 10.8 cm, HeadH: 7.2 cm, FaceH: 4.5 cm.

Provenance not known.

Well under life-size. Plain modius, plain diadem, uraeus, and echeloned tripartite wig. Modius has square hole for lost attribute. No back pillar remains.

CE 1988, 166, 167, 181, cat. no. 63 (late fourth to third century B.C.). PM 8 (1999), 1010, no. 801-809-044 (early Ptolemaic).

A44. Head of queen. New York, Metropolitan Museum of Art 38.10

[No figure]

Third century B.C.

Limestone. H: 11.8 cm, HeadH: 8.4 cm, FaceH: 4.7 cm.

From Abu Rawash. Excavated by Fernand Bisson de la Roque in fill of Late Period rock structure, possibly a crocodile tomb.

Well under life-size. Striated, tripartite wig and double uraeus. Tenon on top for attachment of lost crown. Back abraded. Torso of figure, found at time of excavation, is now missing. No back pillar remains.

Bisson de la Roque 1924, 65–66, pl. 35: 2. *ESLP* 1960, 125–126, 128, 135, 145, 147, 159, 168, cat. no. 98, pl. 92, figs. 244–246 (Arsinoe II, 275–270 B.C.). PM 3^2, 1 (1974), 9 (Abu Rawash, northwest cemetery; Arsinoe II). Quaegebeur 1983, 115–116 (possibly as early as Dynasty 30). *CE* 1988, 166, 172. Goyon and Gabolde 1991, 26–27, fig. 23 (Dynasty 30?). Quaegebeur 1998, 104, cat. no. 80 (c. 275–270 B.C. or reign of Nectanebo II). Walker and Higgs 2001, 44, cat. no. 6 (Arsinoe II, 275–270 B.C.).

A45. Standing queen. Cairo CG 678

[Figure 43]

Third century B.C.

Limestone. H: 66.0 cm (without wooden base), HeadH: c. 14.0 cm, FaceH: 8.0 cm.

Provenance not known.

Under life-size. Tripartite, echeloned wig, vulture cap, and close-fitting sheath dress. Preserved from top of head through most of thighs. Additional attribute atop head broken off. Vulture head damaged and two uraei (four holes above forehead) missing. Left arm under breasts carries lily scepter; right hand flat against thigh. Wears broad collar and bracelets. Back pillar: Reached beyond top of head, but now is broken off. Faint grid(?) lines incised on upper pillar.

Borchardt 1930, 23, pl. 124 (Ptolemaic). Roeder 1932, 18, no. 47 (Ptolemaic). Wildung and Schoske 1984, 154–155, cat. no. 73 (c. 250 B.C.). Capriotti Vittozzi 1998, 62–63, 64, pl. 9a–b. *Gloire* 1998, 171, cat. no. 119 (mid-third century B.C.). PM 8 (1999), 998, no. 801-805-090 (early Ptolemaic).

A46. Head of goddess. Baltimore, The Walters Art Museum 22.417

[Figure 44]

Third century B.C.

Limestone. H: 36.0 cm.

Provenance not known.

Near life-size. Tripartite, echeloned wig and uraeus. Fragmentary modius decorated with uraei supported lost attribute. Left side of wig missing. Back pillar: Reaches height of remaining sculpture and is broken off at top.

INSCRIPTION: Single column of hieroglyphs on back pillar contains fragmentary, divine epithets. I am grateful to Herman De Meulenaere for pointing out to me that the epithets indicate that the Baltimore head is likely a goddess.

Steindorff 1946, 70, cat. no. 225, pls. 38, 118 (Ptolemaic). *ESLP* 1960, 135. PM 8 (1999), 1109, 802-083-070 (Ptolemaic).

A47. Fragmentary queen. Paris, Musée du Louvre E 10957

[Figure 45]

Third century B.C.

Dark stone. H: 39.6 cm.

Provenance not known.

Under life-size. Uraeus, striated, tripartite wig, and broad collar. Added attribute atop head mostly lost. Uraeus and lips abraded. Inlaid eyebrows and eyes missing. Nose broken off. Back pillar: Reaches height of remaining sculpture and is broken off at top.

PM 8 (1999), 937, 801-780-120 (Late Period).

A48. Standing queen. Shigaraki, Miho Museum

[No figure]

Third century B.C.

Dark stone. H: 159.5 cm.

Provenance not known.

Slightly over life-size(?). Plain diadem tied at back, double(?) uraeus, echeloned tripartite wig, and sheath dress. Preserved from head through ankles. Break at top indicates former presence of additional attribute. Left arm under breasts holds lily scepter. Right hand flat at side. Damage to nose, lips, and chin. Back pillar: Square top ends at armpits.

Miho Museum: South Wing (Shigaraki, 1997), 34–37, cat. no. 13, entry by Arielle P. Kozloff (Arsinoe II, 270–246 B.C., usurped from Queen Tiy statue of New Kingdom). Capriotti Vittozzi 1998, 56–58. PM 8 (1999), 1000, no. 801-805-255 (probably Arsinoe II, early Ptolemaic).

GROUP B: PTOLEMIES V–VI

B1. Head of king. Berlin, Ägyptisches Museum 14568

[Figures 46–47]

Attributed to Ptolemy V or VI.

Egyptian alabaster. H: 10.4 cm, HeadH: 4.8 cm, FaceH: 3.2 cm.

Provenance not known.

Well under life-size. Double crown, diadem, and Horus sidelock. Short, dense hair covers head. Diadem is tied at back, and there is no uraeus. Damage to left cheek and chin. No back pillar remains.

Kyrieleis 1975, 54, 134, 172, E 1, pl. 41: 1–4. Parlasca 1978, 29 n. 34. *CE* 1988, 152–153, cat. no. 55. Smith 1988, 92–93. A. Grimm, Schoske, and Wildung 1997, 77, cat. no. 59. Derriks 1998, 99–100. *Gloire* 1998, 208, cat. no. 154. G. Grimm 1998, 109, fig. 106a–b. Walker and Higgs 2001, 51, cat. no. 14. (All authors: Ptolemy V.)

B2. Royal male head. Berlin, Ägyptisches Museum 13457

[Figures 48–49]

Attributed to Ptolemy V or VI.

Egyptian alabaster. H: 7.6 cm, HeadH: 7.4 cm, FaceH: 5.3 cm.

Provenance not known.

Well under life-size. Has uraeus and Horus sidelock. Short, dense hair covers head. Hole (Dia: 1.6 cm, D: c. 1.9 cm) on top originally supported additional crown. Uraeus, sidelock, nose, ears, and lips damaged. Back pillar: Trapezoid top at back of head.

Kyrieleis 1975, 54, 134, 172, E 2, pl. 42: 1–2 (Ptolemy V). Parlasca 1978, 29–30, fig. 49 (Ptolemy XIV?). *CE* 1988, 152–153, cat. no. 56 (Ptolemy V). Bothmer 1996, 220–221, fig. 19 (Ptolemy V). Derriks 1998, 99–100 (Ptolemy V). PM 8 (1999), 201, no. 800-942-100 (probably Ptolemy V).

B3. Royal male head. Berlin, Ägyptisches Museum 23140

[Figures 50–51]

Attributed to Ptolemy V or VI.

Egyptian alabaster. H: 9.7 cm, HeadH: 9.1 cm, FaceH: 6.2 cm.

Provenance not known.

Well under life-size. Has plain diadem, uraeus, and Horus sidelock. Short curls of hair cover head. Small hole on top of head (Dia: 0.2 cm, D: c. 0.7 cm) served for attachment of additional crown. Nose and chin gone. Back pillar: Rounded(?) top ends midway up back of head.

Kyrieleis 1975, 54, 134, 172, E 3, pl. 42: 3–4 (Ptolemy V). Parlasca 1978, 28–30, figs. 45–46 (Ptolemy XIII?). *CE* 1988, 153 (Ptolemy V). PM 8 (1999), 201, no. 800-942-130 (probably Ptolemy V).

B4. Statue base dedicated to Ptolemy V and his parents. Alexandria, Graeco-Roman Museum 54

[No figure]

Red granite. H: 42.0 cm, W: 75.0 cm, D: 108.0 cm.

From Alexandria. Tkaczow 1993, 203: "Found in 1902 in the structure of the Arab walls near Rosetta Gate, on the northern side of Horeya."

Statue base block with Greek dedication to Ptolemy V and parents Ptolemy IV and Arsinoe III. Bottom is rough hewn, top is smooth. Much weathering and damage. Upper left-hand corner of inscription destroyed. Perhaps part of a base composed of multiple pieces of stone. Greek or Egyptian style of statues indeterminate. No back pillar remains.

INSCRIPTION: Seven lines of Greek on shorter side: (Statues of) [King] Ptolemy god manifest and of good grace, [and] his parents King Ptolemy and Queen Arsinoe, father-loving gods, (set up by) . . . .ōtes, son of Hōros and his brother Tearoōs, laarchi and commanders of the select indigenous soldiers of the court, for their benefactions to them and their relatives.

OGIS 2 (1905), 471–472, no. 731. Breccia 1911, 15–16, no. 31, pl. 7: 20 (c. 200 B.C.). Breccia 1914, 150, no. 31. *LdR* 4 (1916), 285, no. 39. É. Bernand 1982, 58–59, no. 731 (204–194/193 B.C.). Tkaczow 1993, 203, cat. no. 42 (c. 200 B.C.). É. Bernand 2001, 71–73, no. 26, pl. 11 (204–194/193 B.C.). (All authors: time of Ptolemy V.)

B5. Fragment of dedication to Ptolemy V (present location not known)

[No figure]

Limestone. Measurements not known.

Provenance not known. Rubensohn 1913, 159: "Ich sah es flüchtig bei einem Händler im Fayûm."

Greek-inscribed panel with dedication to Ptolemy V, of which only left and upper portions are preserved. May have belonged to statue base. Greek or Egyptian style of statue indeterminate.

INSCRIPTION: From Greek on fragment: (Statue of) King Ptol[emy, god manifest and of good grace], son of King [Ptolemy and Queen Arsinoe], father-loving gods . . . *toklēs* . . . for [the good].

Rubensohn 1913, 159–160, no. 4. É. Bernand 1981b, 114–115, no. 195 (Ptolemy V).

B6. Head inscribed for Ptolemy VI. Athens, National Archaeological Museum ANE 108

[Figures 52–53]

Granite. H: 62.5 cm, HeadH: c. 30.0 cm, FaceH: 23.5 cm.

Reportedly from sea near Aegina, Greece (Six 1887, 212). Formerly Dimitriou collection.

Over life-size. Double crown, *nemes,* uraeus, and Greek forehead hair. Entire surface weathered. Nose and lips mostly gone. Roughening below sideburns indicates light beard or sideburns extension. Back pillar: Extends through present remains of double crown; triangular(?) top slants inward in profile view and now is broken off.

INSCRIPTION: Back pillar has three columns of hieroglyphs and contains Ptolemy VI's Horus name.

Six 1887. Bissing 1914, nos. 103–104, note 15. *ESLP* 1960, 132. Kyrieleis 1975, 37, 59–62, 174, F 1, pl. 47: 1–3. Smith 1988, 87, 93, 170, cat. no. 71, pl. 46: 2. Tzachou-Alexandri 1995, 165, cat. no. 57: 1. Bothmer 1996, 215–216, fig. 5a–b. Smith 1996, 205–206. Gill 1997, 73. G. Grimm 1998, 116–117, 119, fig. 113a–b. Rogge 1999, 90, 95. (All authors: Ptolemy VI.)

B7. Head of king. Alexandria, Graeco-Roman Museum 3357

[Figures 54–55]

Attributed to Ptolemy VI.

Granite. H: 61.0 cm, HeadH: 52.0 cm, FaceH: 31.0 cm.

From Canopus (Breccia 1926, 59–60, no. 12).

Colossal. Has plain *nemes* surmounted by additional element (a double crown?), the remains of which are indicated by a flat, roughened oval atop head. Greek forehead hair. Nose, parts of ears, and edges of *nemes* wings broken off; uraeus, lips, and chin abraded. Inlaid eyes missing. Back pillar: Trapezoid top reaches to statue's eye level.

Breccia 1926, 59–60, no. 12, pl. 26: 2. *ESLP* 1960, 132. Kyrieleis 1975, 37, 59–62, 174, F 2, pls. 48: 1–2, 49: 1. Smith 1988, 87, 93–94, 170, cat. no. 72, pl. 46: 3–4. Smith 1996, 206, fig. 4. *Gloire* 1998, 214, cat. no. 160. G. Grimm 1998, 116–117, 119, fig. 112a–b. Walker and Higgs 2001, 53–54, cat. no. 19. (All authors except Breccia: Ptolemy VI.)

B8. Head of king. Frankfurt, private collection

[Figures 56–57]

Attributed to Ptolemy VI.

Dark stone. H: 25.5 cm.

From Iseum at Campus Martius, Rome, according to Lembke 1994, 242 ("Hinter S. Maria sopra Minerva gefunden; Ankauf im Herbst 1970").

Life-size(?) head of king with plain *nemes,* uraeus, and Greek forehead hair. Right one-third of face and back of head missing. Nose and lips damaged. No back pillar remains.

Lembke 1994, 242–243, cat. no. 46, pl. 45: 2–3 (Domitian?).

B9. Head of king with scarab. New York, Metropolitan Museum of Art 66.99.166

[Figure 58]

Attributed to Ptolemy VI.

Limestone. H: 11.4 cm, HeadH: 8.3 cm, FaceH: 5.0 cm.

Provenance not known. Formerly Albert Gallatin collection.

Well under life-size. Has plain *nemes,* uraeus, and false beard. Scarab beetle in relief on top. Surface crumbling. Inlaid eyes missing. Nose and false beard mostly broken off. No back pillar remains.

PM 8 (1999), 208, no. 800-942-515 (Ptolemaic).

B10. Fragmentary statue inscribed for Ptolemy VI. Alexandria, Graeco-Roman Museum N.G. 378

[Figure 59]

Granite. H: 98.0 cm.

Possibly from Alexandria (Rowe 1957, 506).

Hieroglyph-inscribed fragment of colossal standing or seated Ptolemy VI wearing *nemes.* Only parts of left back, right shoulder, *nemes* pigtail, and back pillar preserved. Original inscription probably three columns.

INSCRIPTION: Two partial columns of hieroglyphs on back pillar contain portion of Horus name and most of Two Ladies name of Ptolemy VI.

Rowe 1948, 43–44, fig. 8. Rowe 1957, 506. Bothmer 1960, 5 n. 5. (Both authors: Ptolemy VI.)

B11. Torso inscribed for Ptolemy VI. Cairo JE 41218

[No figure]

Limestone. H: 122.0 cm.

From Karnak, according to Cairo Museum Journal d'Entrée.

Over life-size(?). Has broad collar. Head and legs broken off. In storage and therefore inaccessible. Back pillar: Broken off at top and bottom?

INSCRIPTION: Ptolemy VI cartouches on back pillar.

PM 2^2 (1972), 283 (Karnak, exact find spot unknown; Ptolemy VI). Thiers forthcoming (in *BIFAO* or *RdE*).

B12. Statue base inscribed for Ptolemy VI. Alexandria, Graeco-Roman Museum 2

[Figure 60]

Black granite. H: 12.8 cm, W: 28.1 cm, D: 40.4 cm.

Probably from Isis temple at Philae, because G. Maspero acquired the fragment in Aswan on March 10, 1883, where it served as the back of a stone bench for a boutique, and because the inscription cites Isis and Horus, major deities at Philae.

Front part of rectangular base for approximately life-size, standing statue, with remains of left foot (27.0 cm long) and toes of right one. On front, two lines of Greek inscription and third blank one are recessed at slightly lower level than surface below them, indicating partial recarving, perhaps to remove name of original dedicant. Front, left, and right sides are polished; bottom is rough, and back is broken off. No back pillar remains.

INSCRIPTION: Two lines of Greek on front: (Statue of) King Ptolemy, mother-loving god, (set up by) Isis and Horus.

OGIS 1 (1903), 203, no. 122. Breccia 1911, 18, no. 34, pl. 8: 22. *LdR* 4 (1916), 299, no. 44. Wilhelm 1946, 5–10, 12–13. A. Bernand 1969, 113–115, no. 10, pl. 33 (perhaps before king's marriage to Cleopatra II). É. Bernand 1982, 30, no. 122 (before king's marriage to Cleopatra II). PM 8 (1999), 194–195, no. 800-910-010 (probably from Aswan or Philae). (All authors: Ptolemy VI.)

B13. Statue base inscribed for Ptolemy VI, Cleopatra II, and their son. Philae, Isis temple

[No figure]

Granite. Measurements from A. Bernand 1969, 121: H: 55 cm, W: 120 cm, D: 68 cm. Statue support holes are 4 cm deep, and from left to right measure 60 cm × 30 cm; 40 cm × 20 cm; 50 cm × 28 cm.

Found reused as an altar support in Coptic sanctuary on north end of island of el Hesa, south of Philae (Prof. Sayce, "Archaeological News," *AJA* 10 [1895], 384–385). Moved to Isis temple on Philae in late nineteenth century, whence it likely originated.

Block with three rectangular holes for placement of approximately life-size Egyptian statues. Greek/Demotic inscription, with dedication to Ptolemy VI, Cleopatra II, and their son, perhaps partly carved over another, older one, with Isis and Horus replacing original dedicant's name.

INSCRIPTION: On front, three lines of Greek, followed by two lines of Demotic: (Statues of) King Ptolemy and Queen Cleopatra, mother-loving gods, and Ptolemy their son, (set up by) Isis and Horus.

OGIS 1 (1903), 202–203, no. 121. *LdR* 4 (1916), 298, no. 38. Griffith 1931, 129–130. PM 6 (1939), 256 (Philae). Wilhelm 1946, 5–10, 12–13. A. Bernand 1969, 121–126, no. 12, pls. 33–34 (172–146/145 B.C.). É. Bernand 1982, 30, no. 121 (172–146/145 B.C.). (All authors: Ptolemy VI and Cleopatra II.)

B14. Standing statue inscribed for Cleopatra II. Karnak 177 (Caracol R177) + Cheikh Labib 94CL1421

[No figure]

Limestone. Head/torso H: 88.0 cm. Abdomen/thighs H: 99.0 cm.

From Karnak. Karnak 177 found near Roman chapel in front of first pylon of Amun temple (Lauffray et al. 1970, 71).

Over life-size or possibly colossal (not possible to confirm precise scale because statue is in storage and inaccessible). Has echeloned, tripartite wig, diadem, broad collar, and close-fitting, pleated garment with fringed border. Two strands of ribbonlike sash down front of thighs from tie at waist. Preserved in two fragments: head/torso (Cheikh Labib 94CL1421) and abdomen/thighs (Karnak 177). Additional attribute atop head broken off. Face missing. Arms mostly gone. Left hand under breasts holds lily scepter. Broken-off right hand at side held enigmatic object? Back pillar: Extent and top not preserved. I am grateful to Christophe Thiers for information on this statue and its inscription.

INSCRIPTION: Single column of hieroglyphs on back pillar contains royal names and titles associated with Cleopatra II.

Lauffray et al. 1970, 71, pl. 15, fig. 13 (Cleopatra II). Bianchi 1978, 98–99, fig. 65 (Cleopatra II, usurped from New Kingdom statue). Lauffray 1979, 88–89, fig. 67 (Cleopatra III). Bianchi 1980, 11 (Cleopatra II, usurped from New Kingdom statue). Quaegebeur 1983, 113–114 (Cleopatra II). Quaegebeur 1989, 103 (Cleopatra II or III, possibly not usurped). Capriotti Vittozzi 1998, 60–61, pl. 8a (Cleopatra II). Thiers forthcoming (in *BIFAO* or *RdE*).

B15. Fragmentary king. New Haven, Peabody Museum of Natural History, Yale University YPM.256941 (= Yale University Art Gallery 1.1.1953)

[Figure 61]

First half of second century B.C.

Dark stone. H: 44.5 cm, HeadH: 18.6 cm, FaceH: 11.0 cm.

Provenance not known. Formerly collection of Victor Clay Barringer, judge in Alexandria in late nineteenth century.

Under life-size. Plain *nemes* and uraeus. Preserved from top of head through waist. Uraeus, left eye, nose, and edges of *nemes* wings damaged. Inlaid eyes missing. Arms mostly broken off. Back pillar: Square top ends below armpits.

Needler 1949, 130–132, pl. 23: 1–2 (early Ptolemaic). *ESLP* 1960, 141–142, cat. no. 109, pl. 101, figs. 270–271 (c. 220–180 B.C.). Aldred et al. 1980, 160, fig. 142 (c. 200 B.C.). Scott 1986, 165–167, cat. no. 94 (c. 220–180 B.C.). *CE* 1988, 250 (Ptolemaic). Bothmer 1996, 218, fig. 10 (c. 220–180 B.C.). Josephson 1997a, 20 (Ptolemaic). PM 8 (1999), 199, no. 800-940-650 (early to mid-Ptolemaic).

B16. Standing king. Rome, Museo Nazionale 60921

[Figure 62]

First half of second century B.C.

Dark stone. H: 132.7 cm (with base), HeadH: 18.0 cm, FaceH: 11.2 cm. Base: H: 8.0 cm, W: 23.2 cm, D: 51.0 cm.

From Rome, temple of Syrian triad on Janiculum (Nicole and Darier 1909, 17–18).

Under life-size. Plain *nemes,* uraeus, and plain *shendyt.* Objects held in clenched fists inserted in another material. Preserved from top of head through attached base, which has molding inconsistent with Egyptian-style sculpture; it is unclear whether this is original. Broken at neck, waist, knees, ankles, and left foot, and repaired. Inlaid eyes, nose, and lower right half of face missing. Large portion of screen between legs missing. Back pillar: Square top reaches armpit level.

Nicole and Darier 1909, 14, 17–18, 45–48, 83–86, figs. 24–25, pl. 6 (third century B.C.; also quotes É. Naville opinion for Dynasty 30 date). PM 7 (1951), 413–414 (Syrian Sanctuary at Janiculum; Roman). *ESLP* 1960, 142 (Ptolemaic). H. W. Müller 1961, 27 n. 13 (as Museo Nazionale 6092; Augustus?). Roullet 1972, 103, cat. no. 156, pl. 129, fig. 182 (Ptolemaic). *CE* 1988, 251 (Ptolemaic). Duthoy and Frel 1996, 291 (Roman Osiris). Manera and Mazza 2001, 51, cat. no. 10 (photo reproduced in reverse; Ptolemaic).

B17. Fragmentary king. Staatlichen Sammlung Ägyptischer Kunst München ÄS 20

[Figure 63]

First half of second century B.C.

Dark stone. H: 34.0 cm, HeadH: 14.6 cm, FaceH: 9.6 cm.

Provenance not known.

Under life-size. Plain *nemes* and uraeus. Preserved from top of head through pectorals. Uraeus, nose, and lips damaged. Inlaid eyes missing. Left upper arm broken off at shoulder and repaired; same for small piece of right shoulder. Back pillar: Square top reaches armpit height.

ESLP 1960, 142 (Ptolemaic). H. W. Müller 1966, cat. no. 98 (Augustus?). PM 8 (1999), 249, no. 800-950-700 (probably Augustus).

B18. Standing king. Copenhagen, Ny Carlsberg Glyptotek AEIN 929

[Figure 64]

First half of second century B.C.

Dark stone. H: 104.0 cm, HeadH: 15.0 cm, FaceH: 8.2 cm. Base: H: 8.0 cm, W: 17.5 cm, D: 36.4 cm.

Provenance not known. Acquired in 1896 in art market in Egypt.

Under-life-size statue with plain *nemes,* uraeus, and plain *shendyt.* Small, very shallow, circular hole (Dia: c. 2 cm) atop head. Mostly well preserved, except for missing inlaid eyes and crack at shoulder level. Enigmatic objects in hands at sides. Back pillar: Square top reaches armpit level. Incised, slanted, parallel lines on lateral sides of pillar.

Mogensen 1930, 9, pl. 9: A22 (Roman). Koefoed-Petersen 1950, 69, cat. no. 122, pl. 126 (Ptolemaic). *ESLP* 1960, 142 (Ptolemaic). PM 8 (1999), 196, no. 800-932-150 (Ptolemaic).

B19. Head of king. Lyon, Musée des Beaux-Arts H 1701

[Figure 65]

First half of second century B.C.

Graywacke. H: 19.0 cm, HeadH: 13.0 cm, FaceH: 8.4 cm.

Provenance not known. Entered museum's collection between 1803 and 1813.

Under life-size. Plain *nemes* with uraeus. Back of head broken off at downward diagonal from left to right. Uraeus, nose, and *nemes* wings damaged. Modern restoration of nose recently removed. No back pillar remains.

Goyon and Gabolde 1991, 22–27, figs. 19–21 (Nectanebo II?). Galliano 1997, 31 (Nectanebo II?). Josephson 1997a, 19 (third or second century B.C.). PM 8 (1999), 160, no. 800-871-100 (probably Nectanebo II or early Ptolemaic).

B20. Head of king. Brooklyn Museum of Art 16.169

[Figures 66–67]

First half of second century B.C.

Limestone. H: 21.0 cm, HeadH: 16.6 cm, FaceH: 10.5 cm.

Provenance not known. Perhaps from Upper Egypt, based on statement in letter of Charles Edwin Wilbour, who was in Akhmim when he obtained the head (Capart 1936, 544).

Under life-size. Banded *nemes* and uraeus. Uraeus, ears, and nose damaged. Left back of head broken off. No back pillar remains.

Capart 1936, 544 (Seti).

B21. Head of king. Rome, Museo Barracco 32

[Figure 68]

First half of second century B.C.

Granite. H: 17.0 cm, HeadH: not preserved, FaceH: 8.3 cm.

Provenance not known. Reportedly from Tiber River, Rome (Giovanni Barracco, *Catalogo del Museo di scultura antica* [Rome, 1910], 17).

Under life-size. Plain *nemes* and uraeus. Likely from sphinx because of slight remains of shoulders at back. Top left of head and *nemes* wing broken off. Surface abraded. Inlaid eyes and nose tip missing.

Bissing 1914, nos. 103–104, note 7 (Ptolemaic). H. W. Müller 1961, 27 n. 13 (Augustus?). Roullet 1972, 104, cat. no. 159, pl. 131, fig. 184 (Ptolemaic). Lollio Barberi et al. 1995, 158, cat. no. 18 (Ptolemaic). Sist 1996, 79 (first half of Ptolemaic Period).

B22. Head of king. Alexandria, Graeco-Roman Museum 28103

[Figure 69]

First half of second century B.C.

Limestone. H: 20.1 cm, HeadH: 15.7 cm, FaceH: 10.1 cm.

From Canopus (Breccia 1932, 17–18, no. 10).

Under life-size. Plain *nemes* and uraeus. From sphinx, given the slight horizontal projection (from pigtail?) in back. Nose, mouth, and chin damaged.

Breccia 1932, 17–18, no. 10, pl. 9: 32 (second or first century B.C.). Needler 1949, 131 n. 2, 132 n. 3 (late Ptolemaic).

B23. Standing dyad. London, British Museum EA 27390

[Figure 70]

First half of second century B.C.

Limestone. H: 39.0 cm, FaceH (king): 3.1 cm.

Provenance not known.

Well under life-size dyad of standing king with plain double crown, uraeus, and plain *shendyt* on right and crocodile-headed deity on left. Figures hold enigmatic objects in hands at sides. Well preserved, except upper right corner of back slab is broken off. Slab reaches to tops of crowns.

CE 1988, 106, 148, cat. no. 16 (third to second century B.C.). *Gloire* 1998, 179, cat. no. 128 (third to second century B.C.). PM 8 (1999), 195, no. 800-930-500 (mid-Ptolemaic).

B24. Head of king. Brooklyn Museum of Art 1995.28

[Figure 71]

First half of second century B.C.

Limestone. H: 31.8 cm, HeadH: c. 25.0 cm, FaceH: 14.8 cm.

Provenance not known.

Life-size. Banded *nemes* and uraeus. On top of head are remains of round tenon for attachment of additional attribute. Downward direction of *nemes* pigtail at back indicates head is from nonsphinx statue. Damage to uraeus, eyes, ears, nose, and lips. No back pillar remains.

Apollo 115 (May 1982), 3 (dealer advertisement; third to second century B.C.). Bothmer 1987, 88–92, cat. no. 35 (c. 150–100 B.C.). "Recent Acquisition," *Newsletter: The Brooklyn Museum* (Jul.–Aug. 1995), 7 (Ptolemaic). PM 8 (1999), 211, no. 800-942-710 (Ptolemaic).

B25. Face of king. Naples, Museo Archeologico Nazionale 432

[Figures 72–73]

First half of second century B.C.

Marble. Incorrectly published as limestone. H: 17.5 cm, FaceH: 10.0 cm.

Provenance not known.

Under life-size. Has frontlet, tabs, but no uraeus. Some slight chips, but otherwise well preserved. Not hollowed out. No grid lines. Top and back left rough.

Cantilena and Rubino 1989, 54–55, cat. no. 3.4 (Late Period).

B26. Head of king. Bloomington, Indiana University Art Museum 62.225

[Figures 74–75]

First half of second century B.C., Ptolemy VI?

Limestone. H: 55.0 cm, HeadH: 42.0 cm, FaceH: 27.0 cm.

Provenance not known. Reportedly from Sheikh Abada (Eisenberg 1960, 3).

Colossal. Plain *nemes* and uraeus. Surface abraded. Uraeus, nose tip, and ears damaged. Some repair filler on right side of neck. No back pillar remains.

Eisenberg 1960, 3, cat. no. 1, pl. 1 (early Ptolemaic, Ptolemy III?).

B27. Face of king. Alexandria, Graeco-Roman Museum 3511

[Figures 76–77]

First half of second century B.C., Ptolemy VI?

Marble. H: 60.0 cm, FaceH: 35.0 cm.

Provenance not known. Gift of Pasha Tigrane (Botti 1900, 479, no. 25).

Colossal face of king with partial frontlet and tabs. Back partly hollowed. Multiple small drill holes (c. 0.2 cm in diameter) on top left surface. Weathered and chipped. Plaster fill at right top, back, and bottom of neck.

Botti 1900, 479, no. 25 (Ptolemaic).

B28. Head of queen. New York, private collection

[Figure 78]

First half of second century B.C.

Quartzite. H: 16.0 cm, HeadH: 10.8 cm, FaceH: 6.8 cm.

Provenance not known.

Under life-size. Plain tripartite wig, uraeus(?), and uraeus modius. Midway across top of modius, there is a break line parallel to the front, likely the remains of an additional headdress. Surface worn. Inlaid eyes missing and nose broken off. Back pillar: Extended through broken off attribute atop head.

CE 1988, 59, 117, 130, 148, 166–167, 176, cat. no. 62, color pl. 13 (c. 280–270 B.C.). PM 8 (1999), 1013, no. 801-809-260 (early Ptolemaic).

B29. Standing queen. Turin, Museo Egizio 1386

[No figure]

First half of second century B.C.

Sandstone. H: 101.2 cm, HeadH: 20.0 cm (chin damaged), FaceH: 12.5 cm (chin damaged).

Provenance not known.

Fragment (head through knees) of under-life-size statue with tripartite, echeloned wig, necklace, and pleated garment with fringed border. Broken at waist and repaired. Nose gone, lips worn flat, and chin broken off. Part of left forearm and elbow restored. Wears plain diadem with loopless uraeus; tie at back. Unpolished round area on top of head indicates original presence of added attribute. Right hand under breasts grasps lily scepter, while left hand at side holds *ankh*. Back pillar: Square top ends below armpits.

Curto, Donadoni, and Leospo 1989, 181, 184, fig. 274 (third century B.C.). Capriotti Vittozzi 1998 (Cleopatra II or III?). PM 8 (1999), 1001, no. 801-805-280 (early Ptolemaic).

B30. Head of queen. St. Petersburg, Hermitage 3099

[No figure]

First half of second century B.C.

Dark stone. H: 12.5 cm.

From Panticapeion (modern Kerch, Ukraine). Chance find, according to Turaev (1911, 27). Formerly Novikoff collection.

Under life-size(?). Tripartite, echeloned wig, plain diadem, and uraeus. Uraeus, nose, and lips abraded. Back pillar: None remaining?

PM 7 (1951), 400 (from Panticapeion; not attributed). *ESLP* 1960, 135 (240–200 B.C.?). Lapis and Mat'e 1969, 126–127, cat. no. 143.

GROUP C: PTOLEMY VIII

C1. Head of king. Brussels, Musées Royaux d'Art et d'Histoire E. 1839

[Figures 79–80]

Attributed to Ptolemy VIII. Jubilee type?

Dark stone. H: 47.0 cm.

Provenance not known. Purchased in art market, 1905.

Near life-size. Wears plain double crown with uraeus. Nose and left ear mostly gone. Uraeus, lips, and chin damaged. Fragmentary back pillar narrows as it extends through remains of double crown.

ESLP 1960, 177 (Ptolemaic). Kyrieleis 1975, 64, 174, G 2, pls. 52: 4, 53: 1–2 (Ptolemy VIII). *CE* 1988, 62, 106, 143, 145, 148–149, 154, 176, 184, 249, 251, cat. no. 53 (third to second century B.C.). Smith 1988, 87, 93–94, 170, cat. no. 73, pl. 47: 1–2 (Ptolemy VIII). Bothmer 1996, 220–221, fig. 20 (Ptolemy VIII). Smith 1996, 207–208, fig. 6 (Ptolemy VIII). Josephson 1997a, 15 n. 107, 16 nn. 111 and 115, 18 n. 130 (Ptolemy VIII). *Gloire* 1998, 215, cat. no. 161 (Ptolemy VIII). G. Grimm 1998, 122–123, fig. 118a–b (Ptolemy VIII). PM 8 (1999), 202–203, no. 800-942-190 (probably Ptolemy VIII). Rogge 1999, 86, 90, 95 (Ptolemy VIII). Walker and Higgs 2001, 56–57, cat. no. 22 (170–116 B.C.).

C2. Fragmentary king. Vienna, Kunsthistorisches Museum ÄS 5780

[Figures 81–82]

Attributed to Ptolemy VIII. Inaugural type?

Granodiorite. H: 92.0 cm. FaceH: 33.0 cm.

Provenance not known. Anton Ritter von Laurin, diplomat and collector, reportedly dug up sculpture in garden of his house in Alexandria in mid-nineteenth century with J8 (Rogge 1999, 96).

Fragment (head through part of chest) of colossal royal bust with plain *nemes,* uraeus, Greek forehead hair, and Horus sidelock. Square hole atop flattened crown indicates original presence of another attribute, perhaps the double crown. *Nemes,* uraeus, nose, lips, and chin abraded and broken. Fat folds on neck. Rogge 1999, 96: "Weisse Reste von Kalkmörtel besonders in den Augen und den Haaren." Back pillar: Narrows as it reaches shoulder level and blends smoothly into back of *nemes.*

Satzinger 1987, 68–69 (first century A.D.?). Derriks 1998, 100. Rogge 1999, 76–77, 90, 94–99, 125 (second/first century B.C. [or first century A.D.?]).

C3. Medinet Madi sphinxes

[No figure]

Second half of second century B.C.

Limestone. Various measurements.

From Medinet Madi. Excavated by Achille Vogliano in situ, lining processional way of Ptolemaic addition to Renenutet temple.

Various types of sphinxes found. Some have royal male heads with *nemes* and Greek forehead hair, and some have female heads with corkscrew locks; there are also Greek-style sphinxes and recumbent lions. As of December 1998, many sphinxes still in situ, but unfortunately much abraded. Two over-life-size examples with heads preserved strongly resemble Milan sphinx head (C4).

INSCRIPTION: Some sphinx bases have Demotic dedications to Renenutet or Sobek, but do not mention any royal names. Uncertain when inscriptions were made (Vogliano 1939a, 89; É. Bernand 1981b, 66). In addition, separately worked base of one sphinx has Roman Period(?) Greek dedication to Anubis (Vogliano 1936, 54, cat. no. 10; É. Bernand 1981b, 92–93, cat. no. 171).

Vogliano 1936, 17, pls. 1–3, 5, 9 (not attributed). Vogliano 1937, pl. 1. Vogliano 1938b, 538–543 (Ptolemy VIII). Vogliano 1939a, 88–89 (Ptolemy VIII). Vogliano 1939b, pls. 128, 130. Vogliano 1942, 18–19, pl. 19 (Ptolemy VIII), pl. 21 (Cleopatra VII?). Kyrieleis 1975, 75, 118–119, 177, 184, H 16, H 17, M 3, pls. 67: 5, 101: 3 (Ptolemy IX and Cleopatra III?). É. Bernand 1981b, 62–66. Kiss 1998, 173 (late Ptolemy).

C4. Head of king. Milan, Museo Archeologico E.0.9.40012 (formerly E. 913)

[Figure 83]

Attributed to Ptolemy VIII.

Limestone. H: 50.0 cm.

From Medinet Madi. Excavated by Achille Vogliano in pile of rubble in Middle Kingdom portion of Renenutet temple (Vogliano 1937, 57–58).

Over-life-size sphinx head with banded *nemes,* uraeus, and Greek forehead hair. Surface pitted and discolored. Nose broken off and left ear mostly gone.

Vogliano 1937, 57–58, pl. 43 (Ptolemaic). Vogliano 1938a, 32–33, cat. no. 8 (Ptolemaic). Vogliano 1942, pl. 19 (Ptolemy VIII). Smith 1988, 87, 97, 171, cat. no. 82, pl. 50: 6–7 (second or first century B.C.).

c5. Head of king. Athens, National Archaeological Museum ANE 88

[Figures 84–85]

Attributed to Ptolemy VIII.

Granite. H: 19.3 cm, HeadH: 17.8 cm, FaceH: c. 11.5 cm.

Provenance not known. Formerly Dimitriou collection.

Under-life-size, unfinished head with plain *nemes* and Greek forehead hair. Round chiseled area on top and rectangular extension over front of *nemes* probably indicate the original presence of a blocked-out (not completed) uraeus and additional attribute(?). Surface rough, particularly on top and back of *nemes*. Chin is dimpled (damage only?). Nose broken. No back pillar remains.

Kyrieleis 1975, 75, 176–177, H 11, pl. 66: 1–2 (late Ptolemaic). Kiss 1984, 35–37, 130, figs. 38–39 (Augustus). Tzachou-Alexandri 1995, 165, cat. no. 56: 1 (Ptolemaic). Kiss 1998, 177 (Augustus). PM 8 (1999), 249, no. 800-951-050 (probably Augustus).

c6. Head of king. Washington, D.C., Byzantine Collection, Dumbarton Oaks 48.10

[Figures 86–87]

Attributed to Ptolemy VIII.

Dark stone. H: 7.0 cm.

Provenance not known.

Well under life-size. Greek hair covers head. Has space for diadem. No uraeus. Nose bridge damaged. No back pillar remains.

Handbook of the Byzantine Collection (Dumbarton Oaks, 1967), 7, cat. no. 21 (fifth century A.D.). Vikan 1995, 1–3, cat. no. 1, figs. 1A–D (Ptolemy II?).

c7. Head of king. Athens, Benaki Museum 22586

[Figures 88–89]

Attributed to Ptolemy VIII.

Dark stone. H: 6.6 cm.

Provenance not known. Purchased in Alexandria.

Well under life-size. Greek hair covers head. Rolled diadem. No uraeus. Various surface scratches. Nose tip damaged. Back pillar: None remaining?

Kyrieleis 1975, 74–75, 177, H 14, pl. 67: 6–7 (as inv. no. 22588; late Ptolemy). Vikan 1995, 1–3, figs. 1.1a–b (Ptolemy II?).

c8. Head of king. Vienna, Kunsthistorisches Museum ÄS 5787

[Figures 90–91]

Attributed to Ptolemy VIII.

Diorite. H: 15.8 cm. FaceH: 8.2 cm.

Provenance not known. Formerly Miramar collection (Rogge 1999, 89).

Under life-size. Plain *nemes,* uraeus, and Greek forehead hair. Remains of slight edge on left front top indicate the original presence of additional crown, possibly the double crown. Nose and *nemes* wings broken off. Abraded back pillar originally extended beyond preserved height of head.

Bissing 1914, nos. 103–104, last page ("Alexander"). PM 8 (1999), 210, no. 800-942-629 (late Ptolemaic). Rogge 1999, 89–93, 95, 125 (late second or first half of first century B.C., Ptolemy X?).

c9. Head of king. Tübingen, Ägyptologisches Institut der Universität 1460

[Figures 92–93]

Attributed to Ptolemy VIII.

Limestone. H: 13.0 cm.

Provenance not known. Gift of Laura Sachs to Linden Museum in Stuttgart in 1912. Acquired by Egyptological Institute in Tübingen in 1965.

Under life-size. Remains of Greek hair cover head. Had diadem(?). Top of head missing. Nose and lips damaged. Back pillar: None remaining?

Brunner-Traut and Brunner 1981, 307 (Ptolemy V or VII?).

c10. Head of king. Copenhagen, Ny Carlsberg Glyptotek AEIN 294

[Figures 94–95]

Attributed to Ptolemy VIII. Jubilee type?

Dark stone. H: 27.2 cm, HeadH: c. 23.9 cm, FaceH: c. 16.8 cm.

Provenance not known. Acquired in Cairo in 1890s; reportedly from Auguste Mariette's excavations at Saqqara Serapeum.

Life-size. Has Greek hair covering head, wide diadem, and uraeus. Hair and space for diadem are unpolished. Diadem augmented in another material? Damage to top of head and pitting on face. Inlaid eyes, nose, and chin missing. Abraded back pillar perhaps reached almost to top of head.

Mogensen 1930, 9, pl. 9: A23 (Roman?). Koefoed-Petersen 1950, 74, cat. no. 134, pl. 141 (first century A.D.). *ESLP* 1960, 177 (late Ptolemy). Kyrieleis 1975, 74, 177, H 13, pl. 67: 1–2 (late Ptolemy). Krug 1978, 18–19, figs. 34–35 (Ptolemy XI). Maehler 1983, 10 (Ptolemy IX). Smith 1988, 87, 97, 170–171, cat. no. 78, pl. 49: 3–4 (Ptolemaic). Nielsen and Østergaard 1997, 54–55, cat. no. 24 (first century B.C. to first century A.D.). PM 8 (1999), 204, no. 800-942-250 (1868 auction description does not match head; probably Ptolemy XI).

c11. Head of king. Paris, Musée du Louvre Ma 970

[Figures 96–97]

Attributed to Ptolemy VIII. Jubilee type?

Dark stone. H: 38.0 cm, HeadH: 32.5 cm, FaceH: 24.1 cm.

Provenance not known. Reportedly found near Forum, Rome (Hamiaux 1998, 81).

Over life-size. Has Greek hair covering head, wide diadem, and uraeus. The diadem, likely originally augmented in another material, varies in width from 4.8 cm in front to 1.9 cm in back. Has light beard indicated by roughening. Top of head damaged. Nose, lips, and chin mostly gone. Perhaps faint remains of square back pillar top on neck at back.

Kyrieleis 1975, 70–71, 175, H 2, pls. 58, 59: 1–2 (Ptolemy X?). *CE* 1988, 139. Smith 1988, 87, 96–97, 170, cat. no. 76, pl. 48: 5–6 (later second to first century B.C.). Pasqua 1995, 38–40, no. 4, figs. 5–6 (Ptolemy X?). Hamiaux 1998, 80–81, cat. no. 82 (Ptolemy X?).

c12. Standing king. Amsterdam, Allard Pierson Museum 7780

[Figures 98–99]

Attributed to Ptolemy VIII.

Marble. H: 73.0 cm, HeadH: 11.6 cm, FaceH: 7.7 cm.

Provenance not known. Formerly Friedrich Wilhelm von Bissing collection, Munich and Museum Scheurleer, The Hague.

Under life-size. Plain *nemes,* uraeus, and *shendyt.* Enigmatic objects in hands at sides. Preserved from top of head through portions of legs. Right quarter of face and nose gone. Large chip on right front of *nemes* repaired. Back pillar: Trapezoid top ends halfway up back of head. Round hole drilled into pillar at hip level.

Bissing 1914, nos. 103–104, note 14 (late Ptolemaic). Van Haarlem 1986, 25–27 (Ptolemaic). PM 8 (1999), 195, no. 800-932-050 (Ptolemaic).

c13. Head of king. Alexandria, Graeco-Roman Museum 362

[Figure 100]

Attributed to Ptolemy VIII.

Yellow quartzite. H: 57.5 cm, HeadH: 40.0 cm, FaceH: 24.0 cm.

From Canopus (Breccia 1926, 58, no. 7). Entered museum collection in 1891.

Over life-size. Banded *nemes* and uraeus, from sphinx, given angle of pigtail break at back. Nose and right cheek smashed. Left wing of *nemes* restored. Appearance is similar to c14, also from Canopus.

Breccia 1926, 58, no. 7, pl. 26: 1. Vogliano 1937, 58, pl. 46 top (mislabeled as Alexandria 372; Ptolemy VIII). Kyrieleis 1975, 71, 175, H 4, pl. 60: 1–2 (photos reproduced in reverse; late Ptolemy?). Kiss 1984, 22 (Ptolemy X). *CE* 1988, 147 (incorrectly notes that *nemes* tabs are absent). Smith 1988, 87 n. 3 (Ptolemaic). Josephson 1997a, 20 n. 148 (late Ptolemaic).

c14. Head of king. Alexandria, Graeco-Roman Museum 18505

[No figure]

Attributed to Ptolemy VIII.

Light brown quartzite. H: c. 41.0 cm.

From Canopus (Breccia 1926, 58–59, no. 8). Gift of Omar Toussoun.

Colossal. Banded *nemes* and uraeus. Eyes and ears damaged. Nose, *nemes* wings, and lower part of face broken off. Appearance is similar to c13, also from Canopus, and this head may also come from sphinx, though remains do not permit confirmation.

Breccia 1926, 58–59, no. 8, pl. 21: 2 (at right, sitting atop architectural fragment). Vogliano 1937, 58, pl. 46 (bottom; compared to head Vogliano attributes to Ptolemy VIII).

c15. Sphinx. Cairo CG 1166 (JE 32028)

[Figure 101]

Attributed to Ptolemy VIII.

Limestone. H: 38.8 cm, HeadH: 11.2 cm, FaceH: 7.0 cm. Base: W: 23.5 cm, D: 71.0 cm.

From Sanhur, according to Cairo Museum Journal d'Entrée.

Under life-size. Wears plain *nemes,* uraeus, and plain false beard. Some chips and cracks, but generally well preserved. Roughened surface indicates lack of finish or weathering. Tail curls over right haunch.

Borchardt 1934, 87, pl. 165 (Late Period). *ESLP* 1960, 180. *CE* 1988, 229. Franke 1992, fiche 41, no. II/1627 (Late Period).

c16. Head of king. New Haven, Peabody Museum of Natural History, Yale University YPM.264258 (= Yale University Art Gallery 3.1.1953)

[Figure 102]

Attributed to Ptolemy VIII.

Granite. H: 26.0 cm, HeadH: 19.0 cm, FaceH: 12.0 cm.

Provenance not known. Formerly collection of Victor Clay Barringer, judge in Alexandria in late nineteenth century.

Under life-size. Plain *nemes* and uraeus. Surface greatly abraded. Perhaps unfinished. No back pillar remains.

Needler 1949, 132, pl. 24: 2–3 (early Ptolemaic). Scott 1986, 194, cat. no. 140 (Ptolemaic). PM 8 (1999), 207, no. 800-942-500 (Ptolemaic).

C17. Head of king. Vienna, Kunsthistorisches Museum ÄS 8181

[Figures 103–104]

Attributed to Ptolemy VIII.

Limestone. H: 10.7 cm. FaceH: 7.0 cm.

Provenance not known. Acquired from private collection in 1934 (Rogge 1999, 86).

Under life-size. Plain *nemes* and uraeus. Comes from sphinx. Surface abraded.

Demel 1936, 4, figs. 5–6 (early Ptolemaic). PM 8 (1999), 210, no. 800-942-630 (late Ptolemaic). Rogge 1999, 86–88 (second or first century B.C.).

C18. Head of queen. Copenhagen, Ny Carlsberg Glyptotek AEIN 1472

[Figures 105–106]

Attributed to Cleopatra II.

Dark stone. H: 39.0 cm, HeadH: 25.8 cm, FaceH: 19.8 cm.

Provenance not known. Acquired in Rome in 1912.

Near life-size. Plain modius, diadem, and loopless uraeus. The diadem, whose width increases from back to front of head, was perhaps augmented in another material. Squarish hole on top of modius (5.0 cm × 4.7 cm × 5.0 cm deep) supported additional attribute. Has Greek coiffure with bun at back. Irises of eyes are polished. Remains of fat fold on left side of neck. Back pillar: Trapezoid top ends under hair bun.

Koefoed-Petersen 1965, 9 (early first century B.C.). Kyrieleis 1975, 118–119, 184, M 5, pl. 102: 1–2 (Cleopatra I?). Brunelle 1976, 93–94 (second quarter of first century B.C.). Capriotti Vittozzi 1995, 432. Svenson 1995, 88, 232, cat. no. 112, pl. 39 (Cleopatra I). Nielsen and Østergaard 1997, 46–47, cat. no. 18 (Cleopatra I?, second to first century B.C.). PM 8 (1999), 1010, no. 801-809-082 (probably Cleopatra I).

C19. Head of queen. Alexandria, Graeco-Roman Museum 21992

[Figures 107–108]

Attributed to Cleopatra II as *Thea Philometor Soteira.*

Nummulitic limestone. H: 80.0 cm, HeadH: 50.0 cm, FaceH: 32.5 cm.

Provenance not known. Reportedly from Mazarita district of Alexandria. Purchased by museum in 1926.

Colossal. Wears uraeus modius, plain diadem, and uraeus. Square hole (8.8 cm × 8.8 cm) atop modius for insertion of added attribute. Has Greek coiffure with corkscrews, hair knots at sides, and rolled bun at back. Tip of nose and left cheek damaged. Several corkscrew locks partly broken off. Back pillar: Round top almost reaches top of head.

Breccia 1931b, 264–265, no. 8, pl. 29: 1, 3 (Berenice II). Kyrieleis 1975, 119, 184–185, M 10, pl. 103: 4 (late Ptolemaic). Brunelle 1976, 92–93 (second quarter of first century B.C.). Wildung and Grimm 1978, cat. no. 117 (second half of second century or first half of first century B.C.). Tkaczow 1993, 194, cat. no. 22 (second half of third century B.C.?). Svenson 1995, 88, 233, cat. no. 116, pl. 39 (late Ptolemaic). Walker and Higgs 2001, 53, cat. no. 17 (Cleopatra I or II).

C20. Head of queen. Alexandria, Graeco-Roman Museum 25264

[Figures 109–110]

Attributed to Cleopatra II as *Thea Philometor Soteira.*

Dark stone. H: 12.0 cm.

Provenance not known.

Under life-size. Has corkscrew locks and plain, rather wide diadem (full width visible at sides and back, whereas front is partially covered by hair). Hole in plain modius on top of head accommodated another attribute. No uraeus. Has Greek coiffure with hair knots at sides and corkscrews. Chips and scratches on face. Nose broken off. Back pillar: None remaining?

Adriani 1939, 347, fig. 7. Wildung and Grimm 1978, cat. no. 132 (late second to early first century B.C.).

C21. Colossal statues of the Pharos (includes C22–C27)

[Figures 111–115]

Second century B.C.

Granite. Various measurements.

From Alexandria. Found in harbor, near Pharos lighthouse.

Five or six colossal kings and queens. Surfaces substantially weathered and facial features worn. Additional fragments still lie under water. Bases are separately worked and have Greek-style molding. Back pillars: Various.

Frost 1975. Empereur 1996, 967–968, figs. 4–7 (Ptolemaic). Grimal 1996, 567–570 (early Ptolemaic?). La Riche 1996, passim. Corteggiani 1998, 35–40 (Ptolemaic). Empereur 1998, 64–65, 76–81 (Ptolemaic). Yoyotte 1998, 204, 209–210 (Ptolemaic).

C22. Standing king. Alexandria, Kom el-Dikka 1001 + 1999 + 3200

[Figures 111–112]

Attributed to Ptolemy VIII.

Granite. H: 455.0 cm (without head or double crown).

From Alexandria. Found in harbor, near Pharos lighthouse.

Colossal. Has hair, banded *nemes* (and presumably uraeus), plain double crown, Greek forehead hair, and pleated *shendyt*. Preserved from top of double crown through thighs. Broken into at least four pieces: double crown, head, left upper arm, and torso from base of neck through most of thighs. Inlaid eyes missing. Front of head worn off; sides of statue somewhat better preserved. Likely held enigmatic objects in hands at sides. Back pillar: Narrows as it reaches nearly to top of double crown.

Empereur 1996, 967–968, figs. 4, 6 (Ptolemaic). Grimal 1996, 568–570 (early Ptolemaic?). La Riche 1996, 24–27, 41, 45, 72–73, 76, 78–79, 84–85, 88–91, 94, 114–115, 121 (illustrated). Corteggiani 1998, 35–40, fig. 9 (Ptolemy II?). Empereur 1998, 76–77 (Ptolemaic). *Gloire* 1998, 103, 307, cat. no. 64 (first half of third century B.C.?). Yoyotte 1998, 204 n. 18 (face recalls Ptolemy I). Walker and Higgs 2001, 58, cat. no. 24a (116–87 B.C.?).

C23. Head of king. Alexandria, Kom el-Dikka 1321

[Figure 113]

Second century B.C., Ptolemy VI?

Granite. H: 80.0 cm.

From Alexandria. Found in harbor, near Pharos lighthouse.

Colossal. Has *nemes*. Square hole (10 cm × 10 cm × 8 cm deep) atop head accommodated additional crown. Had Greek forehead hair, but now worn off? Short, narrow, Greek-style sideburns next to left ear. Inlaid eyes missing. No back pillar remains.

Empereur 1996, 967–968, fig. 5 (Ptolemaic). Grimal 1996, 569 (early Ptolemaic?). La Riche 1996, 86–87 (illustrated). Corteggiani 1998, 35–40 (as wearing bag wig instead of *nemes;* Ptolemaic). Empereur 1998, 78 (Ptolemaic).

C24. Head of king. Alexandria, Kom el-Dikka 1314

[No figure]

Second century B.C.?

Granite. H: 70 cm.

From Alexandria. Found in harbor, near Pharos lighthouse.

Colossal. Has *nemes*. Virtually no facial markings left. No back pillar remains.

Grimal 1996, 569 (early Ptolemaic?). Corteggiani 1998, 35–40 (Ptolemaic).

C25. Torso of queen. Alexandria, Kom el-Dikka 1005

[Figure 114]

Second century B.C., Cleopatra II?

Granite. H: 125.0 cm.

From Alexandria. Found in harbor, near Pharos lighthouse.

Colossal torso (shoulders through mid-abdomen) wearing draped ensemble (knotted next to right breast?). At back right next to pillar, there is a raised, curved area, perhaps remains of hairstyle. Garment neckline indicated. Arms missing. Back pillar: Narrows near base of neck. Top broken off.

Grimal 1996, 568 (early Ptolemaic?). La Riche 1996, 17–19, 95 (illustrated). Corteggiani 1998, 35–40 (Ptolemaic). Empereur 1998, 77, 80–81 (Ptolemaic). *Gloire* 1998, 104, cat. no. 67 (third century B.C.).

C26. Hips/thighs fragment. Alexandria, Kom el-Dikka 1583

[No figure]

Second century B.C.

Granite. H: c. 110 cm.

From Alexandria. Found in harbor, near Pharos lighthouse.

Colossal. Abdomen and upper thighs of draped standing figure, probably female. Back pillar: Broken off at top and bottom.

Grimal 1996, 569 (as male; early Ptolemaic?). Corteggiani 1998, 35–40 (as male; Ptolemaic).

C27. Standing queen. Alexandria, Maritime Museum

[Figure 115, head/torso only]

Second century B.C., Cleopatra III?

Granite. Hathor headdress: H: 190.0 cm. Head/torso: H: 288.0 cm (HeadH: c. 108.0 cm, FaceH: 79.0 cm). Hips/legs: H: 368.0 cm.

From Alexandria. Found in early 1960s by scuba divers in sea around eastern Pharos point. Hathor headdress (Alexandria, Kom el-Dikka 1017) found in 1995 by Jean-Yves Empereur's underwater expedition.

Colossal. Has Hathor headdress with feathers, corkscrew locks, diadem, and loopless uraeus. Preserved from Hathor headdress through shins. Broken into three pieces: Hathor headdress, head/torso, and hips/legs. Inlaid eyes missing. Wears draped costume knotted between breasts. Single(?) tier of corkscrew locks around head. Fat folds on neck. Arms at sides. *Ankh*-sign or sistrum in left hand. Back pillar: Blends(?) into top of head and has no distinct top.

Frost 1975, 126, fig. 1. Tkaczow 1993, 183, cat. no. 1 (Ptolemaic). Grimal 1996, 567 (early Ptolemaic?). Corteggiani 1998, 36, 39–40, fig. 10 (Arsinoe II?). Empereur 1998, 64–65, 76–77 (Ptolemaic). Walker and Higgs 2001, 58, cat. no. 24b (116–101 B.C.?).

C28. Standing statue inscribed for Arsinoe II (posthumous). New York, Metropolitan Museum of Art 20.2.21

[Figure 116]

Datable to second half of second century B.C.

Limestone. Traces of paint and gilding. H: 38.3 cm, HeadH: 5.4 cm (preserved), FaceH: 3.9 cm. Base: H: c. 3 cm, W: 7.4 cm (at front), 4.5 cm (at back), D: 12.9 cm (right side), 13.2 cm (left side).

Provenance not known.

Well under life-size. Wears draped costume knotted over right breast and carries double cornucopia. No diadem or uraeus, but top of head is broken off, indicating missing additional headdress. Single tier of corkscrews around head. Right hand clenched at side. Bottom of base completed in plaster. Back pillar: Reached beyond top of head, and is now broken off.

INSCRIPTION: Back pillar has one column of hieroglyphs containing partially preserved birth name of Arsinoe II.

ESLP 1960, 126, 145, 158, 159–160, 170, cat. no. 123, pls. 114–115, figs. 307–310 (c. 100 B.C.). Quaegebeur 1971, 209, cat. no. 2. Kyrieleis 1975, 82, 178, J 1, pl. 71: 1–2. Quaegebeur 1983, 115 (doubts third century B.C. date). *CE* 1988, 47, 65, 67, 69, 75, 84, 170–172, 180, 183, 184, 194, 206, 208, 231, 239, 244, cat. no. 66 (270–246 B.C.). Capriotti Vittozzi 1995, 415, 417–418. Svenson 1995, 87–88, 233, cat. no. 118, pl. 38. *Gloire* 1998, 80, cat. no. 39 (third century B.C., after 270 B.C.). Quaegebeur 1998, 75, 86, cat. no. 4 (late second or early first century B.C.). PM 8 (1999), 999, no. 801-805-230 (early Ptolemaic). Walker and Higgs 2001, 166–167, cat. no. 166 (mid-second century B.C.). (All authors: Arsinoe II.)

GROUP D: CLEOPATRA III, PTOLEMIES IX–X

D1. Statue base dedicated to Cleopatra III. Alexandria, Graeco-Roman Museum 20953

[No figure]

Red granite. H: 27.6 cm, W: 81.9 cm, D: 53.5 cm.

From Canopus (Breccia 1926, 53).

Rectangular base for Greek-style statue, with Greek inscription, dedicated to Cleopatra III. Rightmost part of inscription missing. Three round, rough-hewn cavities on top: back left corner (Dia: c. 7 cm, D: c. 2 cm); front, left of center (Dia: c. 20 cm; filled with cement?); and front right corner (Dia: c. 7 cm, D: c. 5 cm). Front is smooth compared to other surfaces.

INSCRIPTION: Two lines of Greek on front: (Statue of) Queen Cleopatra, benefactor goddess, (set up by) Dionysios, the exegetos.

Breccia 1926, 53, no. 7, pl. 19: 4 (Cleopatra III). A. Bernand 1970a, 239, no. 10 (Cleopatra III, 116–101 B.C.).

D2. Statue base dedicated to Ptolemy IX. Rome, Vatican, Museo Gregoriano Egizio 25056

[No figure]

Dark stone. H: c. 38.0 cm, W: c. 76.0 cm, D: c. 55.0 cm.

Provenance not known. Reportedly from Alexandria. Brought to Italy in 1822 by antiquarian Baseggio.

Rectangular statue base for Greek-style statue, with Greek inscription, dedicated to Ptolemy IX. Left one-third of inscription broken off. Two circular holes (Dia: 11 cm and 13 cm, D: c. 5 cm) on top. Traces of molding on left side and back.

INSCRIPTION: Five lines of Greek on longer side: (Statue of) [King] Ptolemy, savior [god], (set up by) Apollonios, son of . . . Philometoreios . . . [kinsman (of the king)] and grand seneschal, for his benefactor.

OGIS 1 (1903), 250–251, no. 169. *LdR* 4 (1916), 362, no. 55. É. Bernand 1982, 33, no. 169. É. Bernand 2001, 88–89, no. 31, pl. 16 (probably 88–80 B.C.). (All authors: Ptolemy IX.)

D3. Head of queen. Alexandria, Graeco-Roman Museum 3267

[Figures 117–118]

Attributed to Cleopatra III.

Limestone. H: 18.0 cm, HeadH: 10.5 cm, FaceH: 7.5 cm.

Provenance not known.

Under life-size. Has single-tier corkscrew locks around head, Hathor horns with sun disk and uraeus, and plain diadem. Nose tip damaged. Front of neck broken off. No back pillar remains.

No bibliography.

D4. Head of queen. Vienna, Kunsthistorisches Museum, Antikensammlung I 406

[Figures 119–120]

Attributed to Cleopatra III.

Basalt. H: 32.5 cm.

Provenance not known. Formerly Miramar collection (Rogge 1999, 118).

Life-size. Plain, rolled diadem, but no uraeus. Double tier of corkscrews around head. Traces of garment edge at base of neck. Fat fold on neck. Inlaid eyes and tip of nose missing. Back pillar: Perhaps slight remains under corkscrews at back (Rogge 1999, 118).

Bissing 1914, no. 112, note 16. Smith 1988, 87, 94–95, 170, cat. no. 74, pl. 48: 1–2 (later second or early first century B.C.). Seipel 1992, 440–441, cat. no. 180 (second century B.C.). Pasqua 1995, 40, no. 5, figs. 7–8 (late second or first century B.C.). Smith 1996, 208–209, fig. 7 (mid- to late second century B.C.). PM 8 (1999), 1012, no. 801-809-210 (mid- to late Ptolemaic). Rogge 1999, 118–123, 125 (late second century, Cleopatra II or III). Walker and Higgs 2001, 60, cat. no. 26 (145–101 B.C.).

D5. Standing queen. New Haven, Yale University Art Gallery 1931.106

[Figures 121–122]

Attributed to Cleopatra III.

Dark stone. H: 48.6 cm, HeadH: 12.0 cm, FaceH: 8.0 cm.

Provenance not known.

Under life-size. Has single tier of corkscrew locks around head, uraeus, and draped costume knotted between breasts. Area above forehead corkscrews damaged: headdress or additional hair? Preserved from top of head through part of hips. Face damaged and nose missing. Back pillar: Trapezoid top ends at level of mouth.

Needler 1949, 136–141, pl. 26: 1–2 (second century B.C. or later). *ESLP* 1960, 158, 160, 169–170, 177, cat. no. 130, pl. 121, figs. 324–326 (c. 80–50 B.C.). Kyrieleis 1975, 119, 184, M 8, pl. 103: 1–2 (first century B.C.?). Scott 1986, 168–169, cat. no. 95 (c. 80–50 B.C.). *CE* 1988, 105, 166, 170, 181, 182–184, 195, 208, 216, cat. no. 74 (second century B.C.). Svenson 1995, 87, 232, cat. no. 113, pl. 38 (late Cleopatra). PM 8 (1999), 1007, no. 801-808-320 (late Ptolemaic).

D6. Head of queen. Alexandria, Graeco-Roman Museum 28107

[Figures 123–124]

Attributed to Cleopatra III.

Dark stone. H: 24.2 cm, HeadH: 16.5 cm, FaceH: 13.5 cm.

From Canopus (Breccia 1932, 17–18).

Near life-size. Plain diadem. Remains of tenon or small modius on top (c. 5 cm in diameter). No uraeus preserved. Single tier of corkscrews surrounds head. Hair not indicated at back. Face battered. Fat folds on neck. No back pillar remains.

Breccia 1932, 17–18, pl. 8: 30 (second or first century B.C.). Kyrieleis 1975, 119, 184, M 9, pl. 103: 3 (first century B.C.?).

D7. Head of queen. Alexandria, Graeco-Roman Museum 18370

[Figures 125–126]

Attributed to Cleopatra III.

Granite. H: 16.0 cm.

From Canopus (Breccia 1926, 60–61, no. 16). Gift of Omar Toussoun.

Under life-size. Has triple layer of corkscrew locks, plain diadem, two loopless uraei, and plain modius. Shallow hole atop modius for attachment of attribute. Diadem disappears under corkscrews at sides of head. Fat fold on right side of neck. Neck broken off at diagonal and repaired with modern base. No back pillar remains?

Breccia 1905, 116, fig. 42a. Breccia 1926, 60–61, no. 16, pl. 28: 2 (Berenice II). Kyrieleis 1975, 118, 183, M 2, pl. 101: 2 (second or first century B.C.). Svenson 1995, 88, 232, cat. no. 115, pl. 39 (Cleopatra II or III). Walker and Higgs 2001, 166, cat. no. 165 (Arsinoe II, first century B.C.).

D8. Head of queen. Paris, Bibliothèque nationale de France 1980–208

[Figure 127]

Attributed to Cleopatra III.

Green flourite, with gold inlays for eyelids. H: 4.5 cm.

Provenance not known.

Well under life-size. Has two(?) tiers of corkscrew locks. Indentation for diadem, perhaps formerly added in another material, has small hole for missing attribute. Uraeus absent. Inlaid eyes missing. No back pillar remains.

Vollenweider 1995, 136–138, cat. no. 127, pl. 69 (Cleopatra IV?). *Gloire* 1998, 160, cat. no. 99 (Cleopatra IV?).

D9. Standing queen. San Jose, Rosicrucian Egyptian Museum RC 1582

[Figures 128–129]

Attributed to Cleopatra III.

Dark stone. H: 105.0 cm.

Provenance not known.

Under life-size. Has plain diadem, loopless triple uraeus, and unpolished, echeloned, tripartite wig. Dimpled chin. Fat folds on neck. Preserved from top of head through ankles. Feet and base restored. Close-fitting sheath dress indicated by hem near ankles. Hands at sides hold enigmatic objects. Attribute on top of head broken off. Back pillar: Square top ends just below armpits. Closely spaced, parallel, diagonal incisions on edge of right lateral side of pillar. Rectangular cut(?) down length of pillar is now filled in.

ESLP 1960, 147 (Cleopatra VII?). Kyrieleis 1975, 119, 184, M 7, pl. 102: 4 (Cleopatra III?). *CE* 1988, 59, 62, 130, 149, 167, 175–176, 194, 249, cat. no. 69 (third century B.C.). Capriotti Vittozzi 1995, 413–417, 427–431 (likely Berenice II). *Gloire* 1998, 175, cat. no. 123 (second century B.C., reign of Ptolemy VIII?). PM 8 (1999), 1001, no. 801-805-270 (Ptolemaic). Walker and Higgs 2001, 162, cat. no. 161 (Cleopatra VII).

D10. Standing queen. St. Petersburg, Hermitage 3936

[No figure]

Attributed to Cleopatra III.

Dark stone. H: 104.7 cm.

Provenance not known.

Under life-size. Has loopless triple uraeus and unpolished, echeloned, tripartite wig. Roughened, rounded break on top of head indicates former presence of additional attribute. Preserved from top of head through attached statue base. Inlaid eyes missing. Double cornucopia in left arm and *ankh*-sign in right hand at side. Earlobes have holes for earrings. Wears sheath dress. Back pillar: Extended through now-broken-off attribute atop head.

ESLP 1960, 126, 147 (Cleopatra VII?). Landa and Lapis 1974, cat. no. 131 (Arsinoe II, third century B.C.). Aldred et al. 1980, 160, 295, fig. 326 (Arsinoe II, c. 200 B.C.). Quaegebeur 1983, 115–117, 121. *CE* 1988, 176 (Ptolemaic). Capriotti Vittozzi 1995, 413–416, 427–431, fig. 3 (likely Berenice II). *Gloire* 1998, 65, 80, cat. no. 38 (c. 200 B.C.). Quaegebeur 1998, 103, cat. no. 78 (late Ptolemaic). PM 8 (1999), 1001, no. 801-805-260 (probably Arsinoe II, early Ptolemaic). Walker and Higgs 2001, 160–161, cat. no. 160 (Cleopatra VII).

D11. Standing queen. Berlin, Ägyptisches Museum 21763

[Figure 130]

Attributed to Cleopatra III.

Dark stone. H: 69.0 cm, HeadH: 10.8 cm, FaceH: 6.6 cm.

Provenance not known. Purchased in 1915.

Under life-size. Plain diadem, loopless uraeus, and plain tripartite wig. Preserved from top of head through ankles. Rectangular hole (1.5 cm × 1.8 cm) atop head, surrounded by circular roughened area, supported now-missing modius and crowning attribute. Wears close-fitting sheath dress with semicircular collar line and slanted sleeve edges at elbows. Enigmatic objects in right and left(?) hands at sides. Back pillar: Trapezoidal top slants slightly inward at top and ends at back of head.

Roeder 1932, 17–18, no. 46 (Ptolemaic). *ESLP* 1960, 117, 146 (Dynasty 30). Priese 1991, 187, cat. no. 110 (Dynasty 30?). A. Grimm, Schoske, and Wildung 1997, 100, cat. no. 74 (early Ptolemaic, c. 300 B.C.). PM 8 (1999), 926, no. 801-775-020 (Dynasty 30).

D12. Head of king. Berlin, Ägyptisches Museum 14079

[Figures 131–132]

Attributed to Ptolemy IX, first rule, 116–107 B.C.

Red granite. H: 26.0 cm.

Provenance not known. Purchased by Friedrich Wilhelm von Bissing in Cairo art market in 1899. Once considered lost, this head was later found again.

Life-size. Has dense Greek hair covering head and thick under-the-chin beard. Diadem perhaps augmented in another material. No uraeus. Nose and back pillar damaged. Back pillar: Square top ends at back of head.

INSCRIPTION: Back pillar reportedly has remains of hieroglyphs containing start of royal titulary (A. Grimm, Schoske, and Wildung 1997, 79). Inscription not visible in recent photo.

Bissing 1914, no. 111 (Roman emperor of third century A.D.). Kyrieleis 1975, 72, 176, H 7, pl. 63: 1–3 (Ptolemy XI). Parlasca 1978, 26 (Ptolemy IX). Kiss 1984, 23, 82, 119, 184, figs. 4, 210–211 (Ptolemy IX). Smith 1988, 87, 96, 170, cat. no. 75, pl. 48: 3–4 (later second or first century B.C.). Smith 1996, 210 (Ptolemies IX–X). A. Grimm, Schoske, and Wildung 1997, 78–79, cat. no. 60 (Ptolemies IX–X). PM 8 (1999), 201, no. 800-942-110 (probably Ptolemy IX).

D13. Head of king. Alexandria, Graeco-Roman Museum 3364

[Figures 133–134]

Attributed to Ptolemy IX, first rule, 116–107 B.C.

Red granite. H: 150.0 cm, HeadH: 58.0 cm, FaceH: 38.2 cm.

From Canopus (Breccia 1926, 60, no. 13). Gift of A. Ruffer.

Colossal. Has Greek forehead hair and long sideburns, banded *nemes,* and large, plain double crown. Right side of *nemes* and right ear badly abraded. Gouges and chip marks all over. Inlaid eyes and nose missing. Back pillar: Narrows as it ascends, ending in triangular top midway through red crown.

Dutilh 1905, 49–50, fig. 16 (Ptolemy IV). Breccia 1926, 60, no. 13, pl. 26: 4 (Ptolemy IV). Kyrieleis 1975, 37, 44–46, 171, D 2, pl. 33: 1–2 (Ptolemy IV). Smith 1988, 87, 97, 171, cat. no. 80, pl. 49: 6 (Ptolemaic). Bothmer 1996, 220–221, fig. 18 (Ptolemy IV). *Gloire* 1998, 209, cat. no. 155 (Ptolemy IV). G. Grimm 1998, 100, fig. 99 (Ptolemy IV).

D14. Standing king. Cairo 13/3/15/3

[Figures 135–137]

Attributed to Ptolemy X, recut from Ptolemy IX.

Dark stone. H: 96.3 cm, HeadH: 18.5 cm, FaceH: 12.8 cm.

Provenance not known. Michalowski (1935, 73 n. 3) speculates that the statue was found at Karnak, since Alexandre Barsanti of the Antiquities Service worked exclusively in Karnak during the period he sent the statue to Cairo. Cairo Journal d'Entrée: "Sent in by Barsanti to have a base made. Probably found in the last two years" (i.e., within two years of the journal entry on March 13, 1915).

Under life-size. Plain *nemes,* Greek forehead hair, and plain *shendyt,* but no uraeus. Front of *nemes,* forehead hair, and jawline show signs of reworking. Traces of beard remain.

Preserved through mid-thighs. Remains of tenon (Dia: c. 7 cm) atop head for attachment of lost attribute. Forehead damaged and nose missing. Enigmatic objects in hands at sides. Fragmentary back pillar extends to neck and may have continued partway up *nemes.* Top perhaps conical or triangular.

Bissing 1914, nos. 103–104 (early Ptolemaic). Michalowski 1935, 73–88, fig. 6, pls. 1–2 (Augustus). *ESLP* 1960, 177 (Marc Antony?). G. Grimm 1975, 3, 19, cat. no. 14, pls. 16–19 (Marc Antony?). Wildung and Grimm 1978, cat. no. 130 (Marc Antony?). Strocka 1980, 179, 180. H. Jucker 1981, 676–677, pls. 10–12: 8a–e (Marc Antony). Kiss 1984, 31–32, 37, 126, figs. 25–26 (Augustus). Heinen 1995, pls. 4–5 (Marc Antony?). Bianchi 1996, 206–207 (lists Mendes as provenance; perhaps Marc Antony). *Gloire* 1998, 285, cat. no. 229 (Marc Antony). G. Grimm 1998, 140–141, 143, fig. 129a–b (Marc Antony). Kiss 1998, 177 (Octavian). PM 8 (1999), 248, no. 800-950-100 (probably Augustus or Marc Antony). Tiradritti 1999, 390 (40–30 B.C.). Hölbl 2000, 7, 13, fig. 4 (Marc Antony as Osiris). Walker and Higgs 2001, 172–173, cat. no. 171 (Ptolemy XV?).

D15. Head of king. Paris, Musée du Louvre E 8061

[Figure 138]

Attributed to Ptolemy IX, second rule, 88–80 B.C.

Dark stone. H: 6.8 cm, FaceH: 3.4 cm.

Provenance not known.

Well under life-size. Plain blue crown with uraeus. Back pillar: Elongated trapezoid top nearly reaches top of blue crown.

INSCRIPTION: A few hieroglyphs on back pillar: sky sign, and below it, sun disk with two pendant uraei holding *ankh*-signs.

ESLP 1960, 90–92, 134, 177, cat. no. 73, pl. 69, figs. 177–180 (Nectanebo I). Aldred 1962, 209 (later Ptolemy, Ptolemy V). H. W. Müller 1970, 89–90, 92–94, 97–99, figs. 1–2, 9 (Nectanebo I). Krug 1978, 23 (Bernard V. Bothmer: very late Ptolemy). Parlasca 1978, 26 (Ptolemy X). *CE* 1988, 130, 143, 194, 228, 249, cat. no. 48 (Nectanebo I). Myśliwiec 1988, 71, 79, 91 (Nectanebo I). Josephson 1997a, 13–17, 45, pl. 4c (Ptolemy X?). Josephson 1997b, 14–15, fig. 15 (Ptolemy X). PM 8 (1999), 208, no. 800-942-550 (late Ptolemaic). Walker and Higgs 2001, 62, cat. no. 30 (Ptolemy X?).

D16. Face of king. Staatlichen Sammlung Ägyptischer Kunst München ÄS 5339

[Figures 139–140]

Attributed to Ptolemy IX, second rule, 88–80 B.C.

Plaster. H: 28.0 cm, FaceH: c. 14.5 cm.

Provenance not known.

Life-size. Has partial crown without uraeus, hollowed out in back. No grid lines visible. Face noticeably crooked: left eye and left side of mouth are higher than counterparts on right. Many small folds around small eyes, including slight bags underneath, and perhaps fat fold at top of neck. Large crack on left side of face repaired. Chips on right eyebrow, nose tip, and both cheeks. Right ear missing.

H. W. Müller 1970, 90–99, figs. 5–8 (Nectanebo I). Parlasca 1978, 26, fig. 36 (Ptolemy X). Altenmüller and Hornbostel 1982, 86–87, cat. no. 36 (Nectanebo I). *CE* 1988, 130, 143. Myśliwiec 1988, 71, 79 (Nectanebo I). A. Grimm, Schoske, and Wildung 1997, 76–77, cat. no. 58 (Ptolemy X, c. 100 B.C.). Josephson 1997a, 13–17, 45, pl. 5b (Ptolemy X?). PM 8 (1999), 161, no. 800-871-250 (Nectanebo I or Ptolemy X).

D17. Standing king. London, British Museum EA 1209

[Figures 141–142]

Attributed to Ptolemy IX, second rule, 88–80 B.C.

Granite. H: 92.5 cm, HeadH: 14.5 cm, FaceH: 10.5 cm.

Provenance not known. Oft-cited find spot of Athribis (Tell Atrib) is not assured. Sculpture was acquired from Alexandrian art dealer.

Under life-size. Unfinished. Plain *nemes,* uraeus, and plain *shendyt.* Preserved through ankles. Roughly incised marks on *nemes* pigtail and front of wings. Head proportionally large relative to body. Very full face has heavy chin with dimple. Uraeus and nose damaged. Enigmatic objects in hands at sides. Back pillar: Square top reaches armpit level. Closely spaced, parallel, diagonal incisions on edges of lateral sides of pillar.

The British Museum, *A Guide to the Egyptian Galleries (Sculpture)* (London, 1909), 243–244 (after Dynasty 26). PM 4 (1934), 66 (Athribis, exact find spot unknown). I. Jucker 1975, 23, pl. 9: 1–2 (Ptolemy IV). Russmann et al. 2001, 257–258, cat. no. 143 (Ptolemy IV?).

D18. Head of king. New Haven, Peabody Museum of Natural History, Yale University YPM.264259 (= Yale University Art Gallery 4.1.1953)

[Figures 143–144]

Attributed to Ptolemy X.

Dark stone. H: 37.0 cm, HeadH: 26.0 cm, FaceH: 14.0 cm.

Provenance not known. Formerly collection of Victor Clay Barringer, judge in Alexandria in late nineteenth century.

Life-size. Plain *nemes,* uraeus, and Greek forehead hair. *Nemes* frontlet is roughened, perhaps because it was originally gilded(?). Neck has Adam's apple. Significant damage to uraeus, forehead, right eye, nose, mouth, and chin. Inlaid eyes missing. Upward curve of break in back indicates former presence of back slab or pillar.

Needler 1949, 133–136, pl. 25: 3–4 (second half of third century B.C.?). *ESLP* 1960, 131–133, 148, 177, cat. no. 103, pl. 96, figs. 257–258 (c. 250–200 B.C.). Kyrieleis 1975, 37–38, 44, 136, 170,

C 16, pl. 28: 1–3 (Ptolemy III). Strocka 1980, 180 (questions third-century B.C. date). Kiss 1984, 35, 37, 43, 129, figs. 36–37 (Augustus). Massner 1986, 65–67, pls. 10: 3, 11: 2 and 4 (Claudius). Scott 1986, 170–171, cat. no. 96 (c. 250–25 B.C.). *CE* 1988, 147–148, 157, 249, cat. no. 52 (third century B.C.). Smith 1988, 87, 93, 169, cat. no. 70, pl. 46: 1 (Ptolemy II, III, or IV?). Bothmer 1996, 223–224, fig. 32 (Ptolemy III?). PM 8 (1999), 207, no. 800-942-501 (probably Ptolemy III). Capriotti Vittozzi 2000, 45, pl. 2: 3.

D19. Diademed royal male head. Milan, Museo Archeologico E.0.9.4075

[Figures 145–146]

Attributed to Ptolemy X.

Limestone. H: 21.0 cm, HeadH: 16.3 cm, FaceH: 11.6 cm.

From Medinet Madi. Excavated by Achille Vogliano in refuse heap in Middle Kingdom portion of Renenutet temple (Vogliano 1937, 3).

Under life-size. Has plain diadem tied at back, two streamers falling down neck. No uraeus. Wavy Greek hair covers head. Hair on left back and on either side of nape unfinished. Crack runs vertically up left profile and diagonally across top of head to back right. No back pillar remains.

Vogliano 1937, 3 (head mentioned only as "frammenti di statue"). Vogliano 1938a, 30–31, cat. no. 7 (king or athlete?). Vogliano 1942, pl. 20 (Ptolemaic prince). Smith 1988, 181, residue cat. no. 13 (a Ptolemy?). Leone 1995 (Ptolemy VIII, IX, or XII).

D20. Fragmentary king. Alexandria, Graeco-Roman Museum P. 12072

[Figure 147]

Attributed to Ptolemy X.

Gray granite. H: 65.0 cm, HeadH: 27.3 cm, FaceH: 18.6 cm.

From Sidi-Biche sud, an eastern suburb of Alexandria, toward Canopus, according to Graeco-Roman Museum Journal d'Entrée. Walker and Higgs (2001, 60) list the find spot as Miami area, slightly farther east, and provide a few additional details. Entered museum collection in 1985.

Fragment (head through chest) of life-size king with Greek forehead hair, plain *nemes,* and uraeus, possibly from standing statue. Ears, nose, and lips damaged. Right arm broken off at biceps and left arm at shoulder. Back pillar: Square top reaches armpit level.

Smith 1988, 96 n. 65 (Ptolemies IX–X). Stanwick 1992 (Ptolemy X?). Kiss 1995, 59, figs. 8–9 (Roman). Smith 1996, 209–210 (Ptolemies IX–X). G. Grimm 1998, 124, fig. 119 (Ptolemy X?). Rogge 1999, 90 (Ptolemy X?). Walker and Higgs 2001, 60–61, cat. no. 27 (Ptolemies IX–X).

D21. Head of king. The Manchester Museum 4816

[No figure]

Late second or early first century B.C.

Limestone. H: 24.1 cm.

From Triphis temple at Wannina (Petrie 1909, 14). Information on temple: Di. Arnold 1999, 10, 206, plan 5.

Wears plain *nemes* and uraeus. Only front of life-size(?) head preserved. No Greek hair or other hellenizations. Photos published by Myśliwiec (1973, 43, fig. 4) show more damage to face since excavation publication: right eye and frontlet above it are missing. No back pillar remains.

Petrie 1909, 14, pl. 45 (Ptolemy IX). Bissing 1914, nos. 103–104, note 7 (Ptolemy IX). Parlasca 1967, 179 n. 38 (doubtful of Physkon attribution). Myśliwiec 1973, 43, fig. 4 (Ptolemy IX).

D22. Standing king. Berlin, Ägyptisches Museum 14764

[Figure 148]

Late second or early first century B.C.

Dark stone. *Top part through knees:* H: 66.5 cm, HeadH: 15.2 cm (top partially missing), FaceH: 9.3 cm. *Bottom part below knees, including base:* H: 39.8 cm, Base: H: 6.5 cm, W: 19.0 cm, D: 34.9 cm.

Provenance not known. Oft-cited provenance of Hadrian's Villa at Tivoli is speculative (Raeder 1983, 181, no. IV 2).

Under life-size. Plain *nemes,* uraeus, and plain *shendyt.* Circular roughened area atop head indicates additional element, possibly double crown, broken off. Lower part of figure shows hem of long skirt, and although matching in proportions, it obviously does not belong to original statue. Enigmatic objects in hands at sides. Head and right shoulder broken off and repaired. Back pillar: Tip of triangular or trapezoidal top is now broken off at top of head.

PM 7 (1951), 416–417 (Hadrian's Villa at Tivoli and later Palazzo Sciarra in Rome; Late Period). Roullet 1972, 105, cat. no. 166, pl. 138, fig. 192 (Ptolemaic?). Raeder 1983, 181, no. IV 2. Priese 1991, 190, cat. no. 113 (Ptolemy III?). *Gloire* 1998, 207, cat. no. 153 (Ptolemy III?).

D23. Head of king. Bloomington, Indiana University Art Museum 59.44

[Figure 149]

Late second or early first century B.C.

Granite. H: 24.8 cm, HeadH: 21.0 cm, FaceH: 14 cm.

Provenance not known. Gift of Frederick Stafford.

Near life-size. Plain *nemes* and uraeus. Left top of head and nose missing. Remains of shoulders in back and slight horizontal thrust of *nemes* pigtail break indicate that head is from sphinx (despite H. W. Müller 1959, 7).

H. W. Müller 1959, 7, cat. no. 9, pl. 4 (first century B.C.). PM 8 (1999), 211, no. 800-942-700 (late Ptolemaic).

D24. Head of king. Alexandria, Graeco-Roman Museum 23844

[Figures 150–151]

Late second or early first century B.C.

Granite. H: 25.4 cm, HeadH: 21.2 cm, FaceH: 13.4 cm.

From Canopus (Breccia 1932, 17–18, no. 12). Entered museum collection in 1927.

Life-size. Plain *nemes* with large, circular uraeus loops, probably from sphinx, given remains of right shoulder at back. Left *nemes* wing mostly gone, including left back of head.

Breccia 1932, 17–18, no. 12, pl. 9: 34 (second or first century B.C.). Needler 1949, 131 n. 2, 132 n. 3 (late Ptolemaic). H. W. Müller 1961, 27 n. 12 (Roman?). H. W. Müller 1969, 61 (Roman).

D25. Head of king. Madrid, Museo Arqueológico Nacional 2015

[Figure 152]

Late second or early first century B.C.

Granite. H: 26.0 cm.

Possibly from eastern suburbs of Alexandria toward Canopus (López 1963, 211). Found in nineteenth century.

Life-size. Plain *nemes* and uraeus. Inner edges of upper and lower eyelids recut, but outlines of corneas not altered. Nose mostly gone. No back pillar remains.

ESLP 1960, 162 (late Ptolemaic). López 1963, 211–213, pl. 1: 1–2 (Ptolemy II or III?). Die 1992, 104 (as pedestal 35; Ptolemy II or III).

D26. Standing queen. Paris, Musée du Louvre E 13102

[No figure]

Attributed to Cleopatra III.

Steatite(?) H: 36.5 cm.

Provenance not known.

Well(?) under life-size. Has loopless triple uraeus, echeloned tripartite wig, and sheath dress. Preserved from modius through hips. Uraeus modius has hole for added attribute. Left arm under breasts holds lily scepter. Right arm flat at side. Inlaid eyes missing. Wig, nose, and chin damaged. Back pillar: Square top ends at armpits.

Walker and Higgs 2001, 163, cat. no. 162 (Cleopatra VII).

GROUP E: PTOLEMY XII, CLEOPATRA VII, PTOLEMY XV

E1. Head of king from dyad. Alexandria, Graeco-Roman Museum 11275

[Figures 153–154]

Attributed to Ptolemy XII.

Granite. H: 130.0 cm, FaceH: c. 61.0 cm.

From Hadra, an eastern district of Alexandria. Unearthed near a sizable, poorly documented structure about 1840 by English consul A. C. Harris along with E2.

Colossal royal male head from standing dyad, with goddess (E2) on his right. He has Greek forehead hair and wears plain *nemes* with uraeus, originally surmounted by *hm-hm*-crown. On left lappet, top of *heqa*-scepter is carved in relief. Most of *hm-hm* and uraeus broken off, nose smashed, and lips badly abraded. Much of right *nemes* wing restored. Left leg, including part of plain *shendyt,* also preserved (Alexandria, Graeco-Roman Museum G. 304; 266.0 cm long). Various fragments indicate that dyad was supported by back slab that likely reached at least as high as tops of headdresses of figures.

PM 4 (1934), 3 (Alexandria; not attributed). Van de Walle 1952, 29–31, pl. 7 (Marc Antony(?). *ESLP* 1960, 132–133 (Ptolemy VI?). Kyrieleis 1975, 37, 73–74, 120, 175, H 5, pl. 61: 1–2 (second or first century B.C.). Kiss 1984, 22–23, 119, fig. 3 (Ptolemy XII?). Smith 1988, 87, 97, 171, cat. no. 81, pl. 50: 1, 4–5 (second or first century B.C.?). Tkaczow 1993, 196–197, cat. no. 29 (Ptolemaic). El-Fattah and Gallo 1998, 12 n. 16 (Ptolemy VI?). Kiss 1998, 173–174 (Ptolemy XII).

E2. Goddess from dyad. Musée royal de Mariemont B. 505 (= E. 49)

[Figures 155–156]

Attributed to reign of Ptolemy XII.

Granite. H: 300.0 cm, HeadH: 90.0 cm, FaceH: 62.0 cm. Hands: length: 60.0 cm, W: 30.0 cm.

From Hadra, an eastern district of Alexandria. Unearthed near a sizable, poorly documented structure about 1840 by English consul A. C. Harris along with E1.

Fragment of colossal goddess, preserved from partial Hathor headdress through half of left upper arm. From a dyad with king (E1) to her left. Wears tripartite, echeloned wig, vulture cap, and uraeus modius with Hathor headdress. Small hole in middle of forehead may have held vulture head in another material. Face abraded and nose broken off. Semicircular neckline of garment at base of neck. Pair of clasped hands also preserved.

PM 4 (1934), 3 (Alexandria; not attributed). Van de Walle 1952, 29–31, pls. 6–7 (Cleopatra VII?). *ESLP* 1960, 132–133 (Cleopatra II?). Kyrieleis 1975, 119–120, 185, M 11 (second or first century B.C.).

Smith 1988, 87, 97, 171, cat. no. 81, pl. 50: 1–3 (second or first century B.C.?). Bruwier 1989 (Cleopatra II or III). Derriks 1990, cat. no. 40 (Cleopatra II?). Tkaczow 1993, 196–197, cat. no. 29 (Ptolemaic). El-Fattah and Gallo 1998, 12 n. 16 (Cleopatra II or III?).

E3. Standing statue found with Ptolemy XII inscription, c. 55 B.C. Alexandria, Graeco-Roman Museum 22979

[Figures 157–159]

Limestone. H: 211.4 cm, HeadH: c. 30.0 cm (chin damaged), FaceH: c. 19.0 cm (chin damaged). Base: H: 24.0 cm, W: 54.0 cm, D: 78.0 cm. Based on excavation photographs, Bastianini and Gallazzi (1989, 202) estimate that an inscribed block, possibly part of the statue's base, measured: H: 45.0 cm, W: 90.0 cm, D: 45.0 cm.

From Tebtunis. Found in situ at end of sphinx-lined dromos of Soknebtunis temple. Now-lost limestone block with Greek inscription for Ptolemy XII, which may have belonged to statue's base, found nearby (Bastianini and Gallazzi 1989).

Over life-size. Banded *nemes*, uraeus, and pleated *shendyt*. Rectangular hole cut into top of *nemes* for insertion of attribute. Preserved from top of head through attached statue base. Chest, lengths of both arms, and statue base are damaged. Statue broken at neck, waist, and knees, and mended. Enigmatic objects in hands at sides. Back pillar: Much damaged, but appears to have ended in square(?) top at pectoral level.

INSCRIPTION: Five lines of Greek on front of block, which may be from statue's base: (Statue of) King Ptolemy, great Theos Neos Dionusos, Philopator, and Philadelphos (set up) year 16, 12(th day) of Pharmouthis (April 15, 55 B.C.).

ESLP 1960, 171 (Ptolemy XII?). Parlasca 1978, 26, figs. 37–38 (Ptolemy X). Bastianini and Gallazzi 1989 (Ptolemy XII). Stanwick 1992, 138–139, figs. 8a–b (Ptolemy XII).

E4. Fragmentary standing king inscribed for Ptolemies XII–XV. New York, Metropolitan Museum of Art 1981.224.1

[Figure 160]

Basalt. H: 93.0 cm. Scale slightly smaller than E5.

Provenance not known. Purchase, Lila Acheson Wallace Gift and Rogers Fund, 1981.

Slightly under life-size standing statue of first century Ptolemy in *nemes* (indicated by pigtail in back) and plain *shendyt*. Preserved from abdomen through left thigh and right calf. Likely held enigmatic objects in both hands at sides. Back pillar: Square top ends below armpits.

INSCRIPTION: Hieroglyphs on back pillar contain Horus, throne, and birth names of a late Ptolemy, with identical throne name on belt. Names could belong to Ptolemy XII, XIII, XIV, or XV.

Russmann et al. n.d., 8–9 (80–30 B.C.). PM 8 (1999), 195, no. 800-926-600 (Ptolemy XII or XV). Milleker 2000, 86–87, 207, figs. 64–65 (80–30 B.C.).

E5. Fragmentary standing king. New York, Metropolitan Museum of Art 1981.224.2

[No figure]

First century B.C.

Basalt. H: 79.0 cm. Scale slightly larger than E4.

Provenance not known. Purchase, Lila Acheson Wallace Gift and Rogers Fund, 1981.

Slightly under life-size standing king in *nemes* (evidenced by plain lappets) and plain *shendyt*. Preserved from right shoulder through knees. Appears unfinished because front wrap edge of *shendyt* is not carved. Enigmatic objects in hands at sides. Back pillar: Square top ends below armpits.

Russmann et al. n.d., 7–8 (332–30 B.C.). PM 8 (1999), 197, no. 800-932-610 (Ptolemaic). Milleker 2000, 86–87, 207, figs. 66–67 (Ptolemaic).

E6. Head of king. Turin, Museo Egizio Suppl. 18350

[Figures 161–162]

Attributed to Ptolemy XII.

Granite. H: 15.0 cm.

Provenance not known.

Under life-size. Has thin, plain diadem, but no uraeus. Curly Greek hair covers head. Nose missing. Back pillar: No remains?

Kyrieleis 1975, 16, 19–23, 37, 167, B 7 (as Munich private collection), pl. 12: 3–4 (Ptolemy II?). Curto 1984, 296, 358. Curto, Donadoni, and Leospo 1989, 180, 183–184, fig. 272 (early Ptolemaic).

E7. Standing king. Paris, Musée du Louvre A 28 (N 28)

[Figure 163]

Attributed to Ptolemy XII.

Dark stone. H: 82.0 cm, HeadH: 21.2 cm, FaceH: 13.6 cm.

Provenance not known.

Near life-size. Wears plain *nemes*, uraeus, and plain *shendyt*. Irregular bumps atop *nemes* may indicate former presence of additional crown. Preserved from top of head through mid-thighs. Nose missing. Arms at sides. Left forearm and part of upper arm broken off. Back pillar: Conical top blends into back of *nemes*.

ESLP 1960, 162 (late Ptolemaic). *CE* 1988, 156–157, 189, cat. no. 59 (first century B.C.). Berman and Letellier 1996, 88–89, 98, cat. no. 28 (first century B.C.). Josephson 1997a, 20. Pfrommer 1999, 12–14, fig. 15 (second or first century B.C.?). PM 8 (1999), 197, no. 800-932-700 (late Ptolemaic). Walker and Higgs 2001, 54–55, cat. no. 20 (mid- to late second century B.C.).

E8. Head of king. Alexandria, Graeco-Roman Museum 425

[Figure 164]

Attributed to Ptolemy XII.

Dark stone. H: 28.2 cm, HeadH: 23.2 cm, FaceH: 13.9 cm.

From Kafr Dawar, about 20 km south of Alexandria, according to Graeco-Roman Museum Journal d'Entrée. Gift of A. Lascaris.

Life-size. Plain *nemes* and uraeus. Uraeus badly abraded and nose mostly gone. No back pillar remains.

Botti 1900, 354, no. 26 (not attributed). *ESLP* 1960, 162 (late Ptolemaic). H. W. Müller 1961, 27 n. 12 (Roman?).

E9. Bust of king. Birmingham Museums and Art Gallery B.67'71

[Figures 165–166]

Attributed to Ptolemy XII.

Plaster. H: 23.6 cm.

From North Saqqara. Part of cache of plaster objects found in clean sand outside Mastaba 3518 at sacred animal necropolis (Emery 1970, 10–11).

Well under life-size. Has double crown, but no uraeus. Slight damage to nose, lips, and cheeks, but virtually intact. Details of crown's tabs, ears, and nose are not fully worked out. Faint, vertical, red(?) line runs down front center of crown. Base is marked with irregular incisions and smoothing marks. Bottom slants upward, right to left. Hastings 1997, 62, cat. no. 232: "Eyes are outlined in black."

Emery 1970, 10. Hastings 1997, 62, cat. no. 232, pl. 61 (Late Period).

E10. Head of king. Brooklyn Museum of Art 37.1489E

[Figures 167–168]

Attributed to Ptolemy XII.

Limestone. H: 36.3 cm, HeadH (with crown): 33.0 cm, FaceH: 9.6 cm.

Provenance not known. Formerly Dr. Henry Abbott collection. Reported Thebes provenance cannot be relied upon because Dr. Abbott built his collection via purchases from antiquities dealers, though Upper Egyptian provenance is plausible based on the attributes and sculptural style.

Under life-size. Wears double crown, diadem, uraeus, and false beard. Three folds of draped costume preserved on left shoulder. Tied ends of diadem carved in relief on either side of back pillar. Front of false beard broken off. Back pillar: Elongated triangular top reaches top of double crown.

Catalogue . . . Henry Abbott . . . 1854, 72, cat. no. 1115 (not attributed). *Catalogue . . . Historical Society* 1915, 68, cat. no. 1111 (not attributed). PM 8 (1999), 202, no. 800-942-158 (probably late Ptolemaic or Roman).

E11. Fragmentary queen. Alexandria, Graeco-Roman Museum 3222

[Figure 169]

First century B.C.

Black granite. H: 53.6 cm, HeadH: 22.4 cm, FaceH: 13.3 cm.

From Fouah (south of Rosetta), according to Graeco-Roman Museum Journal d'Entrée.

Fragment (head through top of abdomen) of life-size queen wearing plain diadem with loopless uraeus over unpolished, echeloned, tripartite wig, and probably modius on top of head. Wears fringed garment, knotted at center of chest, over plain undergarment. Uraeus, nose, and lips damaged. Back of left shoulder missing. Back pillar: Reached beyond top of head, and now broken off. Elongated, smooth, vertical depression in middle of pillar.

ESLP 1960, 135 (240–200 B.C.). Capriotti Vittozzi 1998, 64–65. Walker and Higgs 2001, 169, cat. no. 168 (first century B.C.).

E12. Standing queen. Leiden, Rijksmuseum van Oudheden F 1938/7.20

[Figure 170]

First century B.C.

Limestone. H: 83.0 cm, HeadH: 11.2 cm, FaceH: 6.7 cm.

Provenance not known.

Under life-size. Has echeloned, tripartite wig, combination crown of Arsinoe II (including vulture cap), and double uraeus. Preserved from crown through partial shins. Right side particularly abraded. Figure faces left and is not perpendicular to back pillar. No indication of garment. Left hand clenched at side (right hand broken off). Vulture head(?) on forehead and nose broken. Thick back pillar reached beyond top of crown, and is now broken off.

Quaegebeur 1983, 109–124, figs. 1–4 (Arsinoe II, early Ptolemaic?). *CE* 1988, 180–181, cat. no. 72 (Cleopatra II or III?). Quaegebeur 1998, 78–79, 103, cat. no. 77 (third or second century B.C.). PM 8 (1999), 998–999, no. 801-805-205 (Arsinoe II, Cleopatra II, III, or VII).

E13. Head of queen. Brooklyn Museum of Art 71.12

[Figures 171–172]

Attributed to Cleopatra VII.

Marble(?). H: 13.7 cm, HeadH: 11.0 cm, FaceH: 7.2 cm.

Provenance not known.

Under life-size. Has single tier of corkscrew locks around head, plain diadem, and loopless triple uraeus. Additional attribute on top of head broken off; it was not a modius, because right and back edges of break are straight lines. Fat folds on neck. Inlaid eyes missing. Back pillar: Square top surface slants upward slightly as it extends over back of head, apparently to join now-broken-off attribute.

Die Weltkunst 40 (1970), 1082 (dealer advertisement; Berenice II). "Additions to the Museum Collections, Department of Ancient Art," *BMA* 12 (1970–1971), 20–21 (third century B.C.). Bothmer 1996, 218, fig. 12 (Ptolemaic). PM 8 (1999), 1009, no. 801-809-040 (early Ptolemaic). Walker and Higgs 2001, 164, cat. no. 163 (Cleopatra VII).

E14. Standing queen. New York, Metropolitan Museum of Art 89.2.660

[Figure 173]

Attributed to Cleopatra VII.

Marble(?). H: 62.2 cm, HeadH: 10.7 cm, FaceH: 6.1 cm.

Provenance not known. Gift of Joseph W. Drexel, 1889.

Under life-size. Has single tier of corkscrew locks around head, plain diadem, and triple uraeus with loops. Preserved from top of head through just above ankles. Wears draped costume knotted between breasts and carries single cornucopia. Additional attribute atop head broken off. Right hand flat at side. Back pillar: Reached beyond top of head, and is now broken off.

INSCRIPTION: Cleopatra cartouche on right biceps is likely a modern addition. Typically, such cartouches would be written from a viewer's right to left when placed on a statue's right shoulder (Kozloff and Bryan 1992, 173, fig. 14a). In addition, a shoulder cartouche would be highly unusual for a Ptolemaic royal statue (a fragmentary wooden queen in a private collection has a Cleopatra cartouche on its right shoulder, but the authenticity of the work is questionable; photos appear in the Corpus of Late Egyptian Sculpture).

ESLP 1960, 126, 135, 145–147, 159, 160, 167, 170, 177, 181, cat. no. 113, pl. 105, figs. 281–283 (Cleopatra II, c. 170–160 B.C.). Kyrieleis 1975, 118, 183, M 1, pl. 101: 1 (second or first century B.C.). Quaegebeur 1983, 113 (perhaps Cleopatra II?). *CE* 1988, 176 (Ptolemaic). Capriotti Vittozzi 1995, 431–433 (likely Cleopatra I). Svenson 1995, 87–88, 228, cat. no. 94, pl. 38 (Cleopatra I?). PM 8 (1999), 1000, no. 801-805-235 (Ptolemaic). Walker and Higgs 2001, 165, cat. no. 164 (Cleopatra VII).

E15. Head of king. Bologna, University Collection, Museo Civico Archeologico KS 1803

[Figures 174–175]

Attributed to Ptolemy XV.

Gabbro. H: 12.0 cm, FaceH: c. 6.3 cm.

Provenance not known.

Under life-size. Has uraeus and narrow diadem decorated with diagonal incisions. Wavy Greek hair covers head. Back pillar: Trapezoid top reaches midway up back of head.

ESLP 1960, 177 (c. 60–30 B.C.). Kyrieleis 1975, 75, 177, H 19 (Ptolemaic). Pernigotti 1980, 76–77, cat. no. 40, pls. 111–112 (mid-first century B.C.). Kiss 1984, 47, 49, 143, figs. 81–82 (Nero). Govi et al. 1990, 199, cat. no. 152 (mid-first century B.C.). Bothmer 1996, 218, fig. 11 (c. 60–30 B.C.). PM 8 (1999), 201, no. 800-942-150 (late Ptolemaic).

E16. Standing king. Brooklyn Museum of Art 54.117

[Figures 176–177]

First century B.C.

Attributed to Ptolemy XV.

Brown graywacke. H: 30.2 cm, HeadH: 7.9 cm, FaceH: 5.1 cm.

Provenance not known.

Well under life-size. Has plain diadem, uraeus (apparently without loops, though area is damaged), and plain *shendyt*. Wavy Greek hair covers head. Preserved through midthighs. Diadem, like hair, has rough surface. Drilled chin dimple. Inlaid eyes missing and nose smashed. Enigmatic objects in hands at sides. Back pillar: Trapezoid top ends midway up back of head.

Cooney 1956, 19–20, cat. no. 22, pls. 39–40 (c. 80–30 B.C.). *ESLP* 1960, 133, 176–177, 179, cat. no. 135, pl. 127, figs. 338–339 (c. 60–30 B.C.). Kyrieleis 1975, 75, 177, H 18 (Ptolemaic). *CE* 1988, 249 (Ptolemaic). Bothmer 1996, 223–225, fig. 34 (Ptolemy XV?). PM 8 (1999), 196, no. 800-932-070 (late Ptolemaic).

E17. Royal male head. Athens, National Archaeological Museum ANE 1632

[No figure]

Attributed to Ptolemy XV.

Dark stone. H: 16.0 cm, HeadH: 13.0 cm, FaceH: 10.0 cm.

Provenance not known?

Under life-size. Has plain diadem, but no uraeus. Wavy Greek hair covers head. Square hole and flattened area atop head for added attribute, perhaps double crown. Face well preserved. No back pillar remains. I am grateful to Bernard V. Bothmer for calling my attention to this head.

No bibliography.

E18. Head of king. New York, Harmon Fine Arts/ Leonard Stern

[Figure 178]

Attributed to Ptolemy XV.

Limestone. H: 23.0 cm.

Provenance not known. Reportedly from Fayoum.

Near life-size. Wears *kausia,* uraeus, and plain diadem tied in back. Wavy Greek hair under *kausia* at front, sides, and back. Inlaid eyes and eyebrows gone. Nose, chin, and surface of back pillar broken off. Back pillar: Elliptical top reaches partway up rear of head.

Bianchi 1992a (Alexander the Great). Bothmer 1996, 219–220, fig. 17 (mid-first century B.C.). Josephson 1997a, 19–21, pl. 7c–d (Ptolemy Philadelphos?, son of Cleopatra VII and Marc Antony). G. Grimm 1998, 143, 145, fig. 131 (Caesarion?). Pfrommer 1999, 140–142, fig. 193 (Caesarion or a son of Cleopatra VII and Marc Antony). PM 8 (1999), 217, no. 800-942-980 (late Ptolemaic).

E19. Head of king. Alexandria, Graeco-Roman Museum 28163

[Figures 179–180]

Attributed to Ptolemy XV.

Granite. H: 17.5 cm, HeadH: 14.7 cm, FaceH: 8.9 cm.

From Canopus (Breccia 1932, 17–18).

Under life-size. Plain *nemes,* uraeus, and Greek forehead hair. Nose, lips, and chin very damaged. No back pillar remains.

Breccia 1932, 17–18, pl. 9: 33 (second or first century B.C.). Kyrieleis 1975, 75, 177, H 20, pl. 67: 4 (Ptolemaic). Stanwick 2000 (Ptolemy XV).

E20. Head of king. Alexandria, Graeco-Roman Museum P. 1798

[Figures 181–182]

Attributed to Ptolemy XV.

Limestone. H: 30.4 cm, HeadH: 25.6 cm, FaceH: 16.5 cm.

From Ras el-Soda, an eastern suburb of Alexandria toward Canopus. According to museum Journal d'Entrée, head was found by chance at site and came from a sphinx (though head shows no such indications). Entered museum collection in 1939.

Life-size. Plain *nemes* and uraeus(?) with Greek forehead hair and beard. Square hole (2.7 cm × 3.0 cm × c. 5 cm deep) on top of head for addition of another headdress. Right half of face obliterated. Mouth and nose completely gone. No back pillar remains.

Stanwick 2000 (Ptolemy XV).

E21. Head of king. New York, private collection

[Figure 183]

First century B.C.

Granite. H: 31.0 cm, HeadH: 23.0 cm, FaceH: 15.0 cm.

Provenance not known.

Life-size. Has plain *nemes* and uraeus. Remains of shoulder on left back indicate that head is from sphinx. Top of head abraded. Uraeus, nose, and chin broken off.

PM 8 (1999), 216, no. 800-942-902 (mid-Ptolemaic).

E22. Dendera treasure horde. Now in Cairo Museum

[Figures 184–186]

Mostly made of precious metals. *Silver sphinx (JE 46392),* H: 15.8 cm (with base), HeadH: 5.5 cm, FaceH: 3.0 cm, W: 7.5 cm, D: 26.0 cm. *Gilded stone sphinx (JE 46393),* H: 24.0 cm (with base), HeadH: 5.7 cm, FaceH: 3.5 cm, W: 12.8 cm, D: 43.0 cm. *Gilded silver, seated goddess (JE 46382),* H: 40.0 cm, HeadH: 5.5 cm, FaceH: 2.8 cm.

From Dendera. Found in 1918 near sacred lake within enclosure wall to southwest of Hathor temple (Cauville 1987, 116).

A collection of objects from a temple treasure, including statues of deities, ritual vessels, ritual instruments, jewelry, coins, mirrors, and royal male sphinxes, both with a banded *nemes* and uraeus. Well under life-size silver sphinx (JE 46392) has tenon atop head, formerly inlaid eyes, and broad collar. Well under life-size gilded stone sphinx (JE 46393) has faintly incised Middle Kingdom royal titulary on chest and between forepaws. Well under life-size seated goddess (JE 46382) has double crown, diadem, uraeus, echeloned, tripartite wig, broad collar, and sheath dress. Her clenched right hand on lap once held a scepter(?), as indicated by centered hole in fist, whereas left hand is flat on lap. Inlaid eyes preserved, but seat missing. Abdalla (1995, 22–26) shows 48 Cairo Museum acquisition numbers for the horde, and provides the most complete published list.

Cauville 1987, 116, pls. 15–19. Abdalla 1995, 22–26.

GROUP F: PTOLEMAIC, DATE UNCERTAIN

F1. Fragmentary standing king. Berlin, Ägyptisches Museum 8810

[Figure 187]

Inscribed for Ptolemy XII?

Black granite. H: 59.5 cm, W: 25.8 cm, D: 36.2 cm.

Possibly from Ptah temple at Memphis, because fragment was purchased in nearby Giza in 1886 and because back pillar's hieroglyphic inscription mentions Memphite form of Ptah (*Ptḥ rsj jnb.f,* "Ptah-south-of-his-wall").

Near-life-size fragment of standing king in draped costume. Preserved from upper thighs through ankles. Back pillar: Extent and top not preserved.

INSCRIPTION: Three columns of hieroglyphs on back pillar, containing the birth name of a Ptolemy.

Ausführliches 1899, 324 (Ptolemy [IX] Soter II). Bothmer 1959, 107 n. 26 (Ptolemy XII). Bianchi 1976b, 71–76, cat. no. V A, pl. 26: 35, 27: 36 (Ptolemy IV). PM 3², 2 (1981), 864 (Mitrahineh; Ptolemy XII). *CE* 1988, 67.

F2. Falcon statue with standing male. Edfu, in front of pylon of Horus temple

[Figure 188]

First century B.C.?

Granite. H: c. 210 cm (with restored base). H of human figure: 79.0 cm.

From Edfu. Now placed on left side of entranceway through Horus temple pylon decorated under Ptolemy XII. Published record lacks documentation that this was original placement.

Over-life-size falcon with plain double crown standing protectively over an under-life-size standing figure of king(?) in draped garment. Figure may have had hair and diadem (definitely not a *nemes,* or red, white, or double crown). Right arm held at side. Left arm held over abdomen. Statue abraded. Feet and base of falcon partially broken off and restored.

PM 6 (1939), 121 (Edfu, entrance of Ptolemy XII pylon; not attributed). *CE* 1988, 67 (nature of figure is equivocal).

F3. Queen's headdress. Petrie Museum of Egyptian Archaeology, University College London 14521

[Figure 189]

Ptolemaic Period.

Limestone. H: 51.3 cm, W: 21.5 cm, D: 18.7 cm.

From Koptos. Excavated by W. M. Flinders Petrie between second and third pylons of Min temple.

Headdress from statue: Hathor horns framing sun disk with three uraei, the whole surmounted by two feathers. Top horizontal surface of headdress not polished. Back pillar: Square top reaches top of feathers.

INSCRIPTION: Two columns of hieroglyphs on back pillar contain royal titles associated with Arsinoe II and later queens.

Petrie 1896, 21–22, pl. 26: 3 (probably Arsinoe II). *LdR* 4 (1916), 241, I (Arsinoe II). PM 5 (1937), 123 (found between second and third pylons, Ptolemaic temple; Arsinoe II). Quaegebeur 1971, 209, cat. no. 4 (Arsinoe II). H. Stewart 1983, 38, cat. no. 146, pl. 28 (as marble; almost certainly Arsinoe II). Quaegebeur 1998, 74, 103, cat. no. 79 (date uncertain). Gabolde, Galliano et al. 2000, 77, cat. no. 41 (Ptolemaic). Walker and Higgs 2001, 171, cat. no. 170 (Cleopatra VII?).

F4. Head of queen. Copenhagen, Ny Carlsberg Glyptotek IN 586

[Figures 190–191]

Second or first century B.C.

Dark stone. H: 23.5 cm, HeadH: 21.5 cm, FaceH: 14.4 cm.

Provenance not known. Purchased in art market in Paris.

Life-size. Has plain diadem and Greek coiffure with bun at back. No uraeus extant. Hair over forehead and lower right side of face damaged. Inlaid eyes and nose missing. Broken off, metal dowel(?) in middle of top of head. Back pillar: Round top reaches nearly to top of head.

D. B. Thompson 1973, 90, pl. 71c (Arsinoe III). Kyrieleis 1975, 107–108, 110, 183, L 8, pl. 98: 3–4 (Arsinoe III). *CE* 1988, 177–179, 189, 220, cat. no. 71 (Arsinoe III). Pasqua 1995, 36–37, no. 2, figs. 2–3 (Arsinoe III). Nielsen and Østergaard 1997, 44–45, cat. no. 17 (posthumous Arsinoe III, second century B.C.). PM 8 (1999), 1010, no. 801-809-080 (probably Arsinoe III).

F5. Fragmentary queen. Turin, Museo Egizio 1385

[Figures 192–193]

Identity uncertain. Perhaps Cleopatra VII.

Dark stone. H: 54.0 cm, HeadH: 18.5 cm, FaceH: 11.2 cm.

Provenance not known.

Fragment (head through waist) of under-life-size queen with echeloned tripartite wig, vulture cap, and loopless triple uraeus. Unpolished oval area atop head indicates former presence of added attribute. Upper neck bulges with fat fold. Collar line indicates close-fitting sheath dress. Uraei, eyes, and lips abraded, and nose mostly gone. Back pillar: Square top ends just below armpits.

Roeder 1932, 18, no. 48 (Ptolemaic). *ESLP* 1960, 134, 147 (Ptolemaic). Kyrieleis 1975, 119, 184, M 6, pl. 102: 3 (Cleopatra I–VI). Curto 1984, 292, 294, 358. *CE* 1988, 176. Curto, Donadoni, and Leospo 1989, 182–184, fig. 275 (end of third century B.C.). Capriotti Vittozzi 1995 (Berenice II). Svenson 1995, 87, 232, cat. no. 114 (Cleopatra III?). PM 8 (1999), 1008, no. 801-808-420 (probably Berenice II, time of Cleopatra VII). Walker and Higgs 2001, 168–169, cat. no. 167 (Cleopatra VII?).

GROUP G: ROMAN

G1. Royal male head. Alexandria, Goddio 1015

[No figure]

Attributed to Augustus.

Granite. H: 80.0 cm.

From Alexandria. Found in eastern Alexandrian harbor, near site of Augustus' Caesareum, by Franck Goddio's underwater archaeological team.

Colossal head of king with plain *nemes,* uraeus, and Roman forehead hair. Uraeus greatly worn, nose missing, and chin damaged. Break atop head perhaps indicates former presence of added attribute (double crown?). Single hole drilled above each ear at juncture of frontlet to *nemes*-headdress. Surface greatly weathered from extended submersion in water. Back pillar: Trapezoid top reaches bottom edge of *nemes.*

Kiss 1998, 175–177, photos 79–81 (Augustus). Pfrommer 1999, 17–18, fig. 25 (probably early Ptolemaic). Walker and Higgs 2001, 174, cat. no. 172 (Ptolemy XV?).

G2. Standing emperor. Cairo CG 701

[Figures 194–196]

Attributed to Augustus.

Granite. H: 280.0 cm, HeadH: c. 39 cm, FaceH: 26.0 cm.

From Karnak. (Strocka 1980, 177, summarizes bibliography.)

Over-life-size standing statue of king with plain *nemes,* uraeus, Roman forehead hair, and additional missing element on top, perhaps the double crown. Wears plain *shendyt.* Enigmatic objects in hands at sides. Broken through left knee and right shin and repaired. Ankles, feet, and base restored. Back pillar: Triangular or trapezoidal top reaches beyond top of head.

Bissing 1914, nos. 103–104 (early Ptolemaic). Borchardt 1930, 44, pl. 129 (Ptolemaic or later). Michalowski 1935, 75–76, fig. 1 (early Roman). *ESLP* 1960, 133 (after 200 B.C.). PM 2² (1972), 283 (Karnak, exact find spot unknown; Alexander II). G. Grimm 1975, 3, 18–19, cat. no. 13, pls. 14–15 (late second to early first century B.C.). I. Jucker 1975, 23, pls. 6: 3, 7: 4–5 (posthumous Ptolemy III, late Ptolemaic). Kyrieleis 1975, 57–58, 173, E 11, pl. 45: 2–4 (Ptolemy V?). Parlasca 1978, 26–27, figs. 41–43 (Ptolemy X). Aldred et al. 1980, 161, 296, fig. 329 (c. 150 B.C.). Strocka 1980 (Augustus, Actium type). Fittschen and Zanker 1985, 2 n. 7 (Augustus, Actium type). Smith 1988, 92 n. 35 (Augustus). Boschung 1993, 202, cat. no. 268 (falsely assigned to Augustus). Heinen 1995, pls. 10–11 (Octavian-Augustus?). G. Grimm 1998, 157, 161–162, fig. 151 (Octavian, 30–29 B.C.). Hölbl 2000, 12, 19, fig. 10 (Augustus, Actium type).

G3. Standing emperor. Mantua, Museo Civico di Palazzo Te 98

[No figure]

First century A.D.?

Marble (Donatelli 1983, 47: "Marmo Italiano"). H: 57.0 cm.

From Rome (Donatelli 1983, 47).

Under life-size. Has plain *nemes,* uraeus, and Roman forehead hair. Chin is cleft. Tip of nose missing. Enigmatic objects in hands at sides. Back pillar: Conical(?) top reaches midway up back of head.

Kyrieleis 1975, 75, 178, H 21 (Ptolemaic). Bergmann and Zanker 1981, 350, fig. 24 (Domitian). Donatelli 1983, 47–49, cat. no. 14 (first century A.D.). Kiss 1984, 46, 49, 142, fig. 80 (Nero). *CE* 1988, 249 (Roman). Kiss 1995, 58 (Nero).

G4. Fragmentary emperor. Paris, Musée du Louvre E 27418

[No figure]

First century A.D.?

Marble(?). H: 28.0 cm, HeadH: 9.7 cm, FaceH: 6.3 cm.

Provenance not known. Acquired in 1986.

Under life-size. Has banded *nemes,* uraeus, and Roman forehead hair. Adam's apple indicated. Preserved from top of head through portion of rib cage. Arms mostly missing. Back pillar: Extends into fragmentary attribute atop head; top broken off.

Ziegler 1990, 84 (first century A.D.). Kiss 1995, 57–58, figs. 6–7 (Nero). Berman and Letellier 1996, 92–93, 98, cat. no. 30 (probably Nero). PM 8 (1999), 249, no. 800-950-800 (probably Nero).

G5. Standing dyad. Maamura (present location unknown)

[No figure]

First century A.D.?

Limestone. Leclant 1956, 263: "calcaire très dur." Fragment of male's legs: H: 160.0 cm. Fragment of male's abdomen: H: 120.0 cm. Female: H: 150.0 cm, D: 53.0 cm. Base: D: 181.0 cm.

From Maamura. Found in 1954 on beach near ruins of Egyptian temple enclosure (Farid 1955, 69; Leclant 1956, 262–263).

Colossal dyad of nude male figure with small female figure behind his advanced left leg, her right leg forward. Female has corkscrew locks, draped ensemble knotted between breasts, and *ankh*-sign(?) in left hand. Three fragments preserved: right half of male's abdomen (pubic hair, right testicle, and portion of penis) and part of his right thigh; male's right shin and knee attached to mostly preserved figure of female; and base with four feet. Fragmentary back pillar visible on remains of base.

Bothmer 1955, 3 (not dated). Farid 1955, 69, fig. 40 (not dated). Bothmer 1956, 9 (Ptolemaic). Leclant 1956, 262–263, pl. 53 (not dated). A. Bernand 1970a, 289–290 (not dated). Walters 1988, 9 n. 24 (early Roman).

G6. Standing emperor. Rome, Museo Nazionale 129.270

[No figure]

First century A.D.?

Red granite. Curto 1978, 57: "Granito rosa di un tipo simile a quello di Assuan, ma, ci sembra, piuttosto di cava italiana." H: 131.0 cm, HeadH: 19.0 cm, FaceH: 11.0 cm. Base: H: c. 11.0 cm, W: c. 41.5 cm, D: c. 42.5 cm.

From near Rome (Curto 1978, 57).

Under-life-size statue of emperor with small female figure attached to his left leg. Male has left leg forward and female her right one. Preserved from top of head through attached base. Broken at ankles and repaired. Male has plain *nemes,* loopless uraeus, and Roman forehead hair, and is nude except for lion's skin(?) draped over back and fastened in front. Whole male figure leans forward slightly. Right hand at side holds an enigmatic object(?). Left arm bent at elbow, held forward, and broken off. Left foot turned out, not parallel (Cairo JE 66753, H: 51.5 cm, granite king with *nemes* and *shendyt* from Tuna el-Gebel has similar turnout). Female has corkscrew locks and wears draped ensemble knotted between breasts. Face missing. No back pillar on the male figure, though a screen of stone remains between his legs and behind the female.

Curto 1978, 57–61, pls. 17–19 (Nero?). Kiss 1984, 48 (not Nero). Manera and Mazza 2001, 112, cat. no. 81 (photo reproduced in reverse; first century A.D., Nero?).

G7. Royal male head. Paris, Musée du Louvre A 35 (N 36)

[No figure]

First or second century A.D.?

Dark stone. H: 31.6 cm, HeadH: 23.0 cm, FaceH: 14.2 cm.

Provenance not known.

Life-size. Plain *nemes,* uraeus, and Roman forehead hair. Formerly inlaid eyes. Cleft chin. Robert S. Bianchi (*CE* 1988, 249–250, cat. no. 137) convincingly demonstrated that the head is Roman, despite earlier attributions to Ptolemies. He cited the distinctive uraeus shape, depiction of the hair, general style, and technical execution. Small area on top of head, lower part of nose, parts of *nemes* wings and lappets, and bottom of neck repaired. No back pillar remains. An under-life-size standing statue of ruler or divinity from Canopus (Alexandria 22829, H: 42 cm; Breccia 1932, 15, pl. 7: 23) has a similar face and also dates to Roman Period (although *Gloire* [1998, 212, cat. no. 158] suggests Ptolemy VI).

Bissing 1914, end of nos. 103–104 (Ptolemaic). Kyrieleis 1975, 75, 177, H 12, pl. 66: 3–4 (late Ptolemy?). Parlasca 1978, 27 (Ptolemy X). *CE* 1988, 184, 249–250, 251, cat. no. 137 (first century A.D.). Smith 1988, 87, 97, 170, cat. no. 77, pl. 49: 1–2 (Ptolemaic). Kiss 1995, 57, figs. 4–5 (Domitian?). Yoyotte et al. 1997, 60–61, cat. no. 39 (first century A.D.).

G8. Head of emperor. Hermopolis Magna (el-Ashmunein)

[No figure]

Second century A.D.?

Granite. Measurements not known (Bailey et al. 1991, 57: "colossal").

Provenance not known? Bailey et al. 1991, 57: "For several years stood outside the Antiquities Department's storeroom at el-Ashmunein."

Over life-size or colossal. Has *nemes,* Roman beard, and mustache(?) (not clear from published photo). Preserved from middle of face through portion of chest. Back pillar: Unknown.

INSCRIPTION: Unknown.

Bailey et al. 1991, 57, pl. 110c (Hadrian).

G9. Standing emperor. Naples, Museo Archeologico Nazionale 1060

[No figure]

Second century A.D.?

Dark stone. H: 42.3 cm, HeadH: 11.5 cm, FaceH: 6.5 cm.

Provenance not known. Possibly purchased in Alexandria, because sculpture appears in sketch made by French artist/antiquarian L. S. Fauvel, probably during 1789 stay in Alexandria (Beschi 1983, 12, pl. 4: 5).

Under life-size. Plain *nemes* with uraeus, Roman forehead hair, and natural beard. Preserved from top of head through thighs. Arms at sides. Significant abrasion and damage. Five holes drilled through figure: one below each ear, one on either side of waist, and one in crotch. Back pillar: Round top ends at top of head.

Beschi 1983, 12, pl. 4: 5 (top row, right of center). Cantilena and Rubino 1989, 60, cat. no. 5.2 (Roman).

G10. Head of emperor. Alexandria, Graeco-Roman Museum 3233

[No figure]

Attributed to Caracalla.

Gray granite. H: 29.8 cm, HeadH: 23 cm (not fully preserved), FaceH: 20.5 cm (with beard).

From Tanis. Excavated in great Amun temple (Mariette 1887, 16, no. 15).

From life-size(?) statue. Rectangular hole on top of head (6 cm × 10 cm × 4.2 cm deep) likely secured an added headdress. Roman hair and beard. Nose smashed. Back pillar: Reached at least partway through missing added headdress.

Wildung and Grimm 1978, cat. no. 172. H. Jucker 1981, 721–722, pls. 56–57, figs. 52a–c. Kiss 1984, 81, 89, 90, 93, 183, figs. 207–208. Fittschen and Zanker 1985, 107, no. 40. É. Bernand 1998, 166–167, photo 68. (All authors: Caracalla.)

G11. Standing emperor. Cairo CG 702

[No figure]

Attributed to Caracalla.

Quartzite. H: 142.0 cm, HeadH: 29.0 cm, FaceH: 18.0 cm.

From Mendes. Excavated by Édouard Naville in Banebdjedet temple.

Unfinished and over life-size. Plain *nemes,* Roman forehead hair and beard, and plain *shendyt.* No uraeus. Additional attribute is missing, as indicated by round hole atop head. Hands at sides hold enigmatic objects. Preserved through portion of thighs. Back pillar: Thick pillar curves inward toward top of *nemes.*

Naville 1894, 18 (Apries recut to Caracalla). Borchardt 1930, 44, pl. 130 (Roman). PM 4 (1934), 36 (Mendes; Caracalla). Graindor n.d., 144–145, cat. no. 79, pl. 70 (Caracalla). De Meulenaere and MacKay 1976, 201, no. 82 (probably Caracalla). H. Jucker 1981, 721, pl. 56, fig. 51 (Caracalla). Kiss 1984, 81, 89, figs. 205–206 (Caracalla). Fittschen and Zanker 1985, 107, no. 37 (Caracalla). É. Bernand 1998, 153, 167, photo 66 (Caracalla). Hölbl 2000, 34–35, 42, fig. 29a–b (Caracalla).

G12. Standing emperor. Cairo CG 703 (= JE 31621)

[No figure]

Second or early third century A.D.

Granite. H: 275.0 cm.

From Sheikh Fadl, near Beni Masar (Borchardt 1930, 44). Site information: Di. Arnold 1999, 209.

Colossal. Has double crown, plain *nemes,* uraeus, Roman forehead hair, moustache, and beard, and plain *shendyt.* Arms at sides. Preserved through ankles. Back pillar: Reaches two-thirds up *nemes.*

Borchardt 1930, 44–45, pl. 130 (Roman). PM 4 (1934), 126 (Sheikh Fadl; Roman). McCann 1968, 128, cat. no. 3, pl. 23 (Septimius Severus). H. Jucker 1981, 721 n. 205 (Caracalla). Kiss 1984, 74–75, 80, 88, 175, fig. 188 (Septimius Severus). Fittschen and Zanker 1985, 107, no. 38 (Caracalla). Hölbl 2000, 34, 42, fig. 28 (Antoninus Pius or Septimius Severus).

G13. Standing emperor. Giza antiquities storeroom

[No figure]

Attributed to Caracalla.

Red granite. H: 85.0 cm.

From Terenouthis. Found in the Nile by fisherman (Hawass 1997).

Over life-size. Has banded *nemes,* uraeus, and Roman forehead hair and beard. Additional attribute atop head missing. Preserved from top of head through most of torso. Back pillar: Narrows as it ascends back of head.

INSCRIPTION: Fragmentary single column of hieroglyphs on back pillar.

Hawass 1997 (Caracalla).

G14. Head of emperor. Philadelphia, University of Pennsylvania Museum of Art and Archaeology E 976

[No figure]

Attributed to Caracalla.

Granite. H: 51.0 cm.

From temple dedicated to Hathor/Isis and Min at Koptos (Petrie 1896, 23).

Colossal. Plain diadem with uraeus. Roman hair covers head. Roman beard. Irises and pupils are scored. Tip of nose damaged. Additional attribute on top of head missing. Back pillar: Reached at least as far as top of head.

Graindor n.d., 145–146, cat. no. 80, pl. 71a–c. PM 5 (1937), 132 (Koptos). Kiss 1984, 82, 89, 93, 95, 184, fig. 209. Fittschen and Zanker 1985, 107, no. 39. *CE* 1988, 254–255, cat. no. 140. É. Bernand 1998, 160, 167, photo 67. (All authors: Caracalla.)

GROUP H: DATE UNCERTAIN

H1. Bologna, Museo Civico Archeologico KS 1803 bis, provenance not known, formerly Fava collection, H: 14.0 cm. Under-life-size granite head of king in plain *nemes* with uraeus. Some aspects have unusual renderings, particularly very rounded top of *nemes,* depiction of eyes, and flattening of ears against *nemes* wings. Pernigotti 1980, 74, cat. no. 36, pls. 103–104 (second half of third century B.C.). Govi et al. 1990, 181–182, cat. no. 127 (second half of third century B.C.). PM 8 (1999), 201–202, no. 800-942-151 (early Ptolemaic).

H2. Cambridge, Fitzwilliam Museum E.2.1995, provenance not known, purchased in art market, H: 9.4 cm. Dark stone fragment (head through shoulders) of well under life-size king wearing plain *nemes* and uraeus. Ovoid facial shape, flat *nemes* crown, and depiction of facial features recall H10. Remaining areas of chest are unusually flat. Vertical depression down center of back is unusual. PM 8 (1999), 199–200, no. 800-940-810 (probably Ptolemy IV or V).

H3. Cambridge, Harvard University Art Museums 1943.1041, provenance not known, Grenville Lindall Winthrop Bequest, formerly Borelli Bey collection, Alexandria, H: 26.3 cm. Fragment (head through chest) of under-life-size king wearing plain *nemes* and uraeus. Material uncertain. Statue appears unfinished because surface is unpolished and some details of ears and nose are not fully worked out. Fleshy face, single-arc eyebrows in low relief, slanted, delicately rimmed eyes, and protruding lips resemble Group A examples. Some details, however, are unusual: large uraeus, sketchily rendered ears, and V-shaped ridge on neck and top of chest. PM 8 (1999), 198, no. 800-940-100 (probably early Ptolemaic).

H4. Hannover, Kestner-Museum 1959.42, provenance not known, H: 37.8 cm. Over-life-size limestone head of king with plain *nemes* and uraeus. Facial shape and features do not match sculptures ascribed to Ptolemaic Period. Unusual details: high placement of uraeus, distinctive shape of eyes with notched tear ducts, slanted, leftward angle of nose, and natural forms of lips. Woldering 1961, 30, cat. no. 25, pl. 25 (sixth century B.C.). PM 8 (1999), 204, no. 800-942-280 (Ptolemaic).

H5. Hannover, Kestner-Museum 1959.62, provenance not known, H: 20.2 cm. Under-life-size limestone head of king with plain *nemes* and uraeus. Two facial details particularly do not match other Egyptian-style Ptolemies: incised line defining top edge of upper eyelid, which does not join tear ducts or outer canthi, and highly naturalistic lips. Sculpture resembles H11 in these details. Woldering 1961, 30, cat. no. 32, pl. 32 (late Ptolemaic).

H6. Hannover, Kestner-Museum 1976.62, provenance not known, H: 27.7 cm. Under-life-size dark stone head of king with plain *nemes* and uraeus. Prominent Adam's apple. Bulky proportions of face and its features do not correspond to Ptolemaic types. Some details of *nemes* are poorly articulated, including loops of uraeus and flattened edge on top of left wing. Notchings of both tear ducts and outer canthi are unusual. PM 8 (1999), 205, no. 800-942-290 (probably early Ptolemaic).

H7. Hildesheim, Pelizaeus-Museum, provenance not known, H: 6.4 cm. Well under life-size Egyptian alabaster head of king with plain *nemes* and uraeus. Full face with downturned lips and heavy double chin resembles Group C and D Physkons, though selected details are unusual: concave, smooth depression under frontlet across forehead and up left side; slanted eyes with incised cosmetic lines and prominent tear ducts; squat nose with wide base and incised philtrum; and naturalistic lips. PM 8 (1999), 205, no. 800-942-320 (mid-Ptolemaic).

H8. London, British Museum EA 1641, provenance not known (Budge 1914, 24: "Found under the ruins of a small building of Ptolemy XIII"), H: 64.0 cm. Dark stone king (head through chest) wearing a *nemes* and uraeus. Treatment of pleating the lappets, but leaving the rest of the *nemes* plain, is highly unusual. There are odd asymmetries. Face vaguely resembles Group A types, but is nonetheless very different, particularly in the shaping of the cosmetic extensions and in the articulations of the brow, nose, and mouth. Uraeus is anomalous. PM 8 (1999), 198–199, no. 800-940-610 (Ptolemaic). Walker and Higgs 2001, 40–41, cat. no. 3 (Ptolemy I).

H9. Musée royal de Mariemont Ac. 69/25, provenance not known, H: 34.0 cm. Near-life-size limestone head of king in plain *nemes* with uraeus(?). Face and its features do not find any parallels among those attributed to the Ptolemaic Period. *Cahiers de Mariemont* 1 (1970), 59–60, cat. no. 10 (third century B.C.).

H10. Munich, Staatlichen Sammlung Ägyptischer Kunst München ÄS 5302, provenance not known, H: 29.3 cm. Under-life-size dark stone head of king in plain *nemes* with uraeus. Ovoid facial shape and flat surfaces around nose are atypical. Other differentiating details: flatness of *nemes* crown, T-shaped eyebrows with dip at nose root, rounded eyeballs, raised triangular join between lower lip and the surface of chin, and rounded, vertical peak down center front of neck. Depiction of facial features recalls H2. H. W. Müller 1966, cat. no. 94 (second century B.C.). PM 8 (1999), 206, no. 800-942-450 (Ptolemaic).

H11. Munich, Staatlichen Sammlung Ägyptischer Kunst München ÄS 5526, provenance not known, reportedly from Behnasa (H. W. Müller 1961, 25 n. 1), H: 25.0 cm. Under-life-size limestone head of king with plain *nemes* and uraeus. Two facial details are particularly atypical: incised line defining top edge of upper eyelid, which does not join tear ducts or outer canthi, and highly naturalistic lips. Sculpture resembles H5 in these details. Other distinctive elements are extra-wide philtrum and crooked line of *nemes* frontlet, which slants downward right to left. H. W. Müller 1961, 25–31, fig. 13 (later third century B.C.). H. W. Müller 1966, cat. no. 96 (250–200 B.C.).

H12. New York, Metropolitan Museum of Art 1971.10, provenance not known, H: 35 cm. Unfinished limestone standing king wearing plain *nemes,* uraeus, and plain *shendyt.* The uraeus is only blocked out and no frontlet or tabs are indicated. Sculpture resembles others in sculptors' studies/votives category (Appendix A), but execution of various details are unusual, particularly *nemes* proportions, facial contours, shapes of eyes and mouth, and appearance of the pectorals. PM 8 (1999), 197, no. 800-932-600 (Ptolemaic).

GROUP J: MISCELLANEA

J1. Alexandria, Graeco-Roman Museum 28104, provenance not known, H: 22.7 cm. Badly damaged dark stone fragment consists of head and left shoulder of under-life-size king in plain *nemes* with uraeus, from seated or standing statue. Facial features too damaged for proper assessment. Possibly Ptolemaic. No bibliography.

J2. Copenhagen, Ny Carlsberg Glyptotek AEIN 926, provenance not known (acquired in the late nineteenth century in the art market in Athens), H: 13.8 cm. This under-life-size, dark stone head wearing a plain *nemes* but no uraeus has been attributed to Ptolemy I (Nielsen and Østergaard 1997, 48, cat. no. 19; PM 8 [1999], 204, no. 800-942-260) or Vespasian (Kiss 1995, 59–60, figs. 10–11). The rendering of the *nemes* (highly rounded crown, wide frontlet, and triangular tabs) and the advanced age clearly shown in the face (bags under the eyes, sunken cheeks, and skin wrinkles) are anomalous relative to other Ptolemaic royal representations. Date and identity are uncertain.

J3. Copenhagen, Ny Carlsberg Glyptotek AEIN 933, provenance not known (acquired in 1896 in art market in Rome through Helbig and reportedly found in area of Iseum at Campus Martius in Rome), H: 47.0 cm. This over-life-size, dark stone male head with Greek hair, diadem, and hole for attachment of missing uraeus(?) is sometimes associated with Ptolemy III (Nielsen and Østergaard 1997, 50–51, cat. no. 21) or Alexander the Great (Koefoed-Petersen [1965, 10–12] proposes a Hadrianic representation of Alexander). A flat edge at the juncture of hairline and forehead likely indicates that the upper part of the face is recut, whereas the nose and lower part of the face are definitely restored (Lembke 1994, pl. 40: 2–3). Other scholars are cautious in suggesting a date (Smith 1988, 87, 97, 171, cat. no. 79, pl. 49: 5; and Lembke 1994, 234–235, cat. no. 29, pl. 40: 2–3). Given the extensive reworking, the head is not considered here.

J4. Naples, Museo Archeologico Nazionale, no no., provenance not known, H: 25.5 cm. The face of this near-life-size head of a king appears repolished because of its smooth surface relative to that of the *nemes*. The lower part of face, particularly lips, chin, and jaw line, are perhaps recut. Though sometimes considered to be Ptolemaic (H. W. Müller 1961, 26 n. 5), the dark stone head has also been published as Dynasty 26 (PM 8 [1999], 161, no. 800-871-300). Given the modern(?) repolishing, the head is not considered here.

J5. Rome, Museo Nazionale 49597, provenance not known (bought in antiquarian market in Rome), H: 21.0 cm. This under-life-size, granite, male head with Greek hair is sometimes questioningly attributed to an early Ptolemy (Kiss 1975, 295, pl. 86d; *Museo Nationale Romano: Le sculture,* vol. 1, 9, 1 [Rome, 1987], 40–42, cat. no. R22). There is no diadem, however, and a cut channel along the hairline and the highly polished face suggest a recutting (Roberta Belli Pasqua, in Anderson and Nista 1989, 79–81, cat. no. 11). Therefore, the sculpture is not considered here.

J6. Toronto, Royal Ontario Museum 910.75, provenance not known, H: 65.0 cm. Near-life-size granite bust of queen with echeloned, tripartite wig, plain diadem, loopless uraeus, and plain modius. This sculpture is usually attributed to the Ptolemaic Period: *ESLP* 1960, 121, 134–135, 145, 147, cat. no. 105, pl. 98, figs. 261–262 (240–200 B.C.); *CE* 1988, 181, cat. no. 73 (second century B.C.); and PM 8 (1999), 1007, no. 801-808-400 (early Ptolemaic). The queen, however, displays several unusual features: the facial profile is flat and receding, and the wig lappets are concave in profile. The date is uncertain.

J7. Vienna, Kunsthistorisches Museum ÄS 8, provenance not known (acquired in Egypt in 1821), H: 16.8 cm. This under-life-size, dark gray-and-white-speckled porphyry male head with hair and headband has been attributed to Ptolemy IV (Rogge 1999, 82–85; PM 8 [1999], 210, no. 800-942-627) based on a comparison to a Greek-style bronze bust in the British Museum assigned to the same ruler (London, British Museum GR 1772.3-2.11). The Vienna head's facial features, however, do not conform to any royal types examined in this study, particularly the relatively heavy upper eyelids. A private person with a headband may be represented, particularly because no uraeus or other royal attribute is present.

J8. Vienna, Kunsthistorisches Museum ÄS 79 and 80, reportedly unearthed by Anton Ritter von Laurin in Alexandria with C2 (Rogge 1999, 77), H: 57.0 cm and 58.0 cm, respectively. These two colossal heads of kings with banded *nemes,* uraeus, and formerly inlaid eyes have been published as fourth or third century B.C. (Rogge 1999, 75–81). The weathered and battered condition of these nummulitic limestone sculptures makes assessment difficult, though the broad faces with single-arc eyebrows, slanted eyes, broadly flaring frontal nose outlines, and puckered mouths with large corner drill holes certainly belong in the fourth century or early Ptolemaic Period.

ABBREVIATIONS

ÄAT Ägypten und Altes Testament.

AfP *Archiv für Papyrusforschung und verwandte Gebiete.*

AJA *American Journal of Archaeology.*

Alexandria Submerged Franck Goddio et al., eds., *Alexandria: The Submerged Royal Quarters* (London, 1998).

Alexandrianism *Alexandria and Alexandrianism* (Malibu, 1996).

AM *Mitteilungen des Deutschen Archäologischen Instituts, Athenische Abteilung.*

AncSoc *Ancient Society.*

ANRW *Aufstieg und Niedergang der römischen Welt.*

AntJ *The Antiquaries Journal.*

AntK *Antike Kunst.*

Archives Marie-Françoise Boussac and Antonio Invernizzi, eds., *Archives et sceaux du monde hellénistique, BCH*, suppl. 29 (Athens, 1996).

ArtB *The Art Bulletin.*

AS Archäologische Studien.

ASAE *Annales du Service des antiquités de l'Égypte.*

AW *Antike Welt.*

BASP *The Bulletin of the American Society of Papyrologists.*

BCH *Bulletin de correspondance hellénique.*

BClevMus *The Bulletin of the Cleveland Museum of Art.*

BdE Bibliothèque d'étude. Institut français d'archéologie orientale (Cairo).

BES *Bulletin of the Egyptological Seminar.*

BICS *Bulletin of the Institute of Classical Studies of the University of London.*

BIFAO *Bulletin de l'Institut français d'archéologie orientale.*

BiOr *Bibliotheca orientalis.*

BJRylLib *Bulletin of the John Rylands Library.*

BKP Beiträge zur klassischen Philologie.

BMA *The Brooklyn Museum Annual.*

BMMA *Bulletin of the Metropolitan Museum of Art.*

BMonMusPont *Bollettino. Monumenti, musei e gallerie pontificie.*

BMRAH *Bulletin des Musées royaux d'art et d'histoire, Bruxelles.*

BMusHongr *Bulletin du Musée hongrois des beaux-arts.*

BMusLyon *Bulletin des musées et monuments lyonnais.*

BSAA *Bulletin de la Société archéologique d'Alexandrie.*

BSFE *Bulletin de la Société française d'égyptologie.*

BSRAA *Bulletin de la Société royale d'archéologie d'Alexandrie.*

CAA Corpus Antiquitatum Aegyptiacarum (Mainz).

CAH The Cambridge Ancient History.

CDD Janet H. Johnson, ed., "The Chicago Demotic Dictionary," unpublished manuscript, University of Chicago. Citations are from draft dated Jan. 14 or 15, 2001.

CdE *Chronique d'Égypte.*

CE Robert S. Bianchi, ed., *Cleopatra's Egypt: Age of the Ptolemies* (Brooklyn, 1988).

CGA Catalogue général des antiquités égyptiennes du Museé d'Alexandrie.

CGC Catalogue général des antiquités égyptiennes du Museé du Caire.

DAIK Deutsches Archäologisches Institut, Abteilung Kairo.

DPA Herwig Maehler and Volker Michael Strocka, eds., *Das ptolemäische Ägypten. Akten des internationalen Symposions 27.–29. September 1976 in Berlin* (Mainz, 1978).

EPRO Études préliminaires aux religions orientales dans l'empire romain.

ESLP Bernard V. Bothmer et al., *Egyptian Sculpture of the Late Period, 700 B.C. to A.D. 100* (Brooklyn, 1960).

EtTrav *Études et travaux. Studia i prace. Travaux du Centre d'archéologie méditerranéenne de l'Académie des sciences polonaise.*

FIFAO Fouilles de l'Institut français d'archéologie orientale.

Gloire Jean-Yves Empereur et al., *La gloire d'Alexandrie* (Paris, 1998).

GM *Göttinger Miszellen.*

HSCP *Harvard Studies in Classical Philology.*

Hundred-Gated Thebes S. P. Vleeming, ed., *Hundred-Gated Thebes: Acts of a Colloquium on Thebes and the Theban Area in the Graeco-Roman Period,* PLB 27 (Leiden, 1995).

IntJNautA *International Journal of Nautical Archaeology.*

JARCE *Journal of the American Research Center in Egypt.*

JbBerlMus *Jahrbuch der Berliner Museen.*

JdI *Jahrbuch des Deutschen Archäologischen Instituts.*

JEA *The Journal of Egyptian Archaeology.*

JHS *Journal of Hellenic Studies.*

JJurP *Journal of Juristic Papyrology.*

JKSW *Jahrbuch der Kunsthistorischen Sammlungen in Wien.*

JNES *Journal of Near Eastern Studies.*

JPKS *Jahrbuch der preussischen Kunstsammlungen.*

JRS *The Journal of Roman Studies.*

JSSEA *Journal of the Society for the Study of Egyptian Antiquities.*

JWalt *The Journal of the Walters Art Gallery.*

LÄ Wolfgang Helck and Wolfhart Westendorf, eds., *Lexikon der Ägyptologie,* vols. 1–7 (Wiesbaden, 1975–1992).

LdR 4 Henri Gauthier, *Le livre des rois d'Égypte,* vol. 4 (de la XXVe dynastie à la fin des Ptolémées), MIFAO 20 (Cairo, 1916).

MAAR *Memoirs of the American Academy in Rome.*

MÄS Münchner Ägyptologische Studien.

MDAIK *Mitteilungen des Deutschen Archäologischen Instituts, Abteilung Kairo.*

MEFR *Mélanges d'archéologie et d'histoire de l'École française de Rome.*

MIFAO Mémoires publiés par les membres de l'Institut français d'archéologie orientale du Caire.

MMJ *Metropolitan Museum Journal.*

MonPiot *Monuments et mémoires: Fondation Eugène Piot.*

NARCE *Newsletter of the American Research Center in Egypt.*

OBO Orbis biblicus et orientalis.

OEAE Donald B. Redford, ed., *The Oxford Encyclopedia of Ancient Egypt,* vols. 1–3 (Oxford, 2001).

OGIS Wilhelmus Dittenberger, *Orientis Graeci inscriptiones selectae,* vols. 1–2 (Leipzig, 1903–1905).

OLA Orientalia Lovaniensia Analecta.

OxfJA *Oxford Journal of Archaeology.*

PLB Papyrologica Lugduno-Batava.

PM 1–7 Bertha Porter and Rosalind L. B. Moss, *Topographical Bibliography of Ancient Egyptian Hieroglyphic Texts, Reliefs, and Paintings,* vols. 1–7 (Oxford, 1927–1981).

PM 8 Jaromir Malek, Diana Magee, and Elizabeth Miles, *Topographical Bibliography of Ancient Egyptian Hieroglyphic Texts, Statues, Reliefs, and Paintings,* vol. 8 (objects of provenance not known) (Oxford, 1999).

Quaegebeur Studies Willy Clarysse, Antoon Schoors, and Harco Willems, eds., *Egyptian Religion—The Last Thousand Years: Studies Dedicated to the Memory of Jan Quaegebeur,* vols. 1–2, OLA 84–85 (Louvain, 1998).

RA *Revue archéologique.*

RdE *Revue d'égyptologie.*

RdL *La revue du Louvre et des musées de France.*

RendLinc *Atti dell'Accademia nazionale dei Lincei. Rendiconti.*

RIA *Rivista dell'Istituto nazionale d'archeologia e storia dell'arte.*

RT *Recueil de travaux relatifs à la philologie et à l'archéologie égyptiennes et assyriennes.*

SAK *Studien zur altägyptischen Kultur.*

SASAE Supplément aux annales du Service des antiquités de l'Égypte.

SBWien *Sitzungsberichte: Österreichische Akademie der Wissenschaften.* Vienna.

SH Studia Hellenistica.

Studi Adriani 4 Giuseppina Barone and Elena Epifanio, eds., *Alessandria e il mondo ellenistico-romano: Studi in onore di Achille Adriani,* Studi e materiali Istituto di Archeologia Università di Palermo 4, series edited by Nicola Bonacasa and Antonino Di Vita (Rome, 1983).

Wb Adolf Erman and Hermann Grapow, *Wörterbuch der aegyptischen Sprache,* vols. 1–5 (Leipzig, 1926–1931).

ZÄS *Zeitschrift für ägyptische Sprache und Altertumskunde.*

ZPE *Zeitschrift für Papyrologie und Epigraphik.*

BIBLIOGRAPHY

Abdalla, Aly. 1995. "Finds from the Sebbakh at Dendera." *GM* 145:19–28.

Adriani, Achille. 1939. "Sculture del Museo Greco-Romano VI." *BSRAA* 33:336–349.

———. 2000. *La tomba di Alessandro: Realtà ipotesi e fantasie.* Rome.

Albersmeier, Sabine, and Martina Minas. 1998. "Ein Weihrelief für die vergöttliche Arsinoe II." In *Quaegebeur Studies* 1:3–29.

Aldred, Cyril. 1957. Review of Cooney 1956. *AJA* 61:290–291.

———. 1962. Review of *ESLP. AJA* 66:207–209.

———. 1980. *Egyptian Art.* London.

Aldred, Cyril, et al. 1980. *L'Égypte du crépuscule.* Paris.

Alexandria and Alexandrianism. 1996. Malibu. [Abbreviated *Alexandrianism.*]

Altenmüller, Hartwig, and Wilhelm Hornbostel. 1982. *Das Menschenbild im Alten Ägypten: Porträts aus vier Jahrtausenden.* Hamburg.

Anderson, Maxwell L., and Leila Nista, eds. 1989. *Radiance in Stone: Sculptures in Colored Marble from the Museo Nazionale Romano.* Rome.

Andrews, Carol. 1994. *Amulets of Ancient Egypt.* Austin, Tex.

Arnold, Dieter (Di.). 1994. *Lexikon der ägyptischen Baukunst.* Zurich.

———. 1999. *Temples of the Last Pharaohs.* New York.

Arnold, Dorothea (Do.). 1996. "The Workshop of the Sculptor Thutmose." In *The Royal Women of Amarna,* 41–83. New York.

Aufrère, Sydney. 2000. *Le propylône d'Amon-Rê-Montou à Karnak-Nord.* MIFAO 117. Cairo.

Aufrère, Sydney, and Jean-Claude Golvin. 1997. *L'Égypte restituée III: Sites, temples et pyramides de Moyenne et Basse Égypte de la naissance de la civilisation pharaonique à l'époque gréco-romaine.* Paris.

Ausführliches Verzeichnis der ägyptischen Altertümer und Gipsabgüsse. 1899. Berlin.

Bagnall, Roger S. 1997. "The Fayum and Its People." In *Ancient Faces: Mummy Portraits from Roman Egypt,* ed. Susan Walker et al., 17–20. London.

———. 1998. "Cults and Names of Ptolemais in Upper Egypt." In *Quaegebeur Studies* 2:1093–1101.

———. 2001. "Archaeological Work on Hellenistic and Roman Egypt, 1995–2000." *AJA* 105:227–243.

Bailey, Donald M. 1984. "Glass Plaques from a Foundation Deposit at Canopus, Egypt." *AntJ* 64:389–393.

Bailey, Donald M., et al. 1991. *Excavations at El-Ashmunein IV: Hermopolis Magna: Buildings of the Roman Period.* London.

Barguet, Paul. 1953. *La stèle de la famine, à Séhel.* BdE 24. Cairo.

Barone, Giuseppina, and Elena Epifanio, eds. *Alessandria e il mondo ellenistico-romano: Studi in onore di Achille Adriani.* 1983. Studi e materiali Istituto di Archeologia Università di Palermo 4. Series edited by Nicola Bonacasa and Antonino Di Vita. Rome. [Abbreviated *Studi Adriani* 4.]

Bastianini, Giorgio, and Claudio Gallazzi. 1989. "Un' iscrizione inedita di Tebtynis per una statua controversa di Tolomeo XII." *Quaderni ticinesi di numismatica e antichità classiche* 18:201–209.

Beckerath, Jürgen von. 1999. *Handbuch der ägyptischen Königsnamen.* MÄS 49.

Bell, Lanny. 1985. "Luxor Temple and the Cult of the Royal *KA.*" *JNES* 44:251–294.

———. 1997. "The New Kingdom 'Divine' Temple: The Example of Luxor." In *Temples of Ancient Egypt,* ed. Byron E. Shafer, 127–184. Ithaca, N.Y.

Bennett, Chris. 1997. "Cleopatra V Tryphaena and the Genealogy of the Later Ptolemies." *AncSoc* 28:39–66.

Bergmann, Marianne. 1998. *Die Strahlen der Herrscher: Theomorphes Herrscherbild und politische Symbolik im Hellenismus und in der römischen Kaiserzeit.* Mainz.

Bergmann, Marianne, and Paul Zanker. 1981. "'Damnatio Memoriae.' Umgearbeitete Nero- und Domitiansporträts." *JdI* 96:317–412.

Berman, Lawrence M., and Bernadette Letellier. 1996. *Pharaohs: Treasures of Egyptian Art from the Louvre.* Cleveland.

Bernand, André. 1969. *Les inscriptions grecques de Philae.* Vol. 1. Paris.

———. 1970a. *Le Delta égyptien d'après les textes grecs.* Vol. 1. MIFAO 91. Cairo.

———. 1970b. *Le Delta égyptien d'après les textes grecs.* Vol. 3. MIFAO 91. Cairo.

———. 1992a. *La prose sur pierre dans l'Égypte hellénistique et romaine.* Vol. 1. Paris.

———. 1992b. *La prose sur pierre dans l'Égypte hellénistique et romaine.* Vol. 2. Paris.

———. 1998. *Alexandrie la grande.* New ed. Paris.

Bernand, Étienne. 1975. *Recueil des inscriptions grecques du Fayoum.* Vol. 1. Leiden.

———. 1981a. *Recueil des inscriptions grecques du Fayoum.* Vol. 2. BdE 79. Cairo.

———. 1981b. *Recueil des inscriptions grecques du Fayoum.* Vol. 3. BdE 80. Cairo.

———. 1982. *Inscriptions grecques d'Égypte et de Nubie: Répertoire bibliographique des OGIS.* Paris.

———. 1998. "Epigraphical Documents and Caracalla in Egypt." In *Alexandria Submerged,* 143–167.

———. 1999. *Inscriptions grecques d'Hermoupolis Magna et de sa nécropole.* BdE 123. Cairo.

———. 2001. *Inscriptions grecques d'Alexandrie ptolémaïque.* BdE 133. Cairo.

Beschi, Luigi. 1983. "L. S. Fauvel ad Alessandria." In *Studi Adriani* 4:3–12.

Bianchi, Robert S. 1976a. "The Striding Draped Male Figure of Ptolemaic Egypt I." Ph.D. dissertation, Institute of Fine Arts, New York University.

———. 1976b. "The Striding Draped Male Figure of Ptolemaic Egypt II." Ph.D. dissertation, Institute of Fine Arts, New York University.

———. 1978. "The Striding Draped Male Figure of Ptolemaic Egypt." In *DPA,* 95–102.

———. 1980. "Not the Isis Knot." *BES* 2:9–31.

———, ed. 1988. *Cleopatra's Egypt: Age of the Ptolemies.* Brooklyn. [Abbreviated *CE.*]

———. 1992a. "Alexander the Great as a Kausia Diadematophoros from Egypt." In *The Intellectual Heritage of Egypt,* ed. Ulrich Luft, 69–75. Budapest.

———. 1992b. "Collecting and Collectors, Egyptian Style." *BClevMus* 79:144–151.

———. 1996. *Splendors of Ancient Egypt from the Egyptian Museum, Cairo.* London.

Bissing, Friedrich Wilhelm von. 1914. *Denkmäler ägyptischer Sculptur.* 2 vols. Munich.

Bisson de la Roque, Fernand. 1924. *Rapport sur les fouilles d'Abou Roasch (1922–1923).* FIFAO 1, 3. Cairo.

Bol, Peter C., ed. 1994. *Forschungen zur Villa Albani: Katalog der antiken Bildwerke.* Vol. 4. Berlin.

Borchardt, Ludwig. 1925. *Statuen und Statuetten von Königen und Privatleuten im Museum von Kairo.* Vol. 2. CGC 381–653. Berlin.

———. 1930. *Statuen und Statuetten von Königen und Privatleuten im Museum von Kairo.* Vol. 3. CGC 654–950. Berlin.

———. 1934. *Statuen und Statuetten von Königen und Privatleuten im Museum von Kairo.* Vol. 4. CGC 951–1294. Berlin.

Boschung, Dietrich. 1993. *Die Bildnisse des Augustus.* Berlin.

Bothmer, Bernard V. 1955. "Delta Sites IV." *NARCE,* no. 19 (Oct. 20):2–5.

———. 1956. "Delta Sites V." *NARCE,* no. 22 (June 30):4–12.

———. 1959. "La tête égyptienne d'Auxerre." *La revue des arts* 9:98–108.

———. 1960. "The Philadelphia-Cairo Statue of Osorkon II." *JEA* 46:3–11.

———. 1987. "Egyptian Antiquities." In *Antiquities from the Collection of Christos G. Bastis,* 1–106. Mainz.

———. 1996. "Hellenistic Elements in Egyptian Sculpture of the Ptolemaic Period." In *Alexandrianism,* 215–230.

Bothmer, Bernard V., et al. 1960. *Egyptian Sculpture of the Late Period, 700 B.C. to A.D. 100.* Brooklyn. [Abbreviated *ESLP.*]

Botti, Giuseppe. 1900. *Catalogue des monuments exposés au Musée Gréco-Romain d'Alexandrie.* Alexandria.

———. 1902. "Bulletin épigraphique." *BSRAA* 4:85–107.

Botti, Giuseppe, and Pietro Romanelli. 1951. *Le sculture del Museo Gregoriano Egizio.* Vatican City.

Boussac, Marie-Françoise. 1989. "Cachets de la collection Benaki." *BCH* 113:325–334.

Boussac, Marie-Françoise, and Antonio Invernizzi, eds. 1996. *Archives et sceaux du monde hellénistique. BCH,* suppl. 29. Athens. [Abbreviated *Archives.*]

Bowman, Alan K. 1986. *Egypt after the Pharaohs.* Berkeley.

Breccia, Evaristo. 1905. "Antiquités découvertes à Maamourah par S. A. le prince Omar Pacha Toussoun." *BSRAA* 8:107–117.

———. 1907. "Les fouilles dans le Sérapéum d'Alexandrie en 1905–1906." *ASAE* 8:62–76.

———. 1911. *Iscrizioni greche e latine.* CGA 1–568. Cairo.

———. 1914. *Alexandrea ad Aegyptum.* Bergamo.

———. 1926. *Monuments de l'Égypte Gréco-Romaine.* Vol. 1. Bergamo.

———. 1931a. "Note epigrafiche." *BSRAA* 26:276–294.

———. 1931b. "Sculture inedite del Museo Greco-Romano." *BSRAA* 26:258–270.

———. 1932. *Le Musée Gréco-Romain, 1925–1931.* Bergamo.

Bricault, Laurent. 1999. "Sarapis et Isis, sauveurs de Ptolémée IV à Raphia." *CdE* 74:334–343.

———. 2000. "Un phare, une flotte, Isis, Faustine et l'annone." *CdE* 75:136–149.

Brunelle, Edelgard. 1976. *Die Bildnisse der Ptolemäerinnen.* Frankfurt.

Brunner, Hellmut. 1984. "Textliches zur Frage des Porträts in Ägypten." *SAK* 11:277–279.

Brunner-Traut, Emma, and Hellmut Brunner. 1981. *Die ägyptische Sammlung der Universität Tübingen.* Mainz.

Bruwier, Marie-Cécile. 1989. "Deux fragments d'une statue colossale de reine ptolémaïque à Mariemont." *CdE* 64:25–43.

Bruyère, Bernard. 1952. "Note 15: Manteau macédonien." In *Rapport sur les fouilles de Deir el Médineh (1935–1940),* FIFAO 20, 3:129–137. Cairo.

Budge, E. A. Wallis. 1914. *Egyptian Sculptures in the British Museum.* London.

Burstein, Stanley M., ed. and trans. 1985. *The Hellenistic Age from the Battle of Ipsos to the Death of Kleopatra VII.* Translated Documents of Greece and Rome 3. Cambridge.

Cantilena, Renata, and Paola Rubino, eds. 1989. *La collezione egiziana del Museo Archeologico Nazionale di Napoli.* Naples.

Capart, Jean, ed. 1936. *Travels in Egypt [December 1880 to May 1891]: Letters of Charles Edwin Wilbour.* Brooklyn.

Capriotti Vittozzi, Giuseppina. 1995. "Un busto di regina tolemaica al Museo di Torino: Note sull'iconografia di Berenice II e di Cleopatra I." *RendLinc,* ser. 9, vol. 6:409–438.

———. 1998. "Una statua di sovrana al museo di Torino: La tradizione del Nuovo Regno nell'iconografia delle regine tolemaiche." *Vicino Oriente* 11:53–66.

———. 2000. "Note sull'immagine di Alessandro Magno in Egitto." In *Atti del V Convegno Nazionale di Egittologia e Papirologia, Firenze, 10–12 dicembre 1999,* ed. Simona Russo, 27–53. Florence.

Catalogue of a Collection of Egyptian Antiquities, the Property of Henry Abbott, M.D., Now Exhibiting at the Stuyvesant Institute, no. 659 Broadway, New York. 1854. New York.

Catalogue of the Egyptian Antiquities of the New York Historical Society. 1915. New York.

Cauville, Sylvie. 1987. "Les statues cultuelles de Dendera d'après les inscriptions pariétales." *BIFAO* 87:73–117.

Chabân, Mohammed. 1910. "Monuments recueillis pendant mes inspections." *ASAE* 10:28–30.

Chassinat, Émile. 1910. *Le mammisi d'Edfou.* Vol. 1. MIFAO 17. Cairo.

———. 1934. *Le temple de Dendara.* Vol. 2. Cairo.

Chaveau, Michel. 2000. *Egypt in the Age of Cleopatra.* Trans. David Lorton. Ithaca, N.Y.

Clarysse, Willy. 1993. "Egyptian Scribes Writing Greek." *CdE* 68:186–201.

———. 2000. "Ptolémées et temples." In *Le Décret de Memphis,* ed. Dominique Valbelle and Jean Leclant, 41–65. Paris.

Clarysse, Willy, Antoon Schoors, and Harco Willems, eds. 1998. *Egyptian Religion—The Last Thousand Years: Studies Dedicated to the Memory of Jan Quaegebeur.* Vols. 1–2. OLA 84–85. Louvain. [Abbreviated *Quaegebeur Studies.*]

Clayton, Peter, and Martin Price, eds. 1988. *The Seven Wonders of the Ancient World.* London.

Cooney, John D. 1953. "Egyptian Art in the Collection of Albert Gallatin." *JNES* 12:1–19.

———. 1956. *Five Years of Collecting Egyptian Art, 1951–1956.* Brooklyn.

Corteggiani, Jean-Pierre. 1998. "Les *Aegyptiaca* de la fouille sous-marine de Qaïtbay." *BSFE,* no. 142 (June):25–40.

Criscuolo, Lucia. 1995. "L'epigrafia greca a Tebe." In *Hundred-Gated Thebes,* 21–29.

Curto, Silvio. 1978. "Statua egittizzante nel Museo delle Terme." *SAK* 6:57–61.

———. 1984. *L'antico Egitto nel Museo Egizio di Torino.* Turin.

———. 1985. *Le sculture egizie ed egittizzanti nelle Ville Torlonia in Roma.* EPRO 105. Leiden.

Curto, Silvio, Sergio Donadoni, and Enrichetta Leospo. 1989. *Monumental Art.* Milan.

Daumas, François. 1952. *Les moyens d'expression du grec et de l'égyptien comparés dans les décrets de Canope et de Memphis.* SASAE 16.

Davoli, Paola. 1998. *L'archeologia urbana nel Fayyum di età ellenistica e romana.* Missione Congiunta delle Università di Bologna e di Lecce in Egitto Monografie 1. Naples.

Demel, Hans. 1936. "Einige ägyptische Porträtköpfe der Spätzeit." *JKSW* 10:1–8.

De Meulenaere, Herman. 1960. "Les monuments du culte des rois Nectanébo." *CdE* 35:92–107.

———. 1999. "The Karnak Cachette." In *Egyptian Treasures from the Egyptian Museum in Cairo,* ed. Francesco Tiradritti, 334–341. New York.

De Meulenaere, Herman, and Bernard V. Bothmer. 1969. "Une tête d'Osiris au Musée du Louvre." *Kêmi* 19:9–16.

De Meulenaere, Herman, and Pierre MacKay. 1976. *Mendes.* Vol. 2. Warminster.

Depauw, Mark. 1997. *A Companion to Demotic Studies.* Papyrologica Bruxellensia 28. Brussels.

Derriks, Claire. 1990. *Choix d'oeuvres 50: Egypte.* Mariemont.

———. 1998. "Une tête d'enfant isiaque: Hypothèse ou certitude?" In *Quaegebeur Studies* 1:91–103.

Desroches Noblecourt, Christiane, et al. 1981. *Un siècle de fouilles françaises en Égypte, 1880–1980.* Cairo.

Die, María del Carmen Pérez. 1992. "Egipto y Próximo Oriente." In *Museo Arqueológico Nacional: Guía General,* 1: 89–112. Madrid.

Dils, Peter. 1998. "La couronne d'Arsinoé II Philadelphe." In *Quaegebeur Studies* 2:1299–1330.

Dittenberger, Wilhelmus. 1903–1905. *Orientis Graeci inscriptiones selectae.* Vols. 1–2. Leipzig. [Abbreviated *OGIS.*]

Donatelli, Laura. 1983. *La raccolta egizia di Giuseppe Acerbi.* Mantua.

Donohue, A. A. 1988. Xoana *and the Origins of Greek Sculpture.* Atlanta.

Drenkhahn, Rosemarie. 1995. "Artisans and Artists in Pharaonic Egypt." In *Civilizations of the Ancient Near East,* Vol. 1, ed. Jack M. Sasson et al., 331–343. New York.

Dunand, Françoise. 1973. *Le culte d'Isis dans le bassin oriental de la Méditerranée.* Vol. 2. EPRO 26. Leiden.

———. 1980. "Fête, tradition, propagande: Les cérémonies en l'honneur de Bérénice, fille de Ptolémée III, en 238 a.C." In *Livre du Centenaire 1880–1980,* MIFAO 104, 287–301. Cairo.

Duthoy, Françoise, and Jiri Frel. 1996. "Observations sur le sanctuaire Syrien du Janicule." In *Orientalia Sacra Urbis Romae: Dolichena et Heliopolitana,* 289–303. Rome.

Dutilh, E.D.J. 1905. "A travers les collections du Musée Greco-Romain d'Alexandrie." *BSRAA* 7:48–54.

Eaton-Krauss, Marianne. 2001. "Artists and Artisans." In *OEAE* 1:136–140.

Edgar, Campbell Cowan. 1906a. "Planches XXII–XXVIII." In *Le Musée Égyptien: Recueil de monuments et de notices sur les fouilles d'Égypte,* Vol. 2, publ. by G. Maspero, 57–62. Cairo.

———. 1906b. "Report on an Excavation at Toukh el-Qaramous." *ASAE* 7:205–212.

———. 1906c. *Sculptors' Studies and Unfinished Works.* CGC 33301–33506. Cairo.

Eingartner, Johannes. 1991. *Isis und ihre Dienerinnen in der Kunst der römischen Kaiserzeit. Mnemosyne* suppl. 115. Leiden.

Eisenberg, Jerome M. 1960. *A Catalog of Late Egyptian and Coptic Sculptures.* New York.

Emery, Walter B. 1970. "Preliminary Report on the Excavations at North Saqqâra, 1968–9." *JEA* 56:5–11.

Empereur, Jean-Yves. 1996. "Alexandrie (Égypte)." *BCH* 120: 959–970.

———. 1998. *Alexandrie redécouverte.* Paris.

Empereur, Jean-Yves, et al. 1998. *La gloire d'Alexandrie.* Paris. [Abbreviated *Gloire.*]

Erichsen, Wolja. 1954. *Demotisches Glossar.* Copenhagen.

Erman, Adolf, and Hermann Grapow. 1926–1931. *Wörterbuch der aegyptischen Sprache.* Vols. 1–5. Leipzig. [Abbreviated *Wb.*]

Farid, Chafik. 1955. "Fouilles près d'Alexandrie." *La revue du Caire* 33, no. 175:69.

el-Fattah, Ahmed Abd, and Paolo Gallo. 1998. "Aegyptiaca Alexandrina: Monuments pharaoniques découverts récemment à Alexandrie." In *Alexandrina,* Études Alexandrines 1: 7–19. Cairo.

Favard-Meeks, Christine. 1991. *Le temple de Behbeit el-Hagara.* Hamburg.

———. 1998. "Mise à jour des ouvrages de Flinders Petrie sur les fouilles de Tanis." In *Tanis: Travaux récents sur le tell Sân el-Hagar. Mission française des fouilles de Tanis, 1987–1997,* ed. Philippe Brissaud and Christiane Zivie-Coche, 101–178. Paris.

Fay, Biri. 1996. *The Louvre Sphinx and Royal Sculpture from the Reign of Amenemhat II.* Mainz.

Fazzini, Richard A. 1975. *Images for Eternity: Egyptian Art from Berkeley and Brooklyn.* Brooklyn.

Fazzini, Richard A., et al. 1989. *Ancient Egyptian Art in the Brooklyn Museum.* Brooklyn.

Felgenhauer, Annette. 1996. *Ägyptische und ägyptisierende Kunstwerke.* Kassel.

Fischer, Henry G. 1975. "An Elusive Shape within the Fisted Hands of Egyptian Statues." *MMJ* 10:9–21.

Fittschen, Klaus. 1983. "Zwei Ptolemäerbildnisse in Cherchel." *Studi Adriani* 4:165–171.

Fittschen, Klaus, and Paul Zanker. 1985. *Katalog der römischen Porträts in den Capitolinischen Museen und den anderen kommunalen Sammlungen der Stadt Rom.* Vol. 1. Kaiser- und Prinzenbildnisse. Mainz.

Fotopoulos, Dionissis, and Angelos Delivorrias. 1997. *Greece at the Benaki Museum.* Athens.

Franke, Detlef. 1992. *Photographs of Egyptian Art and of Egypt: The Hans Wolfgang Müller Archive.* Leiden.

Fraser, P. M. 1951. "A Syriac *Notitia Urbis Alexandrinae.*" *JEA* 37:103–108.

———. 1957. "Mark Antony in Alexandria—A Note." *JRS* 47:71–73.

———. 1960. "Inscriptions from Ptolemaic Egypt." *Berytus* 13:123–161.

———. 1972a. *Ptolemaic Alexandria.* Vol. 1. Oxford.

———. 1972b. *Ptolemaic Alexandria.* Vol. 2. Oxford.

Friedman, Florence D. 1994. "Aspects of Domestic Life and Religion." In *Pharaoh's Workers: The Villagers of Deir el Medina,* ed. Leonard H. Lesko, 95–117. Ithaca, N.Y.

Fröhlich, Brigitte. 1998. *Die statuarischen Darstellungen der hellenistischen Herrscher.* Antiquitates 14. Hamburg.

Frost, Honor. 1975. "The Pharos Site, Alexandria, Egypt." *IntJNautA* 4:126–130.

Gabolde, Marc, Geneviève Galliano, et al. 2000. *Coptos: L'Égypte antique aux portes du désert.* Lyon.

Gallazzi, Claudio. 1989. "Fouilles anciennes et nouvelles sur le site de Tebtynis." *BIFAO* 89:179–191.

Galliano, Geneviève. 1997. *Les Antiquités: Guide des collections. Musée de Beaux-Arts de Lyon.* Lyon.

Gallo, Paolo. 1990. "Quelques monuments royaux provenant de Behbeit el-Hagar." *BIFAO* 90:223–228.

Gauthier, Henri. 1916. *Le livre des rois d'Égypte.* Vol. 4 (de la XXVe dynastie à la fin des Ptolémées). MIFAO 20. Cairo. [Abbreviated *LdR* 4.]

Gauthier, Henri, and Henri Sottas. 1925. *Un décret trilingue en l'honneur de Ptolémée IV.* Cairo.

Geraci, Giovanni. 1995. "*Praefectus Alexandreae et Aegypti:* Alcune riflessioni." *Simblos* 1:159–175.

Gill, David, Lin Foxhall, and Hugh Bowden. 1997. "Classical and Hellenistic Methana." In *A Rough and Rocky Place: The Landscape and Settlement History of the Methana Peninsula, Greece,* ed. Christopher Mee and Hamish Forbes, 62–76. Liverpool.

Giuliani, Luca. 1986. *Bildnis und Botschaft: Hermeneutische Untersuchungen zur Bildniskunst der römischen Republik.* Frankfurt.

Goddio, Franck, et al., eds. 1998. *Alexandria: The Submerged Royal Quarters.* London. [Abbreviated *Alexandria Submerged.*]

Goedicke, Hans. 1994. *Comments on the "Famine Stela."* San Antonio, Tex.

Govi, Cristiana Morigi, et al. 1990. *Il senso dell'arte nell'antico Egitto.* Milan.

Goyon, Jean-Claude, and Marc Gabolde. 1991. "Trois pièces de Basse Époque et d'Époque Ptolémaïque au Musée des Beaux-Arts de Lyon." *BMusLyon,* nos. 3–4:2–27.

Graindor, Paul. N.d. *Bustes et statues-portraits d'Égypte romaine.* Cairo.

Grenier, Jean-Claude. 1989. "Notes isiaques I (1–6)." *BMonMusPont* 9, 1:5–40.

———. 1993. *Museo Gregoriano Egizio.* Rome.

Griffith, Francis Llewellyn. 1931. "Four Granite Stands at Philae." *BIFAO* 30:127–130.

Grimal, Nicolas. 1996. "Fouilles sous-marines à l'est du fort Qaitbay, 1995." *BIFAO* 96:563–570.

Grimm, Alfred, Sylvia Schoske, and Dietrich Wildung. 1997. *Pharao: Kunst und Herrschaft im Alten Ägypten.* Munich.

Grimm, Günter. 1974. *Die römischen Mumienmasken aus Ägypten.* Wiesbaden.

———. 1975. *Kunst der Ptolemäer- und Römerzeit im Ägyptischen Museum Kairo.* Mainz.

———. 1998. *Alexandria: Die erste Königsstadt der hellenistischen Welt.* Mainz.

Haas, Christopher. 1997. *Alexandria in Late Antiquity: Topography and Social Conflict.* Baltimore.

Habicht, Christian. 1980. "Bemerkungen zum P. Haun. 6." *ZPE* 39:1–5.

Hall, Emma Swan. 1986. *The Pharaoh Smites His Enemies: A Comparative Study.* MÄS 44. Berlin.

Hamiaux, Marianne. 1998. *Musée du Louvre: Les sculptures grecques II: La période hellénistique (IIIe–Ier siècles avant J.-C.).* Paris.

Handler, Susan. 1971. "Architecture on the Roman Coins of Alexandria." *AJA* 75:57–74.

Hastings, Elizabeth Anne. 1997. *The Sculpture from the Sacred Animal Necropolis at North Saqqâra, 1964–1976.* London.

Hawass, Zahi. 1997. "A Statue of Caracalla Found in the Nile by a Fisherman." In *Ancient Egypt, the Aegean, and the Near East: Studies in Honour of Martha Rhoads Bell,* Vol. 1, ed. Jacke Phillips et al., 227–233. San Antonio, Tex.

Hazzard, Richard A. 1995. *Ptolemaic Coins: An Introduction for Collectors.* Toronto.

Heinen, Heinz. 1995. "Vorstufen und Anfänge des Herrscherkultes im römischen Ägypten." In *ANRW* 2, 18.5: 3144–3180. Berlin.

———. 1998. "Eine Darstellung des vergöttlichten Iulius Caesar auf einer ägyptischen Stele?" In *Imperium Romanum,* ed. Peter Kneissl and Volker Losemann, 334–345. Stuttgart.

Helbig, Wolfgang. 1963. *Führer durch die öffentlichen Sammlungen klassischer Altertümer in Rom, 1: Die Päpstlichen Sammlungen im Vatikan und Lateran.* 4th ed. Edited by Hermine Speier. Tübingen.

———. 1972. *Führer durch die öffentlichen Sammlungen klassischer Altertümer in Rom, 4: Die Staatlichen Sammlungen.* 4th ed. Edited by Hermine Speier. Tübingen.

Helck, Wolfgang, and Wolfhart Westendorf, eds. 1975–1992. *Lexikon der Ägyptologie.* Vols. 1–7. Wiesbaden. [Abbreviated *LÄ.*]

Hill, Marsha. 2000. "Ancient Egyptian Royal Bronzes, with Special Attention to the Kneeling Pose." Ph.D. dissertation, Institute of Fine Arts, New York University.

Hodel-Hoenes, Sigrid. 2000. *Life and Death in Ancient Egypt: Scenes from Private Tombs in New Kingdom Thebes.* Translated by David Warburton. Ithaca, N.Y.

Hoffmann, Friedhelm. 2000. *Ägypten. Kultur und Lebenswelt in griechisch-römischer Zeit: Eine Darstellung nach den demotischen Quellen.* Berlin.

Hölbl, Günther. 1997. "Zur Legitimation der Ptolemäer als Pharaonen." In *Selbstverständnis und Realität: Akten des Symposiums zur ägyptischen Königsideologie in Mainz 15.–17. 6. 1995,* ed. Rolf Gundlach and Christine Raedler, ÄAT 36, 1: 21–34. Wiesbaden.

———. 2000. *Altägypten im römischen Reich: Der römische Pharao und seine Tempel.* Vol. 1. Mainz.

———. 2001. *A History of the Ptolemaic Empire.* Translated by Tina Saavedra. London.

Hornemann, Bodil. 1951–1969. *Types of Ancient Egyptian Statuary.* Vols. 1–7. Copenhagen.

Hostens-Deleu, Ria. 1977. "Beeldhouwersmodellen in de Egyptische Afdeling van de Koninklijke Musea voor Kunst en Geschiedenis." *BMRAH* 49:5–65.

Huss, Werner. 1991. "Die in ptolemaiischer Zeit verfassten Synodal-Dekrete der ägyptischen Priester." *ZPE* 88:189–208.

———. 1994. *Der Makedonische König und die ägyptischen Priester. Historia* Einzelshriften 85.

———. 2001. *Ägypten in hellenistischer Zeit: 332–30 v.Chr.* Munich.

Hutmacher, Rudolf. 1965. *Das Ehrendekret für den Strategen Kallimachos.* BKP 17. Meisenheim.

Iside: Il mito, il mistero, la magia. 1997. Edited by Ermanno A. Arslan. Milan.

Jéquier, Gustave. 1921. *Les frises d'objets des sarcophages du Moyen Empire.* MIFAO 47. Cairo.

Johansen, Flemming S. 1987. "The Portraits in Marble of Gaius Julius Caesar: A Review." In *Ancient Portraits in the J. Paul Getty Museum* 1:17–40. Malibu, Calif.

Johnson, Carl Garth. 1995. "Ptolemy V and the Rosetta Decree: The Egyptianization of the Ptolemaic Kingship." *AncSoc* 26:145–155.

Johnson, Janet H. 1984. "Is the Demotic Chronicle an Anti-Greek Tract?" In *Grammata Demotika: Festschrift für Erich Lüddeckens zum 15. Juni 1983,* ed. Heinz-Josef Thissen and Karl-Th. Zauzich, 107–124. Würzburg.

Johnson, Janet H., ed. "The Chicago Demotic Dictionary." Unpublished manuscript, University of Chicago. Citations are from draft dated Jan. 14 or 15, 2001. [Abbreviated CDD.]

Josephson, Jack A. 1995. "A Fragmentary Egyptian Head from Heliopolis." *MMJ* 30:5–15.

———. 1997a. *Egyptian Royal Sculpture of the Late Period, 400–246 B.C.* DAIK 30. Mainz.

———. 1997b. "*Egyptian Sculpture of the Late Period* Revisited." *JARCE* 34:1–20.

Jucker, Hans. 1981. "Römische Herrscherbildnisse aus Ägypten." In *ANRW* 2, 12.2:667–725.

Jucker, Ines. 1975. "Zum Bildnis Ptolemaios' III. Euergetes I." *AntK* 18:17–25.

Kaiser, Werner. 1990. "Zur Büste als einer Darstellungsform ägyptischer Rundplastik." *MDAIK* 46:269–285.

Karlshausen, Christina. 1998. "L'iconographie des barques processionnelles divines à la Basse Époque: Tradition et innovations." In *Quaegebeur Studies* 2:859–873.

Kerkeslager, Allen. 1998. "The Apology of the Potter: A Translation of the Potter's Oracle." In *Jerusalem Studies in Egyptology,* ed. Irene Shirun-Grumach, 67–79. Wiesbaden.

Kessler, Dieter. 2000. "Das hellenistische Serapeum in Alexandria und Ägypten in ägyptologischer Sicht." In *Ägypten und der östliche Mittelmeerraum im 1. Jahrtausend v. Chr.,* edited by Manfred Görg and Günther Hölbl, 163–230. Wiesbaden.

Kiss, Zsolt. 1975. "Notes sur le portrait impérial romain en Egypte." *MDAIK* 31:293–302.

———. 1984. *Études sur le portrait impérial romain en Egypte.* Warsaw.

———. 1995. "Quelques portraits impériaux romains d'Egypte." *EtTrav* 17:53–71.

———. 1998. "The Sculptures." In *Alexandria Submerged,* 168–188.

Koefoed-Petersen, Otto. 1950. *Catalogue des statues et statuettes égyptiennes.* Copenhagen.

———. 1965. "Deux portraits gréco-égyptiens de la Glyptothèque Ny-Carlsberg." *BSFE* 44:9–12.

Koenen, Ludwig. 1968. "Die Prophezeiungen des 'Töpfers.'" *ZPE* 2:178–209.

———. 1993. "The Ptolemaic King as a Religious Figure." In *Images and Ideologies: Self-Definition in the Hellenistic World,* ed. Anthony W. Bulloch et al., 25–115. Berkeley.

Kozloff, Arielle P., and Betsy M. Bryan. 1992. *Egypt's Dazzling Sun: Amenhotep III and His World.* Cleveland.

Krug, Antje. 1978. "Die Bildnisse Ptolemaios' IX., X. und XI." In *DPA,* 9–24.

Kyrieleis, Helmut. 1975. *Bildnisse der Ptolemäer.* Berlin.

———. 1990. "Bildnisse des Kaisarion zu Siegelabdrücken aus Nea Paphos." In *Akten des XIII. Internationalen Kongresses für klassische Archäologie: Berlin 1988,* 456–457. Mainz.

———. 1996. "Ptolemäische Porträts auf Siegelabdrücken aus Nea Paphos (Zypern)." In *Archives,* 315–320.

Lampela, Anssi. 1998. *Rome and the Ptolemies of Egypt: The Development of Their Political Relations, 273–80 B.C.* Helsinki.

Lanciers, Eddy. 1991. "Die ägyptischen Priester des ptolemäischen Königskultes." *RdE* 42:117–145.

Landa, N., and I. Lapis. 1974. *Egyptian Antiquities in the Hermitage.* Leningrad.

Lapis, Irma Alexandrovna, and Militsa Edvinovna Mat'e. 1969. *Drevneegipetskaia skul'ptura v sobranii Gosudarstvennogo Ermitazha.* Moscow.

La Riche, William. 1996. *Alexandria: The Sunken City.* London.

La Rocca, Eugenio. 1984. *L'età d'oro di Cleopatra: Indagine sulla Tazza Farnese.* Documenti e ricerche d'arte alessandrina 5. Rome.

Laubscher, Hans Peter. 1991. "Ptolemäische Reiterbilder." *AM* 106:223–238.

Lauer, J., and C. Picard. 1955. *Les statues ptolémaïques du Serapieion de Memphis.* Paris.

Lauffray, Jean. 1979. *Karnak d'Égypte: Domaine du divin.* Paris.

Lauffray, Jean, et al. 1970. "Rapports sur les travaux de Karnak." *Kêmi* 20:57–99.

Leahy, Anthony. 1992. "Royal Iconography and Dynastic Change, 750–525 B.C.: The Blue and Cap Crowns." *JEA* 78: 223–240.

Leclant, Jean. 1956. "Fouilles et travaux en Égypte, 1954–1955." *Orientalia* 25:251–268.

Legrain, Georges. 1894. *Collection H. Hoffmann III: Catalogue des antiquités égyptiennes.* Paris.

———. 1904. "Rapport sur les travaux exécutés à Karnak du 28 septembre 1903 au 6 juillet 1904." *ASAE* 5:265–280.

———. 1905. "Renseignements sur les dernières découvertes faites à Karnak." *RT* 27:61–82.

Lembke, Katja. 1994. *Das Iseum Campense in Rom: Studie über den Isiskult unter Domitian.* Heidelberg.

———. 1998. "Die Sphingenallee von Saqqara und ihre Werkstatt." *MDAIK* 54:267–273.

Lenger, Marie-Thérèse. 1964. *Corpus des ordonnances des Ptolémées.* Brussels.

———. 1990. *Corpus des ordonnances des Ptolémées: Bilan des additions et corrections (1964–1988): Compléments à la bibliographie.* Brussels.

Leone, Anna. 1995. "Nuove acquisizioni sul tempio di Medinet Madi: Un ritratto 'idealizzato' di principe tardo-tolemaico." *RIA* ser. 3, 18:129–137.

Liepsner, Thomas F. 1980. "Modelle." *LÄ* 4:cols. 168–180.

Lise, Giorgio. 1979. *Museo archeologico raccolta egizia.* Milan.

Lloyd, Alan B. 1982a. "Nationalist Propaganda in Ptolemaic Egypt." *Historia* 31:33–55.

———. 1982b. "The Inscription of Udjaḥorresnet: A Collaborator's Testament." *JEA* 68:166–180.

———. 2000. "The Ptolemaic Period (332–30 B.C.)." In *The Oxford History of Ancient Egypt,* ed. Ian Shaw, 395–421. Oxford.

Lollio Barberi, O., et al. 1995. *Le antichità egiziane di Roma imperiale.* Rome.

López, Jesús. 1963. "Dos estatuas egipcias del Museo Arqueológico Nacional." *Ampurias* 25:211–217.

Lucas, Alfred. 1989. *Ancient Egyptian Materials and Industries.* 4th ed. Rev. by J. R. Harris. London.

Maehler, Herwig. 1983. "Egypt under the Last Ptolemies." *BICS* 30:1–16.

Maehler, Herwig, and Volker Michael Strocka, eds. 1978. *Das ptolemäische Ägypten. Akten des internationalen Symposions 27.–29. September 1976 in Berlin.* Mainz. [Abbreviated *DPA.*]

Malaise, Michel. 1966. "Sésostris, pharaon de légende et d'histoire." *CdE* 41:244–272.

———. 1999. "L'étymologie égyptienne du toponyme 'Canope.'" *CdE* 74:224–230.

Malaise, Michel, and Jean Winand. 1993. "La racine *grb* et l'Amon-*grb.*" *CdE* 68:12–28.

Malek, Jaromir, Diana Magee, and Elizabeth Miles. 1999. *Topographical Bibliography of Ancient Egyptian Hieroglyphic Texts, Statues, Reliefs, and Paintings.* Vol. 8 (objects of provenance not known). Oxford. [Abbreviated PM 8.]

Manera, Fausta, and Claudia Mazza. 2001. *Le collezioni egizie del Museo Nazionale Romano.* Rome.

Marangou, Lila. 1971. "Ptolemäische Fingerringe aus Bein." *AM* 86:163–171.

Mariette, Auguste. 1887. "Fragments et documents relatifs aux fouilles de Sân." *RT* 9:1–20.

Massner, Anne-Kathrein. 1986. "Ägyptisierende Bildnisse des Kaisers Claudius." *AntK* 29:63–67.

Maystre, Charles. 1992. *Les grands prêtres de Ptah de Memphis.* OBO 113. Freiburg.

McCann, Anna Marguerite. 1968. *The Portraits of Septimius Severus (A.D. 193–211). MAAR* 30. Rome.

McKenzie, Judith. 1990. *The Architecture of Petra.* British Academy Monographs in Archaeology 1. Oxford.

Merkelbach, Reinhold. 1995. *Isis regina—Zeus Sarapis: Die griechisch-ägyptische Religion nach den Quellen dargestellt.* Stuttgart.

Meyboom, Paul G. P. 1995. *The Nile Mosaic of Palestrina: Early Evidence of Egyptian Religion in Italy.* Religions in the Graeco-Roman World 121. Leiden.

Michalowski, Kazimierz. 1935. "Un portrait égyptien d'Auguste au Musée du Caire." *BIFAO* 35:73–88.

Milleker, Elizabeth J., ed. 2000. *The Year One: Art of the Ancient World East and West.* New York.

Milne, Joseph Grafton. 1916. "Ptolemaic Seal Impressions." *JHS* 36:87–101.

Minas, Martina. 2000. *Die hieroglyphischen Ahnenreihen der ptolemäischen Könige.* Aegyptiaca Treverensia 9. Mainz.

Mogensen, Maria. 1930. *La Glyptothèque Ny Carlsberg: La collection égyptienne.* Copenhagen.

Montet, Pierre. 1958. "Un chef-d'oeuvre de l'art gréco-égyptien: La statue de Panemerit." *MonPiot* 50:1–10.

Mørkholm, Otto. 1991. *Early Hellenistic Coinage from the Accession of Alexander to the Peace of Apamea (336–186 B.C.).* Edited by Philip Grierson and Ulla Westermark. Cambridge.

Müller, Hans Wolfgang. 1955. "Der Torso einer Königsstatue im Museo Archeologico zu Florenz." In *Studi Rosellini* 2: 181–221. Pisa.

———. 1959. *Antike Kunstwerke: Nachlass Dr. Jacob Hirsch II: Teil und anderer Besitz.* Auction catalog, Ars Antiqua. Lucern.

———. 1961. *Die Sammlung Wilhelm Esch, Duisburg: Werke altägyptischer und Koptischer Kunst.* Munich.

———. 1966. *Die ägyptische Sammlung des Bayerischen Staates.* Munich.

———. 1969. *Der Isiskult im antiken Benevent und Katalog der Skulpturen aus den ägyptischen Heiligtümern im Museo del Sannio zu Benevent.* MÄS 16. Berlin.

———. 1970. "Bildnisse König Nektanebos' I. (380–362 v. Chr.)." *Pantheon* 28:89–99.

Müller, Wilhelm Max. 1920. *The Bilingual Decrees of Philae.* Egyptological Researches 3. Washington, D.C.

Myśliwiec, Karol. 1973. "A Contribution to the Study of the Ptolemaic Royal Portrait." *EtTrav* 7:41–51.

———. 1988. *Royal Portraiture of the Dynasties XXI–XXX.* Mainz.

———. 1992. "A Lower Egyptian Sculptor's 'School' of the Late Dynastic–Early Ptolemaic Period." In *Cult and Ritual in the Ancient Near East,* ed. H.I.H. Prince Takahito Mikasa, 61–80. Wiesbaden.

Nachtergael, Georges. 1999. "Graffites du Sarapieion de Memphis." *CdE* 74:344–356.

Naville, Édouard. 1885. *The Store-City of Pithom and the Route of the Exodus.* London.

———. 1894. *Ahnas el Medineh (Heracleopolis Magna).* London.

Naville, Édouard, and Francis Llewellyn Griffith. 1890. *The Mound of the Jew and the City of Onias.* London.

Needler, Winifred. 1949. "Some Ptolemaic Sculptures in the Yale University Art Gallery." *Berytus* 9:129–141.

Nicholson, Paul T., and Ian Shaw, eds. 2000. *Ancient Egyptian Materials and Technology.* Cambridge.

Nicole, Georges, and Gaston Darier. 1909. "Le sanctuaire des dieux orientaux au Janicule." *MEFR* 29:3–86.

Nielsen, Anne Marie, and Jan Stubbe Østergaard. 1997. *Hellenism: The Eastern Mediterranean in the Hellenistic Period.* Copenhagen.

Nock, Arthur Darby. 1930. "*Sunnaos Theos.*" *HSCP* 41:1–62.

Oates, John F. 1995. *The Ptolemaic Basilikos Grammateus. BASP* suppl. 8. Atlanta.

Ockinga, Boyo. 1984. *Die Gottebenbildlichkeit im Alten Ägypten und im Alten Testament.* ÄAT 7. Wiesbaden.

O'Connor, David, and David P. Silverman, eds. 1995. *Ancient Egyptian Kingship.* Leiden.

Onasch, Christian. 1976. "Zur Königsideologie der Ptolemäer in den Dekreten von Kanopus und Memphis (Rosettana)." *AfP* 24/25:137–155.

Pantos, P. A. 1985. *Ta Sphragismata tēs Aitōlikēs Kallipoleōs.* Athens.

Parlasca, Klaus. 1967. "Ein verkanntes hellenistisches Herrscherbildnis." *JdI* 82:167–194.

———. 1973. "Osiris und Osirisglaube in der Kaiserzeit." In *Les syncrétismes dans les religions grecque et romaine. Colloque de Strasbourg (9–11 juin 1971),* 95–102. Paris.

———. 1976. "Bildnisse des Ptolemaios Apion." In *Festschrift für Gerhard Kleiner,* 95–99. Tübingen.

———. 1978. "Probleme der späten Ptolemäerbildnisse." In *DPA,* 25–30.

Parlebas, Jacques. 1973. *Antiquités égyptiennes.* Strasbourg.

Pasqua, Roberta Belli. 1995. *Sculture di età romana in "basalto."* Rome.

Pensabene, Patrizio. 1983. "Lastre di chiusura di loculi con *naiskoi* egizi e stele funerarie con ritratto del museo di alessandria." In *Studi Adriani* 4:91–119.

———. 1993. *Elementi architettonici di Alessandria e di altri siti egiziani.* Repertorio d'arte dell'Egitto greco-romano, ser. C, 3. Rome.

Peremans, Willy. 1982. "Sur le bilinguisme dans l'Égypte des Lagides." In *Studia Paulo Naster Oblata II: Orientalia Antiqua,* ed. Jan Quaegebeur, 143–154. Louvain.

Pernigotti, Sergio. 1980. *La statuaria egiziana nel Museo Civico Archeologico di Bologna.* Bologna.

Pestman, P. W. 1995. "Haronnophris and Chaonnophris: Two Indigenous Pharaohs in Ptolemaic Egypt (205–186 B.C.)." In *Hundred-Gated Thebes,* 101–137.

Petrie, W. M. Flinders. 1889. *Tanis.* Part 1, *1883–4.* London.

———. 1896. *Koptos.* London.

———. 1909. *Memphis.* Vol. 1. London.

Petrie, W. M. Flinders, et al. 1915. *Heliopolis, Kafr Ammar and Shurafa.* London.

Pfrommer, Michael. 1987. *Studien zu Alexandrinischer und grossgriechischer Toreutik frühhellenistischer Zeit.* Berlin.

———. 1999. *Alexandria: Im Schatten der Pyramiden.* Mainz.

Plantzos, Dimitris. 1992. "*Ektheōsis Arsinoēs:* On the Cult of Arsinoe Philadelphos." *Archaiognōsia* 7:119–133.

———. 1996a. "Female Portrait Types from the Edfu Hoard of Clay Seal Impressions." In *Archives,* 307–313.

———. 1996b. "Ptolemaic Cameos of the Second and First Centuries B.C." *OxfJA* 15, no. 1:39–61.

———. 1999. *Hellenistic Engraved Gems.* Oxford.

Pollini, John. 1999. Review of Boschung 1993. *ArtB* 81:723–735.

Porter, Bertha, and Rosalind L. B. Moss. 1927–1981. *Topographical Bibliography of Ancient Egyptian Hieroglyphic Texts, Reliefs, and Paintings.* Vols. 1–7. Oxford. [Abbreviated PM 1–7.]

Priese, Karl-Heinz, ed. 1991. *Das Ägyptische Museum Berlin.* Berlin.

Quaegebeur, Jan. 1971. "Ptolémée II en adoration devant Arsinoé II divinisée." *BIFAO* 69:191–217.

———. 1980. "The Genealogy of the Memphite High Priest Family in the Hellenistic Period." In *Studies on Ptolemaic Memphis,* SH 24, 43–81. Louvain.

———. 1983. "Trois statues de femme d'époque ptolémaïque." In *Artibus Aegypti: Studia in honorem Bernardi V. Bothmer a collegis amicis discipulis conscripta,* ed. Herman De Meulenaere and L. Limme, 109–127. Brussels.

———. 1989. "The Egyptian Clergy and the Cult of the Ptolemaic Dynasty." *AncSoc* 20:93–116.

———. 1998. "Documents égyptiens anciens et nouveaux relatifs à Arsinoé Philadelphe." In *Le culte du souverain dans l'Égypte ptolémaïque au IIIe siècle avant notre ère. Actes du colloque international, Bruxelles 10 mai 1995,* ed. Henri Melaerts, SH 34, 73–108. Louvain.

Quirke, Stephen, and Carol Andrews. 1989. *The Rosetta Stone: Facsimile Drawing with an Introduction and Translations.* New York.

Rabe, Hugo, ed. 1926. *Aphthonii Progymnasmata.* Rhetores Graeci 10. Leipzig.

Raeder, Joachim. 1983. *Die statuarische Ausstattung der Villa Hadriana bei Tivoli.* Frankfurt.

Raue, Dietrich. 1999. *Heliopolis und das Haus des Re.* Berlin.

Redford, Donald B. 1986. *Pharaonic King-Lists, Annals and Day-Books: A Contribution to the Study of the Egyptian Sense of History.* Mississauga, Ontario.

———, ed. 2001. *The Oxford Encyclopedia of Ancient Egypt.* Vols. 1–3. Oxford. [Abbreviated *OEAE.*]

Reisner, George A. 1931. *Mycerinus: The Temples of the Third Pyramid at Giza.* Cambridge.

Reymond, Eve A. E. 1981. *From the Records of a Priestly Family from Memphis.* Vol. 1. Wiesbaden.

Ridgway, Brunilde Sismondo. 1990. *Hellenistic Sculpture I: The Styles of ca. 331–200 B.C.* Madison, Wis.

———. 2000. *Hellenistic Sculpture II: The Styles of ca. 200–100 B.C.* Madison, Wis.

Robins, Gay. 1994. *Proportion and Style in Ancient Egyptian Art.* Austin, Tex.

Rochette, Bruno. 1996. "Sur le bilinguisme dans l'Égypte Gréco-Romaine." *CdE* 71:153–168.

Rodin collectionneur. 1967. Paris.

Roeder, Günther. 1932. *Statuen ägyptischer Königinnen im Anschluss an den Torso Amon-erdas II. in Sydney untersucht.* Leipzig.

———. 1941. "Lebensgrosse Tonmodelle aus einer altägyptischen Bildhauerwerkstatt." *JPKS* 62:145–170.

———. 1959. *Hermopolis, 1929–1939.* Hildesheim.

Roehrig, Catharine H. 1999. "Reserve Heads: An Enigma of

Old Kingdom Sculpture." In *Egyptian Art in the Age of the Pyramids,* 73–81. New York.

Rogge, Eva. 1999. *Statuen der 30. Dynastie und der ptolemäisch-römischen Epoche.* CAA, Kunsthistorisches Museum, Wien, Ägyptisch-Orientalische Sammlung 11. Mainz.

Rose, Charles Brian. 1997. *Dynastic Commemoration and Imperial Portraiture in the Julio-Claudian Period.* Cambridge.

Roullet, Anne. 1972. *The Egyptian and Egyptianizing Monuments of Imperial Rome.* EPRO 20. Leiden.

Rowe, Alan. 1946. "Discovery of the Famous Temple and Enclosure of Serapis at Alexandria." *ASAE* suppl. 2:1–70.

———. 1948. "Two Ptolemaic Statues Found in Tolmeita." *ASAE* suppl. 12:1–84.

———. 1957. "A Contribution to the Archaeology of the Western Desert: IV. The Great Serapeum of Alexandria." *BJRylLib* 39:485–512.

Rubensohn, Otto. 1913. "Neue Inschriften aus Ägypten." *AfP* 5:156–169.

Russmann, Edna R. 1974. *The Representation of the King in the XXVth Dynasty.* Brussels and Brooklyn.

———. 1989. *Egyptian Sculpture: Cairo and Luxor.* Austin, Tex.

———. 1997. "Vulture and Cobra at the King's Brow." In *Chief of Seers: Egyptian Studies in Memory of Cyril Aldred,* ed. Elizabeth Goring, Nicholas Reeves, and John Ruffle, 266–284. London.

Russmann, Edna R., et al. N.d. "Egyptian Art." In *Notable Acquisitions 1981–1982: The Metropolitan Museum of Art,* 6–9. New York.

———. 2001. *Eternal Egypt: Masterworks of Ancient Art from the British Museum.* Berkeley.

Saatsoglou-Paliadeli, Chryssoula. 1993. "Aspects of Ancient Macedonian Costume." *JHS* 113:122–147.

Sabottka, Michael. 1989. "Das Serapeum in Alexandria." Ph.D. dissertation, Technischen Universität Berlin.

Saleh, Mohamed, and Hourig Sourouzian. 1987. *Official Catalogue: The Egyptian Museum Cairo.* Mainz.

Sambin, Chantal, and Jean-François Carlotti. 1995. "Une porte de fête-sed de Ptolémée II remployée dans le temple de Montou à Médamoud." *BIFAO* 95:383–457.

Samuel, A. E. 1993. "The Ptolemies and the Ideology of Kingship." In *Hellenistic History and Culture,* ed. Peter Green, 168–210. Berkeley.

Satzinger, Helmut. 1987. *Museum: Ägyptisch-Orientalischen Sammlung Kunsthistorisches Museum Wien.* Munich.

Sauneron, Serge. 1960. "Un document égyptien relatif à la divinisation de la reine Arsinoé II." *BIFAO* 60:83–109.

Schäfer, Heinrich. 1986. *Principles of Egyptian Art.* 2d ed. Edited by Emma Brunner-Traut. Translated and edited by John Baines. Oxford.

Schmidt, Inga. 1995. *Hellenistische Statuenbasen.* AS 9. Frankfurt and New York.

Schmidt-Dounas, Barbara. 1994. "Statuen hellenistischer Könige als Synnaoi Theoi." *Egnatia* 4:71–141.

Scott, Gerry D., III. 1986. *Ancient Egyptian Art at Yale.* New Haven.

Seidel, Matthias. 1996. *Die königlichen Statuengruppen I: Die Denkmäler vom Alten Reich bis zum Ende der 18. Dynastie.* Hildesheim.

Seif, Hakim Effendi Abou. 1921. "Une petite trouvaille à Karnak de modèles de sculpture." *ASAE* 21:214–221.

Seipel, Wilfried. 1992. *Gott Mensch Pharao.* Vienna.

Sethe, Kurt. 1904. *Hieroglyphische Urkunden der griechisch-römischen Zeit.* Vol. 1. Leipzig.

Seyrig, Henri. 1968. "Un petit portrait royal." *RA:* 251–256.

Sharpe, Samuel. 1855. *Egyptian Inscriptions from the British Museum and Other Sources (Second Series).* London.

Shaw, Ian, and Paul Nicholson. 1995. *The Dictionary of Ancient Egypt.* London.

Shore, Arthur Frank. 1979. "Votive Objects from Dendera of the Graeco-Roman Period." In *Glimpses of Ancient Egypt: Studies in Honour of H. W. Fairman,* ed. John Ruffle, G. A. Gaballa, and Kenneth A. Kitchen, 138–160. Warminster.

Simpson, R. S. 1996. *Demotic Grammar in the Ptolemaic Sacerdotal Decrees.* Oxford.

Sist, Loredana. 1996. *Museo Barracco: Arte egizia.* Rome.

Six, J. 1887. "Ein Porträt des Ptolemaios VI Philometor." *AM* 12:212–222.

Smith, R.R.R. 1988. *Hellenistic Royal Portraits.* Oxford.

———. 1991. *Hellenistic Sculpture.* London.

———. 1996. "Ptolemaic Portraits: Alexandrian Types, Egyptian Versions." In *Alexandrianism,* 203–213.

Sourouzian, Hourig. 1989. *Les monuments du roi Merenptah.* DAIK 22. Mainz.

———. 1994. "Inventaire iconographique des statues en manteau jubilaire." In *Hommages à Jean Leclant,* Vol. 1, BdE 106, 1:499–530.

Spencer, A. J., et al. 1989. *Excavations at El-Ashmunein II: The Temple Area.* London.

Spiegelberg, Wilhelm. 1909. *Ausgewählte Kunst-Denkmäler der aegyptischen Sammlung der Kaiser Wilhelms Universität Strassburg.* Strasbourg.

Spier, Jeffrey. 1989. "A Group of Ptolemaic Engraved Garnets." *JWalt* 47:21–38.

Stanwick, Paul Edmund. 1992. "A Royal Ptolemaic Bust in Alexandria." *JARCE* 29:131–141.

———. 2000. "Two Ptolemies in Alexandria." *BSAA* 46:51–57.

Steindorff, George. 1946. *Catalogue of the Egyptian Sculpture in the Walters Art Gallery.* Baltimore.

Stewart, Andrew. 1990. Review of Smith 1988. *AJA* 94:508–509.

Stewart, H. M. 1983. *Egyptian Stelae, Reliefs and Paintings from the Petrie Collection.* Vol. 3. Warminster.

Strauss, Christine. 1980. "Kronen." *LÄ* 3: cols. 811–816.

Strocka, Volker Michael. 1980. "Augustus als Pharao." In *Eikones: Studien zum griechischen und römischen Bildnis. Fest-*

schrift Hans Jucker, ed. Rolf A. Stucky and Ines Jucker, 177–180. Bern.

Svenson, Dominique. 1995. *Darstellungen hellenistischer Könige mit Götterattributen.* AS 10. Frankfurt.

Tait, W. J. 1982. Review of *DPA. BiOr* 39: cols. 78–87.

Tefnin, Roland. 1991. *Art et magie au temps des Pyramides: L'énigme des têtes dites "de remplacement."* Monumenta Aegyptiaca 5. Brussels.

Thiers, Christophe. 1998. "Une statue de Ptolémée Éuergète Ier." *RdE* 49:259–264.

———. 1999. "Ptolémée Philadelphe et les prêtres de Saïs: La stèle *Codex Ursinianus,* fol. 6 r° + Naples 1034 + Louvre C.123." *BIFAO* 99:423–445.

———. 2000. Review of Henri Melaerts, ed., *Le culte du souverain dans l'Égypte ptolémaïque au IIIe siècle avant notre ère. BiOr* 57: cols. 89–92.

Thissen, Heinz-Josef. 1966. *Studien zum Raphiadekret.* Meisenheim am Glan.

———. 1979. "Demotische Graffiti des Paneions im Wadi Hammamat." *Enchoria* 9:63–92.

Thompson, Dorothy Burr. 1973. *Ptolemaic Oinochoai and Portraits in Faience: Aspects of the Ruler-Cult.* Oxford.

Thompson, Dorothy J. 1988. *Memphis under the Ptolemies.* Princeton.

———. 1993. "From Model Tools to Written Tablets: The Ptolemies in Egypt." *JJurP* 23:149–156.

———. 1994a. "The Later Ptolemies." In *The Last Age of the Roman Republic, 146–43 B.C.* CAH 9, 2d ed., 310–321. Cambridge.

———. 1994b. "Literacy and Power in Ptolemaic Egypt." In *Literacy and Power in the Ancient World,* ed. Alan K. Bowman and Greg Woolf, 67–83. Cambridge.

———. 2000. "Alexandria: The City by the Sea." *BSAA* 46: 73–79.

Tiradritti, Francesco, ed. 1999. *Egyptian Treasures from the Egyptian Museum in Cairo.* New York.

Tkaczow, Barbara. 1993. *The Topography of Ancient Alexandria (An Archaeological Map).* Warsaw.

Tomlinson, Richard. 1996. "Alexandria: The Hellenistic Arrangement." *Quaderni ticinesi di numismatica e antichità classiche* 25:155–167.

Traunecker, Claude. 1979. "Essai sur l'histoire de la XXIXe dynastie." *BIFAO* 79:395–436.

———. 1991. "Observations sur le décor des temples égyptiens." In *L'image et la production du sacré,* 77–101. Paris.

———. 1992. *Coptos: Hommes et dieux sur le parvis de Geb.* OLA 43. Louvain.

Troy, Lana Kay. 1986. *Patterns of Queenship in Ancient Egyptian Myth and History.* Uppsala.

Turaev, Boris. 1911. "Objets égyptiens et égyptisants trouvés dans la russie méridionale." *RA* 18:20–35.

Turner, Eric G. 1984. "Ptolemaic Egypt." In *The Hellenistic World,* CAH 7, part 1, 2d ed., 118–174. Cambridge.

Tzachou-Alexandri, Olga, ed. 1995. *The World of Egypt in the National Archaeological Museum.* Athens.

Van de Walle, Baudoin. 1949. "La 'Cléopâtre' de Mariemont." *CdE* 24:19–32.

———. 1950. "Un nouveau document concernant le prétendu groupe d'Antoine et Cléopâtre." *CdE* 25:31–35.

———. 1952. "Antiquités égyptiennes." In *Les antiquités égyptiennes, grecques, étrusques, romaines et gallo-romaines du Musée de Mariemont,* ed. G. Faider-Feytmans, 15–61. Brussels.

Vandier, Jacques. 1958. *Manuel d'archéologie égyptienne III: Les grandes époques: La statuaire.* Paris.

———. 1961. "Trois statues égyptiennes au Musée du Louvre." *RdL* 11:243–258.

Vandorpe, Katelijn. 1995. "City of Many a Gate, Harbour for Many a Rebel: Historical and Topographical Outline of Greco-Roman Thebes." In *Hundred-Gated Thebes,* 203–239.

———. 1996. "Seals in and on the Papyri of Greco-Roman and Byzantine Egypt." In *Archives,* 231–291.

van Haarlem, Willem. 1986. *Allard Pierson Museum, Amsterdam.* Fasc. 1, CAA. Mainz.

Varga, Edith. 1960. "Contributions à l'histoire des modèles de sculpture en stuc de l'ancienne Égypte." *BMusHongr* 16:3–20.

Varner, Eric R., ed. 2000. *From Caligula to Constantine: Tyranny and Transformation in Roman Portraiture.* Atlanta.

Vassilika, Eleni. 1989. *Ptolemaic Philae.* OLA 34. Louvain.

———. 1995. *Fitzwilliam Museum Handbooks: Egyptian Art.* Cambridge.

Vierneisel, Klaus. 1980. "Die Berliner Kleopatra." *JbBerlMus* 22:5–33.

Vikan, Gary. 1995. *Catalogue of the Sculpture in the Dumbarton Oaks Collection from the Ptolemaic Period to the Renaissance.* Washington, D.C.

Vleeming, S. P., ed. 1995. *Hundred-Gated Thebes: Acts of a Colloquium on Thebes and the Theban Area in the Graeco-Roman Period.* PLB 27. Leiden. [Abbreviated *Hundred-Gated Thebes.*]

Vogelsang-Eastwood, Gillian. 1993. *Pharaonic Egyptian Clothing.* Leiden.

Vogliano, Achille. 1936. *Primo rapporto degli scavi condotti dalla missione archeologica d'egitto della R. Università di Milano nella zona di Madinet Madi (Campagna inverno e primavera 1935–XIII).* Milan.

———. 1937. *Secondo rapporto degli scavi condotti dalla missione archeologica d'egitto della R. Università di Milano nella zona di Madinet Madi (Campagna inverno e primavera 1936–XIV).* Milan.

———. 1938a. *Mostra delle antichità rinvenute nelle campagne d'egitto condotte dalla missione della R. Università di Milano 1934–37 (XII–XV).* Milan.

———. 1938b. "Rapporto preliminare della IVa campagna di scavo a Madinet Madi (R. Università di Milano)." *ASAE* 38:533–549.

———. 1939a. "Madinet Madi: Fouilles de l'Université Royale de Milan." *CdE* 14:87–89.

———. 1939b. "Rapporto preliminare della Va campagna di scavo a Madinet Madi, R. Università di Milano." *ASAE* 39: 687–695.

———. 1942. *Un' impresa archeologica Milanese ai margini orientali del Deserto Libico.* Milan.

Vollenweider, Marie-Louise. 1995. *Camées et intailles. Tome I. Les portraits grecs du Cabinet des médailles. Catalogue raisonné.* Paris.

Vycichl, Werner. 1983. *Dictionnaire étymologique de la langue copte.* Louvain.

Wagner, Guy. 1971. "Inscriptions grecques du temple de Karnak I." *BIFAO* 70:1–38.

Waitkus, Wolfgang. 1997. *Die Texte in den unteren Krypten des Hathortempels von Dendera.* MÄS 47. Mainz.

Walbank, F. W. 1984. "Monarchies and Monarchic Ideas." In *The Hellenistic World,* CAH 7, part 1, 2d ed., 62–100. Cambridge.

Walker, Susan, and Peter Higgs, eds. 2001. *Cleopatra of Egypt: From History to Myth.* London.

Walters, Elizabeth, J. 1988. *Attic Grave Reliefs that Represent Women in the Dress of Isis. Hesperia* suppl. 22.

Weill, Raymond, and Pierre Jouguet. 1934. "Horus-Apollon au Kôm el-Ahmar de Zawiét el-Maietin." In *Mélanges Maspero* 2, MIFAO 67, 81–104. Cairo.

Wildung, Dietrich, and Günter Grimm. 1978. *Götter-Pharaonen.* Mainz.

Wildung, Dietrich, and Sylvia Schoske. 1984. *Nofret—Die Schöne.* Mainz.

Wilhelm, Adolf. 1946. "*Αιγυπτιακα.*" *SBWien* 224:5ff.

Wilkinson, John Gardner. 1843. *Modern Egypt and Thebes.* Vol. 1. London.

Willer, Frank. 1996. "Beobachtungen zur Sockelung von bronzenen Statuen und Statuetten." *Bonner Jahrbuch* 196: 337–370.

Wilson, Penelope. 1997. *A Ptolemaic Lexikon: A Lexicographical Study of the Texts in the Temple of Edfu.* OLA 78. Louvain.

Winnicki, Jan Krzysztof. 1994. "Carrying Off and Bringing Home the Statues of the Gods." *JJurP* 24:149–190.

Winter, Erich. 1978. "Der Herrscherkult in den ägyptischen Ptolemäertempeln." In *DPA,* 147–160.

Woldering, Irmgard. 1961. *Meisterwerke des Kestner-Museums zu Hannover.* Hannover.

Young, Eric. 1964. "Sculptors' Models or Votives?" *BMMA* 22: 247–256.

Yoyotte, Jean. 1958. "Notes de toponymie égyptienne." *MDAIK* 16:414–430.

———. 1959. "Nectanébo II comme faucon divin?" *Kêmi* 15: 70–74.

———. 1998. "Pharaonica." In *Alexandria Submerged,* 199–219.

Yoyotte, Jean, et al. 1997. *Égypte romaine: L'autre Égypte.* Marseille.

Yoyotte, Jean, and Pascal Charvet. 1997. *Strabon: Le voyage en Égypte. Un regard romain.* Paris.

Yoyotte, Jean, and Pierre Chuvin. 1988. "Le Zeus Casios de Péluse à Tivoli: Une hypothèse." *BIFAO* 88:165–180.

Ziegler, Christiane. 1990. *The Louvre: Egyptian Antiquities.* London.

INDEX

Principal discussions are **bolded.** Figure numbers are *italicized.* HdK = head of king. HdQ = head of queen. "–" = no inventory number.

OBJECT INDEX

GENERAL INDEX

SELECT EGYPTIAN AND GREEK WORDS

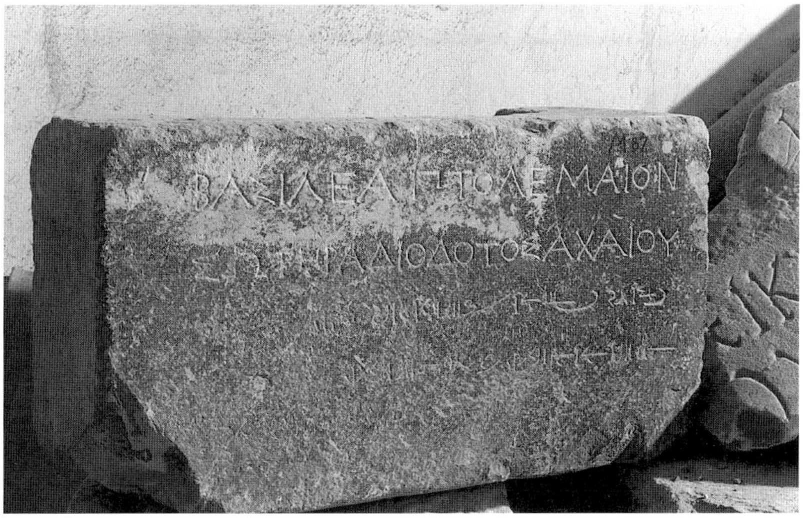

1 [A2] (*left*). Statue base dedicated to Ptolemy I. Alexandria, Graeco-Roman Museum 19 (photo: Centre d'Études Alexandrines).

2–3 [A3] (*below*). Standing statue inscribed for Ptolemy II. Rome, Vatican, Museo Gregoriano Egizio 22681 (photos: Vatican Museums).

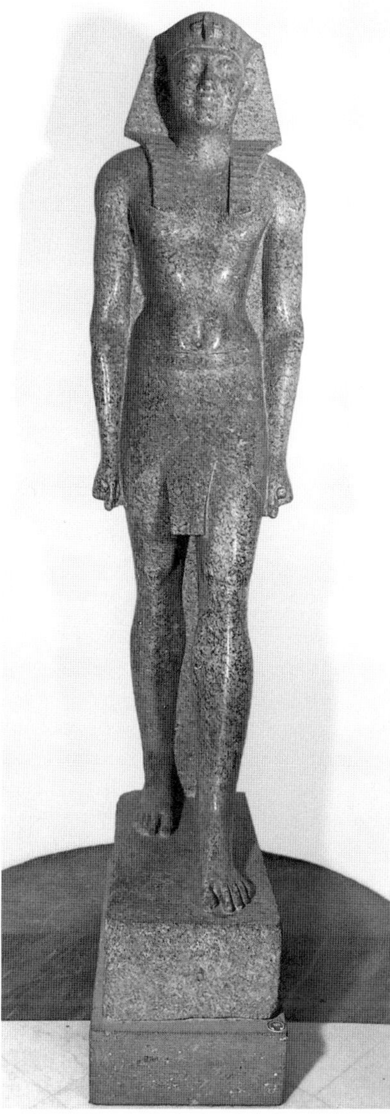

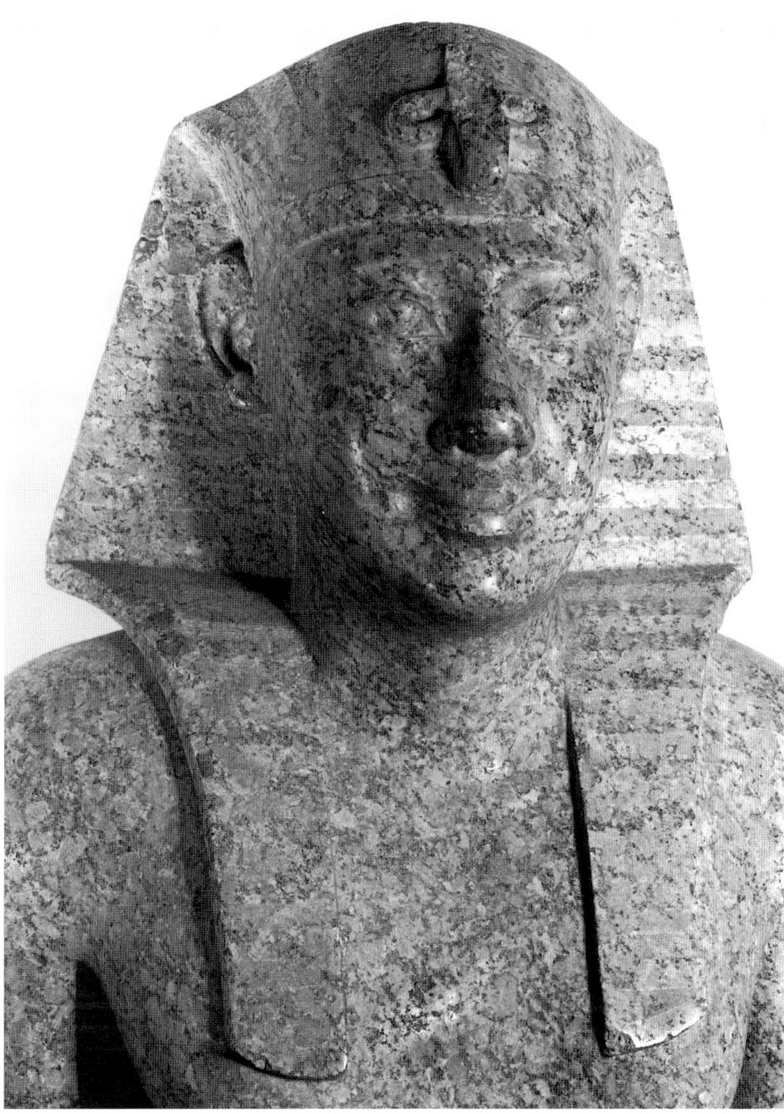

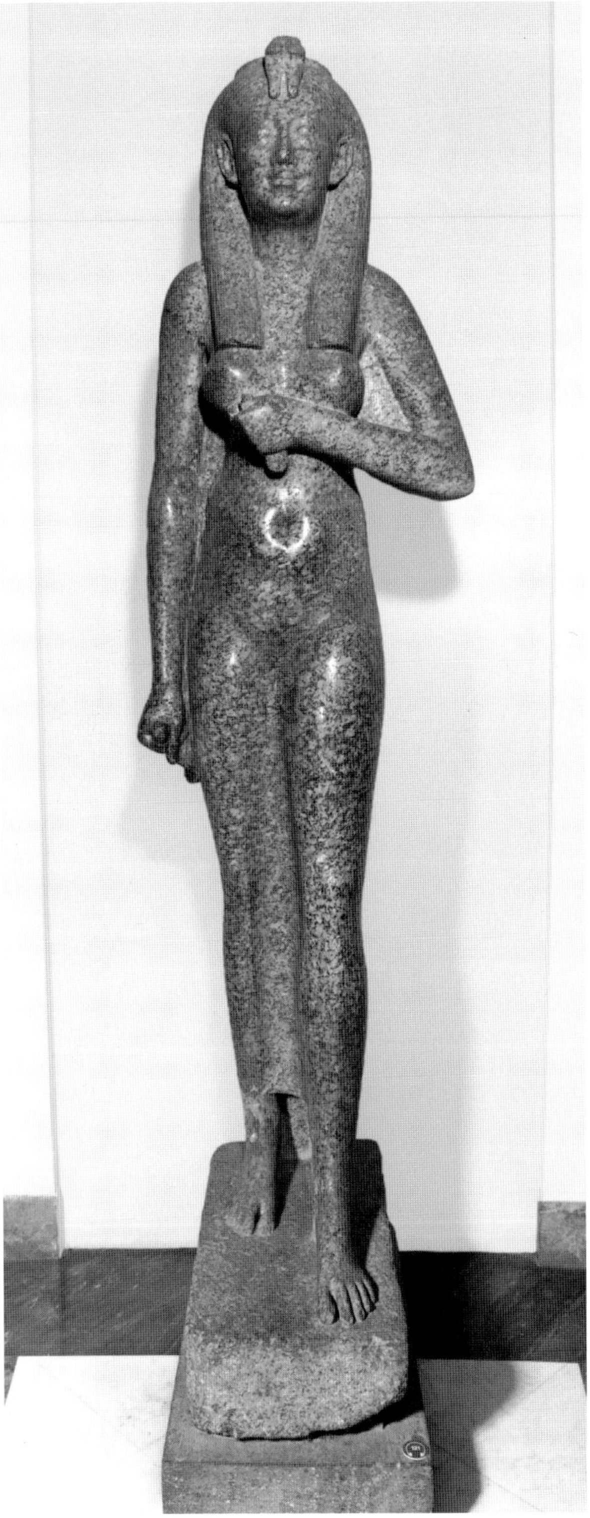

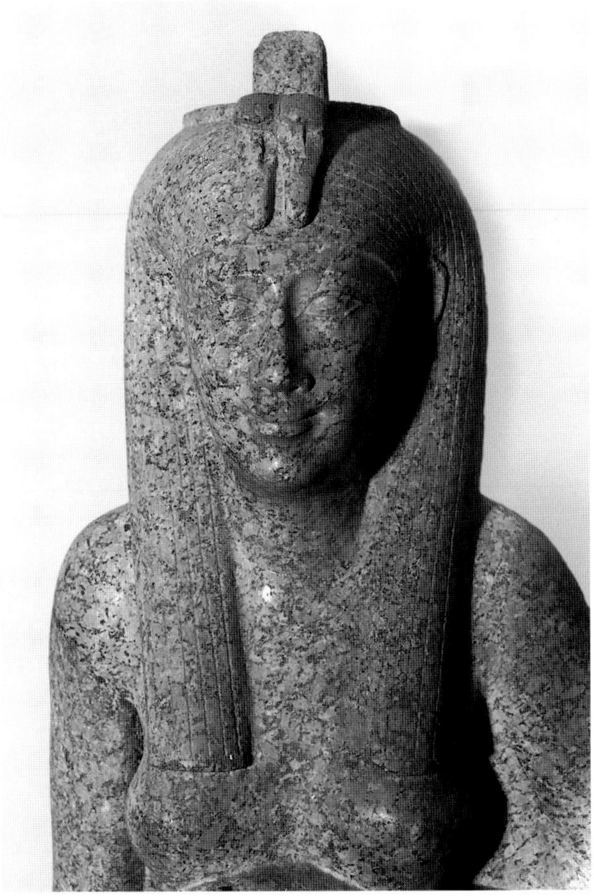

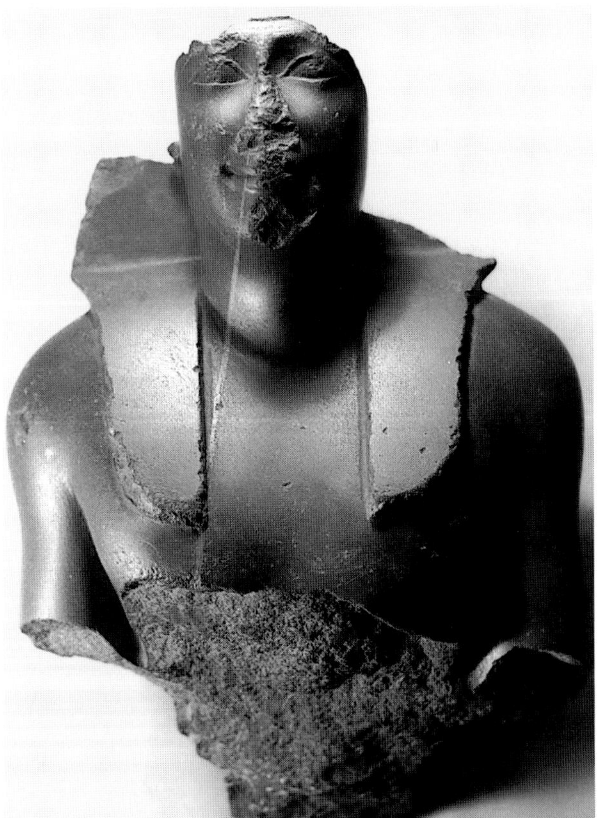

4–5 [A4] (*above, left and right*). Standing statue inscribed for Arsinoe II. Rome, Vatican, Museo Gregoriano Egizio 22682 (photos: Vatican Museums).

6 [A5] (*right*). Fragmentary statue inscribed for Ptolemy II. Collection de l'Institut d'Égyptologie, Université Marc Bloch, Strasbourg 1585 (photo: author).

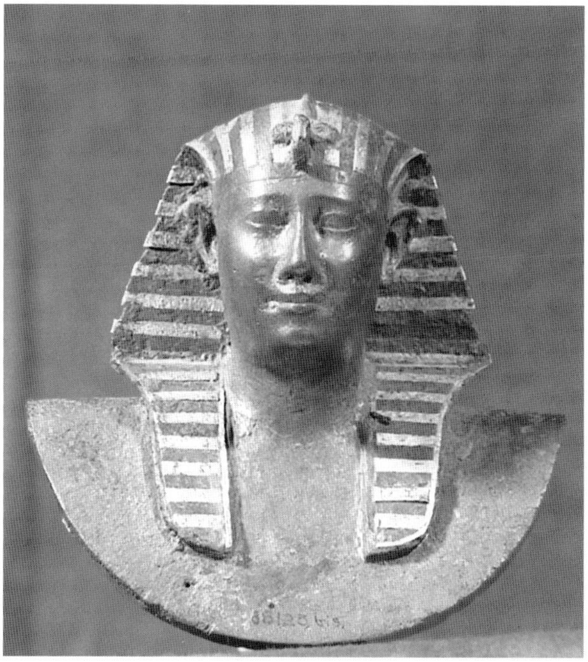

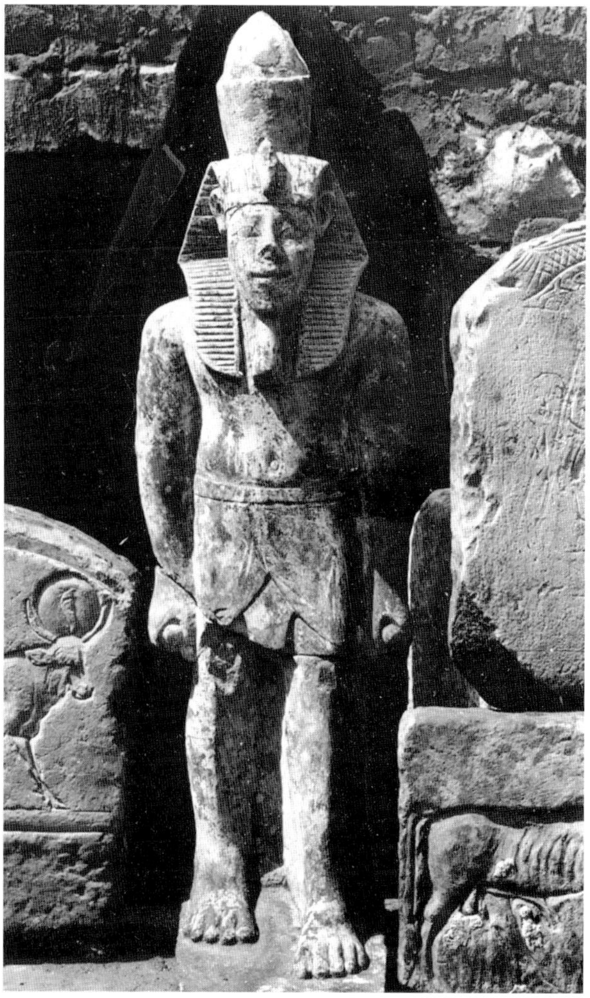

7 [A7] (*above*). Bust of king. Attributed to Ptolemy II. Cairo JE 38123 bis (photo: Sherif Sonbol, Cairo).

8 [A9] (*right*). Standing king. Third century B.C. London, British Museum EA 1190 (photo: ©The Egypt Exploration Society).

9 [A10] (*below*). Fragmentary seated group inscribed for Ptolemy II, Arsinoe II, and Amun. Alexandria, Graeco-Roman Museum 11261 (photo: author).

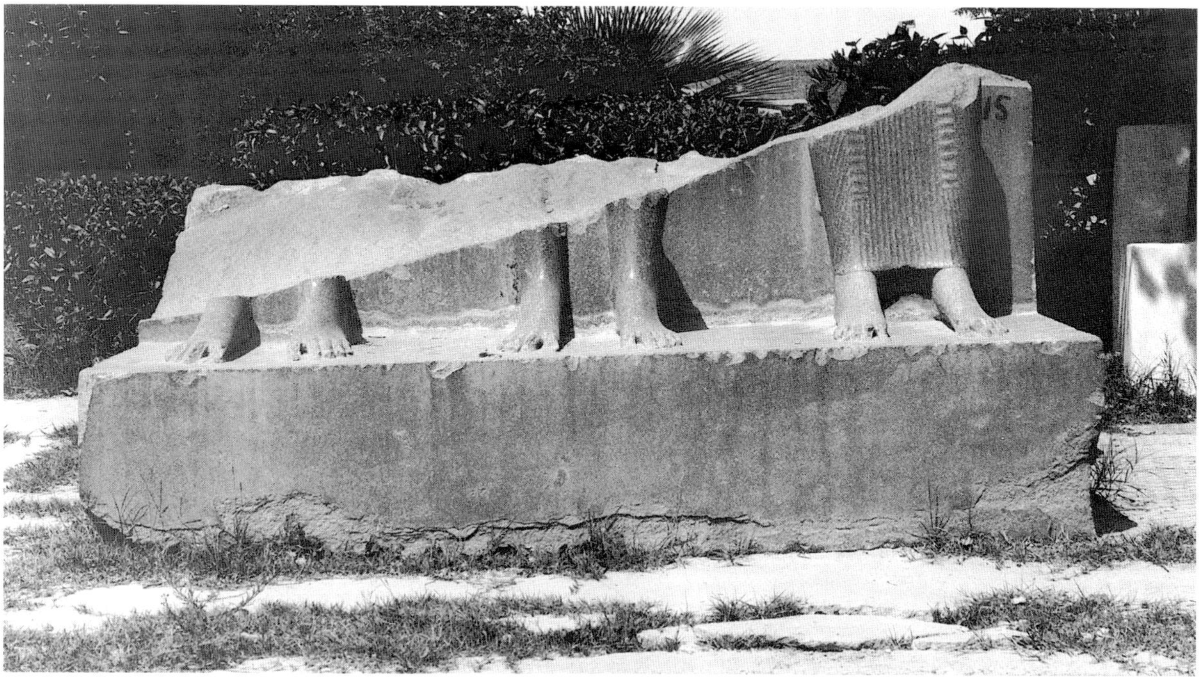

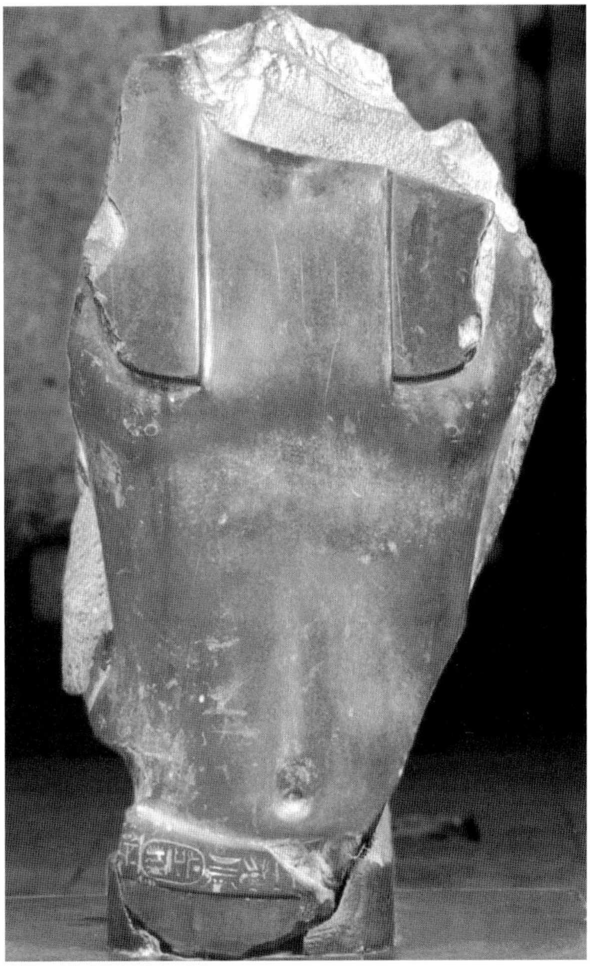

10 [A12]. Torso inscribed for Ptolemy II. Cairo CG 686 (photo: Sherif Sonbol, Cairo).

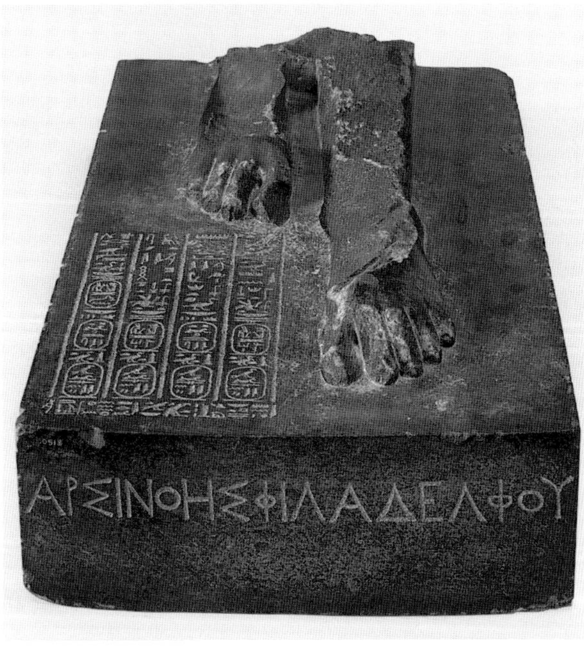

11 [A14]. Statue base inscribed for Arsinoe II. Chicago, Oriental Institute Museum 10518 (photo: courtesy of the Oriental Institute of the University of Chicago).

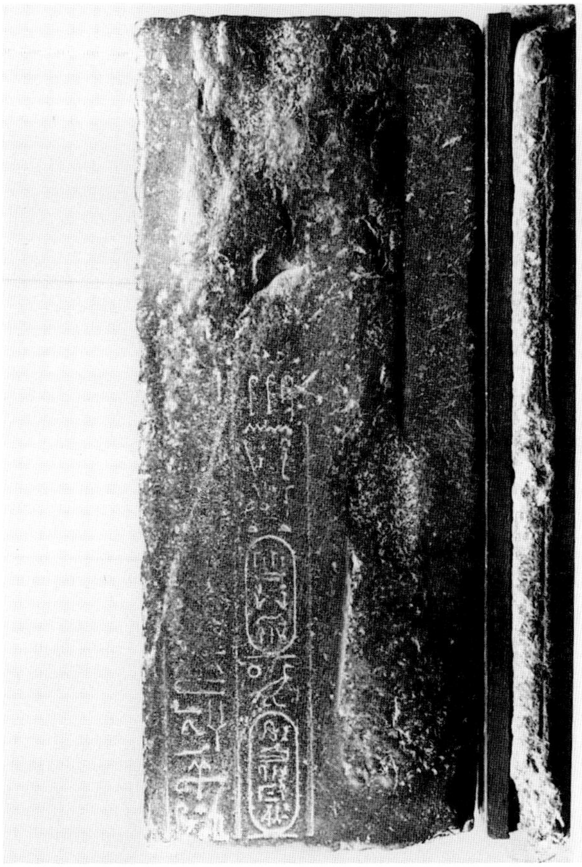

12 [A17]. Statue base inscribed for Ptolemy III (top view). Cairo JE 41439 (photo: Cairo Museum).

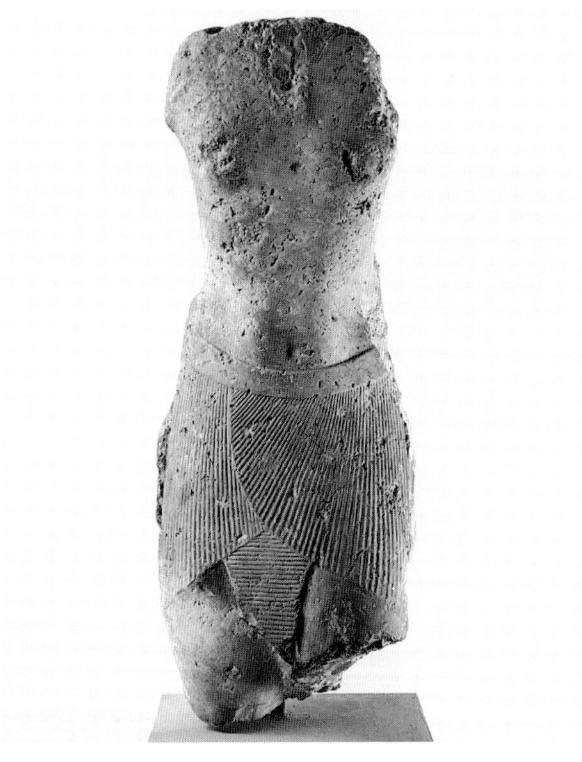

13 [A18]. Fragmentary standing statue inscribed for Ptolemy III. Paris, Musée Rodin Co 1414 (photo: Musée Rodin—Luc and Lala Joubert).

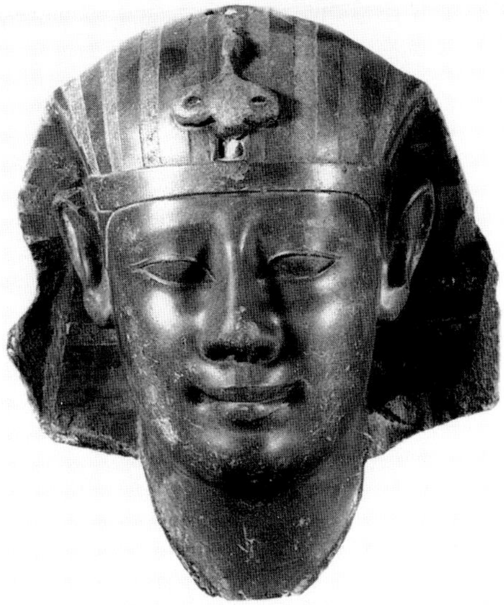

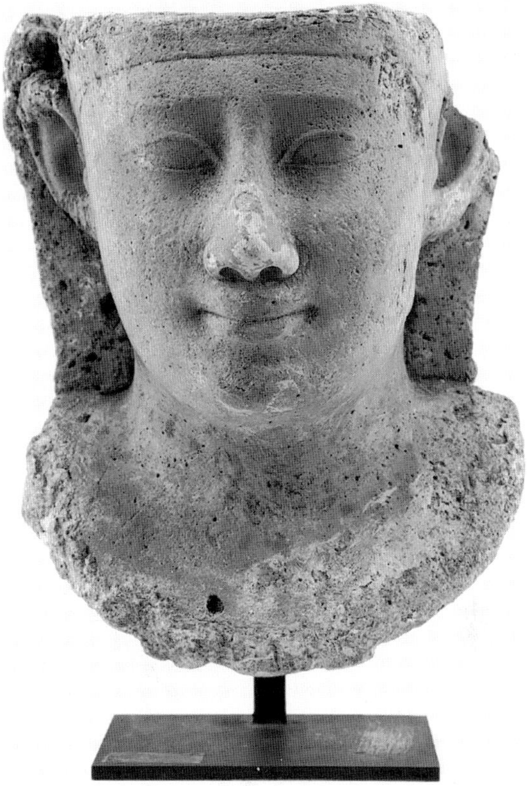

14 [A20] (*above*). Head of king. Late fourth or third century B.C. Turin, Museo Egizio 1399 (photo: ©MBAC—Turin Egyptian Museum).

15–16 [A21] (*right, top and bottom*). Face of king. Late fourth or third century B.C. Paris, Musée Rodin Co 786 (photos: Musée Rodin—Luc and Lala Joubert).

17 [A22] (*below*). Bust of king. Late fourth or third century B.C. New York, Metropolitan Museum of Art 30.8.79 (photo: ©The Metropolitan Museum of Art).

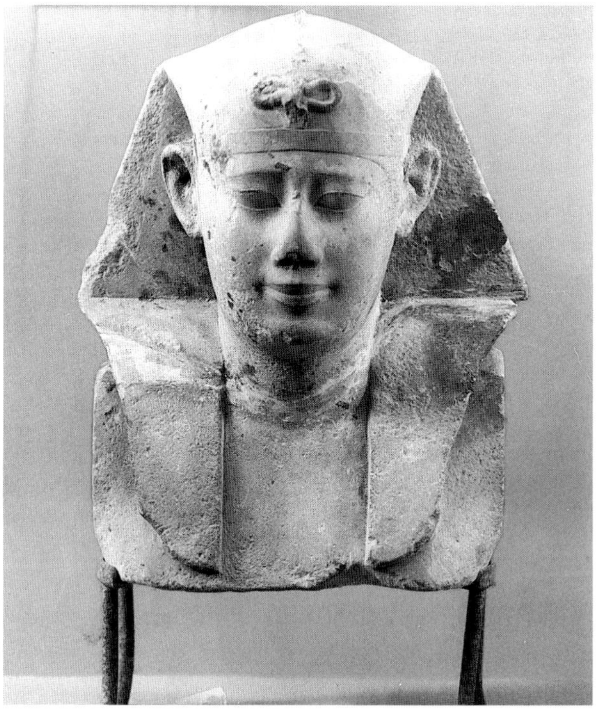

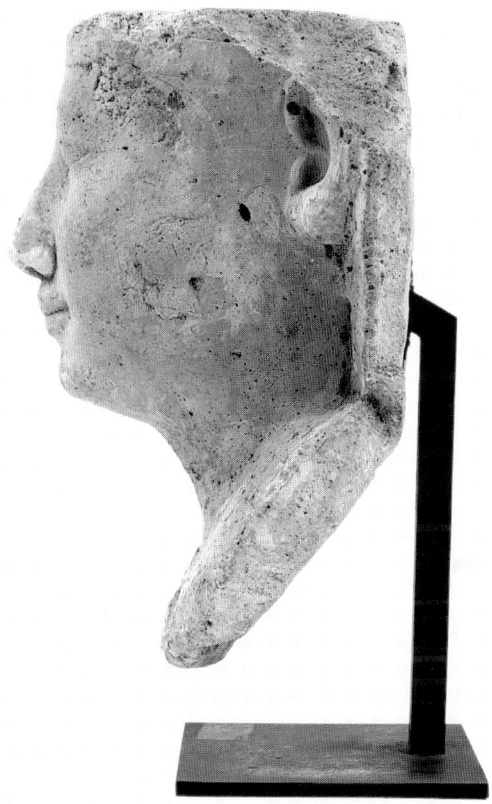

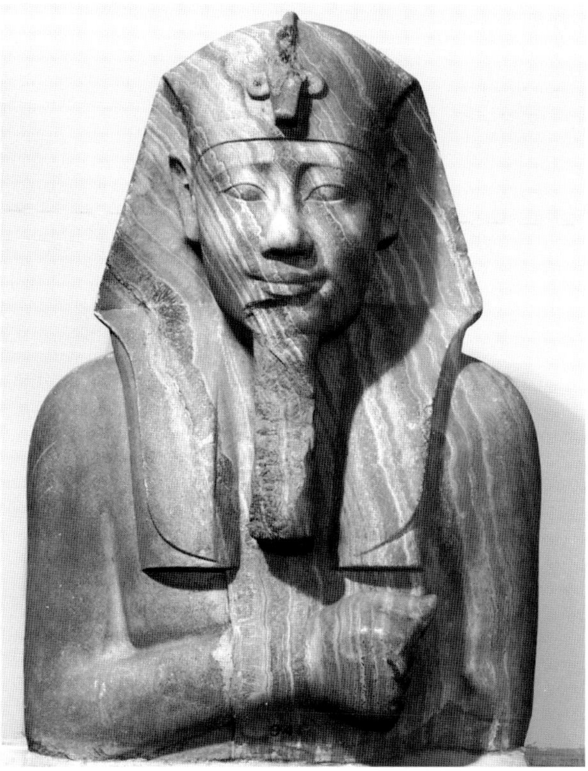

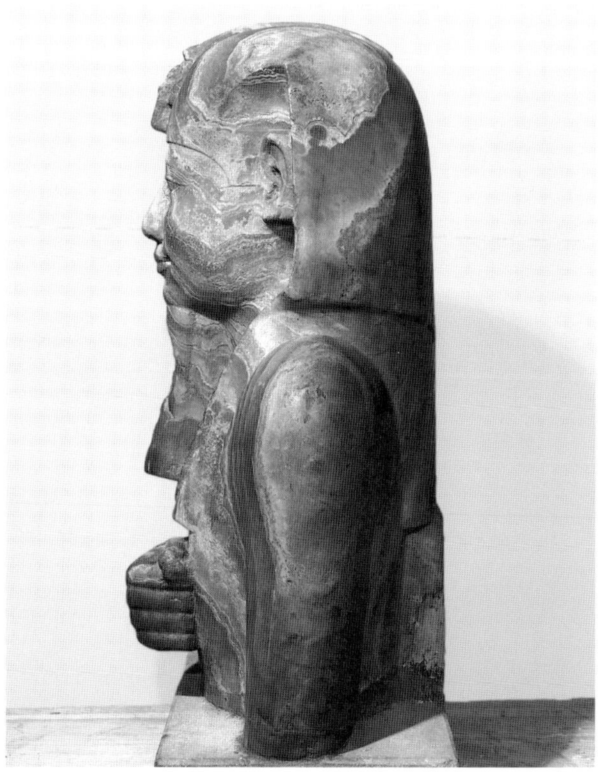

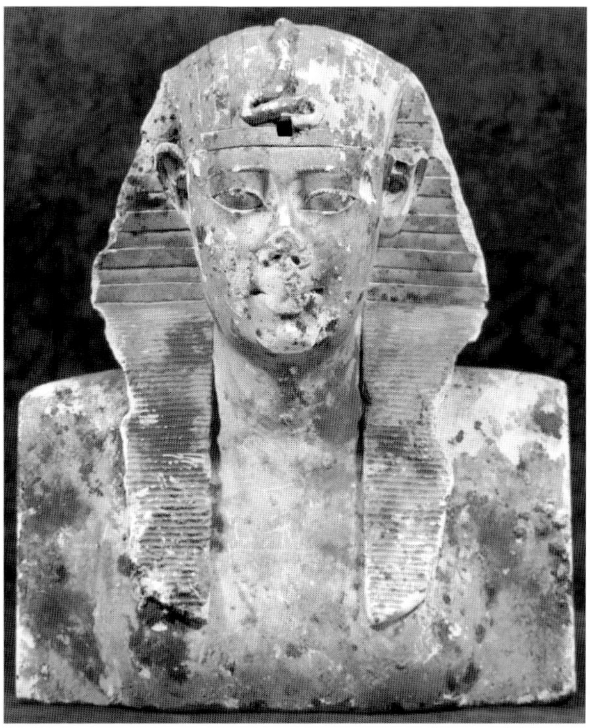

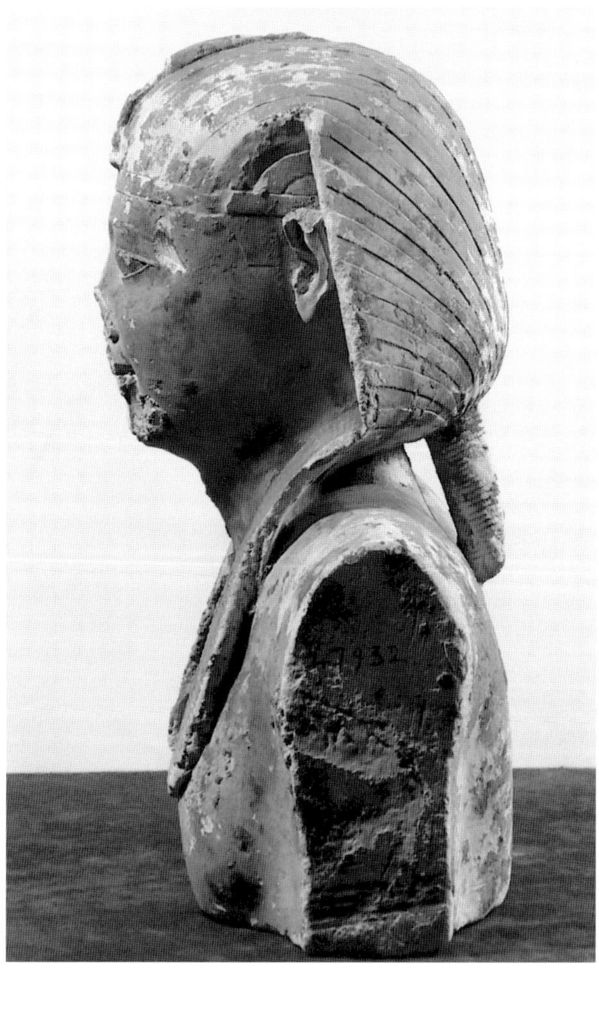

18–19 [A23] (*top*). Fragmentary king. Attributed to Ptolemy II. London, British Museum EA 941 (photos: ©The British Museum).

20–21 [A24] (*above*). Bust of king. Late fourth or third century B.C. Cairo JE 47932 (photos: Sherif Sonbol, Cairo).

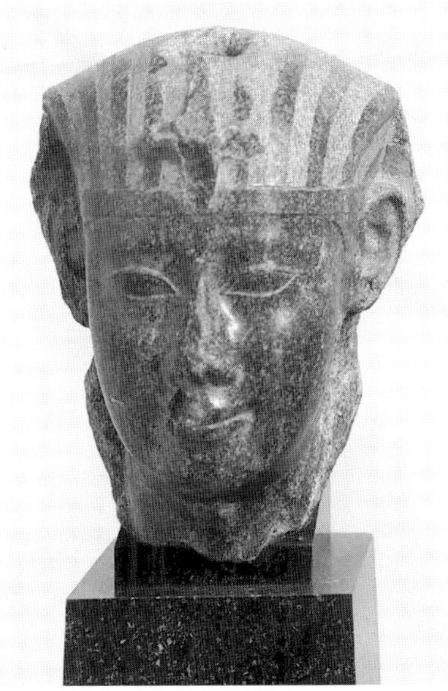

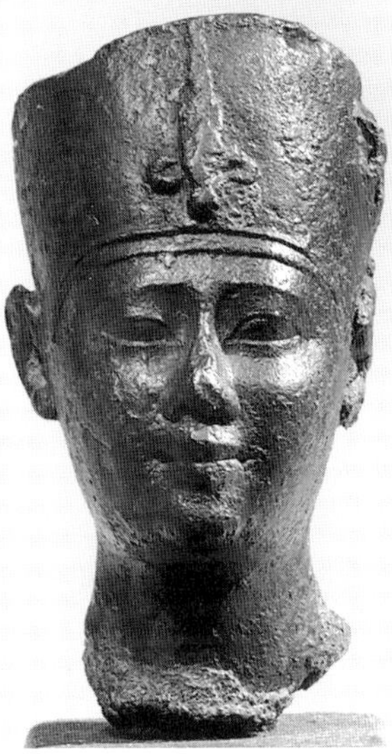

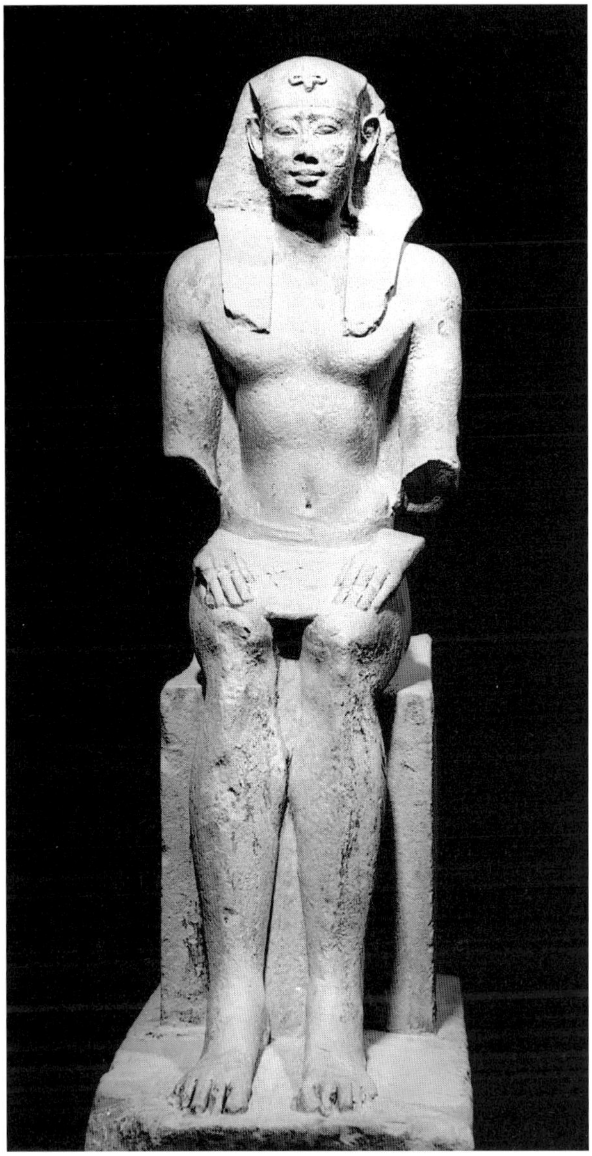

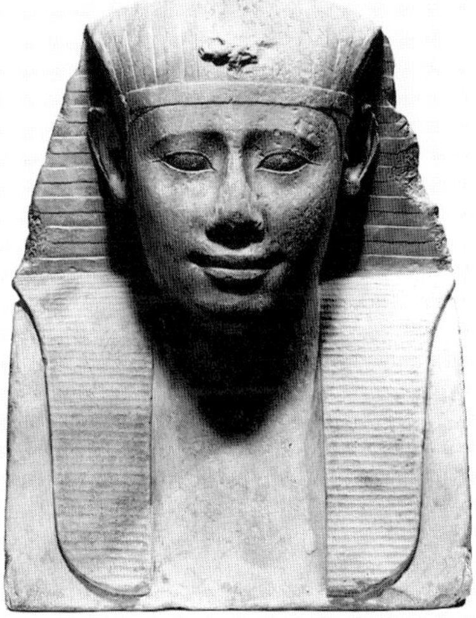

22 [A25] (*top left*). Head of king. Late fourth or third century B.C. Baltimore, The Walters Art Museum 22.109 (photo: ©The Walters Art Museum, Baltimore).

23 [A26] (*above left*). Bronze head of king. Late fourth or third century B.C. New York, Metropolitan Museum of Art 66.99.134 (photo: ©The Metropolitan Museum of Art).

24 [A28] (*above right*). Seated king. Late fourth or third century B.C. Zagazig, Orabi Museum 282 (photo: Grzegorz Wyrzykowski, Polish Center of Mediterranean Archaeology, Cairo).

25 [A29] (*left*). Bust of king. Late fourth or third century B.C. Brooklyn Museum of Art 37.37E, Charles Edwin Wilbour Fund (photo: ©Brooklyn Museum of Art).

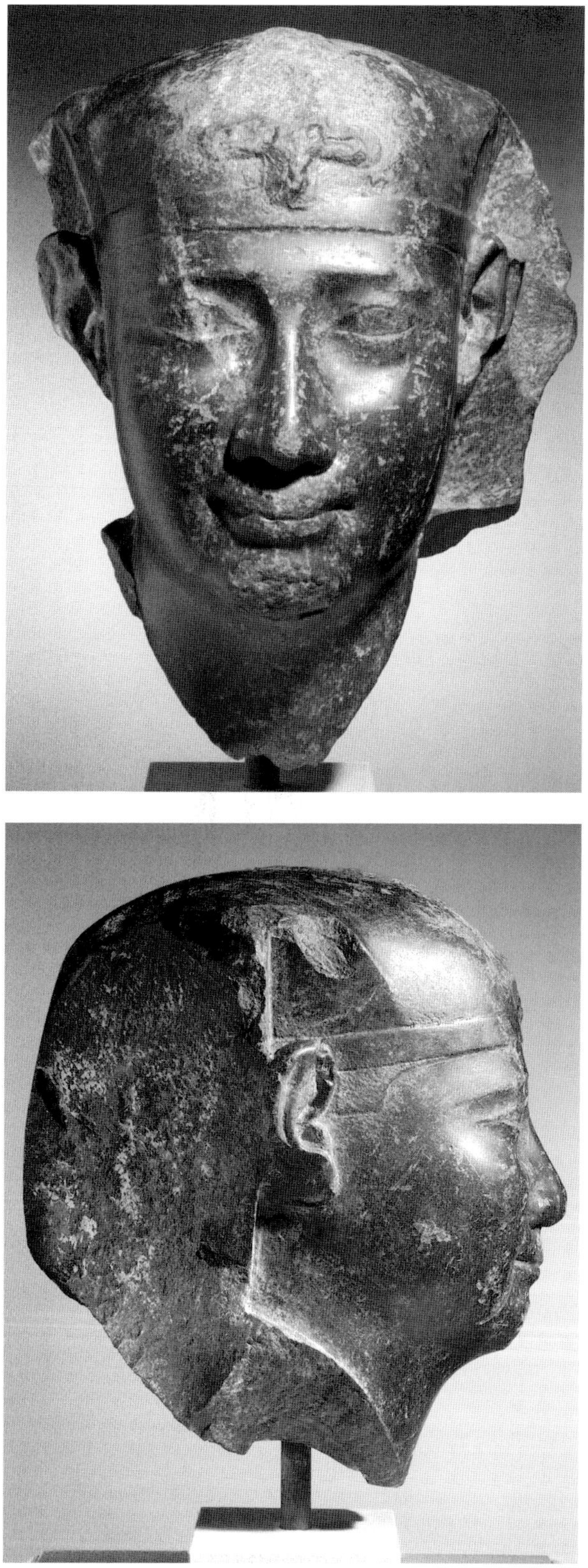

26–27 [A30]. Head of king. Late fourth or third century B.C. Brooklyn Museum of Art 53.75, Charles Edwin Wilbour Fund (photos: ©Brooklyn Museum of Art).

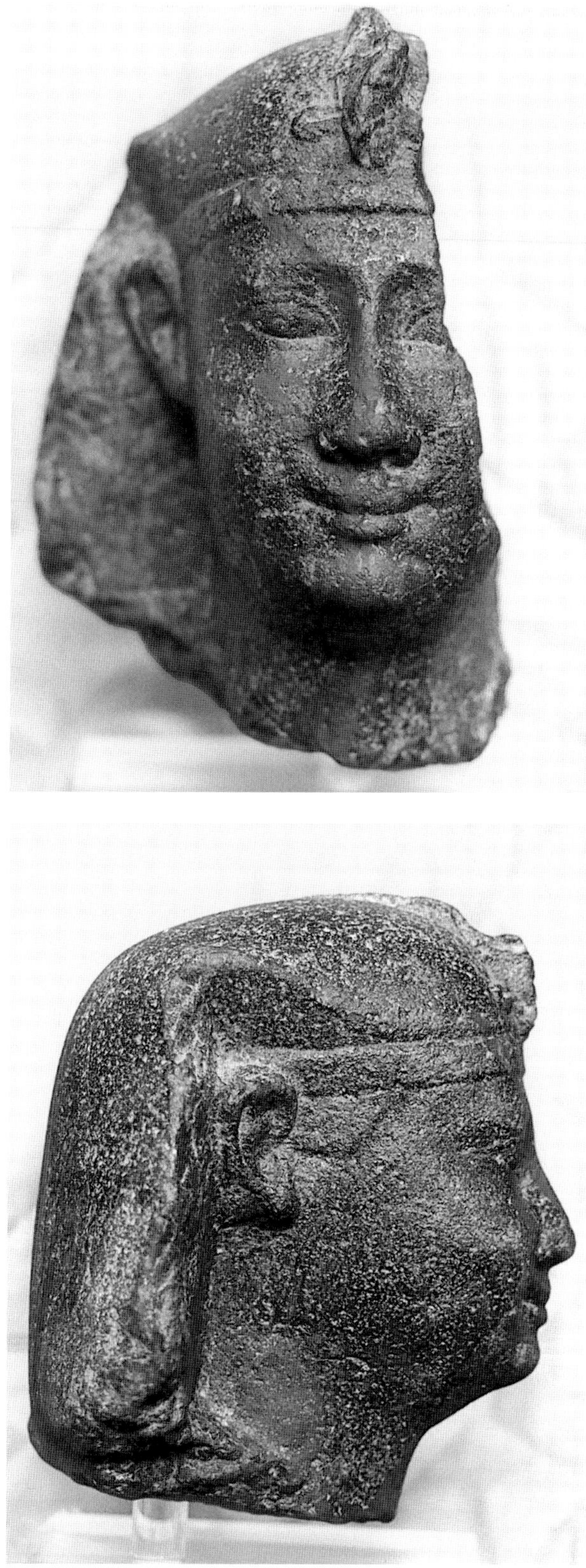

28–29 [A31]. Head of king. Late fourth or third century B.C. Naples, Museo Archeologico Nazionale 321 (photos: author).

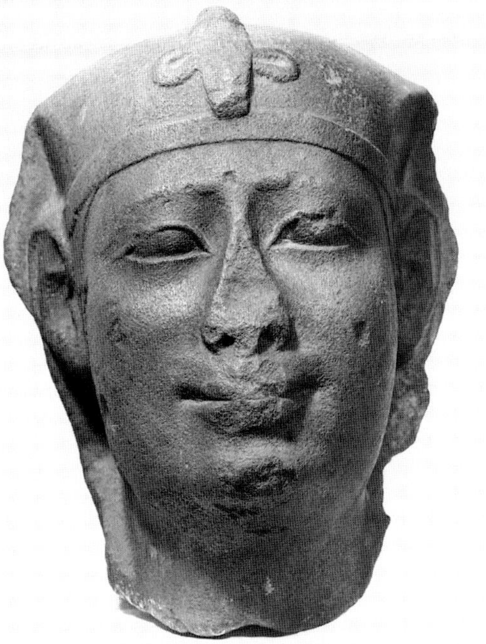

30 [A32]. Head of king. Late fourth or third century B.C. Turin, Museo Egizio 1396 (photo: ©MBAC—Turin Egyptian Museum).

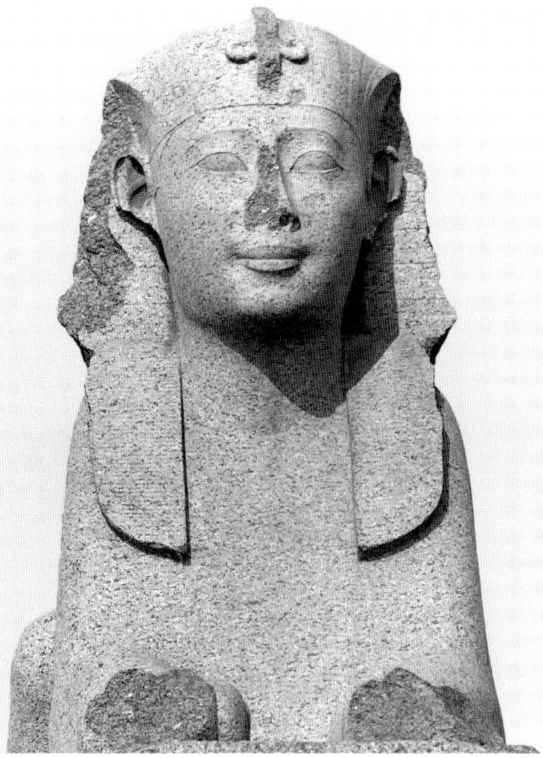

31 [A33]. East sphinx. Late fourth or third century B.C. Alexandria Serapeum (photo: author).

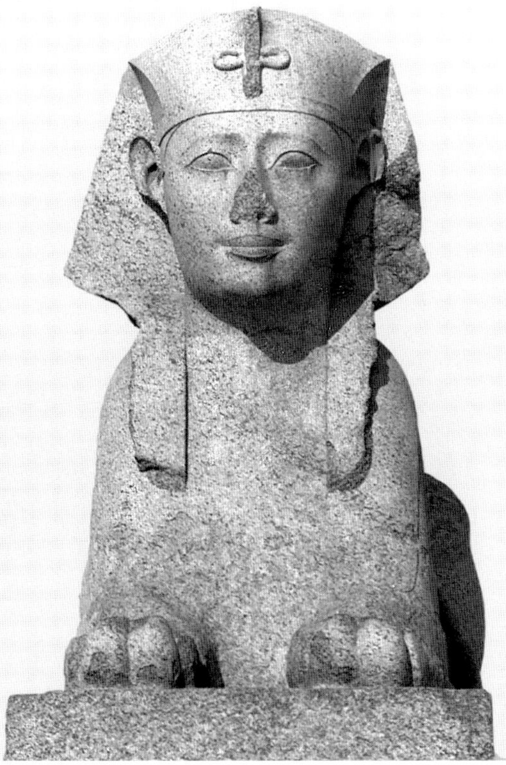

32 [A33]. West sphinx. Late fourth or third century B.C. Alexandria Serapeum (photo: author).

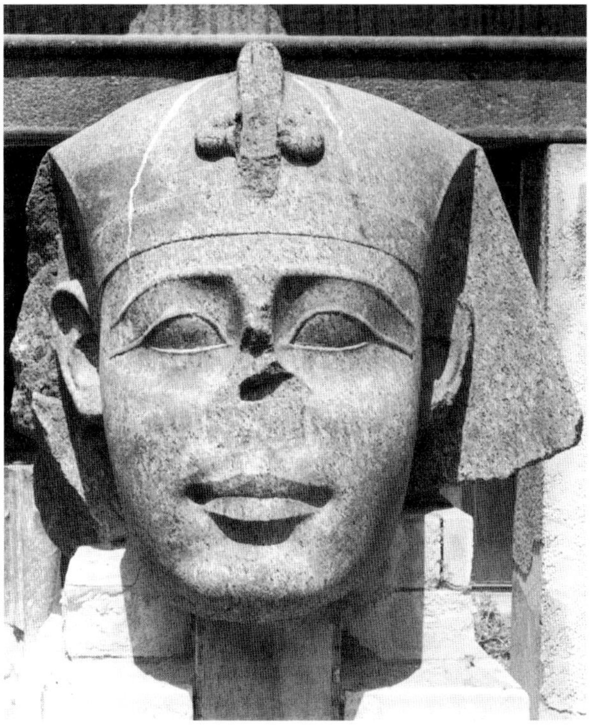

33 [A34]. Head of king. Late fourth or third century B.C. Alexandria, Graeco-Roman Museum 23048 (photo: author).

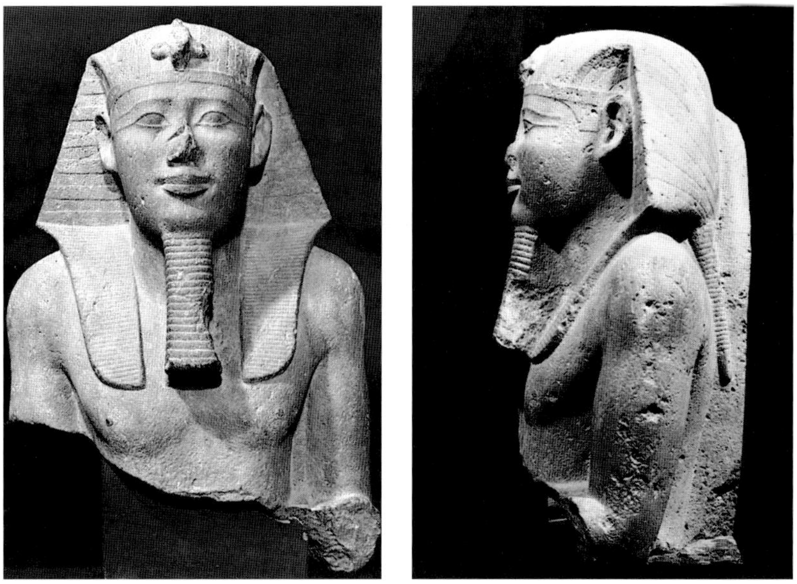

34–35 [A35]. Fragmentary king. Late fourth or third century B.C. Zagazig, Orabi Museum 1411 (photos: Grzegorz Wyrzykowski, Polish Center of Mediterranean Archaeology, Cairo).

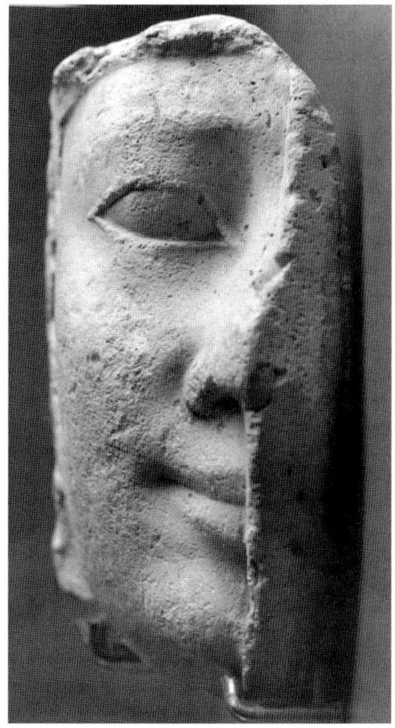

37 [A38]. Half face of king. Late fourth or third century B.C. Amsterdam, Allard Pierson Museum 1937 (photo: author).

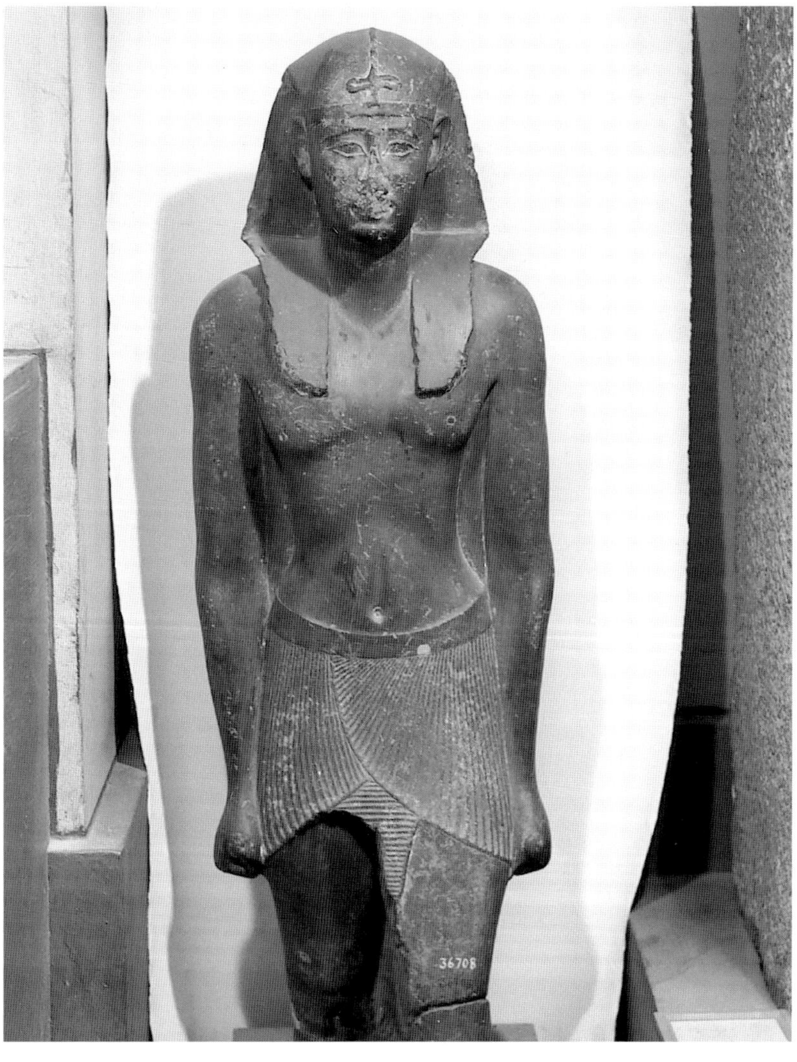

36 [A36]. Standing king. Late fourth or third century B.C. Cairo JE 36708, now in the National Museum, Port Said (photo: courtesy of the National Museum).

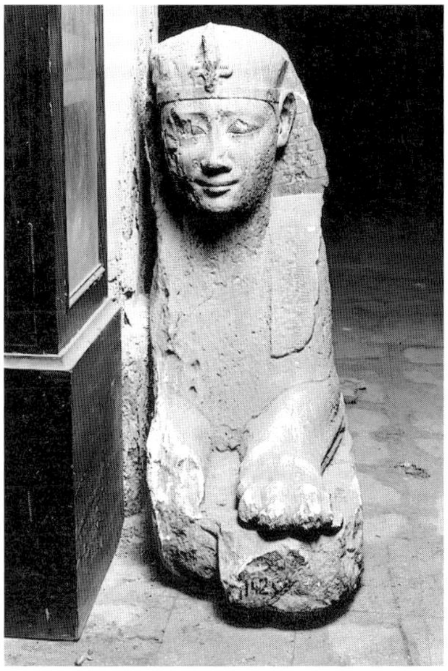

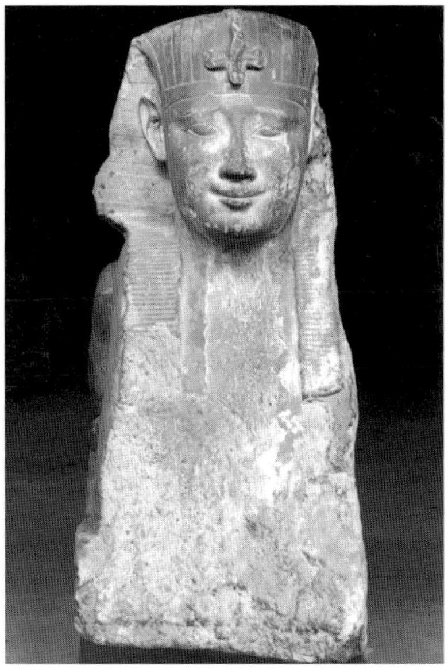

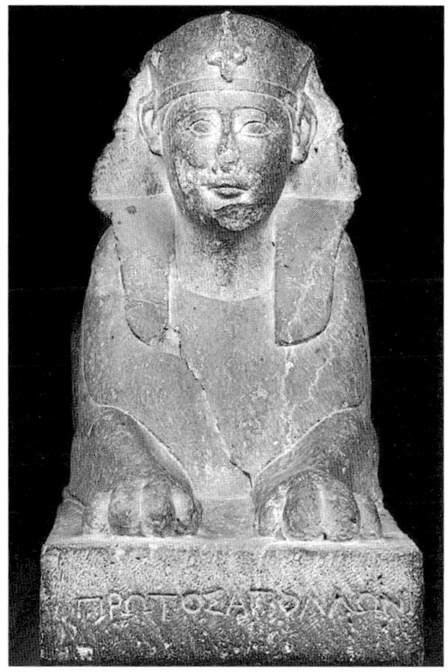

38 [A39] (*top left*). Sphinx. Late fourth or third century B.C. Alexandria, Graeco-Roman Museum 11425 (photo: Centre d'Études Alexandrines).

39 [A40] (*top middle*). Sphinx. Late fourth or third century B.C. Cairo 8/6/25/1 (photo: Sherif Sonbol, Cairo).

40 [A41] (*top right*). Sphinx. Third century B.C. Cairo JE 53104 (photo: Sherif Sonbol, Cairo).

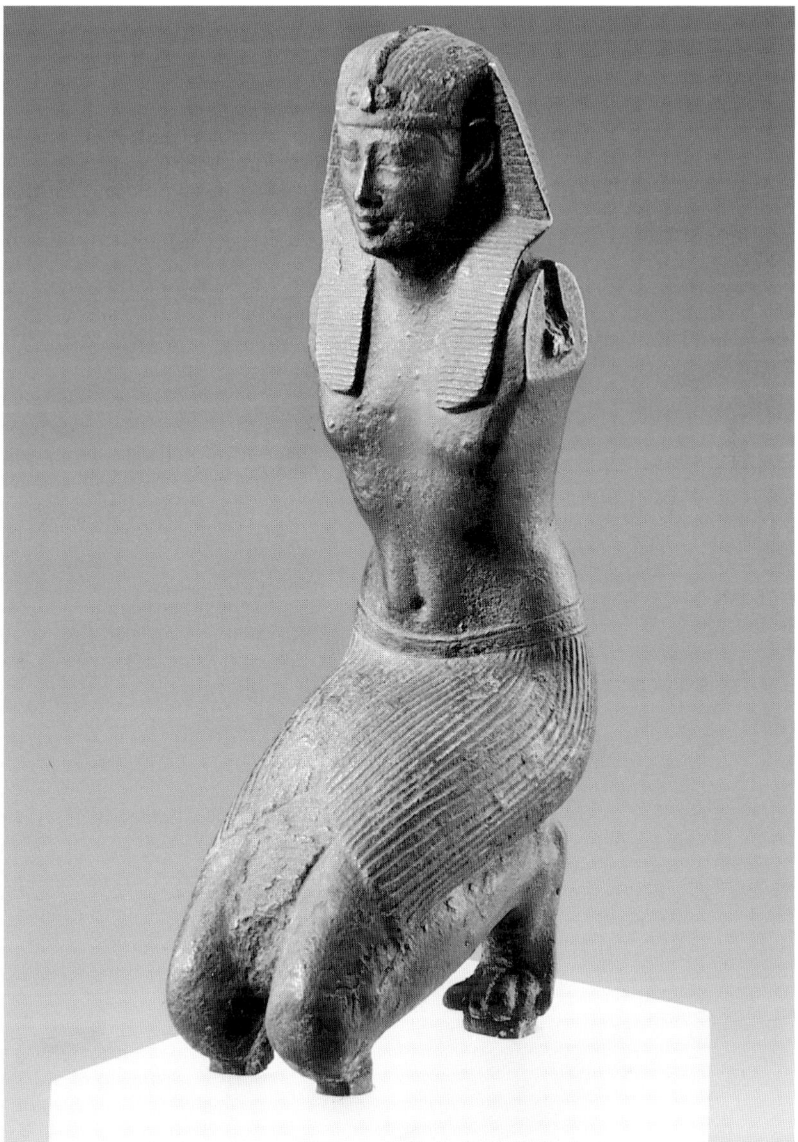

41 [A42] (*right*). Kneeling king. Late fourth or third century B.C. Marseille, Musée d'Archéologie Méditerranéenne 826 (photo: ©Yves Gallois, Acclam).

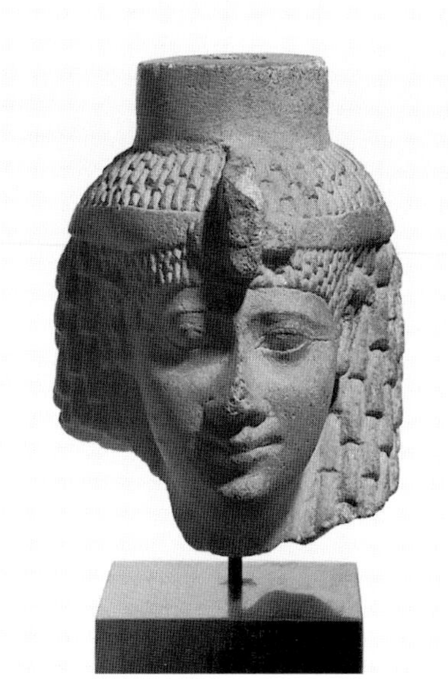

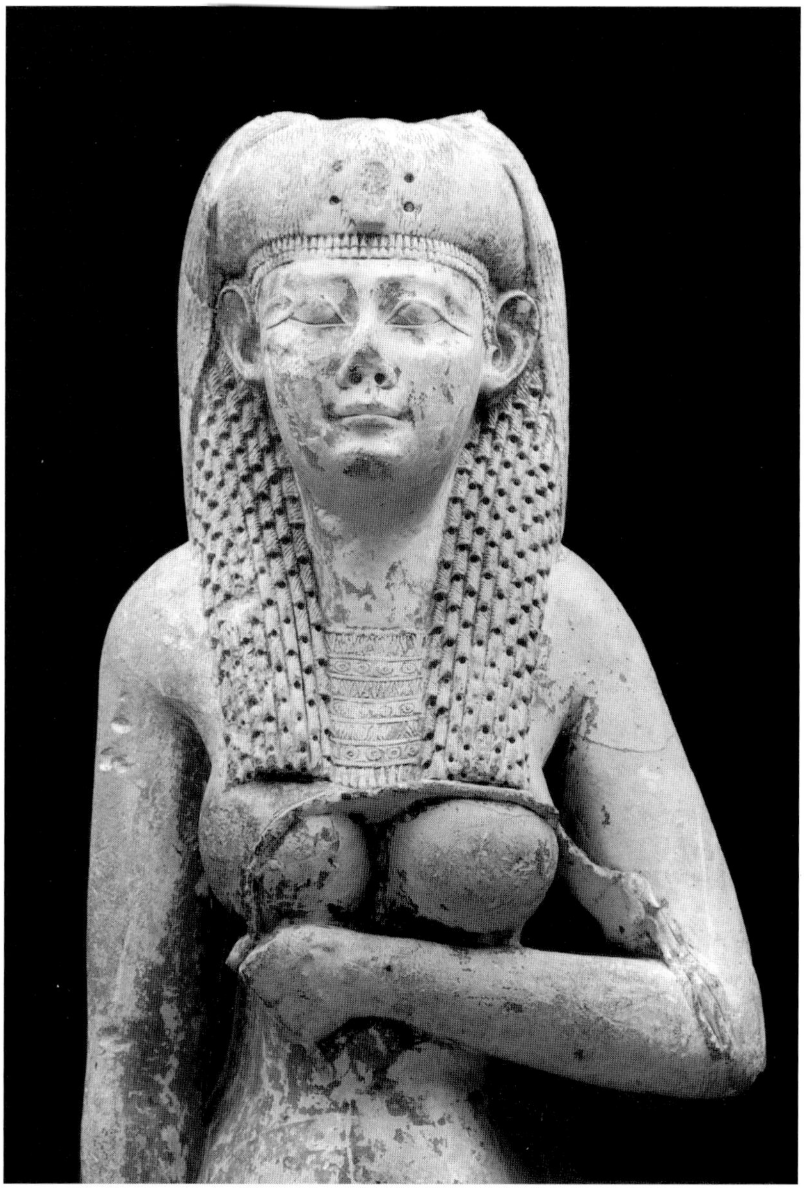

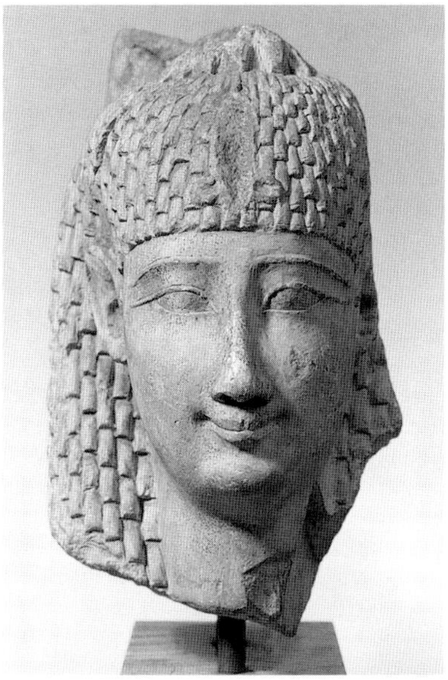

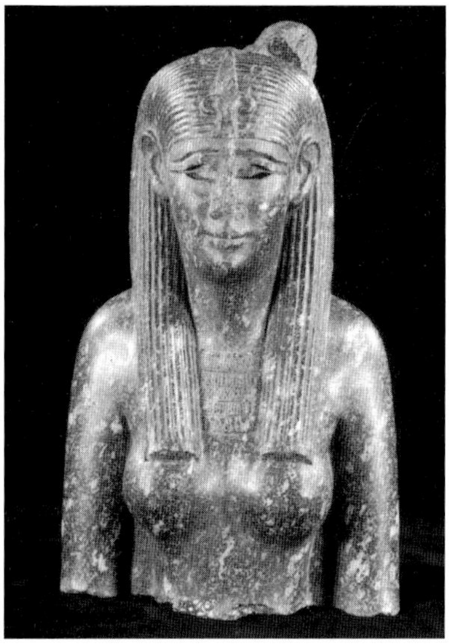

42 [A43] (*top left*). Head of queen. Third century B.C. Brooklyn Museum of Art 86.226.32, Gift of the Ernest Erickson Foundation (photo: ©Brooklyn Museum of Art).

43 [A45] (*above right*). Standing queen (detail). Third century B.C. Cairo CG 678 (photo: Sherif Sonbol, Cairo).

44 [A46] (*above left*). Head of goddess. Third century B.C. Baltimore, The Walters Art Museum 22.417 (photo: ©The Walters Art Museum, Baltimore).

45 [A47] (*left*). Fragmentary queen. Third century B.C. Paris, Musée du Louvre E 10957 (photo: ©Musée du Louvre—Georges Poncet).

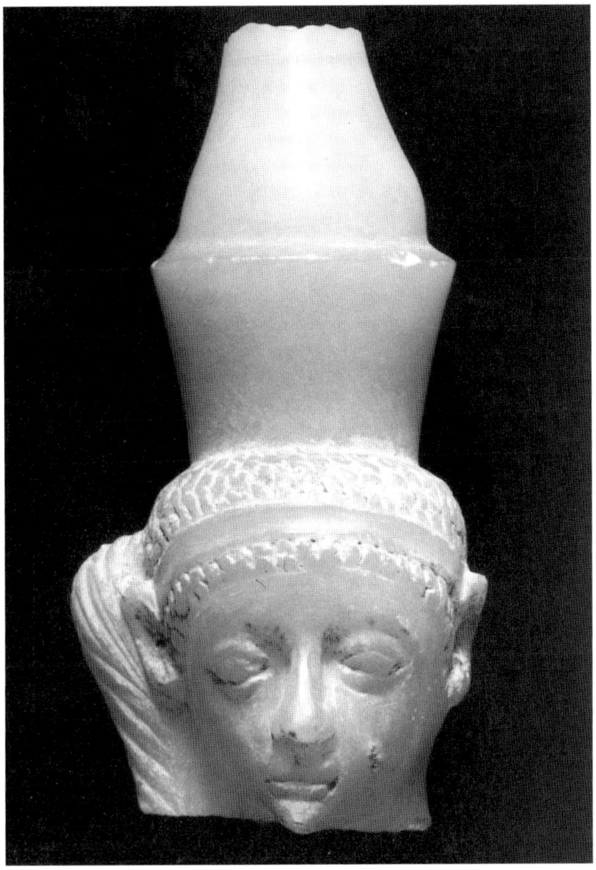

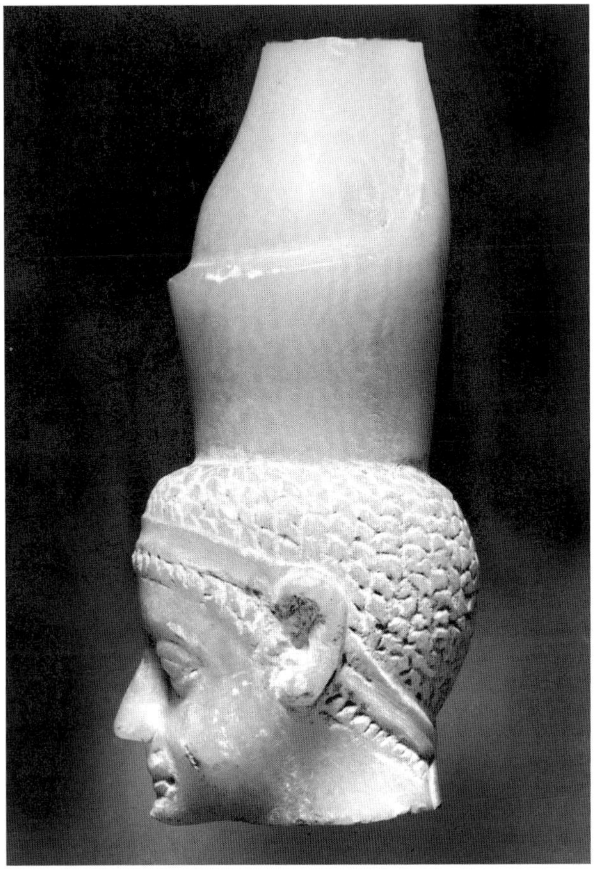

46–47 [B1] (*above*). Head of king. Attributed to Ptolemy V or VI. Berlin, Ägyptisches Museum 14568 (photos: ©Ägyptisches Museum und Papyrussammlung, Staatliche Museen zu Berlin—Preussischer Kulturbesitz, Elsa Postel).

48–49 [B2] (*below*). Royal male head. Attributed to Ptolemy V or VI. Berlin, Ägyptisches Museum 13457 (photos: ©Ägyptisches Museum und Papyrussammlung, Staatliche Museen zu Berlin—Preussischer Kulturbesitz, Jutta Titetz).

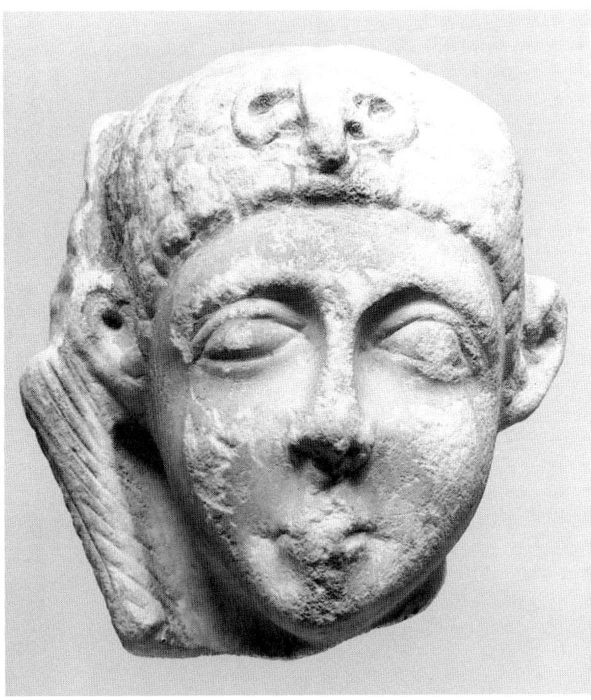

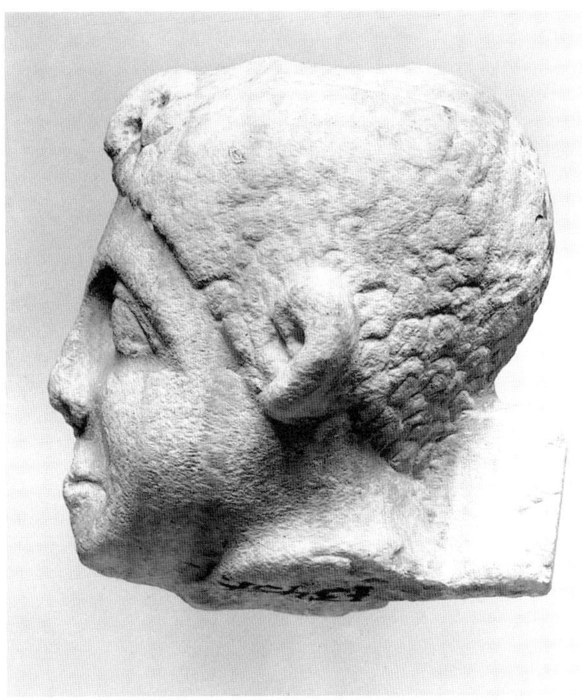

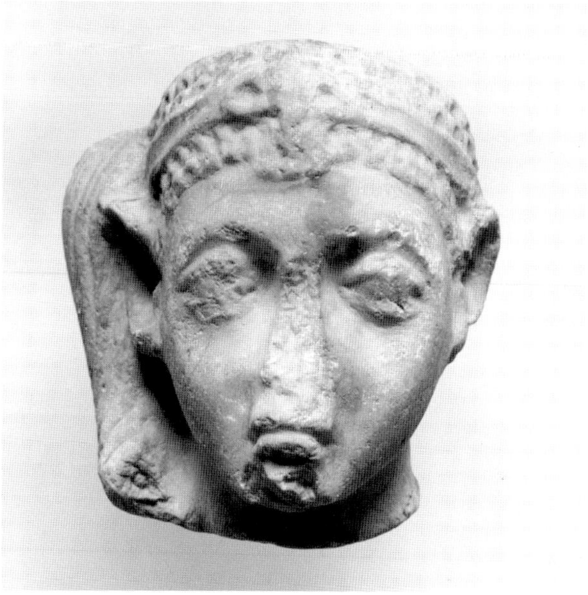

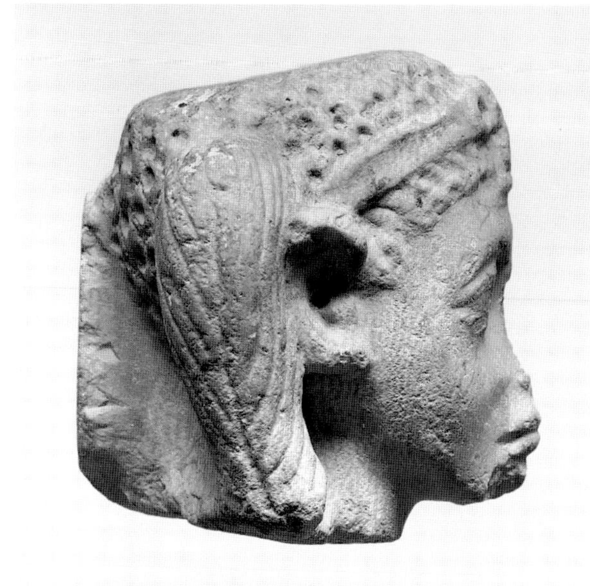

50–51 [B3] (*above*). Royal male head. Attributed to Ptolemy V or VI. Berlin, Ägyptisches Museum 23140 (photos: ©Ägyptisches Museum und Papyrussammlung, Staatliche Museen zu Berlin—Preussischer Kulturbesitz, Jutta Tietz).

52–53 [B6] (*below*). Head inscribed for Ptolemy VI. Athens, National Archaeological Museum ANE 108 (photos: ©National Archaeological Museum).

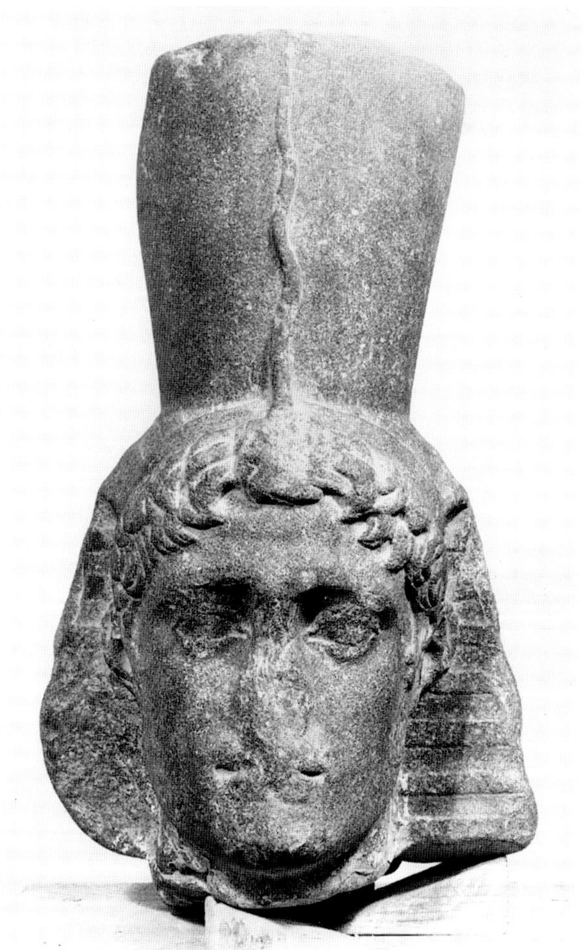

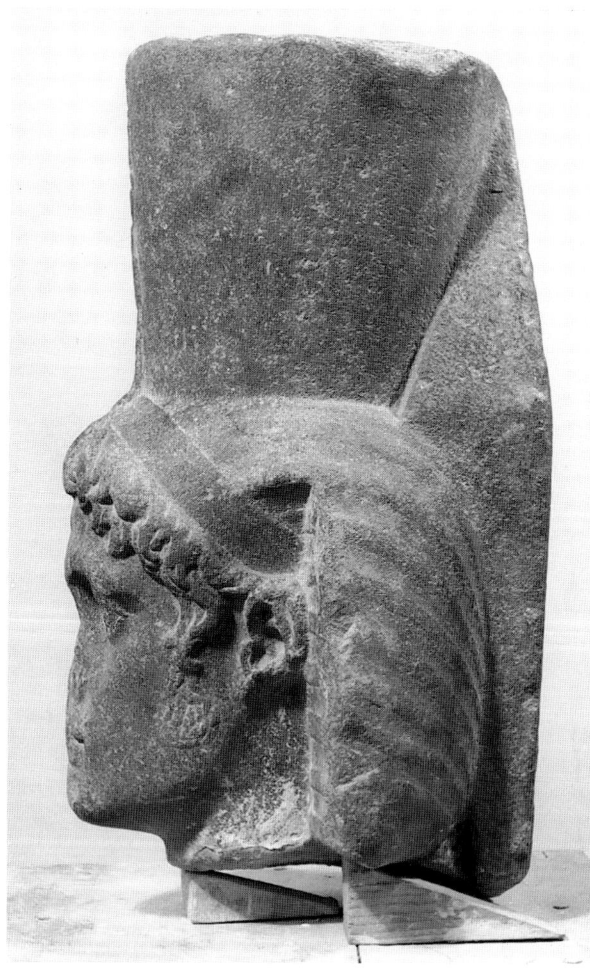

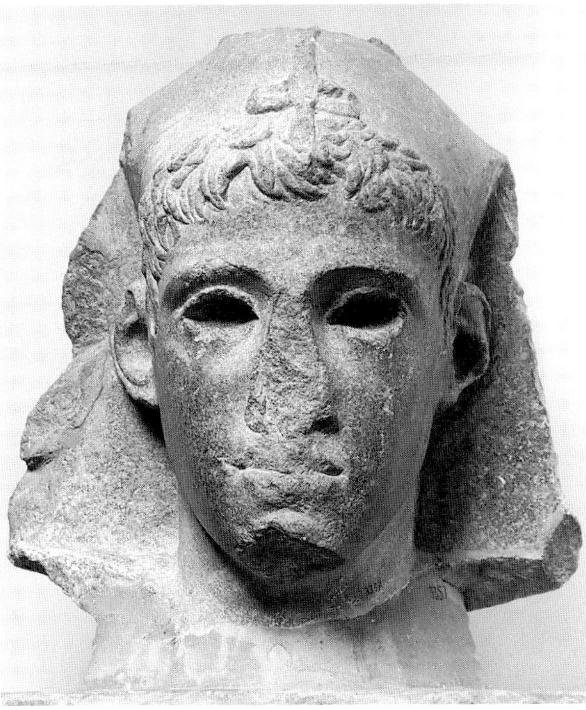

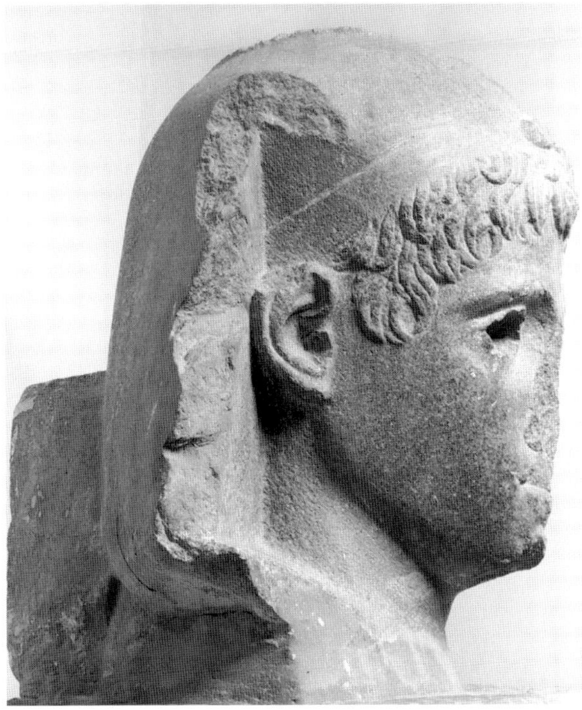

54–55 [B7] (*above*). Head of king. Attributed to Ptolemy VI. Alexandria, Graeco-Roman Museum 3357 (photos: Deutsches Archäologisches Institut, Cairo).

56–57 [B8] (*below*). Head of king. Attributed to Ptolemy VI. Frankfurt, private collection (photos: courtesy Klaus Parlasca).

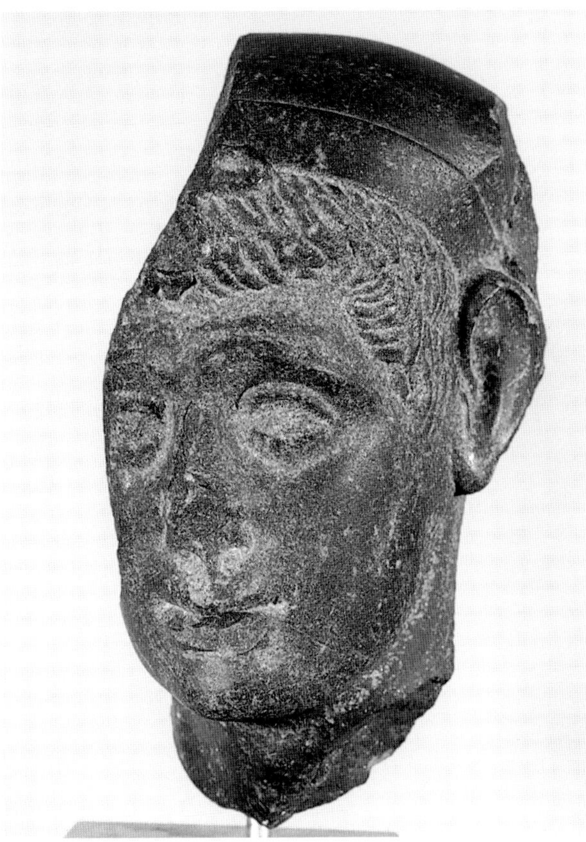

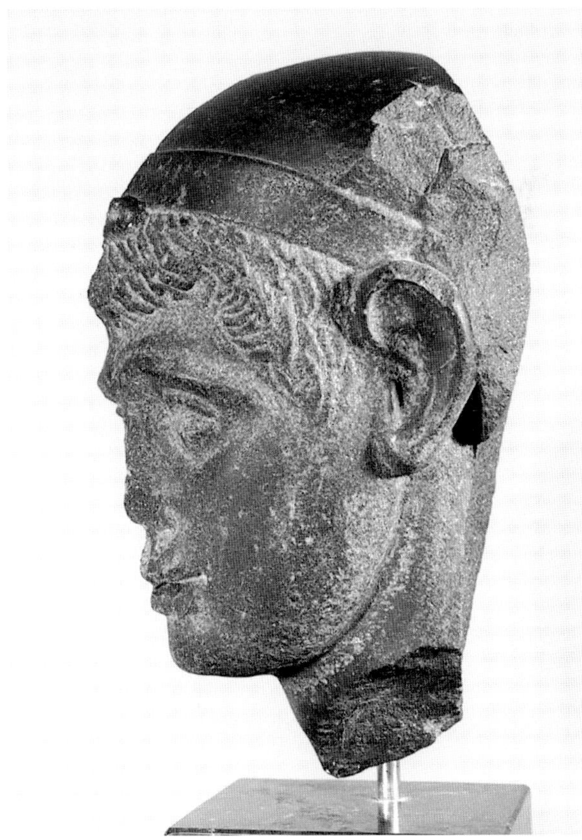

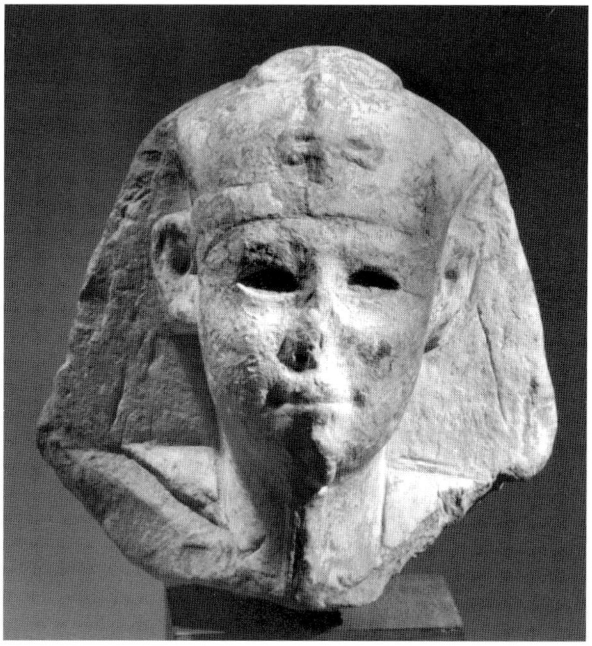

58 [B9] (*above*). Head of king with scarab. Attributed to Ptolemy VI. New York, Metropolitan Museum of Art 66.99.166 (photo: ©The Metropolitan Museum of Art).

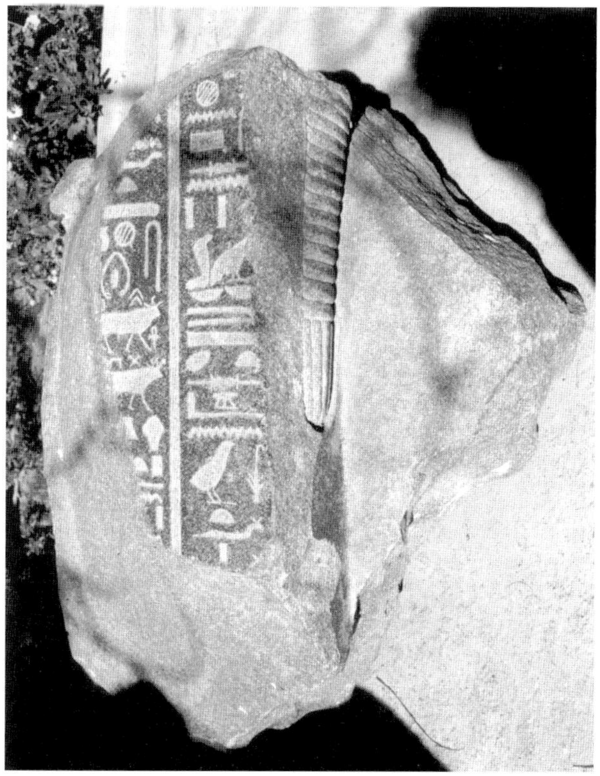

59 [B10] (*above right*). Fragmentary statue inscribed for Ptolemy VI. Alexandria, Graeco-Roman Museum N.G. 378 (photo: Centre d'Études Alexandrines).

60 [B12] (*below*). Statue base inscribed for Ptolemy VI. Alexandria, Graeco-Roman Museum 2 (photo: Centre d'Études Alexandrines).

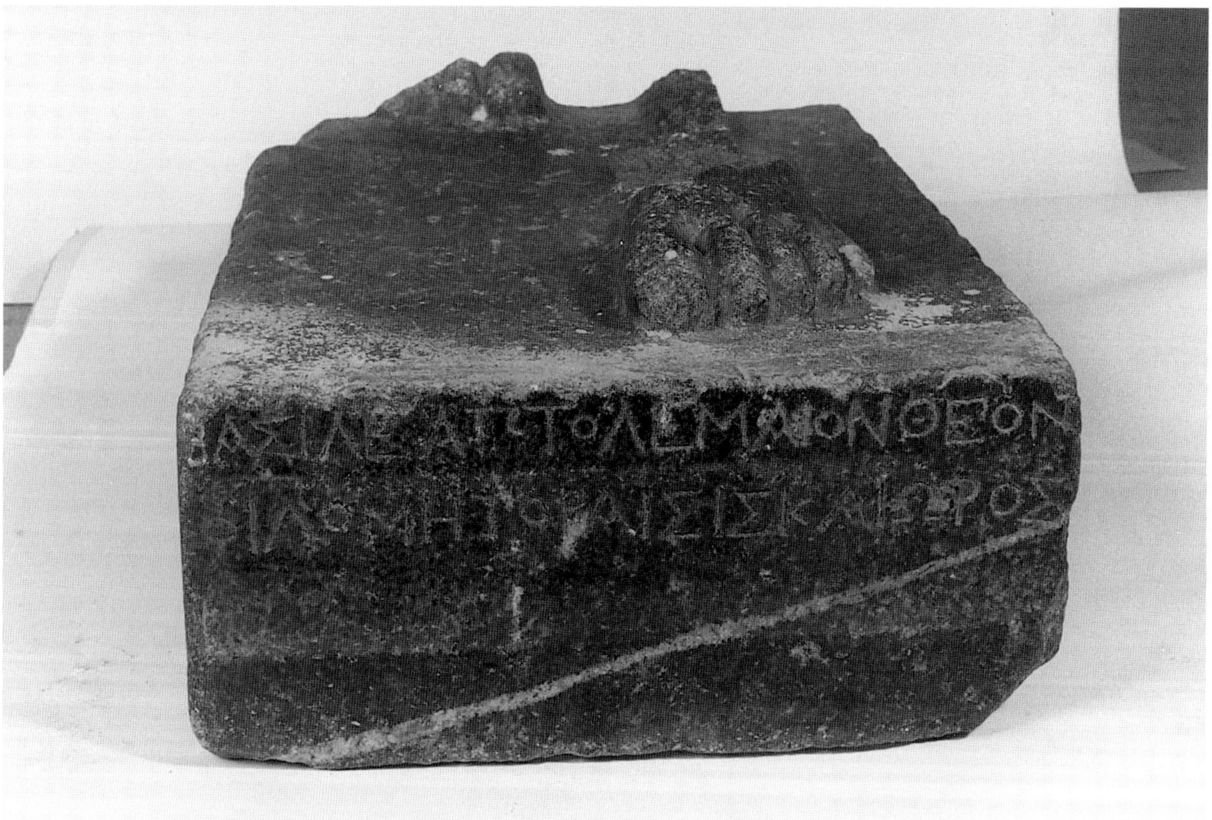

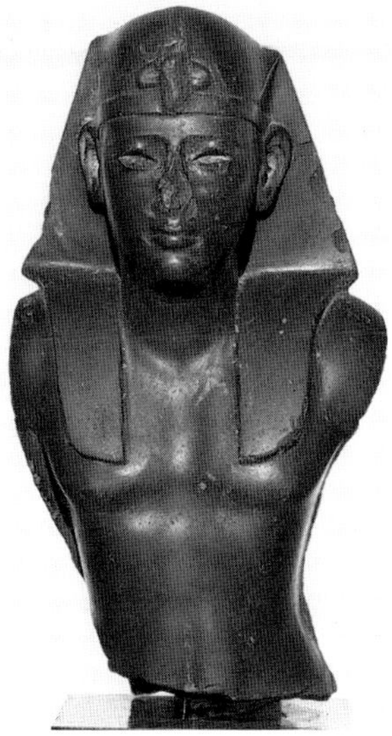

61 [B15]. Fragmentary king. First half of second century B.C. New Haven, Peabody Museum of Natural History YPM.256941 (photo: courtesy of the Peabody Museum of Natural History, Yale University, New Haven, Conn.).

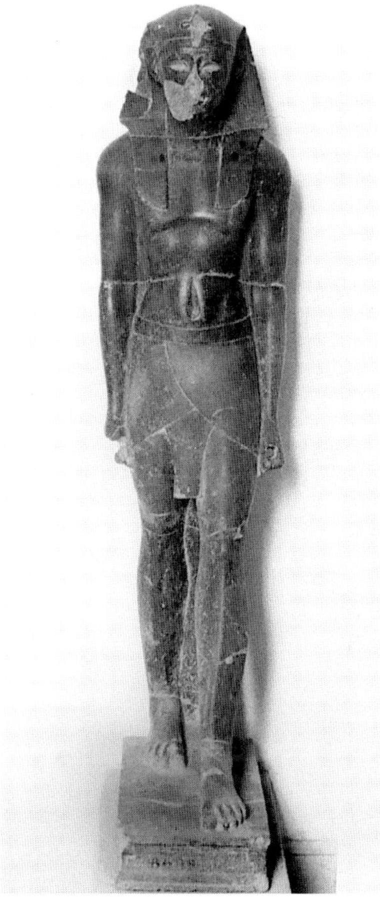

62 [B16]. Standing king. First half of second century B.C. Rome, Museo Nazionale 60921 (photo: courtesy of the Museo Nazionale).

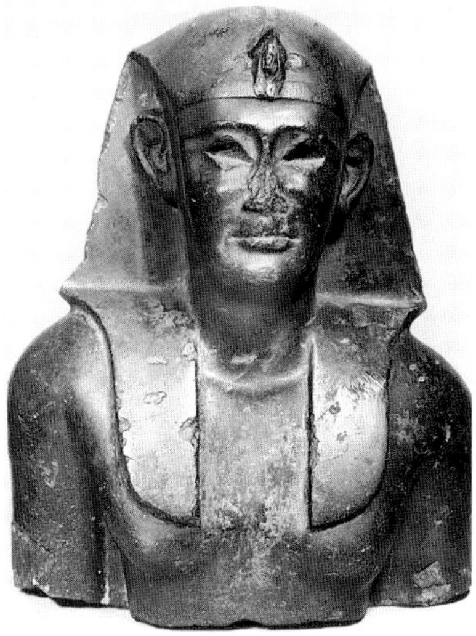

63 [B17]. Fragmentary king. First half of second century B.C. Staatlichen Sammlung Ägyptischer Kunst München ÄS 20 (photo: ©Staatlichen Sammlung Ägyptischer Kunst).

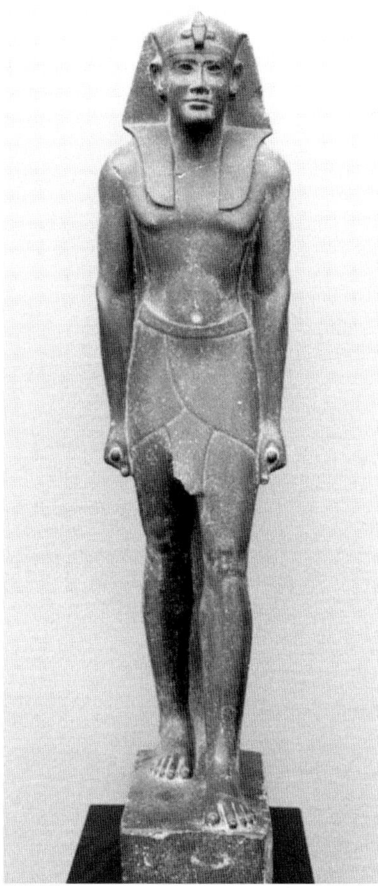

64 [B18]. Standing king. First half of second century B.C. Copenhagen, Ny Carlsberg Glyptotek AEIN 929 (photo: author).

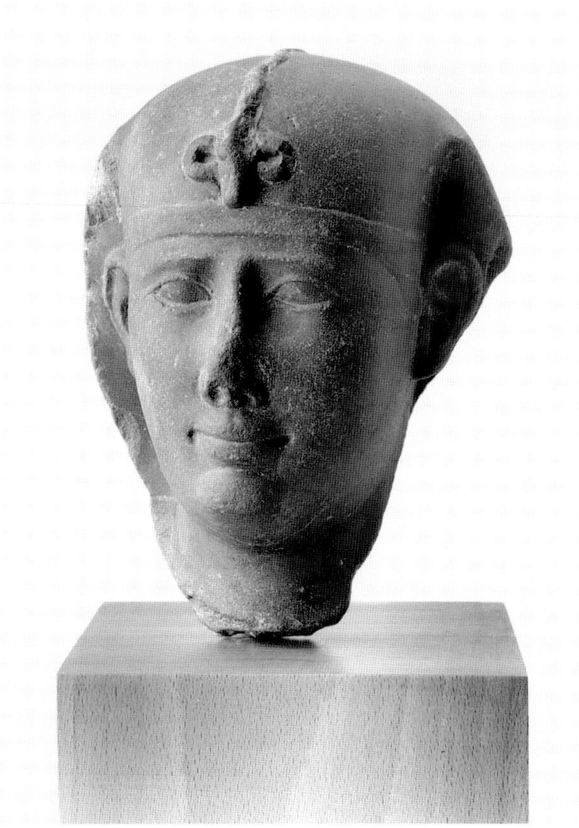

65 [B19]. Head of king. First half of second century B.C. Lyon, Musée des Beaux-Arts H 1701 (photo: ©Réunion des Musées Nationaux/Art Resource, N.Y.).

66–67 [B20]. Head of king. First half of second century B.C. Brooklyn Museum of Art 16.169, Gift of the Estate of Charles Edwin Wilbour (photos: ©Brooklyn Museum of Art).

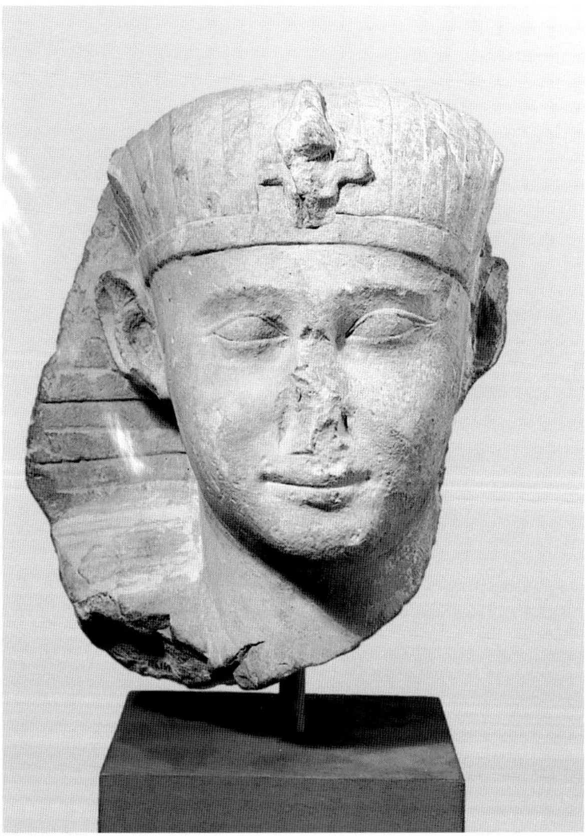

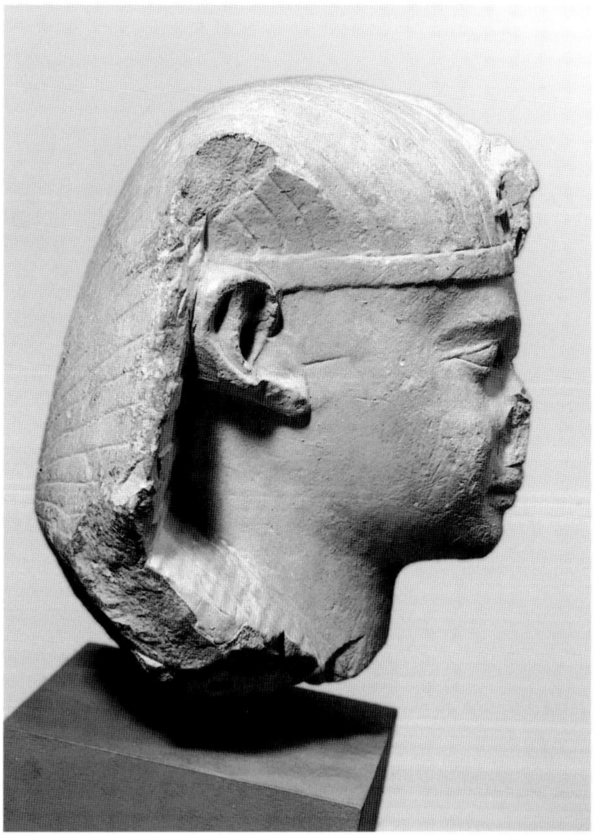

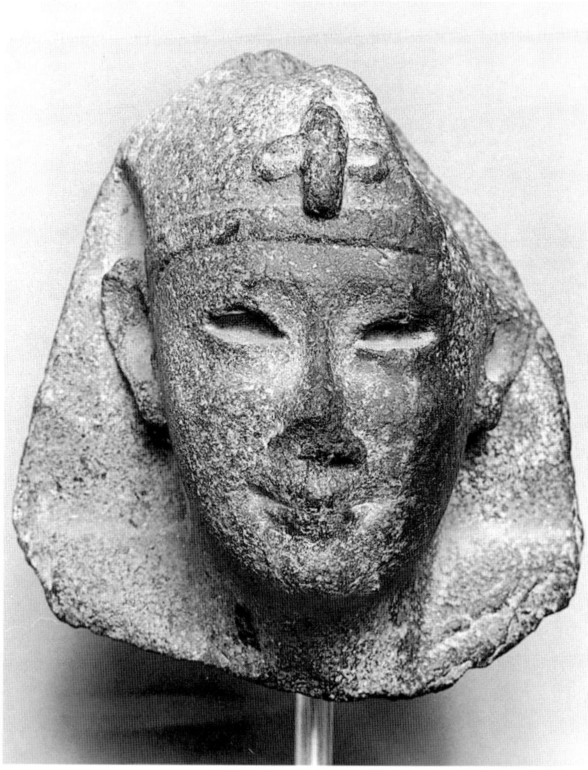

68 [B21]. Head of king. First half of second century B.C. Rome, Museo Barracco 32 (photo: courtesy Museo Barracco).

69 [B22]. Head of king. First half of second century B.C. Alexandria, Graeco-Roman Museum 28103 (photo: Centre d'Études Alexandrines).

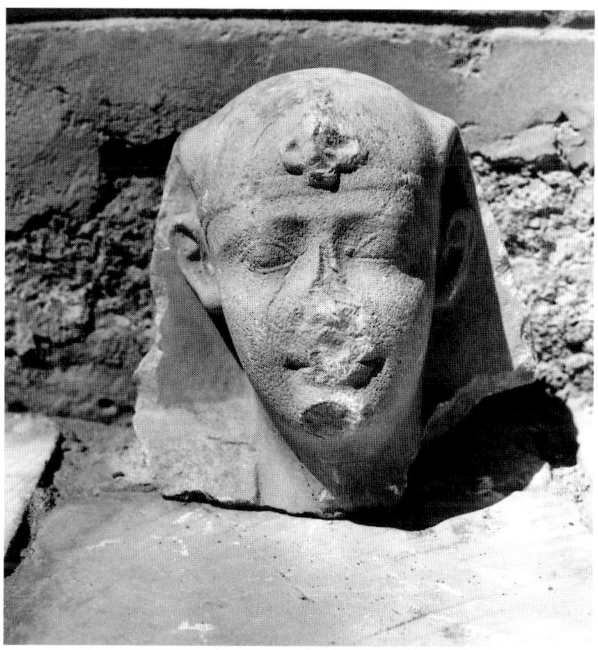

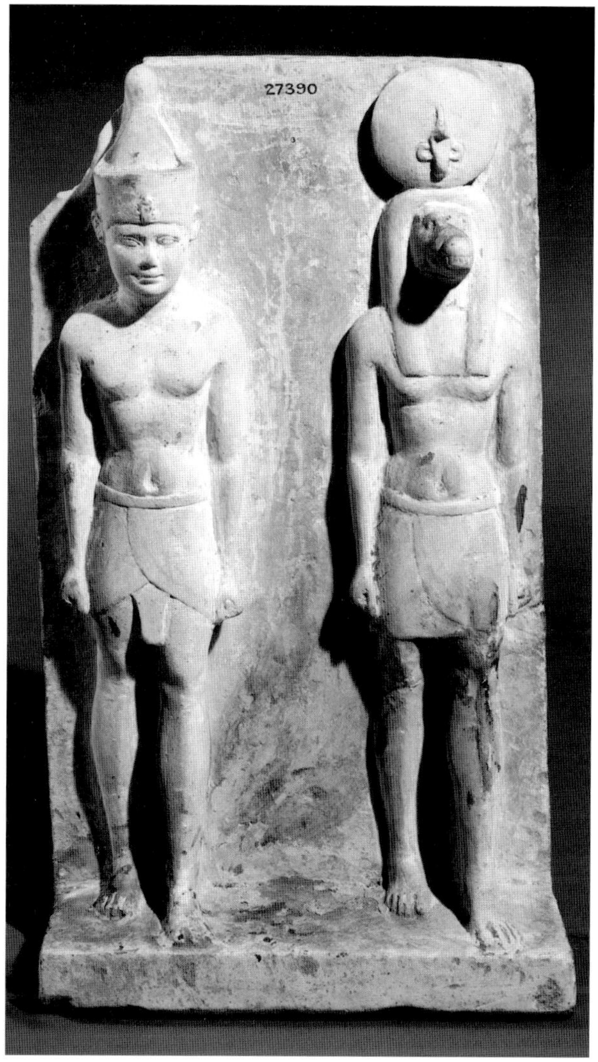

70 [B23]. Standing dyad. First half of second century B.C. London, British Museum EA 27390 (photo: ©The British Museum).

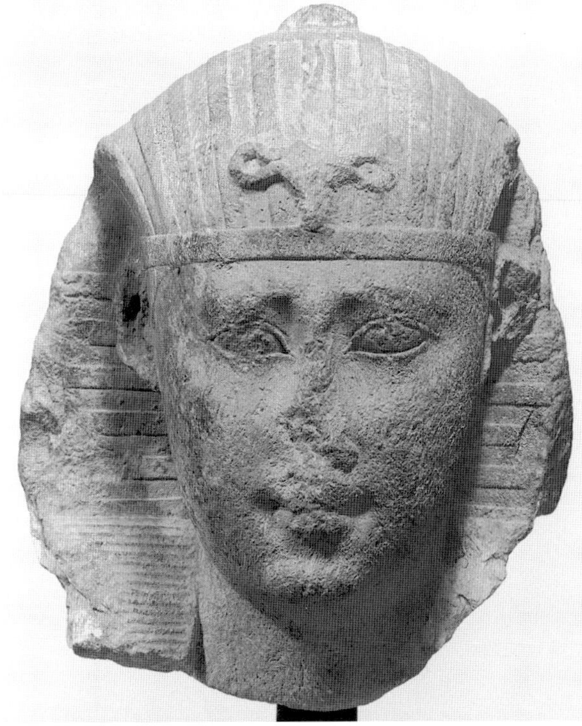

71 [B24]. Head of king. First half of second century B.C. Brooklyn Museum of Art 1995.28, Gift of Christos G. Bastis in honor of Richard Fazzini (photo: ©Brooklyn Museum of Art).

72–73 [B25]. Face of king. First half of second century B.C. Naples, Museo Archeologico Nazionale 432 (photos: author).

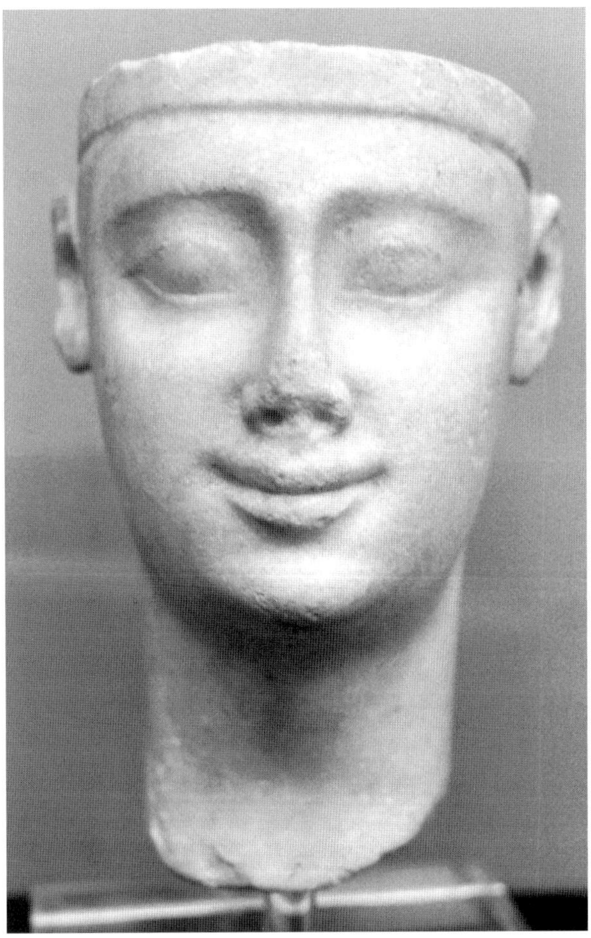

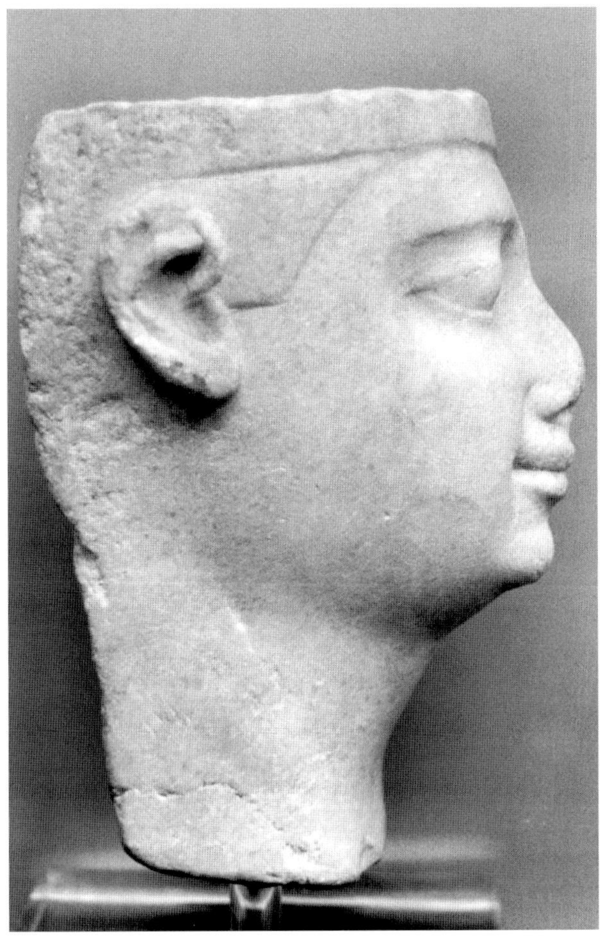

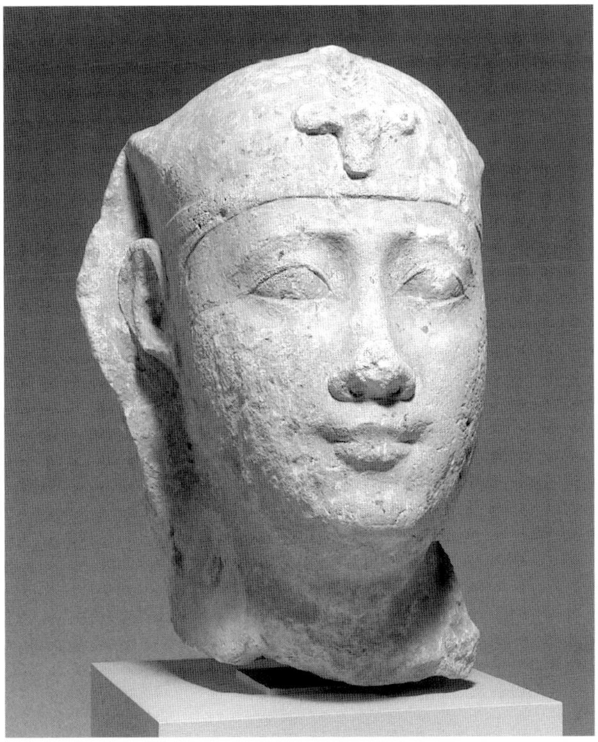

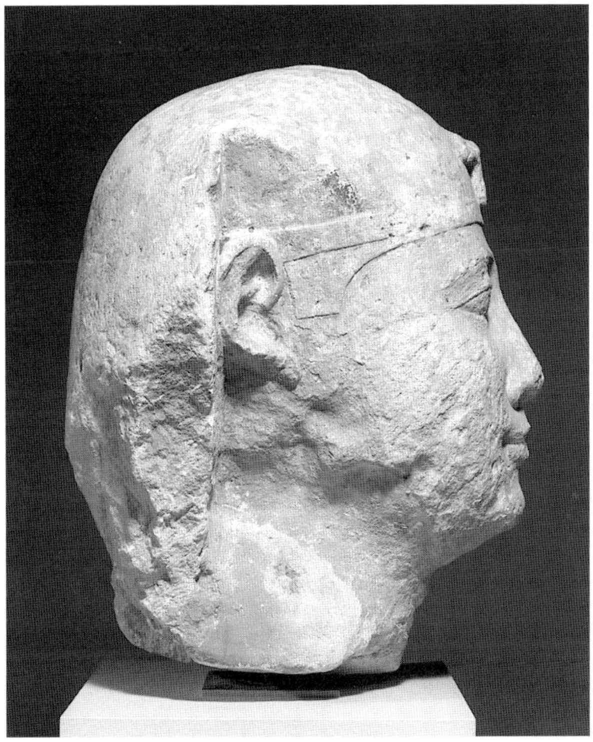

74–75 [B26] (*above*). Head of king. First half of second century B.C., Ptolemy VI? Bloomington, Indiana University Art Museum 62.225 (©Indiana University Art Museum: photographs by: Michael Cavanagh, Kevin Montague).

76–77 [B27] (*below*). Face of king. First half of second century B.C., Ptolemy VI? Alexandria, Graeco-Roman Museum 3511 (photos: Centre d'Études Alexandrines).

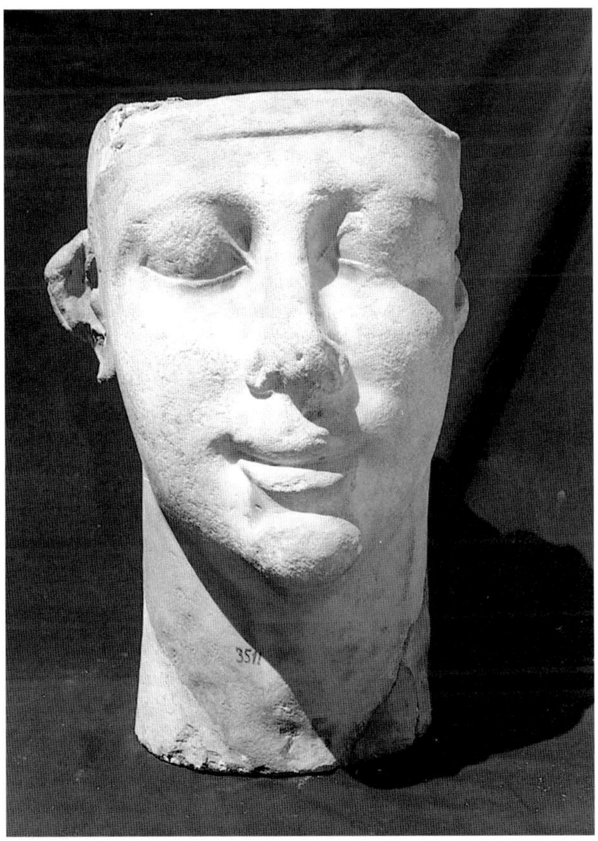

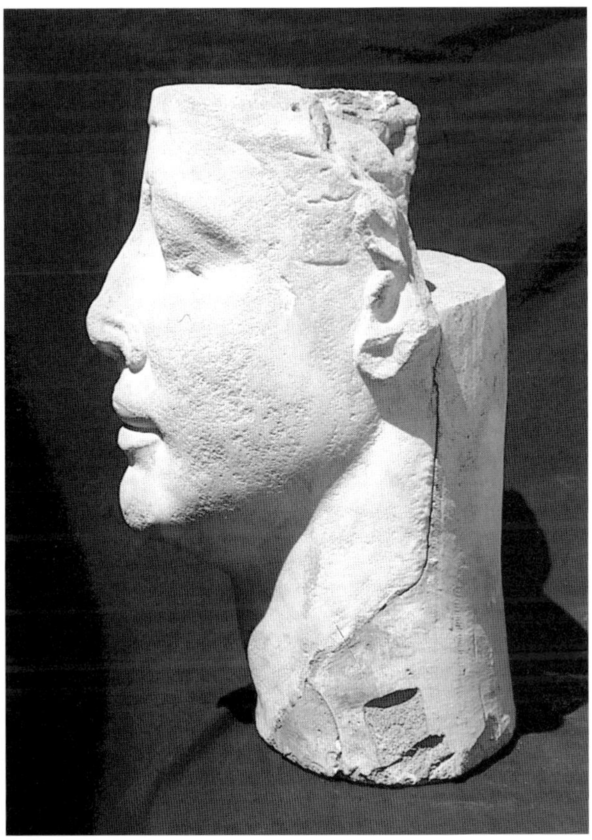

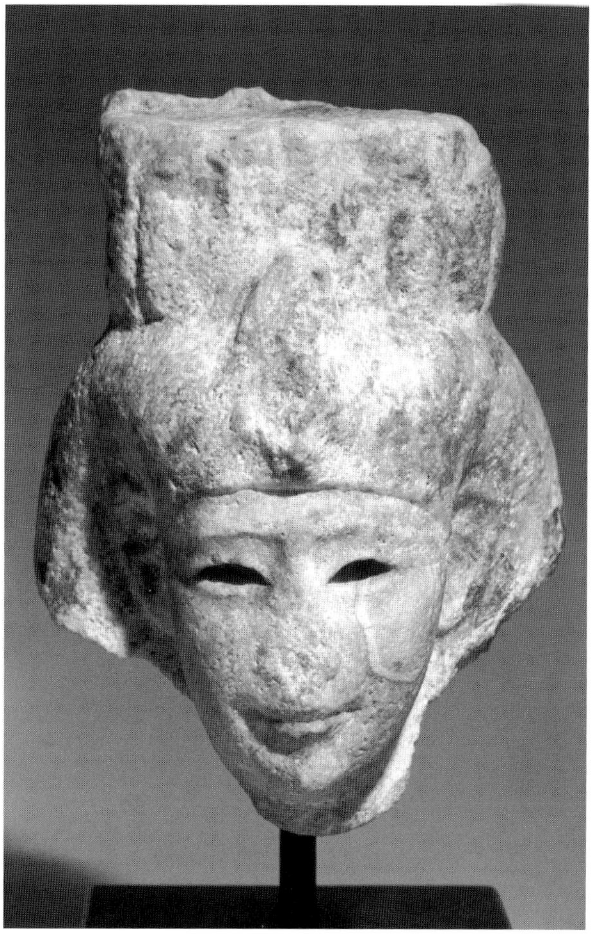

78 [B28]. Head of queen. First half of second century B.C. New York, private collection (photo: courtesy of the owner).

79–80 [C1]. Head of king. Attributed to Ptolemy VIII. Jubilee type? Brussels, Musées Royaux d'Art et d'Histoire E. 1839 (photos: Musées Royaux d'Art et d'Histoire. ©IRPA-KIK, Brussels).

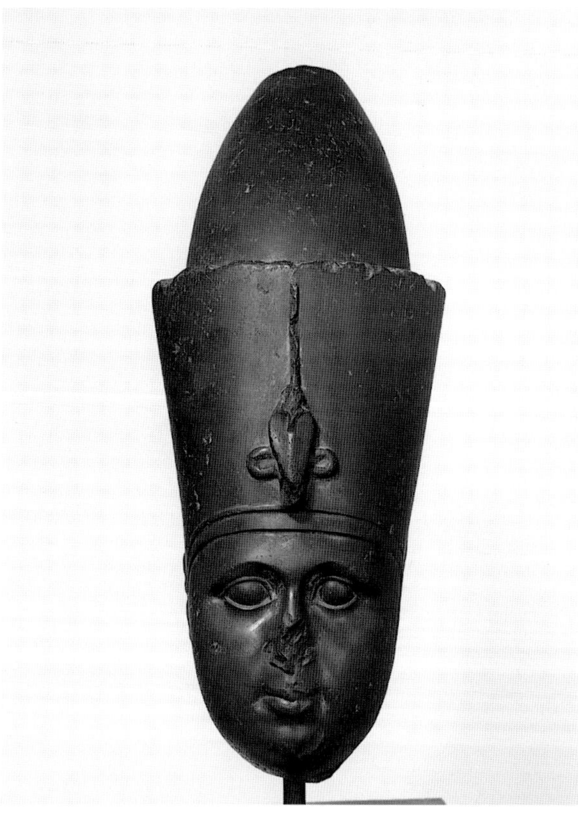

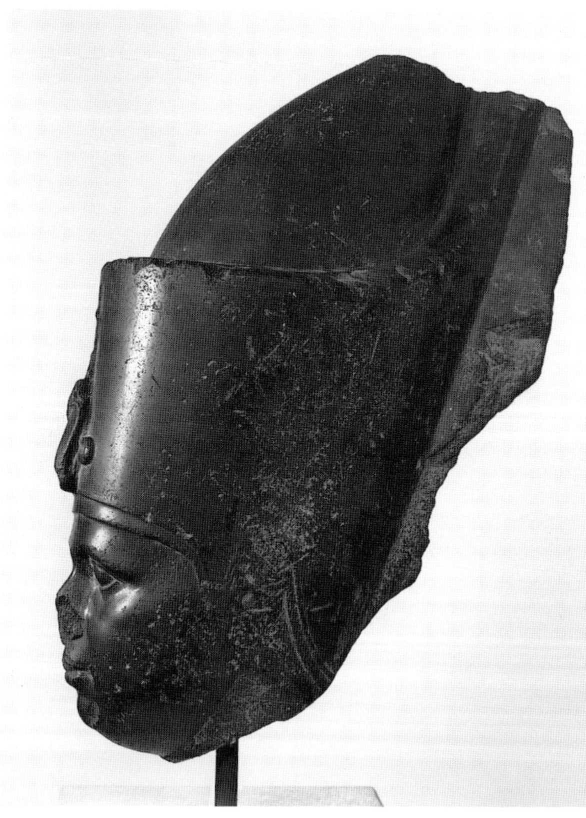

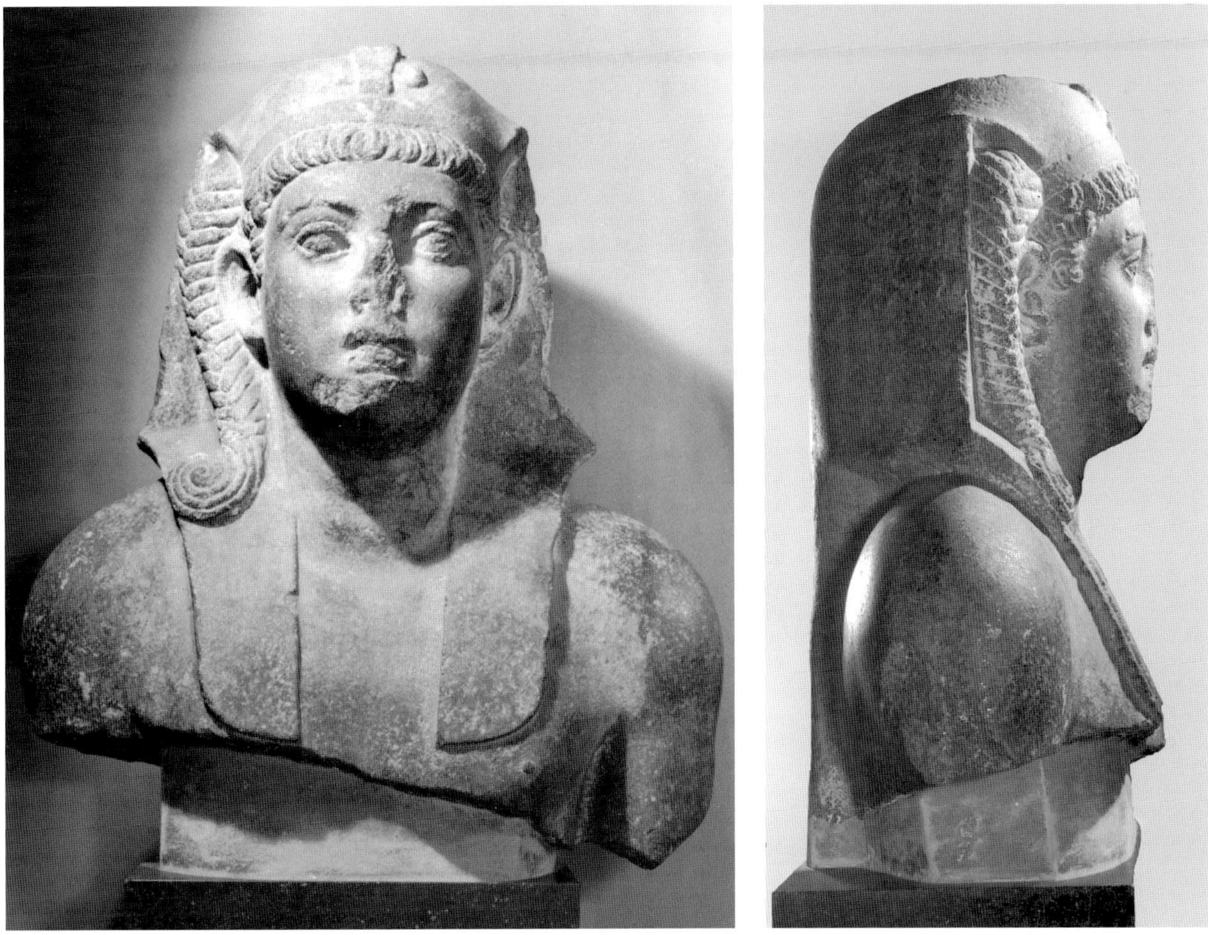

81–82 [C2]. Fragmentary king. Attributed to Ptolemy VIII. Inaugural type?
Vienna, Kunsthistorisches Museum ÄS 5780 (photos: ©Kunsthistorisches Museum, Vienna).

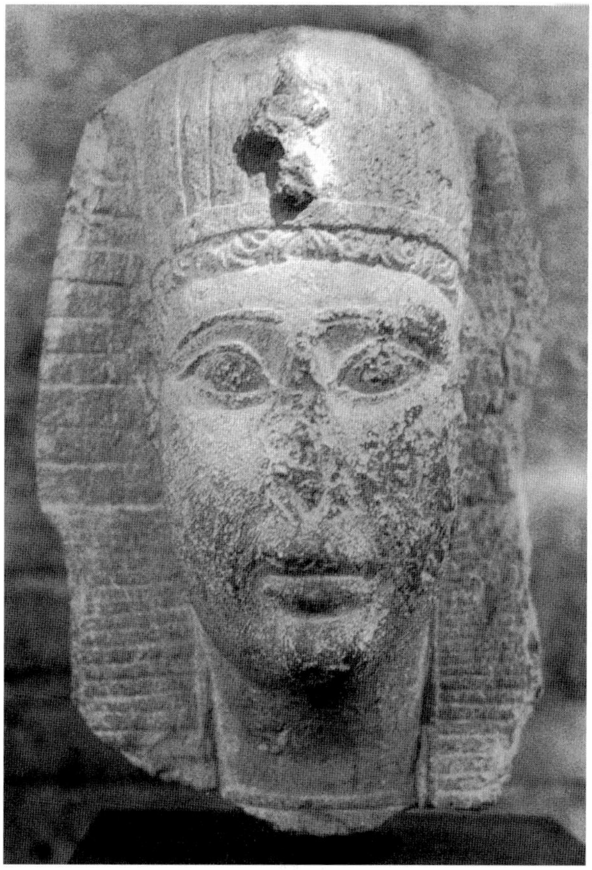

83 [C4]. Head of king. Attributed to Ptolemy VIII. Milan, Museo Archeologico E.0.9.40012 (photo: author).

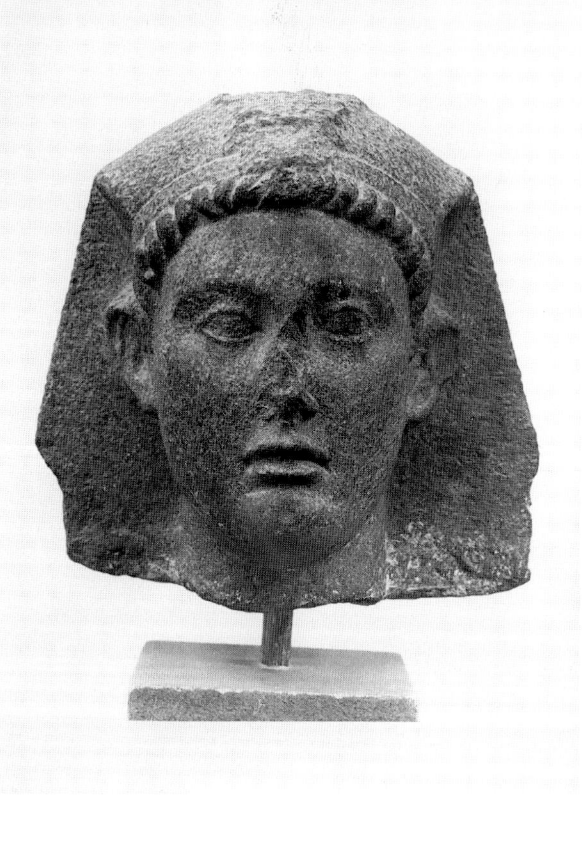

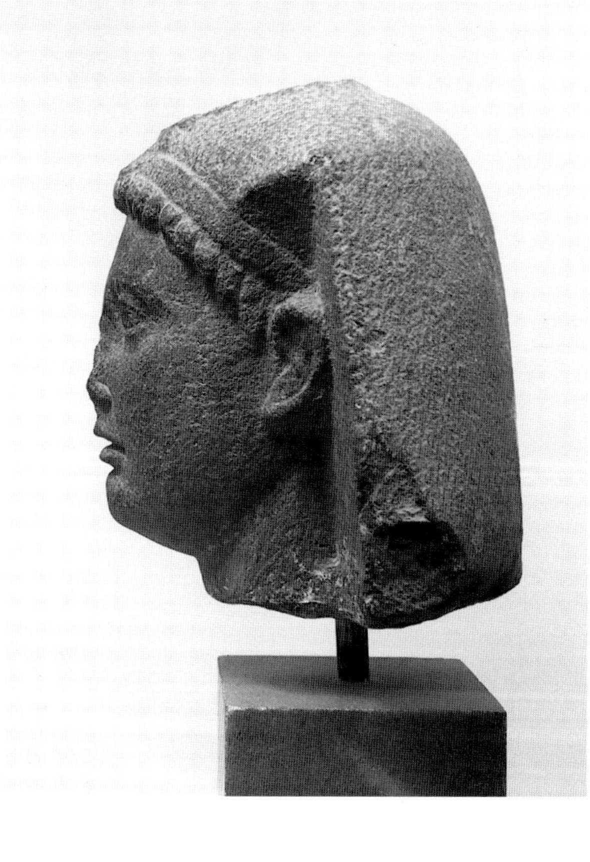

84–85 [C5]. Head of king. Attributed to Ptolemy VIII. Athens, National Archaeological Museum ANE 88 (photos: ©National Archaeological Museum).

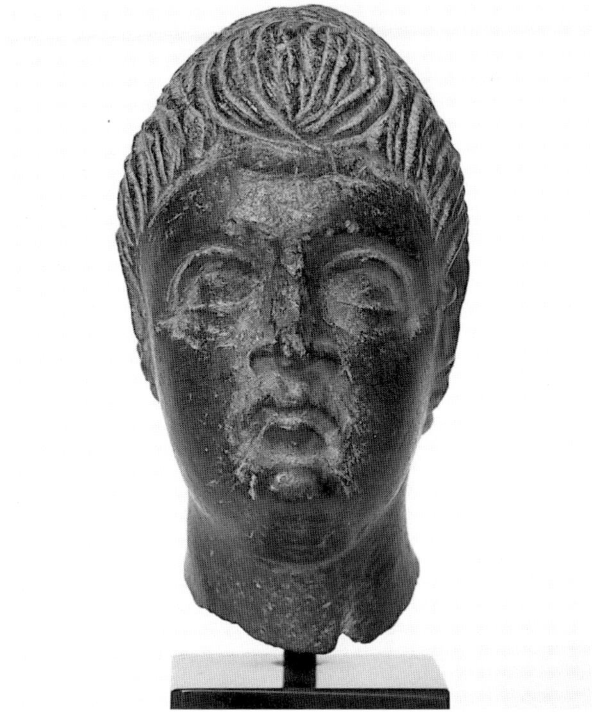

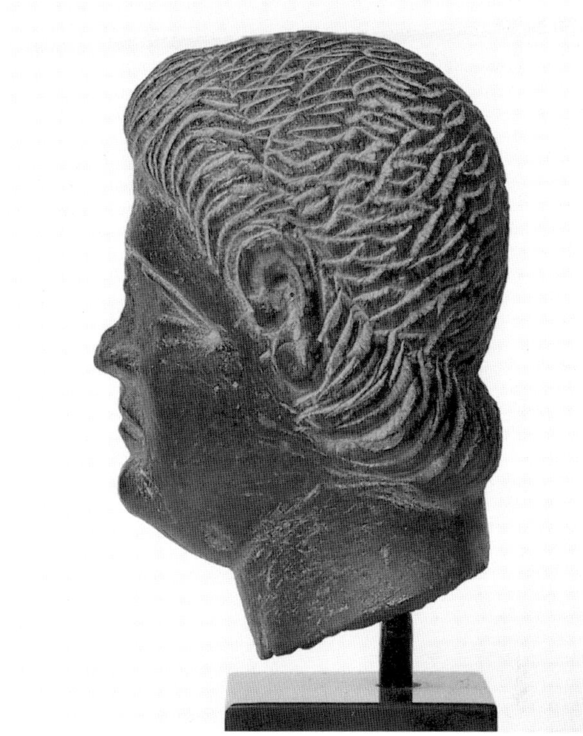

86–87 [C6] (*above*). Head of king. Attributed to Ptolemy VIII. Washington, D.C., Byzantine Collection, Dumbarton Oaks 48.10 (photos: ©Dumbarton Oaks).

88–89 [C7] (*below*). Head of king. Attributed to Ptolemy VIII. Athens, Benaki Museum 22586 (photos: ©Benaki Museum).

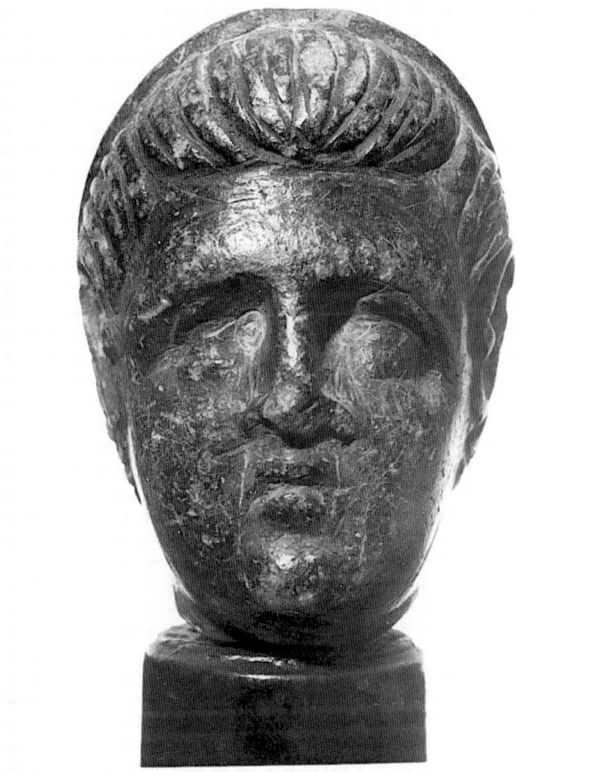

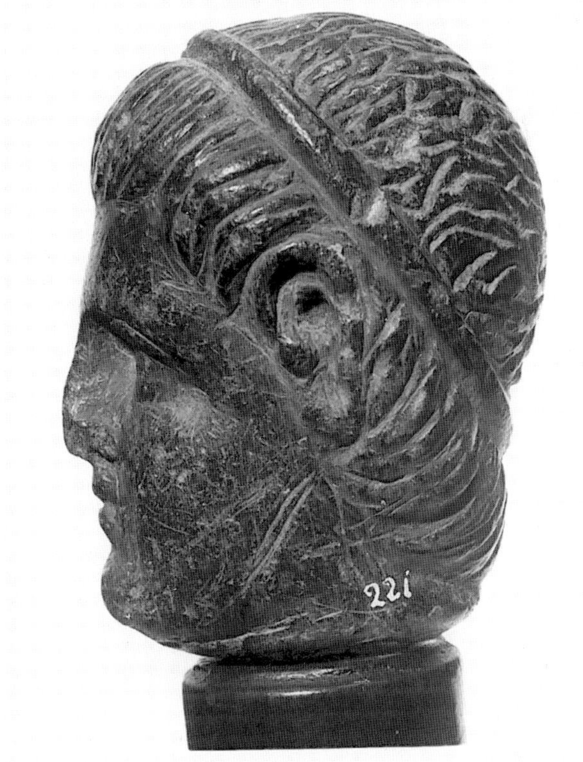

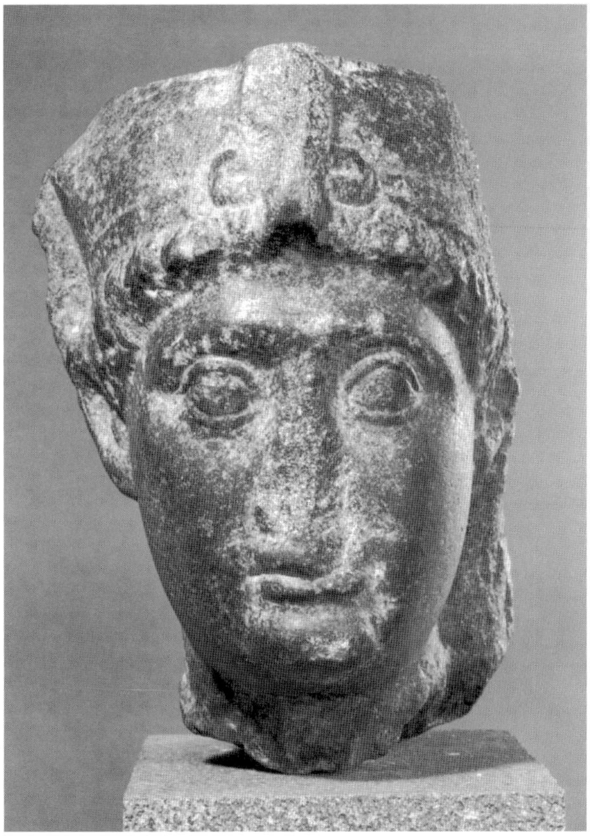

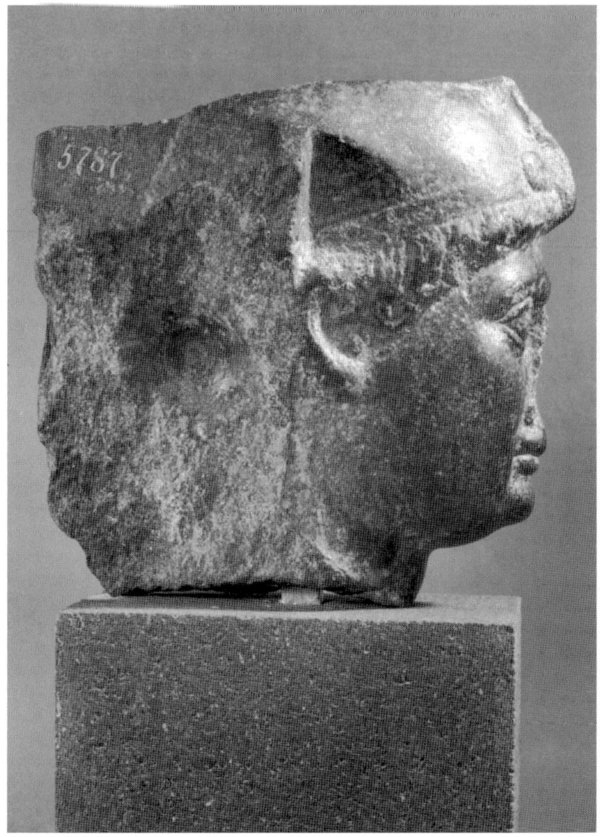

90–91 [C8] (*above*). Head of king. Attributed to Ptolemy VIII. Vienna, Kunsthistorisches Museum ÄS 5787 (photos: ©Kunsthistorisches Museum, Vienna).

92–93 [C9] (*below*). Head of king. Attributed to Ptolemy VIII. Tübingen, Ägyptologisches Institut der Universität 1460 (photos: ©Ägyptologisches Institut der Universität).

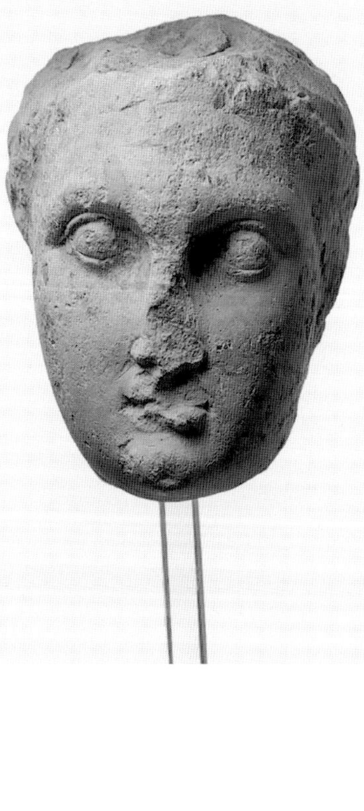

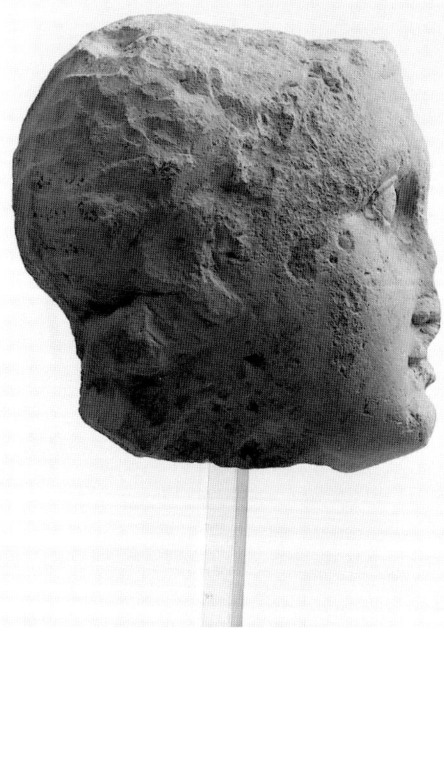

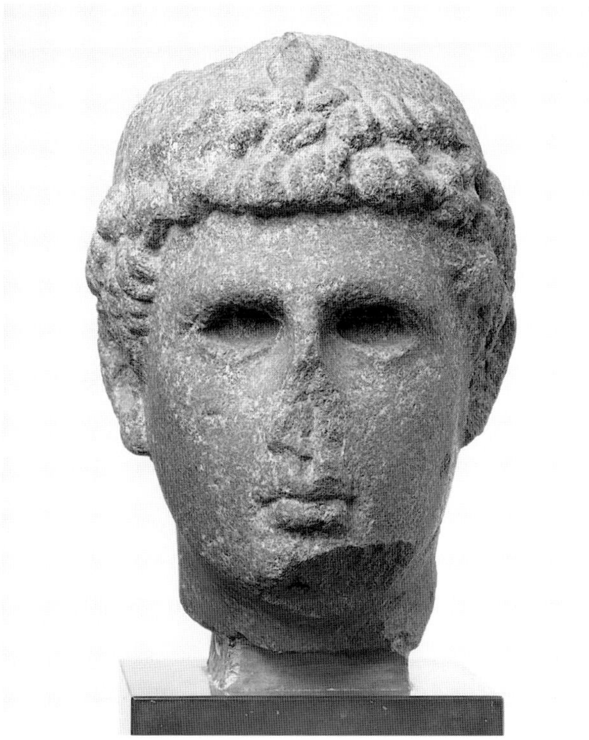

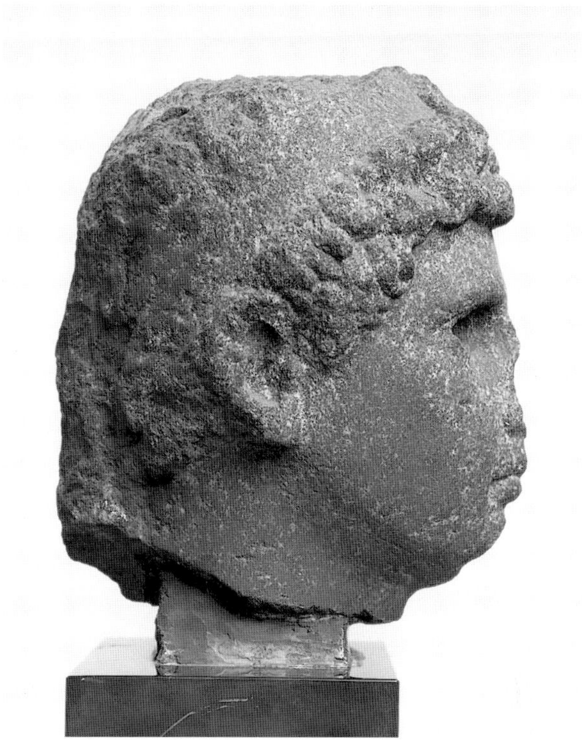

94–95 [C10] (*above*). Head of king. Attributed to Ptolemy VIII. Jubilee type? Copenhagen, Ny Carlsberg Glyptotek AEIN 294 (photos: ©Ny Carlsberg Glyptotek).

96–97 [C11] (*below*). Head of king. Attributed to Ptolemy VIII. Jubilee type? Paris, Musée du Louvre Ma 970 (photos: ©Musée du Louvre—P. Lebaube).

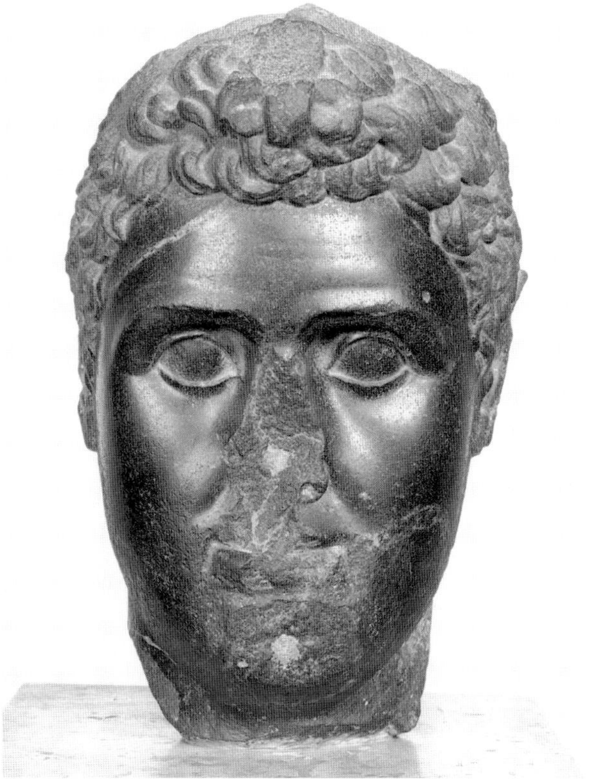

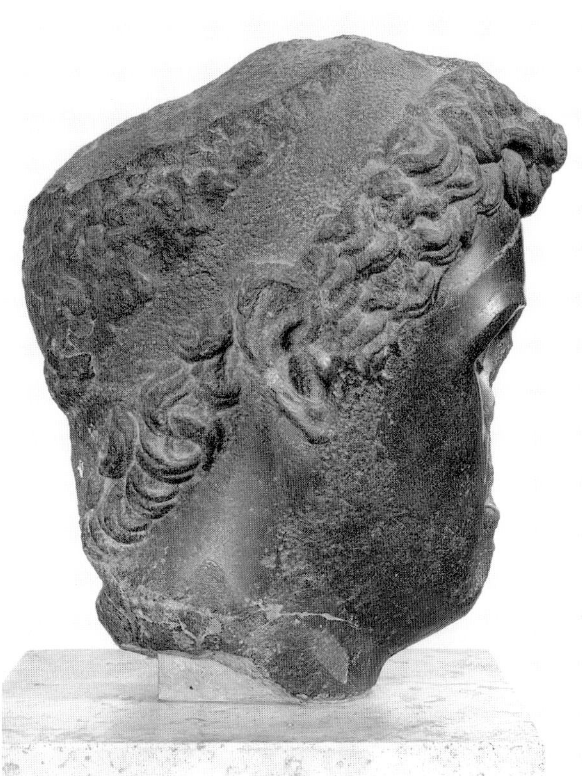

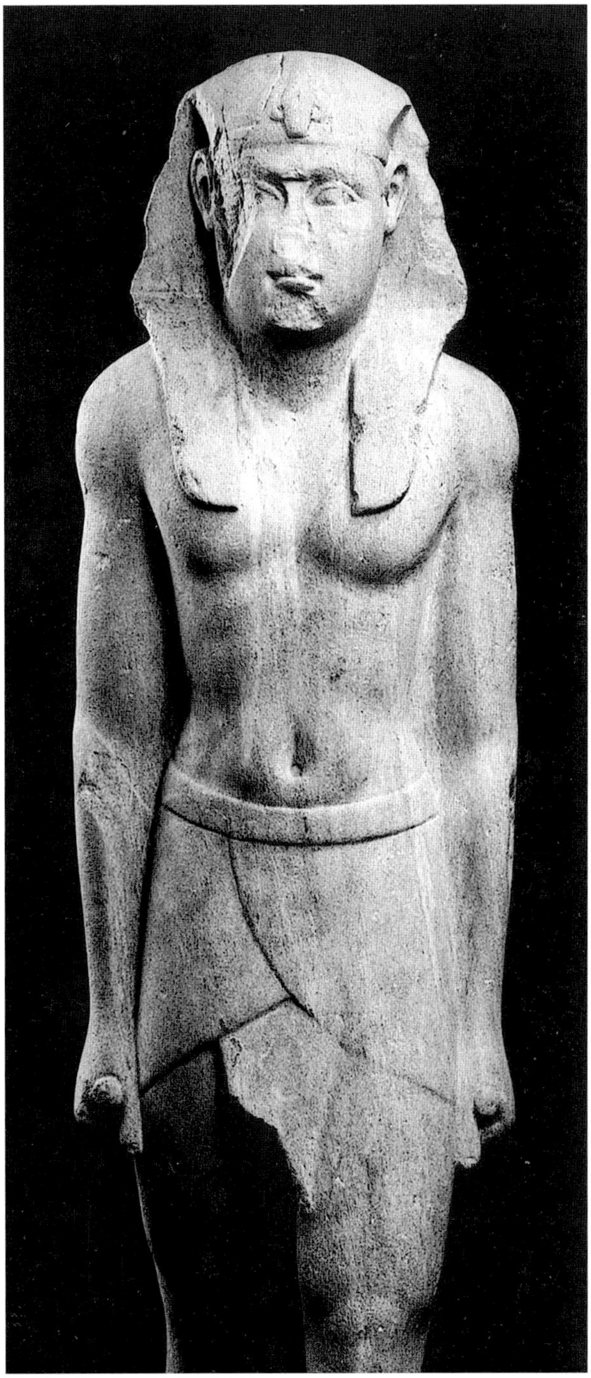

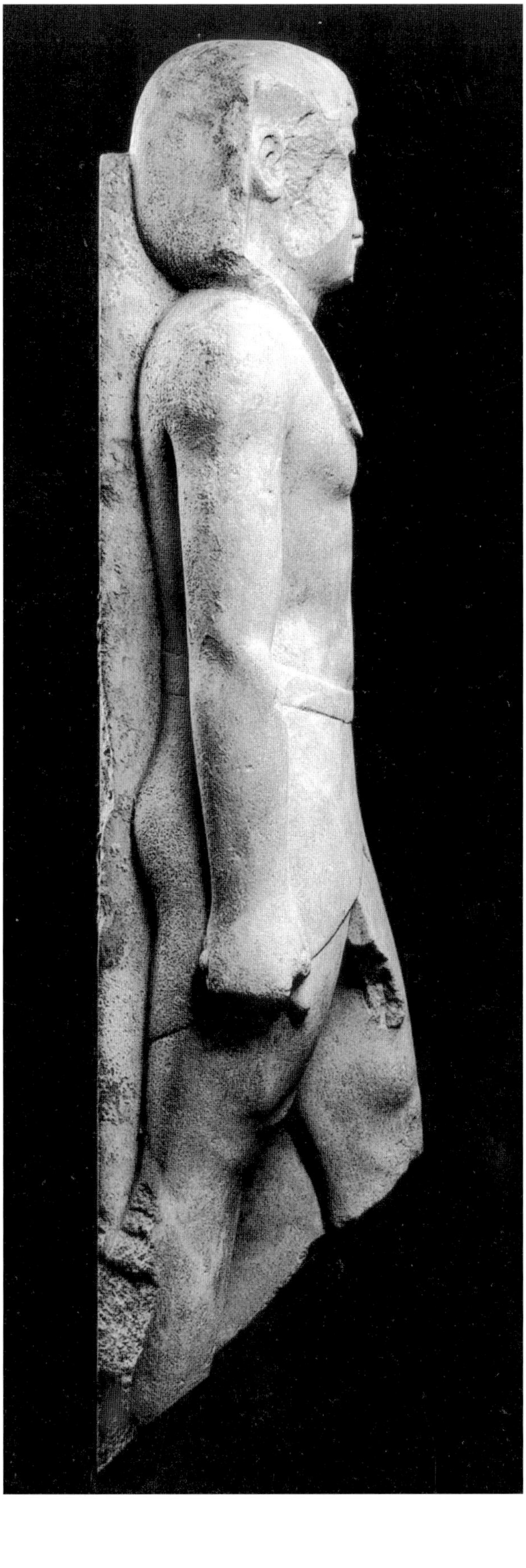

98–99 [C12]. Standing king. Attributed to Ptolemy VIII. Amsterdam, Allard Pierson Museum 7780 (photos: ©Allard Pierson Museum).

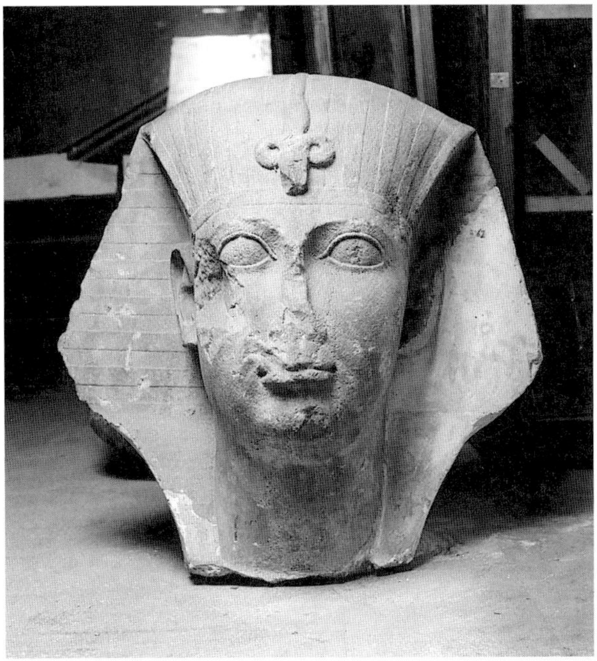

100 [C13]. Head of king. Attributed to Ptolemy VIII. Alexandria, Graeco-Roman Museum 362 (photo: Centre d'Études Alexandrines).

101 [C15]. Sphinx. Attributed to Ptolemy VIII. Cairo CG 1166 (photo: author).

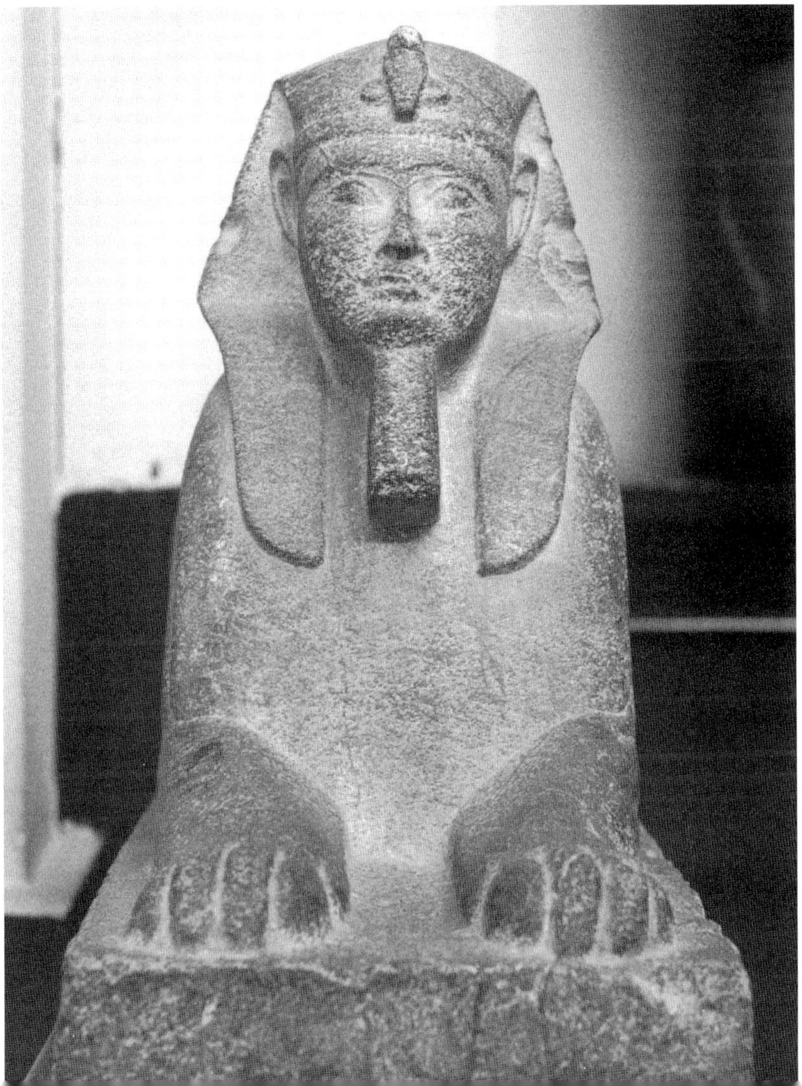

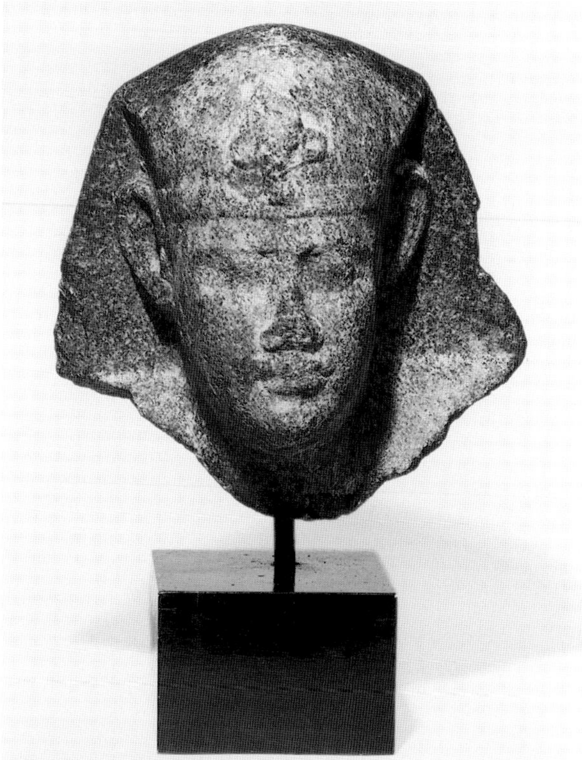

102 [C16]. Head of king. Attributed to Ptolemy VIII. New Haven, Peabody Museum of Natural History YPM.264258 (photo: courtesy of the Peabody Museum of Natural History, Yale University, New Haven, Conn.).

103–104 [C17]. Head of king. Attributed to Ptolemy VIII. Vienna, Kunsthistorisches Museum ÄS 8181 (photos: ©Kunsthistorisches Museum, Vienna).

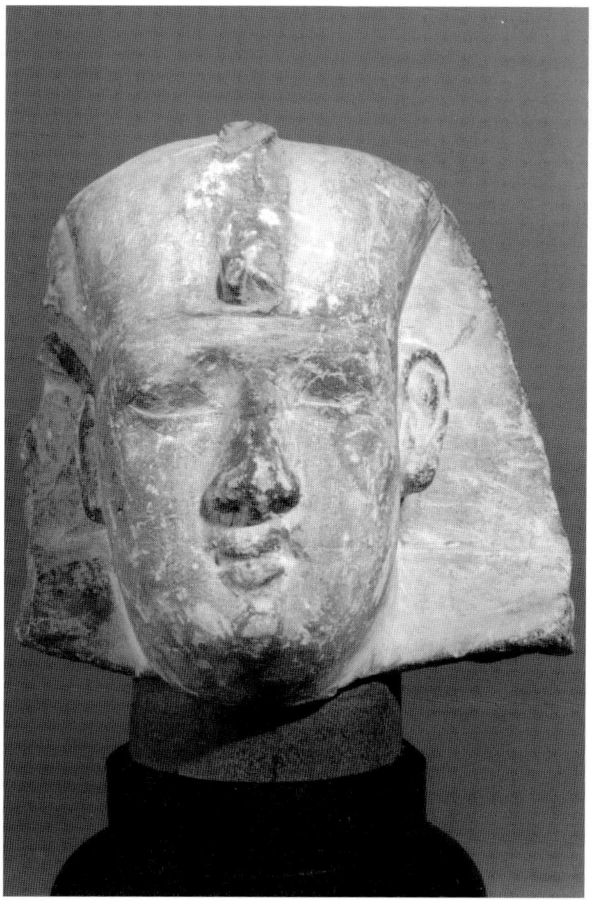

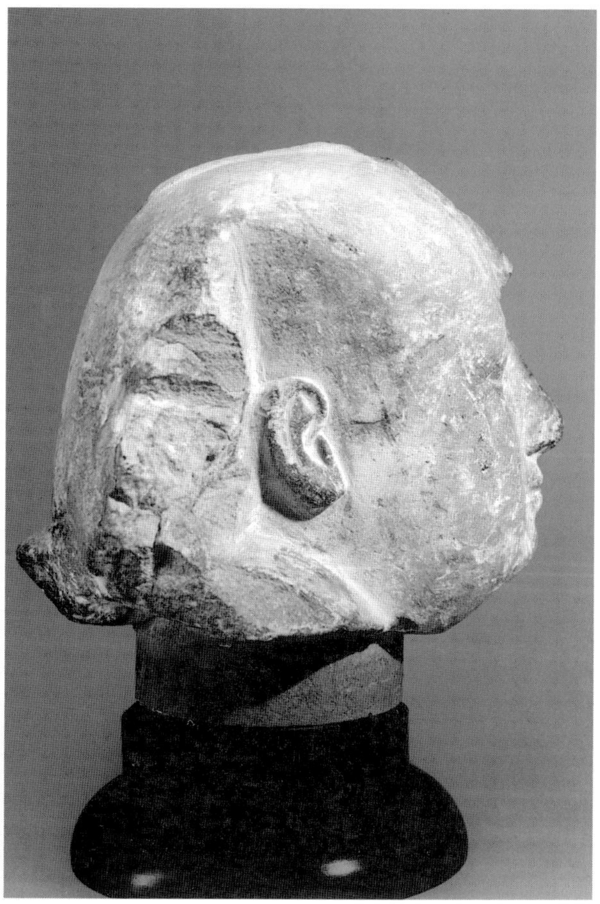

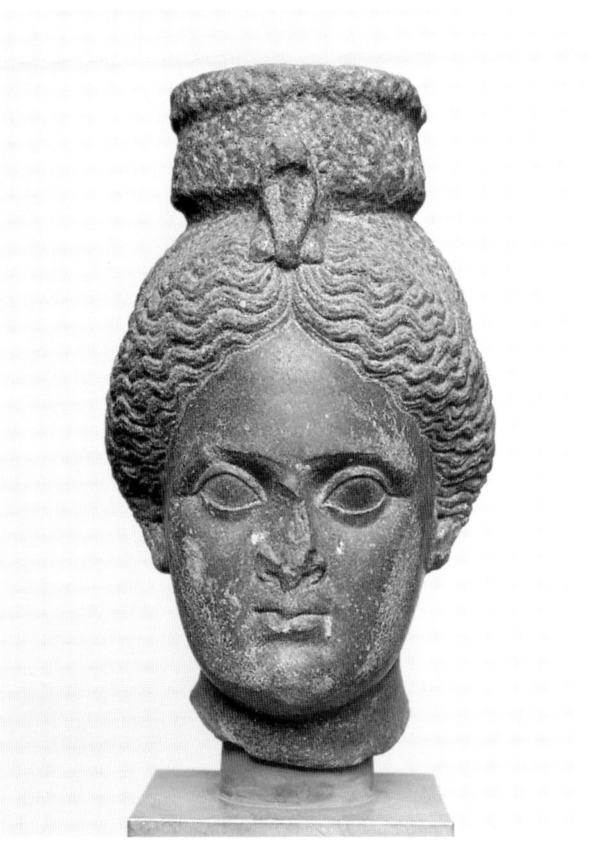

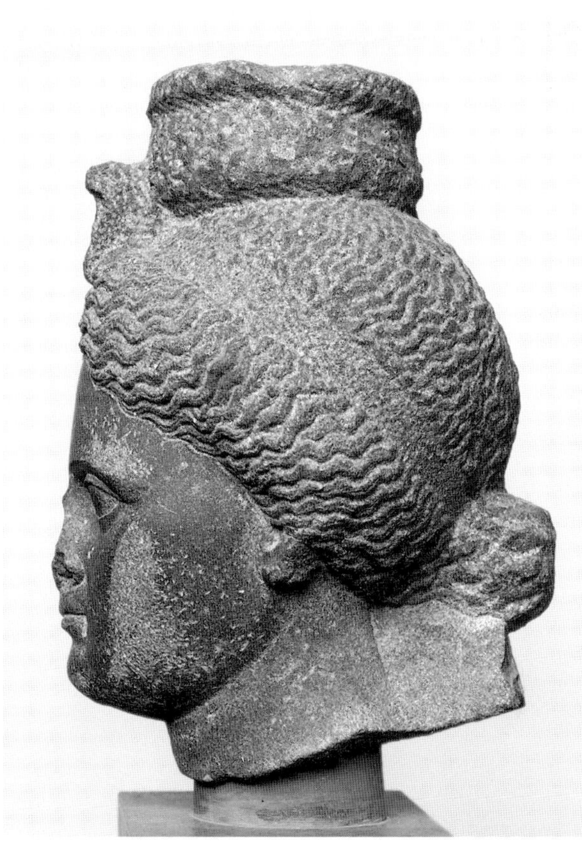

105–106 [C18]. Head of queen. Attributed to Cleopatra II. Copenhagen, Ny Carlsberg Glyptotek AEIN 1472 (photos: ©Ny Carlsberg Glyptotek).

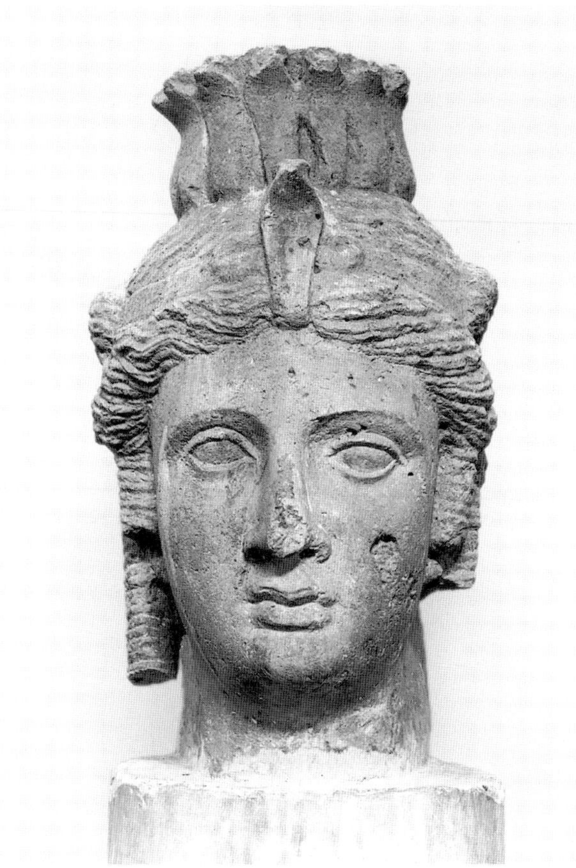

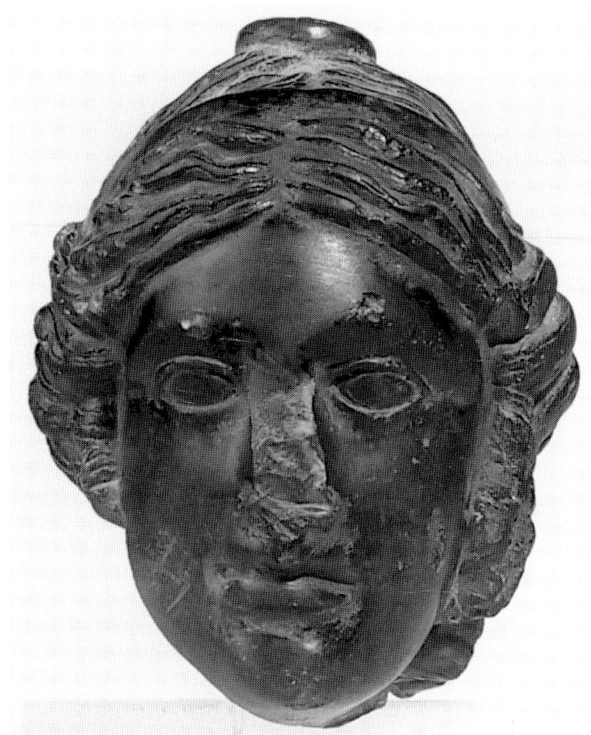

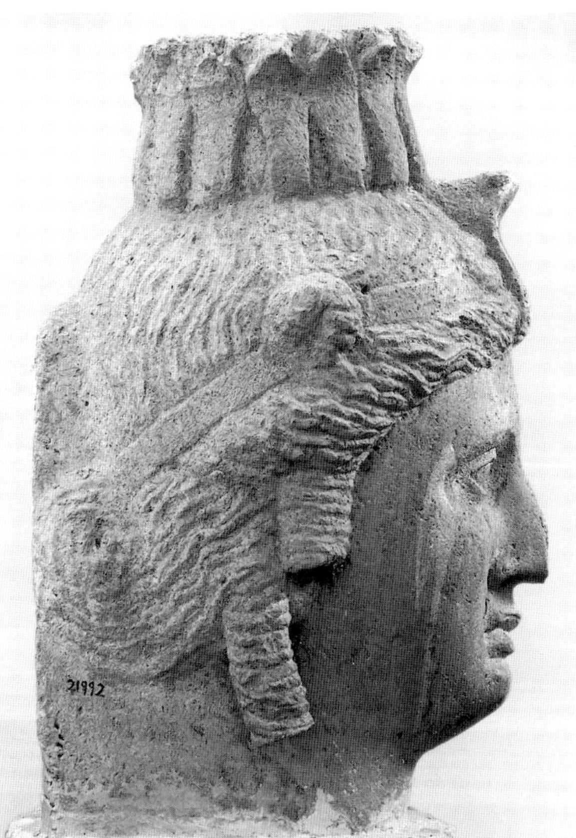

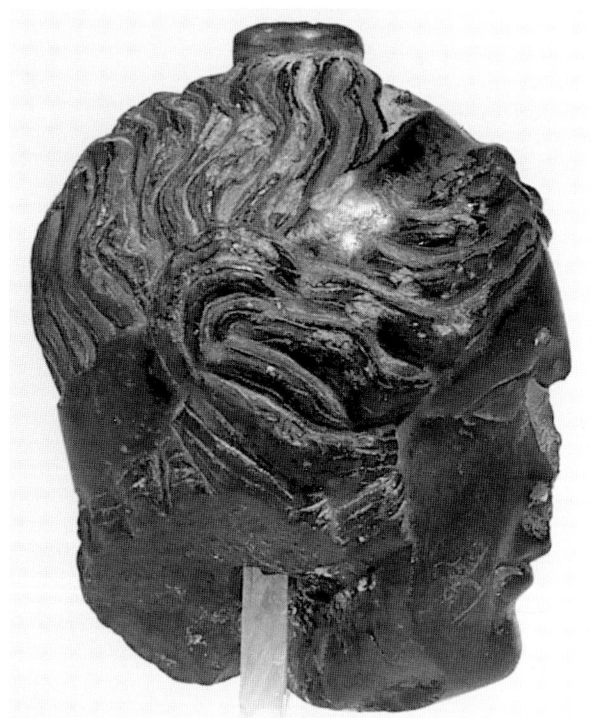

107–108 [C19] (*left*). Head of queen. Attributed to Cleopatra II as *Thea Philometor Soteira*. Alexandria, Graeco-Roman Museum 21992 (photos: Deutsches Archäologisches Institut, Cairo).

109–110 [C20] (*right*). Head of queen. Attributed to Cleopatra II as *Thea Philometor Soteira*. Alexandria, Graeco-Roman Museum 25264 (photos: Centre d'Études Alexandrines).

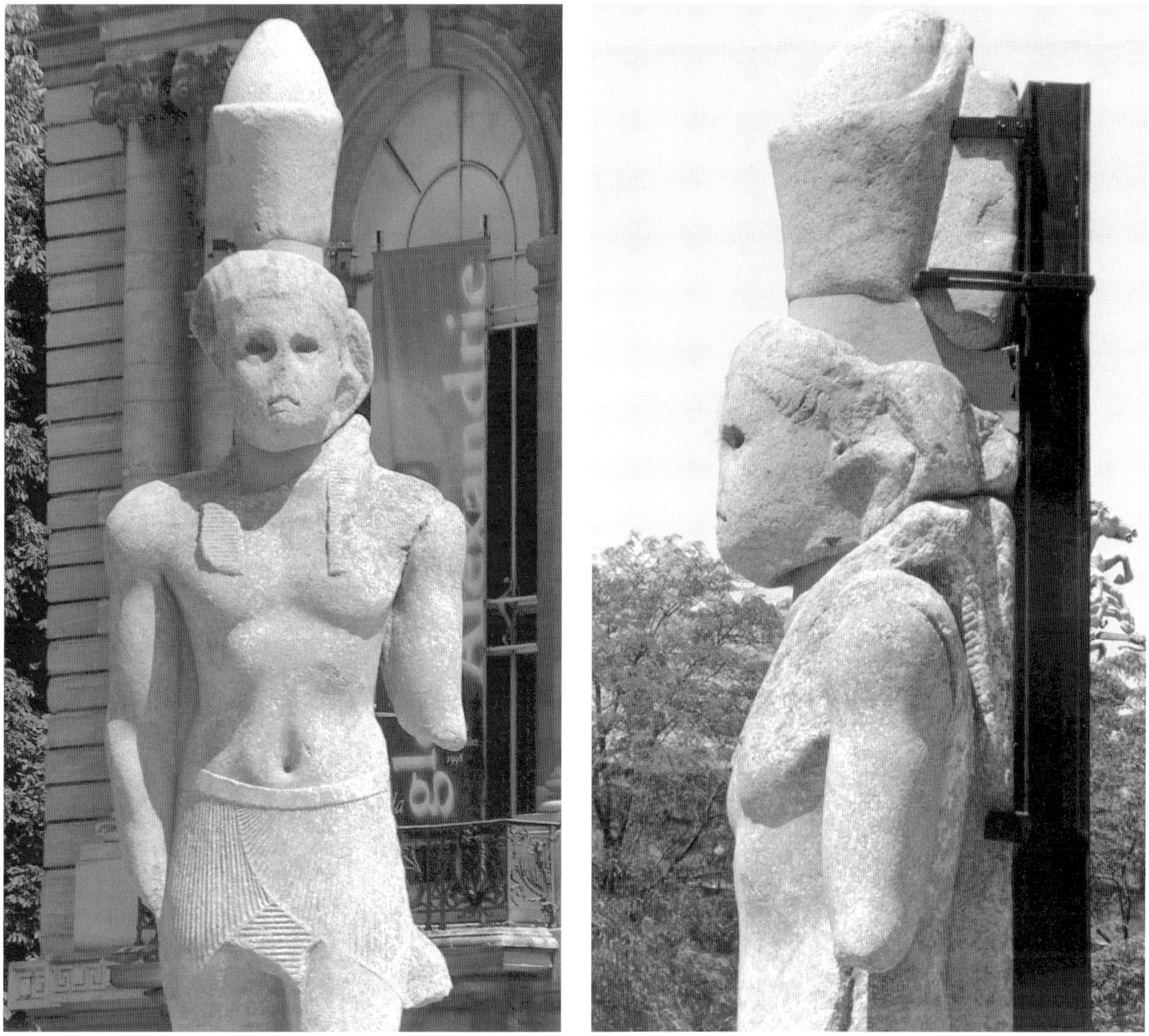

111–112 [C22]. Standing king. Attributed to Ptolemy VIII. Alexandria, Kom el-Dikka 1001 + 1999 + 3200 (photos: author).

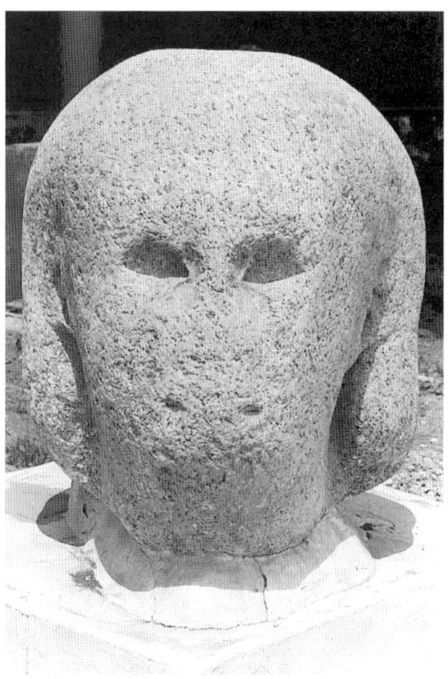

113 [C23]. Head of king. Second century B.C., Ptolemy VI? Alexandria, Kom el-Dikka 1321 (photo: author).

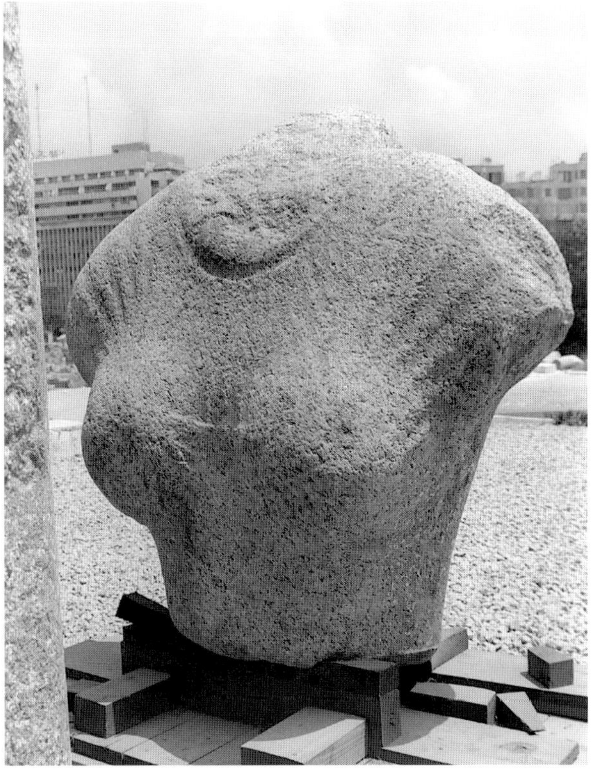

114 [C25] (*left*). Torso of queen. Second century B.C., Cleopatra II? Alexandria, Kom el-Dikka 1005 (photo: author).

115 [C27] (*below left*). Standing queen (upper portion). Second century B.C., Cleopatra III? Alexandria, Maritime Museum (photo: Centre d'Études Alexandrines).

116 [C28] (*below right*). Standing statue inscribed for Arsinoe II (posthumous). Datable to second half of second century B.C. New York, Metropolitan Museum of Art 20.2.21 (photo: ©The Metropolitan Museum of Art).

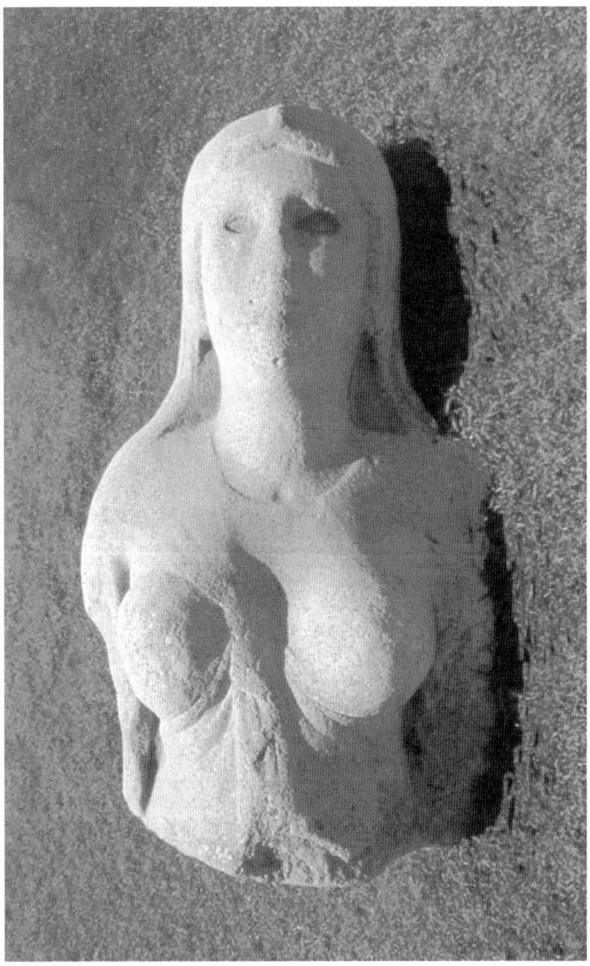

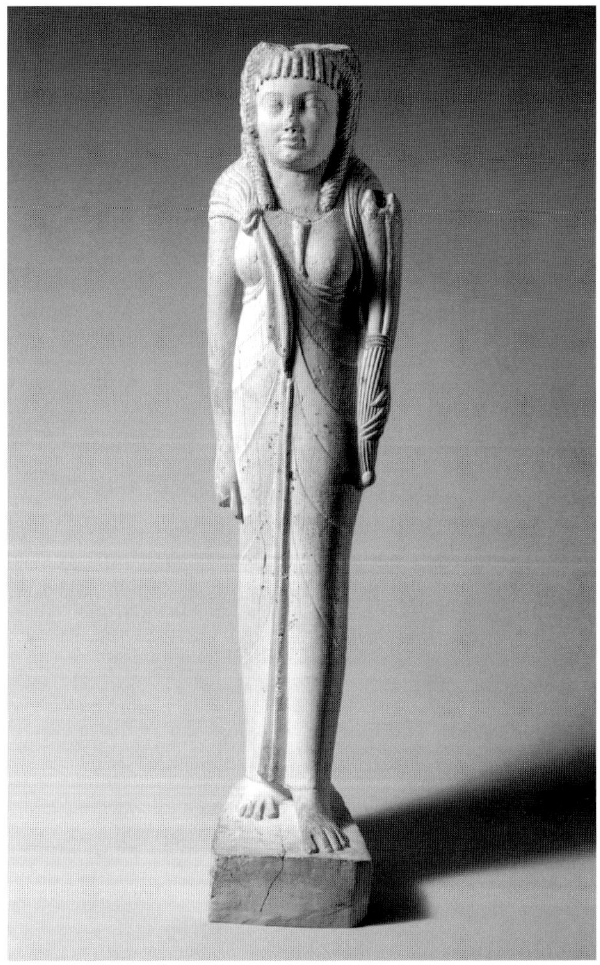

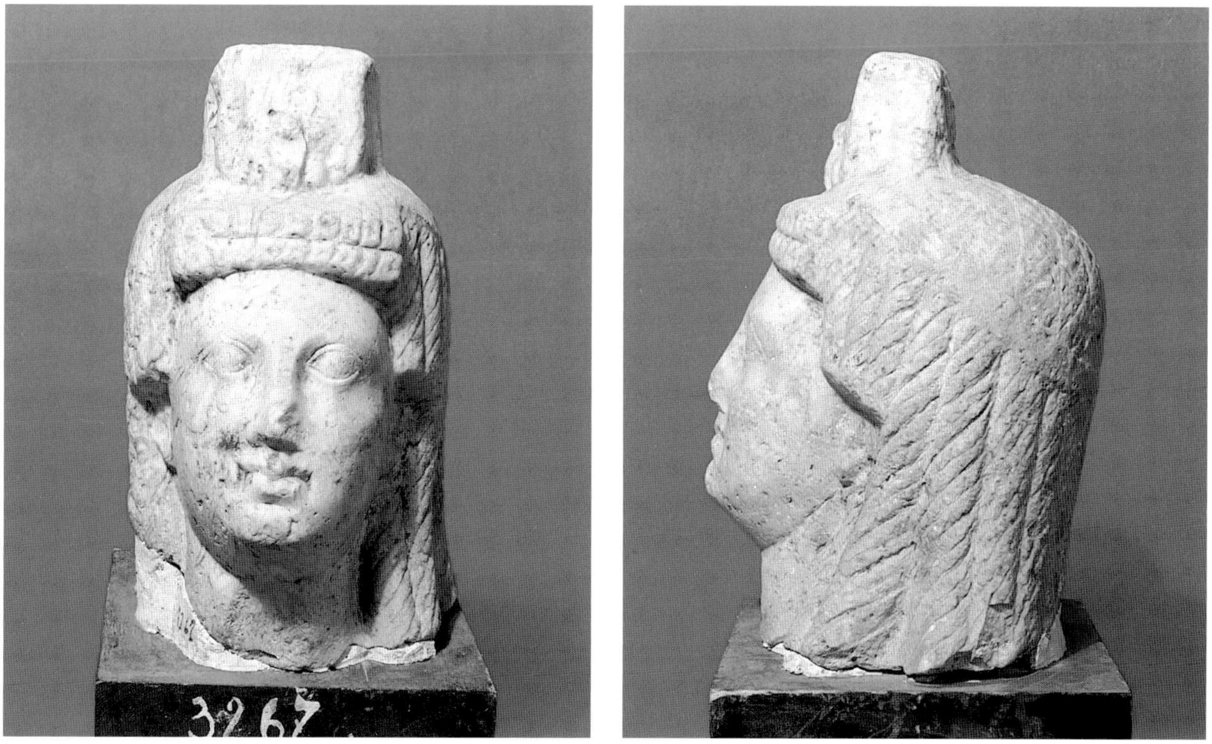

117–118 [D3] (*above*). Head of queen. Attributed to Cleopatra III. Alexandria, Graeco-Roman Museum 3267 (photos: Centre d'Études Alexandrines).

119–120 [D4] (*below*). Head of queen. Attributed to Cleopatra III. Vienna, Kunsthistorisches Museum, Antikensammlung I 406 (photos: ©Kunsthistorisches Museum Wien).

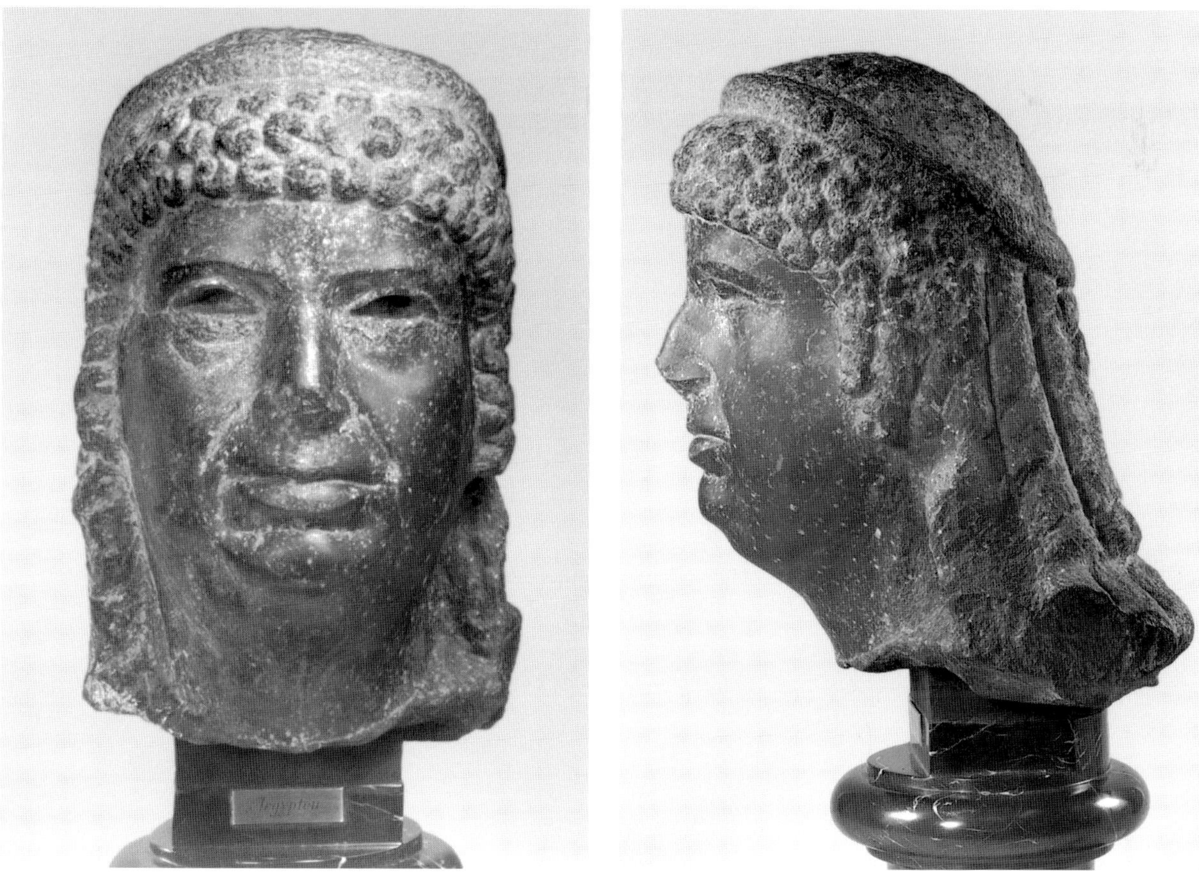

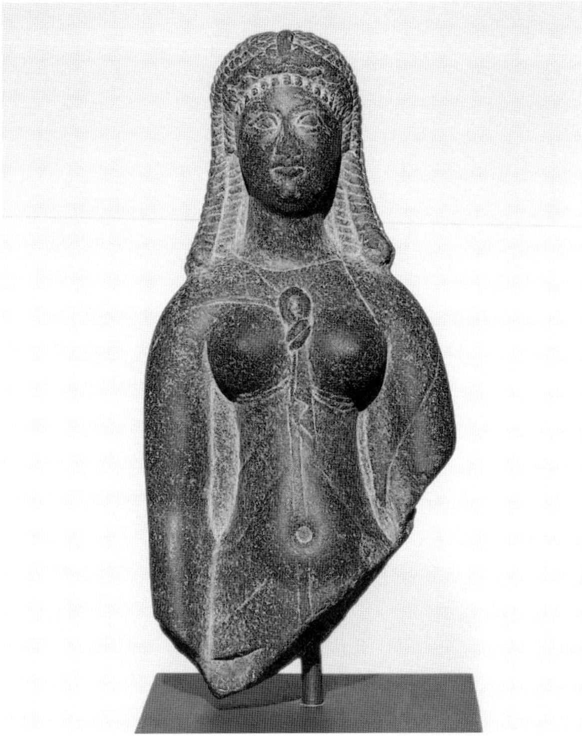

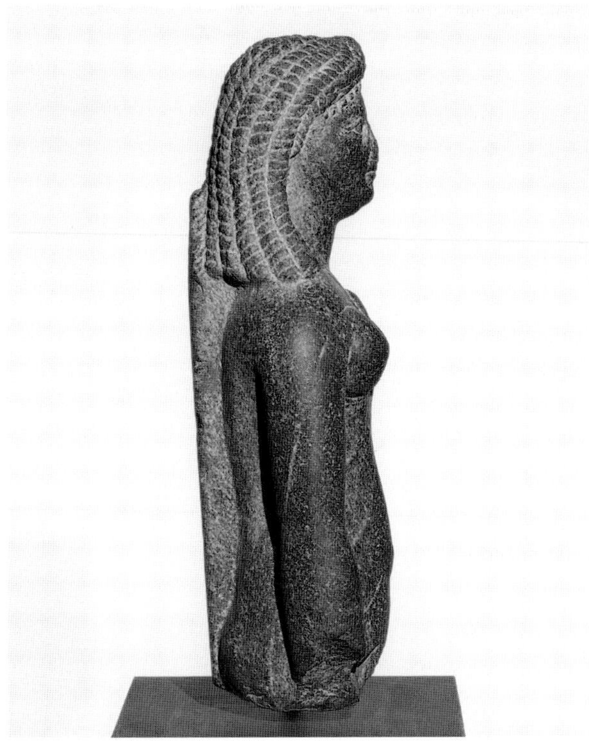

121–122 [D5] (*above*). Standing queen. Attributed to Cleopatra III. New Haven, Yale University Art Gallery 1931.106 (photos: Yale University Art Gallery).

123–124 [D6] (*below*). Head of queen. Attributed to Cleopatra III. Alexandria, Graeco-Roman Museum 28107 (photos: courtesy of the museum).

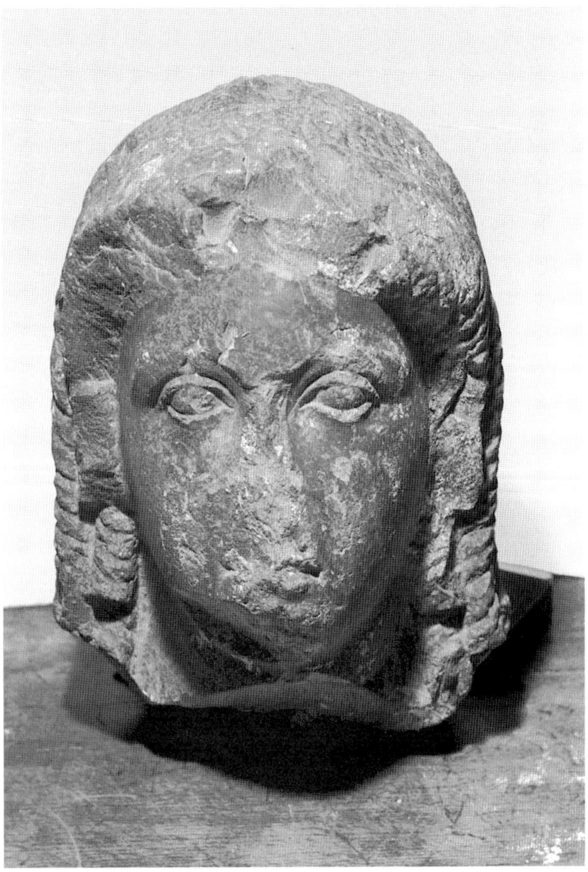

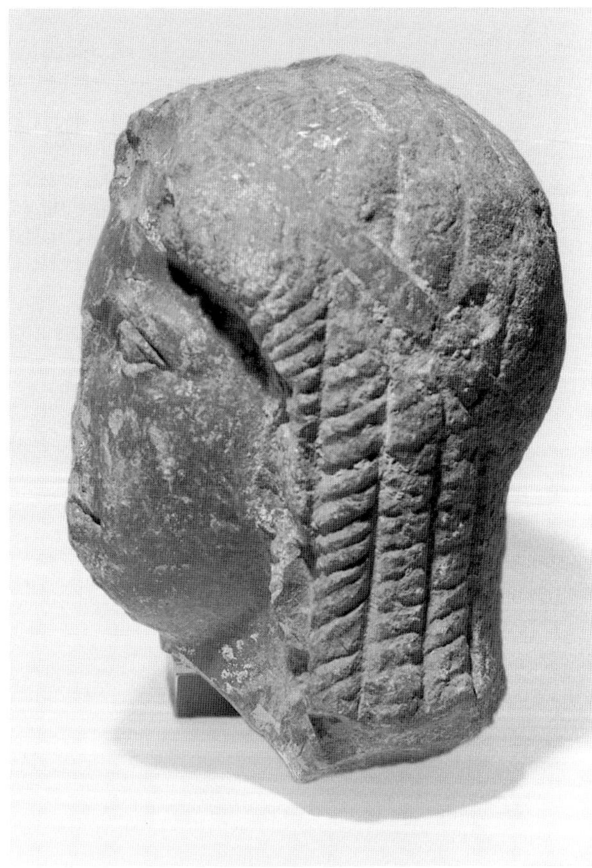

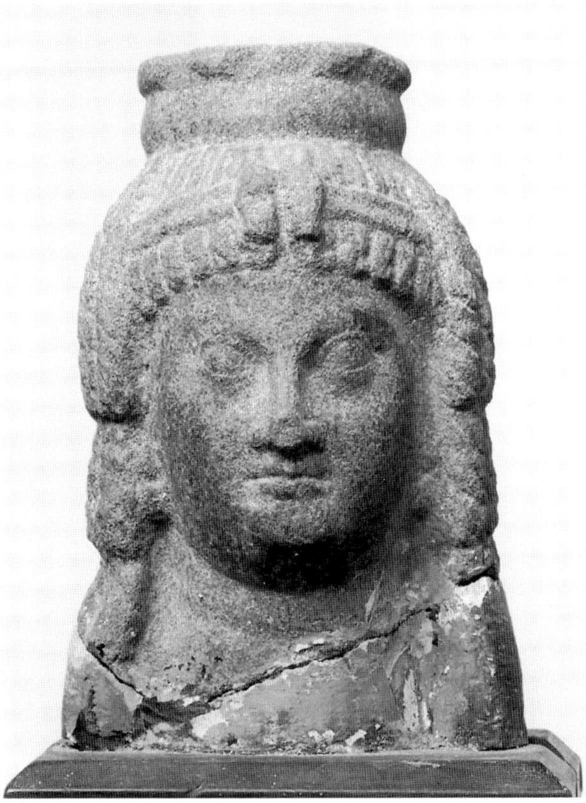

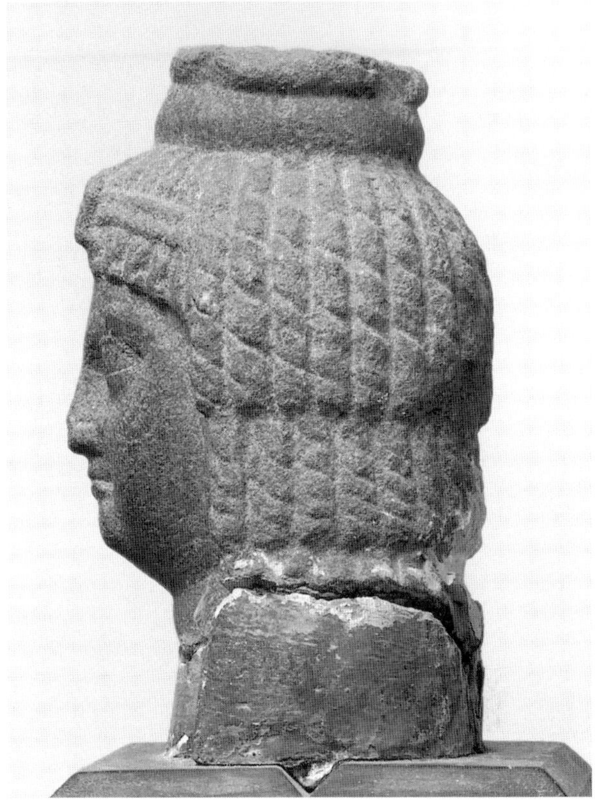

125–126 [D7] (*above*). Head of queen. Attributed to Cleopatra III. Alexandria, Graeco-Roman Museum 18370 (photos: Deutsches Archäologisches Institut, Cairo).

127 [D8] (*right*). Head of queen. Attributed to Cleopatra III. Paris, Bibliothèque nationale de France 1980–208 (photo: Cliché Bibliothèque nationale de France, Paris).

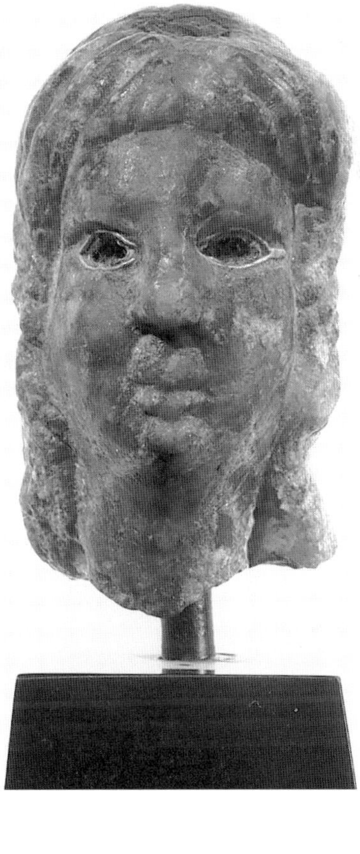

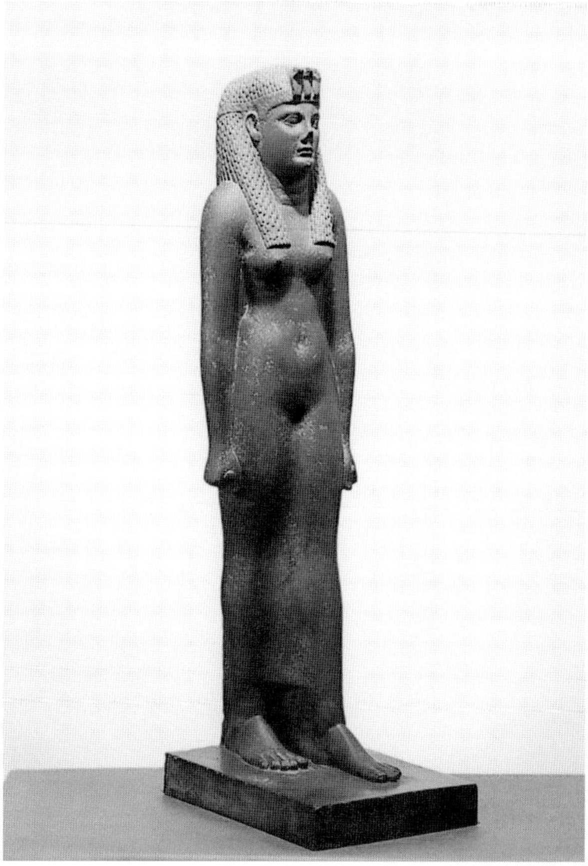

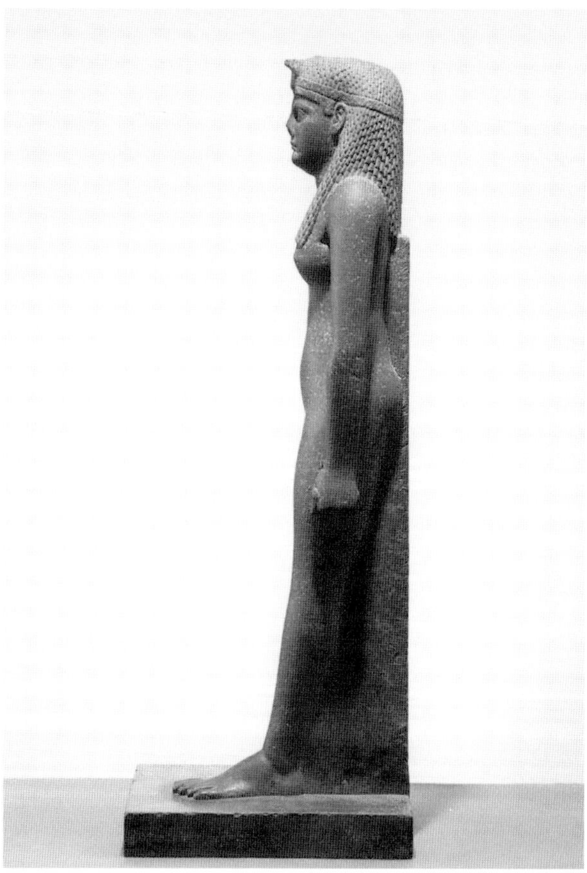

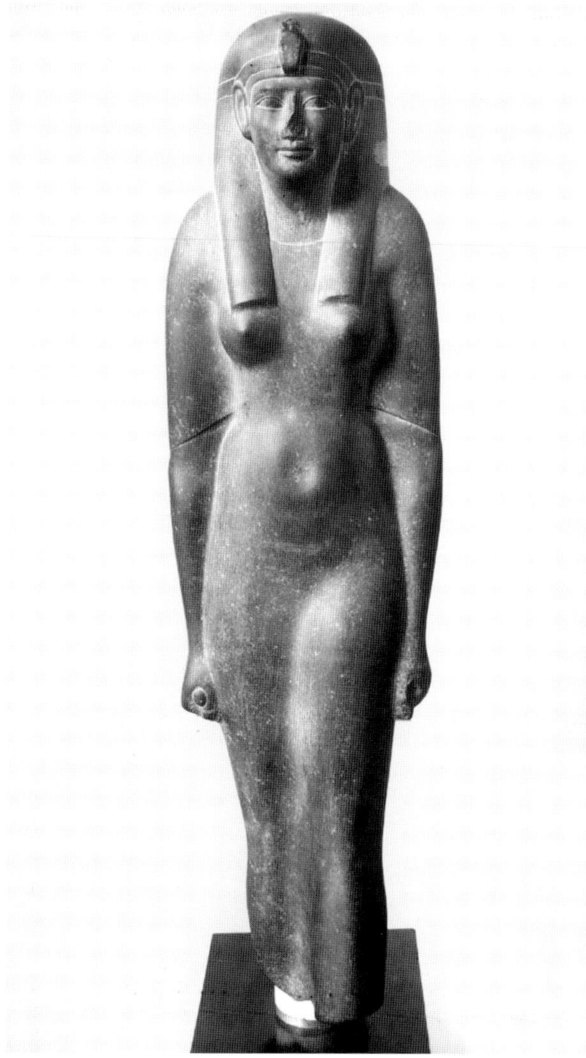

128–129 [D9] (*left*). Standing queen. Attributed to Cleopatra III. San Jose, Rosicrucian Egyptian Museum RC 1582 (photos: ©AMORC).

130 [D11] (*above*). Standing queen. Attributed to Cleopatra III. Berlin, Ägyptisches Museum 21763 (photo: ©Ägyptisches Museum und Papyrussammlung, Staatliche Museen zu Berlin—Preussischer Kulturbesitz).

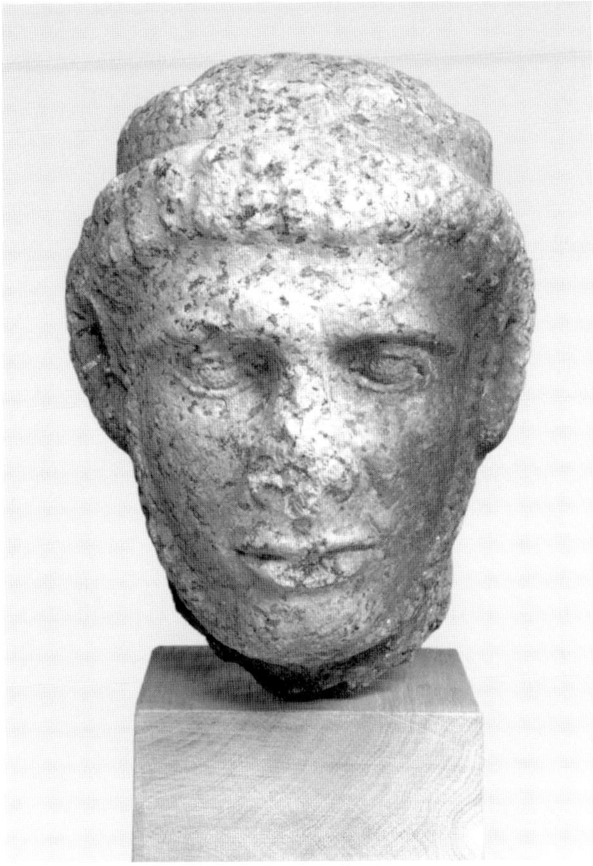

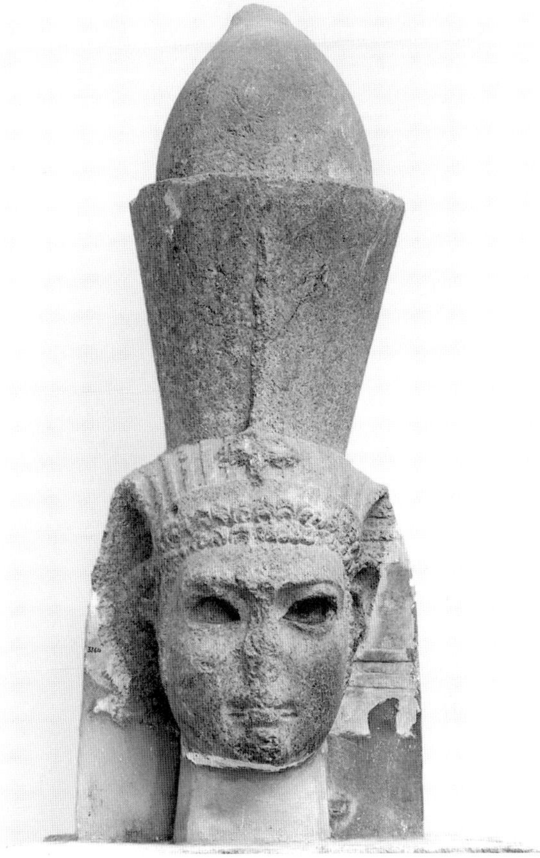

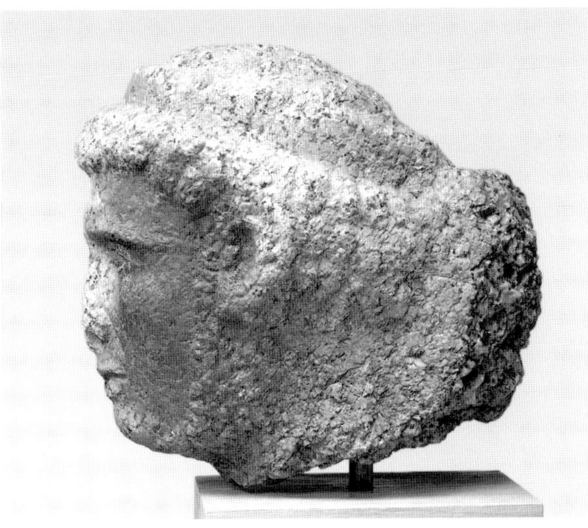

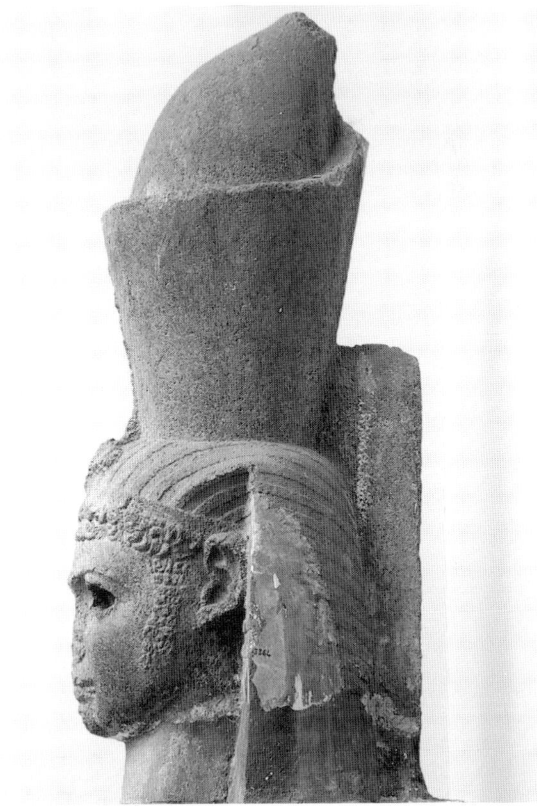

131–132 [D12] (*left*). Head of king. Attributed to Ptolemy IX, first rule, 116–107 B.C. Berlin, Ägyptisches Museum 14079 (photos: ©Ägyptisches Museum und Papyrussammlung, Staatliche Museen zu Berlin—Preussischer Kulturbesitz, Margarete Büsing).

133–134 [D13] (*right*). Head of king. Attributed to Ptolemy IX, first rule, 116–107 B.C. Alexandria, Graeco-Roman Museum 3364 (photos: Deutsches Archäologisches Institut, Cairo).

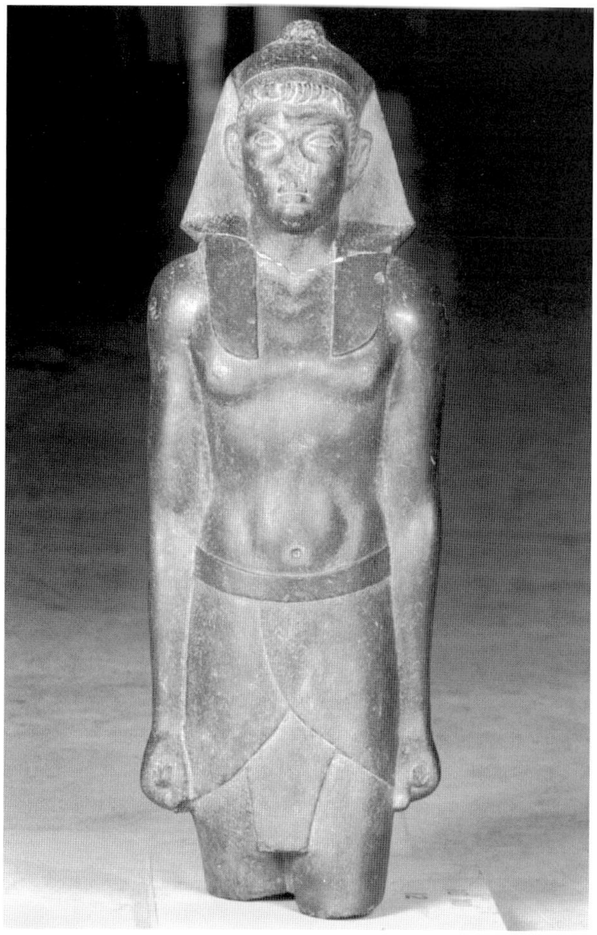

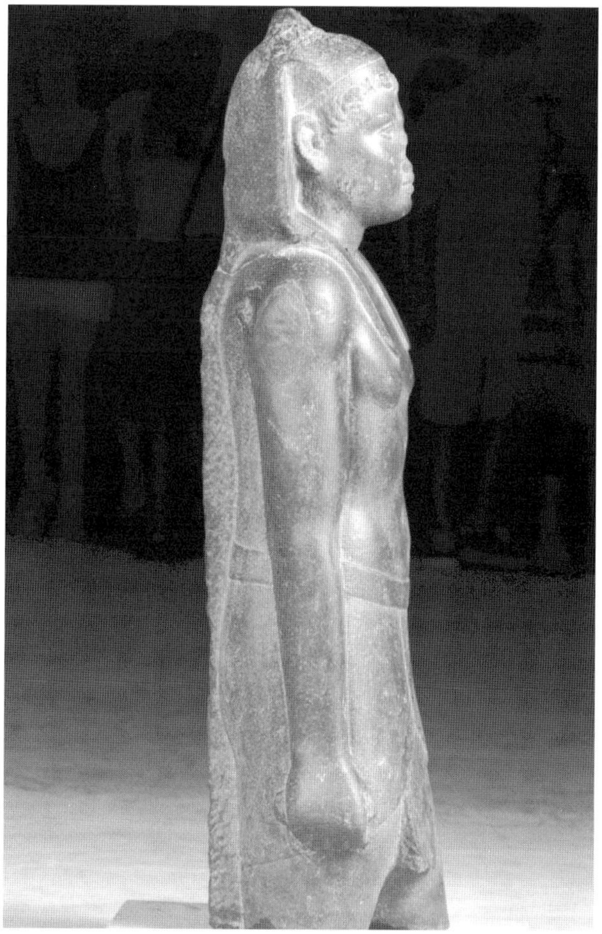

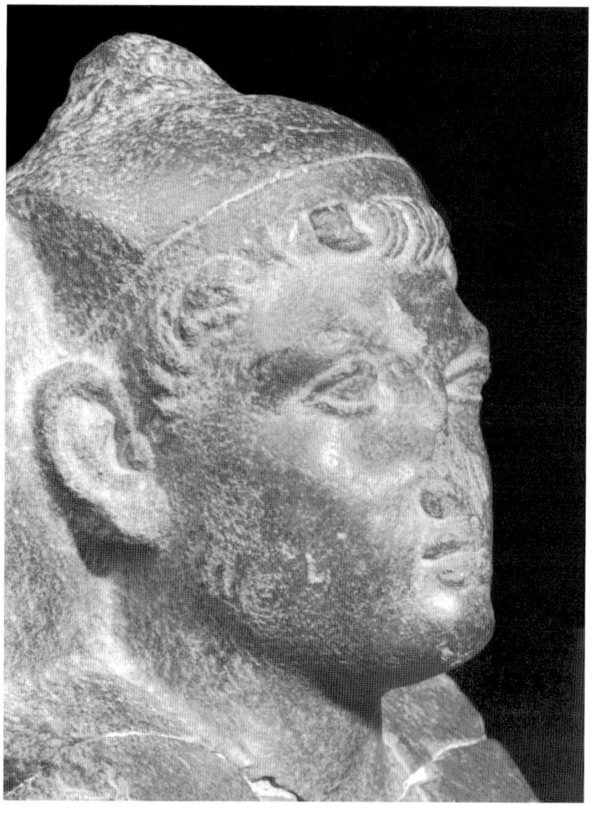

135–137 [D14]. Standing king. Attributed to Ptolemy X, recut from Ptolemy IX. Cairo 13/3/15/3 (photos: Sherif Sonbol, Cairo).

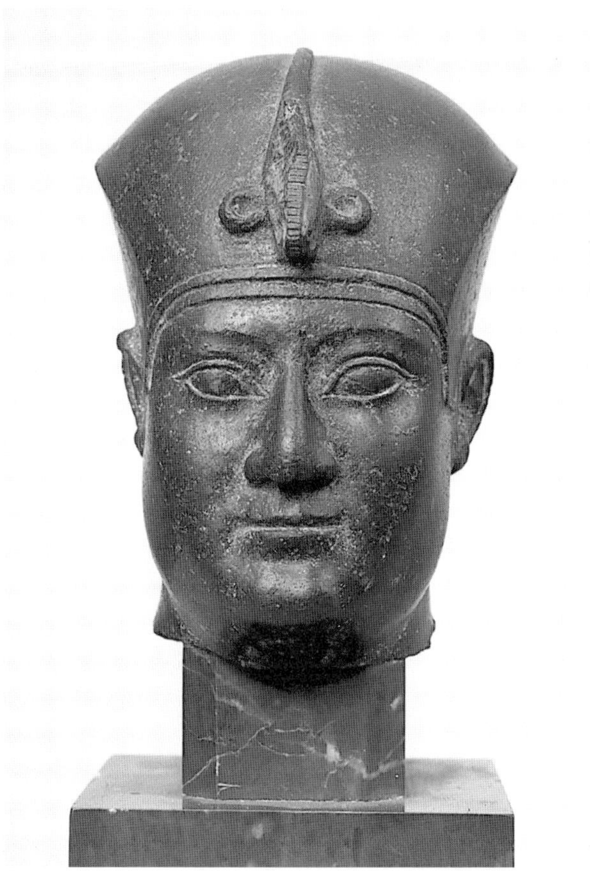

138 [D15]. Head of king. Attributed to Ptolemy IX, second rule, 88–80 B.C. Paris, Musée du Louvre E 8061 (photo: ©Musée du Louvre - M. and P. Chuzeville).

139–140 [D16]. Face of king. Attributed to Ptolemy IX, second rule, 88–80 B.C. Staatlichen Sammlung Ägyptischer Kunst München ÄS 5339 (photo 139: author; photo 140: ©Staatlichen Sammlung Ägyptischer Kunst).

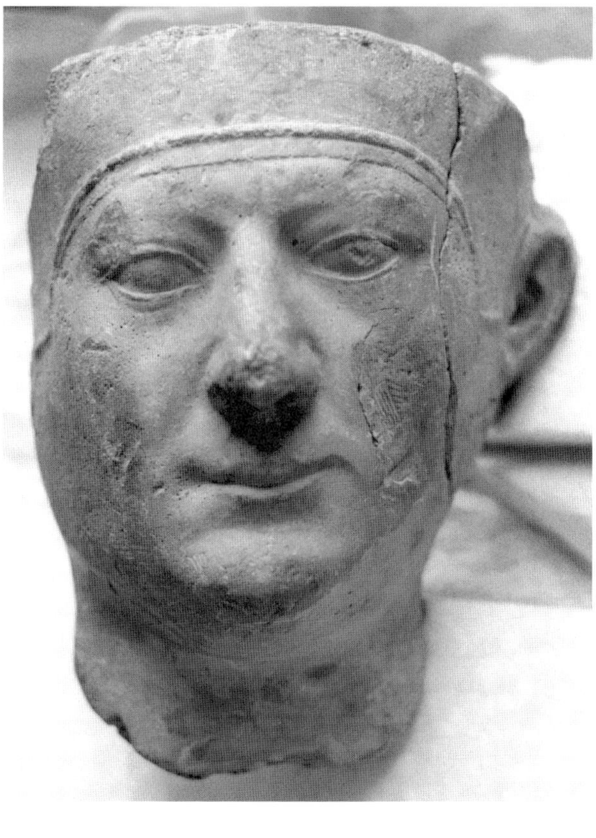

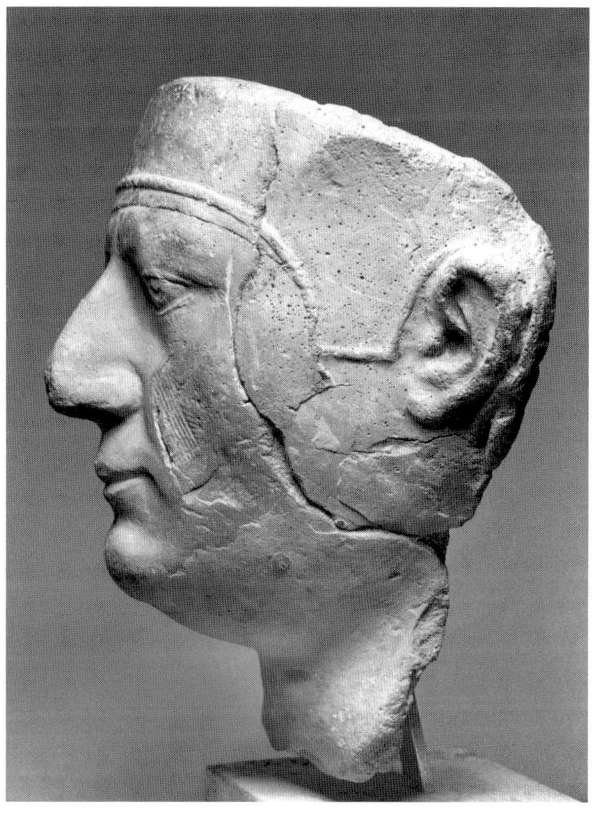

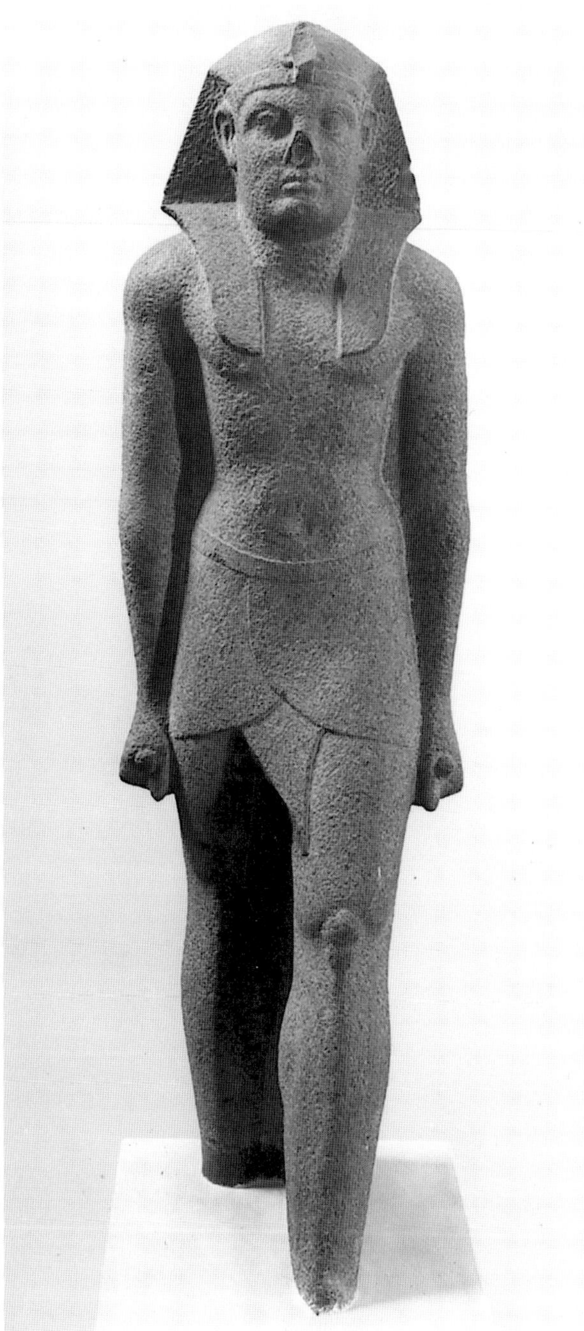
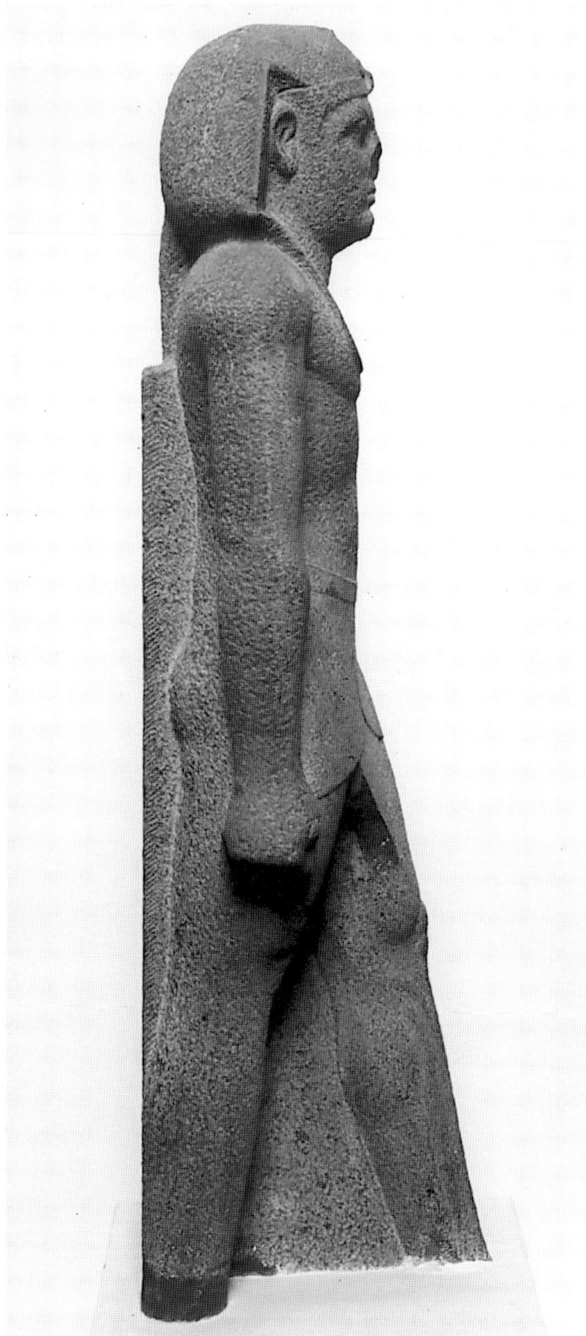

141–142 [D17]. Standing king. Attributed to Ptolemy IX, second rule, 88–80 B.C. London, British Museum EA 1209 (photos: ©The British Museum).

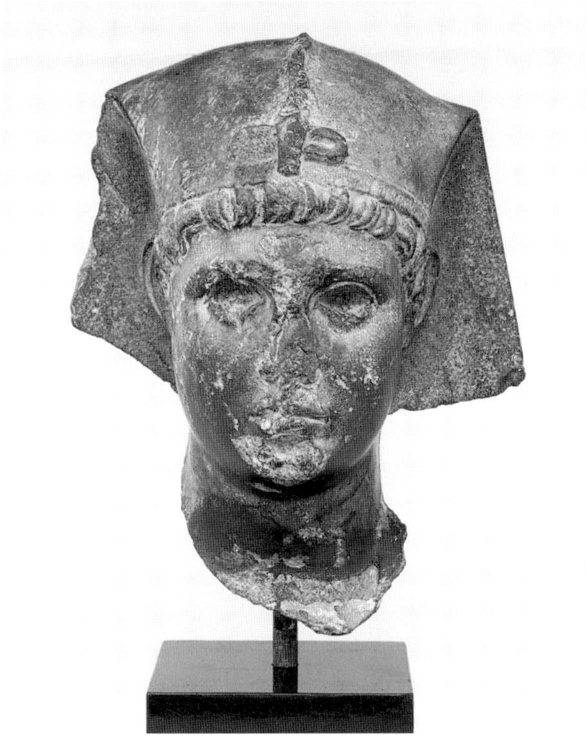

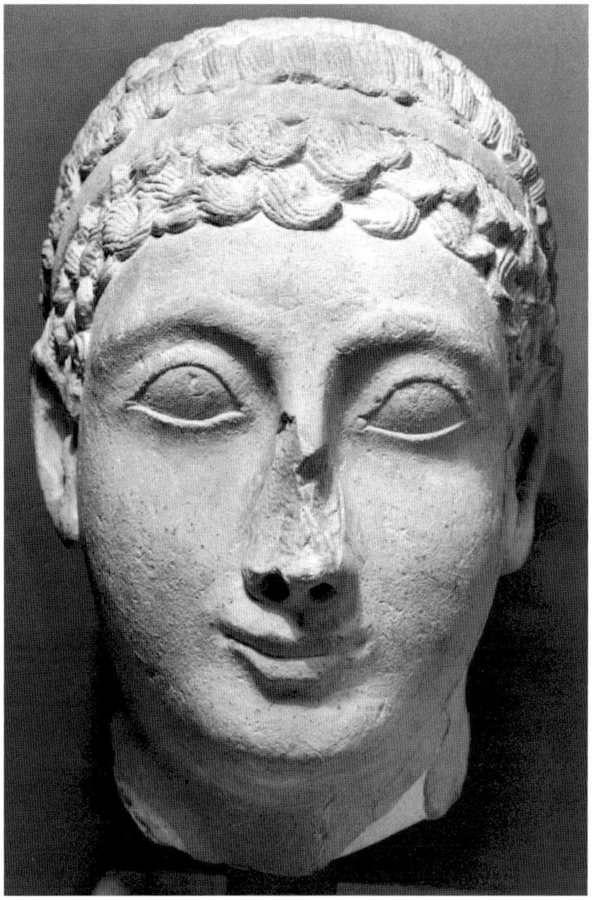

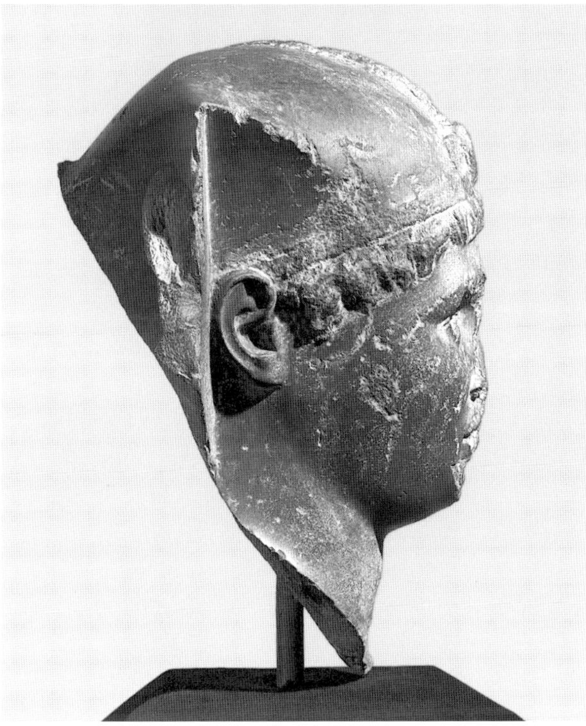

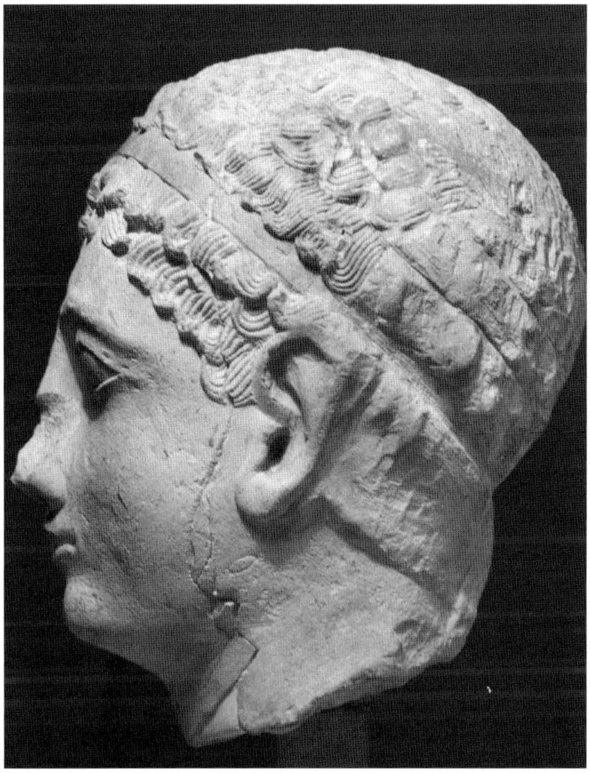

143–144 [D18] (*left*). Head of king. Attributed to Ptolemy X. New Haven, Peabody Museum of Natural History YPM.264259 (photos: courtesy of the Peabody Museum of Natural History, Yale University, New Haven, Conn.).

145–146 [D19] (*right*). Diademed royal male head. Attributed to Ptolemy X. Milan, Museo Archeologico E.0.9.4075 (photos: author).

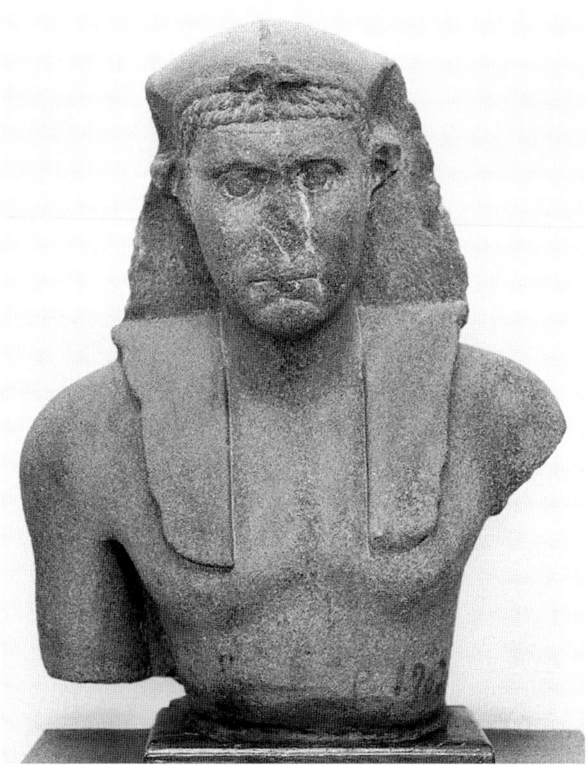

147 [D20]. Fragmentary king. Attributed to Ptolemy X. Alexandria, Graeco-Roman Museum P. 12072 (photo: author).

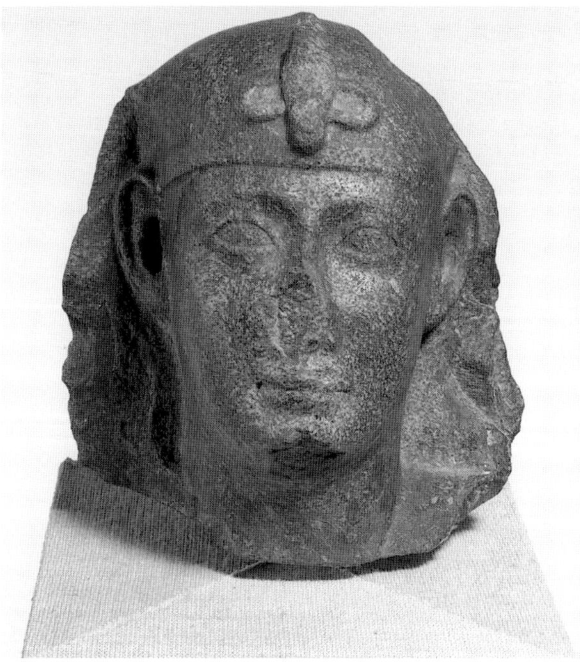

149 [D23]. Head of king. Late second or early first century B.C. Bloomington, Indiana University Art Museum 59.44, gift of Frederick Stafford (©Indiana University Art Museum: photograph by: Michael Cavanagh, Kevin Montague).

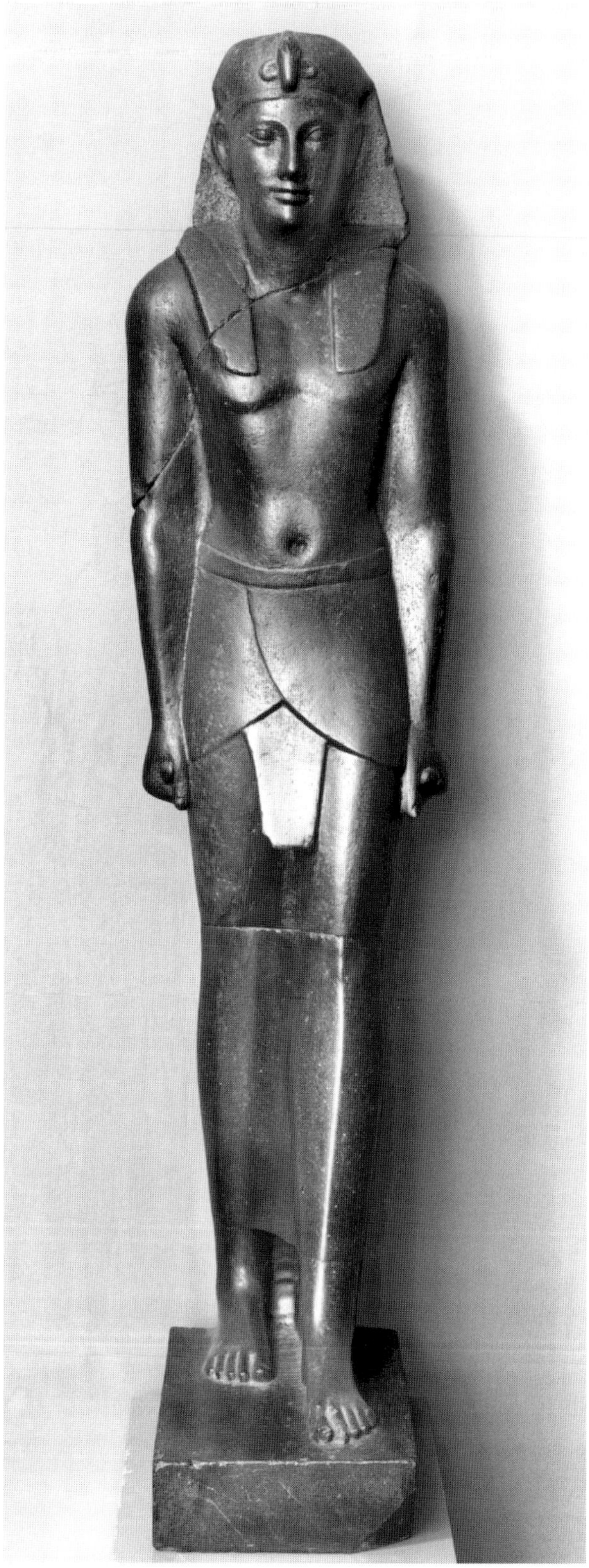

148 [D22]. Standing king. Late second or early first century B.C. Berlin, Ägyptisches Museum 14764 (photo: ©Ägyptisches Museum und Papyrussammlung, Staatliche Museen zu Berlin—Preussischer Kulturbesitz).

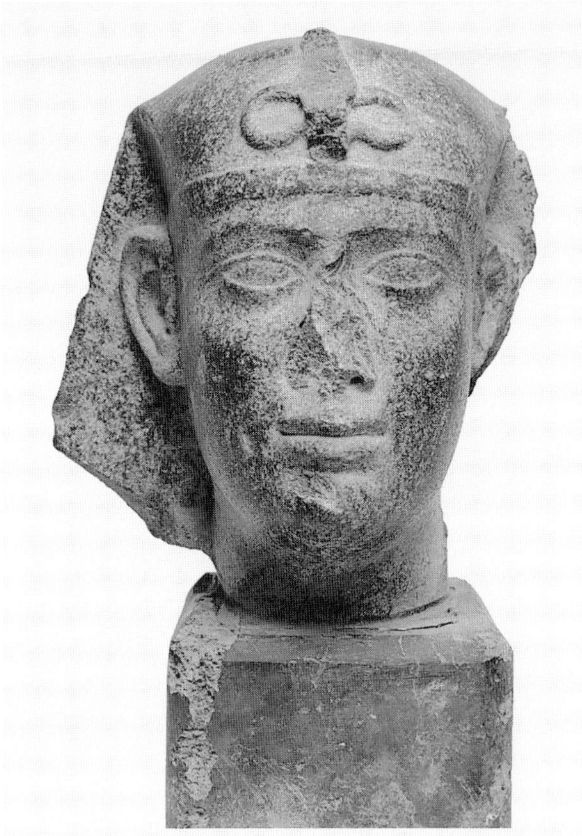

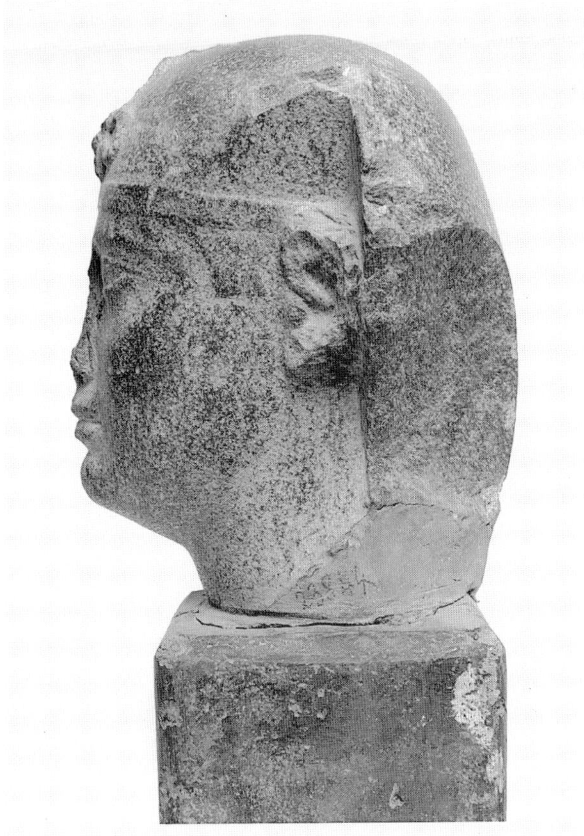

150–151 [D24]. Head of king. Late second or early first century B.C. Alexandria, Graeco-Roman Museum 23844 (photos: Centre d'Études Alexandrines).

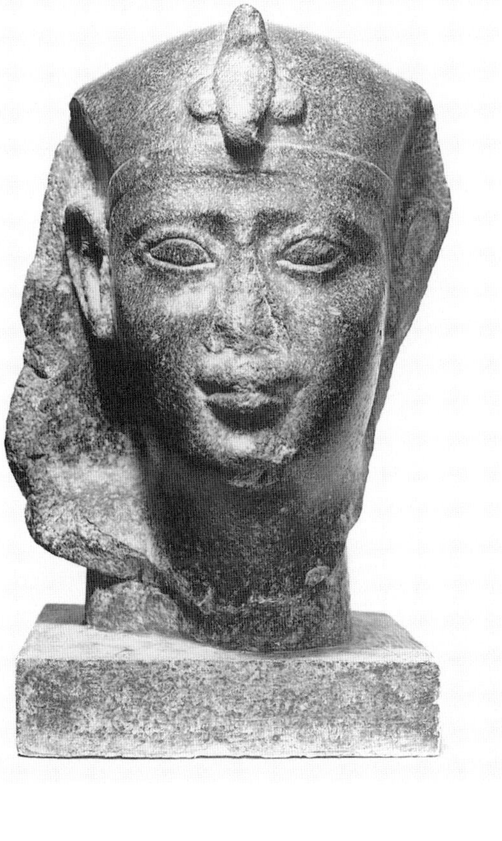

152 [D25]. Head of king. Late second or early first century B.C. Madrid, Museo Arqueológico Nacional 2015 (photo: Archivo Fotográfico, Museo Arqueológico Nacional).

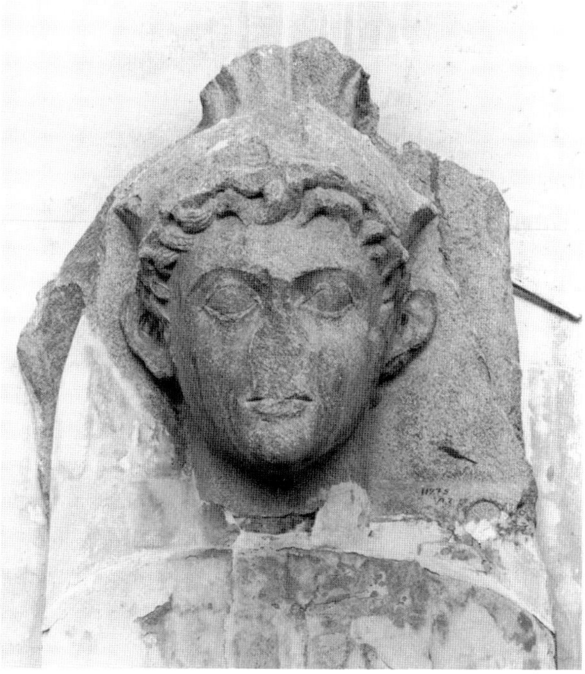

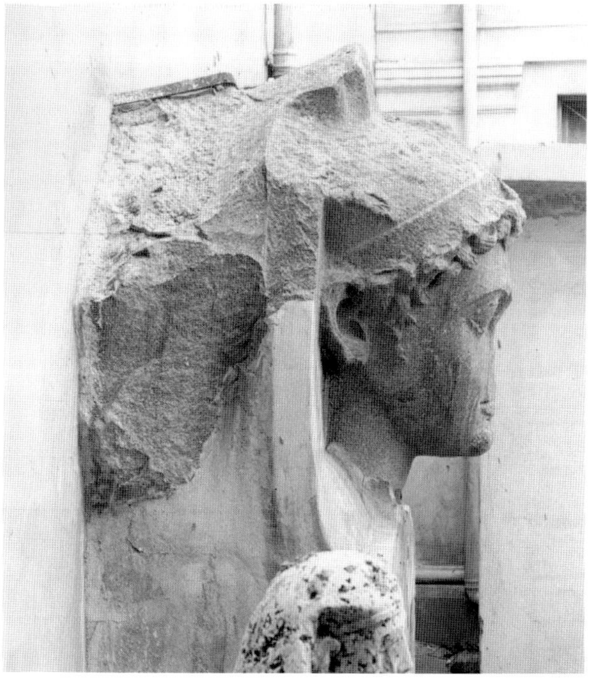

153–154 [E1] (*above*). Head of king from dyad. Attributed to Ptolemy XII. Alexandria, Graeco-Roman Museum 11275 (photos: Deutsches Archäologisches Institut, Cairo).

155–156 [E2] (*below*). Goddess from dyad. Attributed to reign of Ptolemy XII. Musée royal de Mariemont B. 505 (photos: ©Musée royal de Mariemont, Belgique).

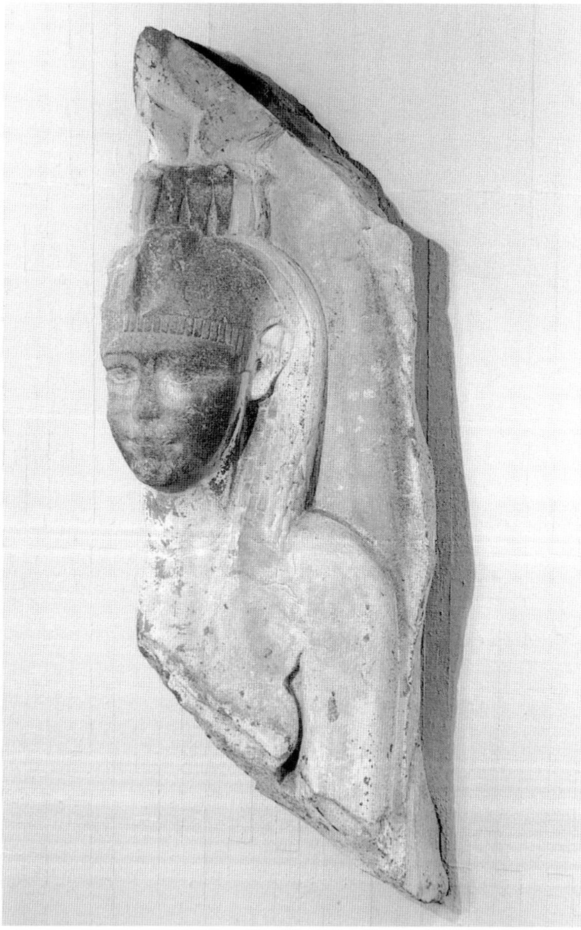

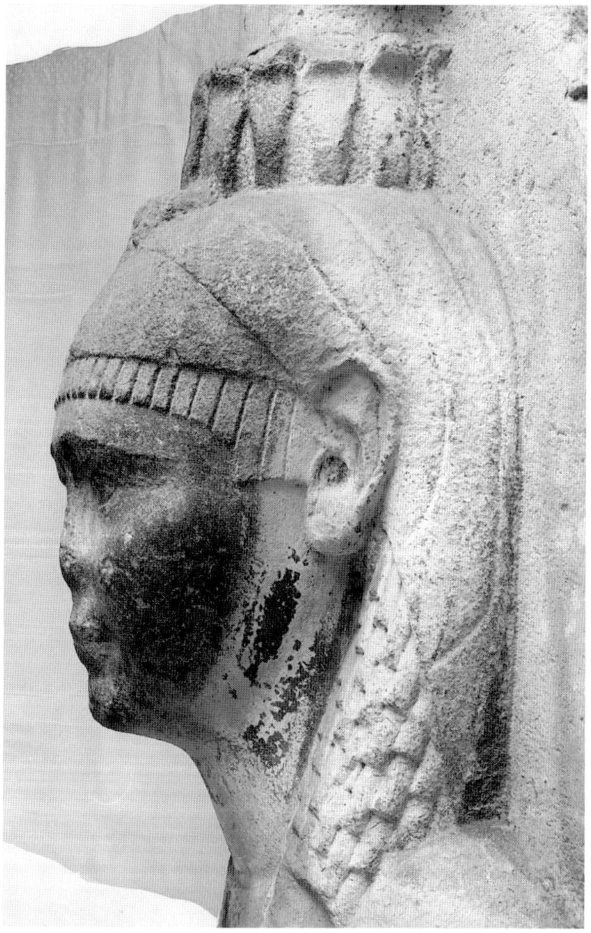

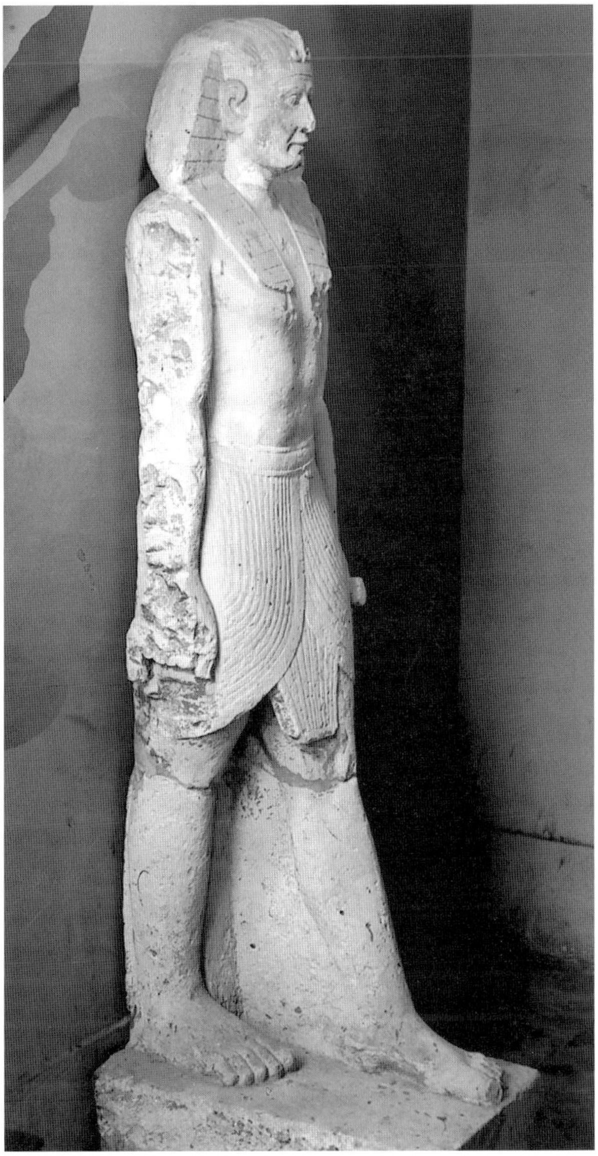

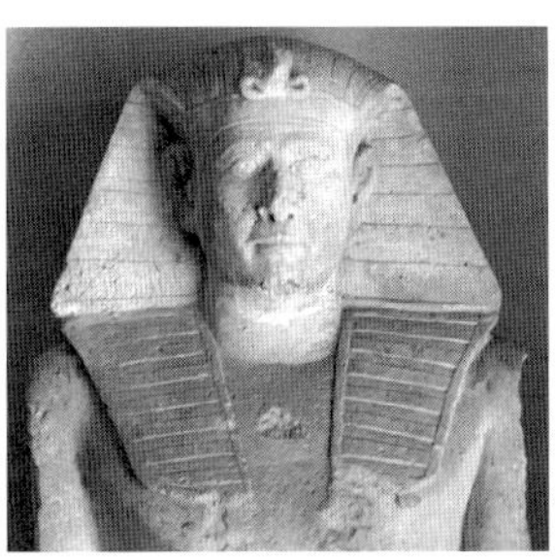

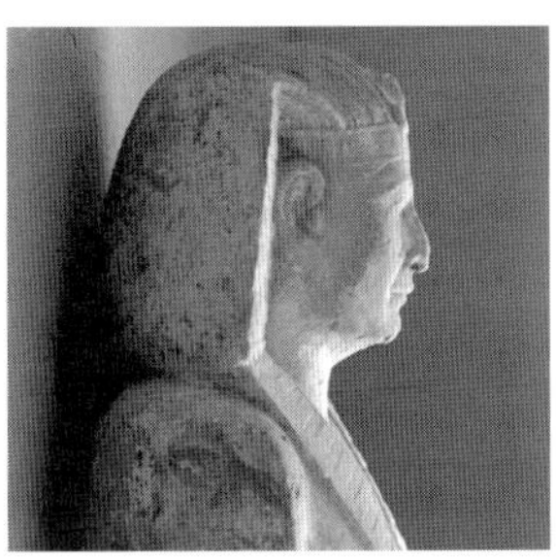

157–159 [E3]. Standing statue found with Ptolemy XII inscription, c. 55 B.C. Alexandria, Graeco-Roman Museum 22979 (photo 157: courtesy of the museum; photos 158–159: Deutsches Archäologisches Institut, Cairo).

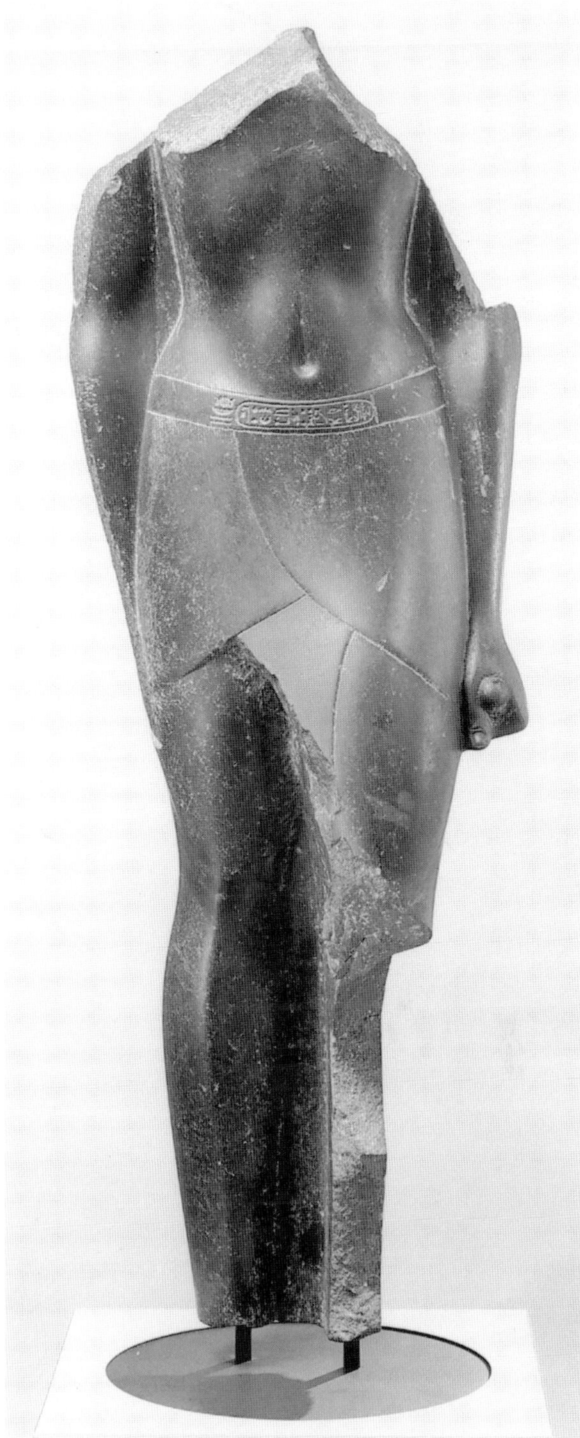

160 [E4]. Fragmentary standing king inscribed for Ptolemies XII–XV. New York, Metropolitan Museum of Art 1981.224.1 (photo: ©The Metropolitan Museum of Art).

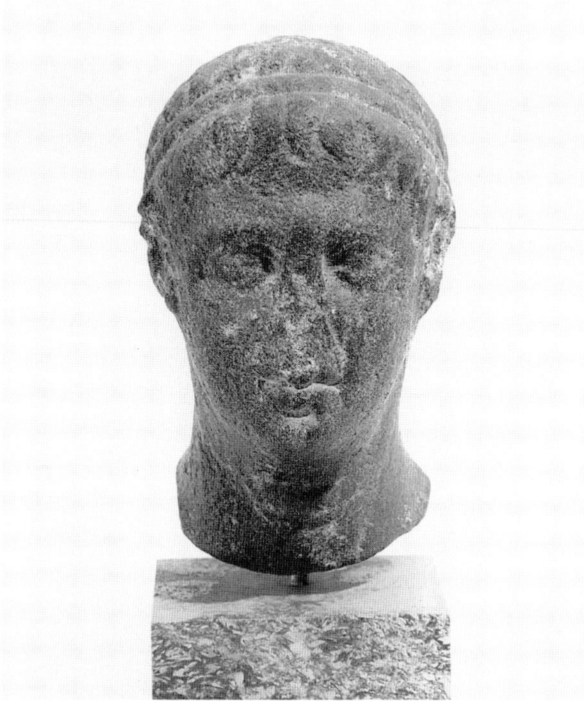

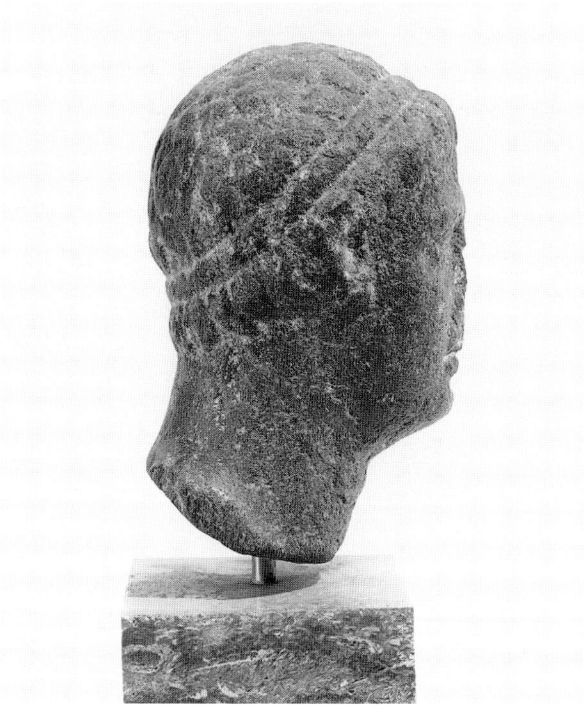

161–162 [E6]. Head of king. Attributed to Ptolemy XII. Turin, Museo Egizio Suppl. 18350 (photos: ©MBAC—Turin Egyptian Museum).

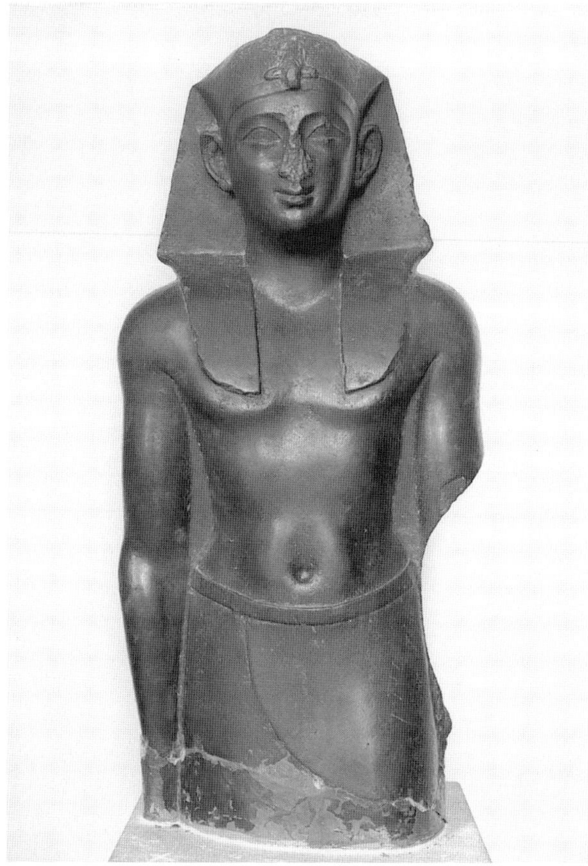

163 [E7]. Standing king. Attributed to Ptolemy XII. Paris, Musée du Louvre A 28 (N 28) (photo: ©Musée du Louvre—M. and P. Chuzeville).

164 [E8]. Head of king. Attributed to Ptolemy XII. Alexandria, Graeco-Roman Museum 425 (photo: Centre d'Études Alexandrines).

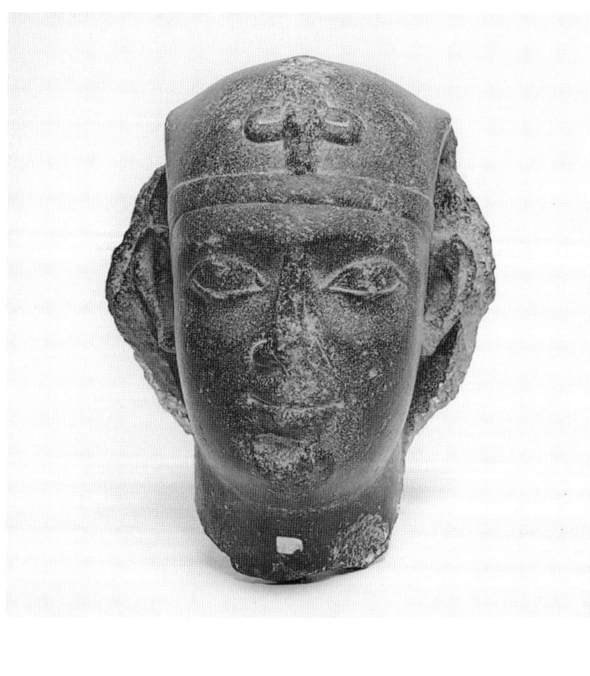

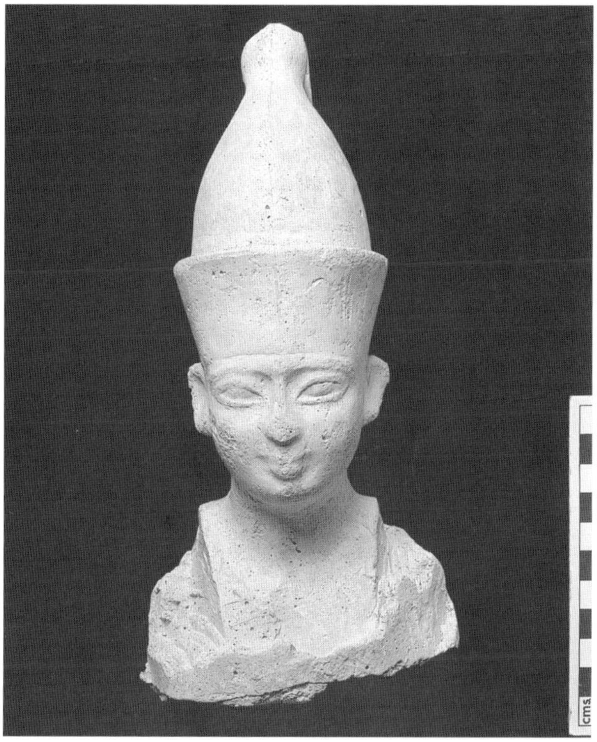

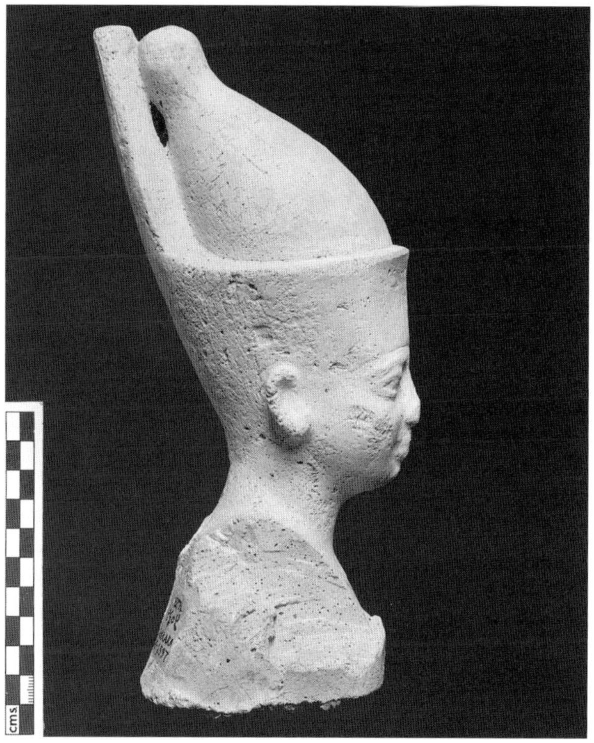

165–166 [E9] (*above*). Bust of king. Attributed to Ptolemy XII. Birmingham Museums and Art Gallery B.67'71 (photos: Birmingham Museums and Art Gallery).

167–168 [E10] (*below*). Head of king. Attributed to Ptolemy XII. Brooklyn Museum of Art 37.1489E, Charles Edwin Wilbour Fund (photos: ©Brooklyn Museum of Art).

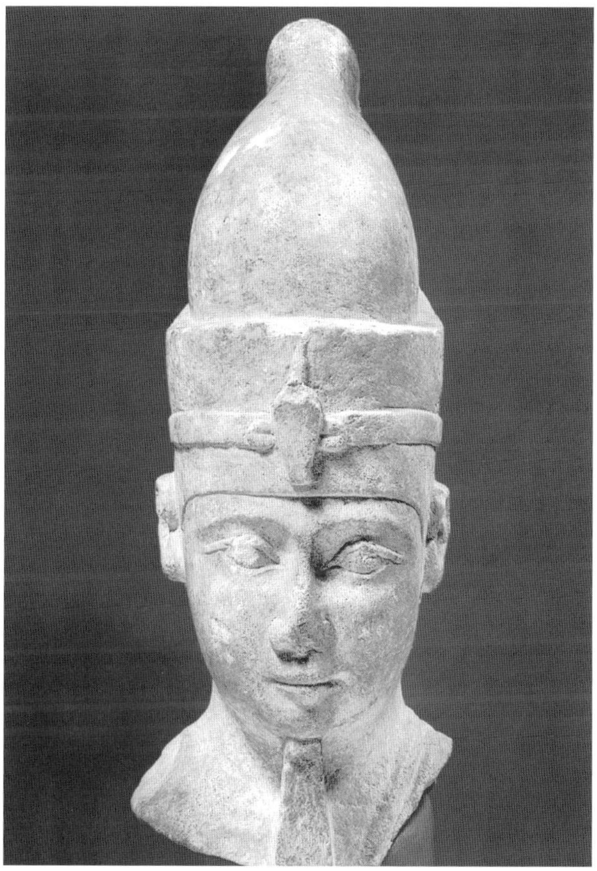

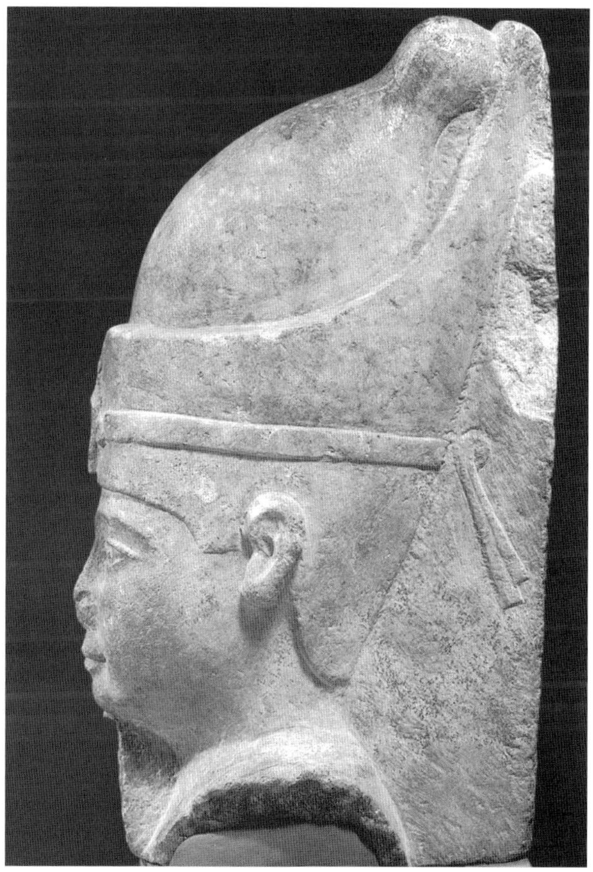

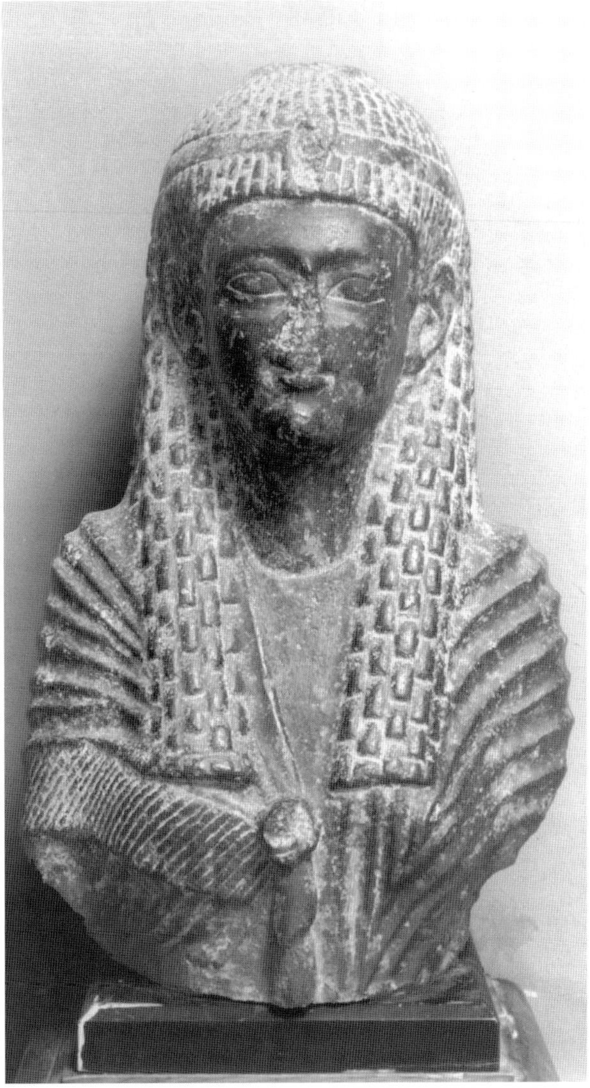

169 [E11]. Fragmentary queen. First century B.C. Alexandria, Graeco-Roman Museum 3222 (photo: courtesy of the museum).

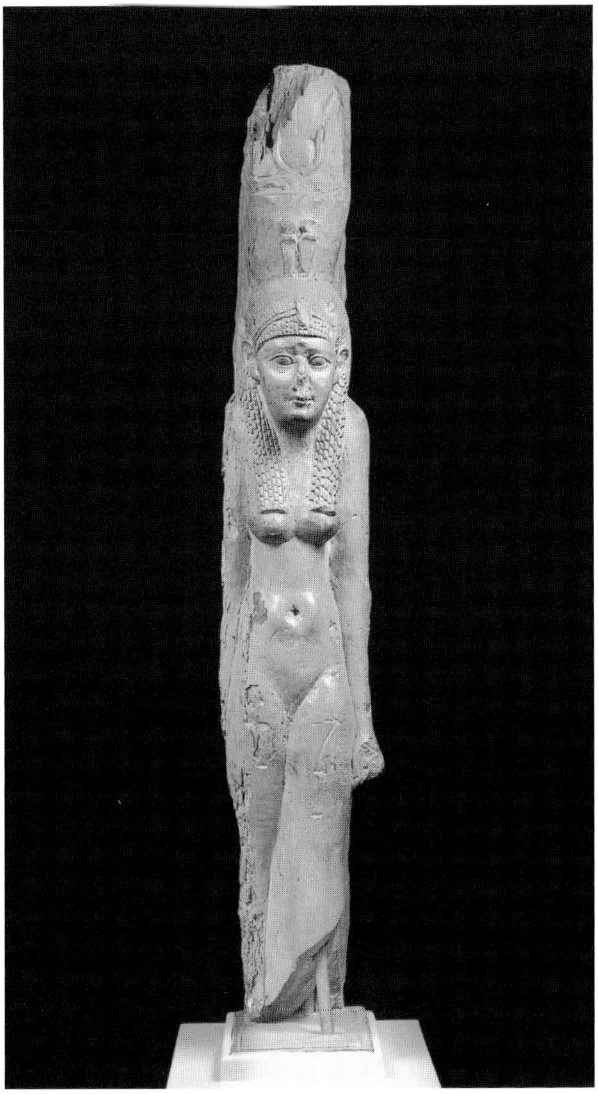

170 [E12]. Standing queen. First century B.C. Leiden, Rijksmuseum van Oudheden F 1938/7.20 (photo: ©Rijksmuseum van Oudheden).

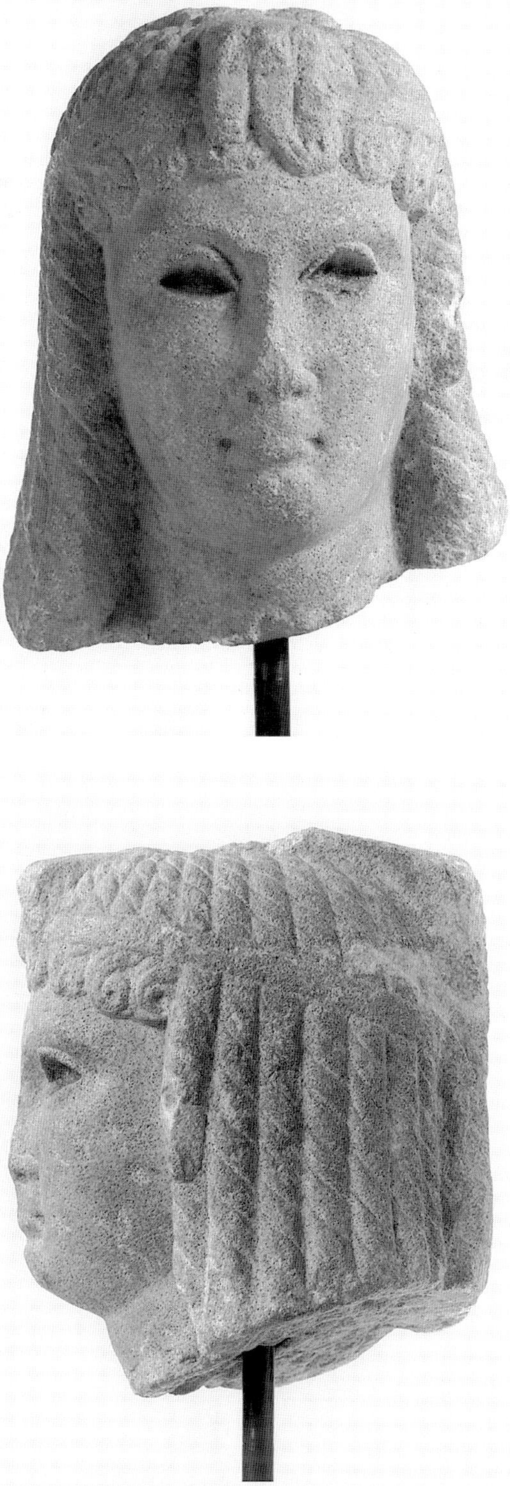

171–172 [E13]. Head of queen. Attributed to Cleopatra VII. Brooklyn Museum of Art 71.12, Charles Edwin Wilbour Fund (photos: ©Brooklyn Museum of Art).

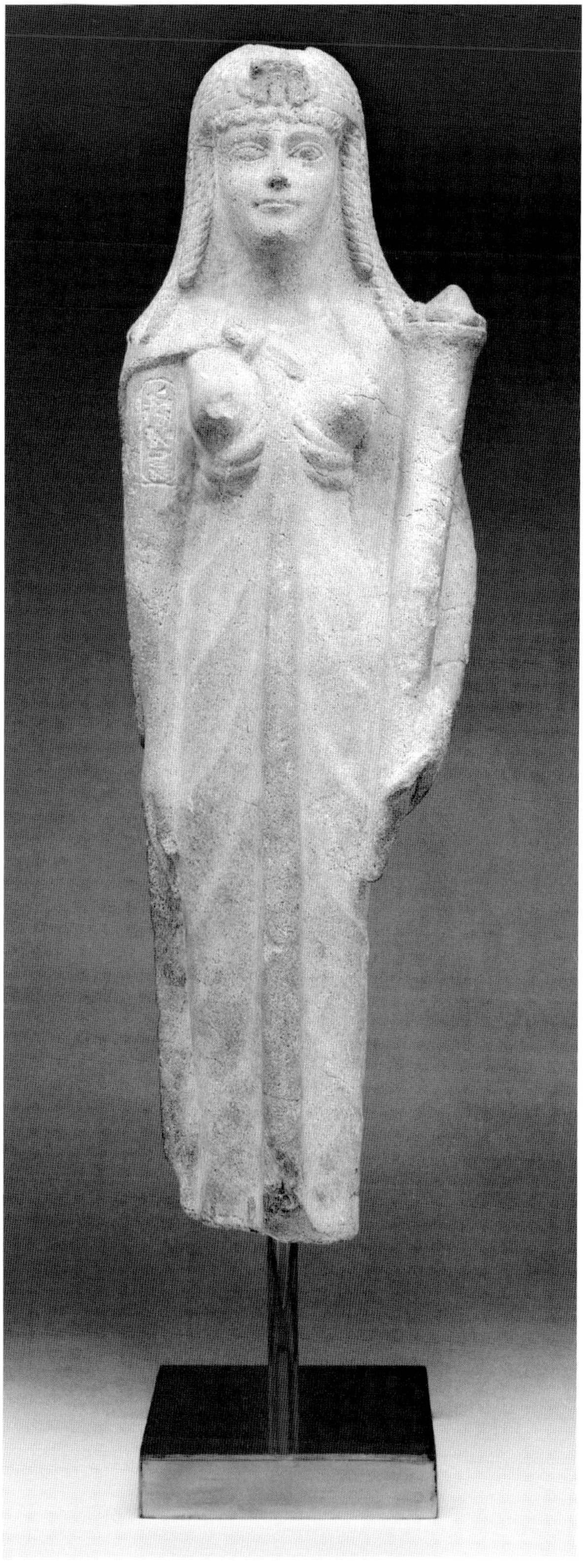

173 [E14]. Standing queen. Attributed to Cleopatra VII. New York, Metropolitan Museum of Art 89.2.660 (photo: ©The Metropolitan Museum of Art).

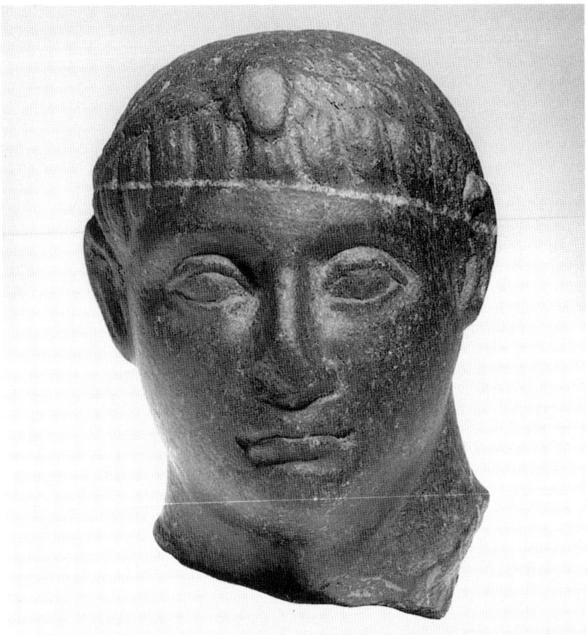

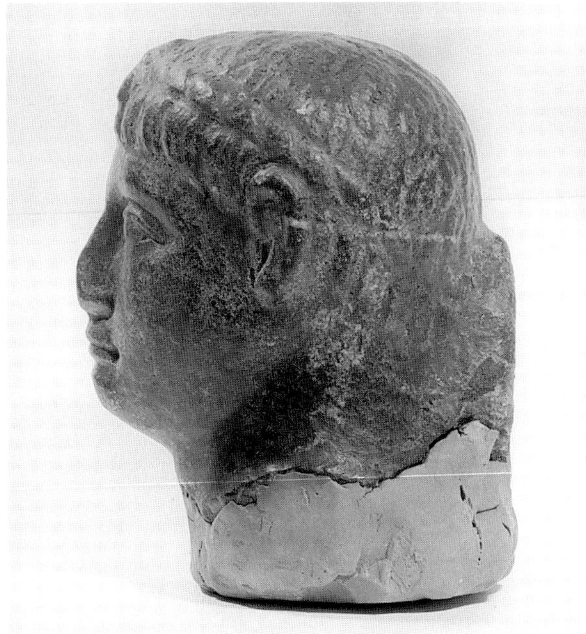

174–175 [E15] (*above*). Head of king. Attributed to Ptolemy XV. Bologna, University Collection, Museo Civico Archeologico KS 1803 (photos: ©Museo Civico Archeologico).

176–177 [E16] (*below*). Standing king. Attributed to Ptolemy XV. Brooklyn Museum of Art 54.117, Charles Edwin Wilbour Fund (photos: ©Brooklyn Museum of Art).

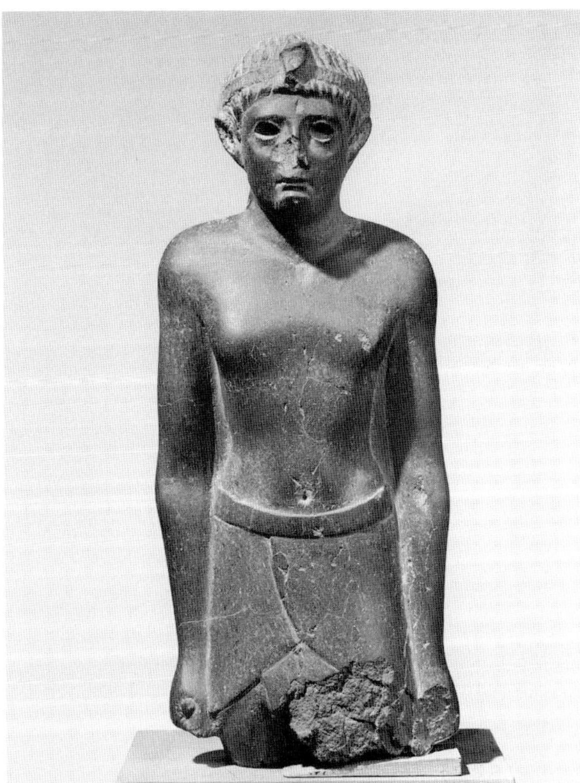

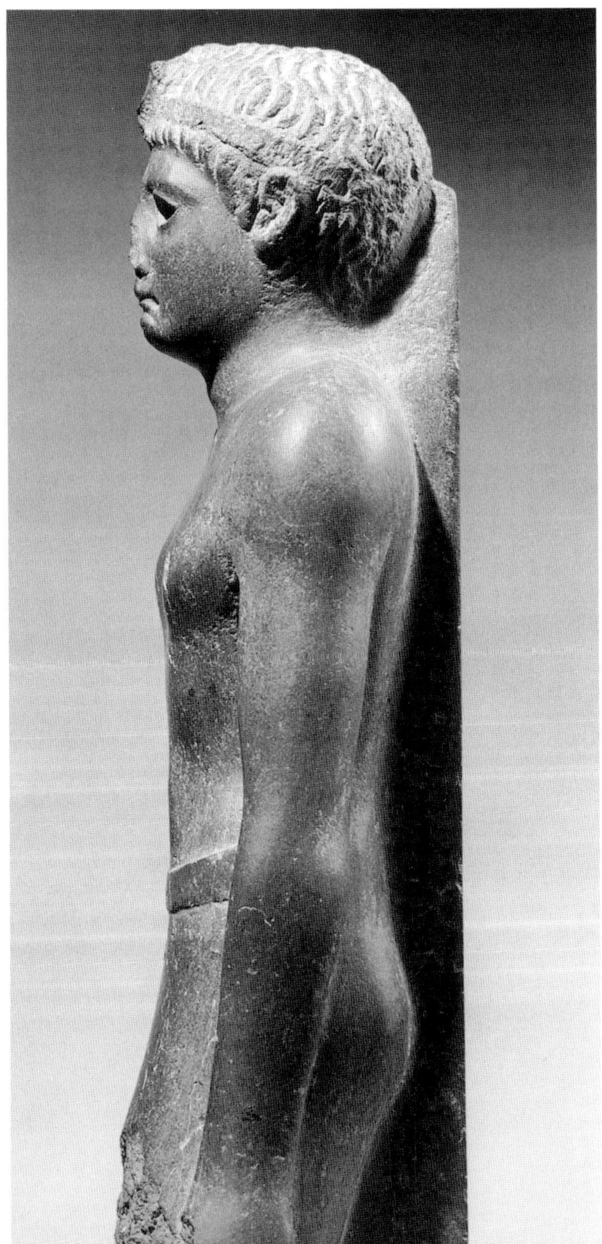

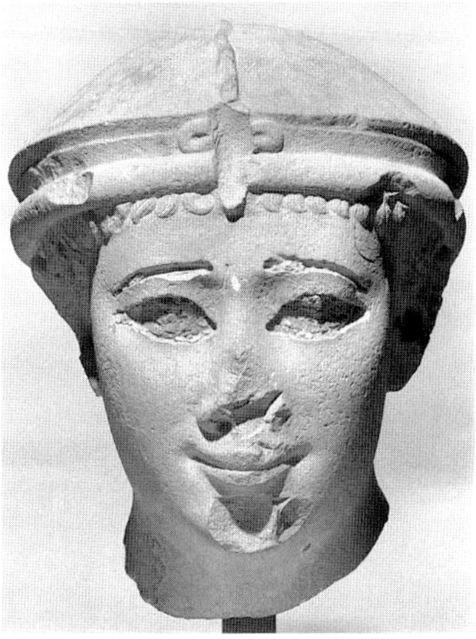

178 [E18]. Head of king. Attributed to Ptolemy XV. New York, Harmon Fine Arts/Leonard Stern (photo: courtesy of the owner).

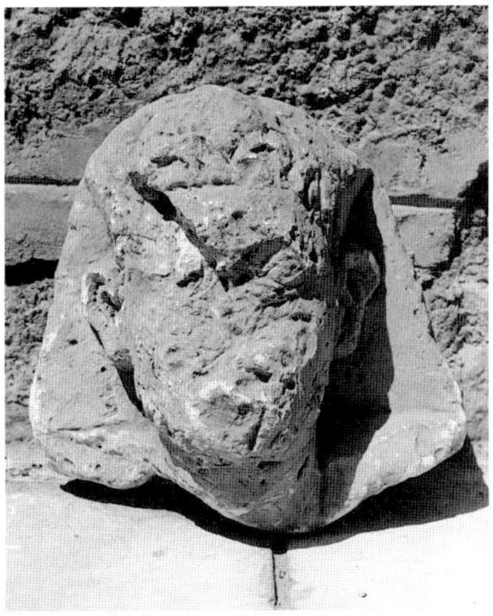

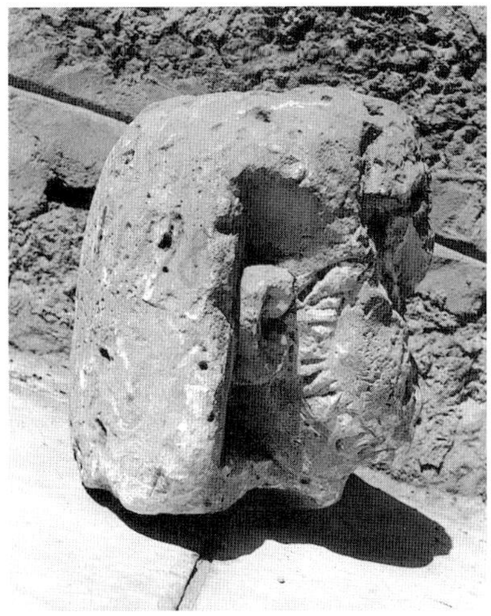

181–182 [E20]. Head of king. Attributed to Ptolemy XV. Alexandria, Graeco-Roman Museum P. 1798 (photos: Centre d'Études Alexandrines).

183 [E21]. Head of king. First century B.C. New York, private collection (photo: author).

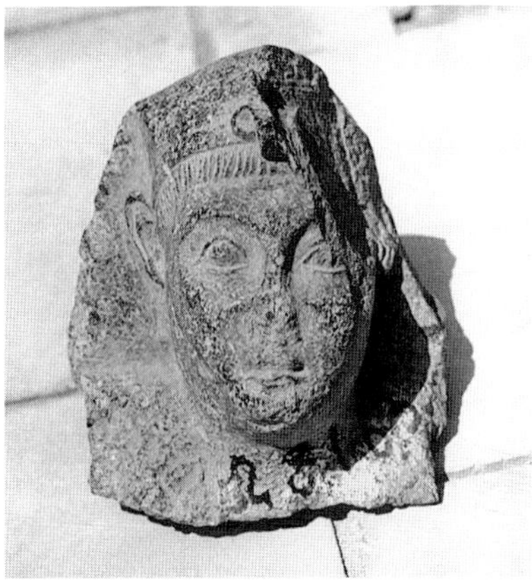

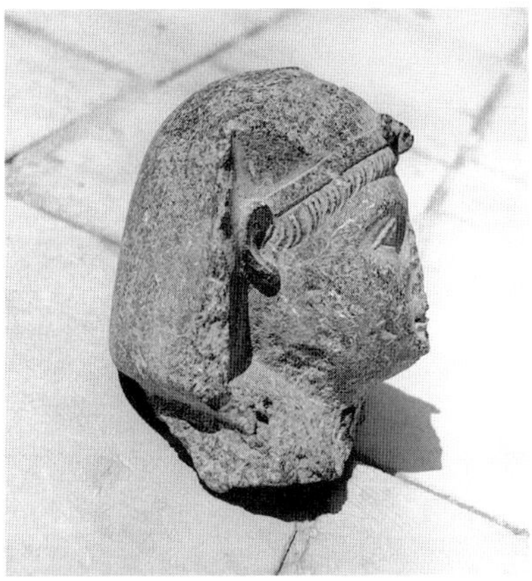

179–180 [E19]. Head of king. Attributed to Ptolemy XV. Alexandria, Graeco-Roman Museum 28163 (photos: Centre d'Études Alexandrines).

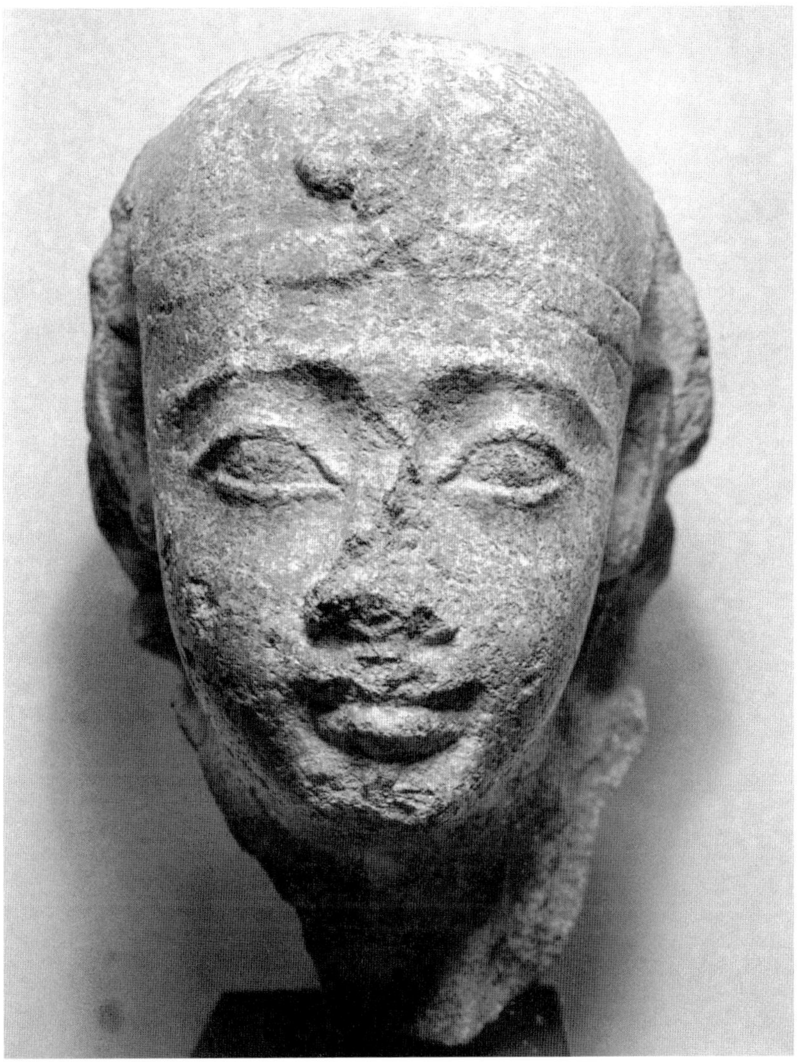

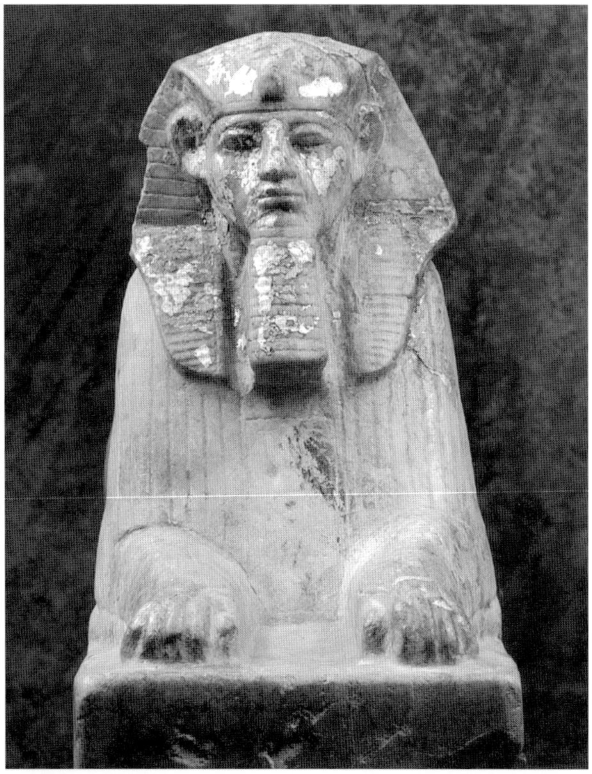

184 [E22] (*left*). Dendera treasure horde. Gilded stone sphinx. Middle Kingdom. Cairo JE 46393 (photo: Sherif Sonbol, Cairo).

185 [E22] (*below left*). Dendera treasure horde. Silver sphinx. First century B.C. Cairo JE 46392 (photo: Sherif Sonbol, Cairo).

186 [E22] (*below right*). Dendera treasure horde. Seated goddess. First century B.C. Cairo JE 46382 (photo: Sherif Sonbol, Cairo).

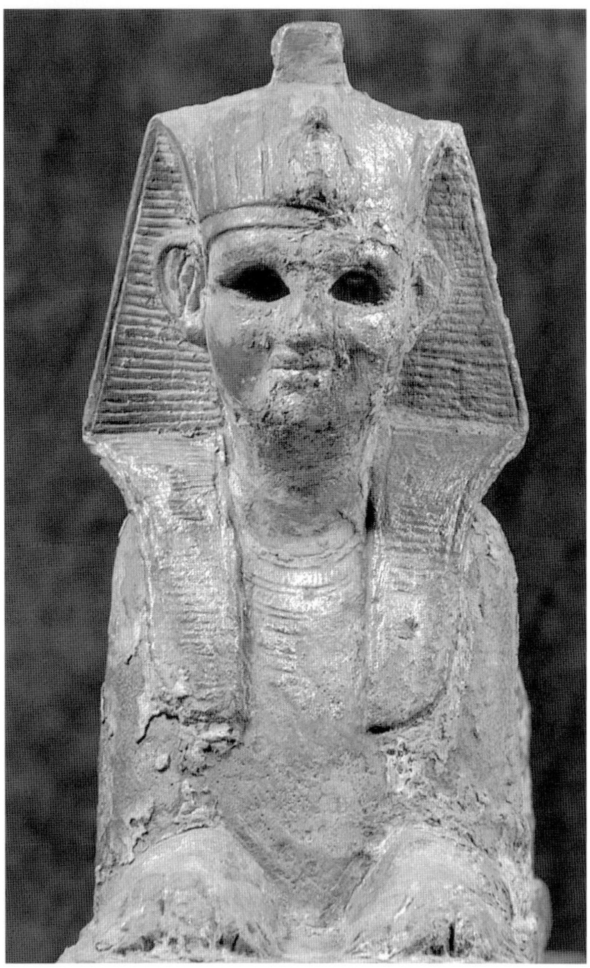

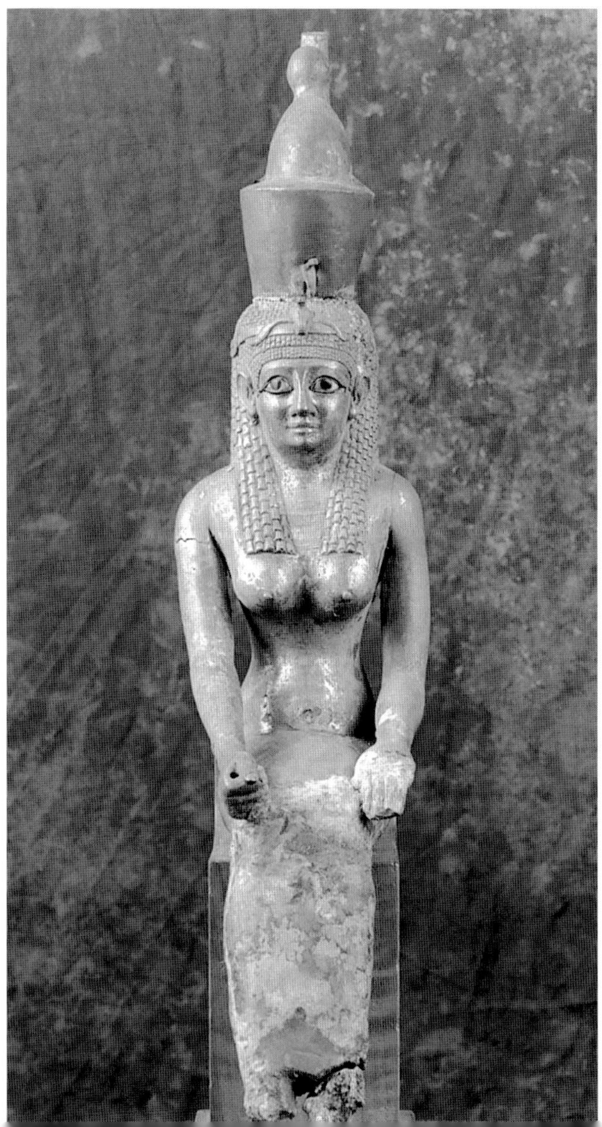

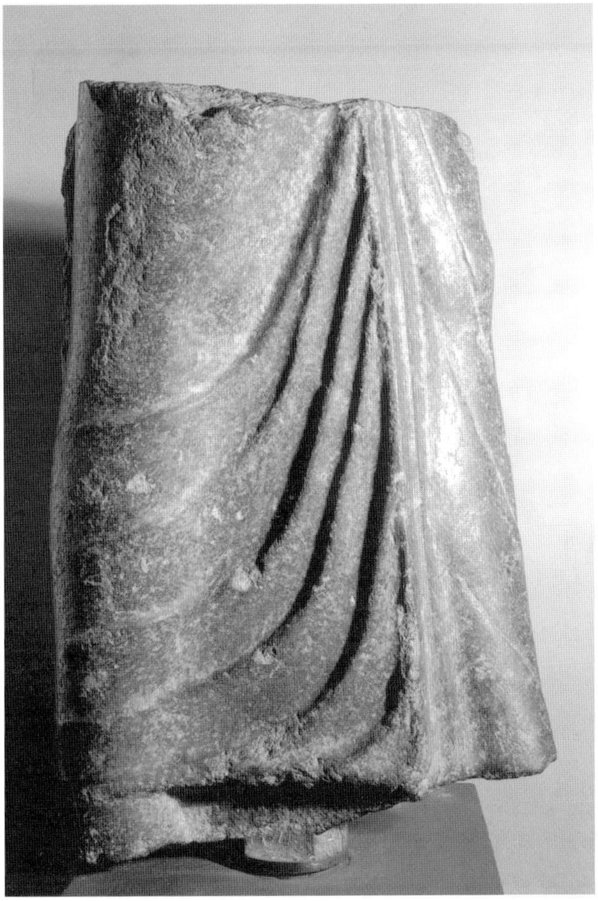

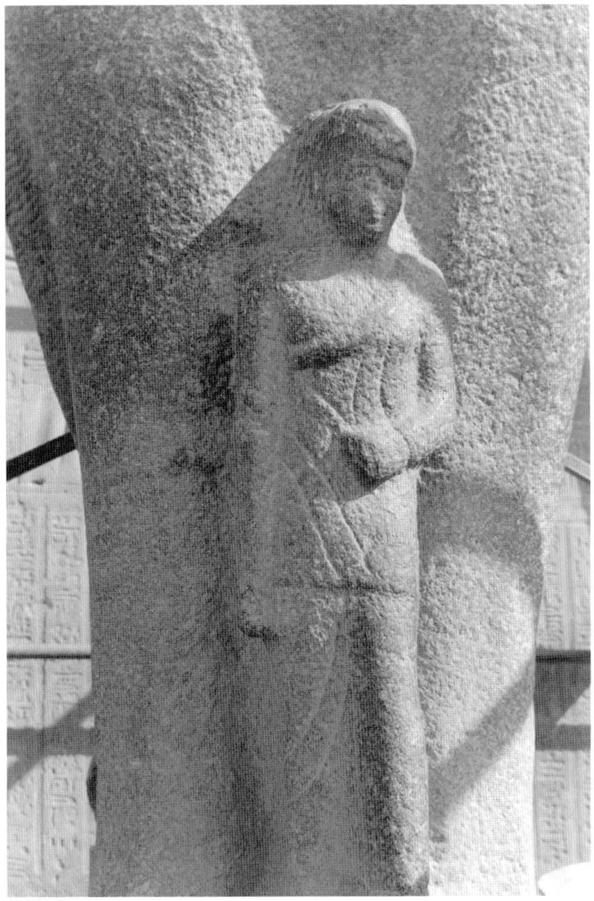

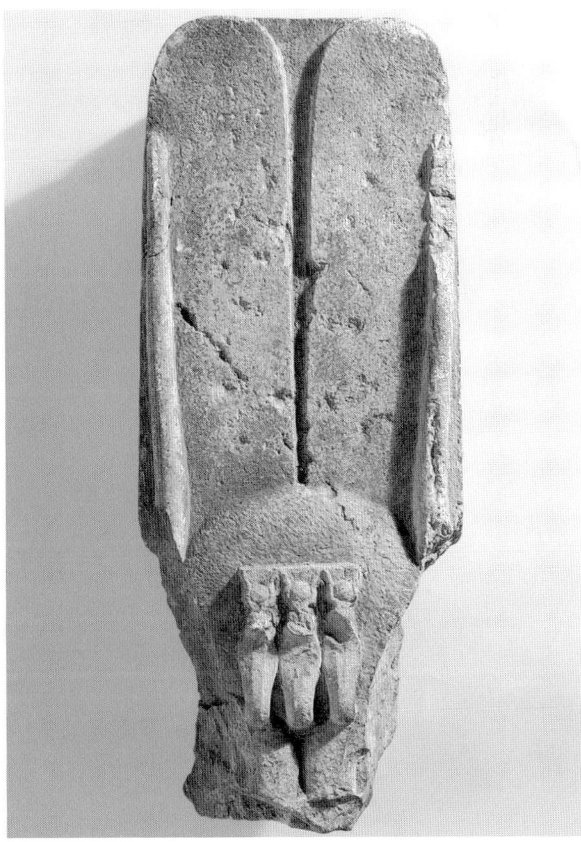

187 [F1] (*above left*). Fragmentary standing king. Inscribed for Ptolemy XII? Berlin, Ägyptisches Museum 8810 (photo: ©Ägyptisches Museum und Papyrussammlung, Staatliche Museen zu Berlin—Preussischer Kulturbesitz).

188 [F2] (*above right*). Falcon statue (detail of standing male underneath). First century B.C.? Edfu, in front of pylon of Horus temple (photo: author).

189 [F3] (*right*). Queen's headdress. Ptolemaic Period. London, Petrie Museum of Egyptian Archaeology, University College London 14521 (photo: ©Petrie Museum of Egyptian Archaeology).

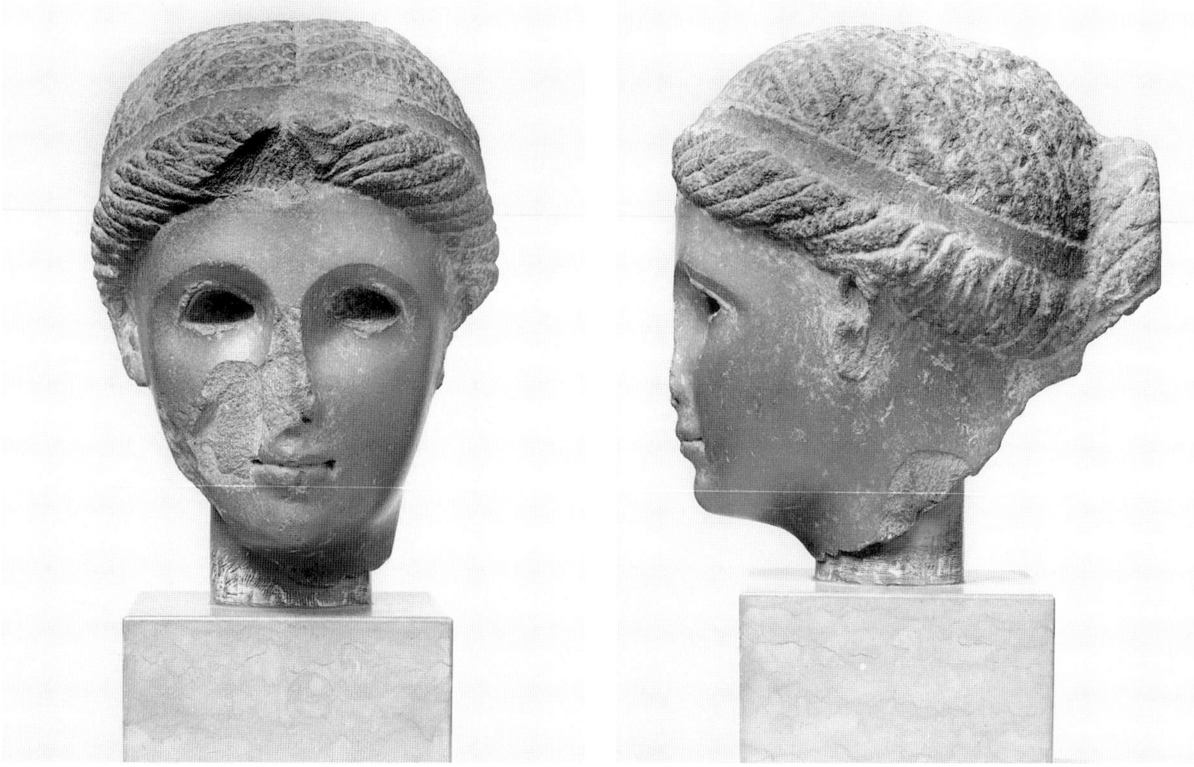

190–191 [F4] (*above*). Head of queen. Second or first century B.C. Copenhagen, Ny Carlsberg Glyptotek IN 586 (photos: ©Ny Carlsberg Glyptotek).

192–193 [F5] (*below*). Fragmentary queen. Identity uncertain, perhaps Cleopatra VII. Turin, Museo Egizio 1385 (photos: ©MBAC—Turin Egyptian Museum).

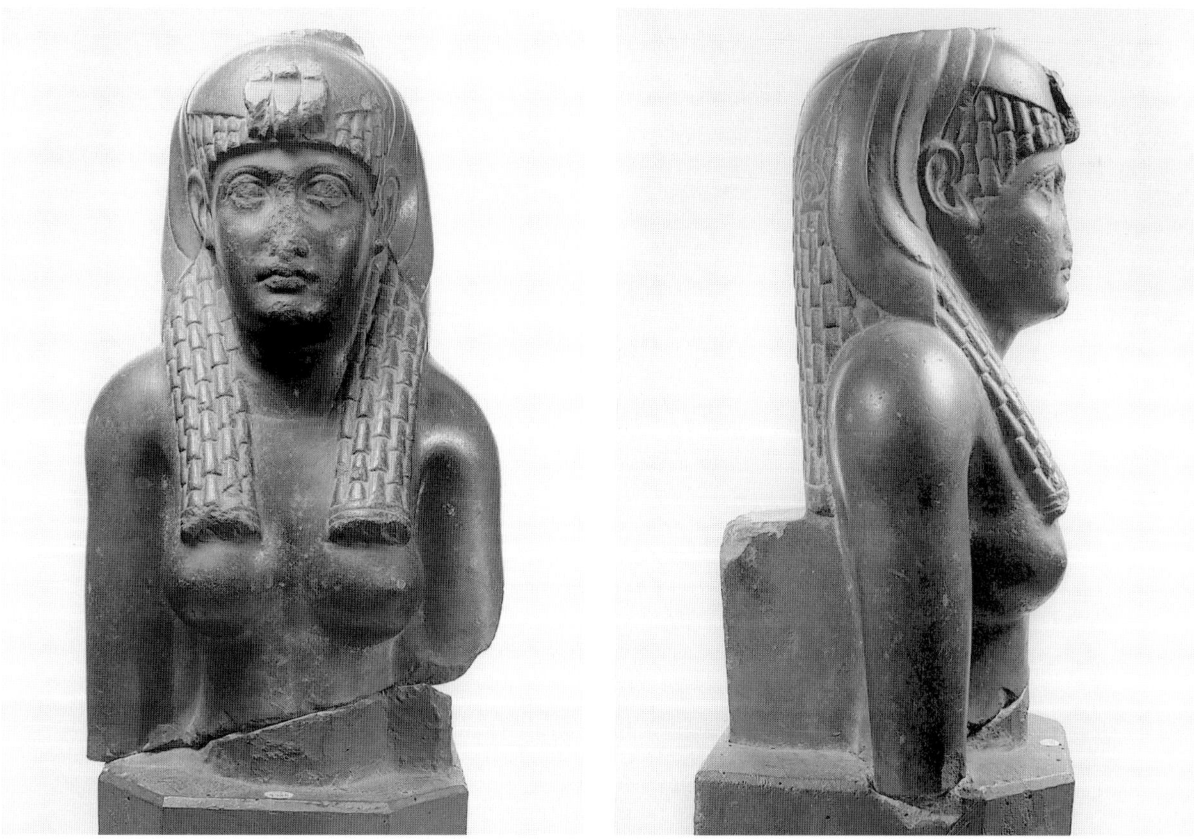

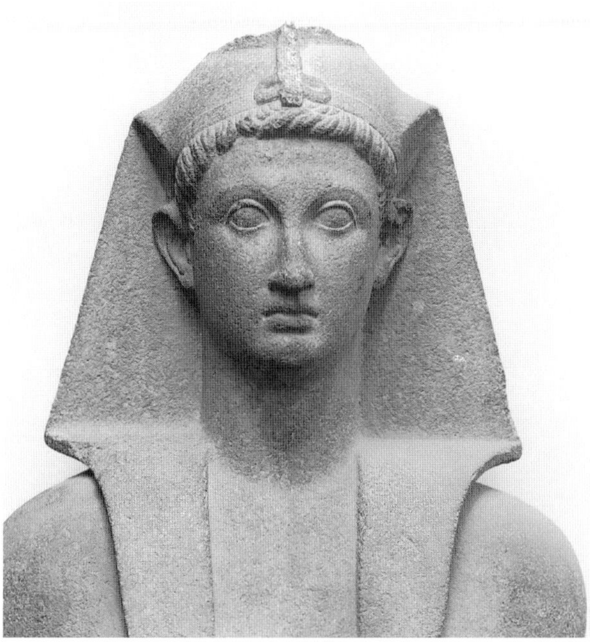

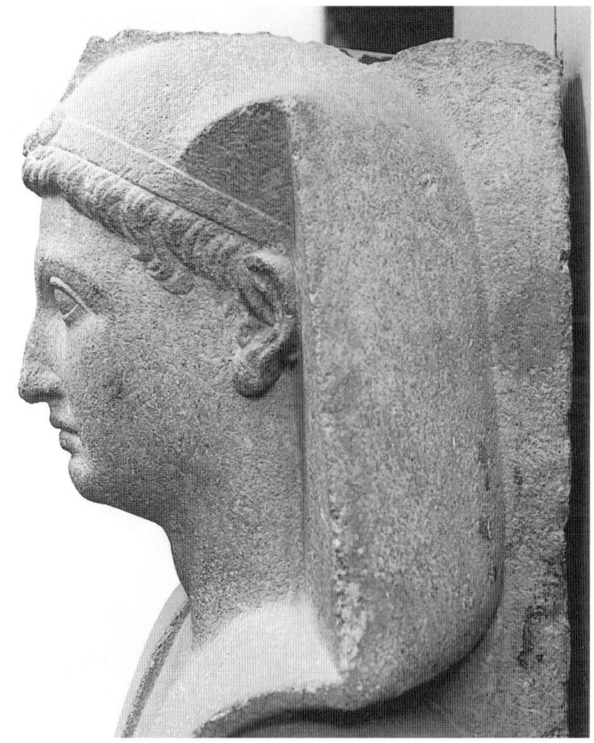

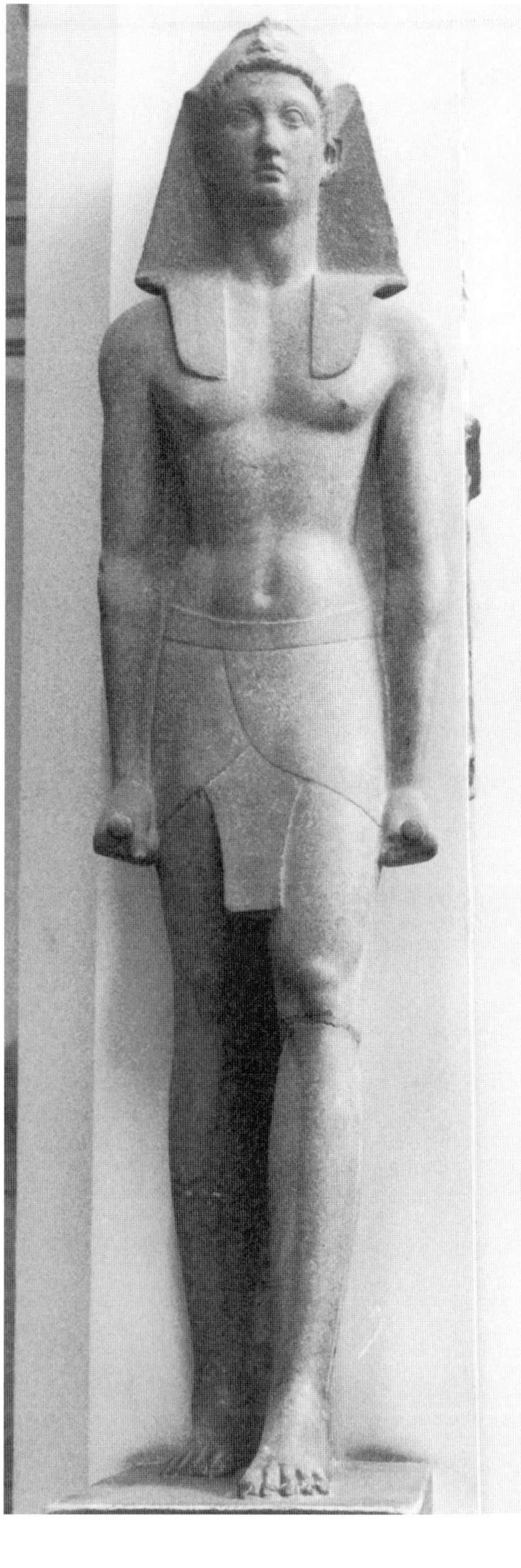

194–196 [G2]. Standing emperor. Attributed to Augustus. Cairo CG 701 (photos 194–195: Deutsches Archäologisches Institut, Cairo; photo 196: author).

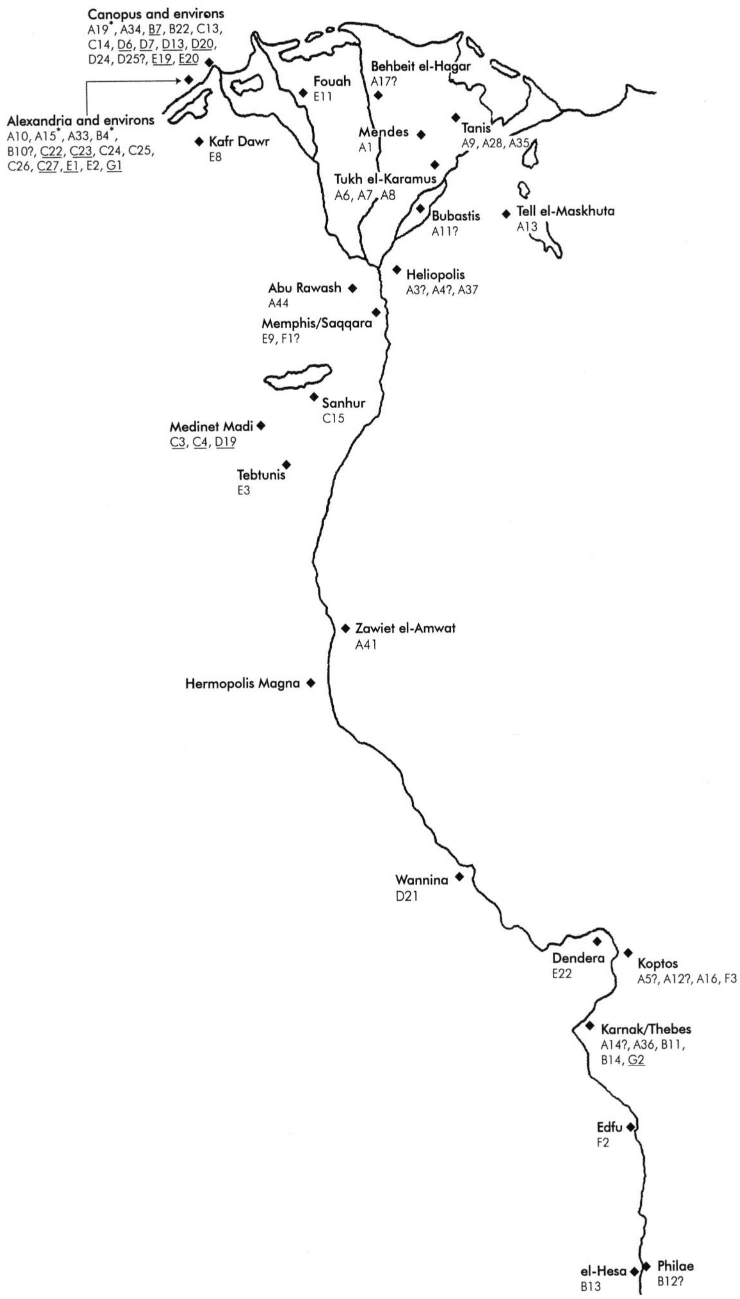

197. Geographic distribution of Egyptian-style, royal Ptolemaic sculptures (and Augustus) in Egypt. Underlined examples have Greek hair. Provenances that are not entirely certain have a question mark (?). An asterisk (*) means that the Greek or Egyptian style of the statue supported by this base is uncertain.

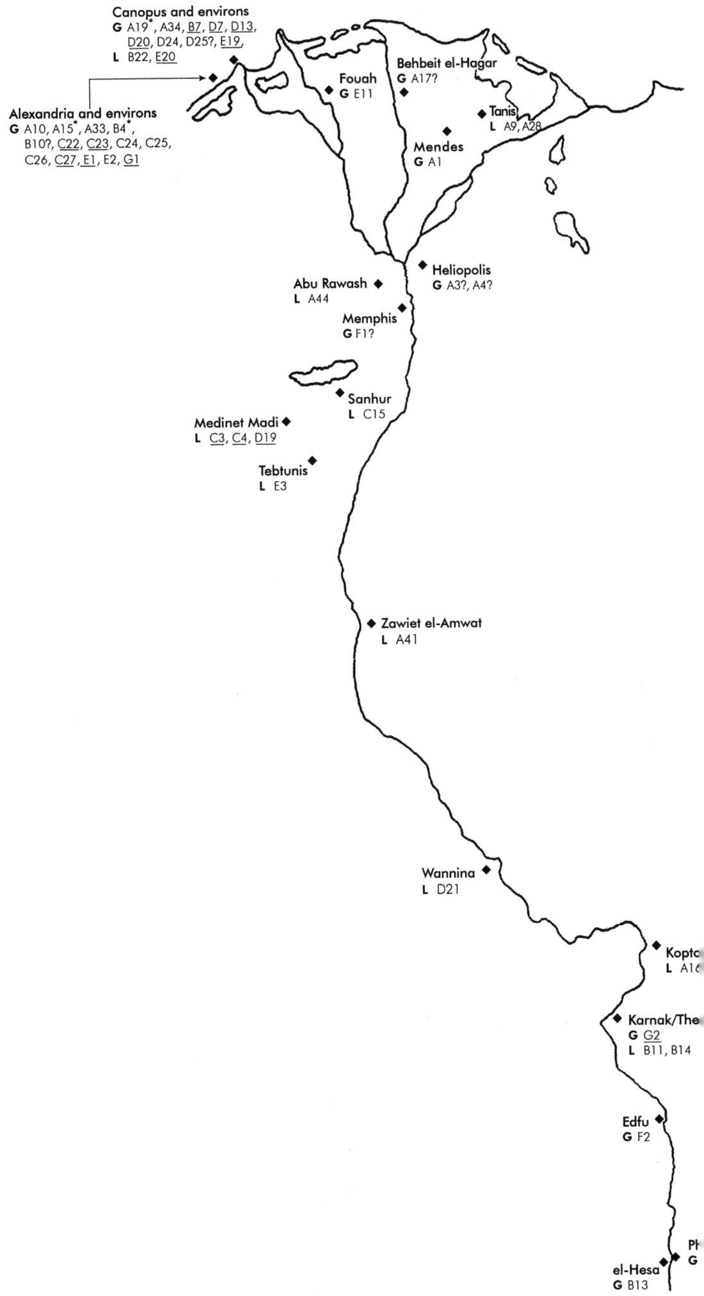

198. Granite (G) and limestone (L) examples of Egyptian-style, royal Ptolemaic sculptures (and Augustus) in Egypt. Underlined examples have Greek hair. Provenances that are not entirely certain have a question mark (?). An asterisk (*) means that the Greek or Egyptian style of the statue supported by this base is uncertain.

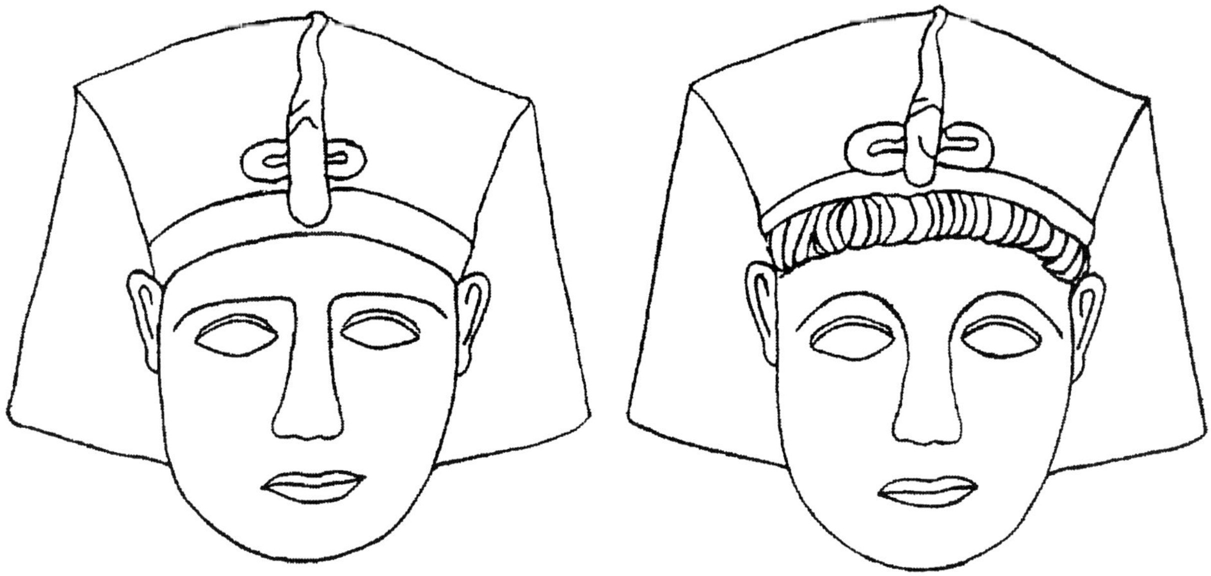

199. Eyebrows in a single arc (left) compared with eyebrows in two semicircles (right) (drawing: ©H. B. Roginski).

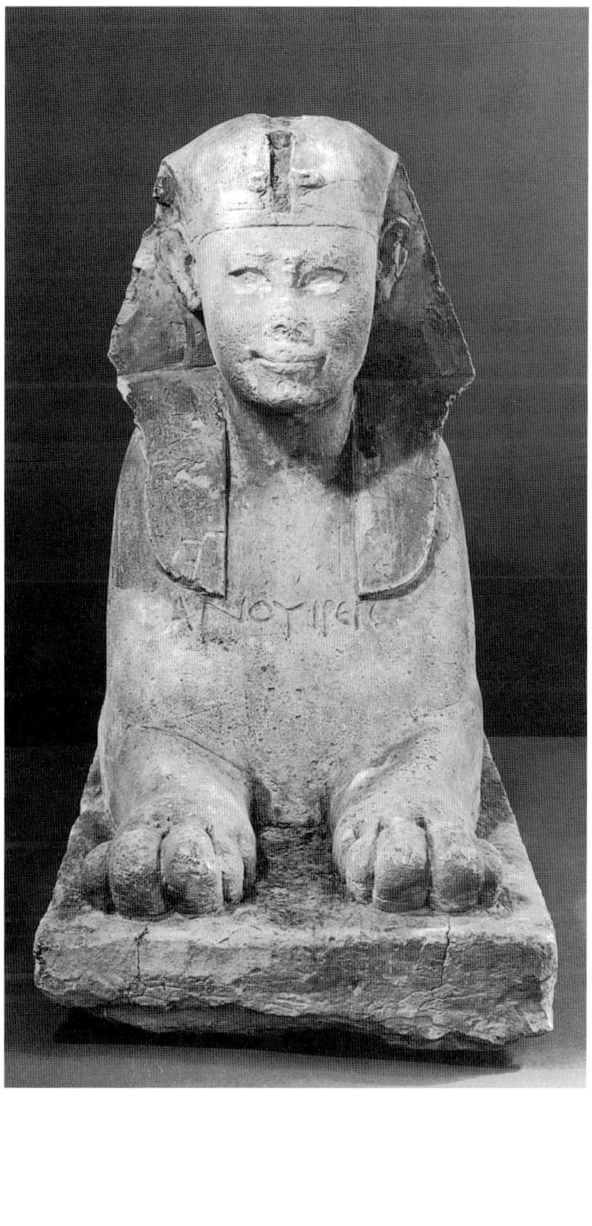

200. Saqqara Serapeum sphinx. Fourth or third century B.C. Vienna, Kunsthistorisches Museum ÄS 5758 (photo: ©Kunsthistorisches Museum, Vienna).

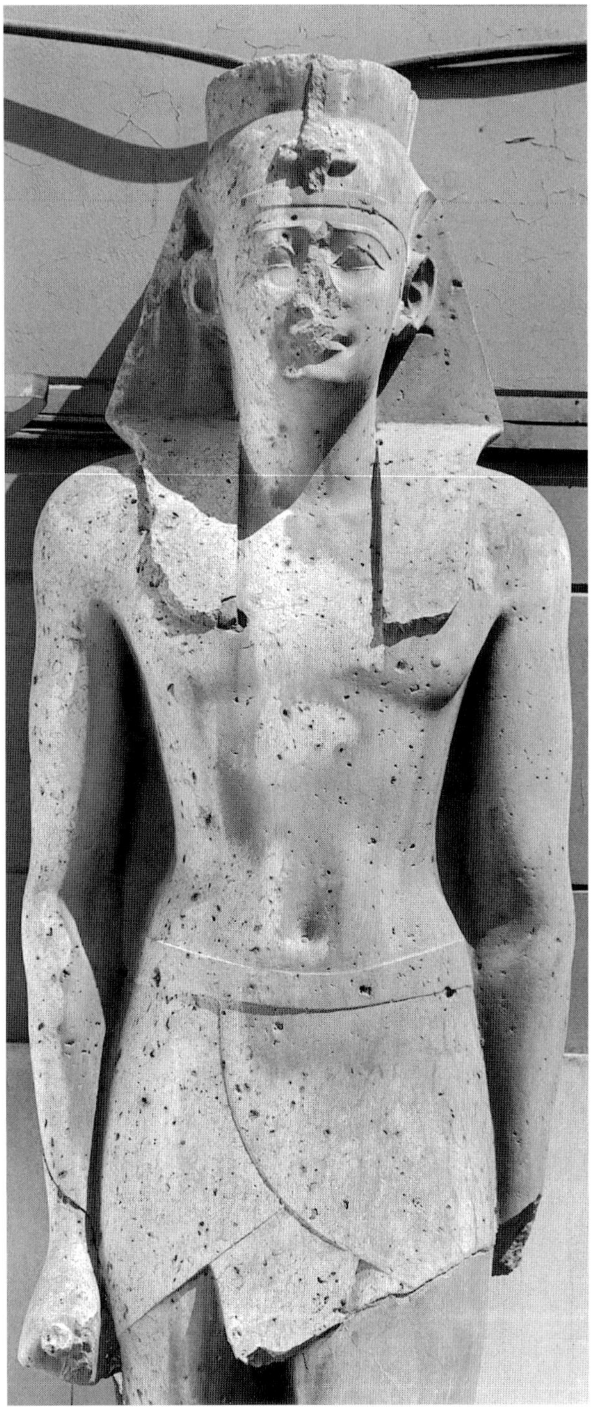

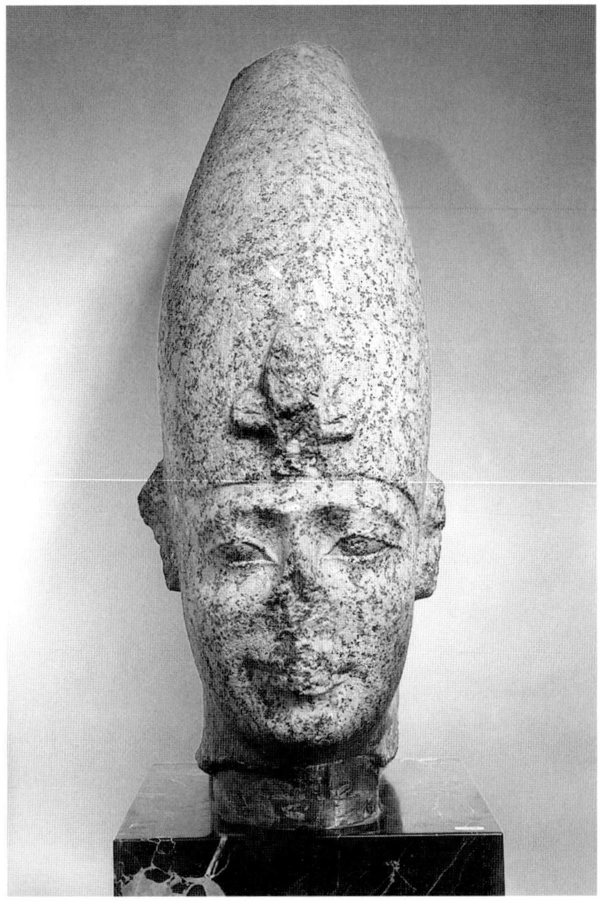

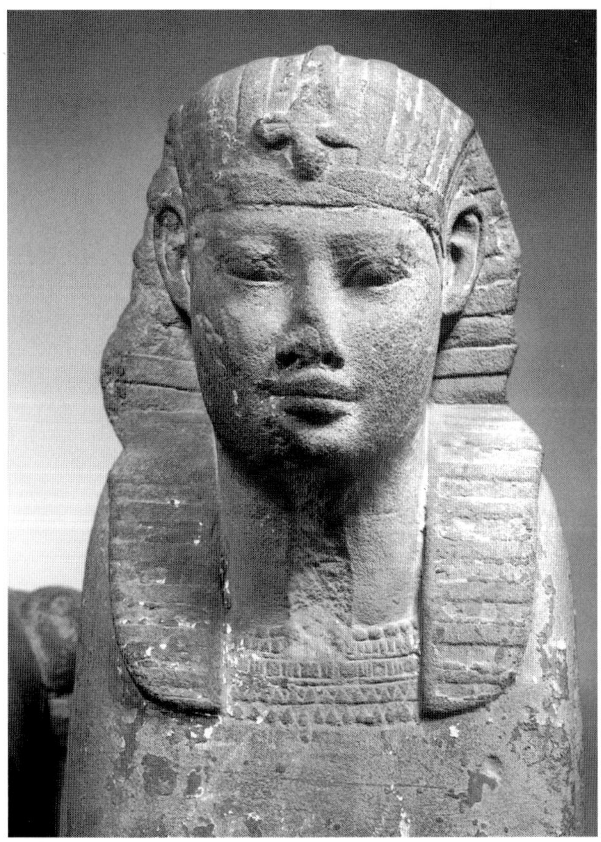

201a (*above*). Standing statue inscribed for Nectanebo I. Cairo JE 87298 (photo: Sherif Sonbol, Cairo).

201b (*above right*). Head inscribed for Nectanebo I. Musée du Louvre E 27124 (photo: ©Musée du Louvre—M. and P. Chuzeville).

201c (*right*). Sphinx inscribed for Nectanebo I (detail). Musée du Louvre A 29 (N 29) (photo: ©Musée du Louvre—M. and P. Chuzeville).

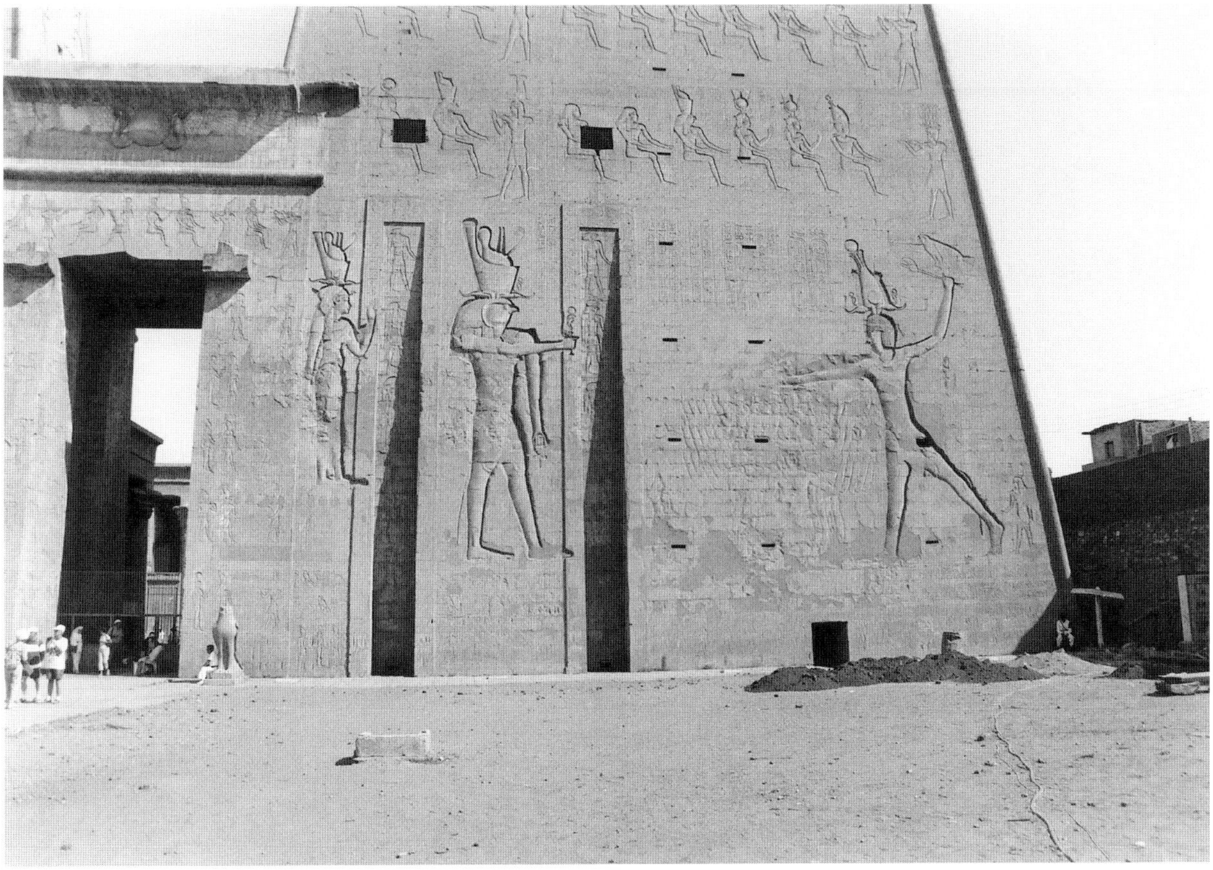

202. (*above*) Pylon of Horus temple, Edfu. Ptolemy XII smites before Horus (photo: author).

203. (*below*) Colonnaded court and first pylon of Isis temple, Philae. Smiting figure of Ptolemy XII on pylon (photo: author).

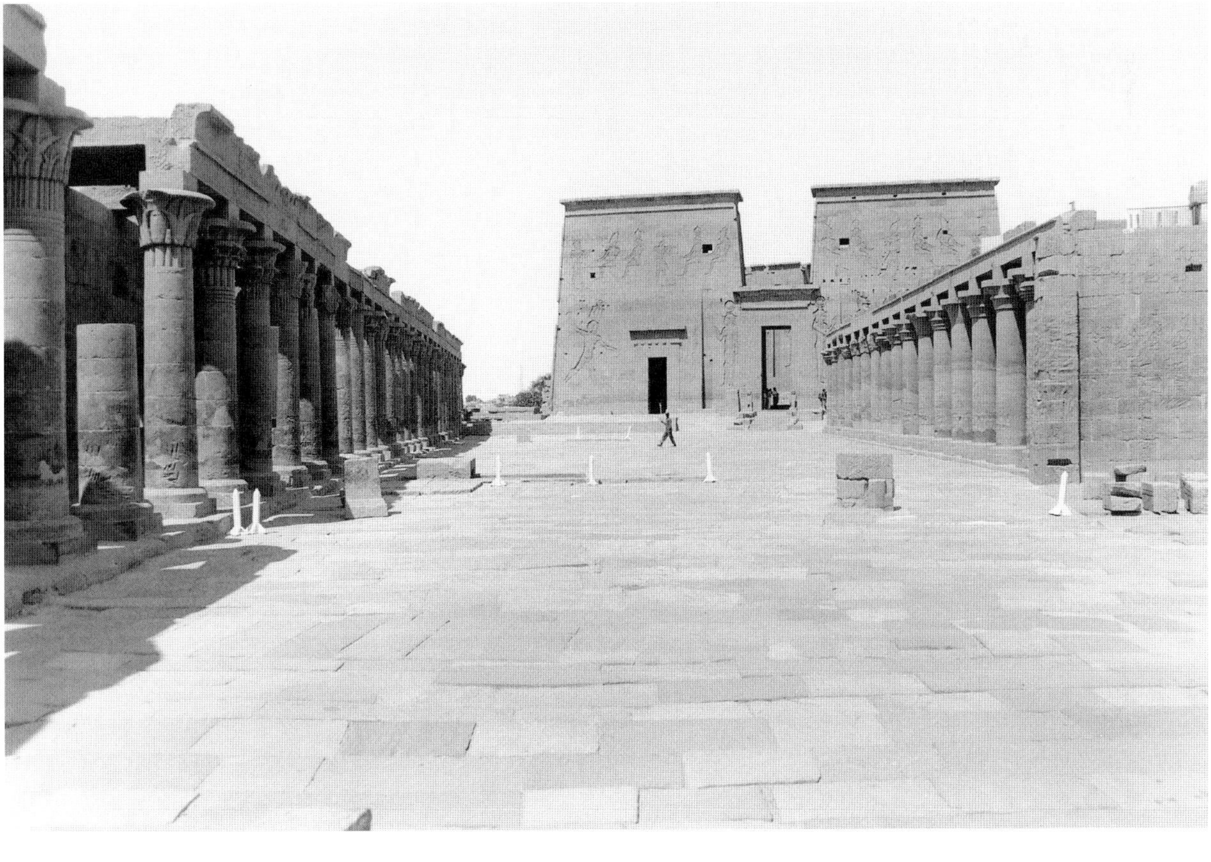

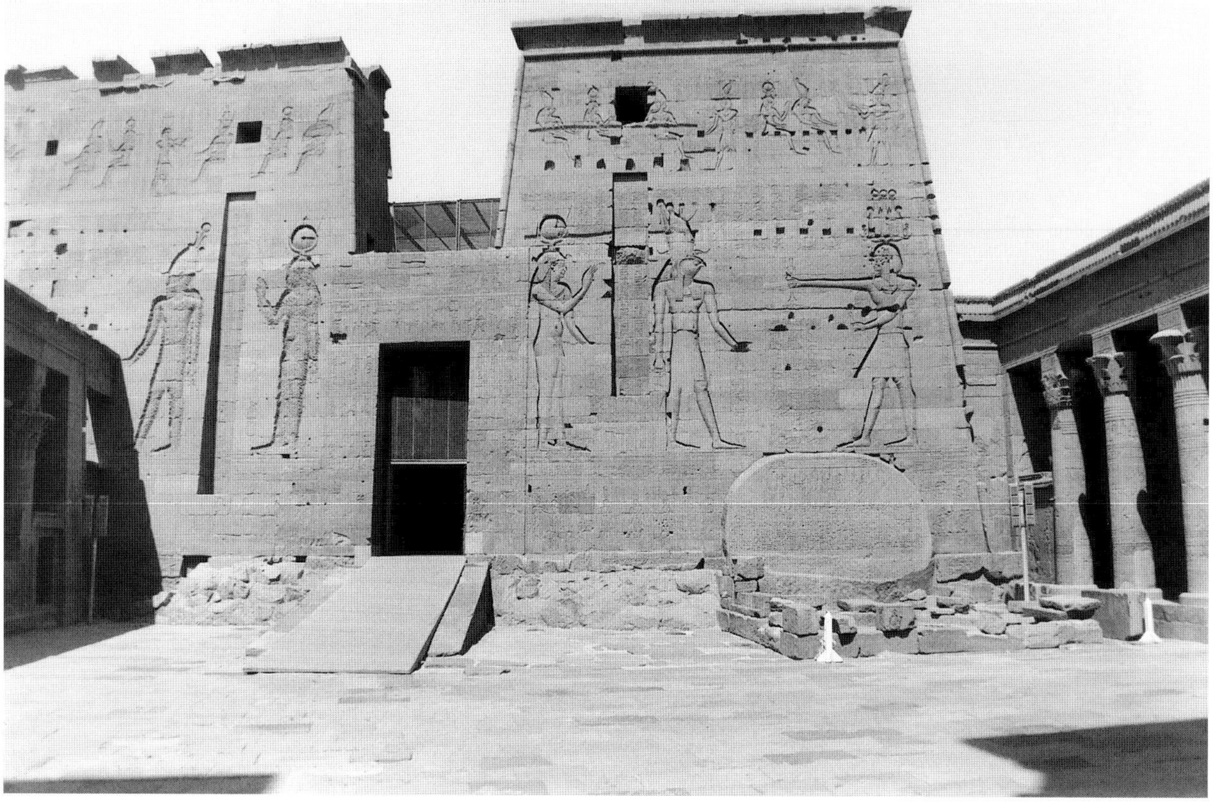

204. (*above*) Second pylon of Isis temple, Philae. Semicircular top of Dodekaschoinos stele below figure of Ptolemy XII (photo: author).

205. (*below*) Ptolemy VI and Cleopatra II receive their right to rule. Haroeris and Sobek temple, Kom Ombo. (photo: author).

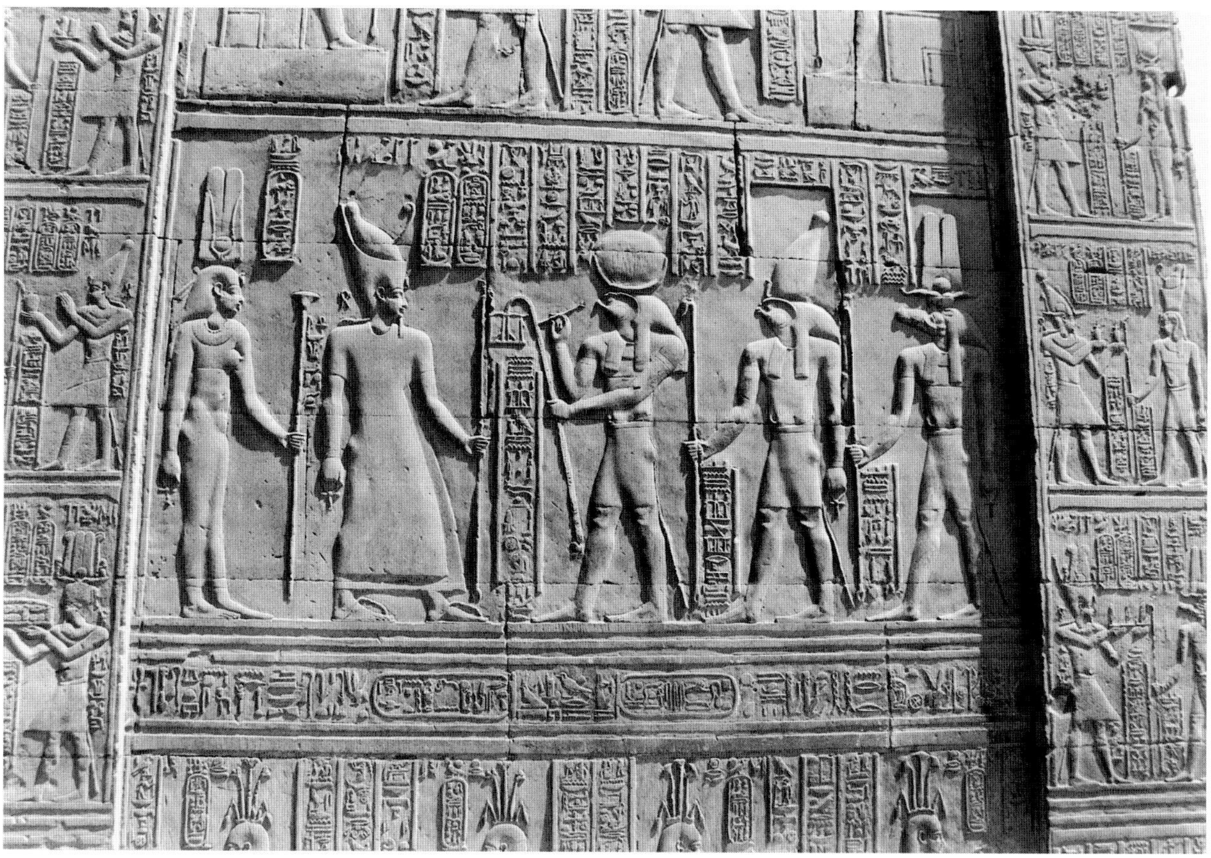

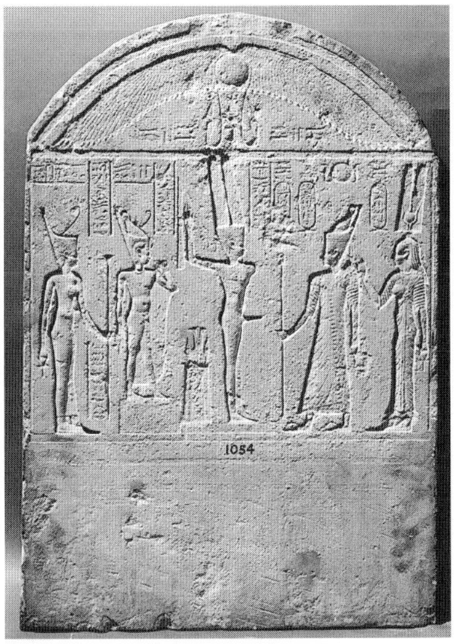

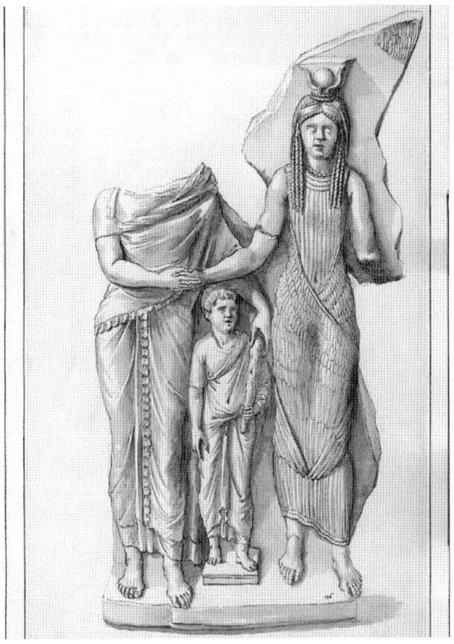

206 (*far left*). Stele of Ptolemy IV and Arsinoe III, Tanis. London, British Museum EA 1054 (photo: ©The British Museum).

207 (*left*). Ptolemaic royal triad. Seventeenth-century drawing of a lost sculpture. Windsor Castle RL 8580, from collection of Cassiano dal Pozzo (photo: The Royal Collection ©2001, Her Majesty Queen Elizabeth II).

208–209 (*below*). Relief plaque, front and back. Baltimore, The Walters Art Museum 22.285 (photos: ©The Walters Art Museum, Baltimore).

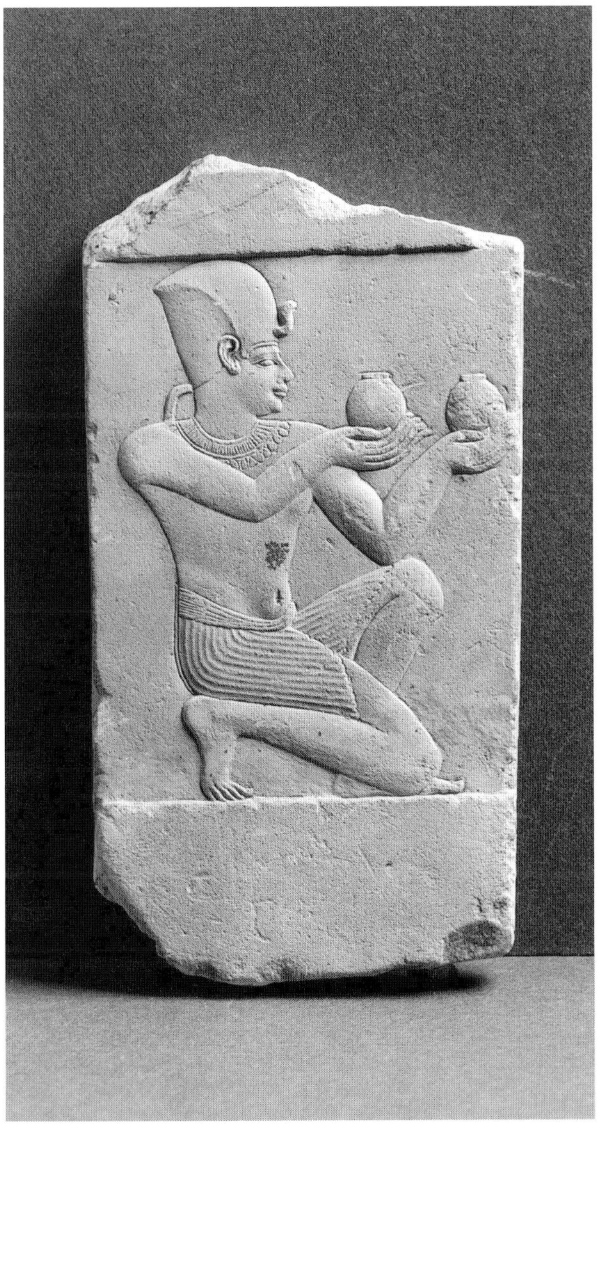

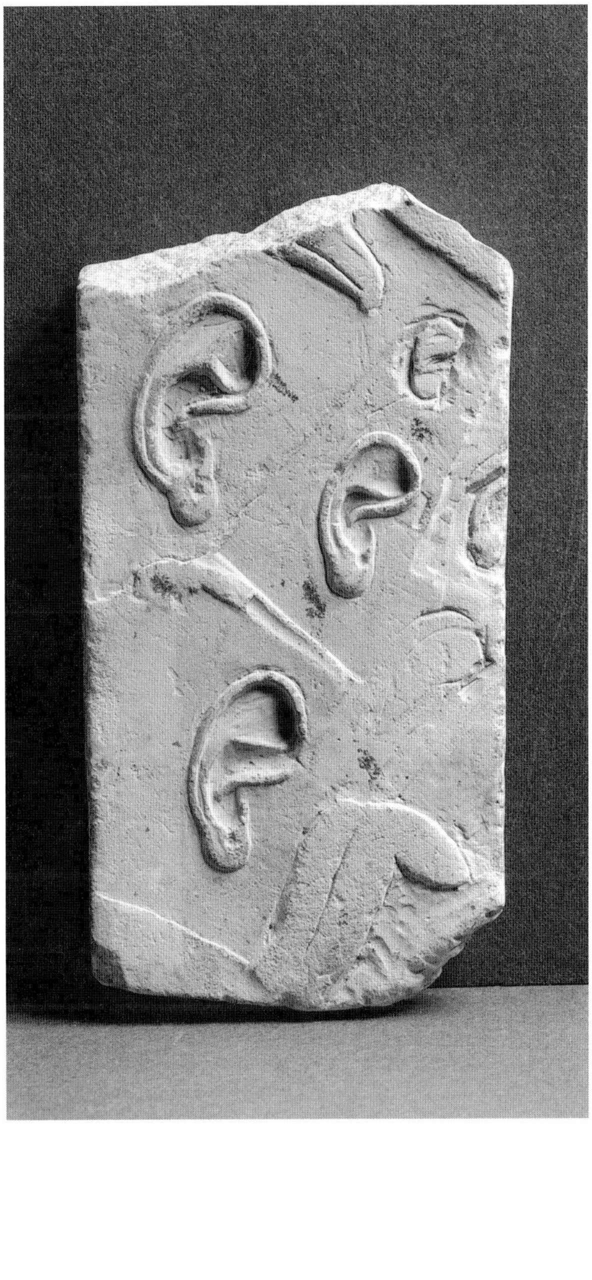

210 (*right*). Lunette of Berenice IV stele from Batn Ihrit (Theadelphia). Cairo JE 40727 (photo: Sherif Sonbol, Cairo).

211 (*below left*). Relief fragment. King's *ka*. Brooklyn Museum of Art 67.69.2, Charles Edwin Wilbour Fund (photo: ©Brooklyn Museum of Art).

212 (*below right*). Head of king. Modern imitation. Brooklyn Museum of Art 54.68, Charles Edwin Wilbour Fund (photo: ©Brooklyn Museum of Art).

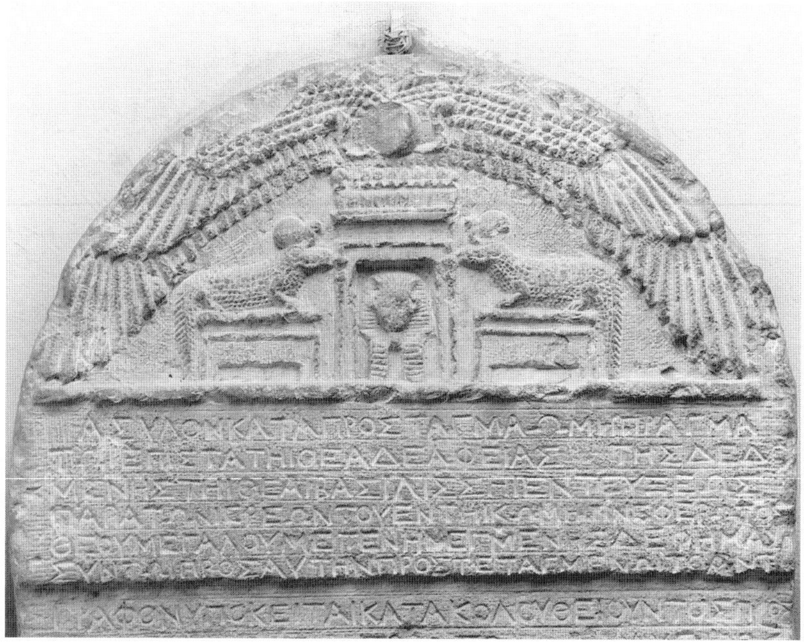

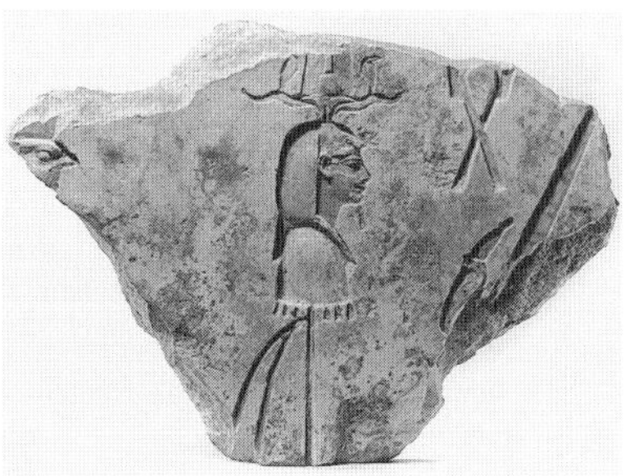

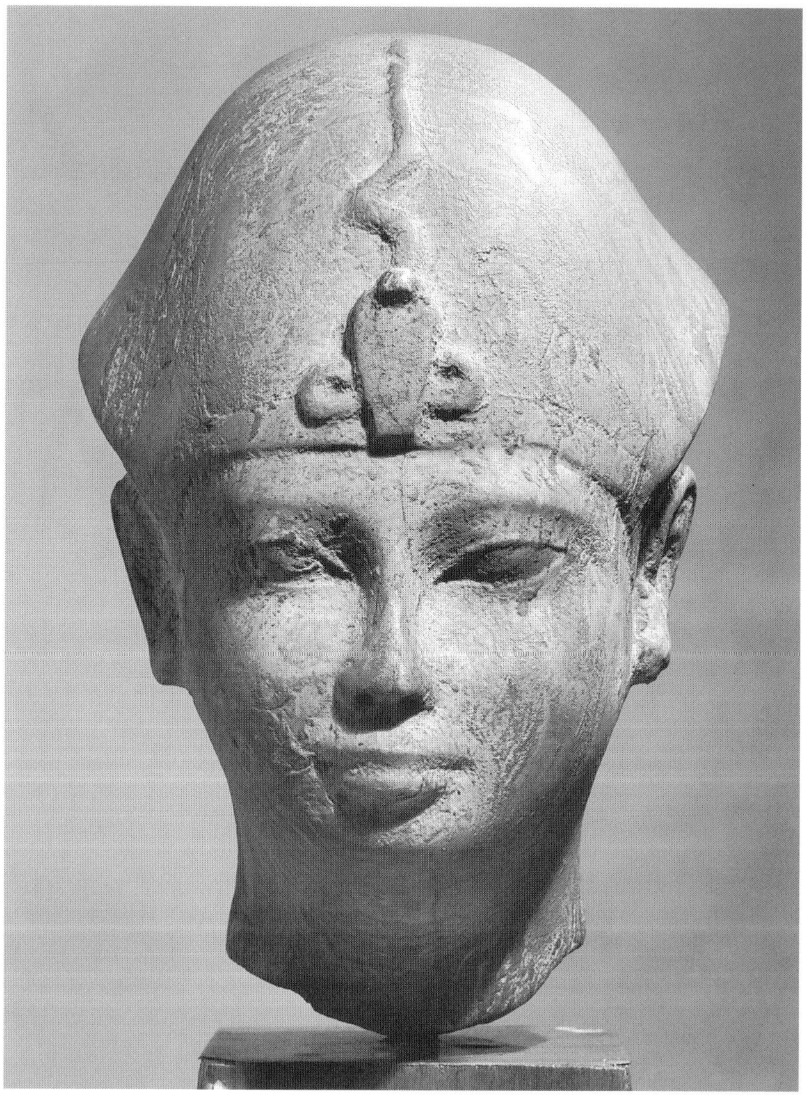

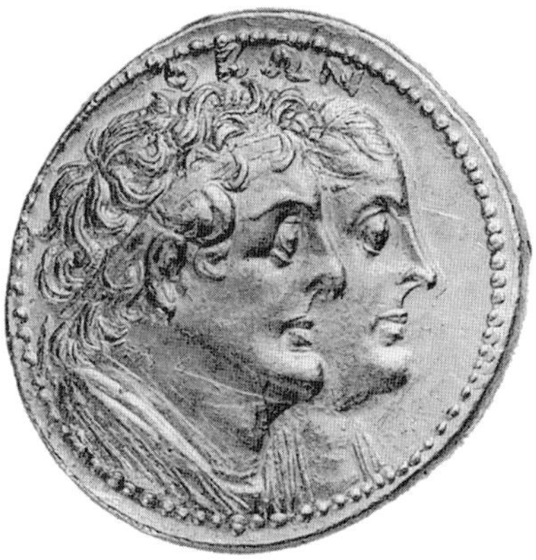

213. Gold octodrachm, Ptolemy I/ Berenice I, Alexandria. New York, American Numismatic Society 1977.158.112 (photo: Sharon Suchma, ©American Numismatic Society).

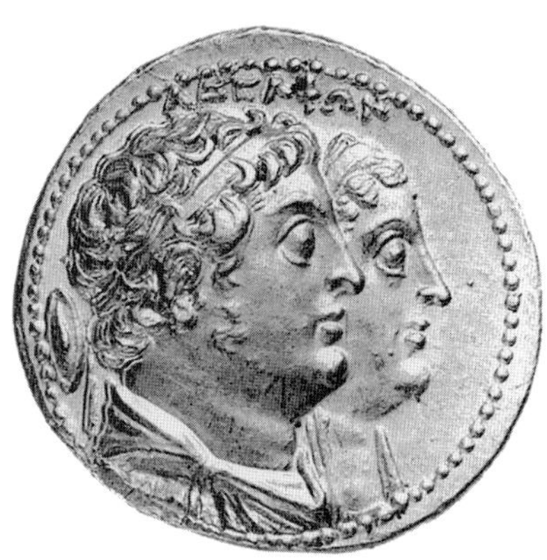

214. Gold octodrachm, Ptolemy II/ Arsinoe II, Alexandria. New York, American Numismatic Society 1977.158.112 (photo: Sharon Suchma, ©American Numismatic Society).

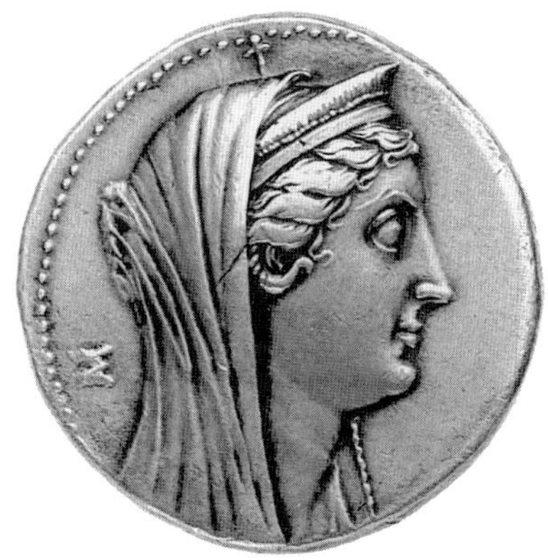

215. Silver decadrachm, Arsinoe II, Alexandria. New York, American Numismatic Society 1974.26.801 (photo: Sharon Suchma, ©American Numismatic Society).

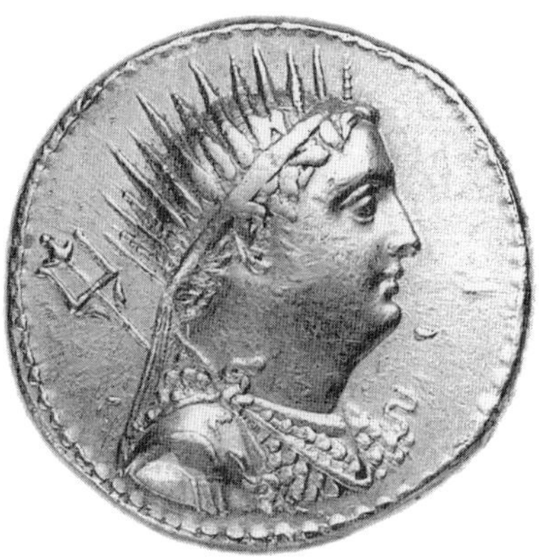

216. Gold octodrachm, Ptolemy III, Alexandria. New York, American Numismatic Society 1980.109.97 (photo: Sharon Suchma, ©American Numismatic Society).

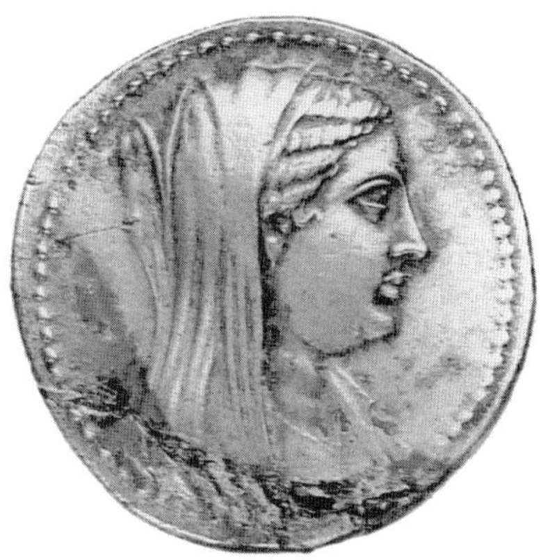

217. Silver pentadrachm, Berenice II, Alexandria. New York, American Numismatic Society 1967.152.626 (photo: Sharon Suchma, ©American Numismatic Society).

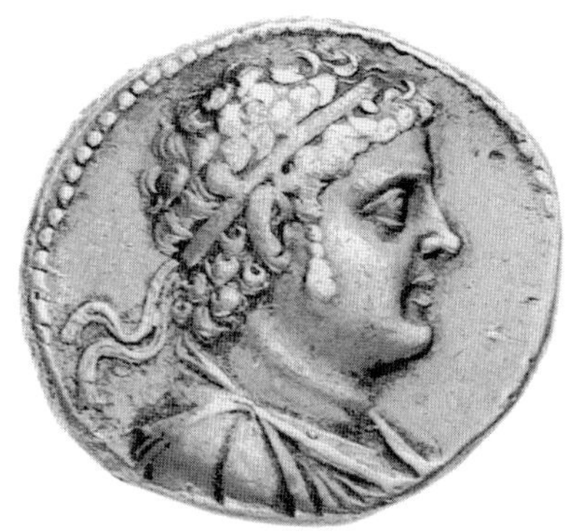

218. Silver tetradrachm, Ptolemy IV, Sidon. New York, American Numismatic Society 1967.152.651 (photo: Sharon Suchma, ©American Numismatic Society).

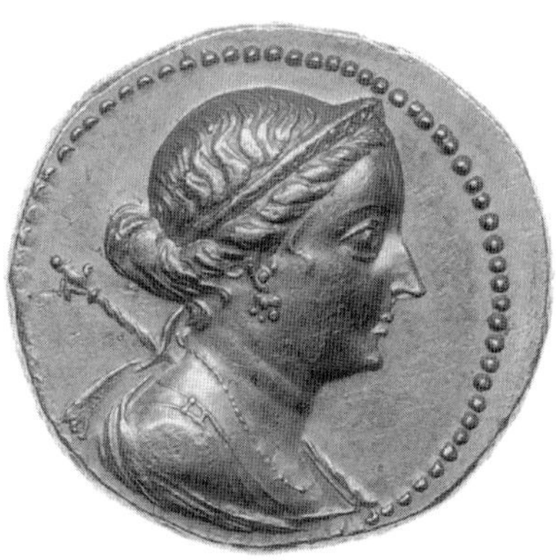

219. Gold octodrachm, Arsinoe III, Phoenicia. Paris, Bibliothèque nationale de France, Fonds général 357 (photo: Cliché Bibliothèque nationale de France, Paris).

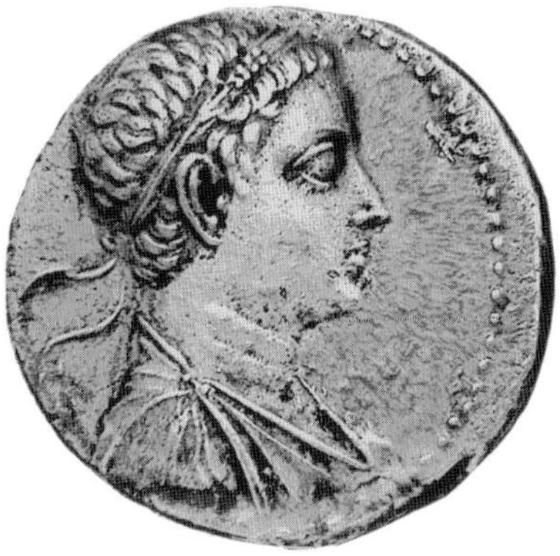

220. Silver tetradrachm, Ptolemy V, Phoenicia(?). New York, American Numismatic Society 1948.19.2423 (photo: Sharon Suchma, ©American Numismatic Society).

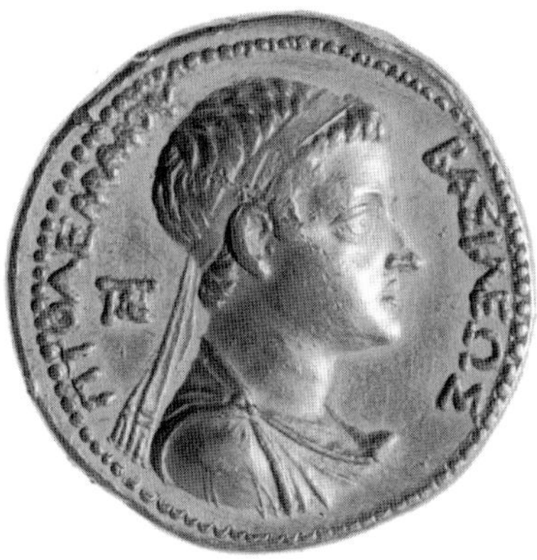

221. Gold octodrachm, Ptolemy VI, Alexandria. London, British Museum 1978-10-21-1 (photo: ©The British Museum).

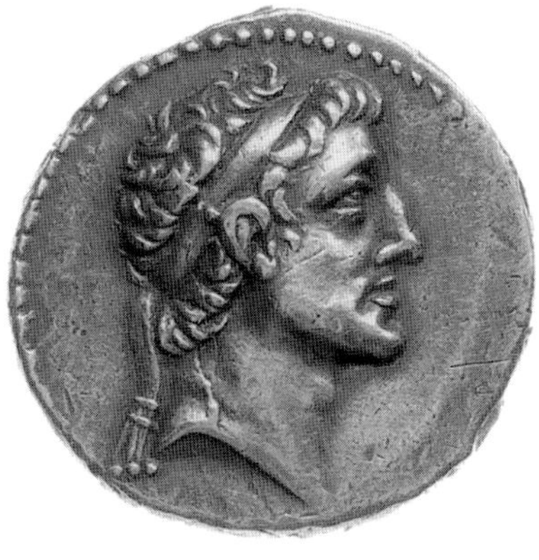

222. Silver tetradrachm, Ptolemy VI, Ake-Ptolemais. Paris, Bibliothèque nationale de France, Fonds général 368 (photo: Cliché Bibliothèque nationale de France, Paris).

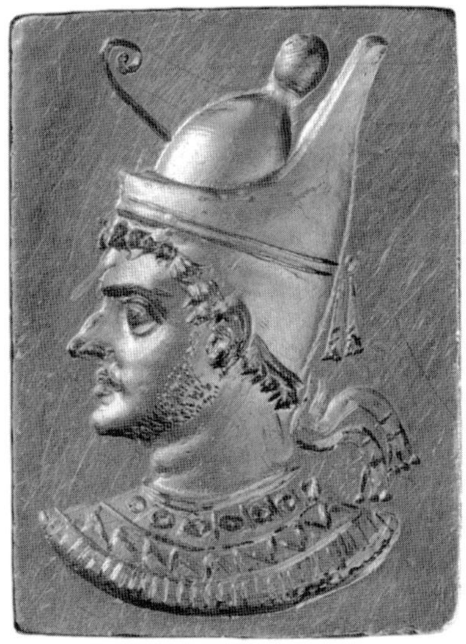

223. Gold ring with bust of a Ptolemy. Paris, Musée du Louvre Bj 1092 (photo: ©Musée du Louvre—M. and P. Chuzeville).

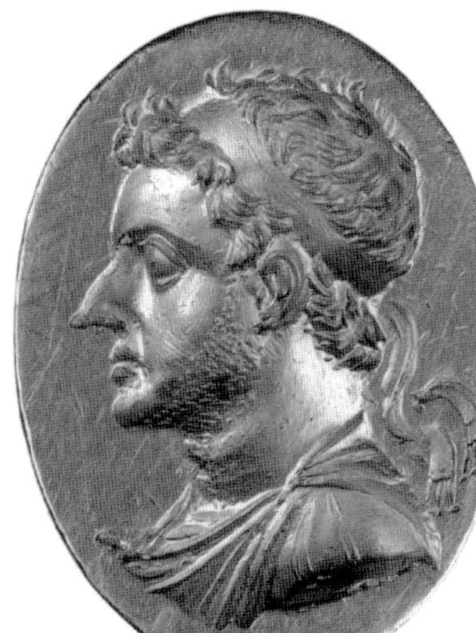

224. Gold ring with bust of a Ptolemy. Paris, Musée du Louvre Bj 1093 (photo: ©Musée du Louvre—M. and P. Chuzeville).

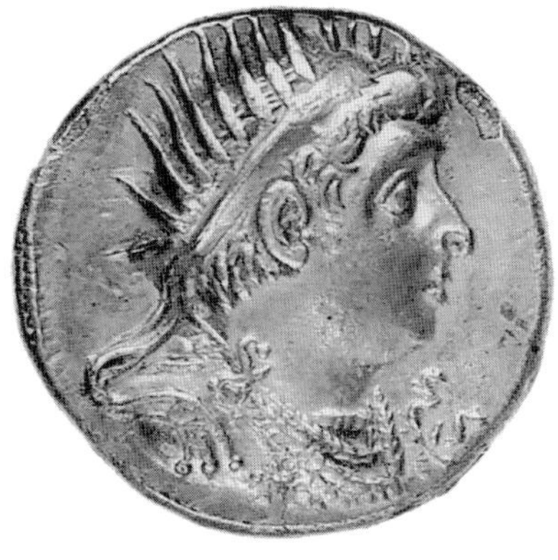

225. Silver didrachm, Ptolemy VIII, Alexandria. New York, American Numismatic Society 1944.100.75452 (photo: Sharon Suchma, ©American Numismatic Society).

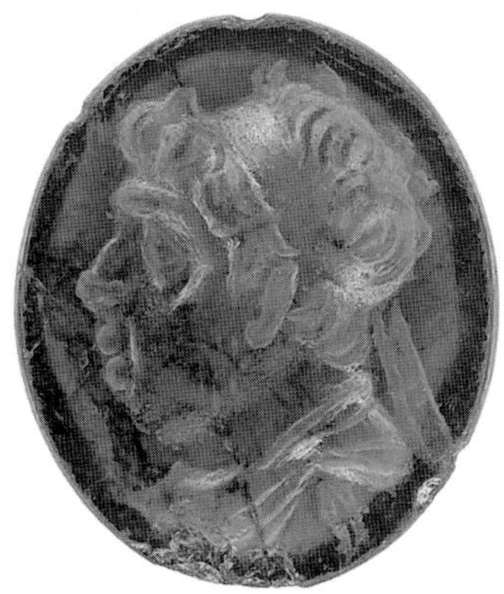

226. Engraved garnet, attributed to Ptolemy VIII. Bloomington, Indiana University Art Museum: Burton Y. Berry Collection 76.85.13 (©Indiana University Art Museum: photograph by: Michael Cavanagh, Kevin Montague).

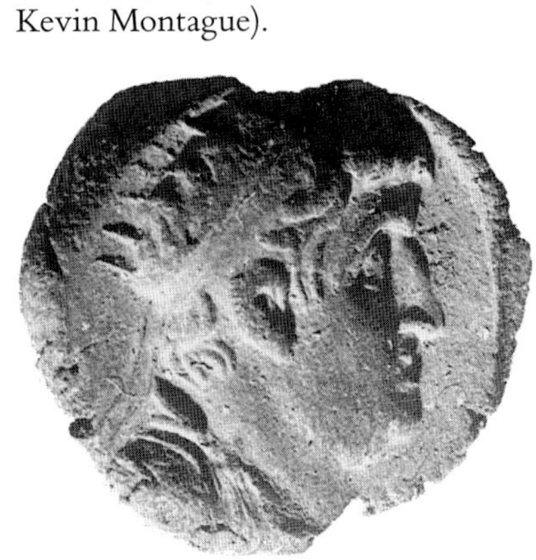

227. Clay sealing, attributed to Ptolemy VIII, Edfu(?). Toronto, Royal Ontario Museum 906.12.141, Milne 1916, cat. no. 161 (photo: courtesy of the Royal Ontario Museum).

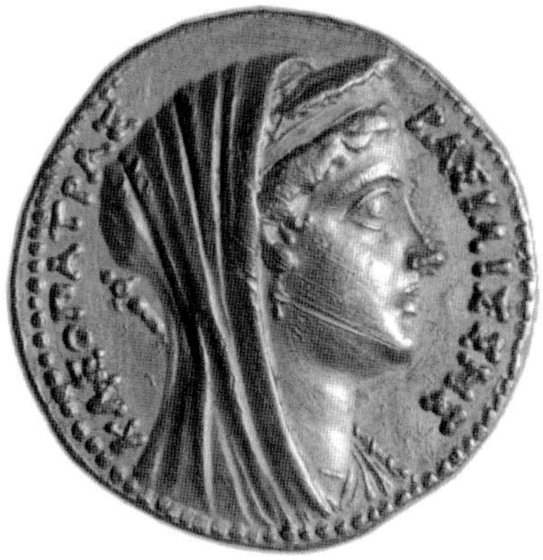

228. Gold octodrachm, Cleopatra I, Alexandria. London, British Museum 1978-10-21-1 (photo: ©The British Museum).

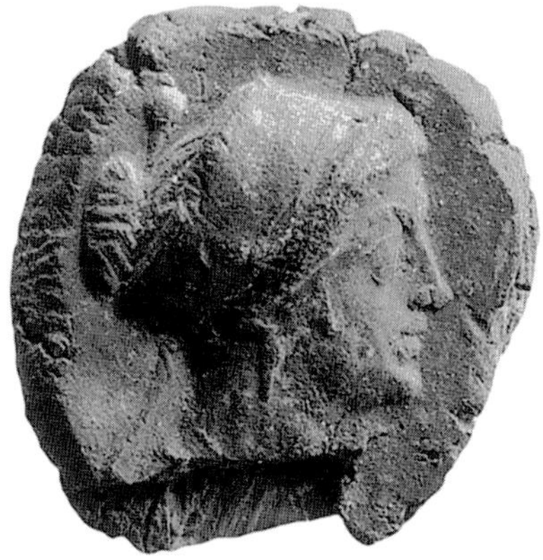

229. Clay sealing, second-century Ptolemaic queen, Edfu(?). Amsterdam, Allard Pierson Museum 2550 (photo: ©Allard Pierson Museum).

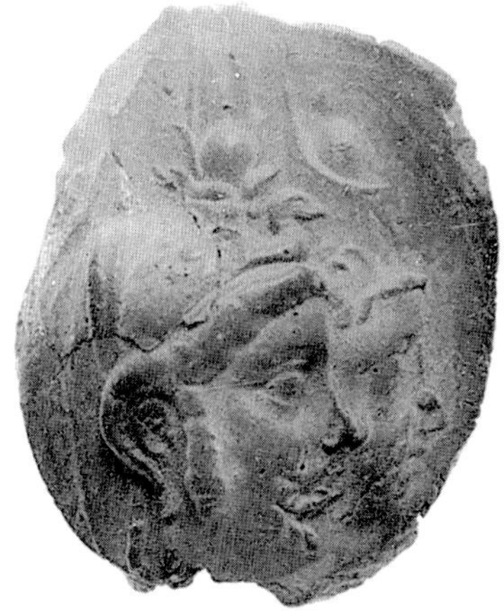

230. Clay sealing, second-century Ptolemaic queen and king, Alexandria. Athens, National Archaeological Museum MN 2447, Benaki Collection (photo: ©National Archaeological Museum).

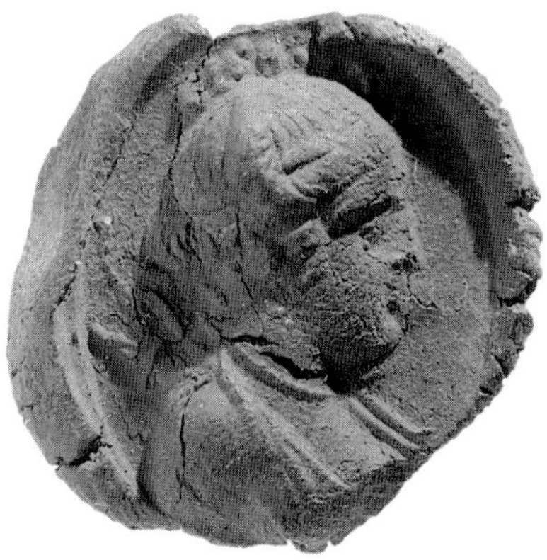

231. Clay sealing, attributed to Cleopatra II, Edfu(?). Toronto, Royal Ontario Museum 906.12.187, Milne 1916, cat. no. 209 (photo: courtesy of the Royal Ontario Museum).

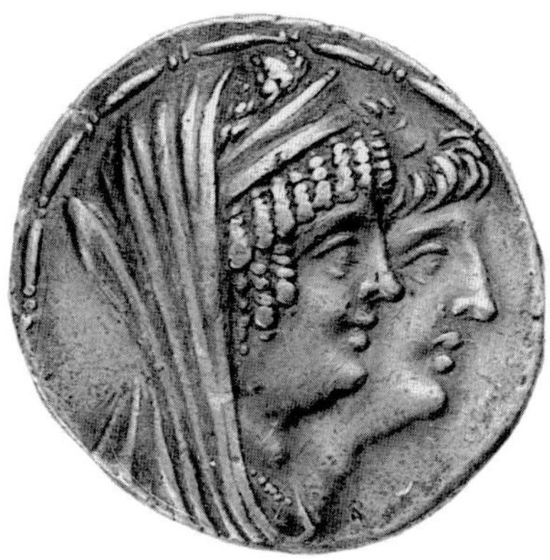

232. Silver tetradrachm, Cleopatra Thea and Antiochus VIII Grypos, Ake-Ptolemais. New York, American Numismatic Society 1948.19.2451 (photo: Sharon Suchma, ©American Numismatic Society).

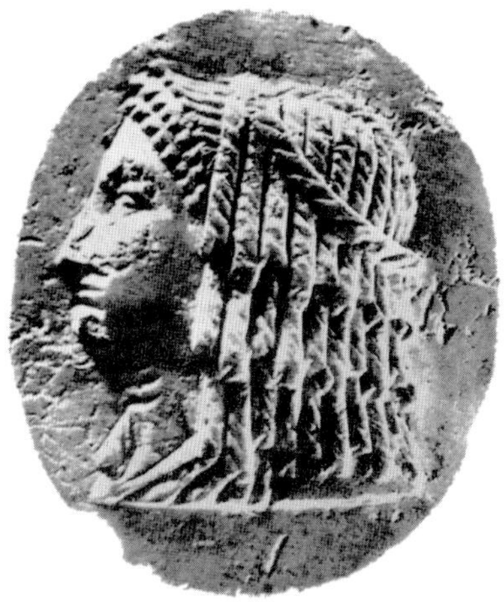

233. Bone ring, attributed to Cleopatra III, Kyreneia. Nicosia, Cyprus Museum J 745 (photo: courtesy of the Cyprus Museum; after *AM* 86 [1971], pl. 81: 4).

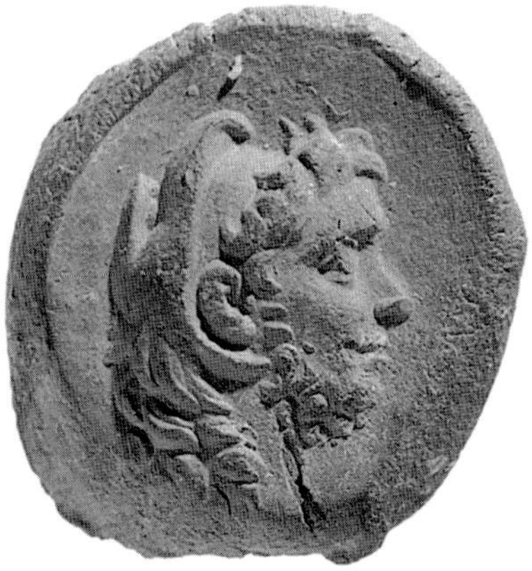

234. Clay sealing, Ptolemy IX, first rule (116–107 B.C.), Edfu(?). Toronto, Royal Ontario Museum 906.12.125, Milne 1916, cat. no. 134 (photo: courtesy of the Royal Ontario Museum).

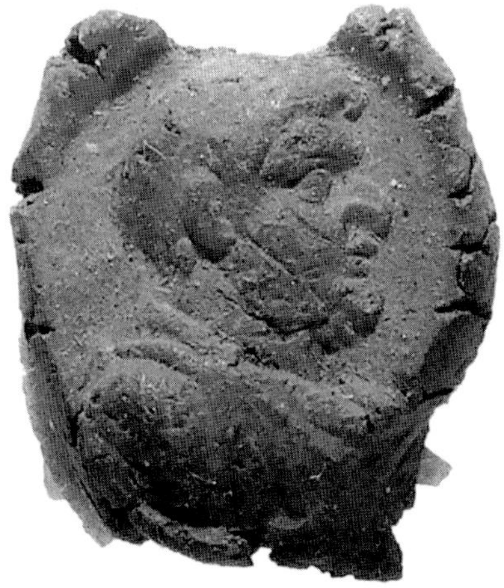

235. Clay sealing, attributed to Ptolemy IX, second rule (88–80 B.C.), Edfu(?). Toronto, Royal Ontario Museum 906.12.121, Milne 1916, cat. no. 125 (photo: courtesy of the Royal Ontario Museum).

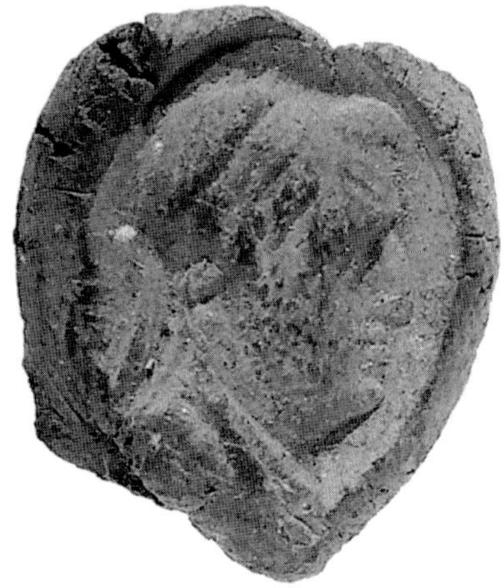

236. Clay sealing, attributed to Ptolemy X, Edfu(?). Toronto, Royal Ontario Museum 906.12.86, Milne 1916, cat. no. 83 (photo: courtesy of the Royal Ontario Museum).

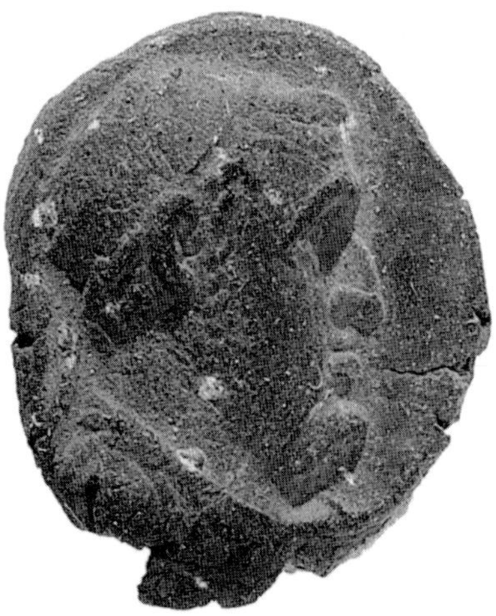

237. Clay sealing, attributed to Ptolemy X, Edfu(?). Toronto, Royal Ontario Museum 906.12.84, Milne 1916, cat. no. 81 (photo: courtesy of the Royal Ontario Museum).

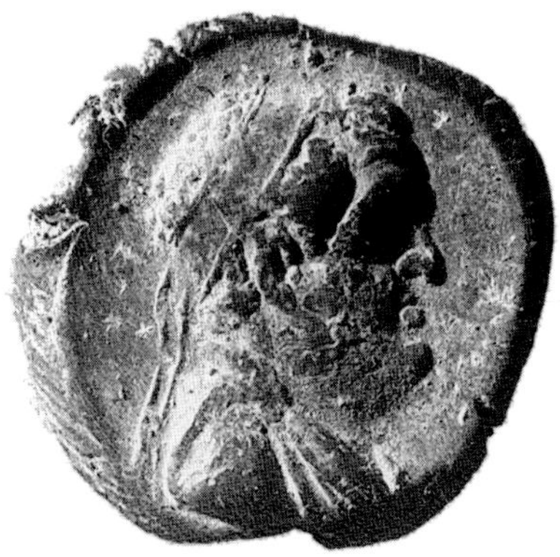

238. Clay sealing, attributed to Ptolemy X, Edfu(?). Toronto, Royal Ontario Museum 906.12.100, Milne 1916, cat. no. 96 (photo: courtesy of the Royal Ontario Museum).

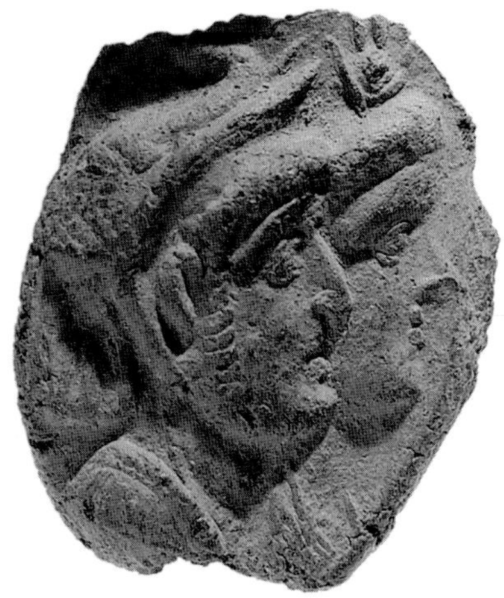

239. Clay sealing, attributed to Ptolemy IX or X and queen, Edfu(?). Toronto, Royal Ontario Museum 906.12.192, Milne 1916, cat. no. 214 (photo: courtesy of the Royal Ontario Museum).

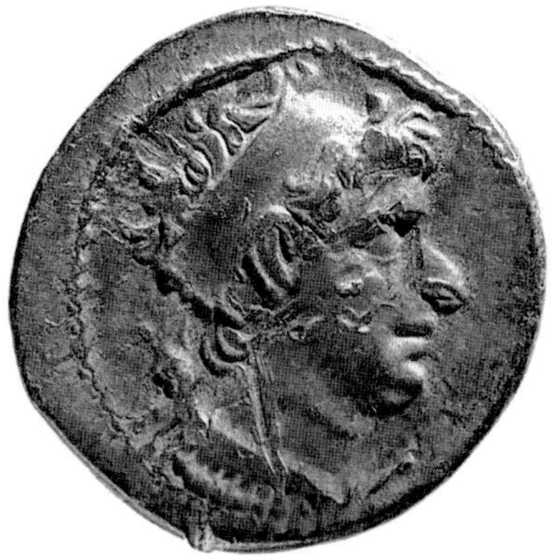

240. Silver drachm with bust of Ptolemy XII, Alexandria(?). Diameter: 17 mm; weight 3.04 gm. Theodora Wilbour Fund, 53.456. Courtesy, Museum of Fine Arts, Boston. Reproduced with permission. ©2000 Museum of Fine Arts, Boston. All Rights Reserved.

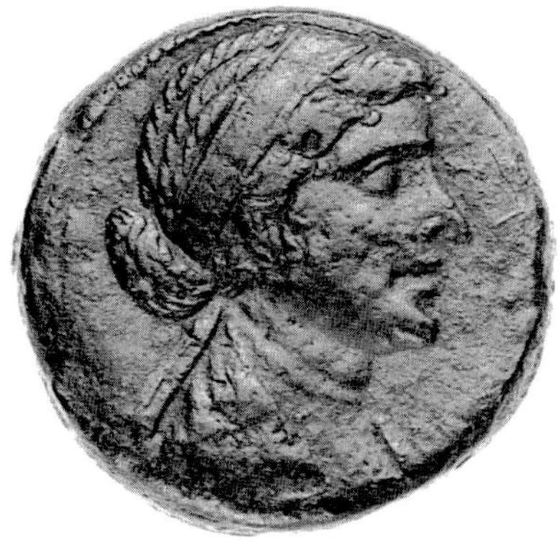

241. Bronze coin, Cleopatra VII, Alexandria. New York, American Numismatic Society 1941.131.1158 (photo: Sharon Suchma, ©American Numismatic Society).

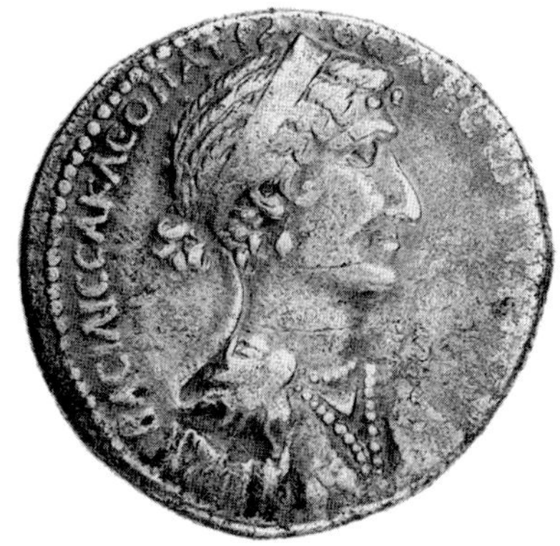

242. Silver tetradrachm, Cleopatra VII, Antioch. New York, American Numismatic Society 1977.158.621 (photo: Sharon Suchma, ©American Numismatic Society).

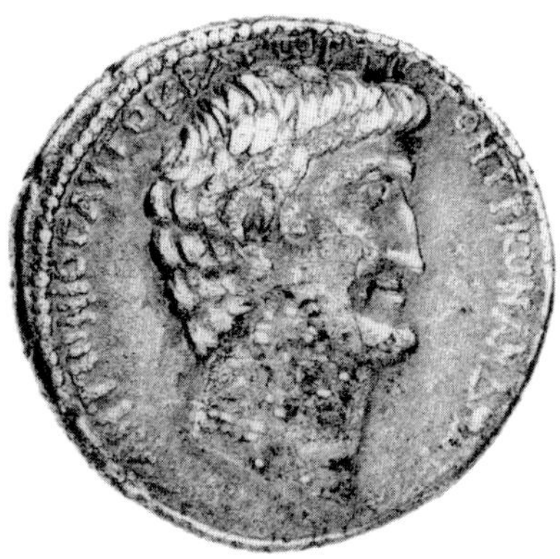

243. Silver tetradrachm, Marc Antony, Antioch. New York, American Numismatic Society 1977.158.621 (photo: Sharon Suchma, ©American Numismatic Society).

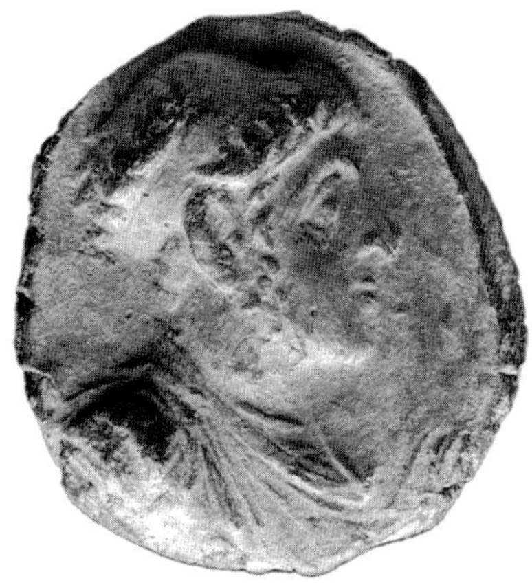

244. Clay sealing, attributed to Ptolemy XV, Tanis. London, British Museum EA 15932 (photo: ©The British Museum).

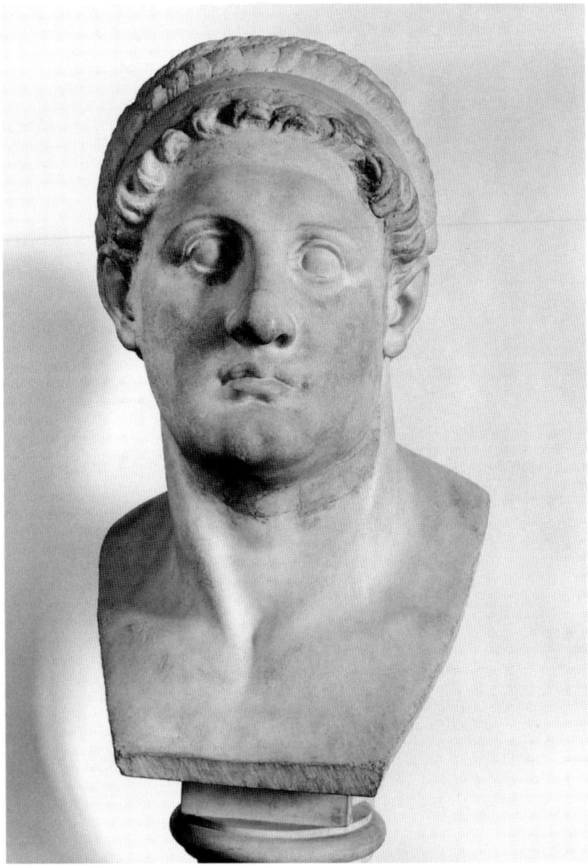

245. Marble head attributed to Ptolemy I. Paris, Musée du Louvre Ma 849 (photo: ©Musée du Louvre—M. and P. Chuzeville).

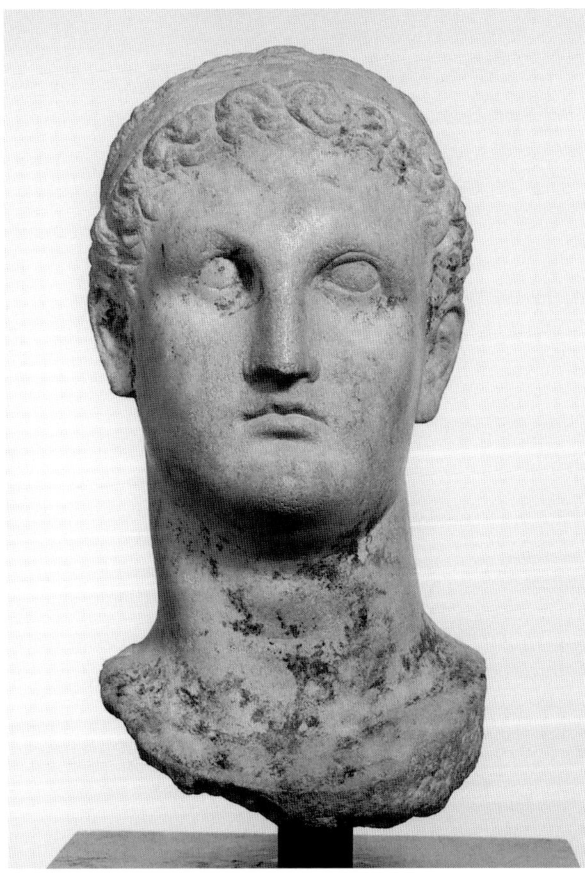

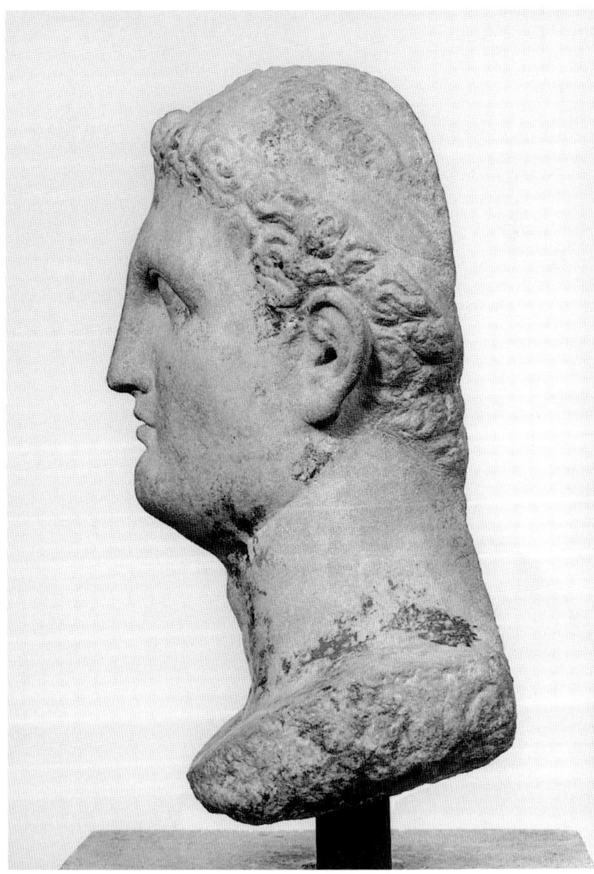

246–247. Marble head attributed to a third-century ruler (Ptolemy II?). Paris, Musée du Louvre Ma 3261 (photos: ©Musée du Louvre—P. Lebaube).

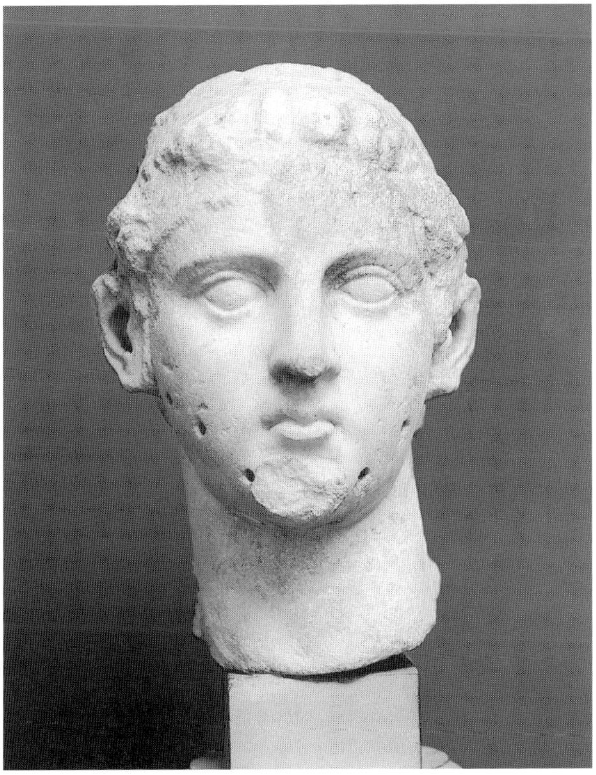

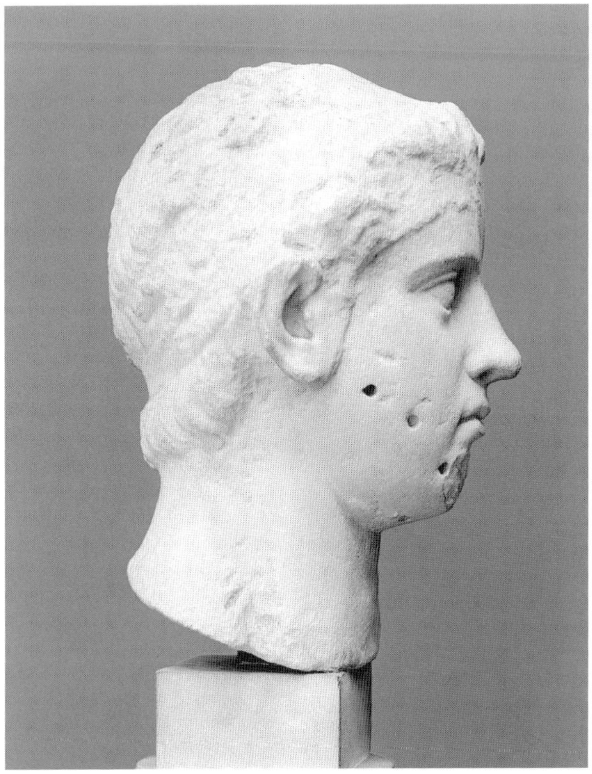

248–249 (*above*). Marble head of Ptolemaic king. Henry Lillie Pierce Fund, 01.8208. Courtesy, Museum of Fine Arts, Boston. Reproduced with permission.

250–251 (*below*). Marble head of Ptolemaic queen. Henry Lillie Pierce Fund, 01.8207. Courtesy, Museum of Fine Arts, Boston. Reproduced with permission.

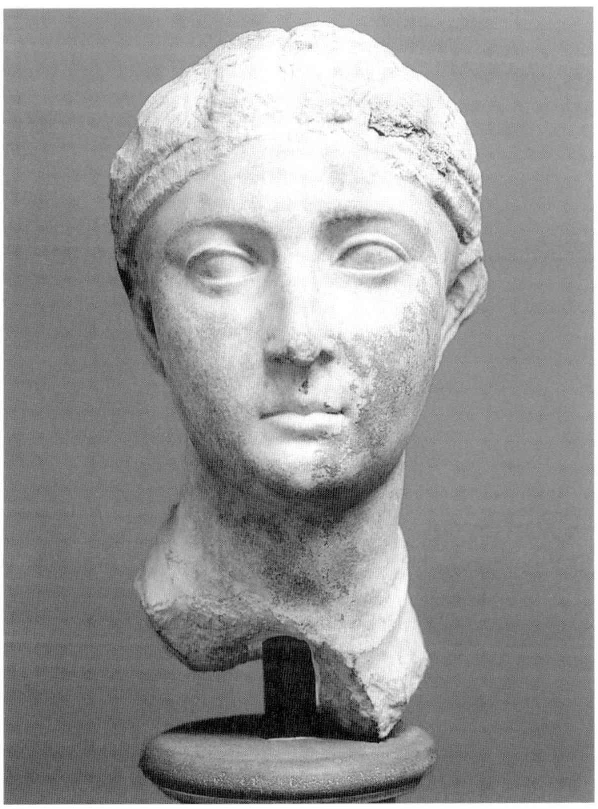

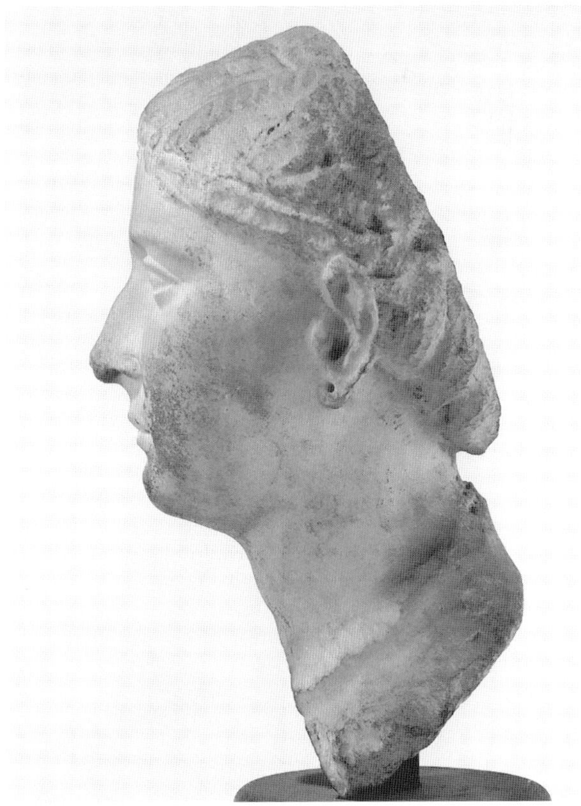

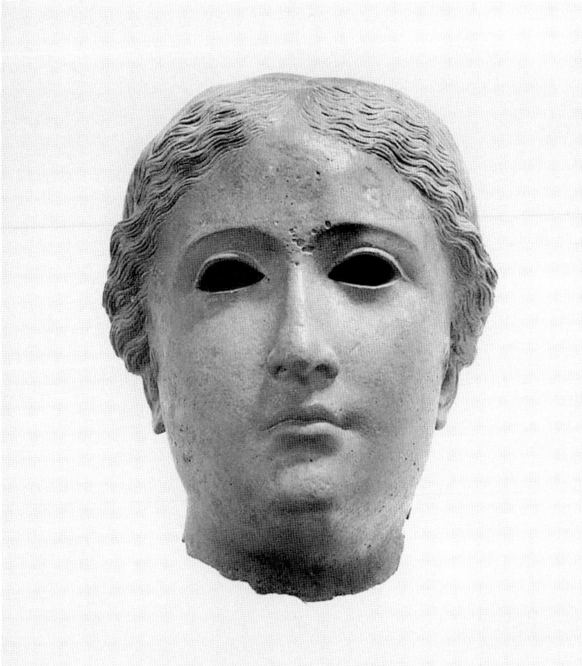

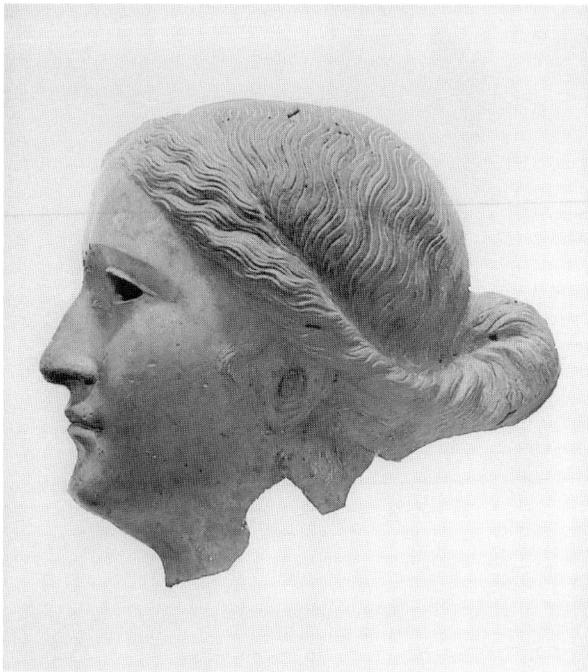

252–253 (*above*). Bronze head attributed to Arsinoe III. Mantua, Museo Civico di Palazzo Te (photos: ©Museo Civico di Palazzo Te).

254–255 (*below*). Marble head attributed to Ptolemy VI. Alexandria, Graeco-Roman Museum 24092 (photos: Deutsches Archäologisches Institut, Cairo).

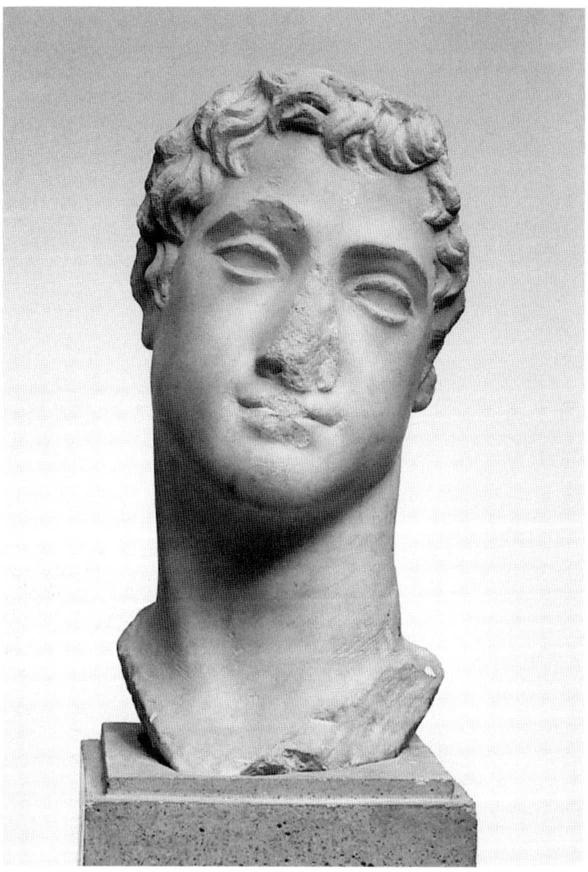

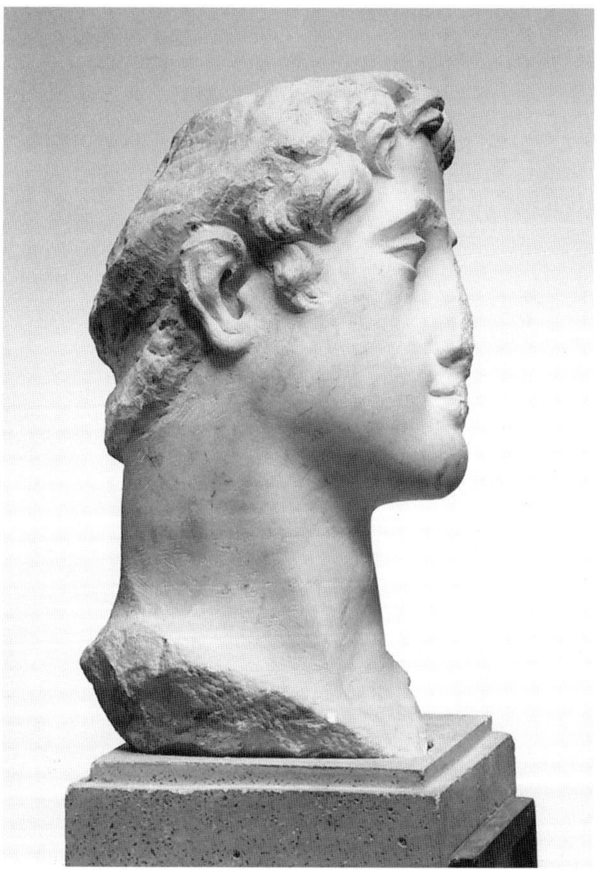

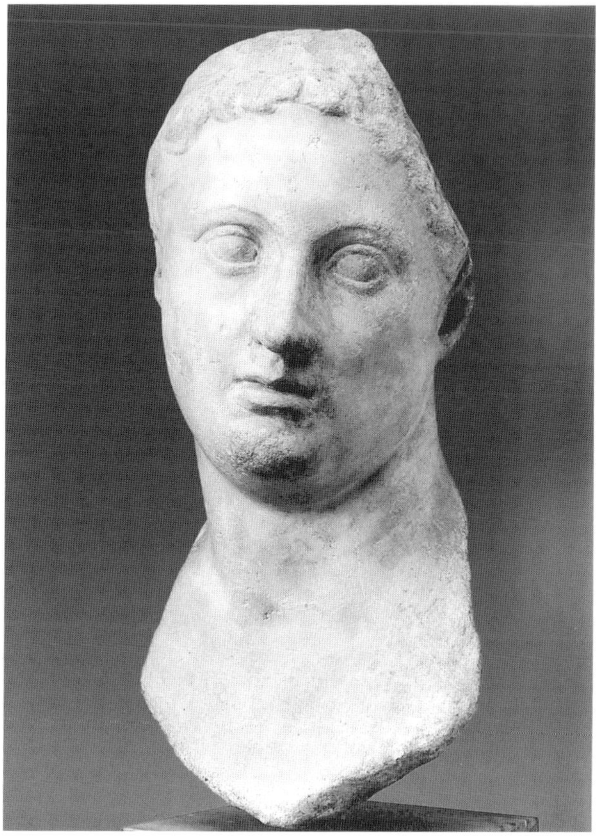

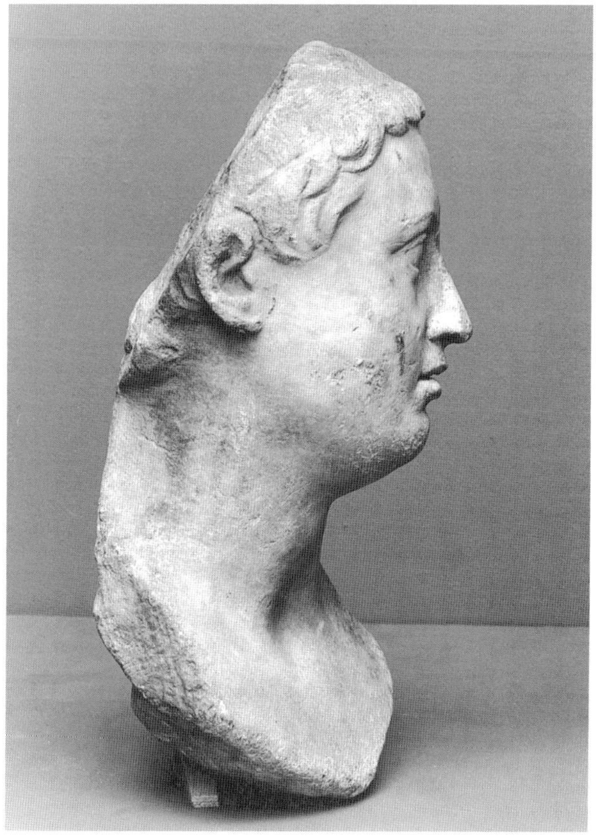

256–257 (*above*). Marble head attributed to Ptolemy VIII. Copenhagen, National Museum, Dept. of Classical and Near Eastern Antiquities ABb 290 (photos: ©National Museum).

258–259 (*below*). Marble head attributed to Ptolemy VIII. New York, William Kelly Simpson collection (photos: Yale University Art Gallery).

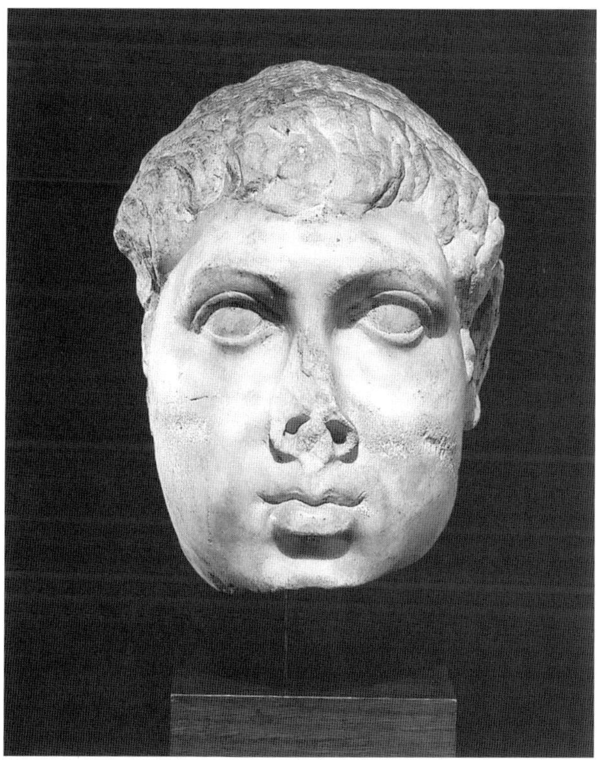

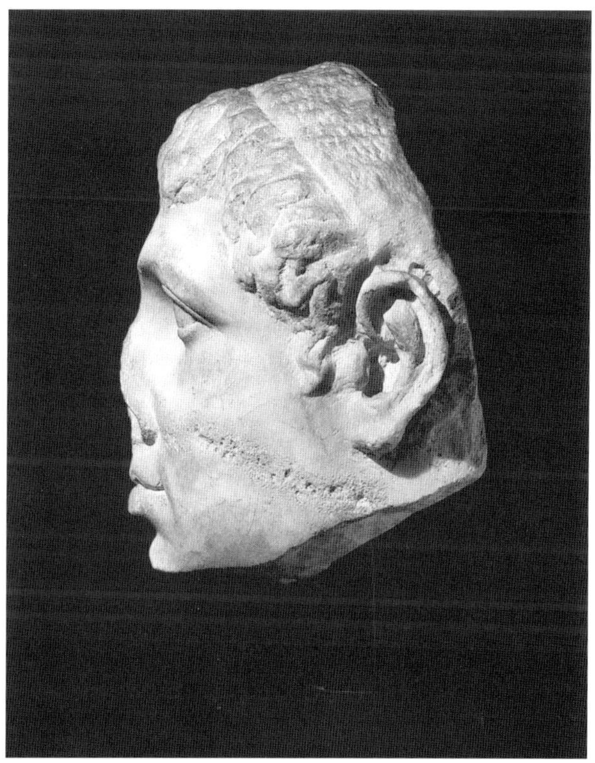

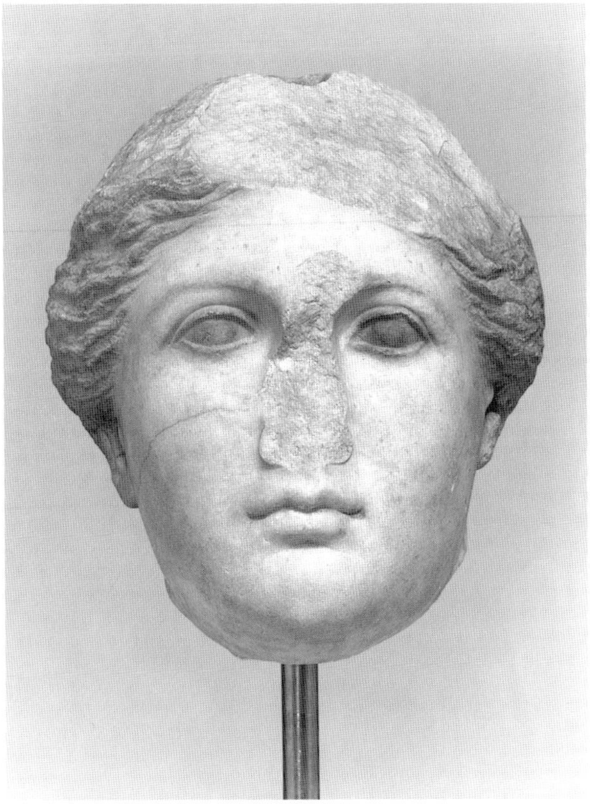

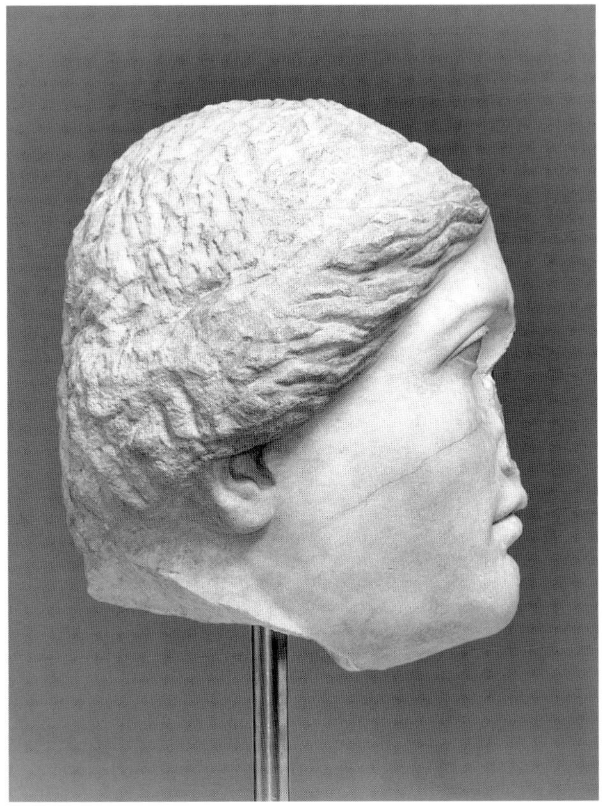

260–261. Marble head of a queen or goddess. Second century B.C.? Kassel, Staatliche Museen, Antikensammlung Sk 115 (photos: ©Staatliche Museen Kassel).

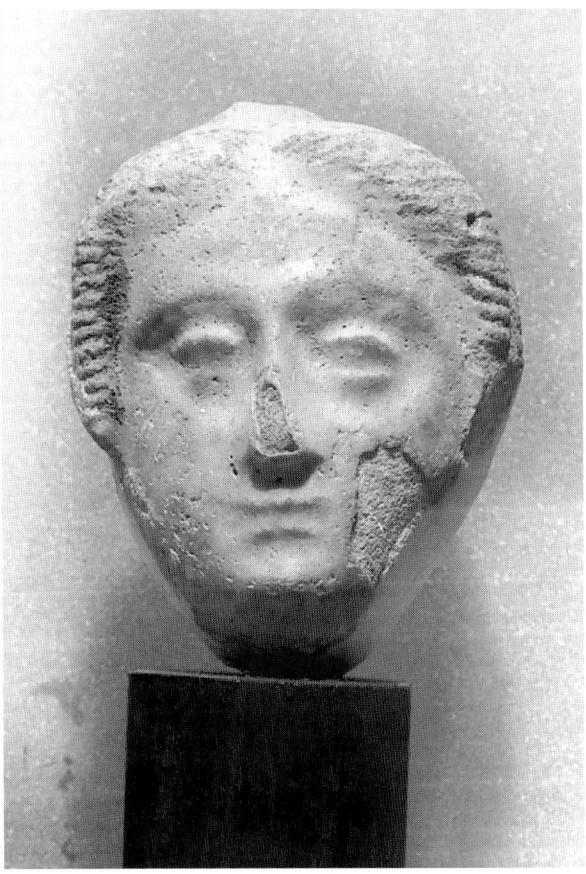

262. Faience head attributed to Cleopatra II. Athens, Benaki Museum 12552 (photo: ©Benaki Museum).

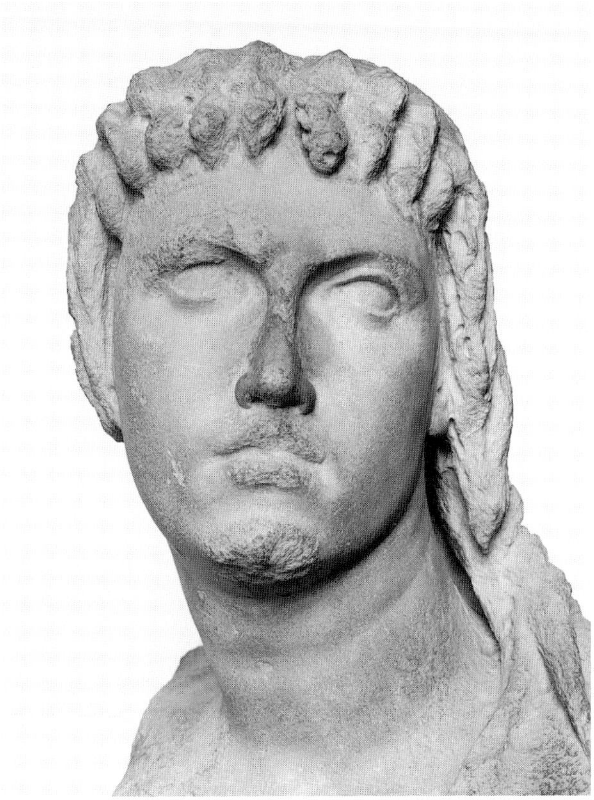

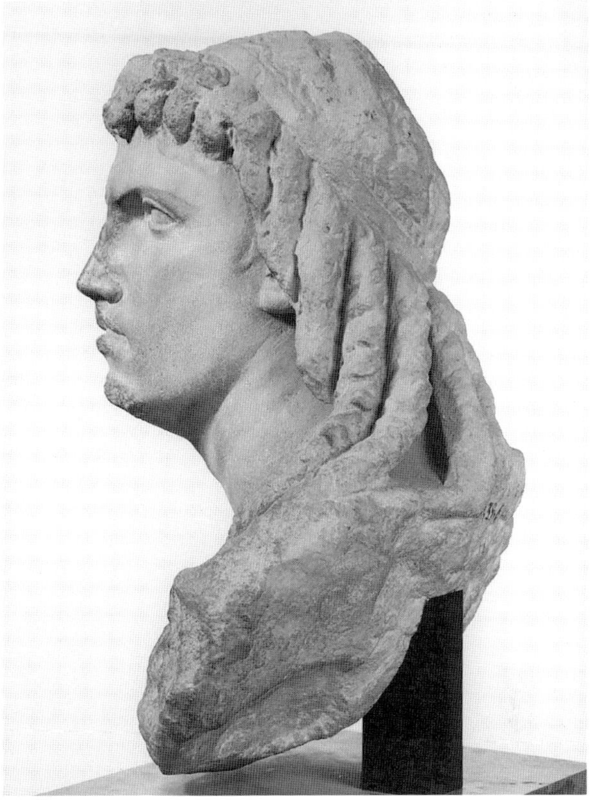

263–264 (*above*). Marble head attributed to Cleopatra III. Paris, Musée du Louvre Ma 3546 (photos: ©Musée du Louvre—M. and P. Chuzeville, P. Lebaube).

265–266 (*below*). Marble and stucco head attributed to Ptolemy IX, Edwin L. Jack Fund, 59.51. Courtesy, Museum of Fine Arts, Boston. Reproduced with permission. ©2000 Museum of Fine Arts, Boston. All Rights Reserved.

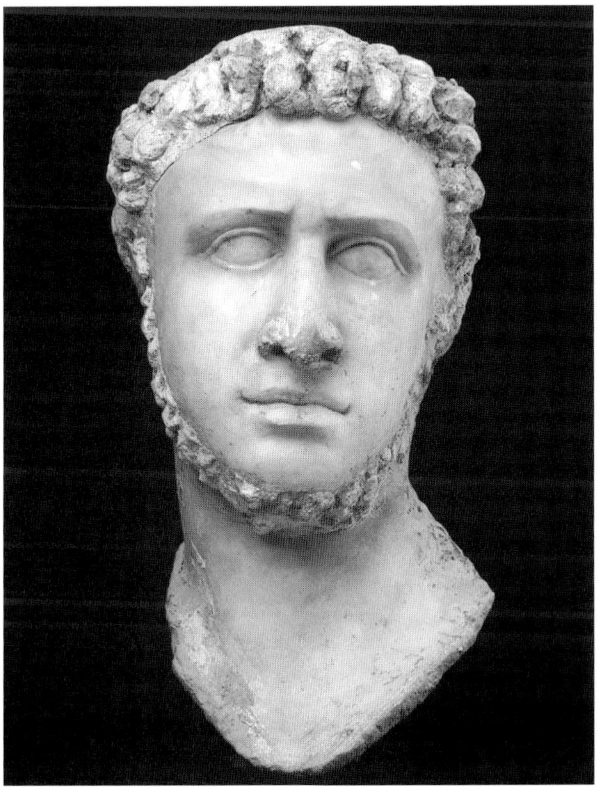

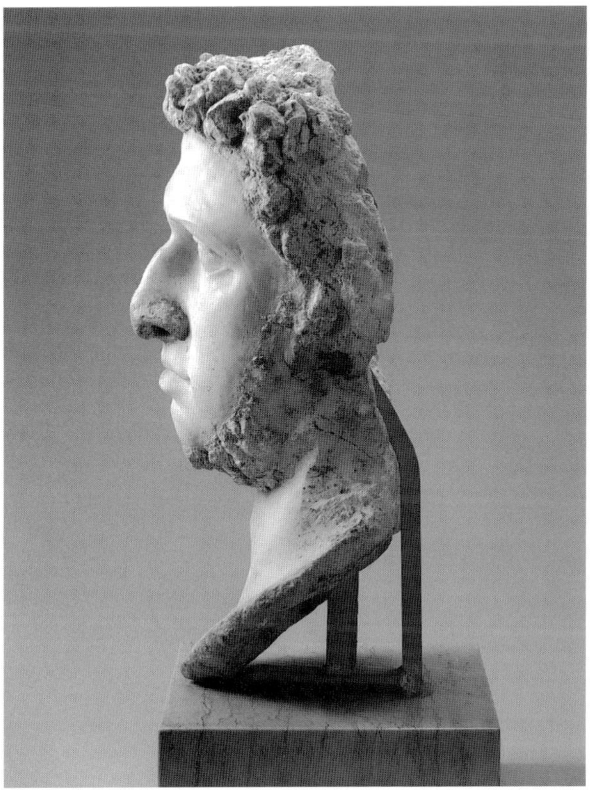

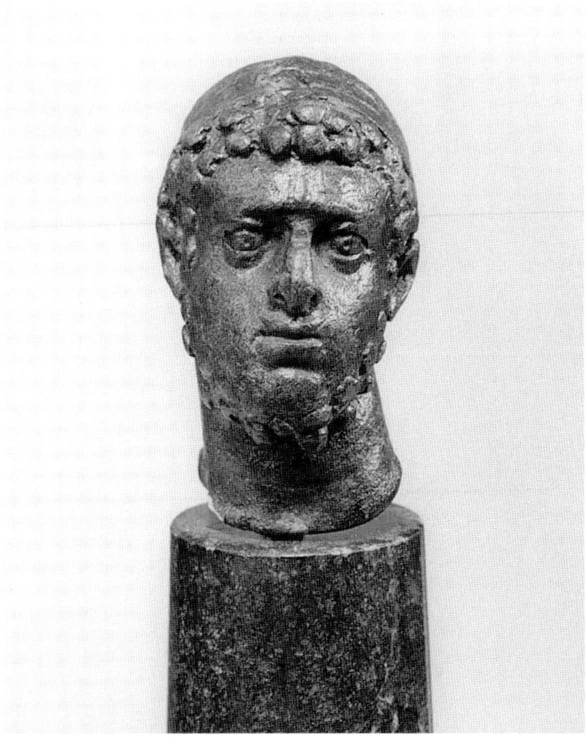

267. Bronze head attributed to Ptolemy IX. Stuttgart, Württembergisches Landesmuseum 3.827 (photo: ©Württembergisches Landesmuseum).

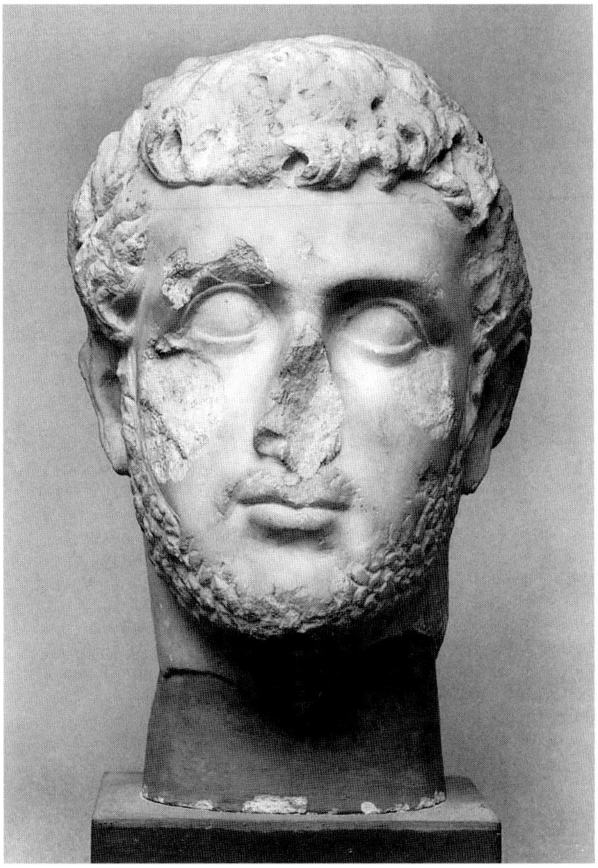

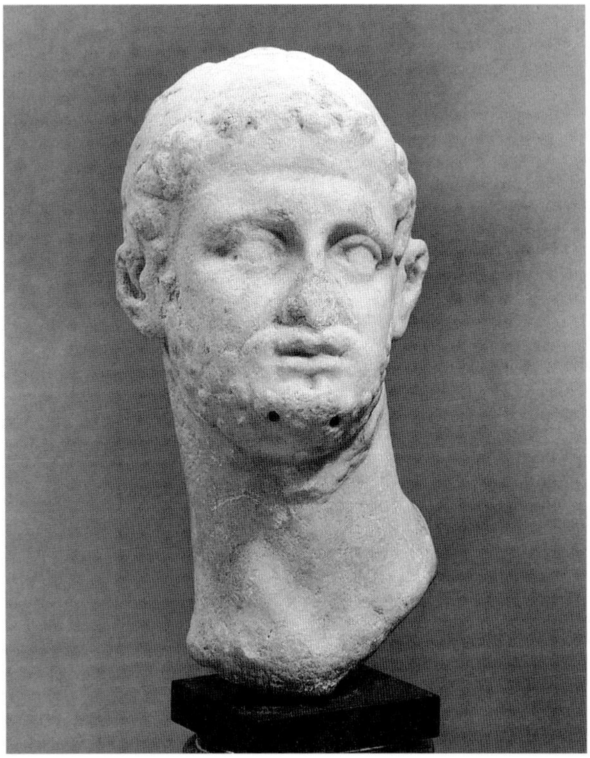

268. Marble head attributed to a late Ptolemy. Stuttgart, Württembergisches Landesmuseum 1.6 (photo: ©Württembergisches Landesmuseum).

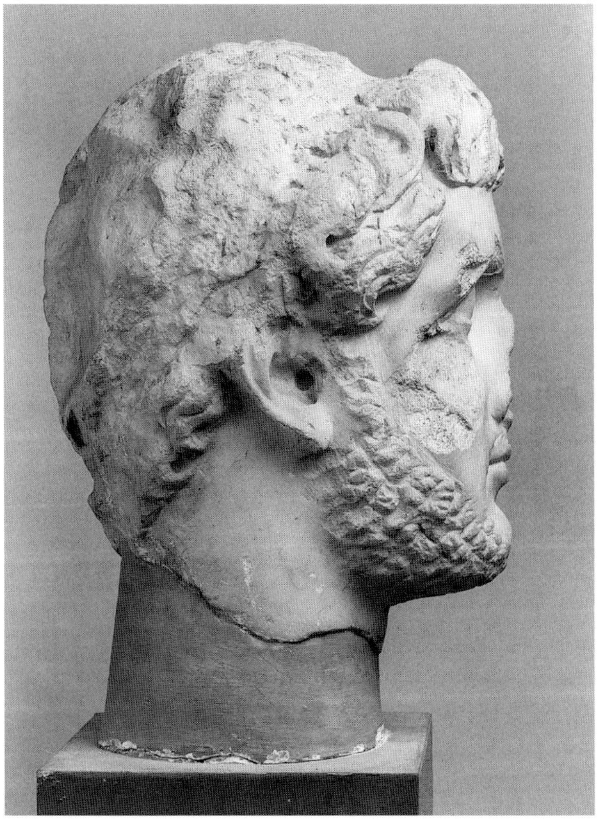

269–270. Marble head attributed a late Ptolemy. Alexandria, Graeco-Roman Museum 24660 (photos: Deutsches Archäologisches Institut, Cairo).

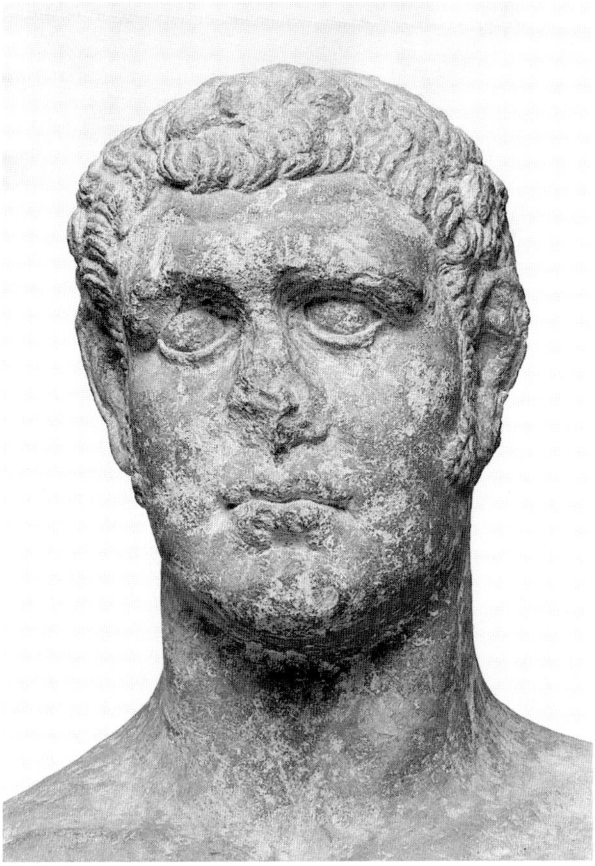

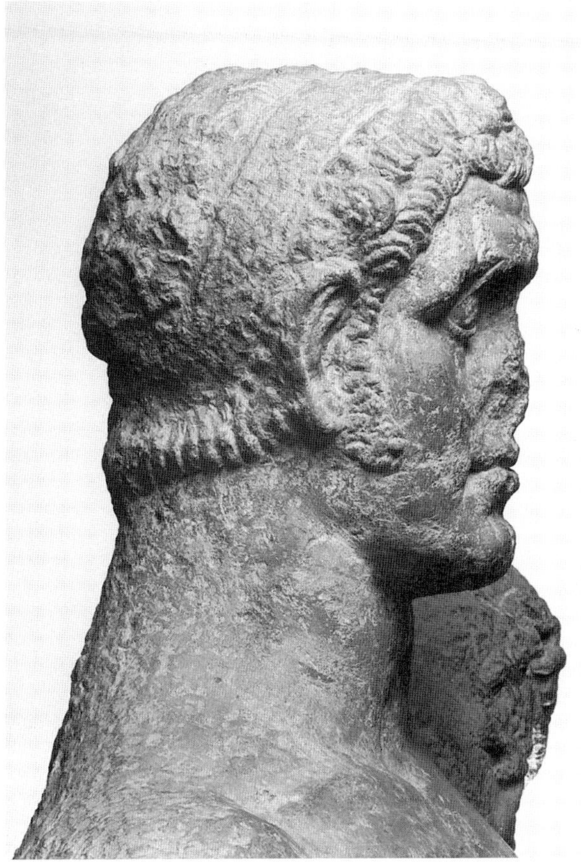

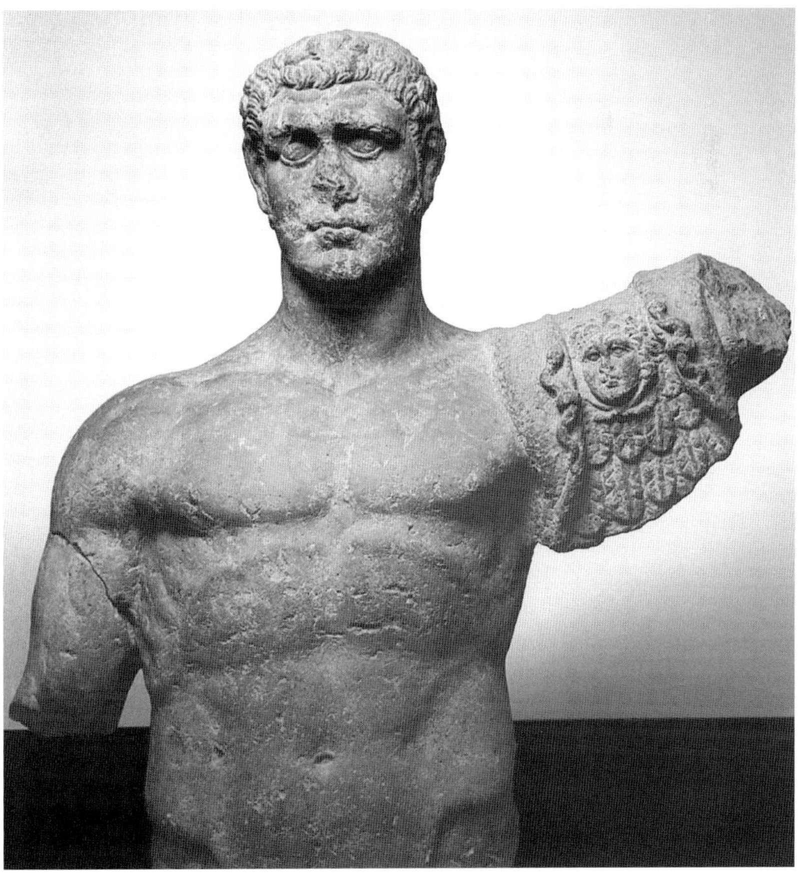

271–273. Limestone statue attributed to Ptolemy X (details of head and chest). Cairo JE 42891 (photos: Deutsches Archäologisches Institut, Cairo).

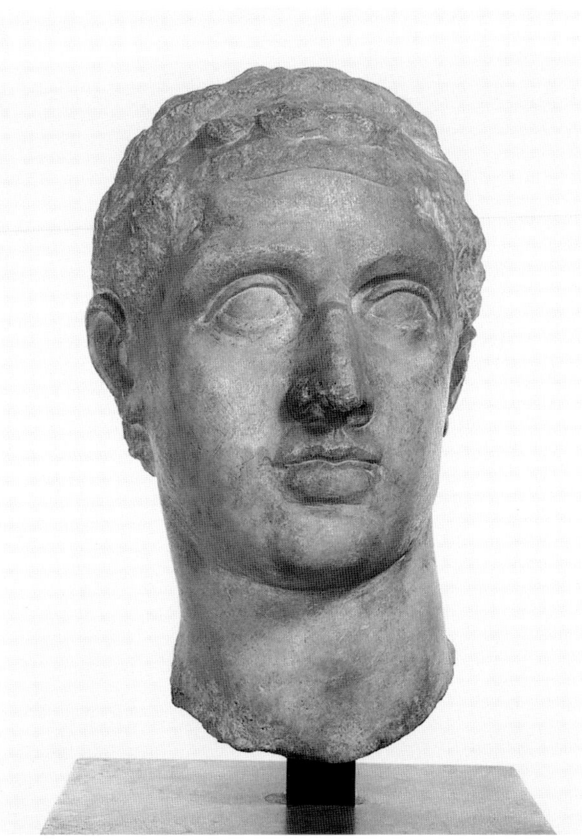

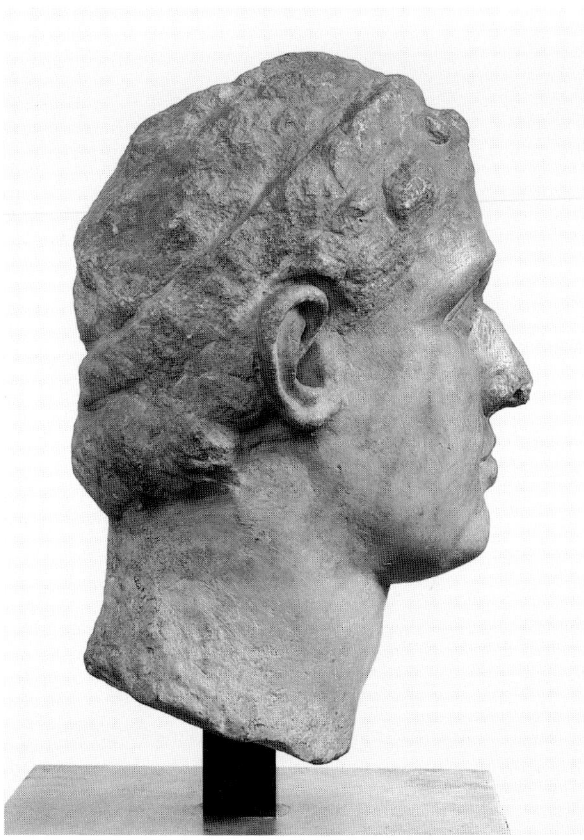

274–275. Marble head attributed to Ptolemy XII. Paris, Musée du Louvre Ma 3449 (photos: ©Musée du Louvre—P. Lebaube).

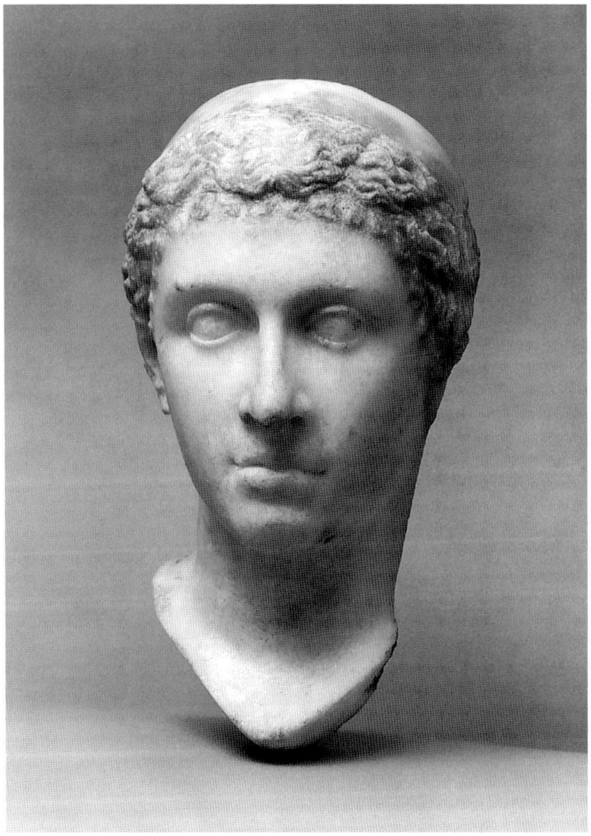

276. Marble head attributed to Cleopatra VII. Berlin, Antikensammlung 1976.10 (photo: ©Antikensammlung, Staatliche Museen zu Berlin—Preussischer Kulturbesitz, Ingrid Geske).

277–278 (*opposite page, top*). Marble head attributed to Cleopatra VII. Rome, Vatican Museums 38511 (photos: Vatican Museums).

279–280 (*opposite page, bottom*). Marble head attributed to Cleopatra VII. Cherchel Museum S 66 (31) (photos: F. Kleinefenn, Paris).

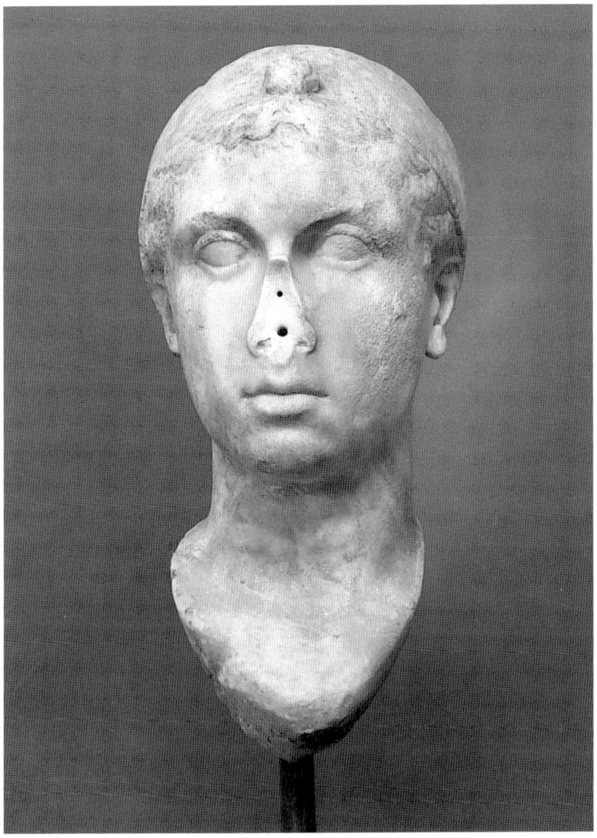

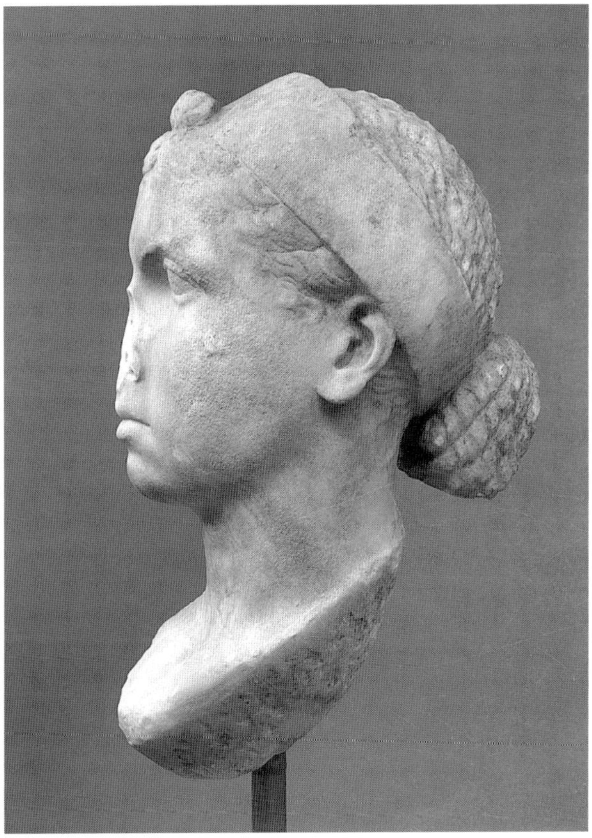

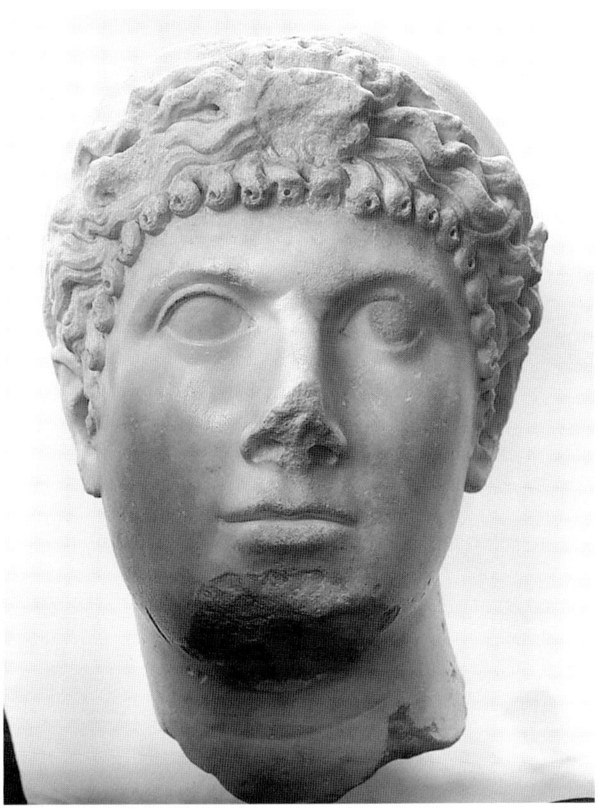

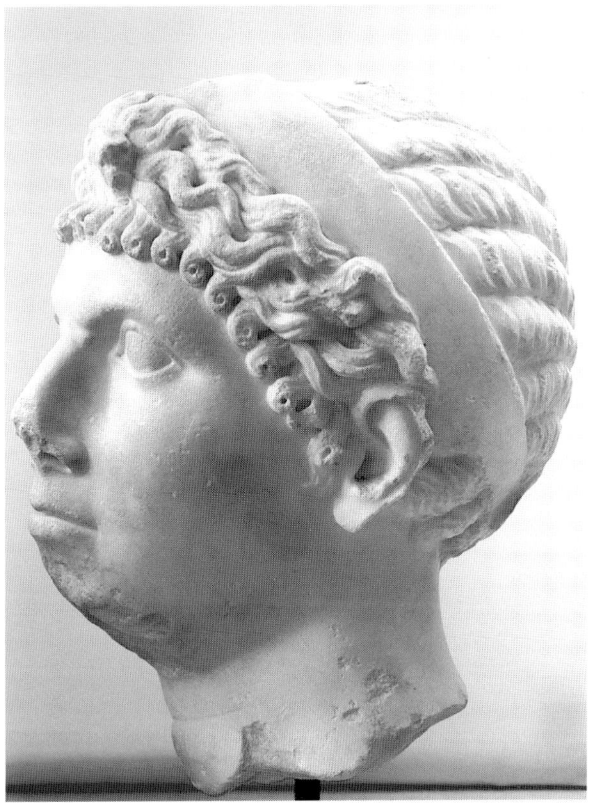

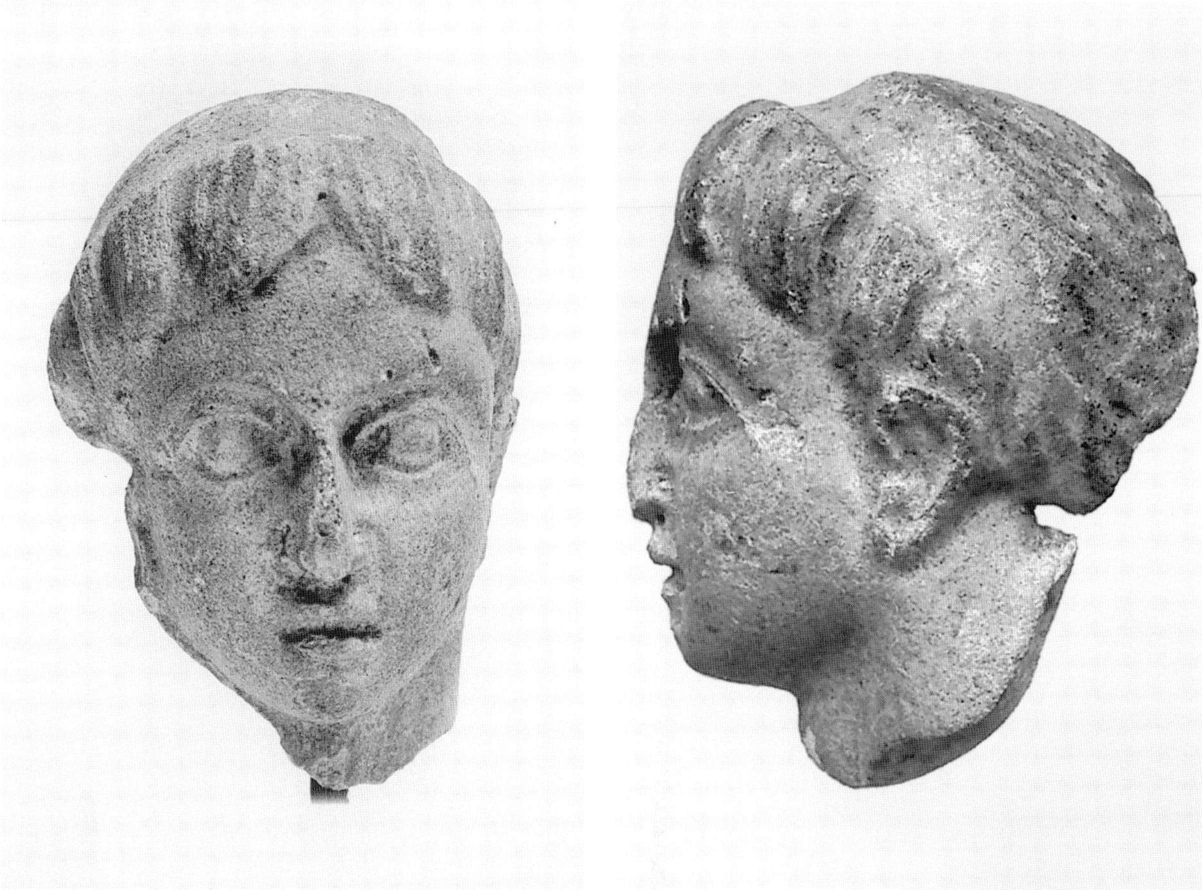

281–282. Faience head attributed to Ptolemy XV. Athens, Benaki Museum 12548 (photos: ©Benaki Museum).